Oxford Practice Grammar
Intermediate

Oxford Practice Grammar

Intermediate

with answers

John Eastwood

OXFORD

UNIVERSITY PRESS

OXFORD
UNIVERSITY PRESS

Great Clarendon Street, Oxford OX2 6DP

Oxford University Press is a department of the University of Oxford.
It furthers the University's objective of excellence in research,
scholarship,
and education by publishing worldwide in

Oxford New York

Auckland Cape Town Dar es Salaam Hong Kong Karachi
Kuala Lumpur Madrid Melbourne Mexico City Nairobi
New Delhi Shanghai Taipei Toronto

With offices in

Argentina Austria Brazil Chile Czech Republic France Greece
Guatemala Hungary Italy Japan Poland Portugal Singapore
South Korea Switzerland Thailand Turkey Ukraine Vietnam

OXFORD and OXFORD ENGLISH are registered trade marks of
Oxford University Press in the UK and in certain other countries

ISBN-13: 978 0 19 430911 0
ISBN-10: 0 19 430911 8

Typeset by Carole White
Illustrated by Oxford Designers and Illustrators
Cover illustration by Joanna Usherwood
Index by Sue Lightfoot

Printed in China

ACKNOWLEDGEMENTS

The author and publisher would like to thank:

All the teachers in the United Kingdom and Italy who discussed
this book in the early stages of its development.

The teachers and students of the following schools who used and
commented on the pilot units of the first edition:
The Bell School of Languages, Bowthorpe Hall, Norwich
The Eckersley School of English, Oxford
Eurocentre, Brighton
Eurocentre, London Victoria
King's School of English, Bournemouth
Academia Lacunza - International House,
San Sebastian, Spain.

The teachers and students of the following schools who used and
commented on the first edition of this book:
Anglo World, Oxford
Central School of English, London
Linguarama, Birmingham.

Thomas Lavelle for his work on the American English appendix.

Rod Bolitho for his valuable advice on what students need from a
grammar book.

The author would also like to thank:

All the staff at Oxford University Press who have been involved
with this book, in particular the editors Stewart Melluish, David
Lott and Helen Ward, who guided Oxford Practice Grammar
through two editions; Glynnis Chantrell and Julia Elliott, who
have handled the integration of Oxford Practice Grammar –
Intermediate into this new series; and Phil Hargraves, who is
responsible for the new design.

Oxford Designers and Illustrators for the illustrations.

And last but not least, my wife Sheila for all her help and
encouragement.

Contents

Introduction

The *Oxford Practice Grammar* is a series of three books, each written at the right level for you at each stage in your study of English. The series is intended for your use either in a classroom or when working independently in your own time.

The books are divided into units, each of which covers an important grammar topic. Each unit starts with an explanation of the grammar and this is followed by a set of practice exercises. Tests at the end of each unit or section of units give the opportunity for more practice and enable you to assess how much you have learned. Answers to the exercises and the tests are given at the back of the book.

You may want to choose the order in which you study the grammar topics, perhaps going first to those giving you problems. (Topics are listed in the Contents page at the front of each book and in the Index at the back.) Alternatively you may choose to start at the beginning of each book and work through to the end.

An interactive CD-ROM is included at each of the three levels, offering alternative ways to practise. You can recognize and correct written mistakes, and you can also take part in spoken dialogues; you can record and listen to your own voice and learn to speak more naturally.

Exam practice

The first level in the series is *Oxford Practice Grammar – Basic.* This is suitable for elementary to pre-intermediate learners, and those working for the PET exam and IELTS. The second is *Oxford Practice Grammar – Intermediate*, for students who are no longer beginners but are not yet advanced in their use of English. It is suitable for those studying for the Cambridge FCE. *Oxford Practice Grammar – Advanced* is for those who have progressed beyond the intermediate level and who wish to increase their knowledge of English grammar and become more confident when using it. It helps students prepare for CAE, CPE, TOEFL, and other advanced-level exams.

The Oxford Practice Grammar – Intermediate is written for intermediate students of English.

The units cover the main areas of English grammar. Special attention is given to those points which are often a problem for learners, such as the meaning of the different verb forms, the use of the passive, the different conditional tenses, or the use of prepositions. Many units contrast two or more different structures, such as the Present Perfect and Past Simple (Units 14 and 15). There are also a number of review units.

The emphasis throughout the book is on the meaning and use of the grammatical forms. The explanations of grammar are descriptions of how English works; they are a guide to help you understand, not rules to be memorized. It is often more effective to look at examples of English rather than to read statements about it, and the grammar explanations are supported by lots of examples of everyday conversational English.

There are also appendices at the back of the book on word formation, the spelling of endings, punctuation, pronunciation, American English, and irregular verbs.

The tests enable you to assess how much you have learned, and they also give you practice in answering the kinds of questions you meet in exams.

An exit test provides an opportunity for more practice, and prepares the student for *Oxford Practice Grammar – Advanced.* The answer key to this exit test refers back to the relevant unit of the book, so if you make a mistake you can read the explanation again.

There is an interactive Oxford Practice Grammar website at www.oup.com/elt/practicegrammar

Key to symbols

The symbol / (oblique stroke) between two words
means that either word is possible. *I may/might go*
means that *I may go* and *I might go* are both
possible. In exercise questions this symbol is also
used to separate words or phrases which are
possible answers.

Brackets ( ) around a word or phrase in the middle
of a sentence mean that it can be left out. *There's
(some) milk in the fridge* means that there are two
possible sentences: *There's some milk in the
fridge* and *There's milk in the fridge*.

The symbol ~ means that there is a change of
speaker. In the example *How are you? ~ I'm fine,
thanks*, the question and answer are spoken by
different people.

The symbol ▷ means that you can go to another
place in the book for more information. ▷7 means
that you can find out more in Unit 7.

The symbol ▶ in an exercise indicates that a
sample answer is given.

For phonetic symbols see page 374.

1 Word classes: nouns, verbs, adjectives, etc.

1 Introduction

Look at the different kinds of word in this sentence.

Pronoun	Verb	Determiner	Adjective	Noun	Preposition	Noun	Adverb
I	*have*	*an*	*important*	*conference*	*at*	*work*	*tomorrow,*

Linking word	Pronoun	Verb	Adverb	Adjective
so	*I*	*am*	*rather*	*busy.*

2 What kind of word?

There are eight different kinds of word in English. They are called 'word classes' or 'parts of speech'. Here are some examples from the conversations in the café. The numbers after the examples tell you which units in the book give you more information.

1 Verb: **have, am, is, would, like, come, are, sitting, look** ▷ 4–75
2 Noun: **conference, work, coffee, party, Saturday, Jessica, friends, corner** ▷ 76–82
3 Adjective: **important, busy, good, cheap** ▷ 104–109
4 Adverb: **tomorrow, rather, really, here** ▷ 113–117
5 Preposition: **at, to, on, in** ▷ 118–125
6 Determiner: **an, this, our, the** ▷ 83–97
7 Pronoun: **I, it, you** ▷ 98–103
8 Linking word: **so, and** ▷ 150–153

3 Words in sentences

Some words can belong to different classes depending on how they are used in a sentence.

VERBS	NOUNS
*Can I **look** at your photos?*	*I like the **look** of that coat.*
*We **work** on Saturday morning.*	*I'll be at **work** tomorrow.*

Practice

A What kind of word? (2)

Read this paragraph and then say which word class each underlined word belongs to. To help you decide, you can look back at the examples in 2.

Andrew didn't go to the café with the other students. Rachel told him they were going there, but he wanted to finish his work. Andrew isn't very sociable. He stays in his room and concentrates totally on his studies. He's an excellent student, but he doesn't have much fun.

▶ to   preposition
▶ café   noun
1 the   ....
2 told   ....
3 they   ....
4 there   ....
5 he   ....
6 finish   ....

7 sociable   ....
8 in   ....
9 and   ....
10 totally   ....
11 an   ....
12 excellent   ....
13 but   ....
14 fun   ....

B What kind of word? (2)

Read this paragraph and then write the words in the spaces below. Write the first three verbs under 'Verb', and so on. Do not write the same word more than once.

Henry thinks Claire is wonderful. He loves her madly, and he dreams of marrying her, but unfortunately he is rather old for her. Today they are at a café with their friends Sarah and Mark, so Henry can't get romantic with Claire. But he might buy her some flowers later.

Verb	Noun	Adjective	Adverb
thinks	Henry		

Preposition	Determiner	Pronoun	Linking word

C Words in sentences (3)

Is the underlined word a verb, a noun or an adjective?

▶ Shall we go for a walk?   noun
▶ Shall we walk into town?   verb
1 Laura wanted to talk to Rita.   ....
2 Laura wanted a talk with Rita.   ....
3 The windows aren't very clean.   ....
4 Doesn't anyone clean the windows?   ....
5 We went to a fabulous show in New York.   ....
6 Laura wanted to show Rita her photos.   ....
7 Henry thought Claire looked beautiful.   ....
8 A strange thought came into Emma's head.   ....
9 Sarah is feeling quite tired now.   ....
10 Studying all night had tired Andrew out.   ....

2 Sentence structure: subject, verb, object, etc.

MIKE AND HARRIET ARE MOVING THEIR PIANO UPSTAIRS.
TOM, MELANIE AND DAVID ARE HELPING THEM.

1 Sentence structure

The parts of a sentence are the subject, verb, object, complement and adverbial. A statement begins with the subject and the verb. There are five main structures which we can use to make a simple statement.

1 | SUBJECT | VERB |
|---|---|
| *My arms* | *are aching.* |
| *Something* | *happened.* |

2 | SUBJECT | VERB | OBJECT |
|---|---|---|
| *I* | *need* | *a rest.* |
| *Five people* | *are moving* | *the piano.* |

The subject and object can be a pronoun (e.g. **I**) or a noun phrase (e.g. **the piano**).

3 | SUBJECT | VERB | COMPLEMENT |
|---|---|---|
| *This piano* | *is* | *heavy.* |
| *It* | *was* | *a big problem.* |

The complement can be an adjective (e.g. **heavy**) or a noun phrase (e.g. **a big problem**). The complement often comes after **be**. It can also come after **appear, become, get, feel, look, seem, stay** or **sound**. For adjectives and word order see Unit 104.2.

4 | SUBJECT | VERB | ADVERBIAL |
|---|---|---|
| *It* | *is* | *on my foot.* |
| *Their house* | *is* | *nearby.* |

An adverbial can be a prepositional phrase (e.g. **on my foot**) or an adverb (e.g. **nearby**).

5 | SUBJECT | VERB | OBJECT | OBJECT |
|---|---|---|---|
| *It* | *'s giving* | *me* | *backache.* |
| *David* | *bought* | *Melanie* | *a present.* |

We use two objects after verbs like **give** and **send** (see Unit 3).

2 Adverbials

We can add adverbials to all the five main structures.

*My arms are aching **terribly**.*   *I **really** need a rest.*
***Of course** this piano is heavy.*   ***Fortunately** their house is nearby.*
***To everyone's surprise**, David **actually** bought Melanie a present **yesterday**.*

▷ 34, 36 Word order in questions   ▷ 113 Adverbs and word order
▷ page 377 **Seem, look**, etc. in American English

Practice

A Parts of the sentence (1)

Mike and Harriet are on holiday. They have written a postcard to David and Melanie. Look at each underlined phrase and say what part of the sentence it is: subject, verb, object, complement or adverbial.

- ▶ We're having <u>a great time</u>. *object*
- 1 <u>The weather</u> is marvellous. ....
- 2 We really <u>enjoy</u> camping. ....
- 3 It's <u>great fun</u>. ....
- 4 We're <u>on a farm</u>. ....
- 5 We like <u>this place</u>. ....
- 6 The scenery is <u>beautiful</u>. ....

B Sentence structure (1)

After moving the piano, the five friends had a rest and a cup of tea.
Look at this part of their conversation and then write the letters a)–e) in the correct place.

- a) David: That was a difficult job.
- b) Tom: <u>I agree</u>.
- c) Mike: I'm on my deathbed.
- d) David: Someone should give us a medal.
- e) Harriet: I've made some more tea.

- ▶ Subject + verb *b*
- 1 Subject + verb + object ....
- 2 Subject + verb + complement ....
- 3 Subject + verb + adverbial ....
- 4 Subject + verb + object + object ....

C Word order (1)

Put the words in the correct order and write the statements.

- ▶ is / Melanie / very nice *Melanie is very nice.*
- 1 football / likes / Tom ....
- 2 an accident / David / had ....
- 3 moved / the piano / we ....
- 4 a tall woman / Harriet / is ....
- 5 sat / on the floor / everyone ....
- 6 gave / some help / Mike's friends / him ....

D Adverbials (2)

These sentences are from a news report. Write down the two adverbials in each sentence. Each adverbial is a prepositional phrase or an adverb.

- ▶ Prince Charles opened a new sports centre in Stoke yesterday. *in Stoke* / *yesterday*
- 1 He also spoke with several young people. ....
- 2 The sports centre was first planned in 1994. ....
- 3 Naturally, the local council could not finance the project without help. ....
- 4 Fortunately, they managed to obtain money from the National Lottery. ....

3 Direct and indirect objects

1 Introduction

*Henry gave **Claire some flowers**.*	*Henry gave **some flowers to Claire**.*
Here the verb **give** has two objects. **Claire** is the indirect object, the person receiving something. **Some flowers** is the direct object, the thing that someone gives.	Here **give** has a direct object (**some flowers**) and a phrase with **to**. **To** comes before **Claire**, the person receiving something.

Here are some more examples of the two structures.

	INDIRECT OBJECT	DIRECT OBJECT		DIRECT OBJECT	PHRASE WITH TO/FOR
Emma gave	**Rachel**	**a CD.**	*Emma gave*	**the CD**	**to Rachel.**
I'll send	**my cousin**	**a postcard.**	*I'll send*	**a postcard**	**to my cousin.**
We bought	**all the children**	**an ice-cream.**	*We bought*	**ice-creams**	**for all the children.**

2 To or for?

We give something <u>to</u> someone, and we buy something <u>for</u> someone.

We can use **to** with these verbs: **bring, feed, give, hand, lend, offer, owe, pass, pay, post, promise, read, sell, send, show, take, teach, tell, throw, write**

> *Vicky paid the money **to** the cashier.* OR *Vicky paid the cashier the money.*
> *Let me read this news item **to** you.* OR *Let me read you this news item.*
> *We showed the photos **to** David.* OR *We showed David the photos.*

We can use **for** with these verbs: **book, bring, build, buy, choose, cook, fetch, find, get, leave, make, order, pick, reserve, save**

> *They found a spare ticket **for** me.* OR *They found me a spare ticket.*
> *I've saved a seat **for** you.* OR *I've saved you a seat.*
> *Melanie is making a cake **for** David.* OR *Melanie is making David a cake.*

3 Give + pronoun

Sometimes there is a pronoun and a noun after a verb such as **give**.
The pronoun usually comes before the noun.

Henry is very fond of Claire. He gave **her some flowers.**	*Henry bought some flowers. He gave* **them to Claire.**
We use **her** because Claire is mentioned earlier. **Her** comes before **some flowers**.	We use **them** because the flowers are mentioned earlier. **Them** comes before **Claire**.

Practice

A Give (1)

Look at the Christmas presents and write sentences about them.
Put one of these words at the end of each sentence: *necklace*, *scarf*, *sweater*, *tennis racket*, *watch*.

► To Mike From Harriet	1 To Melanie From David	2 To Trevor From Laura	3 To Matthew From Emma	4 To Claire From Henry

► *Harriet gave Mike a watch.*
1 ....   3 ....
2 ....   4 ....

B Indirect object or to? (1)

Write the information in one sentence. Put the <u>underlined</u> part at the end of the sentence.
Sometimes you need *to*.

►	Daniel lent something to Vicky. It was <u>his calculator</u>.	→ Daniel *lent Vicky his calculator.*
►	Mark sent a message. It was to <u>his boss</u>.	→ Mark *sent a message to his boss.*
1	Emma sold her bike. <u>Her sister</u> bought it.	→ Emma ....
2	Tom told the joke. He told <u>all his friends</u>.	→ Tom ....
3	Melanie gave <u>some help</u>. She helped her neighbour.	→ Melanie ....
4	Ilona wrote to her teacher. She wrote <u>a letter</u>.	→ Ilona ....

C To or for? (2)

Mark's boss at Zedco is Mr Atkins. He is telling people to do things. Put in *to* or *for*.

►	Give these papers *to* my secretary.	3	Don't show these plans .... anyone.
►	Could you make some coffee *for* us?	4	Leave a message .... my secretary.
1	Book a flight .... me, could you?	5	Fetch the file .... me, could you?
2	Can you post this cheque .... the hotel?	6	Write a memo .... all managers.

D Give + pronoun (3)

Complete each answer using the words in brackets. Sometimes you need to use *to* or *for*.

►	Matthew:	Why is everyone laughing? (a funny story / us)
	Vicky:	Daniel told *us a funny story.*
►	Trevor:	There's some fish left over. (it / the cat)
	Laura:	I'll feed *it to the cat.*
1	Mark:	What are you doing with those bottles? (them / the bottle bank)
	Sarah:	I'm taking ....
2	Trevor:	How are things with you, Daniel? (a job / me)
	Daniel:	Fine. Someone has offered ....
3	David:	What about those papers you found? (them / the police)
	Tom:	Oh, I handed ....
4	Emma:	It's pouring with rain, look. (my umbrella / you)
	Rachel:	It's OK. I'll lend ....

4 Present Continuous

1 Introduction

The Present Continuous means that we are in the middle of an action.

Mark? I'm at the station. **I'm waiting** for the train. Oh, I can hear it. It**'s coming** now.

SARAH'S TRAIN IS LATE, SO SHE IS PHONING MARK.

2 Form

The Present Continuous is the present tense of **be** + an -ing form.

POSITIVE

*I **am looking** OR **I'm looking***
*You/we/they **are looking** OR You/we/they**'re looking***
*He/she/it **is looking** OR He/she/it**'s looking***

NEGATIVE	QUESTION
*I'm **not looking***	*am I looking?*
*you/we/they **aren't looking** OR you're/we're/they're **not looking***	*are you/we/they **looking**?*
*he/she/it **isn't looking** OR he's/she's/it's **not looking***	*is he/she/it **looking**?*

*I'm **getting** the lunch ready.* *The train **is coming**, look.*
*We're **looking** for a post office.* *Rachel **isn't wearing** her new dress.*
*What **are** you **doing**?* *Who **is** Vicky **dancing** with?*

For rules about the spelling of the -ing form see page 370.

3 Use

We use the Present Continuous to say that we are in the middle of an action.
  *I'm **waiting** for the train.* (I'm at the station <u>now</u>.)
  *I'm **getting** the lunch ready.* (I'm in the kitchen <u>now</u>.)
I'm waiting means that I am in the middle of a period of waiting. The wait is not yet over.

We can also use the Present Continuous when we are in the middle of something but not actually doing it at the moment of speaking.
  *I must get back to the office. We're **working** on a new project.*
  *I'm quite busy these days. I'm **doing** a course at college.*

We can use the Present Continuous when things are changing over a long period.
  *The number of cars on the road **is increasing**.*   *The earth **is** slowly **getting** warmer.*

For the future meaning of the Present Continuous see Unit 26.1.
  *I'm **playing** badminton with Matthew **tomorrow**.*

▷ 6 Present Continuous or Simple?   ▷ 7 State verbs and action verbs

Practice

A Form (2)

Look at the pictures and say what people are doing.
Use these verbs: *carry, paint, play, ride, take*
Use these objects: *a bicycle, a parcel, a photo, a picture, basketball*

▶ He's riding a bicycle.

1 ....

2 ....

3 ....

4 ....

B Form (2)

Rachel is in the computer room at college. Complete her conversation with Andrew.
Put in a Present Continuous form of the verb.

Andrew: What (▶) *are you doing?* (you / do)

Rachel: (▶) *I'm writing* .... (I / write) a letter to a friend. He's a disc jockey. Vicky and I
(1) .... (try) to organize a disco.

Andrew: That sounds a lot of work. How (2) .... (you / find) time for your
studies?

Rachel: Well, as I said, Vicky (3) .... (help) me.
(4) .... (we / get) on all right. (5) ....
(we / not / spend) too much time on it. (6) .... (it / not / take) me
away from my studies, don't worry about that. Oh, sorry, (7) ....
(you / wait) for this computer?

Andrew: Yes, but there's no hurry.

Rachel: (8) .... (I / correct) the last bit of the letter. I've nearly finished.

C Use (3)

What can you say in these situations? Add a sentence with the Present Continuous.

▶ A friend rings you up in the middle of *Neighbours*, your favourite soap opera.
Is it important? *I'm watching 'Neighbours'.*

1 A friend is at your flat and suggests going out, but you can see rain outside.
I don't want to go out now. Look, ...

2 A friend rings you up at work.
Sorry, I can't talk now. ....

3 You want to get off the bus, but the man next to you is sitting on your coat.
Excuse me, ...

4 A friend wants to talk to you, but you have just started to write an important letter.
Can I talk to you later? ....

5 You have been ill, but you're better now than you were.
I'm OK now. ....

5 Present Simple

Yes, I **like** this supermarket.
I **think** it's very nice.
Yes, my husband **thinks** so, too.
We always **shop** here. We **come**
here every week. We **live** quite
near, so it **doesn't take**
long to get here.

1 Use

We use the Present Simple for

▶ thoughts and feelings: *I **think** so, I **like** it.*

▶ states, things staying the same, facts and things that are true for a long time: *We **live** quite near* (see Unit 7).

▶ repeated actions: *We **come** here every week.*

and also

▶ in phrases like **I promise, I agree**, etc: *I **promise** I'll pay you back.*

▶ in a negative question with **why** to make a suggestion: *Why **don't** we **go** out?*

For the future meaning of the Present Simple see Units 26 and 27.
  *The new term **starts** next week.*

2 Positive forms

> I/you/we/they **get**
> he/she/it **gets**

In the Present Simple we use the verb without an ending.
  *I **get** the lunch ready at one o'clock, usually.*   *We always **do** our shopping at Greenway.*
  *Most children **like** ice-cream.*   *You **know** the answer.*

But in the third person singular (after **he, she, it, your friend**, etc), the verb ends in **-s** or **-es**. For spelling rules see page 370.
  *It **gets** busy at weekends.*   *My husband **thinks** so, too.*
  *Sarah **catches** the early train.*   *She **faxes** messages all over the world.*

3 Negatives and questions

NEGATIVE	QUESTION
I/you/we/they **do not get** OR **don't get**	**do** I/we/you/they **get**?
he/she/it **does not get** OR **doesn't get**	**does** he/she/it **get**?

We use a form of **do** in negatives and questions (but see Unit 37). We use **do** and **don't** except in the third person singular, where we use **does** and **doesn't**.
  *We **don't live** far away.*   *He **doesn't want** to go shopping.*
  *Do you **live** here? ~ Yes, I do.*   *What **does** he **want**? ~ Money.*

We do not add **-s** to the verb in negatives and questions.
  NOT ~~He doesn't gets~~ and NOT ~~Does he gets?~~

▷ 6 Present Continuous or Present Simple?   ▷ 7 State verbs and action verbs

Practice

A Use (1)

Look at each <u>underlined</u> verb and say what kind of meaning it expresses. Is it a thought, a feeling, a fact or a repeated action?

▶ Matthew <u>loves</u> sport.   a feeling

▶ Sarah often <u>works</u> late at the office.   a repeated action

1 I <u>hate</u> quiz programmes.

2 We <u>play</u> table tennis every Thursday.

3 The computer <u>belongs</u> to Emma.

4 These plates <u>cost</u> £20 each.

5 I <u>believe</u> it's the right thing to do.

6 I'm hungry. I <u>want</u> something to eat.

7 I usually <u>go</u> to work by bus.

8 It's OK. I <u>understand</u> your problem.

B Forms (2–3)

Complete the sentences by putting in the verbs. Use the Present Simple. You have to decide if the verb is positive or negative.

▶ Claire is very sociable. She knows (know) lots of people.

▶ We've got plenty of chairs, thanks. We don't want (want) any more.

1 My friend is finding life in Paris a bit difficult. He .... (speak) French.

2 Most students live quite close to the college, so they .... (walk) there.

3 My sports kit is really muddy. This shirt .... (need) a good wash.

4 I've got four cats and two dogs. I .... (love) animals.

5 No breakfast for Mark, thanks. He .... (eat) breakfast.

6 What's the matter? You .... (look) very happy.

7 Don't try to ring the bell. It .... (work).

8 I hate telephone answering machines. I just .... (like) talking to them.

9 Matthew is good at badminton. He .... (win) every game.

10 We always travel by bus. We .... (own) a car.

C Forms (2–3)

Complete the conversation. Put in the Present Simple forms.

Rita: (▶) Do you like (you / like) football, Tom?

Tom: (▶) I love (I / love) it. I'm a United fan. (1) .... (I / go) to all their games. Nick usually (2) .... (come) with me. And (3) .... (we / travel) to away games, too. Why (4) .... (you / not / come) to a match some time?

Rita: I'm afraid football (5) .... (not / make) sense to me — men running after a ball. Why (6) .... (you / take) it so seriously?

Tom: It's a wonderful game. (7) .... (I / love) it. United are my whole life.

Rita: How much (8) .... (it / cost) to buy the tickets and pay for the travel?

Tom: A lot. (9) .... (I / not / know) exactly how much. But (10) .... (that / not / matter) to me. (11) .... (I / not / want) to do anything else. (12) .... (that / annoy) you?

Rita: No, (13) .... (it / not / annoy) me. I just (14) .... (find) it a bit sad.

6 Present Continuous or Present Simple?

1 Now or sometimes?

I'm speaking to you live from the White House.

KITTY BEAMISH IS A TV REPORTER.

I often **speak** live to the camera, Guy. I **love** that part of the job. News reporting **means** everything to me, you know.

KITTY IS ON GUY'S CHAT SHOW.

PRESENT CONTINUOUS	PRESENT SIMPLE
We use the Present Continuous for something happening now. *I am speaking to you live* means that Kitty is in the middle of a live broadcast. Here are some more examples.	We use the Present Simple for repeated actions. *I often speak live to the camera* means that she does it again and again.
*It's **raining** at the moment.*	*It always **rains** at the weekend.*
*I'm **watching** this programme.*	*I **watch** television most weekends.*
*Look. That man **is taking** a photo of you.*	*He's a photographer. He **takes** lots of photos.*

2 Thoughts, feelings and states

We normally use the Present Simple to talk about thoughts and feelings.
   *I **think** it's a good programme.*   *Kitty **likes** her job.*
We also use it to talk about states (see Unit 7) and permanent facts.
   *Reporting **means** a lot to her.*   *Paper **burns** easily.*
We also use the Present Simple in **I promise, I agree, I refuse,** etc.
   *I **promise** I'll write to you.*   *It's all right. I **forgive** you.*

3 Temporary or permanent?

PRESENT CONTINUOUS	PRESENT SIMPLE
We use the Present Continuous for a routine or situation that we see as temporary (for a short period).	We use the Present Simple for a routine or situation that we see as permanent.
*I'm **working** at a sports shop for six weeks.*	*I **work** at a sports shop. It's a permanent job.*
*At the moment they're **living** in a very small flat.*	*They **live** in a very nice flat.*

4 Always

PRESENT CONTINUOUS	PRESENT SIMPLE
We can use **always** with the Present Continuous to mean 'very often', usually with the added meaning of 'too often'.	**Always** with the Present Simple means 'every time'.
*Tom **is always inviting** friends here.*	*Tom **always invites** us to stay at Christmas.*
(= He invites them very often.)	(= He invites us every Christmas.)
*I'm **always making** silly mistakes.*	*I **always make** silly mistakes in exams.*
(= I make silly mistakes too often.)	(= I make mistakes in every exam.)

Practice

A Present Continuous or Present Simple? (1–2)

At work Mark is talking to Alan in the corridor. Complete their conversation.
Put in the Present Continuous or Present Simple of the verbs.

Mark: (▶) .Are. you. looking... (you / look) for someone?

Alan: Yes, (▶) .I. need....... (I / need) to speak to Neil. He isn't in his office.

Mark: (1) .... (he / talk) to the boss at the moment.
(2) .... (I / think)
(3) .... (they / discuss) money.

Alan: Oh, right. And what about you? (4) .... (you / look) for someone too?

Mark: Yes, Linda. (5) .... (you / know) where she is?

Alan: Oh, she isn't here today. She only (6) .... (work) four days a week.
(7) .... (she / not / work) on Fridays. She'll be here on Monday.

Mark: Thank you. (8) .... (you / know) a lot about Linda.

Alan: Well, most days (9) .... (I / give) her a lift, or
(10) .... (she / give) me one. (11) ....
(she / live) quite close to me. (12) .... (it / save) petrol.

Mark: Yes, of course. Good idea. Yes, (13) .... (I / agree). Well,
(14) .... (I / waste) my time here then. I'll get back to my computer.

B Present Continuous or Present Simple? (1–3)

Complete the sentences. Put in the Present Continuous or Present Simple of the verbs.

▶ .I'm. writing. (I / write) to my parents. .I. write....... (I / write) to them every weekend.

1 .... (it / snow) outside. .... (it / come) down
quite hard, look.

2 Normally .... (I / start) work at eight o'clock, but
.... (I / start) at seven this week. We're very busy at the moment.

3 I haven't got a car at the moment, so .... (I / go) to work on the bus
this week. Usually .... (I / drive) to work.

4 The sun .... (rise) in the east, remember. It's behind us so
.... (we / travel) west.

5 I'm afraid I have no time to help just now. .... (I / write) a report. But
.... (I / promise) I'll give you some help later.

6 .... (I / want) a new car. .... (I / save) up to
buy one.

C Always (4)

Complete the sentences. Use always and the Present Continuous or Present Simple.

▶ Melanie: Tom talks too much, doesn't he?
Rita: Yes, and .he's. always. talking...... about football.

▶ Laura: You forget your keys every time.
Trevor: I try to remember them, but .I. always. forget............. .

1 Claire: Sarah takes the train every day, doesn't she?
Mark: Yes, ...the train.

2 Vicky: Rachel misses lectures much too often in my opinion.
Emma: I agree. .... lectures.

3 Mike: Every time I drive along here, I go the wrong way.
Harriet: But it's very simple, isn't it? Why .... the wrong way?

4 David: Trevor and Laura argue much too often, I think.
Melanie: I know. ....

7 State verbs and action verbs

1 States and actions

STATES	ACTIONS
A state means something staying the same.	An action means something happening.
*The flat **is** clean.*	*I'm **cleaning** the flat.*
*The farmer **owns** the land.*	*The farmer **is buying** the land.*
*The box **contained** old books.*	*He **put** the books in the box.*
State verbs cannot usually be continuous.	Action verbs can be simple or continuous.
NOT ~~The farmer is owning the land.~~	*He **put** / He **was putting** everything away.*

Some state verbs: **be, believe, belong, consist of, contain, depend on, deserve, exist, hate, know, like, love, matter, mean, own, need, prefer, remember, resemble, seem, understand**

2 I think/I'm thinking etc.

Sometimes we can use a verb either for a state or for an action.

STATES (simple tenses)	ACTIONS (simple or continuous)
*I **think** you're right.* (= believe)	*I'm **thinking** about the problem.*
*We **have** three cars.* (= own)	*We're **having** lunch.* (= eating)
*I **come** from Sweden.* (= live in)	*I'm **coming** from Sweden.* (= travelling)
	*I usually **come** on the plane.*
*I **see** your problem.* (= understand)	*Mark **is seeing** his boss.* (= meeting)
*Do you **see** that house?* (= have in sight)	*I **see** Daniel quite often.*
*This picture **looks** nice.*	*I'm **looking** at this picture.*
*She **appears** very nervous.* (= seems)	*She **appeared/was appearing** in a film.*
*The bag **weighed** five kilos.*	*They **weighed/were weighing** my bag.*
*The coat **fits**.* (= is the right size)	*I'm **fitting** a lock to the window.*

These examples with the verb **be** are about how people behave.

PERMANENT QUALITY	TEMPORARY BEHAVIOUR
*Claire **is** a very sociable person.*	*Andrew **is being** very sociable today.*
*That man **is** an idiot.*	*You **are being** an idiot this morning.*
	(= You are behaving like an idiot.)

We use **am/are/is being** only to talk about behaviour, not about other things.
   I'm better now, thanks.   **Are** *you ready?*   **Is** *anyone interested?*

3 I like/I'm liking etc.

We can use some state verbs in the continuous to talk about a short period of time.

PERMANENT STATE (simple tenses)	SHORT PERIOD (continuous)
*I **love/enjoy** parties.*	*I'm **loving/enjoying** this party.*
*I **like** school.*	*I'm **liking** school much better now.*
*Holidays **cost** a lot of money.*	*This trip **is costing** me a lot of money.*

Sometimes we can use either the simple or the continuous with no difference in meaning.
   *You **look** well.* OR *You're **looking** well.*   *We **feel** a bit sad.* OR *We're **feeling** a bit sad.*

Practice

A States and actions (1)

Tom is on the Internet. He's telling people about himself.
Say which verbs express states and which express actions.

▶ I <u>surf</u> the Net most evenings.   action
1 My flat <u>is</u> in the town centre.   ....
2 I <u>drive</u> a taxi in the daytime.   ....
3 I <u>own</u> two cars.   ....
4 I <u>go</u> to lots of parties.   ....
5 I <u>love</u> football.   ....

B I think/I'm thinking etc. (2)

Complete the conversation. Choose the correct form of the verb.

Emma: Hi, Matthew. What (▶) <u>do you look/are you looking</u> at?
Matthew: Oh, hi. These are photos of me when I was a child.
Emma: Oh, look at this one. (1) <u>I think/I'm thinking</u> you look lovely, Matthew.
Matthew: (2) <u>I have/I'm having</u> some more photos here.
Emma: Look at this. Why such a big coat?
Matthew: It was my brother's. That's why (3) <u>it didn't fit/it wasn't fitting</u> properly.
Emma: Oh, (4) <u>I see/I'm seeing</u>. And (5) <u>you have/you're having</u> your tea here. And in this one
           (6) <u>you think/you're thinking</u> about something very serious.
Matthew: This is a photo of the village (7) <u>I come/I'm coming</u> from.
Emma: Oh, that's nice.
Matthew: And I caught this fish, look. (8) <u>It weighed/It was weighing</u> about half a kilo.
Emma: What a nice little boy! And what a sentimental old thing you are now!

C The verb be (2)

Put in the correct form of be.

▶ Daniel is doing some of the work. He 's being .... very helpful at the moment.
▶ I'm .... tired. I want to go home.
1 The children .... very polite today. They don't usually behave so well.
2 I'm afraid Melanie can't come because she .... ill.
3 Of course you can understand it. You .... stupid, that's all.
4 We .... interested in doing a course here.
5 Vicky .... very lazy at the moment. She's done no work at all today.

D I like/I'm liking etc. (3)

Write a sentence which follows on. Choose from these sentences.

I think it's going to be perfect for me.   *And I've still got a chance to win.*
I've never wanted to change it.   *It uses so much petrol.*
It's too expensive to buy.   *I play it every weekend.*

▶ I enjoy the game. I play it every weekend. ....
1 I'm enjoying the game. ....
2 The car costs a lot of money. ....
3 The car is costing a lot of money. ....
4 I'm liking my new job. ....
5 I like my job. ....

Test A: Tenses – present

A

Read the conversation between two students. Then look at the answers below and write the correct answer in each space.

Lisa: Who (▶) ..is..... Michelle talking to?
Amy: I can't see Michelle.
Lisa: You (1) .... looking in the right place. She's over there.
Amy: Oh, that's Adrian. He's new here.
Lisa: Really? Where (2) .... he live? (3) ....
        you know?
Amy: No, I (4) .... know anything else about him.
Lisa: What (5) .... they talking about, I wonder?
Amy: Well, he (6) .... look very interested. He's got a very bored
        expression on his face. And he (7) .... saying anything.

▶	a) are	b) do	c) does	d) is
1	a) aren't	b) doesn't	c) don't	d) isn't
2	a) are	b) do	c) does	d) is
3	a) Are	b) Do	c) Does	d) Is
4	a) aren't	b) doesn't	c) don't	d) 'm not
5	a) are	b) do	c) does	d) is
6	a) aren't	b) doesn't	c) don't	d) isn't
7	a) aren't	b) doesn't	c) don't	d) isn't

B

Read Tessa's postcard to Angela and write the missing words. Use one word only in each space.

We're (▶) ..having..... a great time here. It's beautiful, and the sun (1) ....
shining. Yesterday I went water-skiing! What (2) .... you think of that?

I'm (3) .... at a table in our hotel room and writing a few postcards. The
room is fine, but we (4) .... like the food very much. But it
(5) .... matter because we (6) .... out to a
restaurant every evening.

We're both (7) .... very lazy at the moment. I
(8) .... up quite late in the morning, and Nigel (9) ....
.... up even later. You know of course how much Nigel's work (10) .... to
him and how he's (11) .... talking about it. Well, the holiday is so good that
he's forgotten all about work. So it's the perfect holiday. The only problem is that it's
(12) .... us a lot of money. But we'll worry about that later.

C

Each of these sentences has a mistake in it. Write the correct sentence.

▶ ~~The children is doing their homework now.~~
   The children are doing their homework now.

1 ~~The girls are play tennis at the moment.~~

   ....

2 ~~Both my brothers likes sport.~~

   ....

3   Anna wearing her new coat today.

   ....

4   What colour you like best?

   ....

5   My suitcase is weighing ten kilos.

   ....

6   At the moment I stay at a hotel.

   ....

7   Robert catch the same bus every morning.

   ....

8   What is this word here mean?

   ....

D

Complete the conversations. Put in the correct form of each verb.
Use the Present Continuous or the Present Simple.

▶ A: Is Janet in, please?
   B: Yes, but _I think_ (I / think) she's busy at the moment. _She's washing_ (she / wash)
       her hair.

1 A: .... (I / think) of buying a new computer.
   B: But computers .... (cost) so much money. What's wrong with the
       one we've got?
   A: .... (it / get) out of date now.

2 A: Your new trousers .... (look) nice.
   B: Thank you. The trouble is .... (they / not / fit) properly.
       .... (I / not / know) why I bought them, really.

3 A: What .... (you / do)?
   B: .... (I / weigh) this letter. .... (I / need)
       to know how many stamps to put on it.

4 A: .... (I / think) this road is really dangerous. Look how fast that lorry
       .... (go).
   B: .... (I / agree). People shouldn't go so fast.

5 A: .... (I / like) musicals. And this is a great show, isn't it?
       .... (you / enjoy) it?
   B: Yes, I am. .... (I / love) every minute of it.

6 A: .... (I / always / fall) asleep. I just can't keep awake.
   B: What time .... (you / go) to bed?
   A: About ten o'clock usually. But .... (it / not / make) any difference.

7 A: Could you post the goods to me, please?
   B: Yes, certainly.
   A: .... (I / live) at a guest house at the moment as
       .... (I / look) for a flat. So could you send it to my work address?
   B: Yes, of course. And you'll have the goods by the end of the week,
       .... (I / promise).

8 A: Why .... (you / want) to change the whole plan?
   B: I'm just not happy with it.
   A: And .... (I / not / understand) why ....
       (you / be) so difficult about it.

8 The Past Simple

1 Introduction

> It all **happened** very quickly. The car **came** straight out of the side road, and the van **went** into the back of it. The van driver **didn't have** a chance. It **was** the car driver's fault.

2 Positive forms

A regular past form ends in **-ed**.

> It **happened** very quickly.   The van **crashed** into the car.
> I **posted** the letter yesterday.   We once **owned** a caravan.

For spelling rules, see page 370.

Some verbs have an irregular past form.

> The car **came** out of a side road.   Vicky **rang** earlier.   I **won** the game.
> I **had** breakfast at six.   The train **left** on time.   We **took** some photos.

For a list of irregular verbs, see page 383.

The Past Simple is the same in all persons except in the past tense of **be**.

POSITIVE	
I/he/she/it **was**	I **was** ill last week.
you/we/they **were**	Those cakes **were** nice.

3 Negatives and questions

NEGATIVE	QUESTION
I/you/he/she/it/we/they **did not stop**	**did** I/you/he/she/it/we/they **stop**?
OR **didn't stop**	

> The car **did not stop**.   The driver **didn't look** to his right.
> What **did** you tell **the** police? ~ Nothing.   **Did** you ring home? ~ Yes, I did.

We do not use a past form such as **stopped** or **rang** in negatives and questions.

> NOT ~~The car didn't stopped~~ and NOT ~~Did you rang?~~

We also use **was** and **were** in negatives and questions.

NEGATIVE	QUESTION
I/he/she/it **was not** OR **wasn't**	**was** I/he/she/it?
you/we/they **were not** OR **weren't**	**were** you/we/they?

> I **wasn't** very well last week.   The gates **weren't** open.
> Where **was** your friend last night?   **Was** your steak nice?

4 Use

We use the Past Simple for something in the past which is finished.

> Emma **passed** her exam **last year**.   We **went** to the theatre **on Friday**.   Elvis Presley **died in 1977**.
> I **knew** what the problem **was**.   **When did** you **buy** this car? ~ About **three years ago**.

> ▷ 10 Past Continuous or Past Simple?   ▷ 14–15 Present Perfect or Past Simple?

Practice

A Positive forms (2)

What did Claire do on holiday last month? Look at her photos and use these words:
go out dancing, *have a picnic*, <u>*lie on the beach*</u>, *play volleyball*, *swim in the sea*

▶   1   2   3   4

▶   She lay on the beach. ....

1   3   ....

2   4   ....

B Positive forms (2)

Complete the newspaper story about a fire. Put in the Past Simple forms of the verbs.

Two people (▶) .died.......... (die) in a fire in Ellis Street, Oldport yesterday morning. They
(1).. (be) Herbert and Molly Paynter, a couple in their seventies. The fire
(2) .... (start) at 3.20 a.m. A neighbour, Mr Aziz,
(3) .... (see) the flames and (4) .... (call) the fire
brigade. He also (5) .... (try) to get into the house and rescue his
neighbours, but the heat (6) .... (be) too great. The fire brigade
(7) .... (arrive) in five minutes. Twenty fire-fighters
(8) .... (fight) the fire and finally (9) .... (bring) it
under control. Two fire-fighters (10) .... (enter) the burning building but
(11) .... (find) the couple dead.

C Negatives and questions (3)

Complete the conversation. Put in the Past Simple negatives and questions.

Claire: (▶) .Did you have..... (you / have) a nice weekend in Paris?
Mark: Yes, thanks. It was good. We looked around and then we saw a show.
        (1) .... (we / not / try) to do too much.
Claire: What sights (2) .... (you / see)?
Mark: We had a look round the Louvre. (3) .... (I / not / know)
        there was so much in there.
Claire: And what show (4) .... (you / go) to?
Mark: Oh, a musical. I forget the name. (5) .... (I / not / like) it.
Claire: Oh, dear. And (6) .... (Sarah / enjoy) it?
Mark: No, not really. But we enjoyed the weekend. Sarah did some shopping, too, but
        (7) .... (I / not / want) to go shopping.

9 Past Continuous

1 Introduction

The Past Continuous means that at a time in the past we were in the middle of an action.

> I had a wonderful dream last night. I **was sitting** in a park. The sun **was shining**, and the birds **were singing**. Children **were playing** and **laughing**. It was very peaceful. I didn't want to wake up.

2 Form

The Past Continuous is the past tense of **be** + an -ing form.

POSITIVE

I/he/she/it **was playing**
you/we/they **were playing**

NEGATIVE

I/he/she/it **wasn't playing**
you/we/they **weren't playing**

QUESTION

was I/he/she/it **playing?**
were you/we/they **playing?**

Soft music **was playing**.   People **were walking** in the park.
I **wasn't dreaming**. I really was in New York City.
Why did you give our secret away? What **were** you **thinking** of?
Was Matthew already **waiting** for you when you got there?

3 Use

Read this conversation.

Melanie: *I rang at about three yesterday afternoon, but you weren't in. I didn't know where you were.*
David: *Oh, I **was helping** Mike. We **were repairing** his car. It took ages. We **were working** on it all afternoon.*
Melanie: *It **was raining**. I hope you **weren't doing** it outside.*
David: *No, we were in the garage. So I didn't get wet. But I'm afraid I got oil all over my new trousers.*
Melanie: *Why **were** you **wearing** your new trousers to repair a car?*
David: *I don't know. I forgot I had them on.*

It was raining at three o'clock means that at three o'clock we were in the middle of a period of rain. The rain began before three and stopped some time after three. *We were working all afternoon* means that the action went on for the whole period. David is stressing the length of time that the work went on.

We use the continuous with actions. We do not normally use it with state verbs (see Unit 7). For states we use the Past Simple.

I didn't know where you were. NOT *I ~~wasn't knowing~~ ...*

▷ 10 Past Continuous or Past Simple?

Practice

A Form (2)

Today is the first of January, the start of a new year. Most people are feeling a bit tired.
What were they doing at midnight last night?
Use these verbs: *dance*, *drive*, *listen*, *watch*, *write*
Use these phrases after the verb: *an essay*, *his taxi*, *in the street*, *television*, *to a band*

▶ Claire .was. listening .to a band.
1 Trevor and Laura ....
2 Vicky and Rachel ....
3 Tom ....
4 Andrew ....

B Form (2)

Complete the conversation. Put in the Past Continuous forms.

Jessica: (▶) .I. was. looking................. (I / look) for you, Vicky. I'm afraid I've broken this dish.
Vicky: Oh no! What (1) .... (you / do)?
Jessica: (2) .... (I / take) it into the kitchen. I bumped into
          Emma. (3) .... (she / come) out just as
          (4) .... (I / go) in.
Vicky: I expect it was your fault. (5) .... (you / not / look)
          where (6) .... (you / go).
Jessica: Sorry. I'll buy you another one as soon as I have some money.

C Use (3)

**What can you say in these situations? Add a sentence with the Past Continuous
to say that an action lasted a long time.**

▶ You had to work yesterday. The work went on all day.
   .I. was. working. all. day. ....
1 You had to make phone calls. The calls went on all evening.
   ....
2 You had to wait in the rain. The wait lasted for half an hour.
   ....
3 You had to make sandwiches. This went on all afternoon.
   ....
4 You had to sit in a traffic jam. You were there for two hours.
   ....
5 Your neighbour played loud music. This went on all night.
   ....

10 Past Continuous or Past Simple?

1 Introduction

A reporter is interviewing Mike and Harriet.

Reporter: *Mike and Harriet, tell me what you **saw**.*

Harriet: *Well, when we **were driving** home last night, we **saw** a strange object in the sky.*

Mike: *As we **were coming** down the hill into town, it just suddenly **appeared** in front of us.
We **stopped** the car and **got** out.*

Harriet: *It **was** a very clear night. The stars **were twinkling**.*

Mike: *It **was** a spaceship. It **seemed** quite big. It **had** some strange writing on the side. And a light **was flashing** on the top.*

Harriet: *As we **were watching** it, it suddenly **flew** away and **disappeared**.*

PAST CONTINUOUS	PAST SIMPLE
We use the Past Continuous for an action that we were in the middle of.	We use the Past Simple for a complete action in the past.
We **were driving** home.	We **drove** home.
(We were in the middle of our journey.)	(We finished our journey.)
A light **was flashing**.	The spaceship **flew** away.
We do not normally use the Past Continuous for states. See Unit 7.	We also use the Past Simple (not normally the Continuous) for states. See Unit 7.
NOT *The spaceship was seeming …*	The spaceship **seemed** quite big.
NOT *It was having writing …*	It **had** writing on the side.
NOT *I wasn't knowing …*	I **didn't know** what it was.

2 It happened as I was driving

We often use the Past Continuous and Past Simple together when one (shorter) action comes in the middle of another (longer) one.

*As we **were driving** down the hill, a strange object **appeared** in the sky.*
*While Laura **was sitting** in the garden, it suddenly **began** to rain.*
*You **drove** right past me when I **was waiting** for the bus.*

The appearance of the strange object comes in the middle of the longer action, the drive down the hill.

Longer action: *We were driving down the hill.*
Shorter action: *An object appeared.*

In the three sentences above, the Past Continuous comes after **as**, **while** or **when** (**As** we **were driving** ...). We can also use **when** before the Past Simple.

*We **were driving** down the hill **when** a strange object **appeared** in the sky.*
*David **was making** lunch **when** the phone **rang**.*

But we use two Past Simple verbs for one action after another.

*When we **saw** the spaceship, we **stopped** the car.* (= We saw it and then we stopped.)

3 The sun was shining

PAST CONTINUOUS	PAST SIMPLE
We often use the Past Continuous to describe the background.	We use the Past Simple for actions in a story.
The sun **was shining**.	We **arrived** at the beach.
The stars **were twinkling**.	The aliens **landed** quietly.

Practice

A Past Continuous or Past Simple? (1–2)

David is always having accidents. His girlfriend Melanie is talking about some of the accidents. Write her sentences from these notes. Each sentence has one verb in the Past Continuous and one in the Past Simple.

▶ when / he / carry / a suitcase / he / drop / it / on his foot
   When he was carrying a suitcase, he dropped it on his foot.

▶ he / break / his leg / when / he / ski
   He broke his leg when he was skiing.

1 he / sit down / on a chair / while / I / paint / it
   ....

2 as / he / run / for a bus / he / collide / with a lamppost
   ....

3 his hair / catch / fire / when / he / cook / chips
   ....

4 when / he / hold / a beautiful vase / he / suddenly / drop / it
   ....

5 he / sit / in the garden / when / a wasp / sting / him / on the nose
   ....

B Past Continuous or Past Simple? (1–2)

Put in the correct form of the verb.

Rita: I hear the lights (▶) ...went........... (go) out in your flats last night.

Emma: Yes, (▶) ..I was watching................. (I / watch) a documentary on TV when suddenly
        (1) .... (we / lose) all the power. But
        (2) .... (it / come) on again after about ten minutes.

Vicky: Rachel (3) .... (come) down the stairs when the lights
        (4) .... (go) out. She almost (5) ....
        (fall) over.

Daniel: Matthew and I (6) .... (play) table tennis at the time.

Andrew: (7) .... (I / work) on the computer. (8) ....
        .... (I / lose) a whole hour's work. But this morning (9) ....
        .... (I / get) up early and (10) .... (do) it again.

C Past Continuous or Pasy Simple? (1–3)

Find the second part of each sentence. Put each verb into the correct form.

▶ Vicky (have) a beautiful dream   when she (touch) the wire.
▶ When Andrew (see) the question,   when I (find) a £10 note in it.
1 The train (wait)   when the alarm clock (ring).
2 I (read) a library book   the crowd (rush) in.
3 Sarah (have) an electric shock   he (know) the answer immediately.
4 When the doors (open),   they (see) that the sun (shine).
5 When the campers (wake),   when we (arrive) at the station.

▶ *Vicky was having a beautiful dream when the alarm clock rang.*
▶ *When Andrew saw the question, he knew the answer immediately.*
1 ....
2 ....
3 ....
4 ....
5 ....

Test B: Past Simple and Past Continuous

A

Put in the Past Simple of the verbs in brackets.

▶ The car .stopped........... (stop) at the lights.
1 We .... (leave) the cinema before the end of the film.
2 The streets .... (be) crowded with people.
3 My grandmother .... (die) last year.
4 Everyone .... (have) a marvellous time.
5 We .... (not / like) the food they gave us.
6 Claire .... (go) to Egypt last month.
7 The accident .... (happen) last weekend.
8 It .... (not / be) a very comfortable journey.
9 I .... (know) that ages ago.

B

Write a second sentence so that it has a similar meaning to the first. Use the word in brackets.

▶ There were lights on the spacecraft. (had)
  The spacecraft had lights on it...
1 I had my old coat on. (wearing)
  ....
2 I was on holiday, and you were on holiday, too. (we)
  ....
3 It isn't true that I made a mistake. (didn't)
  ....
4 The boys were in the middle of a game of cards. (playing)
  ....
5 No one told me about the change of plan. (know)
  ....
6 My friend was the winner of the competition. (won)
  ....
7 Is it a fact that the Romans built this wall? (did)
  ....

C

Lorna Bright is a long-distance walker. Look at this part of her diary describing a morning's walk along the coast. Write the missing words. Use one word only in each space.

It was a fine day (▶) .when.... I started out on the last part of my walk around the coast of Britain. The sun was (1) ...., and a light wind (2) .... blowing from the south-west. I was pleased that it (3) .... raining. I knew by now that I (4) .... like rain. In fact I (5) .... it. I (6) .... along the cliff top and then down into the lovely little fishing village of Wellburn, past a café where people (7) .... having morning coffee. Three miles past Wellburn I (8) .... down for five minutes and (9) .... a drink. Now it (10) .... getting warmer, so I (11) .... off one of my sweaters. I (12) .... stop for long because I (13) .... to reach Seabury by lunch-time. (14) .... I finally got there, it (15) .... just after half past twelve.

D

Each of these sentences has a mistake in it. Write the correct sentence.

► The hotel were very quiet.
  The hotel was very quiet.

1 It was peaceful, and the birds were sing.

2 I washed my hair when the phone rang.

3 You came not to the club last night.

4 It taked ages to get home.

5 We tried to keep quiet because the baby sleeping.

6 As I was watching him, the man was suddenly running away.

7 We pass a petrol-station two minutes ago.

8 Everything was seeming OK.

9 Where bought you that bag?

10 When I heard the alarm, I was leaving the room immediately.

E

Complete the sentences. Put in the correct form of each verb. Use the Past Continuous or Past Simple.

► When Martin arrived (arrive) home, Anna was talking (talk) to someone on the phone. Martin started (start) to get the tea.

1 I .... (lie) in the bath when the phone .... (ring). It .... (stop) after a few rings.

2 It .... (be) cold when we .... (leave) the house that day, and a light snow .... (fall).

3 Your friend who .... (come) here the other day .... (seem) very nice. I .... (enjoy) meeting her.

4 When I .... (see) the man, he .... (stand) outside the bank. He .... (have) a black baseball cap on.

5 When I .... (open) the cupboard door, a pile of books .... (fall) out.

6 I .... (walk) along the street when I suddenly .... (feel) something hit me in the back. I .... (not / know) what it was.

7 We .... (go) to London yesterday, but on the way we .... (hear) about a bomb scare in Oxford Street. So we .... (drive) back home straightaway.

8 Something very strange .... (happen) to me on my way home from work yesterday afternoon. I .... (drive) along the bypass at the time. Suddenly I .... (see) my mother in the seat beside me. But she died three years ago.

11 Present Perfect (1)

1 Introduction

The Present Perfect tells us about the past and the present.
The aircraft has landed means that the aircraft is on the ground now.

2 Form

The Present Perfect is the present tense of **have** + a past participle.

POSITIVE

I/you/we/they **have washed** OR *I/you/we/they***'ve washed**
he/she/it **has washed** OR *he/she/it***'s washed**

NEGATIVE	QUESTION
I/you/we/they **haven't washed**	**have** *I/you/we/they* **washed?**
he/she/it **hasn't washed**	**has** *he/she/it* **washed?**

Regular past participles end in -ed, e.g. **washed, landed, finished.**
    *We***'ve washed** *the dishes.*   **Have** *you* **opened** *your letter?*
    The aircraft **has landed** *safely.*   *How many points* **has** *Matthew* **scored?**
    The students **haven't finished** *their exams.*

3 Irregular forms

Some participles are irregular.
    I've **made** *a shopping list.*   *We've* **sold** *our car.*   *I've* **thought** *about it a lot.*
    Have you **written** *the letter?*   *She hasn't* **drunk** *her coffee.*
For a list of irregular verbs see page 383.

There is a Present Perfect of **be** and of **have.**
    The weather has **been** *awful.*   *I've* **had** *a lovely time, thank you.*

4 Use

When we use the Present Perfect, we see things as happening in the past but having a result in the present.
    *We***'ve washed** *the dishes.* (They're clean <u>now</u>.)   *The aircraft* **has landed**. (It's on the ground <u>now</u>.)
    *We***'ve eaten** *all the eggs.* (There aren't any left.)   *They***'ve learnt** *the words.* (They know the words.)
    *You***'ve broken** *this watch.* (It isn't working.)

▷ 12–13 More on the Present Perfect ▷ 14–15 Present Perfect or Past Simple?
▷ page 377 American English

Practice

A Form (2)

Add a sentence. Use the Present Perfect.

▶ I'm tired. (I / walk / miles) I've walked miles.
1 Emma's computer is working now. (she / repair / it) ....
2 It's cooler in here now. (I / open / the window) ....
3 The visitors are here at last. (they / arrive) ....
4 Mark's car isn't blocking us in now. (he / move / it) ....
5 We haven't got any new videos. (we / watch / all these) ....

B Irregular forms (3)

Look at the pictures and say what the people have done.
Use these verbs: *break, build, catch, see, win*
Use these objects: *a film, a fish, a house, his leg, the gold medal*

▶ She's won the gold medal.
1 .... 3 ....
2 .... 4 ....

C Review (1–4)

Trevor and Laura are decorating their house. Put in the verbs. Use the Present Perfect.

Laura: How is the painting going? (▶) Have you finished? .... (you / finish)
Trevor: No, I haven't. Painting the ceiling is really difficult, you know.
(1) .... (I / not / do) very much. And it looks just the
same as before. This new paint (2) .... (not / make) any
difference.
Laura: (3) .... (you / not / put) enough on.
Trevor: (4) .... (I / hurt) my back. It feels bad.
Laura: Oh, you and your back. You mean (5) .... (you / have)
enough of decorating. Well, I'll do it. Where (6) ....
(you / put) the brush?
Trevor: I don't know. (7) .... (it / disappear).
(8) .... (I / look) for it, but I can't find it.
Laura: You're hopeless, aren't you? How much (9) .... (you / do) in here?
Nothing! (10) .... (I / paint) two doors.
Trevor: (11) .... (I / clean) all this old paint around the window. It
looks much better now, doesn't it?
Laura: (12) .... (we / make) some progress, I suppose. Now,
where (13) .... (that brush / go)?
Oh, (14) .... (you / leave) it on the ladder, look.

12 Present Perfect (2): just, already, yet; for and since

VICKY SEES RACHEL OUTSIDE THE CONCERT HALL.

1 Just, already and yet

We can use the Present Perfect with **just**, **already** and **yet**.

Just means 'a short time ago'. Vicky heard about the concert not long ago. **Already** means 'sooner than expected'. They sold the tickets very quickly. We use **yet** when we are expecting something to happen. Vicky expects that Rachel will buy a ticket.

Just and **already** come before the past participle (**heard**, **sold**). **Yet** comes at the end of a question or a negative sentence.

Here are some more examples.
*We've **just come** back from our holiday.*
*I've **just had** an idea.*
*It isn't a very good party. Most people **have already gone** home.*
*My brother **has already crashed** his new car.*
*It's eleven o'clock and you **haven't finished** breakfast **yet**.*
***Has** your course **started yet**?*
But for American English see page 377.

2 For and since

We can use the Present Perfect with **for** and **since**.
*Vicky **has** only **had** that camera **for** three days.*　*Those people **have been** at the hotel **since** Friday.*
*I've **felt** really tired **for** a whole week now.*
*We've **lived** in Oxford **since** 1992.* NOT ~~We live here since 1992.~~
Here something began in the past and has lasted up to the present time.

We use **for** to say how long this period is (**for** three days). We use **since** to say when the period began (**since** Friday).

We use **how long** in questions.
***How long has** Vicky **had** that camera? ~ Since Thursday, I think.*
***How long have** Trevor and Laura **been** married? ~ Oh, for about three years.*

We can also use the Present Perfect with **for** and **since** when something has stopped happening.
*I **haven't seen** Rachel **for** ages. She **hasn't visited** us **since** July.*

▷ 11, 13 More on the Present Perfect　▷ 14–15 Present Perfect or Past Simple?
▷ 17 Present Perfect Continuous or Simple?　▷ 114 **Yet, still** and **already**　▷ 121 **For, since, ago** and **before**

Practice

A Just (1)

Write replies using the Present Perfect and *just*.
Use these past participles: *checked*, *eaten*, *made*, *remembered*, *rung*, *tidied*

▶ We must find out the address. ~ It's all right, I've just remembered it.
1 The children's room looks neat. ~ Yes, they've ....
2 Is Daniel making some coffee? ~ It's ready. ....
3 What happened to that chocolate? ~ Sorry, ...
4 Has Rachel got all the answers right? ~ Yes, ...
5 Have you told your sister? ~ Yes, I've ....

B Just, already and yet (1)

Complete the dialogue. Use the Present Perfect with *just*, *already* and *yet*.

Vicky: (▶) You haven't done your project yet (you / not do / your project / yet), I suppose.
Rachel: No, I haven't. (1) ....
         (I / not / start / it / yet).
Vicky: (2) .... (I / just / see / Andrew), and he says
         (3) .... (he / already / do) about half of it.
Rachel: Well, he works too hard.
Vicky: (4) ....
         (I / not / finish / my plan / yet).
Rachel: (5) .... (you / already / begin) to worry about it,
         haven't you? Take it easy. There's plenty of time.
Vicky: (6) .... (we / already / spend) too long thinking about
         it. (7) .... (I / not / do /
         any real work / yet) and (8) .... (I / just / realize) that
         there are only four weeks to the end of term.
Rachel: OK. (9) .... (I / just / decide) to start next week. Well,
         maybe.

C For and since (2)

Andrew is a very hard-working student. It's midnight and he is still working at his computer.
Write sentences with the Present Perfect and *for* or *since*.

▶ be / at his computer / six hours   He's been at his computer for six hours.
1 not / have / any fun / a long time   ....
2 have / a cold / a week   ....
3 not / see / his friends / ages   ....
4 not / do / any sport / last year   ....
5 be / busy with his studies / months   ....

D For and since (2)

Complete the sentences.

▶ You ought to wash the car. You haven't washed it for .... ages.
▶ I'd better have a shower. I haven't had one since ...... Thursday.
1 I think I'll ring my girlfriend. I haven't .... the weekend.
2 We're going to see some old friends. We haven't .... five years.
3 Let's watch a video, shall we? We haven't .... quite a while.
4 We could have a barbecue. We haven't .... last summer.
5 Shall we play tennis? We haven't .... our holiday.

13 Present Perfect (3): ever, this week, etc.

1 Gone to or been to?

Claire has **gone to** Australia.
Gone there means that she is still there.

Claire has **been to** Australia.
Been there means that the visit is over.

2 Ever and never

Mark: *Where have you been this time, Claire?*
Claire: *I've just come back from the States. Florida.*
Mark: *You get around, don't you? I've **never been** to Florida. Was it good?*
Claire: *It was OK. Not as good as Australia. I might go to Brazil next time. **Have** you **ever been** there?*
Mark: *No, I haven't.*

We can use **ever** and **never** with the Present Perfect. We use **ever** in questions. In *Have you ever been to Brazil?* the word **ever** means 'in your whole life up to the present time'. **Never** means 'not ever'.

Here are some more examples.
   Have *you **ever played** cricket? ~ No,* **never**.   **Has** *Andrew **ever had** any fun? ~ I don't think so.*
   *I've **never ridden** a motorbike in my life.   You've **never given** me flowers before.*
   *This is the most expensive hotel we've **ever stayed** in.*

3 First time, second time, etc.

After **It's/This is the first/second time**, we use the Present Perfect.
   *This is the **first time** we've **been** to Scotland, so it's all new to us.*
   *This is the **second time** Rachel **has forgotten** to give me a message.*
   *I love this film. I think it's the **fourth time** I've **seen** it.*

4 Today, this week, etc.

We use the Present Perfect with **today** and phrases with **this**, e.g. **this morning, this week, this year**.
   *We've **done** quite a lot of work **today**.*
   *I **haven't watched** any television so far **this week**.*
   Have *you **had** a holiday **this year**? ~ No, not yet.*
This year is the period which began in January and has lasted up to the present time.

▷ 14–15 Present Perfect or Past Simple?

A Gone to or been to? (1)

Complete the conversation. Put in *gone* or *been*.

Emma: Hi. Where's Rachel?
Vicky: She's (▶) ..gone.......... to the supermarket to get something for a meal.
Emma: But I've got some chicken for tonight. I've just (1) .... to a
supermarket on my way home, that new place near the station.
Natasha: I haven't (2) .... to that one yet.
Vicky: Where's Jessica? Isn't she here?
Emma: No, she's (3) .... to London. She'll be back tomorrow.

B Ever and never (2)

Write the questions and answers. Use the information in brackets.

▶ Matthew: (sailing?) .Have you ever been sailing?..
Natasha: (no, windsurfing) No, I've never been sailing, but I've been windsurfing.............
1 Laura: (San Francisco?) ....
Mark: (no, Los Angeles) .... ,
but ....
2 Tom: (basketball?) ....
Trevor: (no, volleyball) .... ,
but ....
3 Daniel: ('Hamlet'?) ....
Vicky: (no, 'Macbeth') .... ,
but ....

C First time, second time, etc. (3)

What would you say in these situations? Use *time* and the Present Perfect.

▶ You are watching a cricket match. You have never seen one before.
.This is the first time I've seen a cricket match..
1 You have lost your bank card. It has happened once before.
This is ....
2 The washing machine has broken down. This has happened twice before.
....
3 You are in England for the first time in your life.
....
4 You are staying in a hotel where you once stayed before.
....
5 You have missed the bus. You've done the same thing about four times before.
....

D Today, this week, etc. (4)

Complete the sentences. Use the Present Perfect.

▶ Mark buys a newspaper most mornings, but .he hasn't bought one this morning.....................
1 I see Vicky most days, but ....
2 We go to the club most weekends, but ....
3 We usually have a party each term, but ....
4 Someone usually rings in the evening, but no one ....

14 Present Perfect or Past Simple? (1)

1 I have done or I did?

> We**'ve won** the Cup! It's ours at last!

> Well, we **won** the Cup last year.

The Present Perfect tells us about the past and the present. United have won the Cup, so it's theirs now.	The Past Simple tells us about the past, a time which is finished. Last year is in the past.

We use the Past Simple (not the Present Perfect) to talk about times in the past such as **yesterday**, **last week**, **in 1994**, **a hundred years ago**.

> We **watched** United **last week**. NOT ~~We have watched United last week.~~
> **Long ago** dinosaurs **lived** here. NOT ~~Long ago dinosaurs have lived here.~~

Here are some more examples.

PRESENT PERFECT	PAST SIMPLE
Emma **has packed** her case. (So her things are in the case now.)	Emma **packed** her case **last night**. (Her things may be unpacked now.)
Mike **has repaired** the chair. (So it's all right now.)	Mike **repaired** the chair. (It may be broken again now.)
The plane **has** just **landed**.	The plane **landed ten minutes ago**.
I**'ve turned** the heating on. (It's on now.)	I **turned** the heating on **earlier**, but it's off again now.
I**'ve dropped** my calculator. (It's on the floor now.)	I **dropped** my calculator, but it seems to be OK.

2 I've done it. I did it yesterday.

Trevor: *We**'ve bought** a new car.*
Tom: *Oh, have you? What sort?*
Laura: *An Adagio. We **bought** it last week.*

We often give a piece of news in the Present Perfect, e.g. *We've bought a new car.* (The car is ours now.) We use the Past Simple, e.g. *We bought it last week,* to give details or to ask for details about things such as when and where it happened.

Here are some more examples.

> I**'ve found** my wallet. ~ Oh, good. Where **did** you **find** it?
> Your parcel **has arrived**. The postman **brought** it at eight o'clock.
> They**'ve closed** the factory. ~ Really? When **did** they **do** that?

3 Structures with **for, since** and **last**

PRESENT PERFECT	PAST SIMPLE
We can say that something hasn't happened <u>for</u> a long time or <u>since</u> a specific time in the past.	We can say that it is a long time <u>since</u> something happened or when was <u>the last time</u> it happened.
We **haven't had** a party **for** ages.	It's ages **since** we **last had** a party.
We **haven't had** a party **since** Christmas.	Christmas was **the last time** we **had** a party.

Practice

A I have done or I did? (1)

Put in the correct verb form.

▶ I've done........ (I / do) all the housework. The flat is really clean now.

▶ A young couple bought........ (buy) the house next door. But they didn't live there long.

1 Our visitors .... (arrive). They're sitting in the garden.

2 There's still a problem with the television. Someone .... (repair) it, but then it broke down again.

3 .... (I / lose) my bank card. I can't find it anywhere.

4 The match .... (start). United are playing well.

5 My sister .... (run) away from home. But she came back two days later.

6 Daniel .... (earn) some money last week. But I'm afraid he's already spent it all.

7 .... (we / plant) an apple tree in the garden. Unfortunately it died.

8 Prices .... (go) up. Everything is more expensive this year.

9 Someone .... (turn) on the hi-fi. What's that song called?

10 .... (I / phone) the office at eleven to speak to the manager, but he isn't there today.

11 .... (I / make) a cake. Would you like a piece?

12 The runner Amos Temila .... (break) the world record for the 1500 metres in Frankfurt. Then two days later in Helsinki, Lee Williams ran it in an even faster time.

B I've done it. I did it yesterday. (2)

Things that have happened today are on the radio and TV news.
Give the news using the Present Perfect and Past Simple.

▶ the Prime Minister / visit Luton University / speak to students there / earlier today
  The Prime Minister has visited Luton University. He spoke to students there earlier today.

1 the train drivers / go on strike / stop work / at twelve o'clock
  ....

2 the Queen / arrive in Toronto / fly there / in an RAF aircraft
  ....

3 two men / escape from Parkhurst Prison / get away / during the night
  ....

4 the actor Howard Bates / die in a car accident / his car / crash into a wall
  ....

5 Linda Jones / win the women's marathon / run it / in 2 hours 27 minutes
  ....

C Structures with for, since and last (3)

Complete the conversations.

▶ Mike: This car is filthy. I haven't been to the car wash for about a year.
  Tom: What! You mean it's twelve months since you last went.......... to the car wash?

1 Laura: I haven't used my camera recently. June was the last time I took a photo.
  Trevor: Really? I'm surprised you .... June.

2 Rachel: I haven't seen Andrew for weeks.
  Daniel: Nor me. It's .... him.

3 Tom: What about a game of cards? We haven't played since your birthday.
  David: Really? You mean my birthday .... cards?

4 Emma: I feel terrible. It's three days since I ate anything.
  Vicky: What did you say? You .... three days?

15 Present Perfect or Past Simple? (2)

1 I've been or I was?

PRESENT PERFECT	PAST SIMPLE
We use the Present Perfect for a state which has gone on up to the present. (David is still in hospital.)	We use the Past Simple for a state in the past, in a period which is finished. (David's stay in hospital is over.)
We've lived here for ten years.	*We lived there for ten years.*
(And we still live here.)	(We don't live there now.)

2 Have you (ever) ...? and Did you (ever) ...?

PRESENT PERFECT	PAST SIMPLE
We use the Present Perfect for actions in a period of time up to the present.	We use the Past Simple for actions in the past, a period which is finished.
*This young director **has made** four films so far.* *He has made films* means that it is possible he will make more films.	*The director **made** many films in his long career.* *He made films* means that his career in films is over. He won't make any more.
Here are some more examples.	
***Have** you **ever been** to America? ~ Yes, twice.*	*Did Churchill **ever go** to America? ~ Yes, I think so.*
*I've **played** table tennis before.*	*I **played** table tennis at college.*
*We've **never had** any money.*	*We **never had** any money in those days.*

3 Today, this week, etc.

PRESENT PERFECT	PAST SIMPLE
We use **today** and phrases with **this** for a period up to the present.	We use **yesterday** and phrases with **last** for a past period.
*It **hasn't rained today**.*	*It **rained yesterday**.*
***Have** you **seen this** week's magazine?*	***Did** you **see last** week's magazine?*

But sometimes **today** etc. can mean a past period. Compare:

*I **haven't seen** Rachel **today**.*	*I **didn't see** Sarah at work **today**.*
(It's still daytime.)	(The working day is over.)
***Has** the post **come this** morning?*	***Did** the post **come this** morning?*
(It's still morning.)	(It's later in the day.)

Practice

A I've been or I was? (1)

Complete this letter to a newspaper. Put in the Present Perfect or Past Simple.

A few days ago I (▶) .learned......... (learn) that someone plans to knock down the White Horse Inn. This pub (▶) .has been..... (be) the centre of village life for centuries. It (1) .... (stand) at our crossroads for 500 years. It (2) .... (be) famous in the old days, and Shakespeare once (3) .... (stay) there, they say. I (4) .... (live) in Brickfield all my life. The villagers (5) .... (know) about the plans for less than a week and already there's a 'Save Our Pub' campaign. Last week we (6) .... (be) happy, but this week we're angry. We will stop them, you'll see.

B Have you (ever) ...? and Did you (ever) ...? (2)

Look at each conversation and choose the best sentence, a) or b).

▶ Have you heard about the woman walking across the US? ~ Yes, she's reached the Rockies.
   a) ☑ The walk is continuing.   b) ☐ The walk has finished.
1 Have you ever played beach volleyball? ~ Yes, we played it on holiday.
   a) ☐ The holiday is still going on.   b) ☐ The holiday is over.
2 Did you know old Mr Green? ~ No, I never met him.
   a) ☐ Mr Green is probably alive.   b) ☐ Mr Green is probably dead.
3 Wayne Johnson is a great footballer. ~ Yes, he's scored 200 goals for United.
   a) ☐ Wayne Johnson still plays for United.   b) ☐ Wayne Johnson has left United.

C Today, this week, etc (3)

Put in this, last, today or yesterday.

▶ .Last...... month prices went up, but .this......... month they have fallen a little.
1 It's been dry so far .... week, but .... week was very wet.
2 I went shopping earlier .... and spent all the money I earned ....
3 We didn't have many visitors .... year. We've had a lot more .... year.
4 I don't feel so tired now. We got up quite late .... morning. I felt really tired .... when we got up so early.

D Present Perfect or Past Simple? (Units 14 and 15)

Put in the verbs.

Tom: (▶) .Have you heard....... (you / hear) the news about David?
Harriet: No. (1) .... (what / happen)?
Tom: (2) .... (he / have) an accident. He was walking down some steps. (3) .... (he / fall) and (4) .... (break) his leg.
Harriet: Oh, how awful! When (5) .... (it / happen)?
Tom: Yesterday afternoon. Melanie (6) .... (tell) me about it last night.
Harriet: Last night! (7) .... (you / know) about it last night, and (8) .... (you / not / tell) me!
Tom: Well, (9) .... (I / not / see) you last night. And (10) .... (I / not / see) you today, until now.
Harriet: I hope he's all right. (11) .... (he / have) lots of accidents, you know. (12) .... (he / do) the same thing about two years ago.

Test C: Present Perfect and Past Simple

A

Put in the past participles of the verbs in brackets.

► We've ..found............... (find) all the answers.
1 Have you .... (wash) the car?
2 You haven't .... (eat) very much.
3 They've .... (open) a new supermarket.
4 You've .... (write) it in pencil.
5 I've .... (make) the sandwiches.
6 We've .... (have) our lunch.
7 United have .... (score) a goal.
8 The balloon has .... (land) in a field.
9 Who's .... (break) this glass?
10 It's warm because the heating has .... (be) on.
11 Have you .... (sell) your flat yet?
12 I've .... (finish) that job at last.

B

Complete the second sentence so that it follows on from the first. Use the Present Perfect.

► My hair is tidy now. I ..'ve brushed......... my hair.
1 The door is open. Someone .... the door.
2 This is Oliver's drawing, look. Oliver .... a picture.
3 The calculator is broken. Someone .... the calculator.
4 United are the winners. United .... the game.
5 There's no more wine in the bottle. We .... all the wine.
6 The floor is clean now. I .... the floor.
7 I know my number now. I .... my number by heart.
8 The guests are here now. The guests ....
9 I'm still working on the computer. I .... with the computer yet.

C

Decide which word is correct.

► I'd like to borrow this book. Has Anna read it ..yet.... ?
   a) done   b) for   c) just   d) yet
1 Ben writes very quickly. He's .... finished his essay.
   a) already   b) been   c) for   d) yet
2 What are you going to do? ~ I don't know. I haven't decided ....
   a) just   b) long   c) since   d) yet
3 I've .... to London. I went there in June.
   a) been   b) gone   c) just   d) yet
4 Have you .... done any skiing?
   a) ever   b) for   c) just   d) long
5 My boyfriend hasn't rung .... week.
   a) for   b) last   c) since   d) this
6 I haven't seen that coat before. How .... have you had it?
   a) already   b) for   c) long   d) since
7 The girls have .... to the cinema. They won't be back until ten o'clock.
   a) already   b) been   c) gone   d) just

8 I haven't seen my parents .... last Christmas.
   a) already   b) before   c) for   d) since
9 This is the first .... I've ever lived away from home.
   a) already   b) since   c) that   d) time
10 This programme must be new. I've .... seen it before.
   a) ever   b) never   c) since   d) yet

D

Some of these sentences are correct, and some have a word which should not be there. If the sentence is correct, put a tick (✓). If it is incorrect, cross the unnecessary *have* or *has* out of the sentence and write it in the space.

▶ Susan has lost her keys. She can't find them anywhere.   ✓ ....
▶ Christopher has hurt his hand, but it's OK now.   *has* ....
1 The directors have arrived half an hour ago, but they didn't stay long.   ....
2 It's raining, and Peter has left his umbrella behind, look.   ....
3 It's a long time since your friends have last visited us.   ....
4 None of you have called me for weeks. Aren't we friends any more?   ....
5 We can play tennis now. The others have finished.   ....
6 The company has bought some land, but then it sold it.   ....
7 The computer isn't on now. Someone has turned it off.   ....
8 Tessa has posted the parcel. It's on its way to you.   ....
9 Several bombs have gone off in the city centre. It has happened   ....
   an hour ago.
10 Simon has left. He and Oliver have left after lunch.   ....

E

Put in the Present Perfect or Past Simple of the verbs in brackets.

▶ I 've had .... (have) these shoes since my eighteenth birthday.
▶ I tidied .... (tidy) my desk, but now it's in a mess again.
1 The last time I .... (go) to Brighton was in August.
2 I'd like to meet a ghost, but I .... (never / see) one.
3 I've finished my homework. I .... (do) it before tea.
4 And the race is over! And Micky Simpson .... (win) in a
   record time!
5 I .... (work) for a computer company for a year. That was
   after college.
6 What time .... (you / get) to work this morning?
7 Martin .... (be) to Greece five times. He loves the place.
8 The President .... (come) out of the building and is going to
   make a speech.
9 You won't believe this, but I've got some tickets for the concert. ~ Oh, well done.
   How .... (you / get) them?
10 Of course I can ride a bike. But I .... (not / ride) one for years.
11 Marilyn Monroe .... (be) in about thirty films.
12 .... (you / ever / bake) your own bread? ~ No, but I might try it
   some time.
13 Janet .... (be) very ill three years ago.
14 Rupert has left a message for you. He .... (ring) last night.
15 .... (you / see) the news today? ~ No, not yet. I'll watch it at ten.
16 We moved here in 1993. We .... (be) here a long time now.

16 Present Perfect Continuous

1 Introduction

We use the Present Perfect Continuous for an action (*waiting*). The action happens over a period of time (*for twenty minutes*). Here the period lasts up to the present – they are still waiting now.

2 Form

The Present Perfect Continuous is the present tense of **have** + **been** + an -ing form.

POSITIVE

I/you/we/they **have been waiting** OR I/you/we/they'**ve been waiting**
he/she/it **has been waiting** OR he/she/it'**s been waiting**

NEGATIVE

I/you/we/they **haven't been waiting**
he/she/it **hasn't been waiting**

QUESTION

have I/you/we/they **been waiting?**
has he/she/it **been waiting?**

*We'**ve been standing** here for ages.*   *It **has been raining** all day.*
***Have** you **been waiting** long?*   *Our team **hasn't been doing** very well lately.*

3 Use

We use the Present Perfect Continuous for an action over a period of time leading up to the present (see 1). In these examples the action is still going on.

*We'**ve been waiting** here for twenty minutes.* (We're waiting <u>now</u>.)
*Listen. That burglar alarm **has been ringing** since eight o'clock this morning.*

We must use the perfect in these situations.

NOT ~~We wait here for twenty minutes~~ OR ~~We're waiting here for twenty minutes.~~

We can use the Present Perfect Continuous to talk about repeated actions up to now.

*Natasha **has been playing** the piano since she was four.*

We can also use it to talk about an action which ends just before the present.

*I'**ve been swimming**. That's why my hair is wet.*

4 For, since, how long and recently

We can use the Present Perfect Continuous with **for** and **since** (see Unit 121).

*My sister **has been staying** with me **for** three weeks now.*
*You'**ve been playing** on that computer **since** seven o'clock.*

We use **how long** in questions.

How long have** you **been waiting?

Note also **recently** and **lately**. These both mean 'in the last few days or weeks'.

*I **haven't been feeling** very well **recently**.*   *What **have** you **been doing lately**?*

▷ 17 Present Perfect Continuous or Simple?   ▷ 121 **For** and **since**

Practice

A Form (2)

Put in the verbs. Use the Present Perfect Continuous.

Ilona: Sorry I'm late.

Emma: It's OK. (▶) .I..haven't..been..waiting...... (I / not / wait) long.
What (1) .... (you / do)?

Ilona: I've been with Mrs King. (2) .... (she / help) me with my
English.

Emma: Your English is very good. You don't need lessons, surely.
How long (3) .... (you / study) English?

Ilona: Er, eight years now. But my accent wasn't so good before I came to England.
(4) .... (I / try) to improve it.
I think (5) .... (it / get) better lately.

Emma: Your accent is fine, Ilona. Honestly.

B Use (3)

Say what these people have been doing. Use these verbs: *argue, cook, drive, wait, work*

▶   Andrew is tired because .he's..been..working............. all day.

1   Trevor and Laura are upset because ....

2   David is hot because ....

3   Mark feels very stiff because .... all day.

4   Henry is annoyed. .... a long time for Claire.

C Use (3–4)

**What could you say in these situations? Write sentences with the Present Perfect Continuous and
a phrase with *for*. Use these verbs:** *play, read, swim, talk, travel, work*

▶   A video is on. It began two hours ago, and it hasn't finished yet.
The..video..has..been..playing..for..two..hours. ....

1   Matthew went into the water an hour ago. He doesn't want to come out yet.
....

2   Your friends started their journey around the world three months ago. They've gone about halfway
now.
....

3   Mark got to the office early this morning. Ten hours later he's still there.
....

4   Melanie rang Rita forty minutes ago, and they're still on the phone.
....

5   Trevor has got an interesting book. He started it quite a long time ago. Ask him how long.
....

17 Present Perfect Continuous or Simple?

1 I have been doing or I have done?

Sorry I can't help. I've got oil on my hands.

The car is all right now. We can go into town if you like.

*Mike **has been repairing** the car.*	*Mike **has repaired** the car.*
We use the Present Perfect Continuous for an action happening over a period of time (see Unit 16). We are thinking of Mike doing the repair and getting oil on his hands.	We use the Present Perfect Simple for a complete action (see Unit 11). We are thinking of the finished repair and the result of the repair – that the car is all right now.

Here are some more examples.

OVER A PERIOD (**have been doing**)	COMPLETE (**have done**)
*We**'ve been touring** Scotland.*	*We**'ve finished** our tour of Scotland.*
*A strong wind **has been blowing** all day.*	*The wind **has blown** a tree over.*
*Vicky is out of breath. She**'s been running**.*	*Vicky is here at last. She**'s run** all the way.*
*I**'ve been writing** an essay. I'm tired now.*	*I**'ve written** an essay. I can hand it in now.*
We normally use the continuous form when we say <u>how long</u>.	We normally use the simple form when we say <u>how much/many</u>.
*Rachel **has been playing** music **all day**.*	*Rachel **has played** at least **twenty** CDs.*
*I**'ve been ironing** shirts **since ten o'clock**.*	*I**'ve ironed eight** shirts.*
***How long have** you **been learning** to drive?*	***How many** driving lessons **have** you **had**?*

2 States and actions

We cannot normally use the continuous form with a state verb (see Unit 7).
*I**'ve known** the secret for a long time.* NOT ~~I've been knowing the secret.~~
*My parents **have had** this car for about ten years.*
*We**'ve** never **been** very happy here, I'm afraid.*

Live and **work** (= have a job) can be continuous or simple, with no difference in meaning.
*We**'ve been living** here since 1992.* OR *We**'ve lived** here since 1992.*
*Sarah **has been working** for the company for three years now.* OR *Sarah **has worked** for the company for three years now.*

Practice

A I have been doing or I have done? (1)

Look at these conversations and put in the correct form of the verb.
Use the Present Perfect Continuous or Simple.

▶ Sarah: I feel really tired.
  Mark: It's because you've been doing........ (you / do) too much.
  Sarah: Well, at least I've finished.............. (I / finish) that report now, and I can relax.

1 David: Someone .... (leave) the ladder outside, look.
  Harriet: I expect that's Mike. .... (he / clean) the windows.
          I don't think .... (he / finish) yet.

2 Laura: You've got mud on your shoes.
  Trevor: It's all right, I'll take them off. .... (I / work) in the garden.
  Laura: Yes, it looks a lot tidier. Well done. .... (you / do) a good job.

3 Tom: .... (I / hear) that you and Harriet are building a garage. How long .... (you / do) that?
  Mike: Oh, for about a month now. (we / do) .... about half of it.

B I have been doing or I have done? (1)

What would you ask in these situations? Use the Present Perfect Continuous or Simple.

▶ Your friend is wearing glasses. You've never seen him with glasses on before. Ask him how long …
  How long have you been wearing glasses?

▶ Nick is playing computer games. Ask him how many …
  How many computer games have you played?

1 You meet a group of people walking across country. Ask them how many miles …
  ....

2 Some workmen are digging up the road outside Sarah's house. Ask her how long …
  ....

3 Laura is taking lots of photos of you and your friends. Ask her how many …
  ....

4 You have just woken up from an afternoon sleep and seen that it is raining. Ask your friend how long …
  ....

C I have been doing or I have done? (1–2)

Complete the conversation. Put the verbs in the Present Perfect Continuous or Simple.

Laura: What are you doing, Trevor? (▶) You've been........ (you / be) in here for ages. You're making an awful mess.
Trevor: (1) .... (I / clear) out this cupboard most of the afternoon. There's a lot of old stuff in here. (2) .... (I / find) these, look.
Laura: (3) .... (you / sit) there staring at those old boots for the last five minutes. (4) .... (I / watch) you.
        (5) .... (you / be) in a dream.
Trevor: They're football boots. (6) .... (I / have) them since I was about sixteen. (7) .... (they / be) in here for years.
Laura: Well, throw them away. And what about that tennis racket? Is that yours?
Trevor: No, it must be yours. (8) .... (I / never / have) a tennis racket.

VERBS • PAGE 41

18 Past Perfect

1 Introduction

IN THE CANTEEN AT WORK, MARK IS TELLING A
COLLEAGUE ABOUT THE DREADFUL DAY HE HAD
YESTERDAY.

*I felt really tired when I took the train to work
yesterday because Sarah and I **had been** to a party
the evening before. We **hadn't gone** to bed until
after one. I **hadn't been** on the train long when I
had a bit of a shock. I suddenly realized that I'**d left**
my wallet at home. Then I began to wonder. **Had I
left** it in the office the day before? I just couldn't
remember. I wanted to go back to bed. I felt awful.*

The situation is in the past (*I **took** the train ...
I **felt** tired ...*). When we talk about things <u>before</u>
this past time, we use the Past Perfect.

> *Sarah and I **had been** to a party the evening
> before.*
> *I'**d left** my wallet at home.*

We are looking back from the situation of the
train journey to the earlier actions – going to a
party and leaving home without the wallet.

Here are some more examples of the Past Perfect.

> *It was twenty to six. Most of the shops **had** just **closed**.*
> *I went to the box office at lunch-time, but they **had** already **sold** all the tickets.*
> *By 1960 most of Britain's old colonies **had become** independent.*

As well as actions, we can use the Past Perfect to talk about states.

> *I felt better by the summer, but the doctor warned me not to do too much. I'**d been** very ill.*
> *The news came as no surprise to me. I'**d known** for some time that the factory was likely to close.*

2 Form

The Past Perfect is **had** + a past participle.

> *He **had enjoyed** the party.* OR *He'**d enjoyed** the party.*
> *They **hadn't gone** to bed until late.*   *Where **had** he **put** his wallet?*

For irregular past participles see page 383.

3 Present Perfect and Past Perfect

Compare these examples.

PRESENT PERFECT (before <u>now</u>)	PAST PERFECT (before <u>then</u>)
*My wallet isn't here. I've **left** it behind.*	*My wallet wasn't there. I'd **left** it behind.*
*The match is over. United **have won**.*	*The match was over. United **had won**.*
*That man looks familiar. I've **seen** him somewhere before.*	*The man looked familiar. I'd **seen** him somewhere before.*

▷ 19 Review of the Past Simple, Continuous and Perfect   ▷ 20 The Past Perfect Continuous

Practice

A Past Perfect (1)

Read about each situation and then tick the right answer.

▶ Two men delivered the sofa. I had already paid for it.
Which came first, a) ☐ the delivery, or b) ✓ the payment?

1 The waiter brought our drinks. We'd already had our soup.
Which came first, a) ☐ the drinks, or b) ☐ the soup?

2 I'd seen the film, so I read the book.
Did I first a) ☐ see the film, or b) ☐ read the book?

3 The programme had ended, so I rewound the cassette.
Did I rewind the cassette a) ☐ after, or b) ☐ before the programme ended?

4 I had an invitation to the party, but I'd arranged a trip to London.
Which came first, a) ☐ the invitation, or b) ☐ the arrangements for the trip?

B Past Perfect (1–2)

Add a sentence with the Past Perfect using the notes.

▶ Claire looked very suntanned when I saw her last week.
.She'd just been on holiday.... (just / be on holiday)

1 We rushed to the station, but we were too late.
.... (the train / just / go)

2 I didn't have an umbrella, but that didn't matter.
.... (the rain / stop)

3 When I got to the concert hall, they wouldn't let me in.
.... (forget / my ticket)

4 Someone got the number of the car the raiders used.
.... (steal / it / a week before)

5 I was really pleased to see Rachel again yesterday.
.... (not see / her / for ages)

6 Luckily the flat didn't look too bad when my parents called in.
.... (just / clean / it)

7 The boss invited me to lunch yesterday, but I had to refuse the invitation.
.... (already / eat / my sandwiches)

C Present Perfect and Past Perfect (3)

Put the verbs in the Present Perfect (*have done*) or Past Perfect (*had done*).

▶ It isn't raining now. It 's stopped............. (stop) at last.

▶ We had no car at that time. We 'd sold................(sell) our old one.

1 The park looked awful. People .... (leave) litter everywhere.

2 You can have that newspaper. I .... (finish) with it.

3 There's no more cheese. We .... (eat) it all, I'm afraid.

4 There was no sign of a taxi, although I .... (order) one half an hour before.

5 This bill isn't right. They .... (make) a mistake.

6 I spoke to Melanie at lunch-time. Someone .... (tell) her the news earlier.

7 I was really tired last night. I .... (have) a hard day.

8 Don't you want to see this programme? It .... (start).

9 It'll soon get warm in here. I .... (turn) the heating on.

10 At last the committee were ready to announce their decision. They .... (make) up their minds.

19 Review of the Past Simple, Continuous and Perfect

1 Introduction

Read this true story. It happened some years ago.

> A young man **walked** into a supermarket in Southampton and **put** a few items of food in a basket. He **had chosen** a time when not many people **were shopping** in the store. He **found** a checkout where no one else **was waiting**. When the cashier **had checked** the goods, the man **gave** her a £10 note. When she **opened** the till, the man quickly **snatched** all the money from it and **ran** out of the store before she **realized** what **was happening**. At the time the security guard **was standing** at the other end of the store. When staff **checked** the records in the till, they **found** that the thief **had taken** only £4.37. As he **had left** the £10 note behind, the operation **had cost** him £5.63.

2 Comparison of tenses

We use the Past Simple to talk about the past (see Unit 8).
> He **snatched** the money and **ran** away.

The Past Simple is used for the actions in the story, to tell us what happened next.

We use the Past Continuous (see Unit 9) for something <u>around</u> a past time or a past action.
> At the time of the incident, not many people **were shopping** in the store.

The few customers were in the middle of doing their shopping.

We use the Past Perfect (see Unit 18) for things <u>before</u> a past situation.
> Staff found that the thief **had taken** only £4.37.

The theft of the money happened before they found out how much.

3 Past Simple and Past Continuous

We often use these two forms together when a shorter action comes in the middle of a longer one (see Unit 10.2).
> I **was waiting** at the checkout when I **noticed** a strange-looking man.

Seeing the man came in the middle of the wait.

4 Past Simple and Past Perfect

When we use these two forms together, we use the Past Perfect for what happened earlier.
> A man **walked** into a supermarket. He **had chosen** a quiet time.

The choice of the time came before the arrival in the supermarket.

In this example, one past action followed another.
> He **filled** the basket and **went** to the checkout.

We can also use either **when ... had done**, or **after ... did/had done**.
> **When** he **had filled** the basket, he **went** to the checkout.
> **After** he **had filled** (OR **After** he **filled**) the basket, he **went** to the checkout.

But when one short action comes straight after another, we use the Past Simple for both.
> When she **opened** the till, he **snatched** all the money out of it.

Note the different meanings.
> When I switched the TV on, the programme **started**. I was just in time.
> When I switched the TV on, the programme **had started**. I missed the beginning.

We can use the Past Perfect or the Past Simple with **before** or **until**. There is no difference in meaning.
> The man arrived at the store before it **had opened**/before it **opened**.
> The chairman didn't speak until he **had heard**/until he **heard** all the arguments.

Practice

A Past Simple, Continuous and Perfect (1–4)

Look at these sentences and then tick the right answer.

▶ David and Tom were talking together when a young woman spoke to them.
Which took more time, a) ☑ what David and Tom said, or b) ☐ what the woman said?

1 Mike had put up the tent, but Harriet was still unloading things from the car.
Which finished first, a) ☐ putting up the tent, or b) ☐ unloading?

2 Mark went home and switched off the computer.
What did he do first, a) ☐ go home, or b) ☐ switch off the computer?

3 When Claire arrived, Henry was walking up and down.
Which started earlier, a) ☐ Claire's arrival, or b) ☐ Henry's walking?

4 When Sarah had phoned the office, she drove to the hotel.
Did she phone the office a) ☐ before, or b) ☐ after driving to the hotel?

B Past Simple and Past Perfect (4)

Write the two sentences as one. Use *when* and the Past Perfect in either the first or the second part of the sentence.

▶ I took the book back to the library. I read it.
I took the book back to the library when I'd read it.

▶ The students did the experiment. They wrote a report on it.
When the students had done the experiment, they wrote a report on it.

1 Nick saved enough money. He bought a motorbike.

2 Mark put all the dishes away. He dried them.

3 I looked both ways. I pulled out into the road.

4 The golfers went into the clubhouse. They played the last hole.

C Past Simple, Continuous and Perfect (1–4)

Daniel is telling the story of how he forgot his passport. Put the verbs into the correct form.

(▶) It happened............ (it / happen) last August at the airport. A few weeks before, a group of us
(1) .... (decide) to go to Greece together for a holiday.
(2) .... (we / wait) in the queue at passport control when suddenly
(3) .... (I / realize) that (4) .... (I / forget) my
passport. (5) .... (it / be) quite a shock. (6) ....
(I / hurry) to a phone and (7) .... (ring) my parents.
(8) .... (they / work) in the garden, but luckily my mother
(9) .... (hear) the phone.
(10) .... (they / find) the passport and immediately
(11) .... (drive) to the airport with it. (12) ....
(I / meet) them at the information desk. (13) .... (we / have) no time to talk,
but (14) .... (I / say) goodbye to them earlier that morning.
(15) .... (I / run) all the way to the plane. I was just in time. When
(16) .... (I / get) there, the passengers (17) .... (sit)
in their seats ready for take-off. When (18) .... (they / see) me, everyone
(19) .... (start) clapping.

20 Past Perfect Continuous

1 Introduction

I fell down the steps here and broke my leg. I'd taken a bus into town, and **I'd been swimming** in the pool here.

David is talking about a situation in the past (*I fell and broke my leg*). When we look back to something <u>before</u> this past time, we use the Past Perfect Simple (see Unit 18) or the Past Perfect Continuous.

Past Perfect Simple: *I **had taken** a bus into town.*
Past Perfect Continuous: *I **had been swimming** in the pool.*

We use the Past Perfect Continuous for an action which happened over a period of time. The swimming went on for some time before David broke his leg.

2 Form

The Past Perfect Continuous is **had been** + an -ing form.
  *I **had been waiting** ages.* OR *I'**d been waiting** ages.*
  *I **had not been paying** attention.* OR *I **hadn't been paying** attention.*
  *Was the ground wet? **Had** it **been raining**?*

3 I had been doing or I had done?

Compare the Past Perfect Continuous and Simple.

OVER A PERIOD (**had been doing**)	COMPLETE (**had done**)
*I found the calculator. I'**d been looking** for it for ages.* *Vicky felt tired because she'**d been working** all day.* We are thinking of Vicky's work going on as she got tired.	*I finally bought a new calculator. I'**d looked** everywhere for the old one.* *Vicky felt pleased because she'**d done** so much work.* We are thinking of Vicky's work as complete.

We normally use the continuous form with a phrase saying <u>how long</u>.
  *When the company went bankrupt, it **had been losing** money for months.*
	We normally use the simple form with a phrase saying <u>how much/many</u>.
	  *When the company went bankrupt, it **had lost** over a million pounds.*

We do not normally use the Past Perfect Continuous for states (see Unit 7).
  NOT *He had been seeming unwell.*
	We also use the Past Perfect Simple for states (see Unit 7).
	  *The old man **had seemed** unwell for some time before he died.*

4 Comparison with other continuous forms

Compare the <u>Present</u> Perfect Continuous (**has/have been doing**) and the <u>Past</u> Perfect Continuous.
  *Vicky looks very upset. I think she'**s been crying**.*
  *Vicky looked very upset. I thought she'**d been crying**.*
Compare the Past Continuous (**was doing**) and the Past Perfect Continuous.
  *When I phoned, Natasha **was having** a piano lesson.* (I phoned <u>during</u> the lesson.)
  *When I phoned, Natasha **had been having** a piano lesson.* (I phoned <u>after</u> the lesson.)

Practice

A Form (2)

Complete the conversation. Put in the Past Perfect Continuous of the verbs.

Rachel: How was your job interview?

Vicky: Awful. I felt terribly nervous. (▶) .I'd. been. worrying....... (I / worry) about it all week. And I was tired because (1) .... (I / work) on my project the night before. (2) .... (I / not look) forward to the interview at all.

Rachel: So what happened?

Vicky: The woman interviewing me was half an hour late because (3) .... (she / deal) with an unexpected problem, she said. (4) .... (I / wait) ages, and I'd got even more nervous.

Rachel: How did the interview go?

Vicky: Well, I tried to sound confident. (5) .... (I / read) a book that said that's what you have to do in job interviews. But I don't know if I gave the right answers.

B Form and use (1–2)

Add a sentence with the Past Perfect Continuous to explain why. Look at the pictures to find the reasons.

| ▶ lie/in the sun | 1 cry | 2 drive/too fast | 3 play/with matches | 4 stand/under a tree |

▶ Claire got burnt. _She'd been lying in the sun._

1 Vicky looked upset. ....

2 Henry was stopped by the police. ....

3 The children started a fire. ....

4 A young man was struck by lightning. ....

C Comparison with other tenses (3–4)

Put in the correct form of the verbs.

▶ Tom could hear shouts from the flat next door. His neighbours .were. arguing............ (argue) again.

1 Emma went into the sitting-room. It was empty, but the television was still on. Someone .... (watch) it.

2 I .... (play) tennis, so I had a shower. I was annoyed because I .... (not win) a single game.

3 The walkers finally arrived at their destination. They .... (walk) all day, and they certainly needed a rest. They .... (walk) thirty miles.

4 When I saw Nick last week, he said he .... (stop) smoking. But when I saw him two days later, he .... (smoke) a cigarette. He looked rather ashamed.

5 I really must go and see the dentist. One of my teeth .... (ache) for weeks.

6 When Melanie arrived at David's place, he .... (lie) on the sofa reading a detective novel. He .... (buy) it at the second-hand bookshop, and he .... (read) it for most of the afternoon.

Test D: Tenses – past and perfect

A

Read the conversation. Then look at the answers below and write the correct answer in each space.

Tessa: Hello, Robert. I (▶) ..haven't.............. seen you for ages.
Robert: Hello, Tessa. Great to see you. What have you (1) .... doing lately?
Tessa: (2) .... just started a new job in computer software.
Robert: You (3) .... working for Tuffex Plastics when we last met.
Tessa: That's right. I hadn't (4) .... working there long before I got fed up. I (5) .... realized what a horrible job it would be. But what about you? (6) .... you found a job?
Robert: Well, six months ago I (7) .... working for a car hire company, but then they (8) .... bankrupt. So I'm out of work now. (9) .... been looking around for another job.
Tessa: Well, I'm sure you'll find one soon.

▶	a) didn't	b) hadn't	c) haven't	d) wasn't
1	a) been	b) had	c) has	d) was
2	a) I'd	b) I'll	c) I'm	d) I've
3	a) did	b) had	c) have	d) were
4	a) be	b) been	c) done	d) had
5	a) didn't	b) hadn't	c) haven't	d) wasn't
6	a) Did	b) Had	c) Have	d) Were
7	a) been	b) had	c) have	d) was
8	a) go	b) going	c) gone	d) went
9	a) I'd	b) I'll	c) I'm	d) I've

B

Write a second sentence so that it has a similar meaning to the first. Use the word in brackets.

▶   Susan had a green dress on. (wearing)
     Susan was wearing a green dress. ....

1   The doctor began work at six o'clock and is still working. (has)
    ....

2   Rupert didn't have his credit card. (forgotten)
    ....

3   I didn't want to go without taking a photo. (until)
    ....

4   Nancy has been writing the report. It is finished now. (written)
    ....

5   My wait in the queue has lasted forty minutes so far. (I)
    ....

6   When we arrived, everyone was on the dance floor. (dancing)
    ....

7   The computer has been mine for four years. (had)
    ....

8   In the middle of our lunch there was a knock at the door. (when)
    ....

9   Nigel felt sick from eating too many cakes. (because)
    ....

C

Write the sentences correctly.

▶   I like this CD. ~~I've been having it for ages.~~
     I've had it for ages.

1   It was my first day back at work. ~~I was on holiday.~~

2   I'm quite tired now. ~~I play badminton.~~

3   I had to sit down. ~~I'd been having a shock.~~

4   You need a rest. ~~How much have you been working?~~

5   The robbery happened at midday. ~~Lots of people walked along the street outside.~~

6   My sister speaks good English. ~~She is practising her English since last summer.~~

7   At last I have my qualification. ~~I've been passing my exam.~~

8   Michelle looked really sunburnt. ~~She'd lie in the sun for too long.~~

9   We got to the coach stop at nine yesterday. ~~But the coach has already gone.~~

D

Complete the conversations. Put in the correct form of each verb.

▶   A: Did you buy .... (you / buy) anything at the antiques sale yesterday?
    B: No. I wanted (I / want) to buy some jewellery, but I'd left (I / leave) my credit card at home.

1   A: Are you still copying those addresses?
    B: No, that's all of them. .... (I / finish) now.

2   A: The train is never going to get here.
    B: How long .... (we / wait) now?
    A: At least half an hour. .... (we / be) here since ten to five.

3   A: Did you have a nice chat with Tessa?
    B: No, not really. When .... (we / drink) our coffee, ... (she / hurry) off home.

4   A: It's terrible about that plane crash, isn't it?
    B: Yes, awful. .... (I / have) breakfast when .... (I / hear) the news.

5   A: So you sing in a rock band, do you? How long .... (you / do) that?
    B: Oh, since I was sixteen. .... (we / do) about a dozen concerts.

6   A: Do you know what Polly was so upset about yesterday?
    B: No, I don't. But I'm sure .... (she / cry). Her eyes looked red.
    A: Perhaps .... (she / have) some bad news.

7   A: The shooting was very frightening, I suppose.
    B: It certainly was. When we .... (hear) the shot, we all .... (throw) ourselves to the floor.

21 Review of present and past tenses

1 Introduction

Study the verb forms.

	Claire is ready to go on safari.
Present Continuous:	*She **is waiting** for her guide.*
Present Simple:	*She **goes** on holiday a lot.*
Present Perfect:	*She **has bought** a safari suit.*
Present Perfect Continuous:	*She **has been planning** her trip for months.*
Past Simple:	*She **bought** the suit last week.*
Past Continuous:	*She **was going** past Harrods when she saw it in the window.*
Past Perfect:	*She **had** already **decided** that she needed a safari suit.*
Past Perfect Continuous:	*She **had been looking** for one for a week or two.*

2 I am doing or I do? (Unit 6)

PRESENT CONTINUOUS

We use the Present Continuous for an action now, something we are in the middle of.

> *I **am writing** a letter.*
> *Claire **is wearing** a safari suit.*
> *We**'re getting** lunch now.*

We use the Present Continuous for a feeling over a short period of time.

> *Vicky **is liking** her course much better this year.*

We use the Present Continuous for a temporary situation or routine.

> *I'm very busy at the moment, so I**'m getting up** early this week.*

PRESENT SIMPLE

We use the Present Simple for repeated actions, things that happen again and again.

> *I **write** home every week.*
> *Tom never **wears** smart clothes.*
> *We usually **get** lunch at about one.*

We normally use the Present Simple for thoughts and feelings, and for states and permanent facts.

> *Claire **likes** holidays.*
> *Four times twelve **makes** forty-eight.*

We use the Present Simple for a permanent situation or routine.

> *I usually **get up** quite late.*

3 I have done or I did? (Units 14–15)

PRESENT PERFECT

The Present Perfect tells us about the past and the present.

> *They **have locked** the door. No one can get in.*

We use the Present Perfect for a state which has gone on up to the present.

> *I**'ve known** him for ages. He's an old friend.*

We use the Present Perfect for actions in a period of time up to the present.

> *I **have seen** the carnival several times.*

PAST SIMPLE

The Past Simple tells us about the past, a time which is finished.

> *They **locked** the door at ten o'clock last night.*

We use the Past Simple for a state in the past.

> *I **knew** him when we were at college together.*

We use the Past Simple for actions in the past.

> *I **saw** the carnival several times as a child.*

4 I have been doing or I have done? (Unit 17)

PRESENT PERFECT CONTINUOUS	PRESENT PERFECT

We use the Present Perfect Continuous for an action over a period of time leading up to the present. We are thinking of the action going on.
 	
   Daniel's tired. He's **been working**.
   I've **been reading** all afternoon.
   We've **been staying** here for a week/since
     Thursday.
	We use the Present Perfect Simple for a complete action. We are thinking of the result.
	
	   At least he's **earned** some money.
	   I've **read** 200 pages.

5 I was doing or I did? (Unit 10)

PAST CONTINUOUS	PAST SIMPLE

We use the Past Continuous for an action that we were in the middle of.
 	
   I **was reading** the paper at half past ten.
	We use the Past Simple for a complete action in the past or for a past state.
	
	   I **left** the house at half past ten.
	   Vicky **had** a headache.

We often use the Past Continuous and Past Simple together when a shorter action (simple) comes in the middle of a longer one (continuous).
   We **were looking** for the coffee bar when we **met** Emma.
But we use two Past Simple verbs for one action after another.
   When we **saw** Rachel, she **waved** to us.

6 I did or I had done? (Units 18–19)

We use the Past Simple to talk about a past situation and the Past Perfect for things that happened earlier.
   I **threw** the magazine away. I'd **finished** with it.
   When Sarah **found** the letter, someone **had** already **opened** it.
   When the new people **moved** in, the house **had been** empty for a year.

We can use **when ... had done** to say that one thing finished and then something else happened.
   When we'**d paid** the bill, we **left** the restaurant.
But when one short action comes straight after another, we use the Past Simple for both.
   When the firework **went** off, the dog **ran** away.

Compare these two sentences.
   When we arrived, the others all **left**. (We arrived and then they left.)
   When we arrived, the others **had** all **left**. (They left before we arrived.)

7 I had been doing or I had done? (Unit 20)

We use these forms when we look back from a situation in the past.

PAST PERFECT CONTINUOUS	PAST PERFECT

We use the Past Perfect Continuous for an action over a period of time. We are thinking of the action going on.
 	
   Emma's hand ached because she'**d been using** the
     computer.
   When I finally served the meal, I'**d been cooking**
     for hours.
	We use the Past Perfect Simple for a complete action. We are thinking of the result.
	
	   Her work looked really neat because she'**d used**
	     the computer.
	   I felt quite proud that I'**d cooked** a meal for eight
	     people.

Practice

A Present tenses (1–4)

Complete the sentences using the notes in brackets. The verbs can be Present Continuous (*am doing*), Present Simple (*do*) or Present Perfect (*have done*).

▶ We bought this picture a long time ago. We've had it .... (we / have / it) for ages.
1 Sarah finds her mobile phone very useful. .... (she / use / it) all the time.
2 Vicky doesn't know where her watch is. .... (she / lose / it).
3 We're in the middle of decorating our kitchen, so we can't cook any meals.
   .... (we / get / them) from a take-away restaurant this week.
4 Claire is on a skiing holiday. .... (she / enjoy / it), she says on her postcard.
5 The colour of this paint is absolutely awful. .... (I / hate / it).
6 These figures certainly should add up. .... (I / check / them) several
   times already.
7 Trevor and Laura like Scrabble. .... (they / play / it) most evenings.
8 These flowers are dying. .... (you / not water / them) for ages.

B Present tenses (1–4)

Read about each situation. What else do you say? Use the verb in brackets.

▶ You can't go out with a friend because you have a Saturday job. (work)
   I'm sorry. I work on Saturdays.
1 You have just met a friend you last saw months ago. (not see)
   Hello! How are you? ....
2 Someone has arranged to phone you at this time, and you're ready for the call. (wait)
   I have to stay by the phone. ....
3 Your friend is wearing a very nice jacket you haven't seen before. (like)
   Oh, that's nice. ....
4 You are watching the snow fall. It started yesterday and is still falling. (snow)
   I can't believe it. ....

C Present and past tenses (1–6)

Read about each situation and then tick the right answer.

▶ When we were talking, Tom left the room.
   Which took longer, a) ✓ our conversation, or b) ☐ Tom's departure?
1 Mark has been a member of the golf club for two years.
   a) ☐ He joined the club two years ago and is still a member.
   b) ☐ He was a member of the club for two years but is not a member now.
2 Vicky is watching the weather forecast.
   The weather forecast a) ☐ hasn't started yet, b) ☐ has started but not finished, or
   c) ☐ is over.
3 I've switched off the burglar alarm.
   Do I think that the alarm a) ☐ is off, b) ☐ is on, or c) ☐ may be on or off?
4 I've been studying all afternoon, and I've got a headache.
   Am I thinking of a) ☐ how much I have learned, or b) ☐ the action going on for a long time?
5 We had already travelled some distance when the sun rose.
   Did our journey start a) ☐ before sunrise, b) ☐ at sunrise, or c) ☐ after sunrise?
6 I'm going to work by bus this week.
   a) ☐ I always go to work by bus. b) ☐ My routine is different for this week.

D Present and past tenses (3–6)

Put in a pronoun and the correct form of the verb. Use the Past Continuous (*was doing*), the Past Simple (*did*) or the Present Perfect Continuous (*have been doing*).

▶ Mark: I rang at one, but you weren't in your office.
 Sarah: No, I was having................ (have) lunch.

1 David: You look tired.
 Melanie: Yes, I expect I do. .... (work) all day.

2 Sarah: Is Laura at home?
 Trevor: No, ... (go) out about half an hour ago.

3 Vicky: I haven't finished this letter yet.
 Rachel: It must be a long letter. .... (write) it since lunch-time.

4 Harriet: I see you've got some new neighbours.
 Tom Yes, a young couple. .... (move) in last month.

5 David: Did Tom drive you home?
 Melanie: Yes, ... (stop) and offered me a lift while
 .... (wait) for a bus outside the town hall.

E Present and past tenses (1–7)

Complete the conversation. Choose the correct form.

Melanie: How (▶) are you getting/do you get on in your new job, Nick?
Nick: Oh, so (1) you know/you're knowing about my job as a car salesman.
Melanie: (2) David's told/David told me yesterday.
Nick: Well, I (3) haven't been/wasn't in the job long. (4) I started/I've started on Monday.
Melanie: And how many cars (5) have you been selling/have you sold so far?
Nick: Well, none yet. Give me a chance. Up to now (6) I've been learning/I've learned all the time.
Melanie: David says you (7) had/were having a sports car once.
Nick: I've still got it. (8) I had/I've had it for about five years. (9) I don't often drive/I'm not often driving it because (10) I don't like/I'm not liking getting it dirty. Normally (11) I ride/I'm riding my motorbike. And the car is expensive to run. I (12) bought/had bought it on impulse. I (13) was working/worked on a building site at the time. For several months before I bought it, (14) I'd done/I'd been doing overtime, and when (15) I'd been earning/I'd earned enough to buy a car, it was a really magical moment. Maybe you'd like a ride in it some time?
Melanie: Oh, yes please. That would be lovely.

F Present and past tenses (1–7)

Complete the radio news report. Put in the correct forms of the verbs.

Hello. This (▶) is...... (be) Kitty Beamish. (1) .... (I / speak) to you from Oxford, where the finals of the World Quiz Championships will be held tomorrow. The favourite is Claude Jennings of Cornwall, the man who (2) .... (know) everything. Twelve months ago no one (3) .... (hear) of Claude Jennings, although (4) .... (he / take) part in quiz competitions for years. Now suddenly he is a big star. So far this year (5) .... (he / answer) every single question correctly. And he is popular, too. When (6) .... (he / arrive) here two days ago, hundreds of fans (7) .... (wait) at the station to welcome him. Since his arrival Claude (8) .... (read) encyclopedias in his hotel bedroom. He is clearly the man to watch. And now back to the news desk.

Test E: Tenses – present and past

A

Complete the conversations. Put in the correct form of each verb.

▶ A: Are you ready?
B: I won't be a moment. *I'm doing* (I / do) my hair.

1 A: Could you tell me your address?
B: Well, ... (I / live) in a friend's house at the moment. Luckily
.... (I / find) a place of my own now, but I can't move in until next
week.

2 A: Is this your CD?
B: No, it isn't mine. .... (I / think) ....
(it / belong) to Peter.

3 A: Can I borrow your calculator, please?
B: Well, ... (I / use) it to work out these figures at the moment.
.... (I / want) to finish doing them, now
that .... (I / start).

4 A: Why can't you wash your dirty plates sometimes? ....
(you / leave) them in the sink most of the time.
B: OK, sorry. The last few weeks .... (I / have) so little time.
.... (I / rush) around all the time.

B

Read the story and write the missing words. Use one word only in each space.

One day a man was (▶) *walking* .... past a house in Bournemouth when
he (1) .... a woman's voice shouting for help. The man
(2) .... someone (3) .... probably trying to
murder her. He ran to a phone box and (4) .... the police. The police came
quite quickly, but by now the shouting had (5) .... However, the man
(6) .... quite sure that he (7) .... heard cries for
help. When the police (8) .... on the door, there was no answer. So they
broke down the door and went in. Inside the house was a woman who had just
(9) .... out of the shower. She explained to the police that she had
(10) .... singing along to the Beatles song 'Help!'.

C

Write a second sentence so that it has a similar meaning to the first. Begin with the word
in brackets.

▶ Our trip to Africa was in October. (We ...)
We went to Africa in October. ....

1 We've had ten hours of rain. (It ...)
....

2 It's the right thing to do in my opinion. (I ...)
....

3 Our sofa is in a different place now. (We ...)
....

4 It was breakfast-time when Susan rang. (I ...)
....

5 Their game of badminton is always on Tuesday. (They ...)
....

D

Write the correct answer in each space.

▶ This isn't my first visit to London. *I've been* here before.
  a) I'm   b) I've been   c) I was

1 I've got my key. I found it when .... for something else.
   a) I looked   b) I've looked   c) I was looking

2 Sorry, I can't stop now. .... to an important meeting.
   a) I go   b) I'm going   c) I've gone

3 I can't get Tessa on the phone. .... all afternoon.
   a) I'm trying   b) I try   c) I've been trying

4 The bank told me last week there was no money in my account. .... it all.
   a) I'd spent   b) I spent   c) I was spending

5 There's a new road to the motorway. .... it yesterday.
   a) They'd opened   b) They opened   c) They've opened

E

Some of these sentences are correct, and some have a word which should not be there. If the sentence is correct, put a tick (✓). If it is incorrect, cross the unnecessary word out of the sentence and write it in the space.

▶ Martin has changed his mind about next weekend.   ✓ ....
▶ We ~~were~~ enjoyed the holiday very much.   *were* ....
1 Nancy is practising on the piano.   ....
2 It was lucky that we had been decided to buy our tickets in advance.   ....
3 We were riding our bikes when suddenly I was felt a pain in my leg.   ....
4 We are go camping for three weeks every summer.   ....
5 They have planted some new trees last year.   ....
6 I suddenly realized I had been walking in the wrong direction.   ....
7 Did you know that Anna has been won a prize?   ....
8 No one told me that the goods had arrived the week before.   ....

F

Complete the news report. Put each verb into the correct form.

The actress Vanessa Kemp (▶) *has disappeared* (disappear). Yesterday she
(1) .... (fail) to arrive at the Prince Charles Theatre in London's West End
for her leading role in the comedy 'Don't look now!'. Ms Kemp, who (2) ....
(live) in Hampstead, (3) .... (leave) home at four o'clock yesterday
afternoon for the theatre, a journey she (4) .... (make) several times the
week before. Two people who (5) .... (walk) past her home at the time
(6) .... (see) her leave. But no one (7) .... (see)
her since then. At half past seven she still (8) .... (not / arrive) at the
theatre. At eight o'clock the theatre manager had to break the news to the audience, who
(9) .... (wait) patiently for the play to start. Since yesterday, theatre staff
and friends (10) .... (try) to contact Ms Kemp, but they
(11) .... (have) no success so far. The police
(12) .... (take) the matter seriously, but they
(13) .... (believe) that she is unlikely to be in any danger. Her friends all
(14) .... (want) to hear from her soon.

22 Introduction to the future

1 Present, past and future

Read this paragraph from Rachel's letter to her aunt and uncle.

> *This is my last year at college, so I'll be leaving in June. And I've already got a job! In September I'm starting work at a bank in London. So I'll be free for most of the summer. I'm going to spend six weeks travelling around the US. My friend Vicky is coming with me. (She finishes college at the same time as me.) We're really looking forward to the trip. We might go to Canada too. Vicky has friends in Toronto.*

When we talk about the present or the past, we use verb forms to say what <u>is happening</u> now, what <u>happened</u> yesterday, and so on.

   *Vicky **has** friends in Toronto.*

We know about things in the present and in the past because they are already real. But talking about the future is more of a problem. There is no single form in English that we can always use for the future. There are many different ways of talking about the future, depending on how we see a future event. It may be something that is fairly sure to happen, but on the other hand it may be just a plan or an intention, or it may be something that you think will happen but you can't be sure about.

2 Verb forms used for the future

Here are some examples of verb forms used to express the future.

Be going to	▷ 24	*I'm going to spend six weeks in the US.* (an intention)
Will	▷ 23A	*I'll be free for most of the summer.* (neutral future)
Present Continuous	▷ 26A	*I'm starting work in September.* (an arrangement)
Present Simple	▷ 26B	*She finishes college at the same time.* (a timetable)
Will be doing	▷ 28	*I'll be leaving in June.* (in the course of events)

Very often there is more than one possible form that could be used.

   *She**'ll finish** college in June.*   *She **finishes** college in June.*
   *She**'s finishing** college in June.*   *She**'ll be finishing** college in June.*

Rachel could use any of these in her letter.

3 Will

We often use **will** as a neutral way of expressing the future, but it is not 'the future tense'.
It is only one of the forms we can use. In some situations will is not the right word.

   *After college I**'m going to travel** around the US.*

Here Rachel is saying what she intends to do in the future. We cannot use **will** here.

4 Being sure and unsure

We cannot always be sure about the future. To show that we are unsure we can use **might** or **could** (see Unit 46).

   *We **might** go to Canada.   It **could** snow soon.*

To show how sure or unsure we are, we often use phrases like **I'm sure, definitely, I expect, I (don't) think** and **probably**.

   ***I'm sure** it'll be all right.   We're **definitely** going to be at the meeting.*
   ***I expect** everyone will be going home.   Rachel will **probably** be late.*
   ***I think** I'm going to sneeze.   I **don't think** Tom's coming tonight.*

A Present, past and future (1–2)

Rachel has received a letter from a friend of hers who left college last year.
Find the sentences which refer to the future and write them below.

I'm really enjoying my work at the store. I'm learning lots about the job. Soon they're moving me to another store – in Birmingham. They told me about it last week. I'll be leaving here at the end of the month. I feel a bit sad about that. Luckily they'll find a flat for me.

The time is going very quickly. I've been here three months. The training programme finishes next summer. I like the work, and I want to stay with the company. They'll decide about that next year. I'm just hoping for the best.

▶   *Soon they're moving me to another store – in Birmingham.* ....
1   ....
2   ....
3   ....
4   ....

B Present and future (1–4)

Say if the second sentence is about the present or the future.
Look at the phrases of time such as *at the moment* and *on Friday*.

▶   I'm busy. I'm cooking a meal at the moment.   *present* ....
1   I'm nervous. I'm cooking for ten people on Friday.   ....
2   I don't want to go out. I might watch a video later.   ....
3   There's football on TV tonight. I might watch it.   ....
4   We're off at last. We arrive in New York at seven.   ....
5   This train is never on time. We always arrive late.   ....

C Present and future (1–4)

Read each pair of sentences and then answer the question about them.

▶   a) I'll see you on Thursday.
    b) I saw you on Thursday.
    Which sentence is about the future? .a.................
1   a) I'm going to Manchester. I'm waiting for a connecting train.
    b) I'm going to get a train to Manchester, changing at Birmingham.
    Which is spoken during the journey? ....
2   a) We'll know the results of the tests next week.
    b) We might know the results of the tests next week.
    Which sentence is more certain? ....
3   a) I'm doing two exams this year.
    b) I'm doing some work at the moment.
    In which sentence has the action already started? ....
4   a) What time do we arrive in Swansea?
    b) What time will we arrive in Swansea?
    Which question is more likely if you are travelling by car? ....
5   a) I'm eating at the Thai restaurant tonight.
    b) I'll eat at the Thai restaurant tonight.
    Which would you say if you've booked a table? ....

23 Will and shall

1 Will for the future

> The world leaders **will arrive** here tomorrow. They **will have** plenty to talk about, but they **won't be** here for long – only 24 hours. You**'ll hear** live reports every hour.

We use **will** to say what we know or think about the future. **Will** here has a neutral meaning. It does <u>not</u> express the idea that we have already decided to do something or that we are planning something.

2 Will for instant decisions

We also use **will** for an instant decision, when we decide on something or agree to do it more or less at the moment of speaking.

> *I'm thirsty. I think I'll **make** some tea.*
> NOT *I make some tea.*
> *You've left your computer on. ~ Oh, I'll **go** and switch it off.*
> *We must celebrate. I know, we'll **have** a party.*
> *I don't think I'll **do** any work tonight. I'm too tired.*

We also use it to order things.

> *I'll **have** the ham salad, please.*

We also use **will** in offers and invitations (see Unit 51).

Offer: *I'll **peel** the potatoes. ~ Oh, thank you.*
Invitation: ***Will** you **come** to lunch? ~ Yes, thank you. I'd love to.*
Promise: *I'll **pay** you back next week.*

3 The form of will

The form is **will** or **'ll**.

> *The west **will have** rain tomorrow.*   *You'll **be** late if you don't hurry.*
> ***Will** you **be** at home this evening?*   *The world **will end** in the year 2050.*

The negative is **will not** or **won't**.

> *The cost **will not be** more than £50.*   *I **won't have** time for a meal.*

4 Shall

We can use **shall** for the future, but only in the first person, after **I** or **we**.

> *I **will be**/I **shall be** on holiday in August.*
> *We **will know**/We **shall know** the results soon.*
> But NOT *Everyone shall know the results soon.*

I will and **I shall** have the same meaning here, but **shall** is a little formal. Both **I will** and **I shall** can be shortened to **I'll**, which is pronounced /aɪl/.

> *I'll **be** on holiday in August. (= **I will** OR **I shall**)*

Shall has other meanings. We can use it in offers and suggestions (see Unit 51).

Offer: ***Shall** I **pack** up your shopping for you? ~ Oh, thank you.*
Suggestion: ***Shall** we all **go** out together? ~ Good idea.*

We do not use **shall** in American English (see page 377).

▷ **25 Will and be going to**   ▷ **28 Will be doing**   ▷ **29.1 Will have done**   ▷ **144 Will in conditionals**

A Will for the future and for instant decisions (1–2)

Read the conversations. Which replies are statements about the future and which are instant decisions?

▶ What would you like? ~ I'll have an orange juice, please.   _decision_ ....

1 Shall we go out tonight? ~ I'll be too tired, I think. ....

2 We've lost a tennis ball. ~ I'll help you look for it. ....

3 I'm worried about the exam. ~ Oh, you'll be all right. ....

4 I haven't got any transport. ~ Oh, we'll give you a lift. ....

5 I must fix this shelf some time. ~ We'll be dead before then. ....

B Instant decisions (2)

Say what your decision is in these situations, or what you offer to do.
Use these verbs: *answer, carry, have, post, shut*

▶ You and your friend have come into the room. The window is open, and it is cold.
  I'll shut the window. ....

1 The phone is ringing. You are the nearest person to it.

  ....

2 The choice on the menu is fish or chicken. You hate fish.

  ....

3 You are meeting a friend at the station. He has two suitcases. There's a bag, too.

  ....

4 Your friend has written a letter. You are going to walk into town past the post office.

  ....

C Will and won't for the future (3)

Use the notes to write about what will happen next weekend.

▶ it / be / warm / tomorrow   _It will be warm tomorrow._ ....

1 Tom / watch / the match   ....

2 Harriet's party / be / fun   ....

3 Trevor / not put up / the shelves ....

4 Laura / be / annoyed   ....

5 Andrew / study / all weekend   ....

6 Rachel / not do / any work   ....

D Will and shall (1, 4)

Complete the conversation. Put in *will* or *shall*.

Rachel: What (▶) _shall_ .... we do today?

Vicky: It would be nice to go out somewhere. The forecast says temperatures
  (1) .... rise to thirty degrees.

Jessica: (2) .... we go for a walk?

Rachel: That sounds a bit boring. What about the seaside? We could get a bus.

Jessica: How much (3) .... it cost? I haven't got very much money.

Vicky: It isn't far. It doesn't cost much.

Jessica: Everywhere (4) .... be so crowded today because it's a holiday.
  The journey (5) .... take ages.

Rachel: Come on, Vicky. (6) .... we leave Jessica behind if she's going to
  be so miserable?

24 Be going to

1 Intentions

I think the cat is stuck on the roof. **I'm going to climb** up and have a look.

Be careful, David.

We use **be going to** to talk about something we have decided to do (an intention). David intends to climb up the ladder.

Here are some more examples.
> *I**'m going to watch** the next programme.*
> *Emma **is going to do** an experiment this afternoon.*
> *Rachel and Vicky **are going to spend** six weeks in the States.*

We can use **I'm not going to** for a refusal.
> *I'm sorry, but **I'm not going to walk** half a mile in the rain.*
> (= I don't want to/I'm not willing to walk.)

The Present Continuous can have a very similar meaning to **be going to**. We can often use either form (see Unit 26.1).
> *I**'m going to visit** my friend at the weekend.*
> *I**'m visiting** my friend at the weekend.*

We do not use **will** here.

We can use **be going to** with the verb go (*We**'re going to go** out this evening*), but the Present Continuous is more usual.
> *We**'re going** out this evening.*

2 Form

We use the present tense of **be** + **going to** + a verb.
> *They**'re going to move** house.   Matthew **is going to play** squash.*
> *Vicky **isn't going to have** any lunch.   We **aren't going to** complain.*
> ***Is** Daniel **going to apply** for the job? ~ I think he is.*
> *When **are** you **going to pay** this bill? ~ I don't know. I can't at the moment.*

In informal speech 'going to' is often pronounced /ˈɡənə/.

Oh no! **I'm going to fall.**

3 Predictions

We also use **be going to** for a prediction based on the present situation, when we can see that something is going to happen. The ladder is moving, so David is going to fall.

Here are some more examples.
> *My sister **is going to have** a baby in March.*
> *It's nearly nine now. We**'re going to be** late.*
> *Do you think it**'s going to rain**?*

▷ 25 Will and be going to   ▷ 29.2 Was going to

Practice

A Intentions (1–2)

Look at the pictures and say what is going to happen.
Use these verbs: *answer, catch, have, hit, light*
Use these objects: *the ball, a bath, a bus, the firework, the phone*

▶ They're going to have a bath.

1 ....

2 ....

3 ....

4 ....

B Form (2)

Put in the verbs with *be going to*.

Laura: What are you doing with that camera?

Trevor: (▶) I'm going to take .... (I / take) it to work. (1) ....
(I / lend) it to Phil. (2) .... (he / take) a few photos with it.

Laura: Why can't he buy his own camera?

Trevor: He's got one, but it isn't working properly. (3) .... (it / be)
a while before he can get it repaired.

Laura: Well, how long (4) .... (he / keep) ours? When
(5) .... (we / get) it back?

Trevor: (6) .... (he / have) it over the weekend.
(7) .... (we / get) it back on Monday.

Laura: Well, I hope (8) .... (it / not / get) damaged.

C Predictions (2–3)

What would you say in these situations? Use these words: *be sick, crash, get wet, lose, not stop, rain*

▶ The sky is full of dark clouds.
   It's going to rain.

1 Now it's starting to rain. There's nowhere to shelter, and you haven't got an umbrella.
   ....

2 You feel awful. There's a terrible feeling in your stomach.
   ....

3 You are playing Scrabble. The game is nearly over and you are 100 points behind.
   ....

4 You can see a plane coming down. It's out of control and falling to the ground.
   ....

5 You are waiting for a train. There's one coming, but you don't know if it's the one you want.
   It's travelling very fast.
   ....

25 Will and be going to

1 Introduction

Emma: *It's my birthday soon. **I'll be** twenty next Friday.*

Aunt Joan: *Oh, really? **Are** you **going to have** a party?*

Emma: ***I'm going to have** a meal in a restaurant with a few friends.*

Aunt Joan: *That**'ll be** nice.*

WILL	BE GOING TO
Will has a neutral meaning. We use it to talk about facts in the future. *I**'ll be** twenty next Friday.* *The spacecraft **will come** down in the Pacific Ocean tomorrow morning.*	We use **be going to** for an intention, something we have already decided to do. *We**'re going to have** a meal.* *Tom **is going to sell** his car.*

Will does <u>not</u> express an intention.

> *It's her birthday. She**'s going to have** a meal with her friends.* NOT ~~She'll have a meal.~~

But we often use **be going to** for an intention and **will** for the details and comments.

> *We**'re** all **going to have** a meal. There**'ll be** about ten of us. ~ Oh, that**'ll be** nice.*

As well as **be going to**, we can use the Present Continuous (see Unit 26.1).

> *We**'re going to drive**/We**'re driving** down to the South of France. ~ That**'ll be** a long journey. ~ Yes, it**'ll take** two days. We**'ll arrive** on Sunday.*

2 Decisions and intentions

WILL	BE GOING TO
We use **will** for an instant decision or agreement to do something. *There's a postbox over there. I**'ll post** these letters.* *You still haven't put those shelves up, Trevor. ~ OK, I**'ll do** it tomorrow.* Trevor is deciding now.	**Be going to** means that we have already decided. *I'm going out. I**'m going to post** these letters.* *You still haven't put those shelves up, Trevor. ~ I know. I**'m going to do** it tomorrow.* Trevor has already decided.

3 Predictions

WILL	BE GOING TO
We can use **will** for a prediction about the future. *I think United **will win** the game.* *One day people **will travel** to Mars.*	We use **be going to** for a prediction when we see from the present situation what is going to happen in the future. *There isn't a cloud in the sky. It**'s going to be** a lovely day.* *This bag isn't very strong. It**'s going to break**.*

It is often possible to use either form in a prediction. For example, we can also say *I think United **are going to win** the game.* Usually **be going to** is a little more informal and conversational than **will**.

Practice

A Will and be going to (1–2)

Complete the conversations. Put in *will* or *be going to* with the verbs.

▶ Vicky: Have you got a ticket for the play?
　 Daniel: Yes, I'm going to see........... (see) it on Thursday.
▶ Harriet: The alarm's going. It's making an awful noise.
　 Mike: OK, I'll switch................... (switch) it off.
1 Daniel: Did you buy this book?
　 Matthew: No, Emma did. She .... (read) it on holiday.
2 Laura: Would you like tea or coffee?
　 Sarah: Oh, I .... (have) coffee, please.
3 Trevor: I'm going to miss a good film on TV because I'll be out tonight.
　 Laura: I .... (video) it for you, if you like.
4 Rachel: I'm just going out to get a paper.
　 Emma: What newspaper .... (you / buy)?

B Will and be going to (1–3)

What would you say? Use *will* or *be going to*.

▶ You want to express your intention to look round the museum.
　 Your friend: Do you have any plans for this afternoon?
　 You: Yes, I'm going to look round the museum. ....
1 You hate dogs. Dogs always attack you if they get the chance.
　 Your friend: That dog doesn't look very friendly.
　 You: It's coming towards us. ....
2 You predict the landing of aliens on the earth in the next ten years.
　 Your friend: All this talk about aliens is complete nonsense, isn't it?
　 You: Is it? I think ....
3 You know that your friend's sister has decided to get married.
　 Your friend: Have you heard about my sister?
　 You: Well, I heard that ....
4 You suddenly decide you want to invite Ilona for a meal.
　 Your friend: Did you know Ilona will be in town next weekend?
　 You: No, I didn't. ....

C Will and be going to (1–3)

Complete the news report about the village of Brickfield.
Use *will* or *be going to*. Sometimes either is possible.

We have learned this week that the local council has plans for Westside Park in Brickfield.
The council (▶) is going to sell................ (sell) the land to a builder, Forbes and Son. The plans
are all ready. '(1) .... (we / build) fifty houses,' said Mr Forbes. 'In two
years' time everything (2) .... (be) finished. I'm sure people
(3) .... (like) the houses. Most of them (4) ....
.... (be) for young families. And we intend to take care of the environment.
(5) .... (we / not / cut) down all the trees, only a few of them.'
But people living near the park are angry. 'This is a terrible idea. We're all against it,' said Mrs Mary
Brent. '(6) .... (we / have) a protest march on Saturday. I expect
everyone in Brickfield (7) .... (be) there. We've reached our decision.
(8) .... (we / stop) this plan.'

26 Present tenses for the future

1 Present Continuous for arrangements

Tom: *Are you **doing** anything this evening?*
Nick: *Yes, I'm **going** to an ice hockey match.*
*The Tigers **are playing** the Kings.*
I bought my ticket yesterday.

We use the Present Continuous for what someone has arranged to do in the future.
Here Nick has arranged to go to the match. (He has bought a ticket.)
Here are some more examples.

    *I'm **meeting** Harriet at six o'clock.*   *David **is coming** round later on.*
    *We're **having** a party tomorrow.*   *Sarah **is going** to Paris next week.*

We also use the Present Continuous to talk about things happening now (see Unit 4).
Present: *We're **having** a party **at the moment**.*
Future: *We're **having** a party **tomorrow**.*
Here the phrase of time shows whether we mean the present or the future. But sometimes there is no phrase of time, as when Nick says *The Tigers are playing the Kings*. Here it is clear from Tom's question that the conversation is about a future event.

The Present Continuous for the future and **be going to** (Unit 24.1) have similar meanings.
    *We're **having** a party next week.* (We have made the arrangements.)
    *We're **going to have** a party next week.* (We intend / We have decided to have one.)
Often we can use either form.
    *I'm **meeting**/I'm **going to meet** Harriet at six o'clock.*

2 Present Simple for a timetable

Mark: *What time **does** your **train** leave tomorrow?*
Sarah: *Seven twenty-three in the morning.*
*It **gets** into Paris at eleven twenty-three.*

We can use the Present Simple for the future when we are talking
about a timetable, usually a public one such as a train timetable.
    *The train **leaves** at seven twenty-three tomorrow morning.*
    *The match **starts** at half past seven.*
    *Next Friday **is** the thirteenth.*
    *I've got the tour details here. We **spend** three days in Rome.*
Compare the Present Simple for repeated actions (see Unit 6.1).
    *The train **leaves** at seven twenty-three **every morning**.*

3 Be to and be about to

We use **be to** for a future event that is officially arranged.
It is often used in news reports.
    *The Queen **is to visit** Portugal in November.*
    *The Student Games **are to take place** in Melbourne next year.*
We could also use the Present Continuous here.
    *The Queen **is visiting** Portugal in November.*

We use **be about to** for the very near future.
    *The plane is at the end of the runway. It **is about to take** off.*
    *Do you want to say goodbye to our visitors? They're **about to leave**.*

Practice

A Present Continuous (1)

Read the conversation and say if the verb refers to the present or the future.

Mark: (▶) What <u>are</u> you <u>reading</u>, Claire?

Claire: Oh, it's a guidebook to Brazil. (1) <u>I'm going</u> there next month. (2) My sister and I <u>are having</u> a holiday there. (3) <u>I'm</u> really <u>looking</u> forward to it. (4) We'<u>re spending</u> three weeks in Rio. (5) So I'<u>m finding</u> out about all the things we can do there.

▶ present ....   3 ....

1 ....   4 ....

2 ....   5 ....

B Present Continuous for arrangements (1)

For each situation write a sentence with the Present Continuous. Use the verbs in brackets.

▶   Mike and Harriet have accepted an invitation to Tom's party next week. (go)
    They're going to Tom's party next week. ....

1   Laura has agreed to be in the office on Saturday. (work)

   ....

2   Claire has just bought a plane ticket to Cairo dated 15 May. (fly)

   ....

3   Mark has arranged a meeting with his boss at four o'clock this afternoon. (see)

   ....

4   Matthew and Daniel have booked a tennis court for tomorrow afternoon. (play)

   ....

C Present tenses for the future (1–2)

Put the verbs into the Present Continuous or the Present Simple.

Emma: (▶) Are you doing .... (you / do) anything tonight?

Matthew: Yes, (1) .... (I / go) to the station to meet my friend Richard.

            (2) .... (he / stay) here for the weekend, remember? His train

            (3) .... (get) in at eight fifteen.

Emma: Oh, of course. I'd forgotten about that.

Matthew: Maybe we'll see you later. What (4) .... (you / do) tonight?

Emma: Oh, (5) .... (I / go) to the cinema with Vicky and Rachel and a couple of other people. The film (6) .... (finish) quite early, so (7) .... (we / go) to a pizza place afterwards.

D Be to and be about to (3)

Complete these sentences on the news. Some are spoken by the newsreader in the studio and some by reporters on the spot. Use be to or be about to with the verbs in brackets.

▶   The new museum is to open .... (open) in the autumn.

▶   The Prime Minister is at the microphone now. He is about to start .... (start) speaking.

1   The leading runner is nearly there now. She .... (win) the race.

2   Taxes .... (go) up from next April.

3   The US President .... (visit) Ireland in the new year.

4   The riot isn't over yet, but the police are here. They .... (move) in.

5   The talks on world trade .... (take) place later this year.

27 When I get there, before you leave, etc.

1 Introduction

Mark: *Did I tell you I've got a meeting in Glasgow at nine o'clock tomorrow morning? I'm driving up there overnight.*

Sarah: *You're going to drive all through the night? You're crazy. You'll be exhausted **before you arrive**. Why don't you take a train?*

Mark: *I'll be OK. I'll need the car **while I'm there**. I have to visit some companies in the area. I can sleep **when I get home**.*

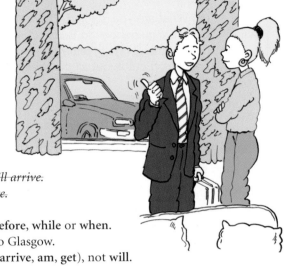

Study these examples.

> *You'll be exhausted **before** you **arrive**.* NOT ~~before you'll arrive.~~
> *I'll need the car **while I'm** there.* NOT ~~while I'll be there.~~
> *I can sleep **when I get** home.* NOT ~~when I'll get home.~~

Each of the sentences has a linking word of time, e.g. **before**, **while** or **when**.
The sentences are about the future, about Mark's trip to Glasgow.
But after the linking words we use the Present Simple (**arrive**, **am**, **get**), not **will**.

We can start the sentence with a linking word.

> ***When I get** home, I can sleep.*

2 Linking words

We use the Present Simple for the future after these linking words of time:
after, as, as soon as, before, by the time, until, when, while.

> *I'm starting a job in sales **after** I **finish** college.*
> ***As soon as** you **hear** any news, will you let me know?*
> *I must get to the bank **before** it **closes**.*
> *They'll have stopped serving meals **by the time** we **get** to the restaurant.*

We also use the Present Simple for the future after **if** (see Unit 144).

> ***If** you **come** in late tonight, please don't make a noise.*

3 Present Perfect

After a linking word of time, we can often use the Present Perfect for the future.

> *I'm starting a job in sales **after** I've **finished** college.*
> ***As soon as** you've **heard** any news, will you let me know?*

Compare ***after** I **finish** college* (see 2). The meaning is the same.

But sometimes there is a difference in meaning between the Present Simple and the Present Perfect.

> *When I **see** the report, I'll make some notes. (I'll do both at the same time.)*
> *When I've **seen** the report, I'll make some notes. (I'll see it and then make notes.)*

4 Present Continuous

We can also use the Present Continuous for the future, especially after **when** and **while**.

> ***When I'm boating** along the canal next week, I might be able to relax.*
> *Mark is going to listen to music **while** he's **driving** to Scotland.*

▷ 26 Present tenses for arrangements and timetables

Practice

A When I get there, before you leave, etc. (1–2)

Comment on the situations. Start each sentence with *when* and the Present Simple.

▶ Claire: I have to call at the travel agency. I'm going to get some holiday brochures.

When Claire calls at the travel agency, she's going to get some holiday brochures.

1 Mark: I want to see the boss. I'm going to discuss my problem.

....

2 Rachel: I'm going to use the computer later. I'm going to send an e-mail.

....

3 Tom: I'm visiting David in hospital. I'm going to tell him about United's win.

....

4 Matthew: I'll be in town tomorrow. I might buy some new trainers.

....

B When I get there, before you leave, etc. (1–2)

Mark and Sarah are continuing the conversation in 27.1. Put in the verbs.
Use *will* or the Present Simple.

Sarah: If (▶) *you take* (you / take) a train, (▶) *it'll be* (it / be) much more comfortable.
If (1) .... (you / need) a car, you can hire one when
(2) .... (you / get) to Glasgow.

Mark: If (3) .... (I / hire) a car, (4) .... (it / be)
too complicated. I'd rather take my own.

Sarah: It's too dangerous. You might fall asleep on the motorway.

Mark: I won't fall asleep. I can play loud music. Anyway, (5) .... (I / get)
there much quicker when (6) .... (there / be) no traffic on the
road. As soon as (7) .... (I / arrive),
(8) .... (I / ring) you, I promise.

Sarah: (9) .... (I / be) worried until (10) ....
(I / hear) from you. But don't ring before (11) .... (I / be) awake in
the morning.

Mark: (12) .... (I / lie) down for a couple of hours before
(13) .... (I / go).

Sarah: Good idea. (14) .... (you / be) exhausted tomorrow if
(15) .... (you / not / get) some sleep this evening.

C Present Perfect and Continuous (3–4)

Join each pair of sentences using the word in brackets.

▶ You can apply for a better job soon. But you need to have more experience first. (when)
You can apply for a better job when you've had more experience.

▶ I'm going to listen to this tape. I'll be travelling on the motorway tomorrow. (as)
I'm going to listen to this tape as I'm travelling on the motorway tomorrow.

1 You shouldn't decide now. You need to think about it first. (until)

....

2 I'll think of you next week. I'll be lying on the beach. (when)

....

3 We can leave in a minute. I need to pay the bill first. (as soon as)

....

4 We can discuss it later. We'll be sitting on the plane together. (while)

....

5 You can use the computer in a minute. I'll have finished with it soon. (when)

....

Test F: The future with **will, be going to** and present tenses

A

Put in the missing words. Use one word only in each space.

▶ I don't want a steak. I think I'll *have* .... the chicken.
1 There's a fireworks display tomorrow. Janet is .... to watch it.
2 We're at that table in the corner. .... you join us?
3 I'm seeing the boss this afternoon. But I must study this report before
   I .... her.
4 There will be drinks at the reception, but there will .... be any food.
5 The European heads of state are .... meet in Brussels on 3 October.
6 It's a lovely day. .... we go for a walk?
7 My birthday .... on a Sunday next year.
8 My brother is engaged. He's .... married in June.
9 You won't be allowed to go to your seat after the play .... started.
10 Martin's got his coat on. I think he's .... to go out.

B

Write the sentences correctly.

▶ I'm hungry. ~~I think I have something to eat.~~
  I think I'll have something to eat. ....

1 You say you're getting a coach at nine. ~~What time is it getting to London?~~
  ....

2 I'll give Polly the news. ~~I'll tell her when I'll see her this evening.~~
  ....

3 Rupert looks really tired. ~~He's about falling asleep.~~
  ....

4 We've arranged to go out. ~~We meet in town later.~~
  ....

5 I'm going to Spain next week. ~~I send you a postcard.~~
  ....

6 I'm going to get to the airport early. ~~I can read a book while I'll be waiting.~~
  ....

7 I feel a bit tired. ~~I go to lie down.~~
  ....

8 Why not come to the party? ~~All your friends shall be there.~~
  ....

9 There's been a bomb warning. ~~No one can go into the building until the police will have searched it.~~
  ....

C

Read the news report and write the missing words. Use one word only in each space.

The Maxi-Shop company is (▶) *going* .... to build a huge new shopping centre on the edge of Millingham, it was announced yesterday. There (1) .... be at least three hundred shops, including some big department stores. When the project (2) .... complete, there (3) .... be hundreds of new jobs for local people. But not everyone is happy. 'We're (4) .... to fight this plan,' said a spokesperson for the local Environment Group. 'Just think what is going (5) .... happen to our countryside. When shopping malls (6) .... covered the whole country, there (7) .... be no green fields left. So we're (8) .... a protest meeting tomorrow evening at the town hall. It (9) .... at half past seven.' Owners of shops in the town centre are also unhappy. 'The new centre (10) .... take our customers away,' said one of them.

D

Look at the answers below and write the correct answer in each space.

▶ A: Let's go to the carnival, shall we?
   B: Yes, good idea. I expect it'll be fun.
   a) it'll be   b) it's   c) it's being

1 A: Could I have a word with you, please?
   B: Sorry, I'm in a big hurry. My train .... in fifteen minutes.
   a) is going to leave   b) leaves   c) will leave

2 A: Have you decided about the course?
   B: Yes, I decided last weekend. .... for a place.
   a) I apply   b) I am to apply   c) I'm going to apply

3 A: I'm trying to move this cupboard, but it's very heavy.
   B: Well, ... you, then.
   a) I help   b) I'll help   c) I'm going to help

4 A: Is the shop open yet?
   B: No, but there's someone inside. I think ....
   a) it opens   b) it's about to open   c) it will open

5 A: Do you mind not leaving your papers all over the table?
   B: Oh, sorry. I'll take them all with me when ....
   a) I go   b) I'll go   c) I'm going

6 A: It's a public holiday next Monday.
   B: Yes, I know. .... anything special?
   a) Are you doing   b) Do you do   c) Will you do

E

Write the sentences using a future form of the verb. Use the word in brackets.

▶ Express your instant decision to take a taxi. (I'll)
   I'll take a taxi.

1 Express your intention to have a rest. (going)

2 Express the idea that the timetable shows the start of term on 6 September. (starts)

3 Predict a world war in five years' time. (there)

4 Express the idea that you and Judy have arranged a game of tennis for tomorrow. (playing)

5 Give your prediction of a probable fall in prices. (probably)

6 Warn your passenger about the car crashing. (going)

28 Will be doing

1 Introduction

Rachel: *Would you like to come to our party tomorrow, Andrew?*

Andrew: *Er, thanks for the invitation, but I've got lots of work at the moment. I'll be working all day tomorrow.*

Rachel: *You won't be working on Saturday evening, surely. Come on, Andrew, take a break. We'll be starting at about ten o'clock.*

We can use **will be** + an -ing form (the Future Continuous) to talk about future actions. There are two different uses.

2 Will be doing for continuous actions

We use the Future Continuous for an action over a period of time.
It means that at some time in the future we will be in the middle of an action.

> *Andrew can't go to the party. He'll be working all day tomorrow.*
> *I'll be out at three o'clock. I'll be playing golf.*
> *When the men leave the building, the police will be waiting for them.*
> *What will we be doing in ten years' time, I wonder?*

Compare the Past Continuous (Unit 9), Present Continuous (Unit 4) and Future Continuous.

Past: *This time **last week** we **were sitting** on the beach.*
Present: ***At the moment** we're **sitting** on the beach.*
Future: *This time **next week** we'll **be sitting** on the beach.*

Compare **will do** and **will be doing** in these sentences.

> *The band **will play** when the President enters.*
> (The President will enter and then the band will play.)
> *The band **will be playing** when the President enters.*
> (The band will start playing before the President enters.)

3 Will be doing for single actions

We also use **will be** + an -ing form for an action which will happen in the course of events because it is part of a plan or part of a schedule of future events.

> *The party **will be starting** at ten o'clock.* (part of the evening's events)
> *The ship **will be sailing** soon.* (part of our journey)

More than one form is often possible. **Will** (Unit 23) or the Present Continuous (Unit 26.1) often have a very similar meaning.

> *The visitors **will be arriving/will arrive/are arriving** later.*

We often use the Future Continuous for something that will happen as part of a routine.

> *I'll call in and see you tomorrow afternoon. I'll **be passing** your house. It's on my way home from work.*
> *Trevor and Laura **will be cleaning** the house tomorrow. They always do it on Sunday.*

We can also use **will be** + an -ing form to ask about someone's plans.

> ***Will** you **be going** anywhere near a chemist's this morning? ~ Yes, why? ~ Could you get me some aspirin, please? ~ Yes, of course.*
> *How long **will** you **be using** this computer? ~ You can have it in a minute.*

Practice

A Will be doing (2)

Complete the conversation. Put in a pronoun and the Future Continuous form of the verb.

Daniel: I'm going to go into business when I leave college. Five years from now
(▶) I'll be running.................... (I / run) a big company. I expect (1) ....
.... (I / earn) lots of money.

Vicky: I don't know what (2) .... (I / do). What about you, Natasha?
What (3) .... (you / do), do you think?

Natasha: I'm too lazy to do any work. I intend to marry someone very rich.
(4) .... (I / give) dinner parties all the time. We'll have a cook
(5) .... (who / do) all the work, of course. And you'll both get
invitations.

Vicky: You're joking, aren't you, Natasha? I expect (6) .... (you / play)
in an orchestra. That's what you really want to do, isn't it?

B Will be doing (3)

Put in the answers. People are saying what they will be doing as part of their routine.

▶   David: When are you going to the club, do you know?
(Nick goes to the club every Friday.)
Nick: I'll be going there next Friday...
1   Vicky: Are you likely to see Ilona in the near future?
(Emma sees Ilona every day.)
Emma: .... tomorrow.
2   Claire: Are you going to France again soon?
(Henry goes to France every summer.)
Henry: ....
3   Jessica: When are you going to play badminton again?
(Matthew plays badminton every weekend.)
Matthew: ....
4   Andrew: When are you next having lunch in the canteen?
(Daniel has lunch in the canteen every day.)
Daniel: ....

C Will be doing (3)

You want to ask a friend to do something for you or to let you do something.
Find out if it is convenient for your friend. Use the verbs in brackets.

▶   You want to have a look at your friend's magazine tonight. (read)
Will you be reading your magazine tonight?...
1   You want your friend to take your library book back today. (go to)
....
2   You want your friend to send your best wishes to Vicky soon. (write to)
....
3   You want to use your friend's calculator this afternoon. (use)
....
4   You want your friend to give a photo to Daniel tomorrow. (see)
....
5   You want your friend to give you a lift to the festival. (drive)
....
6   You want your friend to give a message to her sister soon. (phone)
....

29 Will have done and was going to

1 Will have done

What time will you be home?

I'll have finished here by half past eight, so I should be home about nine.

We use **will have** + a past participle (the Future Perfect) for something that will be over in the future. Sarah is thinking of a future time (half past eight). At half past eight she will be able to say 'I have finished'.

Here are some more examples.

*I like looking at these pictures, but **I'll have had** enough by lunch-time.*
*Trevor and Laura **will have lived** here for four years next April.*
*This chess game is going to last ages. They **won't have finished** it until midnight.*
***Will** you **have read** this book by the time it's due back to the library? ~ Yes. **I'll have finished** it by then.*

We often use the Future Perfect with expressions of time such as **by lunch-time**, **until** midnight, **before** then, **by the time** you have to take it back.

2 Was going to

You still haven't put those shelves up.

Oh, sorry! I **was going to do** it yesterday but I couldn't find any screws.

We can use **be going to** in the past tense to express an intention in the past. Trevor intended to put the shelves up yesterday. Often the intended action did not happen. In fact Trevor did not put the shelves up.

Here are some more examples.

*I **was going to tidy** the flat, but I didn't have time.*
*Daniel **wasn't going to spend** any money, but he saw a jacket he just had to buy.*
*The girls left early. They **were going to catch** the eight o'clock train.*
*So you went to the airport without a ticket. Where **were** you **going to fly** to?*
*The woman walked away just as I **was going to speak** to her. (just as = at the moment when)*

We can also use **was going to** for a prediction in the past.

*I knew something **was going to go** wrong with the plan.*

Would has a similar meaning (see Unit 134.3).

*I knew something **would go** wrong with the plan.*

Practice

A Will have done (1)

Paul wants to be an artist. He's reading about a famous artist called Winston Plummer.

Winston Plummer was a great artist, who had a wonderful career. He won lots of prizes before he was twenty. By the age of twenty-five he had had his own exhibition. He was the subject of a TV documentary by the time he was thirty. By the age of thirty-five he had become world-famous. He made millions of pounds from his pictures before he was forty.

Paul is daydreaming about his own future career. What is he thinking?

▶   I hope *I'll have won lots of prizes* .... before I'm twenty.
1   Perhaps .... my own exhibition by the age of twenty-five.
2   I wonder if .... by the time I'm thirty.
3   Maybe .... by the age of thirty-five.
4   I hope .... by the age of forty.

B Will have done (1)

How good is your maths? Can you work out the answers?

▶   It's quarter to six. Melanie is putting something in the oven.
It needs to be in the oven for an hour and a half. When will it have cooked?
It will have cooked at quarter past seven.

1   It's seven o'clock in the evening, and Andrew is starting to write an essay. He writes one page every fifteen minutes. He plans to finish the essay at midnight. How many pages will he have written?
He will have written .... pages.

2   It's Monday morning, and Sarah is travelling to work. It's twenty miles from her home to the office. How far will she have travelled to and from work by the time she gets home on Friday?

....

3   Matthew is doing press-ups – one every two seconds. How many will he have done after five minutes?

....

C Was going to (2)

Complete the sentences. They are all about being just too late.
Use *was/were going to* with these verbs: *go, get, see, pick*

▶   The train left just as Mike *was going to get* .... on it.
1   I'm afraid the shop closed just as we .... in.
2   The phone stopped ringing just as Melanie .... it up.
3   We .... a film about the Mafia, but the tickets were sold out.

D Was going to (2)

Trevor is always making excuses for not doing things. Complete his sentences.

▶   put up the shelves / not have any screws
Sorry. I was going to put up the shelves, but I didn't have any screws.
1   paint the door / not feel very well
Sorry. ....
2   repair the lamp / forget
Oh, yes. ....
3   wallpaper the bedroom / not have time
Well, ...

30 Review of the future

1 Introduction

CLAIRE IS TALKING TO SARAH OUTSIDE THE TRAVEL AGENT'S.

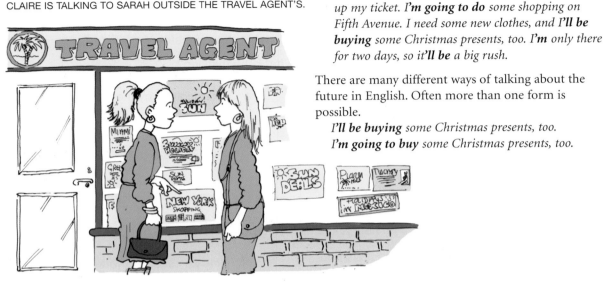

I'm going to New York next week. I'm about to pick up my ticket. I'm going to do some shopping on Fifth Avenue. I need some new clothes, and I'll be buying some Christmas presents, too. I'm only there for two days, so it'll be a big rush.

There are many different ways of talking about the future in English. Often more than one form is possible.

I'll be buying some Christmas presents, too.
I'm going to buy some Christmas presents, too.

2 Talking about the future

How we express future time depends on how we see a future event. Here are some ways of talking about what we think will happen in the future.

The neutral future	*The sun **will rise** at 5.45 am tomorrow.*	▷ 25.1
A prediction	*Claire's trip **will be** a big rush.*	
	*Claire's trip **is going to be** a big rush.*	▷ 25.3
A prediction based on the present	*I'm going to be sick!*	▷ 24.3
A less certain prediction	*I **think** it'll be cold in New York.*	
	*It's **probably going to be** cold in New York.*	▷ 22.4
The very near future	*Claire **is about to pick** up her ticket.*	▷ 26.3
A future action over a period	*Claire **will be shopping** non-stop for two days.*	▷ 28.2
Something that will be over in the future	*The sales **will have finished** by Saturday.*	▷ 29.1

3 Intentions and plans

We often want to talk about our decisions and intentions and what we plan to do in the future.

An instant decision (deciding <u>now</u>)	*It's a lovely coat. It fits Perfectly.*	
	Yes, I'll buy it.	▷ 23.2
An intention (something <u>already</u> decided)	*I'm going to do some shopping.*	▷ 24.1
A less certain decision or intention	*I **think** I'll buy this hat, too.*	
	*I **might go** to a show.*	▷ 22.4
A past intention	*I **was going to buy** a guidebook, but I forgot.*	▷ 29.2
An arrangement	*I'm flying to New York next week.*	▷ 26.1
In the course of events	*I'll be buying some presents, too.*	▷ 28.3
An official arrangement	*The President **is to address** the nation tonight.*	▷ 26.3
A timetable	*I'm in New York for two days next week.*	▷ 26.2

Practice

A Will, will be doing and will have done (2)

Complete the live news report. Put in *will* and the simple, continuous or perfect form of the verb.

The Quiz Marathon (▶) .will..begin............ (begin) in five minutes. (1) ....
(it / be) a big test for the World Quiz Champion, Claude Jennings, (2) ....
(who / answer) questions from a group of quiz writers. Claude (3) ....
(answer) their questions for a very long time. In fact, (4) ....
(he / still / give) answers when the rest of us are in bed tonight. Claude hopes that after 24 hours
(5) .... (he / reply) to about seventeen thousand questions. No meal breaks
are planned, so (6) .... (he / not / eat) anything. If all goes well, his name
(7) .... (be) in the next Guinness Book of Records. Claude has also got a
number of sponsors, and by tomorrow (8) .... (he / earn) at least £10,000 for
charity. Well, (9) .... (we / return) this afternoon for news of how Claude is
getting on. We think that by then (10) .... (he / get) some way past the five
thousandth question.

B The future (2–3)

What do these people say? Pay special attention to the underlined words.

▶ Tom is underlined{predicting} a win for United in their next game.
   Tom: United..will..win..their..next..game...

1 Andrew underlined{intends} to get up early tomorrow.
   Andrew: I ....

2 Vicky's train underlined{timetable} says 'Arrival 10.30'.
   Vicky: The train ....

3 Daniel has underlined{arranged} to see his bank manager tomorrow.
   Daniel: ....

4 Rachel will go out in the underlined{very near} future.
   Rachel: ....

5 There's a crowd of demonstrators in the main square of the capital. The police are arriving.
   Reporter Kitty Beamish is underlined{predicting} trouble.
   Kitty: ....

C The future (2–3)

Complete the conversation. In each sentence choose the best form of the verb to express the
future. Usually more than one answer is possible.

Mark: Hello, Claire. Sarah tells me (▶) .you're..going........................ (you / go) to New York.
Claire: Yes, (1) .... (I / spend) a couple of days there next week.
          (2) .... (I / look) round the shops.
Mark: (3) .... (that / be) exciting.
Claire: Exhausting, you mean. I think (4) .... (I / be) pretty tired when
          I get back.
Mark: (5) .... (you / stay) with friends?
Claire: No, (6) .... (I / stay) at a hotel near Central Park. But
          (7) .... (I / see) my friends. (8) ....
          (I / go) to their apartment for a meal one evening. And it isn't definite yet, but
          (9) .... (we / see) a show.
Mark: And when (10) .... (you / leave)?
Claire: My flight (11) .... (be) on Tuesday morning.
Mark: OK, (12) .... (I / see) you when you get back then.

Test G: Tenses – future

A

Read the telephone conversation. Then look at the answers below and write the correct answer in each space.

Amy: When (►) ..will............. I see you again?
Simon: I don't know. I'm (1) .... to be busy this week. And I'll
        (2) .... going to London on Saturday.
Amy: Oh. But you (3) .... be here for my party, won't you?
Simon: No, I (4) .... get back until Sunday evening.
Amy: I (5) .... going to invite you.
Simon: Well, I'm sorry I can't come.
Amy: What (6) .... you doing in London?
Simon: Oh, I'm just going (7) .... see one or two people. Look, I must
        go. I'm cooking something that I think is (8) .... to boil over.

►	a) am	b) do	c) going	d) will	5	a) be	b) have	c) was	d) will
1	a) being	b) going	c) shall	d) will	6	a) are	b) going	c) to	d) will
2	a) be	b) do	c) for	d) to	7	a) be	b) for	c) is	d) to
3	a) are	b) do	c) was	d) will	8	a) about	b) might	c) probably	d) will
4	a) about	b) aren't	c) be	d) don't					

B

Some of these sentences are correct, and some have a word which should not be there. If the sentence is correct, put a tick (✓). If it is incorrect, cross the unnecessary word out of the sentence and write it in the space.

►	They're probably going to knock the building down.	✓ ....
►	We are be going to get a dog soon.	be ....
1	The bus is leaves at eight twenty.	....
2	The doors of the theatre are about to open.	....
3	The meeting will be start at half past seven.	....
4	The festival is for to take place in June.	....
5	My friend will be calling here tomorrow morning.	....
6	We were going to eat in the restaurant, but it was full.	....
7	I have to register for my course before the classes will begin.	....
8	I will to have finished lunch by two o'clock.	....

C

Put in a form of the verb. Use the Future Continuous (*will be doing*), the Future Perfect (*will have done*) or *was/were going to*.

►   It's quite a long way, isn't it? We'll have walked..... (walk) about five miles by the time we get back, I'd say.
1   It'll be better if you don't ring at one o'clock. We .... (have) lunch then.
2   I .... (drive) over and see you, but there's something wrong with the car.
3   I've got loads of work. I expect I .... (work) all night. And I'm not looking forward to it.
4   I'll have much more time next week because I .... (do) all my exams then.
5   We .... (buy) that computer game, but they don't make it for the kind of computer we've got.
6   I know you'll put on a wonderful show. You .... (have) so much practice by the time you perform it that it's sure to be brilliant.

D

Complete the conversation. Use *will*, *be going to* or a present tense. Choose the best form. Sometimes more than one answer is correct.

Peter: Hello. Where are you going?

Polly: To my evening class. I'm learning Swedish. And next week (►) .I'll have..... (I / have) a chance to speak it for real. (1) .... (I / go) to Sweden for three weeks. (2) .... (I / leave) on Friday. (3) .... (I / visit) some friends there.

Peter: (4) .... (that / be) nice.

Polly: Well, I'd better hurry. My lesson (5) .... (start) at half past seven, and it's twenty-five past now.

Peter: OK. Come and see me when (6) .... (you / get) back from Sweden.

Polly: Thanks. (7) .... (I / send) you a postcard.

E

Write a second sentence so that it has a similar meaning to the first. Use the word in brackets.

►   We have decided to help with the project. (going)
    We are going to help with the project. ....

1   We're willing to wait for you. ('ll)
    ....

2   You can get off this train at Bath. (stops)
    ....

3   My friend intended to meet us. (going)
    ....

4   Adrian's job interview is on 17 October. (having)
    ....

5   Our meal will be over by eight o'clock. (finished)
    ....

6   I think I'm going to go on the trip. (might)
    ....

7   The fire hasn't gone out yet, but it will in a minute. (about)
    ....

F

Choose the correct form.

►   A: I'd better go. I'm cycling home, and I haven't got any lights on my bike.
        B: Oh, yes. <u>It'll be/It'll have been</u> dark soon.

1   A: I hear the rent on your flat is very expensive.
      B: Yes it is. <u>I'll move/I'm going to move</u>, I've decided.

2   A: I'd like a photo of Martin and me.
      B: <u>I'll take/I'm going to take</u> one with your camera, then.

3   A: Have you booked a holiday yet?
      B: Yes, <u>we go/we're going</u> to Spain.

4   A: What's that man doing up there?
      B: Oh no! <u>He'll jump/He's going to jump</u>!

5   A: Can I borrow your bike on Monday?
      B: I'm sorry, but <u>I'll be using/I'll have used</u> it. I always cycle to work.

31 The verb **have**

1 **Have** and **have got**

Look at these examples.

HAVE	HAVE GOT
We **have** three cats.	We'**ve got** three cats.
Emma **has** toothache.	Vicky **has got** blue eyes.
Daniel **doesn't have** a car.	I **haven't got** any money.
Do you **have** the address? ~ Yes, I do.	**Have** you **got** a ticket? ~ No, I haven't.

Here **have** and **have got** mean the same thing. We can normally use either form. But **have got** is more informal. Note that we do not use **have got** in short answers (*No, I **haven't**.*).

2 Forms

	PRESENT TENSE	
	have	have got
POSITIVE	I/you/we/they **have**	I/you/we/they **have got** OR I/you/we/they'**ve got**
	He/she/it **has**	He/she/it **has got** OR He/she/it'**s got**
NEGATIVE	I/you/we/they **don't have**	I/you/we/they **haven't got**
	He/she/it **doesn't have**	He/she/it **hasn't got**
QUESTION	**Do** I/you/we/they **have**?	**Have** I/you/we/they **got**?
	Does he/she/it **have**?	**Has** he/she/it **got**?
	PAST TENSE	
POSITIVE	I/you/he/she/it/we/they **had**	
NEGATIVE	I/you/he/she/it/we/they **didn't have**	
QUESTION	**Did** I/you/he/she/it/we/they **have**?	

We do not often use **had got** in the past tense.

> Tom **had** several jobs to do.   We **didn't have** time to stop.   Why **did** you **have** that funny hat on?

3 The action verb **have**

Here are some examples of **have** as an action verb.

> Mark **has** lunch around one.   I **have** a shower every morning.
> The children **had** a game of cards.   We **had** a wonderful holiday.

Have expresses an action. *Mark has lunch* means that he eats lunch.

With the action verb **have** we cannot use **got** and we cannot use a short form.

> NOT ~~Mark has got lunch around one~~ and NOT ~~I've a shower every morning.~~

The action verb **have** can also be continuous.

> Mark **is having** lunch now.   We **were having** a conversation in English.
> What time **are** you **having** your driving lesson?

In negatives and questions in simple tenses, we use a form of **do**.

> We **didn't have** a very good time.   We **don't have** parties very often.
> Where **do** you **have** lunch?   How often **does** Vicky **have** strange dreams?

In English we often use expressions like **have a talk** instead of a verb like **talk**. Here are some examples.

> Shall we **have a swim**?   I usually **have a rest** in the afternoon.
> I **had a talk** with Daniel.   Trevor and Laura **are having an argument**.

Practice

A Have and have got (1–2)

Look at the pictures and write positive or negative sentences with *have* or *have got*.
Use these objects: *a car, a map, a rabbit, a ticket, an umbrella*

► He's got a ticket. .... OR ..He has a ticket.

1 ....   3 ....
2 ....   4 ....

B Have and have got (1–2)

Complete the dialogue. Put in the negative or question forms.
Use *have got* for the present and *have* for the past.

David: (►) ..Have.......... you ..got............ a bike?
Mike: Yes, but I don't ride it very often.
David: (1) .... it .... lights on?
Mike: Yes, why?
David: Can I leave my bike here and take yours? Mine (2) .... any lights.
It (3) .... any when I bought it. I meant to get some last week, but
I (4) .... time.
Mike: But it's raining now. And you (5) .... a coat. I'll drive you home,
David.

C The action verb have (3)

What does <u>have</u> mean in these sentences? Choose from these verbs: *drink, <u>eat</u>, play, receive, spend*

► Mark never <u>has</u> breakfast.   has = *eats* ....
1 We've just <u>had</u> a game of tennis.   had = ...
2 My father <u>has</u> a cup of cocoa every evening. has = ...
3 We've just <u>had</u> three weeks in Morocco.   had = ...
4 Claire <u>had</u> lots of presents on her birthday. had = ...

D The verb have (1–3)

Complete the conversation. Use *have/have got* or the action verb *have*.

Claire: (►) .You've..got....... (you / have) an empty plate, Henry. Would you like some more food?
Henry: Oh, yes please. I must say, (1) .... (we / have) a great time.
Luckily (2) .... (you / have) lots of room in here.
Claire: Yes, it's a nice big flat, although (3) .... (it / not / have) a balcony.
Mark: How was Brazil? (4) .... (you / have) a good holiday?
Claire: Yes, (5) .... (I / have) a lovely time, thank you.
Henry: (6) .... (you / have) some photos here to show us?
Claire: Yes, you must (7) .... (have) a look at them some time. But I was
so busy doing things (8) .... (I / not / have) time to take very
many.

32 Short forms (**it's**, **don't**)

1 The use of short forms

I've lost my bank card. I **don't** know where it is.

I'll help you look for it. It's probably in your room somewhere.

A short form like **it's** or **don't** stands for the full form **it is** or **do not**. We leave out one or more letters and we write an apostrophe (') instead. We use short forms in conversational English and in informal writing such as a letter to a friend. Short forms are sometimes called 'contracted forms'.

We cannot use a short form when the word is stressed, in a short answer for example.
*Have you looked in this drawer? ~ Yes, I **have**.* NOT ~~Yes, I've.~~
But we can use **n't** in a short answer: *No, I **haven't**.*

2 The most common short forms

Some verbs can have short forms when they come after **I**, **you**, etc.

VERB	SHORT FORMS
am	I'm
are	you're, we're, they're
is/has	he's, she's, it's
have	I've, you've, we've, they've
had/would	I'd, you'd, he'd, she'd, it'd, we'd, they'd
will	I'll, you'll, he'll, she'll, it'll, we'll, they'll
shall	I'll, we'll

A short form can also come after a noun.
*   **Vicky's** lost her bank card. (Vicky **has** ...)   *The* **card'll** *be in here.* (The card **will** ...)

There are also some short forms with question words and with **here**, **there** or **that**.

who's, what's, where's, when's, how's, who'd, who'll, what'll
here's, there's, that's, there'll, that'll, there'd, that'd

There is a negative short form **n't** which can come after some verbs.

aren't, isn't, wasn't, weren't, haven't, hasn't, hadn't, don't /dəʊnt/, doesn't, didn't, won't (= will not),
shan't (= shall not), can't /kɑːnt/, couldn't, mustn't /ˈmʌsnt/, needn't, mightn't, shouldn't, wouldn't, daren't

Sometimes we can shorten either **not** or the verb.
*   *It is* **not** *funny.* → *It* **isn't** *funny.* or *It's* **not** *funny.*
*   *You will* **not** *believe it.* → *You* **won't** *believe it.* OR *You'll* **not** *believe it.*
But we cannot use **n't** after **I**.
*   *I am* **not** *sure.* → *I'm* **not** *sure.* NOT ~~I amn't sure.~~

3 's and 'd

's can be **is** or **has**, and **'d** can be **had** or **would**.
*   *She's short, and she's got fair hair.* (She **is** short ... she **has** got ...)
*   *If I'd known, I'd have told you.* (If I **had** known, I **would** have ...)

Practice

A Short forms (2)

Write the sentences in a more informal style, with short forms.

In a business letter	In a letter to a friend
▶ You are quite right.	You're quite right.
1 It is a difficult problem.	
2 I have seen the results.	
3 I do not have any information.	
4 We have not reached a decision.	
5 I am very excited about it.	
6 You need not decide now.	
7 It is not yet certain.	
8 We will be pleased to see you.	
9 Do not worry.	
10 I would like to buy a new computer.	
11 We are willing to help.	
12 We will not know the result for some time.	

B Short forms (2)

Complete the dialogues. Put in the short form of these phrases:
do not, he is, I am, is not, it is, what is, where is

▶ How are you? ~ .I'm........... fine, thanks.

1 .... your luggage? ~ .... in Los Angeles.

2 Do you like this shirt? ~ No, I .... It .... my style.

3 .... that smell? ~ My husband. .... doing a chemical experiment.

C 's and 'd (3)

Write the forms in full. Use *is*, *has*, *had* or *would*.

▶ What's your name?	What is your name?
1 I'd like a coffee, please.	
2 There's been an accident.	
3 That's correct.	
4 I'd seen the film before.	
5 Who's got the key?	
6 We'd have stopped if we'd seen you.	

33 Emphatic do

1 Introduction

Melanie wants to emphasize the idea that the picture is nice and that she likes it. She wants to say this in a strong and positive way.

NEUTRAL	EMPHATIC
It's nice.	*It **is** nice.*
I like it.	*I **do** like it.*

2 Emphatic forms

Often we can be emphatic by using a full form like **is** or **have**, rather than a short form such as **'s** or **'ve** (see Unit 32). We stress the word when we speak it.

   *Yes, it **is** late. It's half past one in the morning.*   *My goodness you **have** done a lot of work. Well done.*

We can also stress modal verbs such as **will** and **should**.

   *You **will** write to me, won't you?*   *You really **should** drive more carefully. We almost had an accident.*

In the Present Simple we put **do** before the verb.

   *You're so right. I **do** agree with you.*   *Your hair is much too long. You **do** need a haircut.*
   *We **do** hope you can come to our barbecue.*   *I'm getting fed up with those dogs. They **do** make such a noise.*

In the third person singular we use **does**.

   *The city centre **does** get crowded, doesn't it?*
   *Emma says Matthew doesn't care about her, but he says he **does** care.*

We do not add -**s** to the verb.

   *It does **look** nice.* NOT *It does looks nice.*

In the past simple we use **did**.

   *We **did** enjoy the concert. It was really good.*   *You shouldn't have forgotten. I **did** remind you.*
   *Vicky is quite sure that she **did** see a ghost.*

We do not add -**ed** to the verb.

   *We did **enjoy** it.* NOT *We did enjoyed it.*

3 The imperative with do

We can use **do** with an imperative for emphasis.

   ***Do** hurry up, or we'll be late.*   *Oh, **do** be quiet. I'm trying to concentrate.*

Here **do** makes the speaker sound more worried or annoyed. We use this structure only in an informal situation.

But we can also use **do** with an imperative in offers and invitations (see page 122).

   ***Do** have some more soup.*   ***Do** take a seat, won't you?*

Here **do** sounds very polite.

Practice

A Emphatic **do** (1–2)

Put in the emphatic forms of these sentences: *I like my new portrait. I'm smiling.*
It's foggy today. Yes, I'll be late home. Yes, I remembered the water.

▶   Yes, I will be late home.

1 .... 3 ....

2 .... 4 ....

B Emphatic **do** (1–2)

Complete the answers. Use a pronoun + emphatic *do* + a verb.

▶ Tom: Melanie is always helping people, isn't she?

     David: Yes, she does help .... a lot of people.

1 Trevor: How much did that dress cost?

     Laura: Well, ... rather a lot.

2 Jessica: Someone once told me I look like the singer Arlene Black.

     Natasha: Well, ... a bit like her, actually.

3 Daniel: This train doesn't stop at our station.

     Matthew: Are you sure? I think .... there.

4 Nick: Why didn't you go to the match on Saturday?

     Tom: What do you mean? .... to the match.

5 Vicky: Matthew and Emma never quarrel.

     Rachel: Oh yes, ... All the time, in fact.

C Emphatic **do** (1–3)

What would you say? Use *do*, *does* or *did*.

▶ Tell your friend that you worry about your job prospects.

     You know, I do worry about my job prospects. ....

1 Say that you finished the crossword today.

     Actually, ...

2 Admit that your room needs tidying up.

     I'm afraid ....

3 Explain to your teacher that you find the work difficult.

     I'm afraid ....

4 Say that you wanted to give the course up.

     Actually, ...

5 Offer your friend a chocolate.

     Here you are. ....

6 Admit that this place depresses you.

     You know, ...

34 Yes/no questions

1 Use

Are you ready, Vicky?

Yes, nearly. **Has anyone seen my bag?**

Yes, it's on the chair.

Right. **Shall we go then?**

A yes/no question is one that we can answer with **yes** or **no**.

> *Are you ready? ~ **Yes**, nearly./**No**, not quite.*
> *Has anyone seen my bag? ~ **Yes**, it's on the chair./**No**, I don't think so.*

These questions are asking for information. For example, Daniel wants to know if Vicky is ready or not.

Sometimes yes/no questions have other uses, especially questions with modal verbs. For example, when Matthew says *Shall we go then?* he is making a suggestion, not asking for information. Here are some examples of the different uses.

Making a suggestion:	***Shall** we eat out tonight?*
Requesting:	***Can/Could** you write the address down for me, please?*
Offering:	***Can** I carry something for you? ~ No, it's OK, thanks.*
Inviting:	***Would** you like to come to a party? ~ Yes, I'd love to.*
Asking permission:	***May** I use your phone? ~ Yes, of course.*

2 Form

A yes/no question begins with an auxiliary verb. An auxiliary verb is a form of **be** or **have** or a modal verb, e.g. **can**. The auxiliary verb comes before the subject.

AUXILIARY	SUBJECT	VERB		
Is	***it***	*raining?*	STATEMENT:	*It* $\boxed{is}$ *raining.*
Has	***David***	*got a car?*		
Can	***Emma***	*drive?*	QUESTION:	$\boxed{Is}$ *it raining?*

The main verb **be** also comes before the subject in a question.

> ***Is** it cold out there?*   ***Are** you ready?*   ***Was** it easy?*

If there is more than one auxiliary verb, only the first one comes before the subject.

> ***Have** you been working?*   ***Could** we have done better?*

In the Present Simple and Past Simple we use a form of **do**.

AUXILIARY	SUBJECT	VERB		
Do	***the buses***	*run every day?*	STATEMENT:	*They* $\boxed{(do)}$ *run every day.*
Does	***Mark***	*play golf?*		
Did	***you***	*like the concert?*	QUESTION:	$\boxed{Do}$ *they run every day?*

A question cannot begin with an ordinary verb such as **run**, **play** or **like**.

> NOT *Plays Mark golf?* and NOT *Liked you the concert?*

The verb after the subject does not end in **-s** or **-ed**.

> NOT *Does Mark plays golf?* and NOT *Did you liked the concert?*

▷ 35 Answers with **yes** and **no**

Practice

A Use (1)

Write down the use of each question. Choose from these uses:
asking for information (x3), *asking permission, inviting, making a suggestion, offering, requesting* (x2)

▶ Could you post this letter for me?   requesting

▶ Can we get a number 35 bus from this stop?   asking for information

1 Can I help you with those bags?   offering
2 Shall we stop for a rest?   asking permission
3 Is it Tuesday today?   asking for information
4 Could you wait a moment, please?   requesting
5 Would you like to have tea with us?   offering
6 Will your friend be here next weekend?   asking for information
7 May I sit down?   asking permission

B Form (2)

Claude Jennings, the World Quiz Champion, is going to be on Guy's chat show.
Guy is wondering what to ask Claude. Read what Guy is thinking and write down his questions.

▶ (I expect Claude has won lots of prizes.) Have you won lots of prizes?
1 (I wonder if he's a rich man.) Is he a rich man?
2 (Perhaps quizzes are his only hobby.)
3 (I expect he worked hard at school.)
4 (I wonder if he's got any other interests.)
5 (I wonder if it's an interesting life.)
6 (Perhaps his wife asks him quiz questions.)
7 (And maybe he answers questions in his dreams.)

C Yes/no questions (1–2)

What would you say in these situations?

▶ You want to know if Mark has been to Los Angeles. Ask Sarah.
Has Mark been to Los Angeles?

1 You aren't sure if Rachel and Vicky are going to America. Ask them.

2 You want to know if Laura plays tennis. Ask Trevor.

3 You are wondering if Claire enjoyed her holiday. Ask her.

4 You want to suggest to Rachel that you both go for a walk.

5 You need to know if David will be at the club tonight. Ask him.

6 You want to know if the train is on time. Ask Mark.

7 You are wondering if Mike and Harriet go camping. Ask David.

8 You want to ask Matthew if you can borrow his squash racket.

9 You want to know if Nick has got a motor bike. Ask him.

QUESTIONS, NEGATIVES AND ANSWERS   • PAGE 85

35 Short answers, e.g. Yes, it is.

1 Answering yes or no

Look at the answers to these questions.

> *Is it raining?* ~ **Yes.**   *Are we going to be late?* ~ **Yes, we are.**
> *Did you say something?* ~ **No.**   *Did you finish the crossword?* ~ **No, I didn't.**

We can sometimes answer a question with a simple **yes** or **no**, but we often use a short answer like **No, I didn't**. We usually put a comma after **yes** or **no**.

We do not normally use a full sentence, but we can do if we want to add emphasis to the answer.

> *Did you open my letter?* ~ **No, I didn't open your letter.**

Sometimes, to be polite, we may need to add information.

> *Did you get the tickets?* ~ No, I didn't. **There wasn't time, I'm afraid. Sorry.**

2 Form

A positive short answer is **yes** + a pronoun + an auxiliary.

QUESTION		SHORT ANSWER		
Auxiliary			Pronoun	Auxiliary
Are	you working tomorrow?	~ Yes,	I	am.
Has	Emma got a computer?	~ Yes,	she	has.
Will	I need my passport?	~ Yes,	you	will.
Did	they repair your phone?	~ Yes,	they	did.

We can also use the main verb **be** in a short answer.

> **Is** it time to go? ~ **Yes, it is.** *It's ten past eleven.*

Note that in the Present Simple and Past Simple we use a form of **do**.

> **Do** *you like classical music?* ~ *Yes, I* **do**. NOT *Yes, I like.*

A negative short answer is **no** + a pronoun + an auxiliary + **n't**.

QUESTION		SHORT ANSWER		
Auxiliary			Pronoun	Auxiliary + n't
Is	the photocopier working now?	~ No,	it	isn't.
Have	the children gone to sleep?	~ No,	they	haven't.
Will	there be food at the party?	~ No,	there	won't.
Does	this train stop at Derby?	~ No,	it	doesn't.

But note: **No, I'm not.**

> *Are you working tomorrow?* ~ **No, I'm not.** NOT *No, I amn't.*

3 Answering requests, suggestions, offers and invitations

To answer a request, suggestion, etc, we normally use a phrase like **Yes, of course** or **Yes, please** rather than a short answer. If we answer in the negative, we have to give some explanation.

Request:	*Could you help me move these chairs, please?* ~ *Yes, of course.* OR *I'm afraid I'm rather busy.*
Suggestion:	*Shall we have a coffee?* ~ *Yes, OK.* OR *Sorry, I can't. I have to go.*
Offer:	*Can I give you a hand?* ~ *Yes, please. That's very kind of you.* OR *It's OK, thanks. I can manage.*
Invitation:	*Would you like to come to the barbecue?* ~ *Yes, please. I'd love to.* OR *I'd love to, but I'll be away.*

Short negative answers would sound strange or impolite here.

Practice

A Form (2)

It's eleven o'clock, and everyone has arrived at a party. Put in the short answers.

▶ Have you got a drink? ~ _Yes, I have_....., thank you. I've just put it down somewhere.

1 Can you speak Arabic? ~ ...., but not very well.

2 Is it raining outside? ~ .... It's just started.

3 Has David come with you? ~ .... He's in hospital, actually.

4 Did you come by car, Tom? ~ .... It took ages because of all the traffic.

5 Are those people over there your friends? ~ .... I don't know them at all.

6 Do you like England? ~ .... I'm enjoying my stay here.

7 Is your brother here? ~ .... He's away on business at the moment.

8 Have you seen Nick recently? ~ .... I think he's moved away.

B Form (2)

It's one o'clock in the morning, and the party is in full swing.
People are still talking. Put in the short answers.

▶ Are you French? ~ _No, I'm not_....... I'm Italian. I'm from Milan.

1 Will you and Laura be here in August? ~ .... We're going to France.

2 Did you remember to bring the photos? ~ .... I'll give them to you in a minute.

3 Has Rita broken up with her boyfriend? ~ .... It's all over, she told me.

4 Did you see that documentary about the ozone layer on television last night?
~ .... I was working late, unfortunately.

5 Does Laura like these old songs? ~ .... She loves Elvis Presley.

6 Are you and Mike staying the night here? ~ .... We have to get home tonight.

7 Can we afford a taxi? ~ .... It's quite a long way.

8 Are you OK, Vicky? ~ .... I feel really awful.

C Answering questions (1–3)

Which would normally be the best answer?

▶ Are you busy today?
   a) ☐ Yes, busy. b) ☑ Yes, I am.

1 Is it too hot in here for you?
   a) ☐ No, it isn't. b) ☐ No, I'm fine, thanks.

2 Do you know Emma?
   a) ☐ Yes. b) ☐ Yes, we live in the same building.

3 Tell me, did you steal my money?
   a) ☐ No. b) ☐ No, I didn't steal your money.

4 Do you live on the campus?
   a) ☐ Yes, I do. b) ☐ Yes, I live on it.

5 Would you like to come out with us for the day?
   a) ☐ Yes, I would like. b) ☐ Yes, please.

6 Is it the eighteenth today?
   a) ☐ Yes, it is. b) ☐ Yes, it is the eighteenth of November today.

7 Did you bring my CD?
   a) ☐ No. b) ☐ No, sorry. I forgot it.

8 Can I carry your bags?
   a) ☐ No, you can't. b) ☐ It's all right, thanks.

36 Wh-questions

1 Introduction

Reporter Kitty Beamish is interviewing
some guerrilla fighters.

Kitty: Guerrillas:
Why are you fighting?   For our freedom.
What can you do for the people?   We can help them.
When will the war be over?   Very soon.

A wh-question begins with a question word. Question words
are **who**, **what**, **which**, **whose**, **where**, **when**, **why** and **how**.
We use a wh-question to ask for information.

2 Form

Most wh-questions begin with a question word + an auxiliary verb + the subject. (For another form of
wh-question, see Unit 37.) An auxiliary verb is a form of **be** or **have** or a modal verb, e.g. **can**.

QUESTION WORD	AUXILIARY	SUBJECT	VERB
What	is	Kitty	doing?
Where	have	you	put the map?
When	can	we	travel safely?

The main verb **be** also comes before the subject in questions.
    *Where **is** Kitty?*   *How **are** you?*   *What **was** that noise?*
If there is more than one auxiliary verb, only the first one comes before the subject.
    *The guerrillas **have been** hiding.* → *Where **have** the guerrillas been hiding?*
    *I **should have** said something.* → *What **should** I have said?*

In the Present Simple and Past Simple we use a form of **do**.

QUESTION WORD	AUXILIARY	SUBJECT	VERB
Where	do	people	meet?
How	does	the radio	work?
What	did	the guerrillas	say?

An ordinary verb such as **meet**, **work** or **say** cannot come before the subject.
    NOT ~~Where meet people?~~ and NOT ~~How works the radio?~~
The verb after the subject does not end in -s or -ed.
    NOT ~~How does the radio works?~~ and NOT ~~What did the guerrillas said?~~

3 Question phrases

Look at these question phrases with **what** and **how**.
    What time is your friend arriving? ~ Half past eight.   **What colour** is your toothbrush? ~ Yellow.
    What kind of/What sort of club is it? ~ A nightclub.   **How old** is your sister? ~ She's twenty.
    How often do you go out? ~ About once a week, usually.   **How far** is the beach? ~ Only five minutes' walk.
    How long will the meeting last? ~ An hour or so, I expect.   **How many** televisions have you got? ~ Three.
    How much money did you spend? ~ About a hundred pounds.

Practice

A Wh-questions (1–2)

What would you say in these situations?

▶ You are talking to a man at a party. Ask him where he works.
Where do you work?

1 You want to know what the date is today. Ask your friend.

2 You've forgotten when the course finishes. Ask your friend.

3 Your friend is having a party. You'd like to know who he has invited. Ask him.

4 Your favourite band are going to give a concert. Ask how you can get tickets.

5 You are in town with a friend, and you are wondering where the two of you are going to have lunch. What do you ask?

B Question words and phrases (1–3)

Quiz champion Claude Jennings is answering questions. Put in these words and phrases:
how far, how long, how often, how many, what, what colour, what kind, when, where, who

Quiz-master:		Claude:
▶ *What colour*	is the Greek flag?	Blue and white.
1	is Melbourne?	It's in Australia.
2	centimetres are there in a kilometre?	A hundred thousand.
3	did the Second World War end?	In 1945.
4	did Romeo love?	Juliet.
5	is Sirius?	It's a star.
6	is it from Los Angeles to San Francisco?	About 400 miles.
7	are the Olympic Games held?	Every four years.
8	of food is Cheddar?	It's cheese.
9	is a game of rugby?	Eighty minutes.

C Wh-questions (1–3)

Guy is interviewing a guest on his chat show. It's the actress Melissa Livingstone, who is in the TV soap opera 'Round the Corner'. Put in Guy's questions.

▶ Guy: *How often do you record 'Round the Corner'?*
Melissa: Oh, we record it every day. It's a full-time job, you know.

1 Guy: And .... it?
Melissa: In Birmingham, at the BBC studios.

2 Guy: ....
Melissa: How many? Well, let me see, I think we've done a thousand programmes.

3 Guy: ....
Melissa: I'm not going to tell you. How much money I earn is my business.

4 Guy: OK, I'm sorry. ....
Melissa: Oh, a long time ago. I started acting when I was twelve.

5 Guy: ....
Melissa: My plans for the future? I just want to go on with 'Round the Corner'.

37 Subject/object questions

1 Who and what

Who *is interviewing Kitty?*	**Who** *is Kitty interviewing?*
Who and **what** can be the subject of a question. The word order is the same as in a statement.	**Who** and **what** can also be the object. An auxiliary (e.g. **did, will**) comes before the subject.
SUBJECT	OBJECT
Who rang *you?* (Someone rang you.) **Who is helping** *you?* (Someone is helping you.) **What will happen** *next?* (Something will happen next.)	**Who did** *you* **ring?** (You rang someone.) **Who are** *you* **helping?** (You are helping someone.) **What will** *they do next?* (They will do something next.)

Who and **what** can also be the object of a preposition, e.g. **to, with**.
(For prepositions in questions, see Unit 38.) Compare these sentences.

SUBJECT	OBJECT
Who was talking *to you?* (Someone was talking to you.) **What wine goes** *with fish?* (Some wine goes with fish.)	**Who were** *you* **talking** *to?* (You were talking to someone.) **What does** *this colour* **go** *with?* (This colour goes with something.)

2 Which, whose, how many and how much

These words can also be either the subject or the object.

SUBJECT	OBJECT
Which program will work *best?* (One of the programs will work best.) **Whose dog is barking** *over there?* (Someone's dog is barking over there.) **How many people came** *past?* (Some people came past.) **How much oil got** *into the river?* (Some oil got into the river.)	**Which program will** *you* **use?** (You will use one of the programs.) **Whose dog is** *Melanie* **walking?** (Melanie is walking someone's dog.) **How many people did** *you* **see?** (You saw some people.) **How much oil did** *you* **buy?** (You bought some oil.)

A Who and what as subject and object (1)

Read about the situations and answer each question in a single phrase.

▶ The morning after his party, Tom was cleaning up. David came along and took away some empty bottles for him. Nick had just woken up after spending the night on Tom's sofa. He watched them for a while.
   a) Who helped Tom? David................ b) Who did Nick help? No one............

1 Nick wants to marry Rita. She's been out with him a few times, but really she's in love with Tom. Unfortunately he isn't in love with her.
   a) Who is Nick in love with? .... b) Who is in love with Tom? ....

2 Mark met Sarah at the airport. The plane was two hours late. On the way out they passed Mike standing at a bus stop, but they didn't notice him.
   a) Who met Sarah? .... b) What was Mike waiting for? ....

3 There was an accident at the crossroads. A lorry crashed into a van that was waiting at the lights. The van slid forward and crashed into a car. The van driver had to go to hospital.
   a) What hit the van? .... b) What did the van hit? ....

B Who and what as subject and object (1)

People aren't giving you enough information. Ask questions with who or what.

▶ Something has happened. ~ Oh? What has happened?
▶ I've invited someone to tea. ~ Well? Who have you invited?
1 Somebody is having a party. ~ Oh, really? ....
2 I was reading something. ~ Oh? ....
3 I've learnt something. ~ Go on, tell me. ....
4 We should do something. ~ Yes, I know, but ....
5 Someone is looking for you. ~ Oh? ....
6 I'm looking for someone. ~ Maybe I can help. ....
7 Rachel is planning something. ~ Is she? ....
8 Somebody has moved in next door. ~ Oh, really? ....
9 Something is worrying me. ~ Well, tell me. ....
10 I want to meet someone. ~ What do you mean? ....

C Which, whose, how many and how much (2)

Harriet is visiting her grandmother, Mrs Evans. It's Mrs Evans's birthday.
She can't hear very well, and she sometimes gets confused. Complete her questions.

Harriet:	Mrs Evans:
▶ So ten people have sent cards.	Pardon? How many people have sent cards?
▶ I met David's friend yesterday.	What? Whose friend did you meet?
1 You can keep those photos.	Photos? Which ....
2 Those flowers look lovely.	Do they? Which ....
3 Fifty pounds went missing.	Missing? How much ....
4 I passed Mark's house earlier.	Pardon? Whose ....
5 The doctor has four children.	Really? How many ....
6 Doctors earn lots of money.	I don't know. How much ....
7 Mike's uncle has died.	What's that? Whose ....
8 Trevor's wife is coming later.	Oh? Whose ....

38 Prepositions in wh-questions

1 Introduction

What are you looking **for**, Vicky?

My money. I don't know if I've got enough.

What are you worrying **about**? It's free, look.

Daniel and Rachel each ask Vicky a question. In each question, the word **what** is the object of a preposition (**for**, **about**).

> ***What*** *are you looking* ***for****?*
> (You are looking **for something.**)
> ***What*** *are you worrying* ***about****?*
> (You are worrying **about something.**)

The preposition normally comes in the same place as in a statement: **looking for, worrying about.**

> NOT ~~For what are you looking?~~
> NOT ~~About what are you worrying?~~

But in more formal English, the preposition can come before the question word.

> ***In which*** *warehouse were the goods stored?*
> OR ***Which*** *warehouse were the goods stored* ***in****?*

In formal English we use a preposition + whom (not **who**).

> ***From whom*** *did you obtain the information?*
> OR ***Who*** *did you obtain the information* ***from****?*

Here are some more examples of prepositions in wh-questions.

> ***Who*** *are we waiting* ***for****? ~ Rachel.*
> ***What's*** *Nick laughing* ***at****? ~ Oh, one of Tom's jokes.*
> ***Where*** *are you* ***from****?/****Where*** *do you come* ***from****? ~ Sydney.*
> ***What kind of*** *holiday are you interested* ***in****? ~ A package holiday.*
> ***Who*** *did you go out* ***with*** *last night? ~ Just a friend.*

2 What ... for and what ... like

We can use a question with **what ... for** to ask about purpose.

> ***What*** *did you buy this computer magazine* ***for****? ~ To read about business software.*
> ***What*** *are these bricks* ***for****? ~ We're going to build a wall.*
> ***What*** *are they digging the road up* ***for****? ~ They're repairing a gas pipe.*

What ... for means the same as **why**.

> ***Why*** *are they digging up the road? ~ They're repairing a gas pipe.*

We can use **what ... like** to ask if something is good or bad, interesting or boring, etc.

> ***What*** *was the party* ***like****? ~ Oh, we had a great time.*
> ***What's*** *the place* ***like*** *where you live? ~ It's pretty quiet.*

Note also **look like.**

> ***What*** *does your friend* ***look like****? ~ She's very tall and blond.*

But we use **how** to ask about someone's well-being.

> ***How*** *are you? ~ I'm OK, thanks. And you?*
> ***How*** *are you getting on in your new job? ~ I'm really enjoying it.*

Compare these two questions.

> ***How's*** *Melanie? ~ Oh, she's fine, thanks. (She is happy/in good health.)*
> ***What's*** *Melanie* ***like****? ~ She's very nice. (She is a nice person.)*

Practice

A Prepositions in wh-questions (1)

Ask these people questions with *what*.
Use these verbs and prepositions: *look at, look for, point at, talk about, wait for*

2 It's ... erm ... you see ... er ...

▶ What are you looking for?

1 ....

2 ....

3 ....

4 ....

B Prepositions in wh-questions (1)

Put in the question. Use *what* and put the preposition in brackets at the end.

▶ Melanie: Tom is smiling. He's pleased. (about)
   David: Yes, he is. What is he pleased about?
▶ Laura: I'm busy today. I'm getting ready. (for)
   Trevor: What are you getting ready for?
1 Jessica: I've done something awful. I'm ashamed. (of)
   Andrew: ....
2 Trevor: Haven't you heard of Kitty Beamish? She's famous. (for)
   Ilona: No, I haven't. ....
3 Sarah: Mark is annoyed. He's going to complain. (about)
   Claire: ....
4 Matthew: Emma's in a hurry. She's going to be late. (for)
   Daniel: ....
5 Vicky: I don't feel very relaxed. I feel nervous. (about)
   Rachel: ....

C What ... for and what ... like (2)

Trevor has just come home from work. Complete the conversation. Put in *for*, *how*, *like* or *what*.

Trevor: Hello, my love. (▶) How are you?
Laura: Hello. I'm all right, but I'm in a bit of a rush getting ready for the barbecue.
Trevor: Er, I forgot to tell you that I invited two more people.
Laura: (1) .... are you telling me now (2) .... ? I've bought all the food. I just hope
          there's enough. Anyway, who are these people? (3) .... are they (4) .... ?
Trevor: They're friends of Harriet's. They're very nice people. And after all, (5) .... are
          parties (6) .... ? To meet new people.
Laura: It isn't a party, it's a barbecue. (7) .... 's the weather going to be (8) .... ?
Trevor: The forecast said it's going to be perfect. Warm and dry.
Laura: Good. And (9) .... was your day?
Trevor: Oh, not too bad. Busy as usual.

39 Who, what or which?

1 What or which?

We can use **what** or **which** before a noun.

WHAT	WHICH
***What sport** do you play?* ***What books** do you read?* We use **what** when there is a wide choice of possible answers. We ask *What sport?* because there are lots of different sports.	***Which way** do we go here?* ***Which finger** did you break?* We use **which** when there is a limited number of possible answers. We ask *Which way?* because there are only two or three ways to go.
What sport? (Tennis or golf or football or hockey or … ?)	*Which way?* (Right or left?)

After **which** we sometimes say the possible answers.

> ***Which** café did you go to, **Snoopy's, the Coffee Pot or the Tea Gardens**?*
> ***Which** phone shall I use, **this one or the one in the office**?*

Sometimes **what** and **which** are both possible.

> ***What** day/**Which** day is your evening class?*   ***What** train/**Which** train will you catch?*
> ***What** platform/**Which** platform does the train go from?*   ***What** part/**Which** part of Italy are you from?*

2 Patterns with **who, what** and **which**

We can use **who, what** and **which** without a noun.

> ***Who** sent the fax?*   ***What** do you think of our plan?*   ***Which** is quicker, the bus or the train?*

We can use **what** and **which** before a noun, but not **who**.

> ***Which** secretary sent the fax?* NOT ~~Who secretary sent the fax?~~

We can use **which** with **one** or **ones**, or with **of**.

> *You can have a photo. **Which one** would you like?*
> *You can have some of the photos. **Which ones** would you like?*
> ***Which of** these photos would you like?*

But we cannot use **who** or **what** before **of**.

> ***Which of** the secretaries?* but NOT ~~Who of the secretaries?~~

Who always means a person.

> ***Who** did you see?* (a person)

What usually means a thing. It can mean a person only when it comes before a noun.

> ***What** did you see?* (a thing)   ***What** doctor/**What** film did you see?* (a person or a thing)

Which can mean a person or a thing.

> ***Which** doctor/film did you see?* (a person or a thing)

▷ 102 **One** and **ones**

Practice

A What or which? (1)

The questions you are asking have a number of possible answers.
If the list of answers is incomplete, ask a question with *what*. If the list is complete, use *which*.

▶ (Do you play the piano, or the violin, or the guitar, or ...?)
   What musical instrument do you play?
▶ (Did you go to the Little Theatre or the Theatre Royal?)
   Which theatre did you go to?
1 (Did you take the morning flight or the afternoon flight?)
   ....
2 (Did you stay at the Grand Hotel or the Bristol?)
   ....
3 (Do you like classical music, or jazz, or rock music, or ...?)
   ....
4 (Did you buy 'Time' magazine, or 'Newsweek', or a computer magazine, or ...?)
   ....
5 (Do you work for EuroChemicals, or ICM, or SenCo, or ...?)
   ....
6 (Are you learning English, or Spanish, or Arabic, or Japanese, or ...?)
   ....

B What or which? (1)

Rita is moving into a new flat. Trevor has come to see the flat and help her move in.
Complete his questions. Put in *what* or *which*.

▶ Trevor: *What*............ number is this building?
  Rita: Forty-two.
1 Trevor: I didn't realize there were only three floors. .... floor is your flat on?
  Rita: The first floor.
2 Trevor: It's a very nice flat. .... room will be your living-room?
  Rita: This one here, I thought.
3 Trevor: .... colour are you going to paint it?
  Rita: Oh, I don't know yet.
4 Trevor: .... time is your furniture arriving?
  Rita: Three o'clock, they said.
5 Trevor: I'll need some petrol. .... way is the nearest petrol station?
  Rita: Turn left at the end of the street.

C Who, what or which? (2)

Detectives Wilson and Taylor are looking into the murder of Lord Weybridge at his country house.
Put in *who, what* or *which*.

Wilson: (▶) .Which........of the guests in this house is the murderer, do you think, Taylor?
Taylor: I don't know yet. (1) .... had the opportunity? (2) .... of the guests
         had the chance to do it?
Wilson: (3) .... happened after dinner last night? That's what we have to find out.
Taylor: There must be a motive for the murder. (4) .... motive could the murderer have?
Wilson: Love or money – they're the usual motives. (5) .... of them is it, I wonder?
Taylor: (6) .... did Lord Weybridge leave his money to? That's the question, Wilson.

Test H: Questions

A

Put the words in the right order and ask the question.

► everyone / is / ready
  Is everyone ready?

1 been / have / where / you

2 do / postcards / sell / you

3 belong / calculator / does / this / to / who

4 are / here / how / long / staying / you

5 is / like / new / office / what / your

6 are / flights / full / of / the / which

7 carnival / does / start / the / time / what

8 decided / has / holiday / Nancy / on / what

B

Put in the correct question word or phrase.

► *What* .... did you buy? ~ A box of chocolates.
1 .... is this building? ~ It's about two hundred years old.
2 .... does your team play in? ~ Red.
3 .... bag are you carrying? ~ Judy's.
4 .... money do you earn? ~ About £500 a week.
5 .... hand do you write with? ~ My right hand.
6 .... of shop do you work in? ~ A toy shop.
7 .... first stepped on the moon? ~ Neil Armstrong, wasn't it?
8 .... is your mother? ~ She's much better, thank you.
9 .... is it to the post office? ~ About two hundred metres.
10 .... do you take a holiday? ~ Once a year.
11 .... name will you give the baby? ~ We haven't thought of one yet.

C

Write the sentences correctly.

► ~~Would like you to go sailing?~~   *Would you like to go sailing?*
1 ~~Do you be a student here?~~
2 ~~How many cakes have eaten you?~~
3 ~~Enjoyed you your walk?~~
4 ~~Where your friends have gone?~~
5 ~~What kind music do you like?~~
6 ~~Does Peter plays tennis?~~
7 ~~About what are you talking?~~
8 ~~What has it happened?~~

D

Read about each situation and write down the question.

▶ You want to know if it is raining.
  Is it raining?

▶ You need to ask Polly where she lives.
  Where do you live?

1 You would like to ask Nancy where she bought her coat.

2 You want to ask Susan if Amy can swim.

3 You want to ask Simon which band he likes best.

4 On the phone you want to know who you are speaking to.

5 You need to know how much video recorders cost.

6 You are asking permission to come in.

7 You need to find out how long the journey takes.

8 You want to ask Adrian what he locked the door for.

9 You want to ask what happens next.

10 You want to suggest that you all go out together.

E

Write the questions to which the underlined words are the answers.

▶ Christopher is going to London by train.
  How is Christopher going to London?

1 The Smiths have got three cars.

2 Janet works at the supermarket.

3 Andrea is learning English because she will need it in her job.

4 The film was really romantic.

5 The meeting will take place next Tuesday.

6 Tessa switched off the computer.

7 Mr Johnson's burglar alarm was ringing.

8 Anna went to the dance with Martin.

40 Negative statements

1 Use

Christopher Columbus

*Christopher Columbus was a famous explorer. At one time people believed that he had 'discovered' America. We know now this **isn't** true. Columbus **was not** the first European to travel to the New World. We **don't** know who was, but the Vikings had sailed there around the year 1000, and probably others before them. In 1492 Columbus sailed to San Salvador in the Bahamas and to other islands, but he never reached the mainland of North America. He actually thought he was in Asia. He certainly **didn't** discover America.*

We often use a negative statement to correct a mistaken idea, such as the idea that Christopher Columbus discovered America.

2 Negative verb forms

	POSITIVE	NEGATIVE	
be:	*are dancing*	***are not** dancing*	OR ***aren't** dancing*
have:	***have** seen*	***have not** seen*	OR ***haven't** seen*
Modal verb:	***must** stay*	***must not** stay*	OR ***mustn't** stay*

In a negative statement **not** or **n't** comes after the auxiliary verb.
The auxiliary verb is a form of **be**, **have** or a modal verb, e.g. **must**, **can**, **could**.

*The girls **are not** dancing.   The modem **isn't** working properly.*
*I **haven't** seen the new Disney film.   David **hasn't** got a car.*
*I **mustn't** stay long.   You **can't** turn right here.*
*I'm **not** feeling very awake today.*

We write **n't** without a space before it, e.g. **isn't**, **haven't**.

Not or **n't** also comes after the main verb **be**.

*The photos **are not** ready yet.   It **isn't** very warm in here.*

If there is more than one auxiliary verb, we put **not** or **n't** after the first one.

*This plate **hasn't** been washed.   You **shouldn't** have bothered.*

In the Present Simple and Past Simple, we use a form of **do**.

	POSITIVE	NEGATIVE	
Present Simple:	*work*	***do not** work*	OR ***don't** work*
	looks	***does not** look*	OR ***doesn't** look*
Past Simple:	*enjoyed*	***did not** enjoy*	OR ***didn't** enjoy*

*I **don't** work on Saturdays.* NOT ~~I work not on Saturdays.~~
*This part of town **doesn't** look very nice.   I'm afraid we **didn't** enjoy the day very much.*

The verb after **not** or **n't** does not end in **-s** or **-ed**.

NOT ~~It doesn't looks very nice~~ and NOT ~~We didn't enjoyed the day.~~

3 No and not

We can use **no** before a noun or an adjective + noun. The verb is positive.

***No** music is allowed after eleven.* OR *Music is not allowed after eleven.*
*There are **no** new houses in the village.* OR *There aren't any new houses in the village.*

We do not use **no** with a verb.

NOT ~~Music is no allowed~~ and NOT ~~The shops are no open.~~

Practice

A Use (1)

Read the information in 1 about Christopher Columbus.
Then choose a positive or a negative verb.

► Columbus ~~discovered~~/didn't discover America.
1 The first European to sail to the New World was/wasn't Columbus.
2 Europeans had/hadn't been to the New World before Columbus.
3 We know/don't know definitely who first sailed to America.
4 Columbus landed/didn't land on the North American mainland.
5 People's opinion of Columbus has/hasn't changed over the last 500 years.
6 When Columbus landed on San Salvador, he knew/didn't know where he was.
7 It is/isn't true that Columbus travelled across the United States.

B Negative verb forms (1)

Complete the conversation, Put in the negative forms of these words:
can, did, do, does, has, have, is, was, were

Rita: Does anyone live in that house next door?
Melanie: Yes, he's called Jake. He's rather strange. He (►) .hasn't. got a job, but he (1) ....
           be short of money because he's just bought a new car.
Rita: The house (2) .... look very smart.
Melanie: The people who lived there before Jake (3) .... look after it very well. And they
           (4) .... very good at gardening. When Jake bought the house, it had been
           empty for a while. It (5) .... very expensive. But he (6) .... interested
           in doing anything to it, as you can see.
Rita: Is he a friend?
Melanie: No, we aren't really friends. I (7) .... know him very well. I say hello when I see
           him, that's all. I (8) .... seen him for a while, actually.

C Negative verb forms (2)

Vicky and Rachel are good friends, but they are very different kinds of people.
Complete the sentences using a negative.

► Vicky gets upset, but Rachel .doesn't get upset. ....
1 Vicky gets headaches. Rachel is lucky. She ....
2 Rachel can relax. Vicky is different. She ....
3 Rachel missed a lecture yesterday, but Vicky ....
4 Vicky is a nervous person, but Rachel ....
5 Vicky loses things. Rachel ....
6 Rachel was a happy child. Vicky ....
7 Rachel has decided on a career, but Vicky...

D No and not (3)

Complete this paragraph from a travel article. Put in *no* or *not*.

Metropolis is (►) .not............. an attractive town. There are (1) .... parks or gardens in
the city centre. I saw (2) .... interesting buildings, only factories, offices and blocks of flats.
The hotels are (3) .... very good, and there are (4) .... first-class restaurants.
(5) .... tourists visit Metropolis, and I certainly do (6) .... want to go there
again.

41 Negative questions

1 Introduction

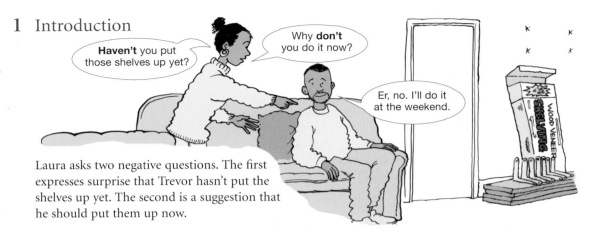

Haven't you put those shelves up yet?

Why **don't** you do it now?

Er, no. I'll do it at the weekend.

Laura asks two negative questions. The first expresses surprise that Trevor hasn't put the shelves up yet. The second is a suggestion that he should put them up now.

2 Form

We make a question negative by putting **n't** after the auxiliary (e.g **have**, **does**).

POSITIVE	NEGATIVE
Have you done it yet?	**Haven't** you done it yet?
What **does** the advert tell you?	What **doesn't** the advert tell you?
Who **eats** meat?	Who **doesn't** eat meat?
What **went** wrong?	What **didn't** go wrong?

3 The use of negative yes/no questions

A negative yes/no question often expresses surprise.
> ***Haven't** you put those shelves up yet?* (= I am surprised that you haven't yet.)
> ***Don't** the children want the ice-cream?* (= I am surprised that they don't want it.)

A question with **can't** can be a complaint or an impolite request.
> ***Can't** you sit down? You're blocking my view.*

We can also use a negative yes/no question instead of a statement and a tag.
> ***Aren't** you a friend of Harriet's?* (= You're a friend of Harriet's, aren't you?)

4 Yes/no answers

The answer **yes** means that the positive is true, and **no** means that the negative is true.
> *Haven't you repaired the car yet? ~ **Yes**, I did it yesterday.*
> *Haven't you repaired the car yet? ~ **No**, sorry. I haven't had time.*

5 The use of negative wh-questions

We can use **Why don't …?** for a suggestion.
> ***Why don't** you put the shelves up now? ~ Well, all right.*
> ***Why don't** we sit on the balcony? ~ Good idea.*

We can use **Why didn't …?** to criticize.
> *We'll have to stand now. **Why didn't** you book seats for us?* (= You should have booked seats for us.)

We can also use a wh-question to ask for information.
> ***Who hasn't** checked their baggage in? ~ Oh, I haven't. Sorry.*
> ***What don't** you understand? ~ This paragraph here.*

Practice

A Negative yes/no questions (2–3)

What would you say in these situations? Use negative yes/no questions.

▶ You are surprised to learn that Rita doesn't like football.
   Don't you like football, Rita?

1 You find it surprising that Melanie can't drive.
   ....

2 It's a surprise that Rachel won't be at the disco.
   ....

3 You find out that surprisingly Nick hasn't got a television.
   ....

B Negative yes/no questions (2–3)

Complete the conversations using the words in the brackets.

▶ Mike: I walked home from the town centre. (take / bus)
   Harriet: You mean you walked all the way? *Didn't you take a bus?*

1 Vicky: I think I'd like to lie down for a while. (feel / well)
   Rachel: Oh, dear. ....

2 Matthew: I'm looking forward to getting the photos you've sent. (arrive / yet)
   Richard: I sent them a week ago. ....

3 David: I saw Rita, but she walked straight past me. (say / hello)
   Melanie: Without speaking to you? ....

4 Andrew: I never sit by the pool. I hate water. (swim)
   Emma: Really? ....

C Yes/no answers (4)

Put in *yes* or *no*.

▶ Didn't Mike stop and give you a lift? ~ *No*........., he didn't, but maybe he didn't see me.
1 Aren't you tired after working all day? ~ ...., I feel fine.
2 Didn't you write the number down? ~ ...., but I've lost the piece of paper.
3 Haven't you got an umbrella? ~ ...., it's here in my bag.
4 Couldn't you get in to the opera? ~ ...., we didn't have tickets.

D Why not? (2, 5)

Reporter Kitty Beamish is investigating an accident at the Magic World theme park. A ride crashed, and people were injured. This is what Kitty has found out.

▶ The people on the ride didn't get enough help.   3 They aren't trained in first aid.
1 The staff didn't know what to do.   4 The ambulance wasn't called immediately.
2 They couldn't stop the ride.   5 The doctor didn't have a mobile phone.

What questions beginning with *why* does Kitty ask?

▶ *Why didn't the people on the ride get enough help?* ....
1 ....
2 ....
3 ....
4 ....
5 ....

42 Question tags, e.g. isn't it?

1 Use

Melanie:	*It's a lovely day, **isn't it?***
Harriet:	*Beautiful. We're having a glorious summer, **aren't we?***
Melanie:	*You haven't heard a forecast for the weekend, **have you?***
Harriet:	*No, I haven't, but I think it's going to stay sunny.*

A question tag is a short question added on to a statement. When a tag is spoken, the voice can go down or up.

FALLING	RISING
It's a lovely day, isn't it? ↘	*You haven't heard a forecast, have you?* ↗
With a falling intonation, the speaker thinks the statement is true. Melanie knows that it is a lovely day, and she is inviting Harriet to continue the conversation. The tag is not really a question.	With a rising intonation, the speaker is less sure. Melanie doesn't know if Harriet has heard a weather forecast or not. The tag is more like a real question.

2 Form

POSITIVE STATEMENT + NEGATIVE TAG	NEGATIVE STATEMENT + POSITIVE TAG
*It **is** very warm, **isn't** it?*	*It **isn't** very warm, **is** it?*
A negative tag is an auxiliary verb + n't + pronoun.	A positive tag is an auxiliary verb + pronoun.
*You've played before, **haven't you?***	*David hasn't got a car, **has he?***
*The children can swim, **can't they?***	*I shouldn't laugh, **should I?***
*It'll be dark soon, **won't it?***	*You aren't ill, **are you?***
*There was a mistake, **wasn't there?***	*The answer wasn't right, **was it?***

The pronoun (**you**, **he**, etc.) refers to the subject of the sentence, e.g. **you**, **David**.

In the Present Simple and Past Simple we use a form of **do**.

*You live near here, **don't you?***	*We don't have to pay, **do we?***
*This coat looks nice, **doesn't it?***	*The shower doesn't work, **does it?***
*I turned right, **didn't I?***	*Your horse didn't win, **did it?***

The answer **yes** means that the positive is true, and **no** means that the negative is true.
> *Mark works for Zedco, doesn't he? ~ **Yes**, he does. (He **works** for Zedco.)*
> *Melanie doesn't eat meat, does she? ~ **Yes**, I think she does. (She **eats** meat.)*
> *Claire is married, isn't she? ~ **No**, of course she isn't. (She **isn't** married.)*
> *Andrew hasn't got many friends, has he? ~ **No**. (He **hasn't** got many friends.)*

3 Requests and suggestions

After a request with an imperative (e.g. **Wait** …), we can use **can you?** or **could you?**
> ***Wait** here a moment, **can you?** **Give** me an example, **could you?***

We can also use **You couldn't …, could you?** or **You haven't …, have you?** for a request.
> ***You couldn't** help me, **could you?** **You haven't** got a pound, **have you?***

After **Don't** … the tag is **will you?**: ***Don't** make any noise, **will you?***

After **Let's** … we use **shall we?**: ***Let's** sit in the garden, **shall we?***

▷ page 378 Question tags in American English

Practice

A Use (1)

Look carefully at each statement and tag. Say if it is more likely to be a comment (with falling intonation) or a question (with rising intonation).

▶ This price list is up to date, isn't it? ~ Yes, it is.   *a question*

1 It was a super show, wasn't it? ~ Great. I really enjoyed it.   ....

2 These sweaters are nice, aren't they? ~ I like this one.   ....

3 We've got time for a coffee, haven't we? ~ A quick one maybe.   ....

4 Let me see, the bus goes at ten past, doesn't it? ~ Quarter past.   ....

B Form (2)

You are at a barbecue. Add tags to help start a friendly conversation.

▶ These sausages are delicious, *aren't they* ? ~ They certainly are.

▶ You haven't lived here long, *have you* ? ~ No, only three months.

1 It's quite a big garden, ... ? ~ Yes, there's plenty of room.

2 There aren't many people here yet, ... ? ~ No, but it's still quite early.

3 You're Rachel's friend, ... ? ~ Yes, I'm Vicky.

4 You came in a sports car, ... ? ~ That's right.

5 These burgers look good, ... ? ~ I can't wait to try them.

6 We can sit on the grass, ... ? ~ I think it's dry enough.

7 The weather forecast wasn't very good, ... ? ~ No, it wasn't.

C Form (2)

Complete the conversation. Put in the question tags.

Emma: You don't really want to go out with me any more, (▶) *do you* ?

Matthew: Of course I do. But I need a bit of time to myself sometimes.

Emma: You get plenty of time to yourself, (1) ....?

Matthew: Emma, you know what I feel for you. I've told you enough times,
          (2) ....?

Emma: Yes, you have. And you're quite happy, (3) ....?
          You don't mind, (4) ....? The situation doesn't bother you,
          (5) ....?

Matthew: Why are we arguing? There's nothing to argue about, (6) ....?

Emma: You can't ever look at things from my point of view, (7) ....?

D Requests and suggestions (3)

What would you say in these situations? Write sentences with a question tag. Use the word in brackets.

▶ You want to look at a newspaper. Daniel might have one, so ask him. (haven't)
  You haven't got a newspaper, have you?

1 Suggest to Vicky that you both listen to some music. (Let's)

  ....

2 Warn David not to do anything silly. (Don't)

  ....

3 You need a train timetable. Emma might have one, so ask her. (haven't)

  ....

4 Ask Rachel to pass you the salt. (Pass)

  ....

43 So/Neither do I and I think so

1 So and neither

Vicky: *I'm hungry.*
Rachel: ***So am I.*** *I haven't eaten anything all day.*
Daniel: ***Neither have I.*** *I didn't have time for breakfast.*

We use **so** after a positive statement and **neither** after a negative one.
> *I'm hungry.* ~ ***So am I.*** (= And I'm hungry./I'm hungry, too.)
> *I haven't eaten.* ~ ***Neither have I.*** (= And I haven't eaten./I haven't eaten either.)

The structure is **so/neither** + an auxiliary + the subject.
The auxiliary is a form of **be** or **have** or a modal verb, e.g. **can.**
> *We're really busy at work.* ~ ***So are we.***
> *Tom has gone to the match.* ~ *And* ***so has Nick.***
> *David can't drive, and* ***neither can Melanie.***

The subject comes at the end. NOT *We're busy.* ~ ~~So we are.~~
In the Present Simple and Past Simple we use a form of **do.**
> *I love old cowboy films.* ~ ***So do I.*** *This phone doesn't work.* ~ ***Neither does this one.***
> *United won, and* ***so did Rangers.***

We can use **nor** instead of **neither.**
> *Emma isn't here tonight.* ***Neither/Nor*** *is Matthew.*

2 I think so, etc.

Vicky: *It's 'Round the Corner' at half past seven, my favourite soap opera. Are we going to be back in time?*
Daniel: ***I think so.*** *We haven't got far to go now.*
Rachel: *We might miss the beginning.*
Vicky: *Oh,* ***I hope not.*** *I want to know if Bernard really did steal the money.*

Here *I think* **so** means 'I think we'll be back in time', and *I hope* **not** means 'I hope we don't miss the beginning'.

We can use **so** after **be afraid, believe, expect, guess, hope, suppose** and **think.**
> *Do you think you'll get the job?* ~ *Well, I* ***hope so.***
> *Are you going on holiday this year?* ~ *Yes, I* ***expect so.***
> *I don't know for sure if Henry is rich, but I should* ***think so.***

But we cannot use **so** after **know** or **be sure.**
> *There's been an accident.* ~ *Yes,* ***I know.*** NOT ~~I know so.~~
> *Are you sure you're doing the right thing?* ~ *Yes,* ***I'm sure.*** NOT ~~I'm sure so.~~

There are two negative structures.

NEGATIVE + **so**	POSITIVE + **not**
Is it raining? ~ *I* ***don't think so.*** *Are you going to the concert?* ~ *I* ***don't expect so.*** With **expect** and **think,** we normally use the negative and **so.**	*Is it raining?* ~ *I* ***hope not.*** *Have we won a prize?* ~ *I'm* ***afraid not.*** With **be afraid, guess** and **hope,** we use the positive and **not.**

We can use **believe** and **suppose** in either structure.
> *Will there be any seats left?* ~ *I* ***don't suppose so.*** OR *I* ***suppose not.***

A So and neither (1)

Andrew has just met Jessica at a party. They are finding out that they have a lot in common.
Put in the structures with *so* and *neither*.

	Andrew:	I haven't been to a party for ages.
▶	Jessica:	Neither have I. I hate crowded rooms.
▶	Andrew:	Yes, so do I. I'm not a party-goer, really.
1	Jessica:	No, ... I can't make conversation.
2	Andrew:	.... You know, I'm a quiet sort of person.
3	Jessica:	And .... I lead a pretty quiet life.
4	Andrew:	Well, ... I haven't got many friends.
5	Jessica:	.... And I would really like a good friend.
6	Andrew:	Oh, ...

B So and neither (1)

Look at the table and complete the sentences.

	Mark	Claire	Melanie	Emma
Music	✓	✗	✗	✓
Travel	✓	✓	✗	✗
Skiing	✗	✓	✓	✗
Cooking	✗	✗	✓	✓

▶ Claire can ski, and so can Melanie.
▶ Mark isn't keen on cooking, and neither is Claire.
1 Melanie doesn't like travelling much, and ....
2 Mark has got lots of CDs, and ....
3 Emma can't ski, and ....
4 Claire isn't a music lover, and ....
5 Melanie cooks quite often, and ....
6 Mark travels quite a lot, and ....

C I think so, etc. (2)

Complete these short conversations. Put in structures with *so* or *not* and use the words in brackets.

	Laura:	Does the library open on Saturdays? (think)
▶	Trevor:	Yes, I think so. But I'm not absolutely certain.
▶	Harriet:	You can't go out for an evening meal wearing shorts. (guess)
	Mike:	I guess not. I'd better put some trousers on.
1	Sarah:	Will there be a lot of people at the concert tonight? (expect)
	Mark:	.... There aren't usually very many.
2	Daniel:	Are you going to apply for the job? (suppose)
	Vicky:	.... It's the only one available.
3	David:	Do you think it's going to rain? (hope)
	Melanie:	Well, ... I'm just about to go out.
4	Nick:	Will the match take place in this weather? (think)
	Tom:	.... In fact, I'm sure it won't.
5	Claire:	Is my coat ready, please? (afraid)
	Assistant:	.... We're having problems with the machine.

Test I: Questions, negatives and answers

A

Read the conversation. Then look at the answers below and write the correct answer in each space.

Judy: (▶) _Shall_............ we go to the party tonight?

Lisa: (1) .... giving a party?

Judy: Susan. You know her, (2) .... you?

Lisa: I'm (3) .... sure. Has she got long dark hair?

Judy: Yes, she (4) .... And she's quite tall. (5) .... you spoken to her?

Lisa: No, I don't think (6) .... But I know who you mean. There are two sisters, Susan and Janet. They're twins, aren't (7) ....?

Judy: Yes, that's right.

Lisa: (8) .... one is Susan?

Judy: Oh, I (9) .... know. They both look the same. I can't always tell them apart.

Lisa: No, (10) .... can I. In any case, I haven't been invited to the party.

Judy: That (11) .... matter.

Lisa: OK. (12) .... go to it then, shall we?

▶	a) Do	b) Shall	c) Would					
1	a) What's	b) Who's	c) Whose		7	a) it	b) not	c) they
2	a) don't	b) know	c) so		8	a) What	b) Which	c) Who
3	a) isn't	b) no	c) not		9	a) don't	b) no	c) not
4	a) got	b) has	c) so		10	a) neither	b) not	c) so
5	a) Haven't	b) Having	c) Not		11	a) doesn't	b) isn't	c) not
6	a) it	b) neither	c) so		12	a) Could	b) Let's	c) Shall

B

What would you say? Use the word in brackets, and use a question form in each sentence.

▶   You want to suggest a game of cards. (have)
    Shall we have a game of cards? ....

1   You are asking Tessa where her house is. (live)

2   You want Janet to tell you what she is thinking. (about)

3   You are inviting a friend to come to your room. (like)

4   You are surprised that your friend missed the football match on television. (watch)

5   You are asking permission to take a photo. (may)

6   You are looking for Polly. You are asking her friend for information. (seen)

7   You are asking Nigel about the number of letters he has written. (how)

8   You are asking Nancy about the people coming to her party. (who)

9   You are asking Martin's wife if he cooks every day or once a week. (often)

10   You are asking about the weather tomorrow. (will)

C

Each of these replies is wrong. Write the correct reply.

▶ Is it going to snow? ~ ~~I'm not thinking it.~~   I don't think so.

1 Has the computer arrived? ~ ~~No, not.~~   ....

2 Don't you like curry? ~ ~~Yes, I hate it.~~   ....

3 Will you be in tonight? ~ ~~Yes, I expect.~~   ....

4 Horrible weather. ~ ~~It isn't very nice, isn't it?~~   ....

5 Would you like a sweet? ~ ~~Yes, right.~~   ....

6 I'm quite tired now. ~ ~~Too am I.~~   ....

7 You might catch my cold. ~ ~~I don't hope to.~~   ....

8 The first train didn't stop. ~ ~~Neither the second.~~   ....

D

Rupert is at a job interview. Someone is asking him questions. Write the questions.

▶ Interviewer: Where do you live?
  Rupert: Oh, I live in Longtown.

1 Interviewer: ....
  Rupert: I'm twenty-three.

2 Interviewer: ....
  Rupert: Yes, I went to college.

3 Interviewer: ....
  Rupert: My interests? I don't have any, really.

4 Interviewer: ....
  Rupert: Which company? Oh, I work for BX Electric.

5 Interviewer: ....
  Rupert: Nothing. There's nothing I don't like about my job.

E

Put in the missing word.

▶ How.... does this phone work? ~ You press this button.

1 The new building looks awful. ~ I agree. It .... look very nice.

2 Could you give me a receipt, please? ~ Yes, of ....

3 This chair isn't very comfortable. ~ And .... is this bed.

4 Didn't you watch 'Frankenstein' last night? ~ .... , I hate horror films.

5 What's this wood .... ? ~ I'm going to make a table.

6 I didn't say the wrong thing, ... I? ~ Well, you weren't very polite.

7 Will there be any free gifts? ~ No, there ....

8 Have they sent you some money? ~ No, I'm afraid ....

9 Don't drop those plates, ... you? ~ OK, I'll be careful.

10 How .... is it to the station? ~ About half a mile.

11 Do those shoes fit you? ~ Yes, I think ....

12 Why .... we have a picnic? ~ Yes, good idea.

13 .... foot is hurting? ~ My right one.

14 I feel a bit cold actually. ~ Yes, ... do I.

15 Who .... eaten their ice-cream? ~ Oh, it's mine. I'm just going to eat it.

16 .... of these magazines would you like? ~ This one, please.

44 Ability: can, could and be able to

Modal verbs

1 Can and can't

Vicky: *How many instruments **can** you play, Natasha?*
Natasha: *Three – the violin, the clarinet and the piano.*
Vicky: *That's terrific. You haven't got a piano here, though.*
Natasha: *No, but I **can** go to the music room in college and play the one in there.*
Vicky: *I'm not musical at all. I **can't** even sing.*

We use **can** to say that something is possible: that someone has an ability (*Natasha **can** play the piano*) or an opportunity (*She **can** go to the music room*). **Can** is usually pronounced /kən/ but sometimes we say /kæn/. The negative is **cannot** /ˈkænɒt/ or **can't** /kɑːnt/.

2 Can and be able to

In the present tense, **be able to** is a little more formal and less usual than **can**.
    *Emma is good with computers. She **can** write/**is able to** write programs.*
But in some structures we always use **be able to**, not **can**.
To-infinitive: *It's nice **to be able to go** to the opera. (NOT ~~to can go~~)*
After a modal verb: *Melanie **might be able to** help us.*
Present Perfect: *It's been quiet today. I**'ve been able to** get some work done.*

For the future we use **can** or **will be able to** but NOT ~~will can~~.
    *If we earn some money, we **can** go/we**'ll be able to** go on holiday next summer.*
    *I'm afraid I **can't** come/I **won't be able to** come to the disco on Friday.*
But to suggest a possible future action, we normally use **can**.
    *Let's have lunch together. We **can** go to that new restaurant.*

3 Could and was/were able to

For ability or opportunity in the past, we use **could** or **was/were able to**.
    *Natasha **could** play (OR **was able to** play) the piano when she was four.*
    *In those days we had a car, so we **could** travel (OR **were able to** travel) very easily.*

To say that the ability or opportunity resulted in a particular action, something that really happened, we use **was/were able to** but not **could**.
    *The plane **was able to** take off at eleven o'clock, after the fog had lifted.*
    *Luckily Mark **was able to** get (OR **succeeded in getting**) the work done in time.*
    *The drivers **were able to** stop (OR **managed to stop** ▷ page 60.3) before they crashed into each other.*

Compare these two sentences.

*The children **could** swim when they were quite young.* (a past ability)	*The children **were able** to swim across the river.* (a past action)

In negative sentences and questions, we can use either form.
    *It was foggy, so the plane **couldn't/wasn't able** to take off.*
    *The pool was closed, so they **couldn't/weren't able** to have a swim.*
    ***Could you/Were** you **able** to describe the man to the police?*

We normally use **could** (not **was/were able to**) with verbs of seeing etc., and with verbs of thinking.
    *We **could see** the village in the distance.*
    *As soon as Harriet opened the door, she **could smell** gas.*
    *I **couldn't understand** what was happening.*

Practice

A Can and can't (1)

Look at the pictures and say what they can or can't do. Use these words: *climb trees*, *juggle*, *lift the weights*, *play the violin*, <u>*walk on his hands*</u>

▶ He can walk on his hands.

1 ....
2 ....

3 ....
4 ....

B Can and be able to (2)

Harriet is visiting David, who hurt himself when he fell off a ladder. Complete the conversation using *can* or a form of *be able to*. Sometimes there is more than one possible answer.

Harriet: Hello, David. I'm sorry I haven't (▶) been able to come .... (come) and see you before. I've been really busy lately. How are you?

David: I'm OK, thanks. (1) .... (I / walk) around now. The doctor says (2) .... (I / go) back to work soon. It'll be nice (3) .... (get) out again. I hate being stuck here like this. I haven't (4) .... (do) anything interesting.

C Could and was/were able to (3)

▶ Which is closer to the meaning of the sentence 'Years ago I could run a marathon'?
   a) ☐ I ran a marathon at one particular time in the past.
   b) ☑ I was once fit enough to run a very long way.

1 Which of these sentences is correct?
   I was ill, so I couldn't go to the party.
   I was ill, so I wasn't able to go to the party.
   a) ☐ Only the first one.   b) ☐ Only the second one.   c) ☐ Both of them.

2 Which is closer to the meaning of the sentence 'Sarah was able to leave work early yesterday'?
   a) ☐ Sarah left work early yesterday.
   b) ☐ Sarah had the opportunity to leave work early yesterday, but we don't know if she took it.

D Could and was/were able to (3)

Put in *could* or *was/were able to*. Sometimes either is possible. Use a negative if necessary.

▶ Suddenly all the lights went out. We couldn't .... see a thing.
1 The computer went wrong, but luckily Emma .... put it right again.
2 There was a big party last night. You .... hear the music half a mile away.
3 I learnt to read music as a child. I .... read it when I was five.
4 People heard warnings about the flood, and they .... move out in time.
5 The train was full. I .... find a seat anywhere.

45 Permission: **can, may, could** and **be allowed to**

1 Asking permission

We use **can**, **could** or **may** to ask for permission.

> **Can** *I use your pen?*
> **Could** *we borrow your ladder, please? ~ Well, I'm using it at the moment.*
> **May** *I see the letter? ~ Certainly.*

Could often sounds more polite than **can**. **May** is rather formal.

2 Giving and refusing permission

To give permission we use **can** or **may** (but not **could**).

> *You* **can** *wait in my office if you like.*
> **Could** *I borrow your calculator? ~ Of course you* **can.**
> *You* **may** *telephone from here.* (a written notice)

May is formal and is not often used in speech.

You may telephone from here

Bicycles must not be left here

To refuse permission we use **can't** or **may not** (but not **couldn't**).

> *Could we picnic here? ~ I'm sorry. I'm afraid you* **can't.**
> *Members* **may not** *bring more than two guests into the club.*

We can also use **must not**.

> *Luggage* **must not** *be left unattended.*

3 Talking about permission

We sometimes talk about rules made by someone else. To do this we use **can**, **could** and **be allowed to**.

We use **can** to talk about the present, and we use **could** for the past.

Present: *Each passenger* **can** *take one bag onto the plane.*
Past: *In the 1920s you* **could** *drive without taking a test.*

We can also use **be allowed to**.

Present: *Passengers* **are allowed to** *take one bag onto the plane.*
Future: **Will** *I* **be allowed to** *record the interview on tape?*
Past: *We* **weren't allowed** *to look round the factory yesterday.*

For a general permission in the past we use either **could** or **was/were allowed to**.

> *I* **could** *always stay/I* **was** *always* **allowed to** *stay up late as a child.*

But to say that the permission resulted in a particular action, something that really happened, we use **was/were allowed to** (but not **could**).

> *I* **was allowed to** *leave work early yesterday.*
> *We* **were allowed to** *go into the control room when we looked around the power station.*

Compare these questions with **may** and **be allowed to**.

ASKING FOR PERMISSION	ASKING ABOUT PERMISSION
May *I take a photo of you?* (= Will you allow it?)	*Are we* **allowed to** *take photos?* (= What is the rule?)

Practice

A Asking permission (1)

How would you ask for permission in these situations?
Use *Can I ...?*, *Could I ...?* or *May I ...?* and these verbs: *borrow, join, look at, use*

▶ You are at a friend's flat. You want to make a phone call.
  Can I use your phone?

1 You need a calculator. The person sitting next to you has got one.

   ....

2 You have gone into a café. Three people who you know from work are sitting at a table. You go over to the table.

   ....

3 You had to go to a lecture, but you were ill. Your friend went to the lecture and took notes. Next day you are well again and you see your friend.

   ....

B Giving and refusing permission (2)

A policeman is telling you what the signs mean. What does he say?
Use *can* and *can't* and these verbs: *drop, go, have, park, play, smoke, turn*

Policeman:
▶ You can't go this way.
▶ You can park here.
1 ....
2 ....
3 ....
4 ....
5 ....

C Be allowed to (3)

Put in the correct forms.

Rita: I hear you've moved into a new flat with a couple of friends.
Emma: Yes, it's a nice flat, but the landlady is really strict. (▶) We aren't allowed to do
       (we / not / allow / do) anything. It was my birthday last month, and
       (1) .... (I / not / allow / have) a party.
Rita: Oh, (2) .... (we / allow / have) parties at our place,
       luckily. (3) .... (we / allow / do) anything, more or
       less. We're hoping to have an all-night party soon, but I'm not absolutely sure if
       (4) .... (we / allow / hold) it.

D May I ...? or Am I allowed to ...? (3)

Are you asking for permission, or are you asking what the rule is? Put in *May I ...?* or
Am I allowed to ...?

▶ May I .... use your computer?
▶ Am I allowed to .... smoke in this cinema?
1 .... cross the road here?
2 .... ask you a personal question?
3 .... rollerblade in this park?
4 .... drive a car without insurance?
5 .... read your magazine?

46 Possibility and certainty: may, might, could, must, etc.

1 May, might and could

Rachel: *Whose bag is that?*
Daniel: *I don't know. It **may** belong to Maria's friend.*
Vicky: *It **might** be a bomb. It **could** explode at any moment.*

We use **may** or **might** to say that something is possible or that it is quite likely.
We can use them for the present or the future.
> It ***may/might*** *be a bomb.* (= Perhaps it is a bomb.)
> I ***may/might*** *go to the disco tomorrow.* (= Perhaps I will go to the disco.)

We can use **could** to say that something is possible.
> *The story **could** be true, I suppose.* (= Possibly it is true.)
> *You **could** win a million pounds!* (= Possibly you will win a million pounds.)

Sometimes **could** means only a small possibility. It is possible (but not likely) that you will win a million pounds.

In some situations we can use **may**, **might** or **could**.
> It ***may/might/could*** *rain later.*

After **may**, **might** or **could** we can use a continuous form (**be** + an -ing form).
> *That man **may/might be watching** us.* (= Perhaps he is watching us.)
> *Sarah **may/might be working** late tonight.* (= Perhaps she will be working late.)
> *I'm not sure where Matthew is. He **could be playing** squash.* (= Possibly he is playing squash.)

2 May, might and could in the negative

The negative forms are **may not**, **might not/mightn't**, and **could not/couldn't**.

MAY NOT AND MIGHT NOT	COULDN'T
Something negative is possible.	Something is impossible.
*Daniel **may not** get the job.*	*Vicky is afraid of heights. She **couldn't** climb onto the roof.*
*Tom **might not** be in.*	*I'm completely unfit. I **couldn't** run a marathon.*
*I **mightn't** finish the marathon tomorrow.*	*(It is impossible for me to run it.)*
(It is possible that I will not finish it.)	

3 Must and can't

MUST	CAN'T
We use **must** when we realize that something is certainly true.	We use **can't** when we realize that something is impossible.
*She isn't answering the phone. She **must** be out.*	*We haven't walked far. You **can't** be tired yet.*
*I had my keys a moment ago. They **must** be here somewhere.*	*Life **can't** be easy when you have to spend it in a wheelchair.*
*Andrew isn't here. He **must** be working in the library.*	*Nick **can't** be touring Scotland. I saw him here this morning.*

▷ 53 **Might/could/must have been**   ▷ page 379 **Mustn't** in American English
▷ 51.1 **Could** in suggestions

Practice

A Might be and might be doing (1)

Vicky and Rachel are at college. They're looking for their friend Natasha. Complete the conversation.
Use *may* or *might* and the verb in brackets. Sometimes you need to use the continuous.

Vicky: I can't find Natasha. Have you seen her?

Rachel: (▶) *She might be* (she / be) in the music room. (▶) *She may be practising* (she / practise).

Vicky: No, she isn't there. I thought (1) .... (she / be) with you.

Rachel: It's a nice day. (2) .... (she / be) on the lawn.
(3) .... (she / sit) out there reading the paper. Or
(4) .... (she / have) a coffee.
(5) .... (you / find) her in the canteen.

Emma: No, I've looked there.

Rachel: Well, here comes Jessica. (6) .... (she / know).

B May and might (1–2)

Add a sentence with *may* or *might* (both are correct).

▶ I'm not sure if it's going to rain. *It might rain.*
▶ I don't know if we'll see an elephant. *We may see one.*
1 I can't say whether Daniel will win. ....
2 I haven't decided if I'm having a holiday. ....
3 I don't know if we'll get an invitation. ....
4 I've no idea whether Sarah will be late. ....
5 I'm not sure if my friends are visiting me. ....

C Mightn't and couldn't (2)

Put in *mightn't* or *couldn't*.

▶ I've got one or two things to do, so I *mightn't* .... have time to come out tonight.
▶ David *couldn't* .... work as a taxi driver. He can't drive.
1 We're going to need lots of glasses. We .... have enough, you know.
2 Mark .... be in the office tomorrow. He thinks he's getting a cold.
3 We .... possibly have a dog, living in a small flat like this.
4 How can you work with all this noise? I .... work in such conditions.
5 Don't come tomorrow because I .... be in. I'm not sure what I'm doing.

D Must, can't and might (1, 3)

A reporter is interviewing Mrs Miles for a TV news programme.
Complete the conversation. Put in *must*, *can't* or *might*.

Mrs Miles: My name's Nora Miles, and I'm going to do a parachute jump.

Reporter: Mrs Miles, you're seventy-three, and you're going to jump out of an aeroplane.
You (▶) *must* .... be mad. You (1) .... be serious.

Mrs Miles: It really (2) .... be wonderful to look down from the sky. I've always wanted to try it.

Reporter: But anything could happen. You (3) .... be injured or even killed. I wouldn't take the risk.

Mrs Miles: Well, young man, your life (4) .... be much fun if you never take risks. You ought to try it. You never know – you (5) ....
enjoy it.

Reporter: Enjoy it? You (6) .... be joking!

47 Necessity: **must** and **have to**

1 Present, past and future

We use **must** and **have to/has to** to say that something is necessary.

> *You'll be leaving college soon. You **must** think about your future.*
> *We're very busy at the office. I **have to** work on Saturday morning.*
> *Mark **has to** get the car repaired. There's something wrong with the brakes.*

When we use the past, or the future with **will**, we need a form of **have to**.

> *Emma **had to** go to the dentist yesterday.* NOT ~~She must go to the dentist yesterday.~~
> *That wasn't very good. We**'ll have to** do better next time.*

And in other structures we also use a form of **have to**, not **must**.

To-infinitive: *I don't want **to have to** wait in a queue for ages.*
After a modal verb: *Emma has toothache. She **might have to** go to the dentist.*
Present Perfect: *Mark **has had to** drive all the way to Glasgow.*

For negatives and questions with **have to/has to** and **had to**, we use a form of **do**.

> *I **don't have to** work on Sundays.*   *Why **does** Andrew **have to** study every evening?*
> ***Did** you **have to** pay for your second cup of coffee? ~ No, I didn't.*

I don't have to work means that it is not necessary for me to work (see Unit 48.2).

2 **Must** or **have to**?

Both **must** and **have to** express necessity, but we use them differently.

MUST	HAVE TO
We use **must** when the speaker feels that something is necessary.	We use **have to** when the situation makes something necessary.
*You **must** exercise.* (I'm telling you.) *We **must** be quiet.* (I'm telling you.)	*I **have to** exercise.* (The doctor told me.) *We **have to** be quiet.* (That's the rule.)
I/we **must** can also express a wish. *I **must** buy a newspaper. I want to see the racing results.* *We **must** invite Claire. She's wonderful company.*	 *I **have to** buy a newspaper. The boss asked me to get one.* *We **have to** invite Trevor and Laura. They invited us last time.*

3 Have got to

Have got to means the same as **have to**, but **have got to** is informal. We use it mainly in the present.

> *I **have to**/I**'ve got to** make my sandwiches.*   *My father **has to/has got to** take these pills.*
> ***Do** we **have to** apply/**Have** we **got to** apply for a visa?*

▷ 48 **Mustn't** and **needn't**

Practice

A Have to (1)

Complete the conversations. Use the words in brackets and a form of *have to*.

▶ Melanie: David's broken his leg. He's had to go .... (he's / go) to hospital.

Harriet: Oh no! How long will he have to stay ..... (will / he / stay) there?

Melanie: I don't know.

1 Claire: I parked my car outside the hairdresser's, and while I was in there, the police took the car away. I've got it back now. But .... (I / pay) a lot of money.

Henry: How much .... (you / pay)?

Claire: Two hundred pounds!

2 Trevor: That door doesn't shut properly. .... (you / slam) it every time.

Laura: .... (you / will / fix) it then, won't you?

3 Jessica: You're always taking exams. Why .... (you / take) so many?

Andrew: .... (I / will / take) a lot more if I want a good job.

4 Mike: We're in a new house now. .... (we / move). The old place was too small.

Nick: Did it take you long to find a house?

Mike: No, we found one easily. .... (we / not / look) very hard. But it was in bad condition. .... (we've / do) a lot of work on it.

5 Nick: My brother .... (start) work at five o'clock in the morning.

Melanie: That's pretty early. What time .... (he / get) up?

Nick: Half past three.

B Must and have to (2)

Write a sentence with *must*, *have to* or *has to*.

▶ The sign says: 'Passengers must show their tickets.'
So passengers have to show their tickets. ....

▶ The children have to be in bed by nine.
Their parents said: 'You must be in bed by nine.' ....

1 Laura has to get to work on time.
Her boss told her: ....

2 The police told Nick: 'You must keep your dog under control.'
So Nick ....

3 The pupils have to listen carefully.
The teacher says: ....

4 The new sign says: 'Visitors must report to the security officer.'
So now ....

C Must or have to? (2)

Put in *must* or *have to/has to*. Choose which is best for the situation.

▶ I have to .... go to the airport. I'm meeting someone.

1 You .... lock the door when you go out. There've been a lot of break-ins recently.

2 Daniel .... go to the bank. He hasn't any money.

3 I .... work late tomorrow. We're very busy at the office.

4 You really .... make less noise. I'm trying to concentrate.

5 I think you .... pay to park here. I'll just go and read that notice.

6 You really .... hurry up, Vicky. We don't want to be late.

7 I .... put the heating on. I feel really cold.

48 Necessity: mustn't, needn't, etc.

1 Mustn't or needn't?

We use **must** to say that something is necessary (see Unit 47).
> You **must** be careful with those glasses.   I **must** remember my key.

Now compare **mustn't** and **needn't**.

MUSTN'T	NEEDN'T
We use **mustn't** /ˈmʌsnt/ to say that something is a bad idea.	We use **needn't** when something is not necessary.
*You **mustn't** drop those glasses. They'll break.*	*You **needn't** wash those glasses. They're clean.*
*I **mustn't** forget my key, or I won't get in.*	*We **needn't** make sandwiches. There's a café.*
*You **mustn't** wear your best clothes. You'll get them dirty.*	*You **needn't** wear your best clothes. You can wear what you like.*

2 Don't have to and don't need to

We can use **don't have to** and **don't need to** when something is not necessary.
The meaning is the same as **needn't**.
> You **don't have to** / **don't need to** wash those glasses. They're clean.
> Mark **doesn't have to** / **doesn't need to** finish the report today. He can do it at the weekend.

For American usage see page 379.

For the past we use **didn't**.
> The food was free. We **didn't have to** pay/We **didn't need to** pay for it.

3 Didn't need to or needn't have?

*Daniel hadn't booked a seat, but luckily the train wasn't full. He **didn't need** to stand.*	*Trevor and Laura booked a table for dinner. But the restaurant was empty. They **needn't have** booked a table.*

DIDN'T NEED TO	NEEDN'T HAVE
We use **didn't need to** when something was not necessary. Standing was not necessary because there were seats.	We use **needn't have** + a past participle for something we did which we now know was not necessary, e.g. booking a table.
*Mark **didn't need** to hurry. He had lots of time. He drove slowly along the motorway.*	*Mark **needn't have** hurried. After driving at top speed, he arrived half an hour early.*
*We **didn't need** to go to the supermarket because we had plenty of food.*	*We **needn't have** gone to the supermarket. We already had a pizza for tonight.*

Sometimes we can use **didn't need to** when the action happened, even though it was not necessary.
> Mark **didn't need to** hurry, but he drove at top speed. He likes driving fast.

Practice

A Must, mustn't or needn't? (1)

Put in *must, mustn't* or *needn't*.

▶ Laura: You <u>needn't</u> take an umbrella. It isn't going to rain.
Trevor: Well, I don't know. It might do.
Laura: Don't lose it then. You <u>mustn't</u> leave it on the bus.

1 Vicky: Come on. We .... hurry. We .... be late.
Rachel: It's only ten past. We .... hurry. There's lots of time.

2 Claire: My sister and I are going a different way.
Guide: Oh, you .... go off on your own. It isn't safe. We .... keep together in a group.

3 David: I'll put these cups in the dishwasher.
Melanie: No, you .... put them in there. It might damage them. In fact, we .... wash them at all. We didn't use them.

4 Secretary: I .... forget to type this letter.
Mark: Yes, it .... go in the post today because it's quite urgent. But the report isn't so important. You .... type the report today.

B Don't have to (2)

An old woman is talking to a reporter from her local newspaper. She is comparing life today with life in the past. Complete her sentences using *don't have to, doesn't have to* or *didn't have to*.

▶ We had to make our own fun in the old days. There wasn't any television then. These days people <u>don't have to make their own fun.</u>

1 There's so much traffic now. You have to wait ages to cross the road. In those days you
   ....

2 I had to work long hours when I was young. But children today have it easy.
   They ....

3 My father had to work in a factory when he was twelve. Just imagine! Today a twelve-year-old child ....

4 There's so much crime today, isn't there? People have to lock their doors now. It was better in the old days when people ....

5 We had to wash our clothes by hand. There weren't any washing-machines, you know. Nowadays people ....

C Didn't need to or needn't have? (3)

Write the sentences using *didn't need to* or *needn't have*.

▶ The previous owners had already decorated the flat, so
   <u>we didn't need to decorate it ourselves</u> (we / decorate / it / ourselves).

1 Luckily we were able to sell our old flat before we bought the new one,
   so .... (we / borrow / any money).

2 It was very hot yesterday, so I watered all the flowers.
   And now it's pouring with rain. .... (I / bother).

3 We've done the journey much more quickly than I expected.
   .... (we / leave / so early).

4 A friend had already given me a free ticket to the exhibition,
   so .... (I / pay / to go in).

5 Service was included in the bill, so ....
   (you / tip / the waiter). It was a waste of money.

49 Should, ought to, had better and be supposed to

1 Introduction

Maybe you **should** ask for your money back, Matthew.

They **ought to** make these things a bit easier for you.

I'd better read the instructions again.

I think this bit **is supposed to** go in here.

2 Should and ought to

We use **should** and **ought to** to say what is the best thing or the right thing to do.
There is no difference in meaning.

> You're not very well. Perhaps you **should** see a doctor.
> Your uncle was very kind to me. I **ought to** write him a letter of thanks.
> People **shouldn't** break/**oughtn't to** break their promises.

We can also use **should** and **ought to** in questions to ask for advice.

> Where **should** I put this picture, do you think?
> It's a difficult problem. How **ought** we **to** deal with it?

After **should** or **ought to** we can use a continuous form (**be** + an -ing form).

> It's half past six already. I **should be cooking** the tea.
> Why are you sitting here doing nothing? You **ought to be working**.

3 Had better

We use **had better** to say what is the best thing to do in a situation.

> It's cold. The children **had better** wear their coats.
> The neighbours are complaining. We**'d better** turn the music down.
> My wife is waiting for me. I**'d better not** be late.

We could also use **should** or **ought to** in these examples, although **had better** is stronger.
The speaker sees the action as necessary and expects that it will happen.

4 Be supposed to

We use **be supposed to** when we are talking about the normal or correct way of doing things.

> The guests **are supposed to** buy flowers for the hostess.
> Look at these cars. This area **is supposed to** be kept clear of traffic.
> The bus driver needs to concentrate. You**'re not supposed to** talk to him.
> How **am** I **supposed to** cook this? ~ It tells you on the packet.

We can use **was/were supposed to** for the past.

> It's eleven o'clock. You **were supposed to** be here at ten thirty, you know.

▷ 52.4 **Shall** used to ask for advice

Practice

A Should and ought to (2)

Put in *should*, *shouldn't*, *ought* or *oughtn't*. (Look for the word *to*.)

Vicky: I can't come out tonight, Rachel. I (▶) ..ought.......... to do some more work. I'm behind with everything. I've got so much to do.

Rachel: You (1) .... worry so much, Vicky. Don't panic. You (2) .... to relax sometimes. You (3) .... take a break.

Vicky: I know I (4) .... panic, but I do. I can't help it.

Rachel: Anyway, you're doing OK, aren't you? Your results have been good. You (5) .... be pleased. You (6) .... to invent problems for yourself.

B Had better (3)

What would you say in these situations? Add a sentence with *'d better* (*not*) and the words in brackets.

▶ Vicky doesn't feel well. She's got a headache. What might you say to her? (an aspirin)
You'd better take an aspirin...

1 You and Daniel are meeting Rachel. You've both arrived, but she isn't there yet. She is usually late. (wait) ....

2 Ilona is leaving her bike outside the swimming-pool. You know it won't be safe if she leaves it unlocked. (lock) ....

3 Some friends are going to visit you today. Your room is in a mess. What do you think? (tidy) ....

4 Nick is giving you a lift in his old sports car. There's a speed limit, and there's a police car behind you. (too fast) ....

5 There's an exam tomorrow. Neither you nor Rachel have done any work for it. (some revision) ....

C Be supposed to (4)

Add a sentence using *be* (*not*) *supposed to* and these words:
leave it outside, report to the police, stand in a queue, take two before meals, watch it

▶ You shouldn't bring your bike in here. You're supposed to leave it outside. ....

1 I've got some pills. ....

2 Foreign visitors can't travel freely here. ....

3 Be careful waiting for a bus in England. ....

4 This film isn't for under-sixteens. ....

D Should, ought to, had better and be supposed to (1–4)

Complete the conversation. Use *should*, *ought to*, *had better* or *be supposed to* and the verbs in brackets. Usually there is more than one correct answer.

Vicky: What time (▶) .are. we. supposed. to. be........................ (we / be) at the coffee morning?

Rachel: The invitation says ten o'clock.

Vicky: Well, it's ten now. (1) .... (we / hurry).
(2) .... (we / not / be) late.

Rachel: Oh, it won't matter if we're a bit late.

Vicky: I think it would be rude, wouldn't it? I don't think people
(3) .... (arrive) late when they've been invited to something.

Rachel: You worry too much. (4) .... (you / not / take) everything so seriously, Vicky. It's a coffee morning, not a job interview.
(5) .... (we / not / get) there exactly on time.

50 Asking people to do things

1 Polite requests

We can use **can** or **could** in a request, when we ask someone to do something.

*   **Can** *you keep me informed? ~ Yes, of course.*
*   **Could** *you lend me ten pounds until tomorrow? ~ Sorry, I haven't got ten pounds.*
*   *I wonder if you **could** explain something to me. ~ I'll try.*

Could is often more polite than **can**.

In a request we can also use **Do you mind …?** or **Would you mind…?** with an -ing form.

*   **Do you mind waiting** *a moment? ~ No, I can wait.*
*   **Would you mind sitting** *in the back? ~ No, not at all.*

We can also use **Would you like to …?**

*   **Would you like to** *lay the table for me? ~ Yes, of course.*

We do not use **Do you like …?** for a request. NOT ~~Do you like to lay the table for me?~~

It is always worth taking the trouble to use one of these request forms in English. We do not normally say ~~Lay the table for me.~~ This can sound very abrupt and impolite without a phrase like **Could you …?**

2 The imperative

We can sometimes use the imperative form to tell someone what to do.

*   **Bring** *another chair.*   **Hurry** *up or we'll be late.*

We form the negative with **don't**.

*   **Don't be** *silly.*   **Don't make** *so much noise.*

We can use an imperative when we are with friends in an informal situation. But we do not use it to tell a stranger what to do in a more formal situation.

*   *Excuse me.* **Could you** *tell me the way to Oxford Street, please?*
*   **Would you mind** *sending me a copy of your catalogue?*
*   NOT ~~Send me a copy of your catalogue.~~

Even people in authority often avoid using the imperative to give orders. Instead they can use **I want/I'd like you to …**, **You must …**, or a polite request form.

Manager:	**I want you** *all to be at the meeting.*
Policeman:	**You must** *wait until you see the green light.*
Doctor:	**Could you** *lie down on the bed, please?*

But we use an imperative in instructions and directions, in offers and invitations, and to express good wishes.

*   **Turn** *right at the crossroads.*   **Have** *a biscuit.*
*   **Enjoy** *your holiday.*

3 Asking for things

We use **Can I/we have…?** and **Could I/we have …?** when we ask someone to give us something.

*   **Can we have** *our room key, please?*   **Could I have** *a receipt, please?*

We can also say *Could you give me a receipt, please?* but we do not use the imperative.

When we ask for something in a shop or a café, we can simply name what we want, but we must say **please**.

*   *A large white loaf,* **please**.   *Two coffees,* **please**.

We can also use **I'd like …** or **I'll have …**

*   **I'd like** *a chicken sandwich, please.*   **I'll have** *a coffee.*

▷ 45 **Can** and **could** for permission   ▷ 52.2 **Would like**

Practice

A Asking people to do things (1–3)

Complete these sentences and write them in: *Can I ... a fork, please? Could ... have a towel, ...?*
Could you ... the ... for me? Would you ... answering the phone?

▶ Could you open the door for me?   2 ....

1 ....   3 ....

B Asking people to do things (1–3)

Mr Atkins is the boss at Zedco. He tells everyone what to do. Complete his sentences. Use these
words: *can, could, have, like, mind, must, want, wonder, would*

▶ Would you .mind............... making some tea, Alan?

1 You .... inform me of any developments.

2 Could I .... the latest sales figures, please?

3 Would you .... to arrange a meeting some time next week, Fiona?

4 I .... everyone to read the report.

5 .... I see the file, please, Mark?

6 .... you mind putting this in writing?

7 I .... if you could translate this letter, Linda.

8 .... you meet our customer at the airport?

C Asking people to do things (1–3)

Read about each situation and then make a request. Use the word in brackets.

▶ It is cold in the restaurant. Ask the waiter to shut the window. (could)
   Could you shut the window, please?

1 You are buying a coat. Ask the assistant for a receipt. (can)
   ....

2 You want to know the time. Ask someone in the street. (could)
   Excuse me. ....

3 You need someone to help you. Ask a friend. (can)
   ....

4 You have bought some food, but you haven't got a bag. Ask the assistant. (could)
   ....

5 You are carrying a tray. Ask someone to clear a space on the table. (mind)
   ....

6 You are on the phone. You want to speak to the manager. (could)
   ....

51 Suggestions, offers and invitations

1 Suggestions

We can use **Shall we ...?** or **Let's** to make a suggestion.

*It's a lovely day. **Shall we** go for a walk? ~ Yes, OK.*
***Let's** play some music. ~ Good idea.*

We can also use **could** for a suggestion.

*We **could** watch this comedy on TV tonight. ~ Well, actually I've seen it before.*
*You **could** invite a few friends around. ~ Yes, why not?*

We can also use **Why don't ...?**

***Why don't** we have a look round the market?*

To ask for a suggestion we use **shall**, **should** or **can**.

*Where **shall/should** we go for our holiday? ~ What about Spain?*
*What **can** I get Claire for her birthday? ~ I've no idea.*

2 Offers

We can use **will** or **can** to offer to do something.

*I'**ll** carry your bag. ~ Oh, thanks.*
*We **can** give you a lift. ~ Oh, that would be great. Thank you.*

We can also use question forms with **shall** or **can**.

***Shall** we pay you the money now? ~ Oh, there's no hurry.*
***Can** I get a taxi for you? ~ Yes, please.*

To offer food or drink, we use **would like**.

***Would** you **like** one of these chocolates? ~ Yes, please. Thank you.*
***Would** anyone **like** more coffee? ~ No, thanks.*

We can also use **Will/Won't you have ...?**

***Will you have** a biscuit? ~ Thank you.*
***Won't you have** something to drink? ~ Not for me, thank you.*

In informal speech we can use the imperative.

***Have** a biscuit. ~ Thank you.*

3 Invitations

The words we use in invitations are similar to those we use in offers of food and drink (see 2).
To invite someone, we often use **Would you like to ...?**

***Would** you **like to** have lunch with us? ~ Yes, I'd love to. Thank you.*

Would like can have a verb with **to** after it, or an object with a noun.

*Would you like **to stay** the night. ~ Oh, that's very kind of you.*
*Would you like **a bed** for the night? ~ Are you sure it's not too much trouble?*

We can also use **Will/Won't you ...?**

***Will you** join us for coffee? ~ Yes. Thanks.   **Won't you** sit down?*

In informal speech we can use the imperative.

***Come** and have coffee with us.   Please **sit** down.*

▷ 52 Will, would, shall and should

Practice

A Suggestions, offers and invitations (1–3)

Put the words in the right order and write in the sentences:

post / for you / I'll / that letter
for a minute / shall / stop / we

have / one of these / won't / you
a game / like / would / you

▶ Won't you have one of these?

1 ....

2 ....

3 ....

B Suggestions and offers (1–2)

Complete the conversation. Put in *could*, *shall*, *will* **or** *would*.

Daniel: Where (▶) .*shall*.......... we have our picnic, then?

Rachel: This looks all right. (1) .... we sit here?

Emma: Oh, I've forgotten the sausages. They're in the car.

Matthew: (2) .... I get them?

Emma: Oh, thanks, Matthew.

Vicky: We (3) .... sit by those trees. It looks nicer over there.

Rachel: No, it's fine here.

Daniel: Yes, it's better here, I think.

Emma: (4) .... you like a sandwich, Vicky?

Vicky: Oh, thank you.

Emma: (5) .... you have one, Rachel?

Matthew: And here are the sausages. (6) .... anyone like one?

C Suggestions, offers and invitations (1–3)

What would you say? There is more than one correct answer.

▶   A friend has called at your flat. Invite him to come in.
     Would you like to come in?

1   Offer your visitor a cup of tea.
     ....

2   You don't know what to say in your letter. Ask your friend for a suggestion.
     ....

3   You are walking in town with a friend. Suggest having a cup of coffee.
     ....

4   A woman you know is afraid to walk home alone. Offer to walk home with her.
     ....

5   You are writing to a friend. Invite her to visit you one weekend.
     ....

52 Will, would, shall and should

1 Will and would for predictions

We can use **will** for a prediction (see Unit 25.3).

> *It's midnight, and Sarah is still working. She'll be tired tomorrow.*
> *We're going to Cornwall for the weekend. ~ That'll be nice.*
> *Wait a minute while I send this e-mail. It won't take long.*

We use **would** for a past prediction or a prediction about a possible situation.

Past: *At midnight Sarah was still working. She **would** be tired the next day.*
Possible: *How about going to Cornwall next weekend? ~ That **would** be nice.*
                *I **wouldn't** enjoy a camping holiday.*

We can use **shall** instead of **will**, and **should** instead of **would**, but only in the first person, after **I** and **we**.

> *I **will/shall** be twenty-five in June.*
> *We **would/should** like to meet your family. But* NOT *~~My friend should like …~~*

Shall and **should** are a little formal here.

2 Would like

We can use **would like**, usually shortened to **'d like**, when we ask for something.

> *I**'d like** a brochure, please.*   *We**'d like** to order our drinks first.*

This is a more polite way of saying *I want a brochure*, for example.

We also use **would like** in offers and invitations.

> ***Would** you **like** a free gift?*   ***Would** you **like** to visit the museum with us?*

3 Decisions and refusals

We can use **will** for an instant decision or for an offer.

Decision: *Tea or coffee? ~ I**'ll** have coffee, please.* (see Unit 23.2)
Offer: *I**'ll** wait for you if you like. ~ Oh, thanks. I won't be long.*

We use **won't** and **wouldn't** for a refusal.

> *The strikers **won't** go back to work until they get a pay increase.*
> *The key went in the lock, but it **wouldn't** turn.*

I won't … is a strong refusal.

> *I **won't** listen to any more of this nonsense.*

4 Shall and should

We use **Shall I …?** in offers and **Shall we …?** in suggestions.

Offer: ***Shall** I wait for you? ~ Oh, thanks. I won't be long.*
Suggestion: ***Shall** we go to the park? ~ Good idea.*

We also use **shall** to ask for a suggestion.

> *What **shall** we have for lunch?*

We use either **shall** or **should** to ask for advice.

> *I'm in terrible trouble. What **shall/should** I do?*

We use **should** to say what is the best thing or the right thing to do.

> *People **should** exercise regularly.*
> *You **shouldn't** spend all your money as soon as you've earned it.*

▷ 23 **Will and shall**   ▷ 49 **Should**   ▷ 51 **Suggestions, offers and invitations**

Practice

A Will and would (1–2)

Complete the conversation. Put in *will*, *won't*, *would* or *wouldn't*.

Emma: We (▶) ..won't.. be here next September. It's hard to believe, isn't it? In a few months our student days (1) .... be over.

Matthew: It (2) .... be long now. I wish I had a job. Then I (3) .... know where I was going.

Emma: Who knows what the future (4) .... bring?

Matthew: Why don't we get married, Emma? Then at least we (5) .... be together.

Emma: I don't think so, Matthew. It (6) .... be a good idea.

Matthew: I couldn't live without you, Emma.

Emma: I really (7) .... like to believe you, Matthew.

B Some other uses of will and would (2–3)

Complete the conversations. Put in *will*, *won't*, *would* or *wouldn't* with these verbs:
eat, give, go, help, let, like, open, stand

▶ Vicky: Have you noticed how thin Jessica has got?
   Rachel: She's on a diet. She ..won't eat.. anything except carrots.

1 Harriet: Mike and I .... you get everything ready.
   Mike: Yes, we're quite willing to lend a hand.

2 Laura: You're late. I thought you were going to leave work early today.
   Trevor: Sorry. The boss .... me go.

3 Mark: Sarah and I .... you a lift, Mike.
   Sarah: Yes, we're going your way.

4 Harriet: I heard Rita has quarrelled with her boyfriend.
   Melanie: That's right. If he's invited to the party, she ....

5 Vicky: I've had enough of table tennis for one day.
   Rachel: OK. Maybe Daniel .... a game with me.

6 Trevor: What's wrong with the washing-machine?
   Laura: When I tried to use it earlier, the door ....

7 Mike: This lamp is always falling over.
   Harriet: It .... up properly.

C Will, would, shall and should (1–4)

What would you say? Use *will*, *would*, *shall* or *should*.

▶ Offer to make the tea.
   Shall I make the tea?

1 Suggest going to the swimming-pool.
   ....

2 Refuse to take any risks.
   ....

3 Say politely that you want a shower.
   ....

4 Tell someone it's best they don't decide in a hurry.
   ....

5 Predict the end of the world in the year 3000.
   ....

53 It may/could/must have been, etc.

1 Introduction

Vicky, Emma and Matthew are at a club in town.

Vicky: *Where's Daniel? He **should have been** here half an hour ago.*
Emma: *He **may have got** lost. It isn't easy to find this place.*
Matthew: *He **could have forgotten** all about it, I suppose.*
Emma: *He **can't have forgotten**. We were talking about it this morning.*
Matthew: *Well, something **must have delayed** him.*

We can use a modal verb with the perfect (**have** + a past participle).
We use this structure to talk about possible past events.

2 May have, might have and could have

We use these forms to say that possibly something happened in the past.

*He **may have got** lost.* (= Perhaps he has got lost.)
*You **might have left** your keys at work.* (= Perhaps you left them at work.)
*Someone **could have stolen** them.* (= It is possible that someone stole them.)

We also use **could have** for an opportunity that we didn't take or a possible result that didn't happen.

*We **could have gone** out somewhere, but we were too tired.*
*You were very lucky. There **could have been** a terrible accident.*

3 May not have, might not have and couldn't have

Compare these different uses.

MAY/MIGHT NOT HAVE	COULDN'T HAVE
Possibly something did not happen.	It is impossible that something happened.
*Daniel **may not have caught** the bus. I expect he missed it.*	*Daniel **couldn't have caught** the bus. It doesn't run on Sundays.*
(Perhaps he didn't catch it.)	(It is impossible for him to have caught the bus.)
*I **might not have locked** the door.*	
(Perhaps I didn't lock it.)	

4 Must have and can't have

Must and **can't** are opposites.

MUST HAVE	CAN'T HAVE
*My watch says it's only ten past two. It **must have stopped**.*	*You've only spent five minutes on that job. You **can't have done** it properly.*
I realize it is certainly true that my watch has stopped.	I realize it is impossible that you did the job properly.

5 Should have and ought to have

We use these forms when someone didn't do the right thing.

*We didn't play very well. We **should have played** better.*
*I got lost. ~ Sorry. I **ought to have drawn** you a map.*
*It was a lovely old building. They **shouldn't have knocked** it down.*

▷ 29.1 **Will have done**   ▷ 46 **May, might, could, must, can't**   ▷ 48.3 **Needn't have**
▷ 49 **Should, ought to**   ▷ 146 **Would have**

Practice

A It may/could/must have been, etc. (2–4)

Look at each conversation and choose the best sentence, a) or b).

▶ Has the car broken down? ~ Well, we may have run out of petrol.

a) ☐ I'm sure there's no petrol left. b) ✓ I think there's no petrol left.

1 You could have had a free holiday. ~ Yes, we could, but the dates weren't convenient.

a) ☐ We had a free holiday. b) ☐ We didn't have a free holiday.

2 Did you record the programme? ~ I can't remember. I might not have done.

a) ☐ I'm not sure if I recorded it. b) ☐ I certainly didn't record it.

3 Can't you find that newspaper? ~ No, someone must have thrown it away.

a) ☐ It was necessary to throw it away. b) ☐ I realize now that it was thrown away.

B Should and ought to (5 and Unit 49.2)

Complete the replies. Use *should/ought to* or *should have/ought to have*.

▶ Rita: Tom's car was stolen. He hadn't locked it.

David: I suppose it's his fault then. *He should have locked it.*

▶ Tom: I can't sleep sometimes. My neighbours play music all night.

Melanie: That's a nuisance. *They shouldn't play music all night.*

1 Mark: The picnickers left litter everywhere.

Sarah: That's awful. ....

2 Emma: Jessica isn't very friendly, is she? She never says hello to people.

Matthew: I know. ....

3 Rachel: I don't think Daniel's going to get that job. He was late for the interview.

Natasha: That can't have looked very good. ....

4 Daniel: Did you see Vicky crossing the road? She didn't look.

Emma: She could have been killed. ....

C It may/could/must have been, etc. (2–5)

Complete the conversation. Use *can't have, might have, must have* and *shouldn't have*.

Harriet: There's a parcel outside. The postman (▶) *must have left* .... (leave) it.

Mike: Well, (1) .... (he / leave) it outside. He isn't supposed to do that. Someone (2) .... (take) it. Why didn't he ring the bell?

Harriet: He always rings. (3) .... (you / be) out when he came.

Mike: I haven't been out. So (4) .... (he / ring) the bell.

D It may/could/must have been, etc. (2–5)

Complete the sentences. The second person agrees with the first. Use *might have, couldn't have*, etc.

▶ Matthew: I'm sure the computer didn't make a mistake. That's impossible.

Emma: No, of course *the computer couldn't have made a mistake.*

1 Mark: I can't see the letter here now. So clearly someone posted it.

Alan: Yes, ...

2 Natasha: It's possible Emma didn't hear the alarm.

Rachel: Well, I suppose ....

3 Sarah: Henry drove at 100 miles an hour. Don't you think that's dangerous?

Mark: Yes, I do. ....

4 Daniel: I just don't believe that Andrew has failed the exam.

Vicky: Andrew? Impossible! ....

Test J: Modal verbs

A

Decide which word is correct.

▶ <u>Could</u> .... I have some more tea, please?
   a) Could   b) Shall   c) Will   d) Would

1   Everyone's asleep. We .... make a noise.
    a) couldn't   b) mustn't   c) needn't   d) wouldn't

2   .... you like to go for a ride with us?
    a) Do   b) Should   c) Will   d) Would

3   I wonder if this is the right way. It .... not be.
    a) can   b) could   c) might   d) must

4   I don't think I want to see this film. ~ Oh, I think you .... enjoy it.
    a) can   b) shall   c) will   d) would

5   I'm quite happy to walk. You .... drive me home.
    a) don't   b) haven't   c) mustn't   d) needn't

6   .... I show you the way? ~ Oh, thank you.
    a) Do   b) Shall   c) Will   d) Would

7   It's late. I think we .... better go.
    a) had   b) have   c) should   d) would

8   We all tried to push the van, but it .... move.
    a) can't   b) couldn't   c) won't   d) wouldn't

B

Some of these sentences are correct, and some have a word which should not be there. If the sentence is correct, put a tick (✓). If it is incorrect, cross the unnecessary word out of the sentence and write it in the space.

▶ I won't be able to come to the meeting. — ✓
▶ We didn't needn't have watered the garden because it's raining. — didn't
1   Would you like to be in the team? — ....
2   Did people have to bring their own sleeping-bags? — ....
3   I could to ski when I was quite young. — ....
4   Would you mind for checking these figures? — ....
5   We may be go swimming tomorrow. — ....
6   I knew that I would be sorry later. — ....
7   If you had fallen, you could have been hurt yourself. — ....
8   We're not supposed to use this entrance. — ....
9   You don't have to do all the work yourself. — ....
10 Anna wasn't be allowed to take photos. — ....

C

Write a second sentence so that it has a similar meaning to the first. Use the word in brackets.

▶ Perhaps Susan knows the address. (may)
   <u>Susan may know the address.</u>

1   We should be careful. (ought)
    ....

2   I managed to finish all my work. (able)
    ....

3   I realize that it was a terrible experience for you. (must)
    ....

4   It's against the rules for players to have a drink. (allowed)

....

5   The best thing for you to do is sit down. (better)

....

6   The report must be on my desk tomorrow morning. (has)

....

7   It is possible that Joanne did not receive my message. (might)

....

8   It's impossible for Martin to be jogging in this weather. (can't)

....

9   Tessa wants a cup of coffee. (like)

....

10   It was not necessary for Nancy to clean the flat. (didn't)

....

D

Say what the speaker is doing. After each sentence write one of the phrases from the box.

asking for advice	giving an order	making a suggestion	refusing permission
asking permission	inviting	offering food	
expressing a wish	making a request	offering to help	

▶   Will you have a piece of cake?   offering food ....
1   May I sit down?   ....
2   You must report to me every day.   ....
3   What jobs should I apply for?   ....
4   Would you like to spend the day with us? ....
5   Shall I do the washing-up?   ....
6   Shall we sit outside?   ....
7   I'm sorry. You can't park here.   ....
8   Could you fill in this form, please?   ....
9   We really must have a nice big party.   ....

E

Here is some information for visitors to New York City.
Write the missing words. Use one word only in each space.

Before you travel to the US, you (▶) ..must.. find out what documents you need. You'll probably
(1) .... to get a visa, but there are different rules for different nationalities.
For example, you (2) .... need to show that you have enough money with you.
But there's one rule you can be sure about: everyone (3) .... to show their
passport. The roads in New York are very busy, but don't worry – you (4) .... get
around cheaply and easily by subway. Remember that you are not (5) .... to
smoke on public transport or in shops. And don't forget either that you are (6) ....
to tip taxi drivers and waiters. New York is not the most dangerous city in the US, but you really
(7) .... walk along empty streets at night. And it is safer if you are
(8) .... to travel around in a group.

54 Passive verb forms

1 Introduction

A passive verb is a form of **be** + a past participle, e.g. **is baked, was worn**. Some participles are irregular (see pages 382–3).

OUR BREAD IS BAKED

HERE

THIS JACKET WAS WORN BY ELVIS PRESLEY

2 Summary of verb tenses

	ACTIVE	PASSIVE
Present Simple:	We **bake** the bread here.	The bread **is baked** here.
Present Continuous:	We **are baking** the bread.	The bread **is being baked**.
Present Perfect:	We **have baked** the bread.	The bread **has been baked**.
Past Simple:	We **baked** the bread yesterday.	The bread **was baked** yesterday.
Past Continuous:	We **were baking** the bread.	The bread **was being baked**.
Past Perfect:	We **had baked** the bread.	The bread **had been baked**.

We form negatives and questions in the same way as in active sentences.

*The bread **isn't baked** in a factory.   The jacket **hasn't been worn** for years.*
*Where is the bread **baked**?   Has the jacket ever **been worn** by anyone else?*

3 The future and modal verbs in the passive

We use **be** + a past participle after **will, be going to, can, must, have to, should**, etc.

*The gates **will be closed** this evening.   This rubbish **should be thrown** away.*
*The machine **has to be repaired**.   The news **might be announced** soon.*
*Seats **may not be reserved**.   How **can** the problem **be solved**?*

	ACTIVE	PASSIVE
Future:	We **will bake** the bread next.	The bread **will be baked** next.
	We **are going to bake** the bread.	The bread **is going to be baked**.
Modal verb:	We **should bake** the bread soon.	The bread **should be baked** soon.
	We **ought to bake** the bread.	The bread **ought to be baked**.

4 The passive with get

We sometimes use **get** in the passive instead of **be**.

*Lots of postmen **get bitten** by dogs.   I'm always **getting chosen** for the worst jobs.*
*Last week Laura **got moved** to another department.*

Get is informal. We often use it for something happening by accident or unexpectedly.

In negatives and questions in the Present Simple and Past Simple, we use a form of **do**.

*The windows **don't get cleaned** very often.   How **did** the painting **get damaged**?*

We also use **get** in these expressions: **get dressed/changed, get washed** (= wash oneself), **get engaged/married/divorced, get started** (= start), **get lost** (= lose one's way).

*Emma and Matthew might **get married**.   Without a map we soon **got lost**.*

Practice

A Present Continuous passive (2)

Look at the pictures and say what is happening. Use these subjects: *the car*, *dinner*, *a flag*, *some houses*, *the seals*. Use these verbs: *build*, *feed*, *raise*, *repair*, *serve*.

▶ *The car is being repaired.*
1 ....
2 ....
3 ....
4 ....

B Passive verb tenses (2)

Complete the information about Barford Hall. Put in the correct form of these verbs.

▶ *build*	2 *use*	4 *not look*	6 *use*
(Past Simple)	(Past Continuous)	(Past Perfect)	(Present Simple)
1 *own*	3 *buy*	5 *do*	
(Present Simple)	(Past Simple)	(Present Perfect)	

The building at the end of the High Street is Barford Hall, which (▶) was built .... in 1827. Today the Hall (1) .... by Bardale Council. It (2) .... as a warehouse when it (3) .... by the Council in 1952, and it (4) .. .. after very well. Since then a lot of work (5) .... on it, and these days the Hall (6) .... as an arts centre.

C The future and modal verbs in the passive (3)

A press conference is being held. Put in the correct form of the verbs.
▶ Reporter: Can this new drug prolong human life?
  Professor: Yes, we believe that human life can be prolonged .... by the drug.
1 Reporter: Are you going to do any more tests on the drug?
  Professor: Yes, further tests .... soon.
2 Reporter: What .... the drug ....?
  Professor: It will be called Bio-Meg.
3 Reporter: Can people buy the drug now?
  Professor: No, it .... by the public yet.
4 Reporter: Do you think the company should sell this drug?
  Professor: Yes, I think Bio-Meg .... to anyone who wants it.

D The passive with **get** (4)

Put in *get* or *got* and the past participle of these verbs: *break*, *change*, *divorce*, *hurt*, *lose*
▶ If we're going out to the theatre, I'd better get changed ....
1 Daniel .... when he tried to break up a fight.
2 I know the way. We won't ....
3 You'd better wrap up the glasses, so they don't ....
4 They were only married a year before they ....

55 Active and passive (1)

1 What is the sentence about?

Compare these two entries in an encyclopedia.

Alexander Graham Bell A British inventor who went to live in Canada and then the USA. Bell invented the telephone.	**Telephone** An apparatus with which people can talk to each other over long distances. The telephone was invented by Alexander Graham Bell.

Look at these two sentences.

ACTIVE	PASSIVE
Bell *invented the telephone.*	***The telephone*** *was invented by Bell.*

The two sentences have the same meaning, but they are about different things. One sentence is about Bell, and the other is about the telephone. Each sentence begins with the subject. The subject is the starting-point of the sentence, the thing we are talking about. The new information about the subject comes at the end of the sentence.

We say *Bell invented the telephone* because we are talking about **Bell**, and the new information is that he invented **the telephone**.	We say *The telephone was invented by Bell* because we are talking about **the telephone**, and the new information is that it was invented by **Bell**.
When the subject is the person or thing doing the action (the agent), then we use an active verb.	When the subject is not the agent (is not doing the action), then we use a passive verb.
ACTIVE	PASSIVE
Bell | *invented the telephone.* ⎯⎯ Subject and agent	*The telephone* | *was invented by* | *Bell* . ⎯⎯ ⎯⎯ Subject Agent
The subject (**Bell**) is the agent.	The subject (**the telephone**) is not the agent. It is the thing that the action is directed at.

2 The passive and **by the police, in 1876,** etc.

In a passive sentence, when we want to say who or what did the action, we use **by**.
 *On our way home we were stopped **by the police**.   The new hospital will be opened **by the Queen**.*
 *The paper was all blown away **by the wind**.*
We can give other details about the action. For example, we can use a phrase saying when or where something happens.
 *The telephone was invented **in 1876**.   The visitors will be driven **to the airport**.*
 *The concerts are usually held **at the university**.*
Sometimes there is no phrase after the verb.
 *A new swimming-pool **is being built**.   All the documents **have been destroyed**.*
For more details see Unit 56.

Practice

A Active or passive verb? (1)

Choose the correct verb forms in this news report about a storm.

Millions of pounds' worth of damage (▶) ~~has caused~~/has been caused by a storm which
(1) swept/was swept across the north of England last night. The River Ribble (2) burst/was burst its
banks after heavy rain. Many people (3) rescued/were rescued from the floods by fire-fighters, who
(4) received/were received hundreds of calls for help. Wind speeds (5) reached/were reached ninety
miles an hour in some places. Roads (6) blocked/were blocked by fallen trees, and electricity lines
(7) brought/were brought down, leaving thousands of homes without electricity. 'Everything possible
(8) is doing/is being done to get things back to normal,' a spokesman (9) said/was said.

B By the police, etc. (2)

In each of these sentences <u>underline</u> who or what is doing the action (the agent).

- ▶ <u>The traffic</u> was all heading out of town.
- 1 The photo was taken by my brother.
- 2 The water was pouring out of the hole.
- 3 A policeman has been murdered by terrorists.
- 4 We were woken by the alarm.
- 5 The guide led a group of tourists around the castle.
- 6 The dog has bitten several people.

C Active and passive (1–2)

You are telling a friend some news. Use the notes and complete the second sentence.
Sometimes you need to use the active and sometimes the passive.

- ▶ (Past Simple: Claire / go / to Florida / last month)
  You remember Claire? She went to Florida last month.
- ▶ (Present Perfect: send / our luggage / to Australia)
  Bad news about our luggage. It's been sent to Australia.
- 1 (Past Simple: Claude Jennings / win / the quiz competition)
  Did you hear about the quiz competition? It ....
- 2 (Past Simple: Mrs Miles / do / a parachute jump / last week)
  You know Mrs Miles? She ....
- 3 (Present Perfect: a bull / attack / David)
  Have you heard about David? He's ....
- 4 (Present Continuous: build / the house)
  Trevor and Laura have bought a house. It's still ....
- 5 (Present Simple: Andrew / like / Jessica)
  Did I tell you about Andrew? He ....
- 6 (Present Perfect: throw away / your stamp collection)
  Bad news about your stamp collection. It's ....
- 7 (Present Perfect: Martians / kidnap / my neighbours)
  Did I mention my neighbours? They've ....
- 8 (Past Simple: five people / see / the ghost)
  Did you hear about the ghost? It ....

56 Active and passive (2)

1 The passive and the agent

In a passive sentence, we sometimes mention the agent (the person or thing doing the action).
We use **by** with the agent.

> *The cheque must be signed **by the manager**.*
> *The medals were presented **by Nelson Mandela**.*

But we mention the agent only if it is important for the meaning of the sentence.
Sometimes we do not mention it.

1 We do not mention the agent if it does not add any new information.

> *All our money and passports were stolen.*
> *A man was arrested last night.*

We do not need to say that the money was stolen 'by a thief' or that the man was arrested 'by the police'.

2 We do not mention the agent if it is not important.

> *The streets are cleaned every day.*
> *Oil has been discovered at the North Pole.*

Who discovered the oil is less important than the fact that it is there.

3 It is sometimes difficult to say who the agent is.

> *This kind of jacket is considered very fashionable these days.*
> *A number of attempts have been made to find the Loch Ness monster.*

2 Empty subjects (**they, people**, etc.)

Compare these two sentences.

ACTIVE	PASSIVE
They *clean the streets every day.*	*The streets are cleaned every day.*

The new and important information is <u>how often</u> the streets are cleaned. We are not interested in saying who cleans them. In the active sentence we can use the 'empty subject' **they**. We sometimes use a sentence with an empty subject instead of the passive, especially in conversation.

We can also use the empty subjects **people, you, one** and **someone**.

ACTIVE	PASSIVE
People *use this footpath all the time.*	*This footpath is used all the time.*
You/One *should check the details.*	*The details should be checked.*
Someone *took my purse.*	*My purse was taken.*

3 When do we use the passive?

We use the passive in both speech and writing, but it is more common in writing.
We see it especially in textbooks and reports. We use it to describe activities in industry,
science and technology, and also for official rules.

> *Bananas **are exported** to Europe.*   *The liquid **is heated** to boiling point.*
> *Payment **can be made** at any post office.*   *Cars left here **will be towed** away.*

In these situations, it is often not important to say who is doing the action, or it is difficult to say.

The passive is also often used in news reports.

> *A number of political prisoners **have been released**.*
> *Talks **will be held** in London next week.*

Practice

A The passive and the agent (1)

Laura is writing to a friend. This is part of her letter.

Someone broke into our house at the weekend. The burglar took some jewellery. But luckily he didn't do any damage. A very nice young police officer interviewed me. Detectives found some fingerprints, and the police computer identified the burglar. Police have arrested a man and are questioning him. But they haven't found the jewellery.

Now complete the passive sentences in this conversation. Use a phrase with *by* only if it adds information.

Laura: Our house (▶) was broken into at the weekend.

Melanie: Oh no!

Laura: Some jewellery (1) .... But luckily no damage (2) ....
           ....

Melanie: Did the police come and see you?

Laura: Yes, they did. I (3) ....

Melanie: I don't suppose they know who did it.

Laura: Well, amazingly they do. Some (4) ...., and
           the (5) ....
           ....
           A man (6) .... and (7) ....

Melanie: Wonderful.

Laura: There's only one problem. The (8) ....

B Active or passive sentence? (1)

Write a paragraph from the notes about the first motor car. Some sentences are active and some are passive. Use a phrase with *by* only if it adds information.

▶	a Belgian called Etienne Lenoir / make / the first motor car	The first motor car was made by a Belgian called Etienne Lenoir. ....
1	but / Lenoir / not produce / many cars / for sale	But Lenoir ....
2	a German called Karl Benz / start / commercial production	Commercial ....
3	people / now / see / Benz / as the father / of the motor car	Benz ....

C Empty subjects (2)

Reply to what people say. Use the subject in brackets.

▶	Daniel:	The bus fares have been increased. (they)	
	Vicky:	What? You mean they've increased the bus fares again!	
1	Melanie:	Bicycles should be used for short journeys. (people)	
	David:	Yes, I agree.	
2	Emma:	A new source of energy has been discovered. (someone)	
	Daniel:	What? Did you say that	
3	Rachel:	This building is going to be knocked down. (they)	
	Vicky:	Well, no one told me that	
4	David:	Eggs shouldn't be kept in a freezer. (you)	
	Tom:	Really? I didn't know	
5	Vicky:	Why isn't litter put in the bin? (people)	
	Emma:	Exactly. Why don't	

57 Special passive structures

1 I was given …

Look at these sentences.

> *Henry gave some flowers to Claire.*   *Henry gave Claire some flowers.*

An active sentence with a verb like **give** can have two different structures (see Unit 3).

If we use a passive sentence, either **some flowers** or **Claire** can be the subject.

***Some flowers** were given to Claire.* This is about the flowers, and it tells us who received them.	***Claire** was given some flowers.* This is about Claire, and it tells us what she received.

It is quite normal in English for a person to be the subject in a passive sentence like the one about Claire.

> ***Mike** was sent tickets for the concert.*   ***My wife** is paid more than I am.*
> ***Andrew** has been awarded a prize for his essay.*

We can use the following verbs in this structure: **allow, award, fed, give, grant, hand, leave** (in a will), **lend, offer, owe, pay, promise, sell, send, show, teach**

2 It is said that …

Henry is in love with Claire.

> ***It is said** that Henry is in love with Claire.*
> (= People say that Henry is in love with Claire.)

We can use the structure **it** + passive verb + clause with verbs of reporting. We use this structure when we cannot say or do not need to say who the speaker is, for example in news reports.

> ***It is thought** that the company is planning a new advertising campaign.*
> ***It was reported** that the President had suffered a heart attack.*
> ***It has been agreed** that changes to the scheme are necessary.*

Here are some verbs we can use in this structure: **agree, allege, announce, assure, believe, consider, decide, expect, explain, hope, know, report, say, suggest, suppose, think, understand**

3 He is said to …

We can also use a subject + passive verb + to-infinitive.

> *Henry **is said to be** in love with Claire.*

This structure is also used in news reports.

> *United **were expected to win**. (= People expected that they would win.)*
> *The company **is thought to be planning** a new advertising campaign.*
> (= Someone thinks that it is planning a new advertising campaign.)
> *The President **was reported to have suffered** a heart attack.*
> (= Someone reported that he had suffered a heart attack.)

We can use the following verbs in this structure: **believe, expect, find, know, report, say, think, understand**

We often use **be supposed to** for things that people say.

> *I might watch this programme. It's **supposed to be** very funny.*

Practice

A I was given ... (1)

Zedco managers are writing a report saying how well the company looks after its employees.
Write sentences from the notes. Put the important <u>underlined</u> information at the end of the sentence.

▶ <u>useful work skills</u> / they are taught to our staff
  Our staff are taught useful work skills. ....

▶ <u>people with initiative</u> / they are given opportunities
  Opportunities are given to people with initiative. ....

1 <u>special training</u> / it is given to new employees
  ....

2 <u>staff who perform well</u> / they are given extra payments
  ....

3 <u>company shares</u> / they are offered to most employees
  ....

4 <u>six weeks' holiday</u> / this is allowed to all Zedco staff
  ....

5 <u>women who leave to have children</u> / they are paid a full salary
  ....

B It is said that ... (2)

Report these rumours. Instead of the active (e.g. *People say ...*) use the passive (e.g. *It is said that ...*).

▶ People say this.

The quiz champion Claude Jennings has lost his memory.

It is said that the quiz champion Claude Jennings has lost his memory. ....

1 Everyone expects this.

The soap opera 'Round the Corner' will end next year.

It is ....
....
....

2 Journalists suppose so.

The footballer Wayne Johnson is earning £10 million a year.

....
....
....

3 Lots of people believe this.

The Prime Minister and his wife have separated.

....
....
....

C He is said to ... (3)

Now report the rumours in Exercise B like this.

▶ *The quiz champion Claude Jennings is said to have lost his memory.* ....

1 The soap opera 'Round the Corner' ....

2 ....

3 ....

58 Have something done

1 Introduction

Compare these situations.

Claire decorated the room.
(She did the work herself.)

*Claire **had** the room **decorated**.*
(A decorator did the work.)

We can use **have** in a passive structure. *Claire had the room decorated* means that she arranged for a decorator to do it for her as a professional service.

2 Form

Look at these examples.

	HAVE	SOMETHING	DONE	
You should	have	your car	serviced	regularly.
Mark usually	has	his suits	cleaned	at Superclean.
We	had	the television	repaired	only last year.
You've	had	your hair	cut.	
Our neighbours are	having	a new garage	built.	
Is Melanie	having	a new cooker	installed?	

Note that we can use the perfect or the continuous (**have had, are having**).

In negatives and questions in simple tenses, we use a form of **do**.
> Mark **doesn't have** his suits cleaned at Fastclean.
> We **didn't have** new windows put in because it was too expensive.
> **Do** you **have** your car serviced regularly?   Where **did** you **have** your hair cut?

3 Get something done

We can also use **get something done**.
> We must **have** another key **made**. OR We must **get** another key **made**.

The sentences have the same meaning, but **get** is more informal than **have**.

Here are some more examples with **get**.
> Laura **got** her shoes **repaired**.   We**'re getting** the carpet **cleaned**.
> Where **did** you **get** your hair **cut**?   **Do** you **get** your heating **checked** every year?

4 Have meaning 'experience'

We can use **have** in this structure with the meaning 'experience something', often something unpleasant.
> We **had** all our money **stolen**.   The car **had** its mirror **pulled** off.

Practice

A Have something done (1–2)

Look at the pictures and say what people are doing or what they did.
Use these phrases: *her photo*, *his windows*, *his car*, *her eyes*, *his hair*
Use these verbs: *clean*, *cut*, *repair*, *take*, *test*

▶ At the moment Trevor .is. having. his. hair. cut. ....

1 Last week Mike ....

2 At the moment Melissa ....

3 Yesterday David ....

4 At the moment Rachel ....

B Have something done (1–2)

Read about each situation and write sentences with *have something done*.

▶ Melanie is paying the man who has repaired her bicycle.
   .Melanie. has. had. her. bicycle. repaired. ....

1 David went to the hospital. A nurse bandaged his arm.

   ....

2 Daniel is going to the dentist. She's going to fill his tooth.

   ....

3 Laura is walking around town while her photos are being developed.

   ....

C Get something done (3)

Look again at Exercise B. The jobs are all done now. Complete the questions using *get*.

▶ Mike: Where .did. you. get. your. bicycle. repaired,. Melanie? ....

1 Harriet: Why ....

2 Emma: Where ....

3 Sarah: Where ....

D Have meaning 'experience' (4)

Say what happened to these people.

▶ Claire (whose luggage was searched in customs)
   .Claire. had. her. luggage. searched. in. customs. ....

1 Tom (whose car was stolen from outside his house)

   ....

2 Rita (whose rent was increased by ten per cent)

   ....

3 David (whose electricity has been cut off)

   ....

59 To be done and being done

1 Active and passive forms

I just want **to sit** here and relax. I really enjoy **having** a lazy time.

And it's nice **to be looked** after. I love **being waited** on.

Compare the active and passive.

	ACTIVE	PASSIVE
to-infinitive: -ing form:	I ought **to meet** Sarah at the airport. I insist on **meeting** you at the airport. (I meet people.)	I hope **to be met** at the airport. I love **being met** at the airport. (People meet me.)

Here are some more examples.

*I want **to play** volleyball. I hope **to be chosen** for the team.*
*The minister agreed **to answer** questions. He agreed **to be interviewed** on television.*
*Why did Tom keep **making** jokes about me? I don't enjoy **being laughed** at.*
*You say you remember **telling** me the news. But I certainly can't remember **being told**.*

An -ing form sometimes comes after a preposition.

*The postman complained **about being attacked** by Nick's dog.*
*Famous people get tired **of being recognized** everywhere they go.*

2 Active forms with a passive meaning

The active -ing form after **need** has a passive meaning.

*The bicycle **needs oiling**. (= The bicycle needs **to be oiled**.)*
*The windows **need cleaning**. (= The windows need **to be cleaned**.)*

We cannot use the passive -ing form here.

NOT ~~The bicycle needs being oiled.~~

We sometimes use an active to-infinitive when we talk about a job **to be done**.

*I've got some letters **to write** today.   We've got this bill **to pay**.*

Here we use the active (**to write**) because the subject of the sentence (**I**) is the person who has to do the job. But if the subject is not a person, then we use the passive infinitive.

*The letters are **to be written** today.   The bill is **to be paid** without delay.*
*All this mess has **to be cleared** away.   The goods have **to be shipped**.*

We can use the structure **be** + to-infinitive to give an order.

*The matter **is to be given** top priority.   You're **not to drive** too fast.*

After the subject **there**, we can use either an active or a passive to-infinitive.

*There are some letters **to write/to be written** today.   There's a bill **to pay/to be paid**.*

▷ 62 Verb + active to-infinitive or -ing form   ▷ 73 Preposition + active -ing form

Practice

A Passive forms (1)

A YOUNG MAN IS APPLYING FOR A JOB.

I hope the company invites me to an interview. I'm worried about them asking me difficult questions. I want them to take me seriously. I hope the company will offer me a job. I don't mind them paying me low wages at first. I'm willing for them to re-train me. I'd enjoy it if they sent me on business trips abroad. I would like the boss to give me a chance.

**Report what the man says. Use the passive
to-infinitive or -ing form.**

▶ He hopes to be invited to an interview.
▶ He's worried about being asked difficult questions.

1 ....
2 ....
3 ....
4 ....
5 ....
6 ....

B Active and passive forms (1)

**TV reporter Kitty Beamish is interviewing some workers who are protesting about not being paid
enough. Complete the workers' statements. Put in an active or passive to-infinitive or -ing form.**

▶ We want to be paid .... (pay) better wages.
1 We don't enjoy .... (use) as cheap labour.
2 We're tired of .... (work) for low wages.
3 We expect .... (treat) like human beings.
4 We don't want .... (give) up all our rights.
5 We hope .... (invite) to a meeting with the management.
6 We insist on .... (take) seriously.

C Active and passive forms (1–2)

Put in an active or passive to-infinitive or -ing form.

Jessica: Are you going to be busy today?
Andrew: Well, I've got a few things (▶) to do .... (do).
         I've got an essay (1) .... (write).
         And this room ought (2) .... (tidy) up a bit.
         This carpet needs (3) .... (hoover).
Jessica: I've got some jobs (4) .... (do), too.
         Most of my clothes need (5) .... (iron).
         And I've got my project (6) .... (finish) off.
         I'm worried about (7) .... (miss) the deadline.
         It has (8) .... (hand) in tomorrow.
         I don't want (9) .... (be) late with it.
Andrew: I don't remember (10) .... (tell) when the project was due in.
Jessica: Why? Haven't you done it yet?
Andrew: Oh, yes. I handed it in ages ago.

Test K: The passive

A

Rewrite these sentences beginning with the underlined words.

▶ Thieves robbed <u>a woman</u>.
  A woman was robbed.

1 They may ban <u>the film</u>.
  ....

2 They offered <u>Nancy</u> a pay increase.
  ....

3 We need to correct <u>the mistakes</u>.
  ....

4 Someone reported that <u>the situation</u> was under control.
  ....

5 They are testing <u>the new drug</u>.
  ....

6 We haven't used <u>the machine</u> for ages.
  ....

B

Read the story and write the missing words. Use one word only in each space.

During periods of terrorist activity, people in Britain are always (▶) *being* warned to look out for bombs. Any bag or parcel without an owner (1) .... seen as a risk to the public. Some time ago a cardboard box was found at the entrance to Bristol Zoo one day. It was noticed (2) .... a visitor and reported to the director. Clearly, if it was a bomb and it went off, people might (3) .... killed. So army bomb experts (4) .... called in, and the box was safely blown up in a controlled explosion. Soon afterwards (5) .... was reported that the box had (6) .... left there by a boy wanting to find a new home for his pet rat. He was tired of the rat, he explained, but he was unwilling to (7) .... it put to sleep by a vet, so he left it in a box outside the zoo. The director of the zoo is thought (8) .... be unenthusiastic about looking after people's unwanted pets. No one knows what the rat thought about (9) .... blown up.

C

Write a second sentence so that it has a similar meaning to the first. Use the word in brackets.

▶ We have to test these products. (be)
  These products have to be tested.

1 Pavarotti sang the song. (by)
  ....

2 Nigel's passport was stolen. (had)
  ....

3 They pay doctors a lot of money. (are)
  ....

4 I hope they'll interview me for the job. (to)
  ....

5 Someone was cleaning the floor. (being)
  ....

6 A mechanic is repairing Judy's car. (having)
  ....

7   Tessa lost her way. (got)

....

8   Everyone agreed that the plan should go ahead. (it)

....

9   When did they decorate your kitchen? (get)

....

10   They say exercise is good for you. (be)

....

D

Which of the two sentences follows on best?

▶   There's going to be a big art exhibition.
a) ☐ A lot of visitors will be attracted to it.   b) ✓ It will attract a lot of visitors.

1   Our neighbours have got a cat and a dog.
a) ☐ A lot of mice are caught by the cat.   b) ☐ The cat catches a lot of mice.

2   Last night Martin dreamt he saw his dead grandmother.
a) ☐ A white dress was being worn by the ghost.   b) ☐ The ghost was wearing a white dress.

3   We've bought a new computer.
a) ☐ It can do the job much more quickly.   b) ☐ The job can be done much more quickly.

4   My grandfather is very ill.
a) ☐ He's being looked after in the local hospital.   b) ☐ The local hospital is looking after him.

5   We've completed the experiment.
a) ☐ The media will publish the results.   b) ☐ The results will be published in the media.

E

Each of these sentences is incorrect. Write the correct sentence.

▶   ~~Those nice glasses got break.~~
Those nice glasses got broken. ....

1   ~~The story was written Agatha Christie.~~

....

2   ~~Baseball do play at this stadium.~~

....

3   ~~This shirt needs iron.~~

....

4   ~~I got cut my hair yesterday.~~

....

5   ~~It believes that there is going to be a war.~~

....

6   ~~My parents divorce themselves last year.~~

....

7   ~~I've got a report to be written.~~

....

8   ~~To the winner was given a prize.~~

....

9   ~~This man on TV supposes to be the tallest person in the world.~~

....

60 Verb + to-infinitive

1 Introduction

I've **decided to have** a round of golf. I've **arranged to play** with someone.

But you **promised to come** shopping this afternoon. I **want to look** for a new sofa.

After some verbs we can use a to-infinitive, e.g. **decided to have, arranged to play**. Here are some more examples.

> *I expect to get my money back.*
> *Sarah agreed to work late at the office.*
> *We can't afford to go to Australia.*
> *Are you hoping to get a job in London?*
> *Melanie has offered to help us when we move house.*

We can put **not** before the to-infinitive.

> *Some people just choose not to get married.*
> *At least I managed not to lose my temper.*

With some other verbs we use an -ing form, not a to-infinitive (see Units 61 and 62).

> *Mark has finished playing golf.*

2 Seem and appear

We can use a to-infinitive after **seem** and **appear**.

> *Sarah seemed to be quite annoyed.*   *The computer program appears to have a bug in it.*
> *The person I spoke to didn't seem to know anything about the company's products.*

We can use a continuous or a perfect to-infinitive.

Continuous: *Andrew seems to be studying even harder these days.*
Perfect: *David appeared to have hurt himself.*

3 Tend, manage and fail

We use **tend to** for things that usually happen.

> *We tend to get up later at weekends.* (= We usually get up later at weekends.)

We use **manage to** for being able to do something.

> *Luckily I managed to find my way here all right.* (= I was able to find my way.)

We use **fail to** for things that don't happen.

> *David failed to pay his electricity bill.* (= David didn't pay his electricity bill.)

4 He promised to go, his promise to go

Some nouns can come before a to-infinitive. Compare these sentences.

Verb + to-infinitive: *Mark promised to go shopping.*
                            But then he arranged to play golf.
Noun + to-infinitive: *Mark forgot about his promise to go shopping.*
                            Sarah found out about his arrangement to play golf.

Here are some nouns we can use: **agreement, arrangement, decision, demand, desire, failure, offer, plan, promise, refusal, tendency, threat**

▷ 61–62 Verb + -ing form   ▷ 65 Verb + object + to-infinitive

Practice

A Verb + to-infinitive (1)

Say what each speaker did. Use these verbs before a to-infinitive: *decide*, *demand*, *offer*, *promise*, *threaten*

▶ Henry: I really must speak to the manager.

Henry demanded to speak to the manager. ....

1 Trevor: I'll put the shelves up soon, I promise.

....

2 Claire: OK, I'll buy both the dresses.

....

3 Melanie: I'll cook the meal if you like.

....

4 Tom: If you don't do your homework, Nick, I'll give you extra exercises.

....

B Seem (2)

Complete the answers using *seem* and a to-infinitive.
(Some of the to-infinitives may be continuous or perfect.)

▶ Vicky: Have Matthew and Emma got over their quarrel?
  Daniel: I think so. *They seem to have got* over it.

▶ Rita: Is Claire in love with Henry?
  Sarah: Probably not. *She doesn't seem to be* .... in love with him.

1 Tom: Do Mike and Harriet really believe there's life on Mars?
  David: Well, yes. .... there is.

2 Victor: Has Ilona's English improved?
  Emma: Yes, ... quite a lot.

3 David: Does Rita like football?
  Tom: I don't think so. .... it much.

4 Natasha: Is Daniel working hard, do you think?
  Rachel: Yes, I think so. .... hard.

5 Sarah: Has Trevor made a good job of those shelves?
  Laura: Not really. .... a very good job of them.

C Verb + to-infinitive (1–4)

Put in the to-infinitive form. (Some may be continuous or perfect.)
Use these verbs: *come*, *find*, *hang*, *have*, *invite*, *leave*, *take*

Harriet: Hello, Nick. You managed (▶) *to find* .... your way then?

Nick: Yes, in the end. It's a bit complicated, isn't it?

Harriet: Well you're here now. Do you want (1) .... your coat up?

Nick: Thank you.

Harriet: I'm glad you decided (2) .... to our party. Everyone seems (3) .... a good time. We tend (4) .... lots of people to our parties.

Nick: Is Tom here?

Harriet: No, he couldn't come. He'd already made an arrangement (5) .... somebody somewhere in his taxi.

Nick: And Rita?

Harriet: Er, she was here, but she appears (6) .... early. I don't know where she's gone. She was with someone.

61 Verb + -ing form

1 Introduction

After some verbs we can use an -ing form, for example, **suggested going**, **enjoy putting**.

*I usually **avoid driving** in the rush hour.*   *We'll have to **practise throwing** the ball into the basket.*
*Have you **finished typing** that letter?*   *Nick says he's **given up smoking**.*

We can sometimes put **not** before an -ing form.

*Imagine **not having** anywhere to live.*

With some other verbs we use a to-infinitive, not an -ing form (see Units 60 and 62).

*I don't **want to put** up a tent in the rain.*

2 Mind

We use **mind** + an -ing form mostly in negative statements and in questions.

*Andrew doesn't **mind having** lots of work. He quite likes it.*
(= He doesn't dislike having lots of work.)
*Do you **mind waiting** a moment? ~ No, that's OK.*
*I wouldn't **mind travelling** around the world some time.*

3 Verbs with can't

Note **can't** or **couldn't** with **help**, **resist**, **face** and **stand**. We can put an -ing form after these verbs.

*I think Tom is very amusing. I **can't help laughing** at his funny stories.*
*The dress was so beautiful that Claire **couldn't resist buying** it.*
*Let's eat out, shall we? I **can't face cooking** a meal today.*
*I never go in the bank if it's busy. I **can't stand waiting** in a queue.*

4 Keep (on) and carry on

We use **keep** or **keep on** + an -ing form to talk about something continuing,
or when it happens again and again.

*Just **keep stirring** the mixture until it boils.*   *Nick **keeps ringing** Rita and asking her out.*
*The runners didn't mind the rain. They just **kept on running**.*

For **continue** see Unit 63.3.

Carry on means something continuing.

*Just **carry on stirring** the mixture until it boils.*

▷ 65.4 Verb + object + -ing form

A Verb + -ing form (1)

Answer the questions using the notes in brackets.

► Mike: Is your car working now? (they / not / finish / repair / it)
   You: No, *they haven't finished repairing it* .... yet.
1 Laura: Have you done the crossword? (I / give up / try)
   You: No, ...
2 Daniel: There's a story here in the paper about a 110-year-old man. (I / can / not / imagine / be)
   You: Good Lord. .... so old.
3 Tom: Do you like football? (I / enjoy / watch / it / on TV)
   You: Well, ...
4 Rachel: Whose idea was it to invite all these people? (suggest / have / a party)
   You: I'm not sure. Someone ....

B Verbs with can't (3)

Use three words from the table to complete each sentence.

1	2	3
can't couldn't	face help resist stand	doing feeling having lying noticing

► Rita said she was OK, but I *couldn't help noticing* .... how upset she looked.
1 I hate holidays by the sea. I .... on a beach all day.
2 I feel really full. I'm afraid I .... a pudding with my lunch.
3 I was so tired yesterday I just .... any housework.
4 Tom's car was stolen, but, as he left it unlocked, I .... it's his own fault.

C Verb + -ing form (1–4)

Some friends have had a meal together in a restaurant. Put in the -ing forms.
Use these verbs: *change, discuss, eat, get, miss, ring, try, wait, walk*

Vicky: Shall we go then?
Rachel: Daniel hasn't finished (►) *eating* .... yet.
Daniel: It's OK. It's just a piece of chocolate.
Matthew: Chocolate? After that enormous meal?
Daniel: I know. I've eaten too much. When I find something new on the menu, I just can't resist
          (1) .... it.
Rachel: How are we getting home?
Vicky: I don't mind (2) .... I feel like some fresh air.
Rachel: You're crazy. It's miles. And we've just eaten.
Matthew: I suggest (3) .... for a taxi. It'll save (4) .... around for a bus.
Emma: Good idea. I couldn't face (5) .... cold again after being in the warm all evening.
Rachel: Yes, the bus journey is too complicated. It involves (6) .... buses in the
          centre. We don't want to risk (7) .... a bus and having to wait half an hour.
Daniel: Or we could take a taxi to the bus station and then get a bus from there.
Matthew: Well, you can carry on (8) .... the problem, but I'm going to ring for a taxi.

62 Verb + to-infinitive or verb + -ing form?

1 Introduction

Some verbs are followed by a to-infinitive, and some by an -ing form.

VERB + TO-INFINITIVE (Unit 60)	VERB + -ING FORM (Unit 61)
*Harriet **decided to have** a party.*	*Harriet **suggested having** a party.*
Decide takes a to-infinitive.	**Suggest** takes an -ing form.

A few verbs take either a to-infinitive or an -ing form (see Units 63–64).
> Laura **started to paint/started painting** a picture.

2 To-infinitive or -ing form?

+ TO-INFINITIVE	+ -ING FORM
These verbs are followed by a to-infinitive.	These verbs are followed by an -ing form.
agree, aim, appear (see 60.2), arrange, ask, attempt, beg, can't afford, can't wait (see 3), choose, claim, decide, demand, desire, expect, fail (see 60.3), guarantee, happen (see 4), help (see 69.3), hope, manage (see 60.3), offer, plan, prepare, pretend, promise, prove (see 4), refuse, seem (see 60.2), tend (see 60.3), threaten, turn out (see 4), undertake, want, wish	admit, avoid, can't face (see 61.3), can't help (see 61.3), can't resist (see 61.3), can't stand (see 61.3), carry on (see 61.4), consider, delay, deny, detest, dislike, enjoy, excuse, fancy (see 3), finish, give up, imagine, involve, justify, keep (on), (see 61.4), mention, mind (see 61.2), postpone, practise, put off, resent, risk, save, suggest, tolerate

3 Can't wait and fancy

If you can't wait to do something, you are eager to do it.
> *I **can't wait to see** the photos you took.* (= I am eager/impatient to see the photos.)

If you fancy doing something, you want to do it.
> *Do you **fancy going** out for a meal?* (= Would you like to go out for a meal?)

Fancy is informal.

4 Happen, turn out and prove

We use **prove to** or **turn out to** when experience shows what something is like.
> *In the end our forecast **proved to be** correct.*
> *Finding Harriet's house **turned out to be** more difficult than Nick had expected.*

Note the meaning of **happen to**.
> *I **happened to see** Sarah in town.* (= I saw Sarah <u>by chance</u> in town.)

5 Two forms together

We can sometimes use more than one to-infinitive or -ing form together.
> *The government decided **to refuse to give** in to the terrorists.*
> *I want **to avoid hurting** anyone's feelings.*
> *The man denied **threatening to kill** a policeman.*

▷ 65 Verb + object + to-infinitive or -ing form   ▷ 70 Verb + preposition + -ing form

Practice

A To-infinitive or -ing form? (1–3)

Complete the conversation. Put in a to-infinitive or -ing form.

Matthew: Are we going to have a holiday this year?

Natasha: Didn't we all decide (▶) .to .spend................... (spend) our holidays on a Greek island?

Matthew: Lovely. I enjoy (▶) .lying...................... (lie) on the beach.
I might manage (1) .... (get) a suntan.

Daniel: I'd love a holiday. I can't wait (2) .... (leave) this place behind.

Emma: I don't fancy (3) .... (stay) in one place all the time.
I really dislike (4) .... (sit) on the beach all day.

Natasha: Well, I don't mind (5) .... (tour) around somewhere.

Emma: Matthew, you promised (6) .... (go) to Scotland with me.
We were planning (7) .... (hire) a car.

Matthew: Scotland? Are you sure? But I couldn't face (8) .... (drive) all the time.

Jessica: I'm afraid I can't afford (9) .... (spend) too much money.

Andrew: And I can't justify (10) .... (take) all that time off from my studies.

B To-infinitive or -ing form? (1–4)

Complete this article from a magazine. Put in the to-infinitive or -ing form of these verbs:
accept, argue, be, find, have, insist, lose, plug, repair, say, take, wait

If you buy something from a shop, a new stereo for example, you usually can't wait (▶) .to .plug.........
it in and put some music on. And of course, you expect (▶) .to .find........ the equipment in working
order. But that doesn't always happen, unfortunately. If the thing doesn't work, you should take it
straight back to the shop. If you delay (1) .... it back, you will risk
(2) .... your rights as a customer. And you should prepare (3) ....
on those rights. You may be one of those people who always avoid (4) .... with
people, but in this case you should be ready for an argument. The assistant may prove
(5) .... a true friend of the customer – it's not impossible – but first he or she
will probably offer (6) .... the stereo for you. That's all right if you don't mind
(7) .... a few weeks, but it isn't usually a good idea. What you should do is politely
demand (8) .... your money back immediately. You may want to accept another stereo
in place of the old one, but you don't have to. You should refuse (9) .... a credit
note. Just keep on (10) .... that you want your money back.

C Two forms together (5)

What might you say in these situations? Write a sentence with both a to-infinitive and an -ing form.

▶ Your decision to change your holiday arrangements might upset Vicky. You won't risk that. You don't want to. What do you say to Rachel?
I don't want to risk upsetting Vicky.

1 You and Melanie want to complain about your meal in a restaurant. You need to see the manager. Melanie won't ask, but you don't mind. What do you say to her?
....

2 Matthew doesn't like the idea of going to Scotland. But he promised. He admitted it. What do you tell Emma?
....

3 The band were playing. They finished just as you arrived. This was quite by chance. What do you tell your friends?
Just as I arrived, ...

63 Like, start, etc.

1 Like, love, prefer and hate

> I **like doing** parachute jumps. This is my third one. I **love to look** down at the fields below.

After **like**, **love**, **prefer** and **hate**, we can use either a to-infinitive or an -ing form. The meaning is the same.

> Mrs Miles **likes to do/likes doing** parachute jumps.
> She **loves to look/loves looking** down at the fields below.
> We always **prefer to stay/prefer staying** in small hotels.
> I **hate to stand/hate standing** up while I'm eating.

But compare these two meanings of the verb **like**.

LIKE TO DO	LIKE DOING

Like takes a to-infinitive when it means that we prefer to do something even though we may not enjoy it.
 	
   I **like to check** my work carefully before I hand it in.
	Like usually takes an -ing form when we use it to talk about hobbies and interests.
	
	   Claire **likes skiing**.
	   I don't **like swimming** much.

2 Would like, etc.

After **would like**, **would love**, **would prefer** and **would hate**, we use a to-infinitive but not usually an -ing form.

> I'd **like to do** a parachute jump one day.   My sister **would love to work** as an artist.
> Mark **would prefer to drive** rather than take the train.   I'm glad I live here. I'd **hate to live** in a big city.

Compare **would like** and **like**.

WOULD LIKE	LIKE
I'd **like to lie** on the beach today. It's too hot to do anything else. I'd **like** means 'I want', but it is more polite (see Unit 52.2).	I **like lying** on the beach. I always spend my holidays sunbathing. I **like** means the same as 'I enjoy'.

3 Start, intend, etc.

We can use either a to-infinitive or an -ing form after these verbs:
begin, **bother**, **continue**, **intend**, **propose** (= intend), **start**

> People **began to leave/began leaving** the theatre before the end of the play.
> Rachel **didn't bother to do/bother doing** the washing-up.
> Do you **intend to make/intend making** a complaint?

The meaning is the same.

We do not usually have two -ing forms together.

> It was **starting to get** dark. NOT ~~It was starting getting dark.~~

Practice

A Like and would like (1–2)

Write in the words. Begin *I like ...* or *I'd like ...*
Use these verbs: *buy, chase, drive, play, see*
Use these objects: *computer games, rabbits, the manager, this car, this tin*

▶ I like playing computer games.

1 ....
2 ....
3 ....
4 ....

B Like, love, prefer and hate (1–2)

Complete the sentences using the words in brackets.

▶ Mark: I've always wanted to visit San Francisco.
   Sarah: Me too. I'd love to visit .... (I'd love) it some time.
1 Harriet: Tom seems to enjoy watching football matches.
   David: Yes, ... (he loves) United play.
2 Trevor: I'm glad I don't work as late as Sarah does.
   Laura: Me too. .... (I wouldn't like) such long hours.
3 Matthew: I think I'll go and see this new film.
   Emma: Can I go with you? .... (I'd like) it, too.
4 Rachel: Do you want to come with me or wait here?
   Vicky: .... (I'd prefer) with you if that's OK.
5 Laura: I think queuing is my least favourite activity.
   Tom: I agree. .... (I hate).
6 Claire: Does Mark cook for you?
   Sarah: No, not often. .... (he doesn't like).
7 Reporter: Have you ever flown in a hot-air balloon?
   Mrs Miles: No, but .... (I'd love) in one someday.
8 Rachel: Did you say you're having your teeth looked at today?
   Emma: Yes, ... (I like) them checked once a year.

C Start, intend, etc. (3)

Complete this news report about a stolen taxi. Put in the to-infinitive or the -ing form of these verbs:
drive, go, lock, make, search. Sometimes more than one answer is possible.

Kevin Paisley, 25, has lost his taxi. It was stolen on Friday afternoon. 'I just went into the newsagent's for a moment,' said Kevin. 'I didn't bother (▶) to lock the car.'
Kevin started (1) .... his own taxi only six months ago. 'I was just beginning (2) .... a profit,' he said. 'I intend (3) ....
... on with my work as soon as I get my taxi back.' The police are continuing (4) ....
.... for the stolen car.

64 Remember, regret, try, etc.

With some verbs, the choice of a to-infinitive or an -ing form depends on the meaning.

1 Remember and forget

*I must **remember to post** this letter today. It's important.*
*The clothes are still dirty because I **forgot to switch on** the machine.*
We use **remember/forget to do** for necessary actions. The remembering is before the action.

*I can **remember posting** the letter. I posted it on Friday morning.*
*I'll never **forget flying** over the Grand Canyon. It was wonderful.*
We use **remember/forget doing** for memories of the past. The action is before the remembering.

2 Regret

*We **regret to inform** you that we are not taking on any new staff at present.*
Regret to do something means to be sorry for something you are doing, e.g. giving bad news.

*I **regret spending** all that money. I've got none left.*
Regret doing something means to be sorry because of something that happened in the past.

3 Try

*I'm **trying to run** this computer program.*
Try to do something means to attempt something, to do your best.

*I **tried clicking** on the box, but it doesn't work.*
Try doing something means to do something which might solve a problem.

4 Stop

*An old man walking along the road **stopped to talk** to us.*
Stop to do something means to stop so that you can do it.

*There's too much noise. Can you all **stop talking**, please?*
Stop doing something means to end an action, to finish doing it.

5 Mean

*I think Nick **meant to break** that glass. It didn't look like an accident.*
Mean to do something is the same as to intend to do it.

*I'm applying for a visa. It **means filling** in this form.*
Means doing something expresses the idea of one thing resulting in another.

6 Go on

*The teacher introduced herself and **went on to explain** about the course.*
Go on to do something means to do something else, to do the next thing.

*The teacher told everyone to be quiet, but they just **went on talking**.*
Go on doing something means to continue doing it.

7 Need

*I **need to clean** my shoes.*
This means that I must clean my shoes, I have to clean them.

*My shoes **need** cleaning.*
This means that my shoes need to be cleaned (see Unit 59.2).

Practice

A Remember and forget (1)

Put in the to-infinitive or the -ing form of the verbs.

Laura: Did you remember (▶) to pick (pick) up those photos today?
Trevor: What photos?
Laura: Oh, no. I can remember (1) .... (mention) it to you only this morning.
Trevor: I can't remember (2) .... (agree) to pick up some photos.
Laura: Well, don't forget (3) .... (call) at the shop for them tomorrow.
You've got a terrible memory. Yesterday you forgot (4) .... (lock) the door.
Trevor: I'm sure I didn't forget (5) .... (lock) it. I can clearly remember
(6) .... (look) for my keys. They were in my pocket.
Laura: You ought to write notes to yourself to remind you.
Trevor: That wouldn't be any good. I'd never remember (7) .... (look) at them!

B Remember, regret, try, etc. (1–7)

Put in the to-infinitive or the -ing form of the verbs.

I used to like going to our local cinema. It was old and rather uncomfortable, but it had character.
Now they've stopped (▶) showing (show) films there. The owner would like to go on
(1) .... (run) the cinema, but he would need (2) .... (make) a lot of
improvements, which would mean (3) .... (spend) tens of thousands of pounds.
I remember (4) .... (watch) the last film at the cinema. It was a murder mystery. It was
five minutes from the end, and we were trying (5) .... (work) out who the murderer was
when suddenly all the lights went out and the film stopped. We sat in the dark for a few minutes, and
then the owner appeared with a torch. 'I regret (6) .... (tell) you,' he said, 'that our
electricity has failed. I don't mean (7) .... (disappoint) you, but I'm afraid we can't
show you the end of the film. We've tried (8) .... (phone) the electricity company, but
they say they can't help.' He went on (9) .... (explain) to the audience how the film
ended. I didn't understand the story. But I don't regret (10) .... (go) to the cinema on
that last evening.

C Remember, regret, try, etc. (1–7)

Write each pair of sentences as one. Use a to-infinitive or an -ing form.

▶ Trevor didn't ring Laura. He forgot.
  Trevor forgot to ring Laura.
▶ Tom and Nick had been playing cards for hours. But they went on with the game.
  Tom and Nick went on playing cards.

1 Harriet didn't think she could move the piano. She didn't even try.
  ....

2 Mike once saw a spaceship. He'll never forget it.
  ....

3 What about painting the walls? They need it.
  ....

4 Natasha was unkind to Jessica. But she didn't mean it.
  ....

5 Andrew was studying. He went on through the night.
  ....

6 When Mark was driving, he needed to make a phone call. So he stopped.
  ....

Test L: Verb + to-infinitive or -ing form

A

Complete the conversations. Put in a to-infinitive or an -ing form.

▶ A: I hear you sometimes sail to France in your boat.
   B: That's right. I really enjoy *sailing* .

1 A: Are you going to organize our trip?
   B: Yes, of course. I've agreed .... it.

2 A: You wear a uniform at work, don't you?
   B: Yes, I have to, although I dislike .... it.

3 A: Do you think they'll approve the plan?
   B: Yes, I'm quite sure they'll decide .... it.

4 A: What time will you be back?
   B: Oh, I expect .... back some time around nine.

5 A: Did I remind you about the dinner tonight?
   B: Yes, thank you. You keep .... me.

6 A: Was your decision the right one, do you think?
   B: Yes, luckily. In the end it proved .... the best thing for everyone.

7 A: Do you still work at the post office?
   B: No, I gave up .... there last year.

8 A: Have ICM bought the company?
   B: Well, they've offered .... it.

9 A: I'm sorry you had to wait all that time.
   B: Oh, it's all right. I didn't mind ....

B

Make sentences from the notes.

▶ Tessa / want / buy / a new coat / soon
   Tessa wants to buy a new coat soon. ....

1 we / must / avoid / waste / so much time

   ....

2 sometimes / a country / refuse / take part / in the Olympics

   ....

3 I / like / see / the Rocky Mountains / some day

   ....

4 I / mean / give / Judy / a nice welcome / yesterday

   ....

5 I / always / like / see / my doctor / once a year

   ....

6 the buses / usually / stop / run / before midnight

   ....

7 I / can't face / get up / at five / tomorrow

   ....

8 last year / we / make / an agreement / work / together

   ....

9 yesterday / you / promise / carry on / shoot / the film

   ....

10 my father / seem / get / better / now

   ....

C

Read the conversation and write the missing words. Use one word only in each space.

Anna: I hear you're preparing to (▶) leave........... for Australia.

Lisa: That's right. And I'm really looking forward to it. I can't (1) .... to get there. I'm hoping (2) .... see all my friends while I'm there. I'm going to enjoy (3) .... them again after so long.

Anna: Martin and I (4) .... like to go away, but we can't manage it this year.

Lisa: There's just one problem that I (5) .... to sort out. My tickets haven't arrived. I've tried to ring the travel agency, but I can't get through. I'm beginning to regret (6) .... going there myself to pick them up.

Anna: I expect they'll be here tomorrow.

Lisa: That's really leaving it to the last minute. It's such a worry.

Anna: Well, I know you. You can't (7) .... worrying, can you?

Lisa: No, I can't. I hope this holiday isn't going to turn out (8) .... be a disaster.

Anna: Of course it isn't. Just keep (9) .... trying to get through.

D

Each of these sentences has a mistake in it. Write the correct sentence.

▶ The man kept ask us for money.   *The man kept asking us for money.*

1 We've finished to decorate the flat.   ....

2 I regret say what I did.   ....

3 Tessa decided go not to work.   ....

4 Do you mind help me?   ....

5 I'm beginning getting worried.   ....

6 I can't afford buy a new car.   ....

7 I hope to avoid to make things worse.   ....

8 Peter seems gone away already.   ....

E

Write a second sentence so that it has a similar meaning to the first. Use the word in brackets.

▶ I wish I hadn't sold my bike. (regret)
I regret selling my bike.

1 The children were eager to see their presents. (wait)

....

2 I hate to get up in the dark. (stand)

....

3 By chance I saw your brother yesterday. (happened)

....

4 The shop usually opens ten minutes late. (tends)

....

5 Would you like to go for a walk? (fancy)

....

6 The police continued to watch the house. (carried)

....

7 Seeing Nelson Mandela will always stay in my memory. (forget)

....

65 Verb + object + to-infinitive or -ing form

1 Introduction

Customer: *None of the things I ordered have arrived. They're three weeks late. I **expect the goods to arrive** on time.*

Mark: *I'm sorry we've **kept you waiting** so long. Can I find out what the problem is and then ring you back?*

Some verbs can take an object + a to-infinitive,
and some take an object + an -ing form.

	VERB	OBJECT		
I	*expect*	*the goods*	*to arrive*	*on time.*
I'm sorry we've	*kept*	*you*	*waiting*	*so long.*

2 Verb + object + to-infinitive

*We **asked the doorman to let** us in.   Nick couldn't **persuade Rita to go** out with him.*
*The hot weather has **caused ice-cream sales to increase**.*
*It **took ages to download** the pictures from the Internet.*
*I didn't **mean my suggestion to be taken** seriously.* (See Unit 59.1.)

Here are some verbs we can use in this structure: **advise, allow, ask, beg, cause, enable, encourage, expect, force, help** (see Unit 69.3), **intend, invite, mean** (= intend), **order, recommend, remind, take** (time), **teach, tell, warn**

3 Want + object + to-infinitive

We can also use an object + a to-infinitive after **want, (would) like, (would) love, (would) prefer** and **(would) hate.**

*Tom **wants United to win**.   We'd **hate the house to be left** empty.*

We can use this structure to give an order (see Unit 50.2).

*I **want everyone to come** here.   I'd **like you to listen** carefully.*

We cannot normally use a that-clause. NOT *I want that everyone comes here.*

4 Verb + object + -ing form

*Andrew is so serious. I can't **imagine him having** a good time.*
*Do you **remember Laura taking** our photo?   A new law has **stopped traffic going** into the city centre.*

Here are some verbs we can use in this structure: **dislike, imagine, involve, keep, mind, prevent** (see Unit 70.3), **remember, risk, stop** (see Unit 70.3)

5 Advise, allow, encourage and recommend

We can use these verbs with an -ing form or with an object + a to-infinitive.

+ -ING FORM	+ OBJECT + TO-INFINITIVE
*They **allow fishing** here.*	*They **allow people to fish** here.*
*I wouldn't **recommend walking** home alone.*	*I would **advise you not to walk** home alone.*

We do not use **suggest** + an object + a to-infinitive.

*I **suggested** to Nick (that) he should leave.* NOT *I suggested Nick to leave.*

Practice

A Verb + object + to-infinitive (2)

Report what people said. Use the verbs in brackets.

► Police to motorists: Take special care. (warn)
  The police warned motorists to take special care.

1 Guy to Kitty: Would you like to come on my chat show? (invite)

   ....

2 Sarah to Mark: Don't forget to get the theatre tickets. (remind)

   ....

3 Dentist to Daniel: You should give up eating sweets. (tell)

   ....

4 Police to gunman: Come out with your hands up. (order)

   ....

B Want and would like (3)

Complete the sentences using *would like* or *don't/doesn't want*.

► Mike won't wear a tie. Harriet is annoyed.
  She would like him to wear a tie .... because they're going to a concert.

1 Mrs Miles is going to do a parachute jump, but her son and daughter don't like the idea.
  They .... because they think it's
  dangerous.

2 Henry is falling in love with Claire, but she's worried about this.
  She .... because she doesn't
  find him attractive.

3 Natasha may not go on holiday with her friends.
  They .... because she's always
  good fun to be with.

C Verb + object + to-infinitive or -ing form (2, 4)

Kitty Beamish is reporting what people have said to her. She combines the two sentences into one.

► 'The lorry skidded. The icy road caused it.'
  The icy road caused the lorry to skid.

► 'The workers might go on strike. The company can't risk that.'
  The company can't risk the workers going on strike.

1 'The suspects might leave the country. The police must stop that.'

   ....

2 'Congress opposed him. The President didn't expect that.'

   ....

3 'The hostages lay down. The terrorists forced them.'

   ....

4 'The pound is falling in value. The government doesn't mind that.'

   ....

D Advise, allow, etc. (5)

Complete this paragraph from a guidebook to London. Use the to-infinitive or the -ing form.

We wouldn't recommend (►) driving .... (drive) into London in the rush hour.
We'd advise you (1) .... (travel) by train.
We'd recommend (2) .... (buy) a special saver ticket, which is cheaper than the full fare.
But the railway companies don't allow you (3) .... (use) saver tickets before ten o'clock.
This is to encourage people (4) .... (take) a later train, which will be less busy.

66 Question word + to-infinitive

1 Introduction

Are you ready, Vicky?

No, not yet. I don't know **what to wear** to this party.

Vicky uses a question word (**what**) and a to-infinitive (**to wear**). She is talking about the best thing to do. **I don't know what to wear** means that I don't know what I <u>should</u> wear.

2 Structures with **what to do, where to go**, etc.

Before the question word we can use a verb such as **ask, decide, discover, discuss, explain, find out, forget, know, learn, remember, say, think, understand, wonder**.

*It was a real problem. I couldn't **think what to do**.*
*We were **wondering where to park** the car.*
*Matthew wants to **know how to work** the computer.*
*Have Trevor and Laura **decided when to have** their barbecue?*

Sometimes there is a verb + object before the question word.
In this structure we can use **advise, ask, show, teach** and **tell**.

*Tom **showed me how to change** a wheel.*
*The guide didn't **tell the tourists when to be** back at the coach.*

Before the question word we can also use the adjectives **clear, obvious** and **sure** and the expressions **have an idea** and **make up your mind**.

*I wasn't **sure who to ask** for help.*   *Claire doesn't **have much idea how to cook**.*

A preposition (e.g. **of**) can come before the question word.

*There's the question **of who to invite** to the reception.*
*You need to be informed **about what to do** in an emergency.*

3 **Why, what, whose, which** and **whether**

We cannot use **why** before a to-infinitive.

*No one could explain **why we had to wait**.* NOT ~~No one could explain why to wait.~~

After **what, which, whose, how many** and **how much**, we can use a noun.

*Sarah and Mark were discussing **what colour to paint** the walls.*
*We wondered **whose story to believe** – both drivers said it wasn't their fault.*
*It's difficult to know **how much luggage to take** with you.*

We can use **whether** but not **if**.

*We'll have to decide **whether to go** ahead with the project (or not).*
NOT ~~We'll have to decide if to go ahead.~~
*Melanie wasn't sure **whether to ring** the doctor or not.*
*I was wondering **whether to order** some tea.*

Practice

A Structures with **what to do**, **where to go**, etc. (2)

Comment on these situations.

▶ How do I switch the computer on? 1 What should I say? 2 Where shall we go? 3 How do I stop?

▶ (not know) He doesn't know how to switch the computer on. ....
1 (can't think) ....
2 (not sure) ....
3 (not know) ....

B Structures with **what to do**, **where to go**, etc. (2)

Look at the questions and then complete the paragraph about a man coming out of prison.
Use a question word and a to-infinitive.

▶ How should he start a new life? 3 How can he find somewhere to live?
1 What can he expect? 4 What should he do?
2 Where should he go? 5 Who can he contact?

This man will have problems when he leaves prison. He needs advice on (▶) how to start ....
a new life. After a long time in prison, he isn't sure (1) .... in the outside
world and he has no idea (2) .... He doesn't know
(3) .... a place to live either. But he won't be completely alone. A social
worker will advise him (4) ...., so he'll know
(5) .... if he needs help.

C Question word + to-infinitive (2–3)

You are finding it very difficult to make your mind up.
Complete your answers to the questions. Use a question word and a to-infinitive.

▶ Rachel: Are you going to buy that sweater?
  You: I don't know whether to buy .... it or not.
▶ Tom: What time do you think we should leave?
  You: I'm not really sure what time to leave ....
1 Daniel: Do you want to do business studies?
  You: I'm wondering .... business studies or statistics.
2 Vicky: How much money should we spend on the present?
  You: I've no idea .... on it.
3 Matthew: Do you intend to join the sports club?
  You: I can't decide .... it or not.
4 Vicky: Which route should we take?
  You: It's difficult to know ....
5 Melanie: Which lottery numbers are you going to choose?
  You: I haven't decided ....

67 Adjective + to-infinitive

1 Introduction

RACHEL IS HAVING A
DRIVING LESSON.

It's **great to be** on the road. This car is **easy to drive**, isn't it?

It's **important to look** in the mirror sometimes. Don't forget to do that.

We can use a to-infinitive (e.g. **to be**)
after an adjective (e.g. **great**).

2 It is easy to drive the car

An adjective + to-infinitive often comes in this structure with **it** + **be**.

    *It's **important to look** in the mirror.*   *It's **lovely to see** you.*
    *It's quite **safe to use** the ladder.*   *It was **silly to make** such a fuss.*

The subject can also be a person.

    *I'm **delighted to see** you.*   *We're **ready to start** now.*

3 The car is easy to drive

Compare these two sentences. They both mean the same thing.

    *It is easy to drive **the car**.*   ***The car** is easy to drive.*

We do not use **it** in the second sentence.

    NOT ~~The car is easy to drive it~~ and NOT ~~The car it is easy to drive.~~

Here are some more examples.

    *Your writing is **difficult to read**.*   *A small car would be **cheap to run**.*
    *The parade was **fascinating to watch**.*   *The ladder is quite **safe to use**.*

We can use this structure with adjectives meaning 'good' or bad', e.g. **awful, bad, exciting, fascinating, good, marvellous, nice, terrible, wonderful**. We can also use it with these adjectives: **cheap, convenient, dangerous, difficult, easy, expensive, impossible, safe, simple**.

4 Certain, sure and likely

We can use a to-infinitive after **certain**, **sure**, **likely** and **unlikely**.

    *United are **certain/sure to win**.* (= They will certainly win.)
    *Sarah is **likely to be** at work.* (= She is probably at work.)

5 For and of

After some adjectives we can use **for** + object + to-infinitive (see Unit 68).

    *It's **important for drivers to take** care.*   *It isn't **safe for children to play** on ladders.*

After an adjective describing how someone behaves (e.g. **polite, silly**), we can use **of**.

    *It was **polite of Emma to write** and thank us.* (Emma was polite.)
    *It was **silly of me to forget** the tickets.* (I was silly.)

   ▷ 68 **For** with the to-infinitive   ▷ 117 **Too** and **enough**

Practice

A It is easy to drive the car (2)

Sarah's job is to write advertisements. She is writing one for Compex computers.
Write sentences with *it* and an adjective followed by a to-infinitive.

▶ Buy a Compex computer. It isn't expensive.
It isn't *expensive to buy a Compex computer.*

1 Using the computer is very simple.
It's very ....

2 Understanding the handbook isn't difficult.
It isn't ....

3 You can run any kind of software. It's easy.
....
....

4 Exploring the world of Compex is absolutely fascinating.
....
....

5 Try the ultimate computer experience. Are you ready?
....
....

B The car is easy to drive (3)

Sarah isn't happy with her ideas for the Compex advertisement.
She is rewriting the first four sentences like this.

▶ A Compex computer *isn't expensive to buy.*
1 The computer ....
2 The handbook ....
3 ....
4 ....

C Certain, sure and likely (4)

Complete the conversation. Make sentences from the notes in brackets.

Nick: Are you going to Mike and Harriet's party?
Tom: Yes, I am. (▶) *It's sure to be a good party*
       (it / sure / be / a good party).
Nick: Will there be a lot of people there?
Tom: Yes, (1) ....
       (it / likely / be / pretty crowded).
Nick: Has Rita been invited, do you know?
Tom: Oh, (2) ....
       (she / certain / be / there).
Nick: I don't know that part of town. Is the house easy to find?
Tom: No, it isn't. Take a map or (3) ....
       (you / unlikely / find / it).

D For and of (5)

Vicky and Rachel are talking about two students they know called Gary and Steve.
Complete the conversation. Put in *for* or *of*.

Vicky: I can't believe that Gary and Steve had a fight in a pub. It was very foolish (▶) *of* them.
Rachel: Yes, it was especially stupid (1) .... them to quarrel about which football team is
         the best. There must be something more interesting (2) .... them to talk about.
Vicky: I blame Steve. It wasn't very sensible (3) .... him to knock Gary's drink over.
Rachel: It was brave (4) .... Daniel to try to stop the fight. It was awful (5) .... him
         to get hit on the head with a chair.

68 For with the to-infinitive

1 Introduction

Sarah: *I'll just ring the office. The boss is waiting for me to ring her back.*

Mark: *I don't think it was a good idea for you to bring that mobile phone on holiday with you, Sarah.*

We can use **for** + object + to-infinitive. Here are some more examples.

	FOR	OBJECT	TO-INFINITIVE
My mother has arranged	*for*	*someone*	*to look after her dog next week.*
It's difficult	*for*	*unskilled people*	*to find work these days.*
The crowd were impatient	*for*	*the match*	*to begin.*
It's a nuisance	*for*	*you*	*to have to wait.*

2 For expressing purpose

We can use this structure to say why something is done (to express purpose). (See also Unit 151.5.)

*Mark photocopied the figures **for the Sales Manager to have** a look at.*

(= He photocopied the figures so that the Sales Manager could have a look at them.)

*The shop provides baskets **for the customers to put** their purchases in.*

*I'd like to put forward a few suggestions **for you to think about**.*

3 Too and enough

We can use **too** and **enough** with this structure.

*The road is **too** busy **for the children to cross** safely.*

*Unfortunately the table was **too** small **for all of us to sit** round.*

*Fortunately the table was big **enough for all of us to sit** round.*

*The guide didn't speak loudly **enough for everyone to hear** clearly.*

4 For and of

FOR	OF
We often use **for** + object + to-infinitive after an adjective.	After an adjective saying how someone behaves, we use **of** + object + to-infinitive.
*Harriet was **anxious for** the party to be a success.*	*It's **kind of** Melanie to put you up for the night.*
*Would it be **possible for** you to move your car, please?*	(Melanie is kind.)
	*It was **clever of** you to work out the answer.*
	(You were clever.)
Some of the adjectives we can use with **for**:	Some of the adjectives we can use with **of**:
anxious, awful, cheap, convenient, dangerous, difficult, eager, easy, exciting, expensive, friendly, good, happy, horrible, impatient, important, interesting, marvellous, necessary, nice, normal, polite, possible, ready, safe, sensible, silly, stupid, terrible, useful, willing, wonderful, wrong	brave, careless, clever, foolish, generous, good, helpful, honest, intelligent, kind, mean, nice, polite, sensible, silly, stupid, wrong
Compare these two sentences.	
*It was good **for** you to come jogging.*	*It was **good of** you to come jogging with me.*
(= It was good for your health.)	(= It was a kind action by you.)

A For with the to-infinitive (1)

The second person agrees with what the first one says. Use *for* and a to-infinitive.

▶ Daniel: Andrew should take it easy. That would be best.
Matthew: Yes, you're right. It <u>would be best for him to take it easy.</u>

1 Trevor: Our new computer should arrive soon. I just can't wait.
Laura: Me neither. I ....

2 Rachel: Matthew shouldn't marry Emma. It would be a mistake.
Vicky: I think so too. ....

3 Customer: Advertisements should tell the truth. It's important.
Mark: I agree. ....

B For expressing purpose (2)

Write the advertisement for a holiday centre.
Match the sentence pairs and write sentences with *for* and a to-infinitive.

<u>There are lots of activities.</u> There's a fun pool. There are quiet areas. There are regular shows. There's a giant roller-coaster.   You can enjoy them. You can relax in them. <u>Guests can take part in them.</u> You can ride on it if you dare. Children can swim in it.

▶ <u>There are lots of activities for guests to take part in.</u>
1 ....
2 ....
3 ....
4 ....

C Too and enough (3)

Add a sentence with *too* or *enough* and: *difficult*, *funny*, *heavy*, *high*, *hot*, *loud*

▶ Mike and Harriet couldn't lift the piano. <u>It was too heavy for them to lift.</u>
▶ Tom won't repeat the joke. <u>It isn't funny enough for him to repeat.</u>
1 Emma can't reach the top shelf. ....
2 We can't understand the poem. ....
3 Not everyone could hear the music. ....
4 The tea had got cold. Daniel couldn't drink it. ....

D For and of (4)

A Japanese company called Sanko is going to open a new factory in a town in England.
Write the sentences from the local newspaper.

▶ marvellous / the town / have / some new jobs
It will <u>be marvellous for the town to have some new jobs.</u>

▶ clever / our local council / bring / Sanko / here
It was <u>clever of our local council to bring Sanko here.</u>

1 difficult / the town / attract / new industry
It has been ....

2 very generous / the council / give / the land / to Sanko
It was ....

3 the company / eager / production / begin / soon
The company ....

69 The infinitive with and without **to**

This is an overview of the different structures with a to-infinitive (e.g. **to do**) and an infinitive without **to** (e.g. **do**).

1 The to-infinitive

We use a to-infinitive:

1 After an adjective (see Unit 67)
   It's **nice to have** a place of your own.   The car is really **cheap to run**.
2 After a noun
   I must take a **book to read**. (= a book that I <u>can</u> read)
   We've got a few **jobs to do**. (= jobs that we <u>must</u> do)
3 With **be able to, be about to, be allowed to, be going to, have to, ought to** and **used to**
   We **aren't allowed to** park here.   The game **is about to start**.
   We**'re going to buy** a camcorder.   You **have to fill** in a form.
4 After some verbs, e.g. **decide, hope, manage, offer** (see Unit 60)
   Tom **decided to leave** early.   I **hope to see** you soon.
   Did you **manage to sort** out the problem?   Henry **offered to pay** for the meal.
5 After some verbs + object (see Unit 65)
   Laura **persuaded Trevor to put** up some shelves.
   I **want you to do** something for me.
6 After **for** + object (see Unit 68)
   We've arranged **for you to visit** our head office.
   It is important **for students to register** with a doctor.
7 After a question word (see Unit 66)
   We don't know **where to leave** our coats.
   This book tells you **how to train** race horses.
8 To say why (see Unit 151.2)
   Mark went out **to play** golf.   I need the money **to pay** the phone bill.

2 The infinitive without **to**

We use an infinitive without **to**:

1 After **can, could, may, might, must, needn't, shall, should, will,** and **would**
   We **could go** to a night club.   I **must speak** to the manager.
   It **might rain** later.   Sarah **will be** away for three days.
2 After **had better** and **would rather**
   It's cold. You**'d better wear** a coat.   I**'d rather listen** to Elvis than the Beatles.
3 After **make** + object and **let** + object
   That programme was funny. It really **made me laugh**.
   Trevor will be here at five. His boss is going to **let him leave** work early.
4 After **see** or **hear** + an object (see Unit 74)
   They **saw the lights come** on.   We all **heard the bomb go** off.

3 Help

An infinitive after **help** can be with or without **to**.
   Can I **help (to) get** the tea?   Vicky **helped** me **(to) choose** a present.

Practice

A The to-infinitive (1)

Comment on these situations. Join each pair of sentences using a to-infinitive.

▶ Mike will give you a lift. He promised.
   You: Mike promised to give me a lift.

1 You want to eat. You must have something.
   You: I must ....

2 You are having a rest. It's nice.
   You: It's ....

3 Will Rita speak to Nick? He wants her to.
   Nick ....

4 Daniel can't repair the video. He doesn't know how to.
   ....

5 Claire and her sister are going to Bali. They have decided.
   ....

6 Melanie is visiting David. She has gone to the hospital.
   ....

7 Vicky is doing some studying. Unfortunately she has to.
   ....

8 Sarah must ring the office. It's important.
   ....

B The infinitive without to (2)

Put in the missing verbs. Usually more than one answer is correct.

▶ I've been repairing the car. I really must wash......... my hands.
1 What's in the letter? Why won't you let me .... it?
2 Did you see that lovely old car .... past a moment ago?
3 It was a terribly sad story. It made me ....
4 I don't want to do anything energetic. I'd rather .... on the beach.
5 It's very cold. I think it might .... for the first time this winter.
6 I keep getting this pain in my leg. I think I'd better .... a doctor.

C The infinitive with and without to (1–2)

Matthew and Emma are at the railway station. Emma is going away for the weekend.
Put in the infinitive of the verbs. You have to decide whether or not you need to.

Matthew: Are you sure you'll (▶) be.................. (be) all right?
Emma: Yes, of course. I'm not a child. I can manage (▶) to look.............. (look) after myself.
Matthew: OK, sorry.
Emma: Some friends have invited me (1) .... (visit) them. I'm not going to the North Pole.
Matthew: It'll be nice for you (2) .... (see) your old friends again. I just know you're going (3) .... (have) lots of fun. Let me (4) .... (buy) you a magazine (5) .... (read) on the train.
Emma: I can't (6) .... (read) when I'm travelling. It makes me (7) .... (feel) sick, even in a train. I'd rather just (8) .... (look) out of the window.
Matthew: OK. Well, you'd better (9) .... (get) in. I think it's about (10) .... (leave). Oh, did I remind you (11) .... (change) at York?
Emma: Yes, Matthew, you did. Don't worry, I won't (12) .... (forget). I know perfectly well how (13) .... (get) there.

70 Verb/adjective + preposition + -ing form

1 Introduction

Claire: *I'm **thinking of going** to Turkey.*
Travel agent: *Are you **interested in travelling** around the country, or would you like to stay in one place?*
Claire: *I don't want to do a lot of travelling.*

Some verbs and adjectives can have a preposition after them (see Units 125–126).
   *I **apologized for** my mistake.   Laura is **keen on** photography.*

Sometimes we can use an -ing form after the preposition.

		PREPOSITION	-ING FORM	
I	*apologized*	*for*	*making*	*a mistake.*
Laura is	*keen*	*on*	*taking*	*photos.*
I'm	*thinking*	*of*	*going*	*to Turkey.*
Are you	*interested*	*in*	*travelling*	*around?*
We're	*tired*	*of*	*not having*	*a place to live.*

We can use **not** before the -ing form, e.g. **not having**.

2 Verb + preposition + -ing form

   *Don't you **believe in discussing** things openly?   Laura doesn't **feel like cooking** tonight.*
   *Unfortunately Tom **insisted on telling** us all about United's win.*
   *I'm **looking forward to seeing** my friends again.*
   *I've **succeeded in getting** hold of the CD I wanted.*
Also: **agree with, apologize for, concentrate on, object to, rely on, think of**

We can use **about** after **ask, complain, dream, speak, talk, think,** and **wonder**.
   *They're **talking about building** a new swimming-pool.*

3 Verb + object + preposition + -ing form

After some verbs we can put an object (e.g. **Matthew**).
   *Emma **accused Matthew of not caring** about her.*
   *Higher prices will **discourage customers from buying**.*
   *The fire-fighters **prevented/stopped the fire (from) spreading**.*
   *The club has **punished its players for fighting** during a match.*
Also: **blame ... for, congratulate ... on, thank ... for**

We can use this structure in the passive.
   ***Matthew was accused** of not caring.   **The customers will be discouraged** from buying.*

4 Adjective + preposition + -ing form

   *People were **annoyed at not being** able to see properly.*
   *I'm **bored with waiting**.   Vicky is **excited about going** to America.*
   *I'm **fed up with living** in this awful place.   Tom is **good at telling** jokes.*
   *The man was found **guilty of stealing** from his employers.*
   *I'm **pleased about/at winning** a prize.*
Also: **capable of, fond of, interested in** (see Unit 71.2), **keen on, tired of**

▷ 125 Adjective + preposition   ▷ 126 Verb + preposition

A Verb + preposition + -ing form (1–2)

Complete the conversation between Claire and her sister Sophie.
Put in the verbs with these prepositions: *for*, *in*, *like*, *of*, *on*

Sophie: Where's that little radio of yours?

Claire: Oh, it got broken. Henry knocked it off the table.
Unfortunately he hasn't succeeded (▶) *in getting* .... (get) it to work again.

Sophie: Oh, what a pity.

Claire: It was only a cheap thing. In fact I'd been thinking (1) .... (buy) a
new one. But Henry not only apologized (2) .... (break) it, he insisted
(3) .... (buy) me a much nicer one. It's in the dining-room.

Sophie: Henry is such a gentleman.

Claire: He didn't really need to buy me a new one, but I didn't feel (4) ....
(argue).

B Verb (+ object) + preposition + -ing form (1–3)

Comment on these situations. Join each pair of sentences using a preposition and an -ing form.

▶ The police prevented the crime. It didn't take place.
The police *prevented the crime from taking place.* ....

1 Laura blamed Trevor. He forgot the tickets.
Laura ....

2 The doctors succeeded. They saved the driver's life.
The doctors ....

3 The customers complained. They didn't receive the goods.
....

4 Emma has accused Matthew. She says Matthew broke his promise.
....

5 Melanie is insisting. She's going to cook a meal for David.
....

6 A new traffic scheme has stopped cars. They can't go into the town centre.
....

7 Everyone congratulated Claude. He won the quiz competition.
....

8 Some football fans were arrested. They attacked a policeman.
....

C Verb/Adjective + preposition + -ing form (1–4)

Complete Emma's letter to her friend Kirsty. Put in a preposition and an -ing form.

Thank you (▶) *for inviting* .... (invite) me to come and see you next month. I'm already
excited (1) .... (see) you again.

You must be very pleased (2) .... (get) the job you wanted. Congratulations.
Personally, I wouldn't be keen (3) .... (travel) forty miles to work.

I apologize (4) .... (not write) sooner, but a week in bed with flu has prevented
me (5) .... (do) anything. I haven't even felt (6) ....
(write) to you until today. I must be getting better because I'm starting to feel bored
(7) .... (do) nothing. I'm thinking (8) .... (go) back to
work tomorrow.

71 Afraid to do or afraid of doing?

1 Afraid

> *David is **afraid to climb** the ladder.*
> (= He <u>doesn't want to climb</u> the ladder because he is afraid.)

> *David is **afraid of falling**.*
> (= He is afraid <u>because he might fall</u>.)

Here are some more examples.

> *I was **afraid to say** anything in front of all those people.*
> *Claire was **afraid to wander** too far from the hotel.*

> *I was **afraid of sounding** foolish, you see.*
>
> *She was **afraid of getting** lost.*

2 Anxious, ashamed and interested

Compare these examples.

> *Zedco are **anxious to increase** their sales.*
> (= They want to increase their sales.)

> *Mark was **anxious about presenting** his report.*
> (= He was worried because he had to present his report.)

> *I'm **ashamed to tell you** what I scored in the test.*
> (= I don't want to tell you because I'm ashamed.)

> *I'm **ashamed of getting** such a low score.*
> (= I'm ashamed because I got such a low score.)

> *I'd be **interested to meet** Laura.*
> (= I want to meet her.)

> *Laura is **interested in painting**.*
> (= It is an interest/a hobby of hers.)

> *I was **interested to hear** Mike's story.*
> (= I found his story interesting.)

3 Structures with sorry

> To apologize for something we are doing, we use a to-infinitive.
> *I'm **sorry to tell** you this, but your test score is rather low.*
> *I'm **sorry to ring** so late, but it's important.*
> To express regret, we also use a to-infinitive.
> *I was **sorry to hear** that Mike's uncle had died.*

> To apologize for something we did, we can use **about** + ing-form.
> *I'm **sorry about making** all that noise last night.*
> (OR *I'm **sorry I made** all that noise last night.*)

Practice

A Afraid (1)

Complete the sentences. Use these words and put the verb into the to-infinitive or -ing form:
dive into the water, *drop them*, *fall*, *move*

► He's afraid to dive into the water.   2   She's afraid ....
1   She's afraid   3   He's afraid ....

B Afraid (1)

Look at what people say and write a comment about each person.
Rewrite the second sentence using *afraid to* or *afraid of*.
► Vicky: There's a large bull in the field. I don't want to open the gate.
Vicky is afraid to open the gate. ....
► Claire: I arrived at the airport in good time. I thought I might get stuck in traffic.
Claire was afraid of getting stuck in traffic. ....
1   Nick: I was going to do a bungee jump yesterday. But I couldn't jump.
....
2   Daniel: The policeman looked angry. I didn't want to argue with him.
....
3   Matthew: I'm keeping my shirt on. I might get sunburnt.
....

C Afraid, anxious, ashamed and interested (1–2)

Complete the conversation. Put in a to-infinitive or a preposition + -ing form.
Laura: I'm ashamed (►) to admit .... (admit) it, but aeroplanes terrify me. I get really anxious
(►) about flying .... (fly). I'm afraid (1) .... (buy) a plane
ticket. I can't stand being on a plane. I'm afraid (2) .... (get) killed. I
feel ashamed (3) .... (be) so silly.
Sarah: Aren't there things you can do to overcome your fear?
Laura: Well, I was interested (4) .... (read) in the paper recently that you
can go on a course that helps you. I'm anxious (5) .... (book) a
place on it very soon.

D Sorry (3)

Complete the conversation. Use a to-infinitive or *about* + -ing form. Look at the information in
brackets.
Alan: I'm sorry (►) to disturb you (I'm disturbing you), but could I just say something? I'm sorry
(1) .... (I was so rude) last night. I didn't mean what I
said.
Mark: Oh, that's OK. I'm sorry (2) .... (I lost my temper).
Alan: Right. OK. And, as I said, sorry (3) .... (I'm interrupting
you).

72 Used to do and be used to doing

1 Used to do

*When I was younger, I **used to be** a singer in a rock band.*

*That was before I became an actress. I **used to travel** around the country doing gigs.*

Used + to-infinitive means that something happened regularly or went on for a time in the past. *I used to travel* means that in the past I regularly travelled, but I no longer do so.

Here are some more examples.

> We **used to play** that game when we were younger.
> Nick **used to smoke**, but he gave it up.   I **used to like** fish, but I never eat it now.
> There **used to be** a dancehall here, but they knocked it down.

We cannot use this structure in the present tense.

> Claire **travels** a lot. NOT ~~Claire uses to travel a lot.~~

We normally use **didn't use to** in negatives and **did ... use to** in questions.

> We **didn't use to have** computers. OR We **never used to have** computers.
> Where **did** people **use to buy** their food before the supermarket was built?
> **Did** you **use to live** in London?

2 Be used to doing

I'm used to driving because I travel a lot in my job. I'm used to travelling around the country.

Be used to + -ing form means that something is familiar and is no longer strange. *I'm used to travelling* means that travelling is no longer strange or difficult because I have done it for so long.

Here are some more examples.

> We**'re used to getting** up early. We do it every day. NOT ~~We're used to get up early.~~
> Sarah **is used to working** late at the office.   Most visitors to Britain **aren't used to driving** on the left.
> I **wasn't used to wearing** glasses. It seemed very strange at first.

We can also say **get used to** to talk about things becoming more familiar.

> It was difficult at first, but Mike soon **got used to working** at night.
> After her husband died, the old woman had to **get used to living** on her own.

Practice

A Used to do (1)

Mrs Bell is a hundred years old. She's the oldest person in the village.
A radio reporter is interviewing her. Put in *used to* with the verb.

Mrs Bell: I've always lived in the village, but not always in this house.

Reporter: Where (▶) .did..you..use..to..live.............................. (you / live)?

Mrs Bell: When I was a girl, we lived at Apple Tree Farm.
(1) .... (we / like) it there.

Reporter: But life was hard, wasn't it?

Mrs Bell: Oh, yes. Things (2) .... (be) different from the
way they are now. In those days (3) ....
(we / not / have) electricity.

Reporter: And (4) .... (you / help) with the farm work?

Mrs Bell: Yes, (5) .... (I / look) after the hens.

B Used to do and be used to doing (1–2)

Look at the pictures and say what the people used to do or are used to doing.
Use these verbs: *climb*, *fly*, *paint*, *play*, *sign*
Use these objects: *autographs*, *badminton*, *mountains*, *pictures*, *planes*

▶ He .used..to..paint..pictures.....................
▶ She`s..used..to..signing..autographs.......... 2 They ....
1 She .... 3 He ....

C Used to do and be used to doing (1–2)

Put in a to-infinitive or to + -ing form. Use the verbs in brackets.

▶ When I was a child, I used .to..dream............ (dream) of being an astronaut.

▶ I'm terribly nervous. I'm not used .to..speaking........ (speak) to a large audience.

1 It took us ages to get used .... (live) in a block of flats.

2 Lots of trains used .... (stop) here, but not many do now.

3 Didn't Nick use .... (work) on a building site?

4 There didn't use .... (be) so many soap operas on television.

5 I'll have an orange juice, please. I'm not used .... (drink) alcohol.

6 David doesn't seem to mind being in hospital. I suppose he's got used ....
(be) there.

7 When Laura was at college, she used .... (have) a picture of Elvis Presley
on her bedroom wall.

73 Preposition or linking word + -ing form

1 Introduction

Rachel: *Shall we have some lunch?*
Jessica: *I usually go for a walk **instead of eating**. I'm on a diet.*
Rachel: *You're joking, aren't you? Since when?*
Jessica: ***Since discovering** I can't get into my old clothes.*
Rachel: *Well, just buy some new ones, then.*

We can use an -ing form after some prepositions (e.g. **instead of**)
or linking words (e.g. **since**).
We cannot use an infinitive. NOT ~~instead of to eat.~~

2 Preposition + -ing form

Here are some more examples.

> ***As a result of losing** my passport, I had to fill in a complicated form.*
> *Vicky and Rachel might go to Canada **as well as travelling** around the US.*
> *You can get skin cancer **from being** in the sun too long.*
> *You aren't **in favour of cutting** down trees, are you?*
> *Sarah went to work **in spite of not feeling** well.*
> *We can't have a party **without making** a bit of noise.*

We can use these prepositions before an -ing form: **against, as a result of, as well as, besides,
by, despite, for, from, how about, in favour of, in spite of, instead of, on, what about, without**

We use **what about/how about** + -ing form to make a suggestion.
> ***How about giving** us some help?*

We use **for** + -ing form to say what we use something for.
> *This cloth is **for cleaning** the floor.*

We use **by** + -ing form to say how someone does something.
> *The thief got in **by breaking** a window.*

We use **on** + -ing form to mean 'as soon as'.
> ***On hearing** the news of David's accident, Melanie burst into tears.*
> (= As soon as she heard the news, ...)

3 Linking word + -ing form

Here are some examples.

> *I always have a shower **after playing tennis**.*
> ***Although hoping** to get the job, Rachel wasn't really expecting to.*
> *Sarah wanted to finish the report **before going** to bed.*
> *The man has been unemployed **since leaving** prison.*
> *You should always lock the door **when leaving** your room.*
> *Mark was listening to the car radio **while sitting** in a traffic jam.*

We can use these linking words before an -ing form: **after, although, before, since, when, while**

A linking word + -ing form can sometimes be a little formal. We can say the same thing like this.
> *I always have a shower **after I've played** tennis.*
> ***Although she was hoping** to get the job, Rachel wasn't really expecting to.*

▷ 70 Verb/Adjective + preposition + -ing form

Practice

A Preposition + -ing form (2)

Complete the sentences using the words in brackets.

▶ Rachel: Do you want to walk? Vicky: Yes, let's not get a bus. (instead of)
Vicky wants to walk instead of getting a bus.

1 Sarah: Did you get through the work? Mark: Yes, I stayed up all night. (by)
Mark got through the work ....

2 Melanie: When do you take the pills? David: The minute I wake in the morning. (on)
David has to take the pills ....

3 Mike: So you got the answer? Harriet: Yes, and I didn't use a calculator. (without)
Harriet got the answer ....

4 Emma: Why the rucksack? Matthew: So I can carry the food. (for)
The rucksack is ....

5 Trevor: Sorry I forgot the sugar. Laura: Well, you had it on your list. (in spite of)
Trevor forgot the sugar ....

6 Mark: Do you have to do the typing? Secretary: Yes, and book some flights. (as well as)
The secretary has to book some flights ....

B Linking word + -ing form (3)

This structure is often used in instructions (sentences which tell people what to do).
Put in *before* or *after* and the -ing form of the verb in brackets.

▶ Replace the top on the bottle after taking .... (take) the medicine.
1 Read the contract through carefully .... (sign) it.
2 You shouldn't have a bath straight .... (eat) a meal.
3 .... (leave) home ring the airport to check that your flight is on schedule.
4 Always put your skis away carefully .... (use) them.
5 Be sure to switch off the electricity .... (change) a fuse.
6 Make sure the safety chain is on .... (open) the door.

C Preposition or linking word + -ing form (2–3)

Ron Mason owns a supermarket business. Write the sentences for a magazine article about his life. Join two sentences into one using the words in brackets.

▶ He saw an empty shop. He was walking around town one day. (while)
He saw an empty shop while walking around town one day.

1 He thought carefully. He decided to buy it. (before)
....

2 He bought the shop. He had little money of his own. (despite)
....

3 He became successful. He gave the customers what they wanted. (by)
....

4 He put the profit back into the business. He didn't spend it on himself. (instead of)
....

5 He was happy. He was running his own business. (when)
....

6 He fell ill. He worked too hard. (as a result of)
....

7 He has made a lot of money. He bought his first shop ten years ago. (since)
....

74 See it happen or see it happening?

1 Introduction

> David fell down the steps.
> Rachel **saw him fall**.

> David was walking with a stick.
> Rachel **saw him walking** across the road.

2 See it happen

After some verbs we can use an object + an infinitive without to.

	VERB	OBJECT	INFINITIVE	
Rachel	*saw*	*David*	*fall*	down the steps.
Vicky	*heard*	*someone*	*close*	the door.
Let's	*watch*	*the parade*	*go*	past.
We all	*felt*	*the house*	*shake.*	

We can use this structure with these verbs: **feel, hear, listen to, notice, see, watch**

3 See it happening

We can also use an -ing form after the object.

	VERB	OBJECT	-ING FORM	
Rachel	*saw*	*David*	*walking*	with a stick.
Can you	*hear*	*someone*	*playing*	the piano?
We	*found*	*Matthew*	*exercising*	in the gym.
I could	*feel*	*an insect*	*crawling*	up my leg.

We can use this structure with these verbs: **feel, find, hear, listen to, notice, see, smell, watch**

4 See it happen or see it happening?

SEE IT HAPPEN	SEE IT HAPPENING
*We saw Trevor **plant** the tree.* (He <u>planted</u> the tree. We saw him do the whole job.) *I watched Nick **light** a cigarette.* *We noticed a young man **sit** down and order a meal.*	*We saw Trevor **planting** the tree.* (He <u>was planting</u> the tree. We saw him in the middle of the job.) *I watched Nick **smoking** a cigarette.* *We noticed a young man **sitting** at the table eating a meal.*

When we talk about a short action, it often does not matter which structure we use.
> *They heard a car **turn/turning** the corner.*   *I didn't see anyone **leave/leaving** any litter.*

Practice

A See it happen (2)

Henry is in court. He is answering questions about a Mr Lewis, who the police suspect of a number of crimes. Add a sentence using the verb in brackets.

▶ And you say a second man came into the restaurant? (see)
Henry: That's right. *I saw him come in.* ....

1   Are you quite certain that Mr Lewis took the envelope? (see)
Henry: Yes, absolutely. ....

2   Then Mr Lewis left the restaurant, did he? (watch)
Henry: He left soon afterwards. ....

3   And he drove away. (hear)
Henry: Yes, he did. ....

B See it happening (3)

Look at the pictures and add a sentence with *I can see/hear/smell ...* and the -ing form of these verbs: *bark, burn, come, ring, wave*

▶

▶ The postman is on his way. *I can see him coming.* ....
1   There's a phone upstairs. ....
2   There's a woman in the boat. ....
3   There are some dogs outside. ....
4   You've forgotten your lunch. ....

C See it happen or see it happening? (4)

There has been a bomb explosion in the city centre. TV reporter Kitty Beamish is asking people about it. What did people see or hear?

▶ Man: The bomb exploded. I heard it. It was a shock.
He heard the bomb explode. ....

▶ Woman: A man was lying in the road. I saw him. He was just lying there.
She saw a man lying in the road. ....

1   Woman: The building shook. I felt it. I couldn't believe it.
....

2   Man: People were shouting. I heard them. There was panic.
....

3   Girl: An alarm was ringing. I could hear it. It went on and on.
....

4   Boys: The police arrived. We saw them. They were over there.
....

5   Man: I saw a woman. She was crying. She was in a terrible state.
....

75 Some structures with the -ing form

1 Two actions at the same time

*All afternoon Claire **lay** in a hammock **reading** a magazine.*

When two things are happening at the same time, we can use a main verb (**lay**) and an -ing form (**reading**). Here are some more examples.

> *We had to **stand** in a queue **waiting** for the bank to open.*
> *You can't **sit watching** television all day.*   *All afternoon, Vicky **lay** on the sofa **thinking** about life.*

We can also use this structure when one action comes in the middle of another. We use the -ing form for the longer action.

> *Matthew **injured** his knee **doing** gymnastics.* (= He injured his knee <u>while</u> he was doing gymnastics.)
> *I **went** to sleep **listening** to the radio.*

2 One action after another

When there are two short actions, one straight after the other, we can use an -ing form for the first action.

> ***Opening** the bottle, Mike poured the drinks.* (= He opened the bottle <u>and then</u> poured the drinks.)
> ***Turning** right into Madison Avenue, the car drove north for two blocks.*

We can also use the perfect -ing form.

> ***Having opened** the bottle, Mike poured the drinks.* (= <u>After opening</u> the bottle, Mike poured the drinks.)

If either of the actions is long, we must use the perfect.

> ***Having photocopied** all the papers, Sarah put them back in the file.*
> ***Having repaired** the car, Tom took it out for a road test.*
> NOT ~~Repairing the car, Tom took it out for a road test.~~

These patterns are typical of written English. In spoken English, to talk about one action after another we use a sentence like this.

> *Tom repaired the car **and then** took it out for a road test.*

3 The -ing form saying why

We can use the -ing form to give a reason.

> *The fans queued for hours, **hoping** to get tickets.*
> (= They queued for hours <u>because</u> they hoped to get tickets.)
> ***Being** the youngest child, Natasha was her father's favourite.*
> ***Not knowing** the way, I had to ask for directions.*

We can also use the perfect -ing form to give a reason.

> ***Having spent** all his money, Daniel couldn't afford a new jacket.*
> *We decided not to travel, **having heard** the terrible weather forecast.*

Practice

A One action in the middle of another (1)

Say what accidents these people had. Use these phrases: *lift weights, light a fire, open a tin, run, ski*
Put the verbs describing the longer action in the -ing form.

▶ Harriet burnt her hand lighting a fire.
1 Matthew ....
2 David ....
3 Vicky ....
4 Trevor ....

B One action after another (2)

Rewrite the **sentences about a detective. Begin with an -ing form**, e.g. *doing* or *having done*.

Mitchell picked up the phone and dialled a number. He let it ring for five long minutes and then slowly replaced the receiver. He took a gun out of the drawer and put it in his briefcase. He left the office and then had to wait a while for the lift. He reached the ground floor and hurried outside to a taxi. The taxi driver pulled out a gun and shot Mitchell.

▶ Picking up the phone, Mitchell dialled a number.
▶ Having let it ring for five long minutes, he slowly replaced the receiver.
1 ....
2 ....
3 ....
4 ....

C The -ing form saying why (3)

Match the two parts and join them using an -ing form, e.g. *doing* or *having done*.

▶ Because she didn't want to be late,Harriet turned on the heating.
▶ As she had worked hard all day,Andrew took it back to the library.
1 Because he had studied the map,   Daniel found it hard to communicate.
2 She felt cold, so   Vicky ran to the bus stop.
3 Because he didn't know French,   Trevor knew which way to go.
4 He had finished the book, so   Sarah was exhausted.

▶ Not wanting to be late, Vicky ran to the bus stop.
▶ Having worked hard all day, Sarah was exhausted.
1 ....
2 ....
3 ....
4 ....

Test M: The infinitive and the -ing form

A

Some of these sentences are correct, and some have a word which should not be there. If the sentence is correct, put a tick (✓). If it is incorrect, cross out the unnecessary word and write it in the space.

▶   I'm used to driving in heavy traffic every day.   ✓

▶   Although ~~of~~ feeling tired, Polly didn't want to go to bed.   of

1   It's important for to sign the form.   ....

2   Peter broke his arm in playing rugby.   ....

3   A woman accused Martin of stealing her money.   ....

4   I wasn't sure whether to write a letter of thanks.   ....

5   Do you remember a young man bumping into you?   ....

6   The girl's parents wouldn't let her to stay out so late.   ....

7   The book is too difficult enough for children to understand.   ....

8   Police found the woman for lying dead on the floor.   ....

9   Cars are always expensive to repair them.   ....

10   The man died as a result of falling asleep while driving.   ....

B

This is an advertisement for the book 'Winning in Business'. Put in the correct form of each verb.

Are you fed up with (▶) _being_ (be) a failure in your job? Wouldn't you rather (▶) _succeed_ (succeed)?
Do you want (▶) _to earn_ (earn) more money? Are you anxious (1) .... (get) ahead? Do you believe in (2) .... (make) the most of your talents? Do you sometimes dream about (3) .... (reach) the top? If the answer is yes, read on. Just imagine yourself (4) .... (run) a big successful company. And now you can do something about it instead of (5) .... (dream). It'll happen if you want it (6) .... (happen). Make it a reality by (7) .... (order) your copy of the best-selling 'Winning in Business'. It has a ten-point plan for you (8) .... (follow). Do it and you're certain (9) .... (be) a success. You'll know what (10) .... (do) in business. You can make other people (11) .... (respect) you and persuade them (12) .... (do) what you want. Experts recommend (13) .... (buy) this marvellous book. You'd better (14) .... (order) your copy today.

C

Combine each pair of sentences. Use a to-infinitive or an -ing form. Sometimes you also need a preposition.

▶   We've advised Nancy. She should get a lawyer.
   We've advised Nancy to get a lawyer.

▶   I'm getting bored. I've been sitting on the beach.
   I'm getting bored with sitting on the beach.

1   We saw Rupert. He was looking in a shop window.

....

2   I remember the clown. He fell over.

....

3   Tessa wasn't sure. Which way should she go?

....

4   The porter just stood there. He expected a tip.

   ....

5   How about it? Shall we go to the barbecue?

   ....

6   Susan is used to it. She's always lived in the country.

   ....

7   I'm afraid. I might hurt myself.

   ....

8   Christopher apologized. He'd forgotten to pay.

   ....

9   The food was too cold. Michelle couldn't eat it.

   ....

10   Polly was silly. She gave away the secret.

   ....

D

Read the story and write the missing words. Use one word only in each space.

Calvin Coolidge was elected US President in 1924. He didn't believe (▶) .in........ doing too much, and his slogan was 'Keep cool with Coolidge'. Soon (1) .... moving into the White House, Coolidge invited some old friends (2).................... have dinner with him there. They were all people he (3) .... to know in the old days, and they were simple country people. They were interested (4) .... see inside the White House, and they were looking forward to (5) .... dinner with the President. They thought it was nice (6) .... him (7) .... invite them. But there was one problem. They weren't used (8) .... attending formal dinners, and they were worried that they wouldn't know (9) .... to behave. They were afraid (10) .... looking foolish. So they decided it would be best (11) .... everyone to copy exactly what Coolidge did.

At last the day came. During the dinner, when Coolidge picked up his knife and fork, everyone did the same. When he drank, everyone drank, and so on. Finally Coolidge decided to amuse himself (12) .... playing a little trick on his visitors. He tipped some coffee into his saucer. Everyone did the same. (13) .... done this, he added a little cream and sugar. Everyone did the same. Then, horrified, they watched Coolidge bend down and (14) .... the saucer on the carpet for his cat.

E

Complete the conversations. Put in the correct form of each verb.

▶   A: I'm annoyed about ..being.................. (be) late.
    B: Well, I told you ..to set.................... (set) off in good time, didn't I?
1   A: Did you accuse Nigel of .... (break) a plate?
    B: Well, it was an accident, but he did break it. I saw him .... (knock) it off the table with his elbow.
2   A: I came here .... (see) Janet. She must have forgotten I was coming.
    B: It seems rather careless of her .... (forget).
3   A: Are you going to have a rest now after .... (do) all the cleaning?
    B: No, I've got an essay .... (write).
4   A: You say you need some advice?
    B: Yes, I'm sorry .... (bother) you, but I don't know
         who .... (ask).
5   A: Do you like Scrabble?
    B: Well, I used .... (play) it quite a lot, but I got fed up with it. I'd rather
         .... (watch) television, actually.

76 **Ship** and **water**: countable and uncountable nouns

1 What is the difference?

a ship   two **boats**   *water*

COUNTABLE	UNCOUNTABLE
A countable noun (e.g **ship**) can be singular or plural. We can count ships. We can say **a ship/one ship** or **two ships**.	An uncountable noun (e.g. **water**) is neither singular nor plural. We cannot count water. We can say **water** or **some water** but NOT ~~a water~~ or ~~two waters.~~
Here are some examples of countable nouns. *We could see a **ship** in the distance.* *Claire has only got one **sister**.* *I've got a **problem** with the **car**.* *Do you like these **photos**?* *I'm going out for five **minutes**.*	Here are some examples of uncountable nouns. *Can I have some **water**?* *Shall we sit on the **grass**?* *The **money** is quite safe.* *I love **music**.* *Would you like some **butter**?*

2 Nouns after **the, a/an** and numbers

There are some words that go with both countable and uncountable nouns. One of these is **the**.
We can say **the ship** (singular), **the ships** (plural) or **the water** (uncountable). But other words go with one kind of noun but not with the other.

COUNTABLE	UNCOUNTABLE
A/an or **one** goes only with a singular noun. *I need **a spoon**.* Numbers above one go only with plural nouns. *We eat **three meals** a day.*	We do not use **a/an** with an uncountable noun. NOT ~~a water~~ and NOT ~~a music~~. We do not use numbers with an uncountable noun. NOT ~~three foods~~

3 Nouns after **some, many/much**, etc.

Some and **any** go with plural or uncountable nouns. We can also use plural and uncountable nouns on their own, without **some** or **any**.

PLURAL	UNCOUNTABLE
*Tom told **some jokes**.* *Do you know **any jokes**?* *Tom usually tells **jokes**.* But NOT ~~He told joke.~~	*We had **some fun**.* *That won't be **any fun**.* *We always have **fun**.*
Many and **a few** go only with plural nouns. *There weren't **many bottles**.* *I made **a few sandwiches**.*	**Much** and **a little** go with uncountable nouns. *I don't drink **much wine**.* *There was only **a little bread** left.*

▷ 79 Agreement   ▷ 85 A/an, one and some   ▷ 95 Many and much

Practice

A What is the difference? (1)

Look at the <u>underlined</u> nouns. Are they are countable or uncountable?

▶ There was a <u>car</u> behind us. *countable*

▶ I never eat <u>meat</u>. *uncountable*

1 Do you play <u>golf</u>? ....

2 I had to wait ten <u>minutes</u>. ....

3 Just tell me one <u>thing</u>. ....

4 <u>Love</u> makes the world go round. ....

5 Good <u>luck</u> in your new job. ....

6 Power stations produce <u>energy</u>. ....

7 I'm taking a <u>photo</u>. ....

8 Would you like an <u>apple</u>? ....

B A and some (2–3)

Laura has been to the supermarket. What has she bought? Use *a* or *some* with these words: *banana, biscuits, butter, cheese, eggs, flowers, lemon, light bulb, mineral water, magazine, soap, wine*

▶ *some flowers* .... 4 ....

▶ *a magazine* .... 5 ....

▶ *some cheese* .... 6 ....

1 .... 7 ....

2 .... 8 ....

3 .... 9 ....

C Countable and uncountable nouns (1–3)

Complete the conversation. Choose the correct form.

Jessica: What are you doing, Andrew?

Andrew: I'm writing (▶) <u>essay/an essay</u>.

Jessica: Oh, you've got (1) <u>computer/a computer</u>. Do you always write (2) <u>essay/essays</u> on your computer?

Andrew: Yes, but I'm not doing very well today. I've been working on my plan for about three (3) <u>hour/hours</u> now.

Jessica: You've got lots of books to help you, though. I haven't got as (4) <u>many/much</u> books as you. That's because I haven't got much (5) <u>money/moneys</u>. Quite often I can't even afford to buy (6) <u>food/a food</u>.

Andrew: Really? That can't be (7) <u>many/much</u> fun.

Jessica: I'd like to get (8) <u>job/a job</u> I can do in my spare time and earn (9) <u>a/some</u> money. I've got (10) <u>a few/a little</u> ideas, but what do you think I should do?

Andrew: I know someone who paints (11) <u>picture/pictures</u> and sells them. Why don't you do that?

Jessica: Because I'm no good at painting.

77 A carton of milk, a piece of information, etc.

1 A carton of milk

a **carton of** milk   two **tins of** soup   a **kilo of** sugar   a **piece/slice of** bread   a **loaf of** bread

Milk, **soup**, etc. are uncountable nouns. We cannot use **a** or a number in front of them. We do not usually say ~~a milk~~ or ~~two soups~~. But we can say **a carton of milk** or **two tins of soup**. Here are some more examples.

CARTON, TIN, ETC.	MEASUREMENTS	PIECE, SLICE, ETC.
a **carton of** orange juice	a **kilo of** cheese	a **piece of** wood
a **tin of** paint	five **metres of** cable	a **piece/slice of** bread
a **bottle of** water	twenty **litres of** petrol	a **piece/sheet of** paper
a **box/packet of** cereal	half a **pound of** butter	a **bar of** chocolate
a **jar of** jam		a **loaf of** bread
a **tube of** toothpaste		
a **glass of** water		
a **cup of** coffee		

We can also use this structure with a plural noun after **of**.

    a **packet of** crisps   a **box of** matches   three **kilos of** potatoes   a **collection of** pictures

2 A piece of information

Advice, information and **news** are uncountable nouns. We cannot use them with **a/an** or in the plural.

    *Can I give you **some advice**?* NOT ~~an advice~~
    *We got **some information** from the tourist office.* NOT ~~some informations~~
    *That's wonderful **news**!* NOT ~~a wonderful news~~

But we can use **piece of**, **bit of** and **item of**.

    *Can I give you **a piece of/a bit of advice**?*
    *There are **two pieces/bits of information** we need to complete the questionnaire.*
    *There's **a bit of/an item of news** that might interest you.*

These nouns are uncountable in English, although they may be countable in other languages:
accommodation, baggage, behaviour, equipment, fun, furniture, homework, housework, litter, luck, luggage, progress, rubbish, scenery, traffic, travel, weather, work

Some countable nouns have similar meanings to the uncountable nouns above.

COUNTABLE	UNCOUNTABLE
*There aren't any **jobs**.*	*There isn't any **work**.*
*It's a long **journey**.*	***Travel** can be tiring.*
*There were **sofas** and **chairs** for sale.*	*There was **furniture** for sale.*
*We've booked a **room**.*	*We've booked some **accommodation**.*
*I've got three **suitcases**.*	*I've got three pieces of **luggage**.*

Practice

A A carton of milk (1)

What did Tom buy at the supermarket? Use *of*.

Milk	0.35	▶	*two cartons of milk*
Milk	0.35	▶	*a kilo of flour*
1 kilo flour	0.85		
Jam	0.95	1	
Matches	0.39	2	
Bread	0.65	3	
Bread	0.65	4	
Chocolate	0.95	5	
5 kilos potatoes	1.59	6	
Breakfast cereal	1.38	7	
Mineral water	0.74	8	
Mineral water	0.74		
Toothpaste	1.89		
Total	£11.48		

B Countable and uncountable nouns (2)

Complete the sentences. Put in *a/an* or *some*.

▶ I really ought to do *some* housework.

1 The people who camped in the field have left .... rubbish.

2 I've been working on the business plan. I've made .... progress.

3 The visitors are here for two nights. They're looking for .... accommodation.

4 That shop has .... nice sofa.

5 You'll have to pay extra for the taxi because you've got .... luggage.

6 The flat is quite empty. I need .... furniture.

7 I can't possibly fit this guitar into .... suitcase.

8 You need .... luck to win at this game.

C Countable and uncountable nouns (2)

You are talking about the holiday you had with a friend. Use these words:
accommodation, awful journey, beautiful scenery, chair, fun, good weather, meal.
You have to decide whether you need to put *a/an* or not.

▶ (It was quite easy to book a place to stay.)
Booking *accommodation* was quite easy.

▶ (There was nothing to sit on in your room.)
But my room wasn't very nice. It didn't even have *a chair* in it.

1 (You were in a beautiful part of the country.)
It was a lovely place, though. There was .... all around us.

2 (The weather was good.)
And we had .... while we were there.

3 (One evening you went to a restaurant with some other people.)
One evening we had .... with some people we met.

4 (You enjoyed yourselves at the disco.)
We went to a disco. We had .... there.

5 (Travelling home was awful.)
We had .... home last Saturday.

78 Nouns that can be countable or uncountable

1 A potato or potato?

Some nouns can be either countable or uncountable. For example, **a potato** is a separate, individual thing, but **potato** cannot be counted.

potatoes

potato

COUNTABLE	UNCOUNTABLE
I'm peeling the **potatoes**.	Would you like **some potato**?
Melanie baked **a cake** for David.	Have **some cake/a piece of cake**.
Vicky was eating **an apple**.	Is there **apple** in this salad?
Someone threw **a stone** at the police.	The house is built of **stone**.
There's **a hair** on your shirt.	I must brush my **hair**. NOT ~~hairs~~

2 A sport or sport?

Often the countable noun is specific, and the uncountable noun is more general.

COUNTABLE	UNCOUNTABLE
Rugby is **a sport**. (= a particular sport)	Do you like **sport**? (= sport in general)
That's **a nice painting** over there.	Paul is good at **painting**.
We heard **a sudden noise** outside.	Constant **noise** can make you ill.
John Lennon had **an interesting life**.	**Life** is complicated sometimes.

3 A paper or paper?

Some nouns can be countable or uncountable with different meanings.

COUNTABLE	UNCOUNTABLE
I bought **a paper**. (= a newspaper)	I need **some paper** to write on.
I'll have **a glass** of orange juice, please.	I bought a piece of **glass** for the window.
Have you got **an iron**? (for clothes)	The bridge is made of **iron**.
I switched all **the lights** on.	There's more **light** by the window.
I've been to France many **times**.	I can't stop. I haven't got **time**.
The journey was **a great experience**.	He has enough **experience** for the job.
I run **a small business**. (= a company)	I enjoy doing **business**. (= buying and selling)
We finally found **a space** in the car park.	There's no **space** for a piano in here.
	There are hundreds of satellites out in **space**.

4 A coffee or coffee?

Words for drink are usually uncountable: *Coffee is more expensive than **tea**.*
But when we are ordering or offering drinks, we can say either **a cup of coffee** or **a coffee**.

   Two coffees, please. (= two <u>cups of</u> coffee)   *Would you like **a beer**?* (= <u>a glass/bottle/can</u> of beer)

Some nouns can be countable when we are talking about a particular kind or about different kinds.
   *Chianti is **an Italian wine**.* (= a <u>kind of</u> Italian wine)
   *The use of **plastics** has greatly increased.* (= the use of different <u>kinds of</u> plastic)

Practice

A   A potato or potato? A sport or sport? (1–2)

Complete the conversations. Choose the correct form.

▶ Can I pick an apple/~~some apple~~ from your tree? ~ Yes, of course.
1 I think sport/a sport is boring. ~ Me too. I hate it.
2 We ought to buy some potato/some potatoes. ~ OK, I'll get them.
3 I think painting/a painting is a fascinating hobby. ~ Well, you're certainly very good at it.
4 Did you hear noise/a noise in the middle of the night? ~ No, I don't think so.
5 Is there cheese/a cheese in this soup? ~ Yes, a little.
6 I had conversation/a conversation with Vicky last night. ~ Oh? What about?
7 Shall I put a chicken/some chicken in your sandwiches? ~ Yes, please.
8 Are you a pacifist? ~ Well, I don't believe in war/a war, so I suppose I am.
9 It isn't fair. ~ No, life/a life just isn't fair, I'm afraid.
10 What's the matter? ~ You've got some egg/some eggs on your shirt.

B   A paper or paper? (3)

Complete the conversations. Put in these nouns: business (x2), experience (x2),
glass, iron, light, paper, space, time. Put a/an or some before each noun.

▶ Harriet: Did you manage to park in town?
  Mike: It took me ages to find _a space_ . And all I wanted was to buy _some paper_ to
           wrap this present in.
1 Sarah: Are you busy tomorrow?
   Mark: I'm meeting someone in the office. We've got .... to discuss.
2 Trevor: Do you think I need to take .... with me for my shirts?
   Laura: Oh, surely the hotel will have one.
3 Vicky: I was going to have some juice, but I can't find ....
   Rachel: If you turned .... on, you might be able to see properly.
4 Claire: I've never met your brother.
   Mark: Oh, he's usually very busy because he runs .... But he's been ill
           recently. The doctor has ordered him to spend .... resting.
5 Daniel: How did your interview go?
   Emma: Well, I didn't get the job. I think they really wanted someone with
           .... of the work, and that's what I haven't got.
           So it was a bit of a waste of time. And the train coming back was two hours late.
           That's .... I don't want to repeat.

C   Countable or uncountable? (1–4)

Complete Claire's postcard to her sister. Choose the correct form.

The island is very peaceful. (▶) Life/~~A life~~ is good here. Everybody moves at a nice slow pace. People
have (1) time/a time to stop and talk. It's (2) experience/an experience I won't forget for a long time.
There aren't many shops, so I can't spend all my money, although I did buy (3) painting/a painting
yesterday. Now I'm sitting on the beach reading (4) paper/a paper. The hotel breakfast is so enormous
that I don't need to have lunch. I've just brought (5) orange/an orange with me to eat later. I've been
trying all the different (6) fruit/fruits grown in this part of the world, and they're all delicious.

79 Agreement

1 Subject and verb

Look at these examples of agreement between the subject (e.g. **the window**) and the verb (e.g. **is**).

SINGULAR	PLURAL
The **window is** open.	The **windows are** open.
She was upset.	The **door and** the **window are** open.
It has been raining.	Her **eyes were** wet.
The **soup tastes** good.	**They have** got wet.
This method **doesn't work**.	The **biscuits taste** good.
	These **methods don't** work.
After a singular or an uncountable noun and after **he**, **she** or **it**, we use a singular verb.	After a plural noun or **they**, and after nouns joined by **and**, we use a plural verb.

2 Everyone, something, every, all, etc.

After **everyone**, **something**, **nothing**, etc, we use a singular verb (see also Unit 103.3).
   Everyone was pleased.   **Something is** wrong.

But compare these examples with **every**, **each** and **all**.

After a phrase with **every** or **each**, we use a singular verb.	After **all** and a plural noun, we use a plural verb.
Every seat has a number.	**All the seats have** a number.
Each door is a different colour.	

3 One of, a number of and a lot of

After **one of …**, we use a singular verb.	After **a number of …**, we normally use a plural verb.
One of the photos **is** missing.	**A number of** questions **were** asked.

After **a lot of …**, the verb agrees with the noun.
   Every year a lot of **pollution is** created, and a lot of **trees are** cut down.

4 Any of, either of, neither of and none of

When a plural noun comes after **any of**, **either of**, **neither of** or **none of**, we can use either a singular or a plural verb.
   Is/Are any of these old maps worth keeping?
   I wonder if **either** of those alternatives **is/are** a good idea.
   Neither of these cameras **works/work** properly.
   None of the plants **has/have** grown very much.

5 An amount + a singular verb

After an amount of money, a distance, a weight or a length of time, we normally use a singular verb.
   Eight pounds seems a fair price.   **A hundred metres isn't** far to swim.
   Ninety kilos is too heavy for me to lift.   **Five minutes doesn't** seem long to wait.
We are talking about the amount as a whole, not the individual pounds or metres.

Practice

A Subject and verb (1)

Mark and Sarah are in an antique shop. Complete the conversation by choosing the correct form of the verb.

Sarah: This table (▶) <u>is</u>/~~are~~ lovely.

Mark: Yes, the wood (1) <u>is/are</u> beautiful, isn't it?

Sarah: The style and the colour (2) <u>is/are</u> both perfect for what we want.

Mark: These chairs (3) <u>looks/look</u> very stylish, too, but they (4) <u>is/are</u> rather expensive.

Sarah: Can you see if the table (5) <u>has/have</u> got a price on?

Mark: Yes, it has. It says it (6) <u>costs/cost</u> £2,000. That's ridiculous.

Sarah: Don't you think prices (7) <u>has/have</u> gone up recently? Those tables we saw last month (8) <u>wasn't/weren't</u> so expensive.

B Everyone, every, etc. and phrases with of (2–4)

Vicky has been to a very grand party. She is telling her parents about it. Put in *was* or *were*.

I really enjoyed the party. It (▶) ..was.... wonderful. Each guest (1) .... welcomed by the hostess in person. All the rooms (2) .... crowded with people. Everyone (3) .... enjoying themselves. A lot of people (4) .... dancing, and a number of people (5) .... swimming in the pool in the garden. All the people there (6) .... very smart. One of the guests (7) .... a TV personality – the chat show host Guy Shapiro. I didn't know many of the guests. None of my friends (8) .... there.

C Agreement (1–4)

The BBC is making a documentary about police work. A policeman is talking about his job. Choose the correct form.

▶ Every policeman <u>is</u>/~~are~~ given special training for the job.

1 No two days are the same. Each day <u>is/are</u> different.

2 But the job <u>isn't/aren't</u> as exciting or glamorous as some people think.

3 Not all policemen <u>is/are</u> allowed to carry guns.

4 A number of police officers here <u>works/work</u> with dogs.

5 An officer and his dog <u>has/have</u> to work closely together.

6 One of our jobs <u>is/are</u> to prevent crime happening in the first place.

7 A lot of crime <u>is/are</u> caused by people being careless.

8 Sorry, I have to go now. Someone <u>has/have</u> just reported a robbery.

D An amount + a singular verb (5)

Combine the questions and answers about travel and holidays into one sentence using *is* or *are*.

▶ Do you know the price of a room? ~ Fifty pounds.
   Fifty pounds is the price of a room.

▶ How many public holidays are there? ~ Ten days in the year.
   Ten days in the year are public holidays.

1 Are you going on a long walk? ~ Fifteen miles.
   ....

2 Who's travelling on the bus? ~ Eight students.
   ....

3 Was someone waiting for the museum to open? ~ Yes, three people.
   ....

4 Do you know the baggage allowance? ~ Twenty kilos.
   ....

80 Singular or plural?

1 Clothes, etc.

Some nouns have only a plural form (with **s**) and take a plural verb.

> The **clothes were** in the dryer. NOT ~~The clothe was ...~~
> The **goods have** been sent to you direct from our factory. NOT ~~The good has ...~~
> My **belongings are** all packed up in suitcases.

> **PLURAL NOUNS**
>
> **arms** (weapons), **belongings** (the things you own), **clothes, congratulations, contents** (what is inside something), **customs** (bringing things into a country), **earnings** (money you earn), **goods** (products, things for sale), **outskirts** (the outer part of a town), **remains** (what is left), **surroundings** (the environment, the things around you), **thanks, troops** (soldiers)

Some nouns have both a singular and a plural form with a difference in meaning.

> **SINGULAR**
>
> Our special price is £10 cheaper than normal. So don't miss this **saving** of £10.
> The storm did a lot of **damage** to buildings.
>
> I've got a **pain** in my back. It really hurts.

> **PLURAL**
>
> My **savings** are in the bank. I'm going to take out all the money and buy a new car.
> The newspaper had to pay £2 million in **damages** after printing untrue stories about a politician.
> I checked the figures carefully three times. I took great **pains** to get them exactly right.

2 News, etc.

Some nouns have a plural form (with **s**) but take a singular verb.

> The **news was** worse than I had expected. NOT ~~The news were ...~~
> **Economics is** a difficult subject. NOT ~~Economics are ...~~

> **NOUNS TAKING A SINGULAR VERB**
>
> The word **news**
> The subjects **economics, mathematics/maths, physics, politics** and **statistics**
> The activities **athletics** and **gymnastics**
> The games **billiards** and **darts**
> The illness **measles**

3 Means, etc.

Some nouns ending in **s** have the same singular and plural form.

> This **means** of transport **saves** energy.
> Both **means** of transport **save** energy.
> This **species** of insect **is** quite rare.
> All these **species** of insect **are** quite rare.

> **NOUNS WITH ONE FORM**
>
> **crossroads, means, series** (e.g. *a series of TV documentaries*), **species** (kind, type)

Works (a factory) and **headquarters** (a main office) take either a singular or a plural verb.

> The steel **works has/have** closed down.

Practice

A Clothes, etc. (1)

Put in the nouns and add -s if necessary.

▶ Claire had to take her luggage through .customs........... (custom).
1 Please accept this gift as an expression of our .... (thank).
2 The woman is demanding .... (damage) for her injuries.
3 The .... (pain) was so bad I called the doctor.
4 The old man carried his few .... (belonging) in a plastic bag.
5 If we pay in cash, we make a .... (saving) of ten per cent.
6 More .... (good) should be transported by rail instead of by road.
7 The gas explosion caused some .... (damage) to the flats.
8 We're going to spend all our .... (saving) on a new car.
9 The company always takes .... (pain) to protect its image.

B News, etc. (2)

Look at each group of words and say what they are part of.
Start your answers like this: *ath..., eco..., geo..., his..., mat..., phy...*

▶ atoms, energy, heat, light   .physics...
1 algebra, numbers, shapes, sums   ....
2 dates, nations, past times, wars   ....
3 the high jump, the long jump, running, throwing ....
4 industry, money, prices, work   ....
5 the climate, the earth, mountains, rivers   ....

C Clothes, news, etc. (1–2)

Choose the correct verb form.

▶ The television news is/~~are~~ at ten o'clock.
1 These clothes is/are the latest fashion.
2 Maths is/are Emma's favourite subject.
3 The troops was/were involved in a training exercise.
4 The contents of the briefcase seems/seem to have disappeared.
5 Darts is/are sometimes played in pubs in England.
6 The athletics we watched was/were quite exciting.
7 The remains of the meal was/were thrown in the bin.

D Clothes, news, means, etc. (1–3)

Complete this email Rachel has received from her sister. Choose the correct forms.

(▶) ~~Thank~~/Thanks for your email. Your news (1) was/were interesting. We must talk soon.
What about us? Well, we're living on the (2) outskirt/outskirts of town, not far from the company
(3) headquarter/headquarters, where Jeremy works. We've spent nearly all our (4) saving/savings on
the house. That wouldn't matter so much if I hadn't crashed the car last week and done some
(5) damage/damages to the front of it. More bills! But at least I wasn't hurt. The house is nice actually,
but the surroundings (6) isn't/aren't very pleasant. We're on a very busy (7) crossroad/crossroads.

I'm doing the course I told you about. Statistics (8) is/are an easy subject, I find, but economics
(9) gives/give me problems!

81 Pair nouns and group nouns

1 Pair nouns

We use a pair noun for a thing made of two parts
which are the same. Some pair nouns are
**binoculars, glasses, jeans, pants, pyjamas,
scissors, shorts, tights, trousers.**

jeans   *scissors*   *glasses*   *binoculars*

A pair noun is plural and takes a plural verb.
> *My **jeans need** washing.* NOT ~~my jean~~
> ***These tights were** quite expensive.* NOT ~~this tight~~
> *We've got **some scissors** somewhere.* NOT ~~a scissor~~

We cannot use **a/an** or a number with a pair noun. But we can use **pair of.**
> *I need **some jeans**.* OR *I need **a pair of jeans**.* NOT ~~a jean~~
> *Laura bought **four pairs of tights**.* NOT ~~four tights~~

2 Group nouns

A group noun can usually take either a singular or a plural verb.
> *The **team was** playing well.* OR *The team **were playing** well.*
> *The **government is** in crisis.* OR *The **government are** in crisis.*

The choice depends on whether we see the group as a whole or as individual people. Often it doesn't matter
whether the verb is singular or plural. But sometimes one form is better than the other.

SINGULAR	PLURAL
*The **family is** a very old and famous one.* *The **orchestra consists** of eighty-six musicians.* When we mean the group as a whole, we use a singular verb.	*The **family are** delighted with their presents.* *The **orchestra don't** know what to play.* When we mean the individual people in the group, we normally use the plural.
We use **it** and **its.** *The **committee has** made **its** decision.*	We use **they, them** and **their.** *The class **will miss their** lessons because **they are** all going on a trip.*

> Some group nouns: **army, audience, band, board, choir, class, club, committee, community, company,
> council, crew, crowd, family, government, group, management, orchestra, population, press**
> (= newspapers), **public, staff, team, union**
> Also: **Harrods, the BBC, the United Nations,** etc. and **England** (the England team), **Manchester United**

3 Police, people and cattle

These nouns have a plural meaning and take a plural verb.
> *The **police have** warned motorists to take extra care.*
> ***People don't** know what the future will bring.*
> *The **cattle are** going to be sold with the farm.*

▷ page 379 Group nouns in American English

Practice

A Pair nouns (1)

Trevor and Laura are shopping for clothes. Choose the correct form.

Trevor: These trousers (▶) ~~is~~/are a bit tight. They (1) doesn't/don't feel very comfortable. And I think the blue ones (2) goes/go better with the jacket.

Laura: That jacket (3) is/are too long.

Trevor: Well, the jeans (4) fits/fit all right. Perhaps I'll buy the jeans instead.

Laura: Yes, the jeans (5) looks/look good on you. I like the style. I think they (6) suits/suit you. Now you get changed while I look for (7) a/some shorts. And I might get (8) a/some skirt.

B Pair nouns (1)

Complete what Rachel says to Vicky.
Put one word in each space.

This old suitcase was in the corridor.
I don't know who left it here. It's been here
for about three days, so I'm having a look
inside. There's a pair (▶) of pyjamas,
(1) .... jeans, two (2) ....
of tights and a (3) .... of sunglasses.
There are (4) .... red shorts, too.

C Group nouns (2)

Complete this TV news report. Choose the correct form of the verb.

Zedco (▶) ~~have~~/has just announced that it made a loss of £35 million last year. The management (1) is/are well aware that they have made mistakes. The press (2) have/has all been printing stories and articles critical of the company. The Zedco board (3) knows/know that they now have some difficult decisions to take. Naturally, the staff (4) is/are worried about their jobs and (5) wants/want a meeting with management as soon as possible. But Chief Executive Barry Douglas says things aren't really so bad. He has said that the company still (6) has/have a great future ahead of it.

D Group nouns (2–3)

Put in a group noun and *is* or *are*. Use these nouns:
cattle, choir, crew, crowd, orchestra, police, population, team

▶ The .crowd .are...... all enjoying the game.
1 This United .... the best one Tom has ever seen.
2 The .... hoping they can take part in a national singing contest.
3 The ship's .... all very tired after a long sea voyage.
4 The .... one of the biggest that has played at one of our concerts.
5 The .... installing cameras to photograph speeding motorists.
6 At the moment beef .... cheap because sales of beef are low.
7 The country's .... growing rapidly because of immigration.

82 Two nouns together

1 Introduction

Look at these phrases.

*a **bread knife*** = a knife for cutting bread   *a **cookery book*** = a book about cookery
*a **bus driver*** = someone who drives a bus   *my **birthday party*** = a party on my birthday
*the **street lights*** = the lights in the street   *a **paper bag*** = a bag made of paper

In English we often use one noun before another like this.

The two nouns are often written as separate words, but we sometimes use a hyphen (-),
or we write them as a single word.

*a **tea break**   at the **tea-table**   a large **teapot***

There are no exact rules about whether we join the words or not. If you are unsure, it is usually safest to
write two separate words.

2 A souvenir shop, etc.

Look at these examples.

*a **souvenir shop*** = a shop selling souvenirs
*an **animal hospital*** = a hospital for animals
*through the **letter-box*** = a box for letters

The first noun is usually singular. There are some exceptions, e.g. *a **sports** club, a **goods** train,*
*a **clothes**-brush, a **sales** conference.*

3 A teacup and a cup of tea

Look at these pictures.

*a **teacup***

*a **cup of tea***

A teacup is a cup for holding tea.	**A cup of tea** is a cup full of tea (see Unit 77.1).

Here are some more examples.

*I picked up a **cigarette packet**.*	*Gary opened a **packet of cigarettes**.*
*I'll wash the **milk bottle**.*	*There's a **bottle of milk** in the fridge.*

4 An -ing form + a noun

We can use an -ing form with a noun.

*a **sleeping-bag*** = a bag for sleeping in   *a **waiting-room*** = a room for waiting in
*a **washing-machine*** = a machine for washing clothes

5 Longer phrases

We can use more than two nouns.

*a **glass coffee-table**   at **Sydney Opera House**   the **bedroom carpet***
*the **winter bus timetable**   our **Assistant Computer Technology Manager***

Practice

A Two nouns together (1)

Say what these things are. For each picture use two of these nouns:

alarm, camera, chair, clock, cycle, luggage, motor, office, racket, television, tennis, trolley

▶ an office chair ....   3 ....
1 ....   4 ....
2 ....   5 ....

B Two nouns together (1–4)

Can you say it a better way? Use two nouns together.

▶ (I read an interesting article in a newspaper yesterday.)
   I read an interesting newspaper article yesterday. ....

1 (Have you got any shirts made of cotton?)
   ....

2 (What shall I do with this bottle that had lemonade in it?)
   ....

3 (Have you got a bag to carry shopping in?)
   ....

4 (Is there a shop that sells shoes near here?)
   ....

5 (I'd like a table in the corner, please.)
   ....

6 (I'll need some boots to climb in.)
   ....

7 (Do you operate computers?)
   ....

C Two nouns together (1–5)

Look at the definitions and write the words.

▶ a station from which trains leave   a train station
▶ a bottle once containing medicine and made of glass   a glass medicine bottle
1 a wall made of stone
2 a centre where information is given to tourists
3 a towel you use after having a bath
4 clothes for working in
5 a block of offices in the centre of a city
6 a graph showing sales
7 a card that gives you credit
8 a race for horses
9 the Director of Marketing
10 a tour by bicycle at the end of the week

Test N: Nouns and agreement

A

Some of these sentences are correct, and some have a word which should not be there. If the sentence is correct, put a tick (✓). If it is incorrect, cross the unnecessary word out of the sentence and write it in the space.

▶ Would you like a piece of chocolate? .....✓.....................
▶ I like ~~a~~ classical music very much. .....a.....................
1 That's a wonderful news! ....
2 Do you own a computer? ....
3 I heard an interesting piece of information today. ....
4 I saw your friend playing a golf. ....
5 There's some luggage in the car. ....
6 I bought a carton of some milk. ....
7 The gates were made of an iron. ....
8 You need an experience to run a business like this. ....

B

Tessa is talking about her shopping trip. Write the missing words. Use one word only in each space.

I spent (▶) _some_ time looking round the shops in Oxford Street yesterday. I spent far too (1) .... money, of course. I bought some (2) .... : three dresses, a sweater, a blouse, two (3) .... of trousers and a skirt. I enjoyed myself – it was great (4) .... The skirt is really nice. A hundred pounds (5) .... quite expensive, but I couldn't resist it. Anyway, it was reduced from a hundred and twenty pounds, so I made a (6) .... of twenty pounds. One of the dresses (7) .... fit, I've discovered, but I can take it back next time I go. I had a wonderful time and bought all these lovely things. But it was very crowded. Everyone (8) .... rushing about. And the traffic (9) .... terrible. I usually have a coffee and a (10) .... of cake, but the cafés were all full, so I didn't bother.

C

Complete the second sentence so that it has a similar meaning to the first. Use the word in brackets.

▶ Could I have some bread, please? (piece)
  Could I have a piece of bread, please? ....

1 All the windows were broken. (every)
  ....

2 The money I earn isn't enough to live on. (earnings)
  ....

3 There were bits of paper everywhere. (litter)
  ....

4 We went to the hotel to get a meal. (food)
  ....

5 Judy bought some binoculars. (pair)
  ....

6 I need a new book of cheques. (cheque)
  ....

7 I'll have some orange juice, please. (glass)
  ....

8 The reporter needed some information. (two)
  ....

D

Each of these sentences has a mistake in it. Write the correct sentence.

▶ ~~Can you lend me some pen to write this cheque?~~
Can you lend me a pen to write this cheque? ....

1 ~~We can't sit here because the grass are wet.~~
....

2 ~~Do you want a butter on your bread?~~
....

3 ~~All my belonging was stolen.~~
....

4 ~~Do you have any informations about hotels?~~
....

5 ~~The police is questioning two men.~~
....

6 ~~Can we have two coffee, please?~~
....

7 ~~The news aren't very good, I'm afraid.~~
....

8 ~~I just want to go into this shoes shop.~~
....

9 ~~It's only a short travel by train.~~
....

E

Choose the correct form.

▶ The house is built of stone/~~a stone~~.
1 Each team <u>wear/wears</u> a different colour.
2 Let me give you <u>an advice/a piece of advice</u>.
3 Everyone was watching <u>the football match/the match of football</u>.
4 We had to take our luggage through <u>customs/a customs</u>.
5 The band <u>is/are</u> proud of their success.
6 I haven't got <u>many/much</u> friends.
7 Three hours <u>is/are</u> long enough to look round the museum.
8 I wear <u>this glass/these glasses</u> when I go out.
9 My father had a job at the <u>steelwork/steelworks</u>.
10 We couldn't find <u>an/any</u> accommodation.
11 Do you eat <u>meat/a meat</u>?
12 The contents of the box <u>was/were</u> thrown away.
13 <u>Noise/A noise</u> woke me up in the middle of the night.
14 Cattle <u>was/were</u> driven hundreds of miles by the cowboys.
15 One of the windows <u>is/are</u> open.
16 What would it be like to travel at the speed of <u>light/a light</u>?
17 Is there a <u>sport club/sports club</u> near here?
18 E-mail is a relatively new <u>mean/means</u> of communication.
19 We make furniture out of many different <u>wood/woods</u>.
20 Someone <u>has/have</u> kidnapped the President!

83 A/an and the (1)

1 Introduction

Read this true story about an American tourist in Britain.

A man *from California was spending* *a month* *in Britain. One day he booked into* *a hotel* *in Cheltenham,* *a nice old town* *in* *the West* *of England. Then he went out to look around* *the place*. *But* *the man* *didn't return to* *the hotel*. *He disappeared, leaving* *a suitcase* *full of clothes behind.* *The police* *were called in, but they were unable to find out what had happened to* *the missing tourist*. *It was* *a mystery*. *But two weeks later* *the man* *walked into* *the police station* *in Cheltenham. He explained that he was very sorry, but while walking around* *the town*, *he had got lost. He had also forgotten* *the name* *of* *the hotel* *he had booked into. So he had decided to continue with his tour of* *the country* *and had gone to visit* *a friend* *in Scotland before returning to pick up* *the case* *he had left behind.*

A/an goes only with a singular noun. With a plural or an uncountable noun we use **some**.	The goes with both singular and plural nouns and with uncountable nouns.
He left ***a case***. (singular)	*He needed* ***the case***. (singular)
He left ***some cases***. (plural)	*He needed* ***the cases***. (plural)
He left ***some luggage***. (uncountable)	*He needed* ***the luggage***. (uncountable)

2 Use

When the story first mentions something, the noun has **a** or **an**.

A man *booked into* *a hotel* *in Cheltenham.*

These phrases are new information. We do not know which man or which hotel.
But when the same thing is mentioned again, the noun has **the**.

The man *didn't return to* *the hotel*..

These phrases are old information. Now we know which man and which hotel – the ones already mentioned earlier in the story. We use **the** when it is clear which one we mean.

A/AN	THE
Would you like to see ***a show***?	*Would you like to see* ***the show***?
(I don't say which show.)	(= the show we already mentioned)
The cyclist was hit by ***a car***.	*Whose is* ***the car*** *outside?*
(I don't say which car.)	('Outside' explains which car I mean.)
In the office ***a phone*** *was ringing.*	*I was in bed when* ***the phone*** *rang.*
(The office has lots of phones.)	(= the phone in my house)
Has Melanie got ***a garden***?	*She was at home in* ***the garden***.
(We do not know if there is one.)	(We know she has one.)
The train stopped at ***a station***.	*Turn left here for* ***the station***.
(We don't know which station.)	(= the station in this town)
We took ***a taxi***.	*We went in* ***the car***. (= my/our car)
We could hear ***a noise***.	*We could hear* ***the noise*** *of a party.*
I wrote the number on ***an envelope***.	*I wrote it on* ***the back*** *of an envelope.*

3 A man/he and the man/someone

We use **a/an** + noun or **someone/something** when we aren't saying which one.	We use **the** + noun or **he/she/it** when we know which one.
A man/Someone *booked into a hotel.*	*The man/He* *didn't return to the hotel.*
He left *a case/something* *behind.*	*The case/It* *contained clothes.*

Practice

A The use of a/an and the (1–3)

Complete this true story. Put in *a/an* or *the*.

(▶) A..... man decided to rob (1) .... bank in the town where he lived. He walked into
(2) .... bank and handed (3) .... note to one of (4) .... cashiers.
(5) .... cashier read (6) .... note, which told her to give (7) .... man some
money. Afraid that he might have (8) .... gun, she did as she was told. (9) .... man
then walked out of (10) .... building, leaving (11) .... note behind. However, he had
no time to spend (12) .... money because he was arrested (13) .... same day. He
had made (14) .... mistake. He had written (15) .... note on (16) .... back of
(17) .... envelope. And on (18) .... other side of (19) .... envelope was his
name and address. This clue was quite enough for (20) .... detectives on the case.

B A man/he and the man/someone (3)

Replace the sentences which contain an <u>underlined</u> word. Use *a/an* or *the* with the word in brackets.

▶   We didn't have much time for lunch. David made <u>something</u> for us. (omelette)
    David made an omelette for us.

1   They ran the race before they held the long jump. Matthew won <u>it</u> easily. (race)
    ....

2   The driver turned left. Suddenly <u>someone</u> ran into the road. (child)
    ....

3   Vicky was lying on the sofa. She was watching <u>something</u> on television. (film)
    ....

4   I had to take a train and then a bus. <u>It</u> was half an hour late. (bus)
    ....

5   A shoplifter tried to steal some clothes. The camera videoed <u>her</u>. (thief)
    ....

C The use of a/an and the (1–3)

Complete the conversations. Put in *a/an* or *the*.

▶   Laura: Look outside. The... sky is getting very dark.
    Trevor: I hope there isn't going to be ..a.... storm.
1   Mike: I'm going out for .... walk. Have you seen my shoes?
    Harriet: Yes, they're on .... floor in .... kitchen.
2   Melanie: Would you like .... tomato? There's one in .... fridge.
    David: Oh, yes, please. I'll make myself .... cheese and tomato sandwich.
3   Sarah: If you're going into .... city centre, can you post these letters for me?
    Mark: Yes, I'll take them to .... main post office.
4   Rita: I've got .... problem with my phone bill. Can I see someone about it?
    Receptionist: Yes, go to .... fifth floor. .... lift is along the corridor.
5   Tom: I didn't know Melanie had .... dog.
    David: It isn't hers. She's just taking it for a walk while .... owner is away.
6   Vicky: I've got .... headache. I've had it all day.
    Rachel: Why don't you go to .... health centre? It's open until six.
7   Andrew: Guess what. I found .... £50 note on the pavement this morning.
    Jessica: You really ought to take it to .... police station, you know.

84 A/an and the (2)

1 Introduction

We use **a/an** and **the** when we aren't saying which one, and we use **the** when we know which one.
> *A tourist arrived in Cheltenham to look around the town.*

Look again at the story and the examples in Unit 83.

2 The sun, etc.

When there is only one of the things we are talking about, we use **the**.
> *The sun was going down.   The government is unpopular.*
> *A drive in the country would be nice.   We shouldn't pollute the environment.*

Normally there is only one sun or one government in the context.
We mean the government of our country and the sun in our solar system.

We normally say: **the country(side), the earth, the environment, the government, the moon, the ozone layer, the Prime Minister, the sea(side), the sky, the sun, the weather**

We also use **the** with **cinema, theatre** and **(news)paper**.
> *Do you often go to the cinema?   I read about the accident in the paper.*

Note that we say **a/the police officer** but **the police**.
> *A police officer came to the hotel.* NOT ~~A police came to the hotel.~~
> *The police came to the hotel.* (= one or more police officers)

3 A nice day, etc.

A phrase which describes something has **a/an**.
> *It was a lovely day.   Cheltenham is a nice old town.*
> *It's a big hotel.   This is a better photo.*

But we use **the** with a superlative.
> *It's the biggest hotel in town.   This is the best photo.*

We also use **a/an** to classify something, to say what kind of thing it is.
> *The play was a comedy.   The man's disappearance was a mystery.*

We use **a/an** to say what someone's job is.
> *My sister is a secretary.   Nick is a car salesman.*

4 A or an?

The choice of **a** or **an** and the pronunciation of **the** depend on the next sound.

a /ə/ or *the* /ðə/ + consonant sound			*an* /ən/ or *the* /ði/ + vowel sound		
a cup	/k/	*the* /ðə/ cup	*an* aspirin	/æ/	*the* /ði/ aspirin
a poster	/p/	*the* /ðə/ poster	*an* egg	/e/	*the* /ði/ egg
a shop	/ʃ/	etc.	*an* Indian	/ɪ/	etc.
a boiled egg	/b/		*an* old photo	/əʊ/	
a record	/r/		*an* umbrella	/ʌ/	

It is the sound of the next word that matters, not the spelling.

a one-way street	/w/	*an* open door	/əʊ/
a uniform	/j/	*an* uncle	/ʌ/
a holiday	/h/	*an* hour	/aʊ/
a U-turn	/j/	*an* MP	/e/

A The sun, etc. (1–2)

Complete these sentences about pollution and the environment. Put in *a/an* or *the*.

▶ There was .a..... programme on television about dangers to .the.... environment.

1 There was also .... article about pollution in .... paper.

2 .... ozone layer will continue to disappear if we don't find .... way to stop it.

3 .... world's weather is changing. Pollution is having .... effect on our climate.

4 Last week .... oil tanker spilled oil into .... sea, damaging wildlife.

5 Some professors have signed .... letter of protest and have sent it to .... government.

6 If .... earth was .... human being, it would be in hospital.

B The use of **a/an** and **the** (1–3)

Complete the conversations. Put in *a/an* or *the*.

▶ David: How was your trip to .the.... coast?

  Trevor: Wonderful. The..... sun shone all day. We had a great time.

1 Henry: Would you like .... cigarette?

  Nick: No, thanks. I've given up smoking. It's .... bad habit.

2 Sarah: What's your brother doing now? Has he got .... good job?

  Laura: Yes, he's .... soldier. He's in .... army. He loves it. It's .... great life, he says.

3 Rita: I went to see Doctor Pascoe yesterday. She's .... best doctor I've ever had.

  Harriet: She's very nice, isn't she? You couldn't meet .... nicer person.

4 Rachel: You were .... long time at .... supermarket.

  Vicky: Yes, I know. There was .... enormous queue. I was thinking of complaining to .... manager.

5 Mark: Why were you late for your meeting?

  Sarah: Well, first I had to go to .... hotel I'd booked into. I took .... taxi from .... airport, and .... driver got completely lost. It was .... terrible nuisance. .... man was .... complete idiot.

6 Matthew: Is this .... book you were telling me about?

  Emma: Yes, it's .... really interesting story.

  Matthew: What did you say it's about?

  Emma: I knew you weren't listening to me. It's .... science fiction story. It's about .... beginning of .... universe.

C A or an? (4)

Put in the abbreviations with *a* or *an*.

▶ a Personal Assistant   a PA ....

▶ a National Broadcasting Company reporter   an NBC reporter ....

1 a Disc Jockey   ....

2 a Very Important Person   ....

3 an Irish Republican Army member   ....

4 a Personal Computer   ....

5 a Los Angeles suburb   ....

6 an Unidentified Flying Object   ....

7 an Annual General Meeting   ....

8 a Member of Parliament   ....

85 A/an, one and some

1 A/an and some

Look at this example.

> Trevor has found **some money** in his old trousers.
> There's **a note** and **some coins**.

We use **a/an** with a singular noun and **some** with a plural or an uncountable noun (see 4).

A + singular noun: **a note**
Some + plural noun: **some coins**
Some + uncountable noun: **some money**

2 A/an and one

A/an and **one** both refer to one thing. Using **one** puts more emphasis on the number.

> Henry gave the taxi driver **a note**. (not a coin)
> Henry gave the taxi driver **one note**. (not two)

We use **one** (not **a/an**) when we mean one of a larger number.

> **One question/One of the questions in the exam** was more difficult than the others.
> The team wasn't at full strength. **One player/One of the players** was injured.

3 A dog = all dogs

We often use a plural noun on its own to express a general meaning (see Unit 86).

> **Dogs** make wonderful pets.   **Oranges** contain vitamin C.

Here **dogs** means 'all dogs, dogs in general'.

These sentences with **a/an** express the same general meaning.

> **A dog** makes a wonderful pet.   **An orange** contains vitamin C.
> **A butcher** is someone who sells meat.   **A kitten** is a baby cat.

A dog here is less usual than the structure with **dogs**, but we often use **a/an** when explaining the meaning of a word, e.g. **a butcher**.

4 Some

Some with a plural noun means 'a number of', and **some** with an uncountable noun means 'an amount of'.

> Claire took **some photos**.   We went out with **some friends**.
> Henry bought **some flowers**.   I had **some chips** with my steak.
> Can you lend me **some money**?   Andrew is doing **some work**.
> Let's play **some music**.   There's **some milk** in the fridge.

Claire took some photos means that she took a number of photos, although we may not know the exact number.

We do not use **some** when we are describing something or saying what kind of thing it is.

> Vicky has **blue eyes**.   Is this **salt or sugar**?
> These are **marvellous photos**.   Those people are **tourists**.

Compare these sentences.

> I had **some chips** with my steak. (a number of chips)
> I had **chips** with my steak. (chips, not potatoes or rice)

▷ 76 Countable and uncountable nouns   ▷ 83–4 A/an and the
▷ 94 Some and any   ▷ 96 All, most and some

Practice

A A/an and some (1)

Paul has painted some pictures for a competition. Say what is in the pictures.
Use *a* or *some* with these words: *birds*, *cat*, *fish*, *flowers*, *fruit*, *luggage*, *people*

▶ ..some people......
▶ .a fish..............
1 ....
2 ....
3 ....
4 ....
5 ....

B A/an and one (2)

Put in *a/an* or *one*.

▶ Have you only got ..one.......... bedroom? I thought you had two.
1 Melanie wanted something to drink. She was looking for .... café.
2 It was Sunday. .... shop was open, but all the others were closed.
3 .... of these photos is of you. Would you like it?
4 Shall I take .... photo of you two together?

C A dog = all dogs (3)

Match each word with the right explanation and write sentences with *a/an*.

carrot	line of people	▶	A carrot is a vegetable...
violin	book of maps	1	....
queue	vegetable	2	....
atlas	tool for digging	3	....
spade	musical instrument	4	....

D Some (4)

What would you say in these situations? Use a noun and decide if you need *some* or not.

▶ You and your friend would like a game of cards, but neither of you has a pack.
   We need .some cards.......... .
▶ You are describing Rachel to someone. Rachel's hair is dark.
   Rachel has .dark hair.......... .
1 You are eating nuts. Offer them to your friend.
   Would you like ....?
2 You want a drink of mineral water. There's a jug on the table, but you don't know what's in it.
   Is there .... in this jug?
3 You've come home from a shopping trip with a few clothes. Tell your friend.
   I've bought ....
4 You are eating some bread that Melanie baked. It's lovely.
   Melanie, this is ....
5 The two women who live next door to you are both studying at the university.
   Tell your visitor. The women next door are ....

86 Cars or the cars?

1 Introduction

I like **ice hockey**. It's my favourite sport. And I like **old cars**. I love driving them.

I like **music**, classical music, I mean. And I love **parties**, of course.

We can use a plural noun (e.g. **cars**, **parties**) or an uncountable noun (e.g. **ice hockey**, **music**) without **the**. *I love parties* means that I love all parties, parties in general.

2 General and specific meanings

GENERAL	SPECIFIC
A plural noun or an uncountable noun on its own has a general meaning.	**The** + plural noun or uncountable noun has a specific meaning.
Cars are expensive to buy.	*The cars had both broken down.*
Elephants are intelligent animals.	*We saw the elephants at the zoo.*
I don't understand computers.	*The computers crashed at work today.*
(= all computers, computers in general)	(= the specific computers at my workplace)
You always need money.	*Laura put the money in her purse.*
Glass is made from sand.	*David swept up the broken glass.*
I'm quite fond of curry.	*The curry was delicious, thank you.*
Natasha is studying music.	*The music was too loud.* (= the music at a
(= all music, music in general)	specific time, at a party for example)

A phrase or clause after the noun often shows that it is specific.
> *Look at **the oil on your sweater**.*   ***The apples you gave me** were nice.*

But the nouns in these sentences have a general meaning.
> *I hate **people who never say hello**.*   ***Life in the old days** was hard.*

Life in the old days is still a general idea, not a specific life.

A phrase with **of** usually takes **the**. Compare these two structures.
> *a book on **Irish history**   a book on **the history of Ireland***

3 Special uses of **the**

We use **the** + singular noun to make general statements about animals and about inventions and discoveries.
> ***The tiger** can swim.*   ***The fly** is a common insect.*
> *Who invented **the camera**?*   ***The electron** is a part of every atom.*

Here **the tiger** means all tigers, tigers in general. We use this structure mainly in written English. In speech, *Tigers can swim* is more usual.

We also use **the** with musical instruments. (But for American English see page 379.)
> *Natasha can play **the piano**, **the violin** and **the clarinet**.*

We do not use **the** with sports.
> *Shall we play **tennis**?* NOT ~~*Shall we play the tennis?*~~

Note that we *listen to the radio* but normally *watch television*.

Practice

A He likes golf (1)

Look at the pictures and say what people like. Use these objects: *art*, *chemistry*, *chips*, *dogs*, *golf*

▶ He likes golf. ....
1 .... 3 ....
2 .... 4 ....

B General and specific meanings (2)

Complete the conversations. Put in the nouns and decide if you need *the*.

▶ Tom: Did you see ..the football.. (football) on television last night?
Melanie: No, I hate ..football.. (football). I was watching ..the news.. (news) on the other channel.
1 Rachel: Did your family have a dog when you were younger?
Vicky: No, thank goodness. I'm afraid of .... (dogs). I didn't
like .... (dogs) that were running around in the park
yesterday. I was afraid they were going to attack me.
2 Melanie: You shouldn't drive so much, Mark. You know that ....
(cars) cause .... (pollution), don't you?
Mark: Yes, but .... (cars) these days are cleaner than they
used to be. Isn't it .... (aeroplanes) that are mainly
responsible for .... (pollution) of the atmosphere?
3 Melanie: I've put some bread out in the garden for .... (birds).
Tom: You like .... (birds), don't you?
Melanie: Yes, I do. I love .... (wildlife), in fact. I'd much rather
live in the country if I could.
4 Laura: You're always reading books about .... (history), aren't
you?
Harriet: It was always my favourite subject. Do you know anything
about .... (history) of this area?
Laura: No, but if you like looking round .... (museums) and
.... (old buildings), we could find out about it together.

C Special uses of the (3)

Put in the correct noun and decide if you need *the*.
Use these nouns: *atom*, *football*, *guitar*, *radio*, *telescope*, *television*

▶ I was listening to a phone-in on ..the radio.......... .
1 Rutherford split .... in 1911.
2 Tom and his friends played .... in the park.
3 Mike is quite musical. He can play ....
4 The children spend a lot of time watching ....
5 Galileo developed .... for use in astronomy.

NOUNS AND ARTICLES • PAGE 203

87 Prison, school, bed, etc.

1 Prison or the prison?

Compare these situations.

*This man is in **prison**. He went to **prison** two years ago.*
We do not use **the** when we are talking about being **in prison** as a prisoner.

*The young woman is in **the prison**. She has gone to **the prison** to visit her father.*
We use **the** when we mean the prison as a specific building. The young woman is **in the prison** as a visitor.

Here are some examples with other buildings.

__School__ is over at half past three.
(= school activities)
*Vicky is at **college**.*
(She is a student there.)
*David is in **hospital**.*
(He is a patient.)
*Melanie is going to **church**.*
(She is going to a service.)

__The school__ is a mile from here.
(= the school building)
*The meeting was at **the college**.*

*Melanie waited in **the hospital** for news.*

*We wanted to look round **the church**, but it was locked.*

We can also use **jail** and **university** in this way. But we do not leave out **the** before other nouns for buildings, e.g. **the cinema, the factory, the house, the library, the office, the pub, the shop, the station.**

2 Bed, home, etc.

Here are some phrases with other nouns.

bed:	*in bed, go to bed* (to rest or sleep)	But *sit on **the** bed, make **the** bed*
home:	*at home, go home, come home, leave home*	But *in **the** house, to **the** house, in **the** home*
sea:	*at sea* (= sailing) *go to sea* (as a sailor)	But *on **the** sea, by **the** sea, at/to **the** seaside, on/to **the** coast*
town:	*in town, go into town, leave town*	But ***the** town centre, **the** city, **the** village*
work:	*at work, go to work, leave work*	But ***the** office, **the** factory*

▷ page 379 American English

A Prison or the prison? (1)

Put in the words in brackets. Decide if you need *the*.

▶ The four members of the gang were sent to .prison...... (prison). Their wives drove together to the..prison. (prison) every week to visit their husbands.

1 Not many people go to .... (church) regularly nowadays. I saw some tourists walking to .... (church) last week, but they only wanted to take photos of it.

2 A group of people came out of .... (cinema), crossed the road and went into .... (pub).

3 When my father was ill and had to go to .... (hospital), my sister went with him in the ambulance. She's a doctor, and she works at .... (hospital).

4 Mark has always known what he wanted to do in life. After leaving .... (school), he took a course in business studies at .... (college).

B Prison, school, etc. (1–2)

Complete this paragraph from a magazine article about Melissa Livingstone.
Put in the words with or without *the*.

Today Melissa Livingstone is a popular actress and star of the TV soap opera 'Round the Corner'. But as a child she was very unhappy. She didn't do well at (▶) .school........ (school) , and she never went to (1) .... (college). Her greatest pleasure was going to (2) ....
(cinema). Her family lived in an unattractive town and their home was next to (3) ....
(station). Melissa's father, Tom, was a sailor, and he spent months at (4) .... (sea).
He was hardly ever at (5) .... (home) and when he was, he didn't do very much.
Sometimes he spent all day in (6) .... (bed). Melissa's mother, Susan, had to get up at five o'clock every day to go to (7) .... (work). When Tom lost his job he stole a gold cup from (8) .... (church) Susan used to go to. He had to go to
(9) .... (prison) for a year. Melissa's mother was horrified at the shame he had brought on the family.

C Prison, school, etc. (1–2)

Complete the sentences. Use *in*, *at* or *to* and these words:
bed, church, college, factory, home, hospital, library, prison, shop, town, work
Decide if you need *the*.

▶ We'll eat out tonight. I'll meet you .in .town............ later.

▶ This sweater was cheap. I bought it .at .the .shop.... by the railway station.

1 The weather was awful. We stayed .... all weekend.

2 Melanie had an early night last night. She was .... at ten.

3 Emma's friend has just had a baby. Emma is going .... to visit her.

4 Vicky's parents are religious. They go .... every Sunday.

5 Laura doesn't like her job. She just goes .... to earn some money.

6 I've read these books. I'm taking them back ....

7 The man who did the robbery is no longer .... He was let out last month.

8 Jessica is a student. She's ....

9 It's very quiet .... when they've turned all the machines off.

88 On Friday, for lunch, etc.

1 Introduction

Henry: *Don't forget we're meeting on **Friday** for **lunch**.*
Sarah: *Of course I haven't forgotten.*
But remind me where we're eating.
Henry: *The Riverside Restaurant. You've been there before.*
*Claire was with us. It was **the Friday** before she*
*went to Australia. We had **a** good **lunch**.*

Phrases of time are usually without **a/an** or **the**.	But we use **a/an** or **the** if there is a phrase or clause after **Friday**, **lunch**, etc.
*We're meeting on **Friday** for **lunch**.*	*It was **the Friday** before she went to Australia.* We normally use **a/an** or **the** if there is an adjective. *We had **a** good **lunch**.*

2 Years, seasons and months

*I was born in **1974**.* *We play cricket **in summer/in the summer**.* ***Winter** always depresses me.* *I start the course in **September**.*	*That was **the year** I was born.* *It was **the winter** of 1995 when things started to go wrong for the company.*

3 Special times

*We go away at **Christmas**.* ***Easter** is early this year.* *I'll be home for **Thanksgiving**.*	*We had **a** wonderful **Christmas**.* *I started work here **the Easter** before last.*

4 Days of the week

*Yes, **Thursday** will be convenient.* *I'll see you on **Tuesday** evening.*	*The storm was on **the Thursday** of that week.* *We went surfing at **the weekend**.*

5 Parts of the day and night

*I can't sleep at **night**.* *I prefer to travel by **day**/by **night**.* *I must get to bed before **midnight**.* *We were on the beach at **sunset**.* *I hope to get there before **dark**.*	*It's warmer in/during **the day**.* *Someone got up in/during **the night**.* *We're meeting in **the morning**.* *They arrived at the hotel in **the evening**.* *It was **a** beautiful **sunset**.* *I couldn't see in **the dark**.*

6 Meals

*I'll see you at **breakfast**.* *We have **supper** at about eight.* *I'm going out after **lunch**.*	*We had **a** quick **breakfast**.* ***The supper** David cooked was excellent.* ***The meal** was very nice.* *We'll need **an** evening **meal**.*

Practice

A On Friday, etc. (2–5)

Complete the conversations. Put in the words and use *a/an* or *the* if you need to.

▶ Rachel: Is it the pop festival on .Friday........... (Friday)?
 Vicky: I think it's .the. .Friday...... (Friday) after that.

1 Henry: Will you be in America for .... (Thanksgiving)?
 Claire: Oh no. That's in .... (November), isn't it?

2 Nick: Are you doing anything at .... (weekend)?
 Tom: Well, I'm going to the match on .... (Saturday), of course.

3 Ilona: Does it snow here at .... (Christmas)?
 Emma: Not often. We haven't had .... (white Christmas) for years.

4 Nick: How long have you lived here?
 Harriet: We came here in .... (summer) of ....
 (1997).

5 Laura: I'd like to look round the castle in .... (afternoon).
 Trevor: Well, it's just a ruin. The building dates from .... (year) 900.

6 Mark: I like driving at .... (night) when the roads are quiet.
 Trevor: Oh, I don't like driving in .... (dark). I'd much rather travel
 during .... (day).

B A/an or the with meals (6)

Laura is talking about the food she and Trevor had on holiday.
Put in the words and use *a/an* or *the* if you need to.

(▶) The .meals......... (meals) we had weren't very good. We had (1) ....
(breakfast) in the hotel, and that wasn't too bad. We usually went out for (2) ....
(lunch) because (3) .... (lunch) they served in the hotel was always the
same. And (4) .... (dinner) we had at the hotel on our first evening was
pretty awful, so we tried a few restaurants. On our last evening we had (5) ....
(marvellous meal) in a Chinese restaurant. I wish we'd discovered the place a bit sooner.

C On Friday, for lunch, etc. (1–6)

Put in the words. Decide if you need to use *the*.

Claire: Hello, Henry. Come in.
Henry: Oh, sorry. You're having (▶) lunch........ (lunch).
Claire: No, this is (1) .... (breakfast). I had a late night. It was long after
 (2) .... (midnight) when I got in.
Henry: Someone told me you're going away after (3) .... (Christmas).
Claire: Yes, I'm going to the Seychelles on (4) .... (Wednesday).
Henry: What a life you lead, Claire. What time do you leave for the airport?
Claire: Oh, in (5) .... (morning) some time. About ten. It's cheaper to fly at
 (6) .... (night), but I decided it would be easier during
 (7) .... (day).
Henry: I can drive you to the airport. I'm usually free on (8) .... (Wednesday)
 mornings. I'd like to see you off.
Claire: That's sweet of you Henry, but I can take a taxi.
Henry: I'll just check in my diary that it isn't (9) .... (Wednesday) of our next
 board meeting. No, it's OK. I can do it. And when will you be back?
Claire: At the beginning of (10) .... (February). The second, I think.

89 Quite a, such a, what a, etc.

1 Introduction

After **quite**, **such** and **what** we can use a phrase with a/an, e.g. *a game*. There is often an adjective as well, e.g. *such a **good** team*.

> **What a** great win that was for United. They're **such a** good team.

> Yes, it was **quite a** game, wasn't it?

2 Very, quite, rather, etc.

A/an goes before **very**, **fairly**, **really**, etc.
> *It's **a very** old house.   It's **a fairly** long walk.*
> *I made **a really** stupid mistake.*

But a/an usually goes after **quite**.
> *It's **quite an** old house.   There was **quite a** crowd .*

A/an can go either before or after **rather**.
> *It's **a rather** old house.* OR *It's **rather an** old house.*

We can also use **very**, **quite**, **rather**, etc. + adjective + plural or uncountable noun.
> *They're **very old houses**.   This is **quite nice coffee**.*

3 So and such a

SO	SUCH A/AN
The structure is **be** + **so** + adjective.	The structure is **such** + **a/an** (+ adjective) + noun.
*The test was **so easy**.*	*It was **such an easy test**.*
NOT *It was a so easy test.*	NOT *It was a such easy test.*
*The hill was **so steep**.*	*It was **such a steep hill**.*
*It's **so inconvenient** without a car.*	*It's **such a nuisance** without a car.*
	We can also use **such** + an adjective + a plural or uncountable noun.
*The weather is **so nice**.*	*We're having **such nice** weather.*
*Tom's jokes are **so awful**.*	*Tom tells **such awful** jokes.*

Note these sentences with **long**, **far**, **many/much** and **a lot of**.

*It's **so long** since I saw you.*	*It's **such a long time** since I saw you.*
*Why are we **so far** from the beach?*	*It's **such a long way** to the beach.*
*There were **so many** people.*	*There were **such a lot of** people.*
*You waste **so much** time.*	*You waste **such a lot of** time.*

We can use this structure with **so** ... (**that**) or **such** ... (**that**).

*Emma was **so angry** with Matthew (that) she threw a plate at him.*	*Vicky got **such a nice** welcome (that) she almost cried.*
*I was **so unlucky** you wouldn't believe it.*	*I had **such** bad luck you wouldn't believe it.*

4 What a

In an exclamation we can use **what a/an** with a singular noun and **what** with a plural or uncountable noun.

+ singular noun:	***What a** goal!*	***What a** good idea!*
+ plural noun:	***What** lovely flowers!*	***What** nice shoes you've got on!*
+ uncountable noun:	***What** rubbish!*	***What** fun we had!*

> ▷ 116 **Quite** and **rather**

Practice

A Very, quite, rather, so, etc. (2–3)

What do you say in these situations?

▶ You're telling someone about the show you saw. It was quite good.
You should go and see it. It's <u>quite a good show</u>.

▶ You are describing Harriet to someone who doesn't know her. She is fairly tall.
Well, Harriet is a <u>fairly tall woman</u>.

1 You're talking about the Savoy Hotel, which is very grand.
Yes, I know the Savoy. It's ....

2 You are talking about your journey. It was quite tiring.
I travelled a long way. It was ....

3 You are telling someone about Claire's flat. It's really big.
I've been to Claire's place. It's ....

4 You are telling a friend about your meal with Tom. It was quite nice.
We went to that new restaurant. We had ....

B So and such (3)

Complete the conversation. Put in *so* or *such*.

Sarah: Sorry I'm (▶) *so* late. We had (▶) *such* a lot to do at work.
Mark: You shouldn't do (1) .... much.
Sarah: The boss gets in (2) .... a panic about things. She makes (3) .... a big fuss.
Mark: Well, you shouldn't be (4) .... willing to work (5) .... long hours. No wonder
         you're (6) .... tired. You'll make yourself ill, you know.

C So ... that and such ... that (3)

Match the sentences and combine them using *so* or *such*.

▶ Sarah was late home.   All the tickets sold out.
▶ Mike hadn't cooked for a long time.   He wouldn't speak to anyone.
1 The piano was heavy.   <u>He'd almost forgotten how to.</u>
2 Tom was annoyed about United losing.   It kept all the neighbours awake.
3 The band was a big attraction.   <u>Mark had already gone to bed.</u>
4 Vicky had a lot of work to do.   Mike and Harriet couldn't move it.
5 The party made a lot of noise.   She was sure she'd never finish it.

▶ <u>Sarah was so late home that Mark had already gone to bed.</u>
▶ <u>Mike hadn't cooked for such a long time that he'd almost forgotten how to.</u>
1 ....
2 ....
3 ....
4 ....
5 ....

D What (4)

Put in *what* or *what a*.

▶ Come into the sitting-room. ~ Thank you. Oh, <u>what a</u> nice room!
1 Vicky believes in ghosts. ~ Oh, ... nonsense she talks!
2 Let's go for a midnight swim. ~ .... suggestion!
3 I think about you all the time, Emma. ~ .... lies you tell me, Matthew.

NOUNS AND ARTICLES • PAGE 209

90 Place names and the

1 Introduction

Man: *Could you tell me where **the Classic Cinema** is, please?*
Rachel: *Yes, it's in **Brook Street**. Go along here and take the second left.*

Whether a name has **the** depends on the kind of place it is – for example, a street (*Brook **Street***) or a cinema (***the** Classic **Cinema***), a lake (***Lake** Victoria*) or a sea (***the** North **Sea***).

Most place names do not have **the**.
  Europe   California   Melbourne
  *Brook **Street**   **Lake** Victoria*
	Some place names have **the** – for example, a name with the word **cinema** or **sea**.
	    *the Classic **Cinema** the North **Sea***

Whether we use **the** can also depend on the structure of the name.

We do not use **the** with a possessive ('s).
 	
  *at **Matilda's** Restaurant*
	We often use **the** in structures with **of**, with an adjective and with plural names.
	  With **of**: *the Avenue **of** the Americas*
	  With an adjective: ***the White** House*
	  With a plural: ***the Bahamas***

2 Continents, countries, islands, states and counties

Most are without **the**.
  *travelling through **Africa***
  *a holiday in **Portugal***
  *on **Jersey**   to **Rhode Island***
  *from **Florida**   in **Sussex***
	Words like **republic** and **kingdom** have **the**.
	  *the Irish **Republic***
	  *the United **Kingdom** (the UK)*
	Plural names also have **the**.
	  the Netherlands the USA
	  the Canary Islands

3 Regions

Regions ending with the name of a continent or country are without **the**.
  ***Central** Asia   **South** Wales*
  ***Western** Australia*
	Most other regions have **the**.
	  the West the Middle East
	  the Riviera the Midlands
	Phrases with **of** have **the**.
	  *the South **of** France*

4 Hills and mountains

Most are without **the**.
  *She climbed (**Mount**) **Everest**.*
  *down **North Hill***
	Hill ranges and mountain ranges have **the**.
	  *skiing in **the Alps***
	  *over **the Rockies***

5 Lakes, oceans, seas, rivers and canals

Only lakes are without **the**.
  *near **Lake Michigan***
  *beside **Coniston Water***
	Seas, oceans, rivers and canals have **the**.
	  *the Mediterranean (**Sea**)*
	  *across **the Atlantic** (Ocean)*
	  *the (**River**) Thames the Suez Canal*

6 Cities, towns, suburbs and villages

Most are without **the**.
*Harehills is a suburb of **Leeds**.*
Houston is west of New Orleans.
We live in North London.

Exceptions are **The Hague** and **The Bronx**.
Note also **the West End** (*of London*).

7 Roads, streets, squares and parks

Most are without **the**.
along Morden Road
in Church Street
on Fifth Avenue
near Berkeley Square
through Central Park

There are a few exceptions.
the High Street   The Avenue
The Strand   The Mall
Main roads and numbered roads have **the**.
the Bath road (= the road to Bath)
the A5   the M6 (*motorway*)

8 Bridges

Most are without **the**.
over Tower Bridge
on Brooklyn Bridge

But there are many exceptions.
across the Golden Gate Bridge
the Severn Bridge (= the bridge over
the River Severn)

9 Stations and airports; important buildings

We do not use **the** with most stations and
airports; with religious, educational and official
buildings or with palaces and houses.
to Waterloo (*Station*)
at Orly (*Airport*)
near St Mary's Church
Merton College   Norwich Museum
Lambeth Palace   Ashdown House

Exceptions are names with **of** or with a noun
(*science*) or adjective (*open*).
at the University of York
in the Palace of Westminster
the Science Museum
the Open University
past the White House

10 Theatres, cinemas, hotels, galleries and centres

A possessive form ('s) is without **the**.
St Martin's (*Theatre*)
at Durrant's (*Hotel*)
In the US, names with **center** are without **the**.
near Lincoln Center

But usually theatres, cinemas, etc. have **the**.
at the Globe (*Theatre*)
the Plaza (*Cinema*)
outside the Dorchester (*Hotel*)
in the Tate (*Gallery*)
the Brunel shopping centre

11 Shops and restaurants

Most shops and restaurants are without **the**.
shopping at Bloomingdale's
at Matilda's Restaurant

Names with a noun (*body, studio*) often have **the**.
at the Body Shop
The Studio Café

Practice

A Place names and **the** (2–6)

How much do you know about geography? Put in these names: *Andes, Brussels, Irish Republic, Italy, Lake Michigan, River Nile, North, Pennsylvania, Tasmania, United Kingdom, West Indies.*
Decide if you need *the*.

▶ Harrisburg is the capital of .Pennsylvania............................... .

▶ Dublin is in .the..Irish..Republic.................... .

1 Chicago lies on the shore of ....

2 Sicily is a part of ....

3 .... are a mountain range in South America.

4 .... is England, Scotland, Wales and Northern Ireland.

5 .... is an island to the south of Australia.

6 Jamaica is an island in ....

7 .... flows through Egypt.

8 .... is the capital of Belgium.

9 Manchester is in .... of England.

B Roads, buildings, etc. (5–10)

Complete these sentences from a guide to London. Put in the words and decide if you need *the*.

▶ The train to Paris leaves from .Waterloo..Station.............. (Waterloo Station).

▶ .The..National..Theatre......... (National Theatre) is south of the river.

1 You can take a trip by boat along .... (Thames).

2 The Serpentine is a lake in .... (Hyde Park).

3 You can get to .... (Heathrow Airport) by underground.

4 Nelson's Column is in .... (Trafalgar Square).

5 Walk a little way along .... (Westminster Bridge).

6 From there you get a view of .... (Houses of Parliament).

7 The Queen lives at .... (Buckingham Palace).

8 Earl's Court is in .... (West London).

9 .... (M1 motorway) goes north from London.

10 .... (Ritz) is a very elegant hotel.

C Roads, buildings, etc. (6–11)

Complete the conversation. Put in the words and decide if you need *the*.

Sarah: We've just been to (▶) .the..States............. (States) – to (1) ....
(New York).

Claire: Oh, really? I was there at Christmas. Were you on holiday?

Sarah: Yes, and we really needed a break. It was wonderful. We saw
(2) .... (Statue of Liberty), and we walked in
(3) .... (Central Park). We did all the sights. We spent a
day in (4) .... (Metropolitan
Museum of Art). And we walked along (5) .... (Broadway)
and around (6) .... (Macy's) department store.

Claire: Where did you stay?

Sarah: In a small hotel near (7) .... (Washington Square), not far from
(8) .... (New York University).

Claire: Last time I was there I stayed at (9) .... (Paramount). It's a nice
hotel close to (10) .... (Broadway).

D Roads, buildings, etc. (9–10)

A woman is asking Trevor the way. Put in the words and decide if you need *the*.

Woman: Excuse me, can you tell me the way to (▶) Millthorpe Station (Millthorpe Station)?

Trevor: Yes, go along here and turn left by (1) .... (Little Theatre) opposite a building called (2) .... (Kingston House). The road is (3) .... (Wood Lane). Go along there, straight across (4) .... (High Street), past (5) .... (Royal Hotel), and you'll see the station in front of you.

Woman: Thank you very much.

E Roads, buildings, etc. (7–11)

Look at the addresses and write the sentences.

Useful addresses for visitors to Seaport	
Seaport Bus Station, Queen's Road	King Edward College, College Road
Grand Theatre, George Street	St John's Church, South Street
Odeon Cinema, The Avenue	Webster's department store, High Street
Clarendon Art Gallery, Newton Lane	Bristol Hotel, Westville Way

▶ Seaport Bus Station is in Queen's Road.

1 The Grand Theatre ....

2 ....

3 ....

4 ....

5 ....

6 ....

7 ....

F Place names and *the* (2–11)

Write the headlines of the articles in this month's edition of 'Holiday', a travel magazine.

▶ walk / along / Princes Street — A walk along Princes Street

▶ holiday / in / Bahamas — A holiday in the Bahamas

1 day / at / Blenheim Palace ....

2 train journey / in / North Wales ....

3 tour / of / White House ....

4 beach / on / Riviera ....

5 shopping trip / to / Harrods ....

6 small town / in / France ....

7 trip / across / Severn Bridge ....

8 walk / around / Lake Windermere ....

9 visit / to / Tower Bridge ....

10 journey / across / Rockies ....

11 look / around / National Gallery ....

12 boat trip / along / Oxford Canal ....

Test O: A/an and the

A

Complete the story about the theft of a river barge. Put in _a, an, one_ or _the_.

This is (▶) .a.. true story about (1) .... man who chose (2) .... worst possible time for his crime. It happened in London in (3) .... summer of 1972. (4) .... man stole a barge on (5) .... River Thames (in case you don't know, (6) .... barge is a river boat used for carrying goods). (7) .... owner of (8) .... barge soon discovered that it was missing and immediately informed (9) .... police so that they could look for it. Normally (10) .... river is quite (11) .... busy place, and it would be difficult to find what you were looking for. On this day, however, there was (12) .... dock strike, and so there was only (13) .... barge on (14) .... river. (15) .... thief was quickly found and arrested.

B

Decide which word or words are correct.

▶ I think that's .an..awful.. thing to say.
a) a awful   b) an awful   c) awful

1 Judy goes to .... on the bus.
a) work   b) a work   c) the work

2 I don't know what to do. It's .... problem.
a) quite difficult   b) a quite difficult   c) quite a difficult

3 .... is my favourite sport.
a) Golf   b) A golf   c) The golf

4 .... starts at nine o'clock.
a) School   b) A school   c) The school.

5 We had .... time at the disco yesterday.
a) really nice   b) a really nice   c) really a nice

6 Nigel opened a drawer and took out ....
a) photos   b) a photos   c) some photos

7 Did you learn to play ....?
a) violin   b) a violin   c) the violin

8 We can finish the rest of the bread for ....
a) breakfast   b) a breakfast   c) the breakfast

9 While I was in hospital, they gave me ....
a) X-ray   b) a X-ray   c) an X-ray

10 I might listen to ....
a) radio   b) radios   c) the radio

11 We need to protect .... from pollution.
a) environment   b) some environment   c) the environment

12 Why do they always play .... music?
a) so terrible   b) such terrible   c) such a terrible

C

**Read the story about a silly mistake and decide if a word needs to go in the space.
If a word is missing, write the word. If no word is missing, write X.**

This is also (▶) .a.... true story. It shows how (▶) ..X.... plans can sometimes go wrong and how (1) .... people can make silly mistakes. This too happened quite (2) .... long time ago – in (3) .... 1979, in fact. The scene was (4) .... old people's home in

(5) .... small town in (6) .... north of England called (7) .... Otley. The owners of the home wanted to put (8) .... fence around it to make it more private. The work began soon after (9) .... Christmas when (10) .... workmen arrived in (11) .... lorry with planks of wood which they put up around the building. 'It was (12) .... very nice fence,' said (13) .... of the old people. But there was (14) .... problem. The workmen forgot to leave a gap for the lorry to drive out through. They had to come back the next day to knock down part of (15) .... fence. '(16) .... a silly mistake!' said another resident. 'It was (17) .... funny we had to laugh. In fact it was (18) .... most fun we've had for a long time.'

D

Some of these sentences are correct, and some have a word which should not be there. If the sentence is correct, put a tick (✓). If it is incorrect, cross the unnecessary word out of the sentence and write it in the space.

▶ The space capsule came down in the Pacific.   ✓ ....
▶ My new job starts in ~~the~~ April.   the ....
1 I was so tired I went to bed at nine.   ....
2 We had a very good lunch in the company canteen.   ....
3 The life just isn't fair sometimes.   ....
4 What the clever children you have!   ....
5 We went out and bought some pictures.   ....
6 Tessa was still working at the midnight.   ....
7 I drive past the hospital every morning.   ....
8 A one boy was much taller than all the others.   ....
9 It costs such a lot of money, you know.   ....
10 I'll meet you outside the National Gallery.   ....
11 Have you any idea who invented the fridge?   ....

E

Complete the conversation. Put in the words and decide if you need *a*, *an*, *some* or *the*.

Martin: I think we ought to book (▶) a holiday .... (holiday). Where shall we go?
Anna: What about (▶) Scotland .... (Scotland)?
I think Edinburgh is (1) .... (beautiful city). I love going there.
Martin: (2) .... (weather) might not be very good. We went there at
(3) .... (Easter), and it was freezing, remember.
Anna: We could have a walk along (4) .... (Princes Street) and up to the castle. And I wanted to go to (5) .... (Royal Scottish Museum), but we never found time.
Martin: Can't we go somewhere different?
Anna: We could spend some time in (6) .... (Highlands), I suppose.
Martin: When I go on holiday, I want to do something more relaxing than climbing
(7) .... (mountains). And I find it pretty boring.
Anna: How can you say such (8) .... (thing)?
Martin: Actually, I'd prefer somewhere warmer and by (9) .... (sea).
I think (10) .... (Corfu) would be nice. We might get
(11) .... (sunshine) there. I just want to lie on a beach.
Anna: Martin, you know I'm not at all keen on (12) ....
(beach holidays).

91 This, that, these and those

1 Introduction

> I'm just having a look at **this** printout. **These** figures aren't very good.

> **That** table is nice, isn't it?

> I don't like **those** chairs.

We use **this** and **these** for things near the speaker (**this** printout **here**). This goes with a singular or uncountable noun, e.g. **this report**. These goes with a plural noun, e.g. **these results**.

We use **that** and **those** for things further away (**that** table **there**). That goes with a singular or uncountable noun, e.g. **that furniture**. Those goes with a plural noun, e.g. **those curtains**.

We can leave out the noun if the meaning is clear.
> *I'm just having a look at **this**.*　　*That's nice, isn't it?*
> *Last month's figures were bad, but **these** are worse.*

2 Places and people

When we are in a place or a situation, we use **this** (not that) to refer to it.
> *There's a wonderful view from **this** office. Just come to the window.*
> ***This** party isn't much fun, is it? Shall we go home?*

We can use **this** to introduce people and **that** to identify people.
> *Jake, **this** is my friend Rita.*　　*That's Andrew over there.*

On the phone we can use **this** to say who we are and **this** or **that** to ask who the other person is.
> *Hello? **This** is Laura speaking. Who's **this/that**, please?*

3 Time

This/these can mean 'near in time' and that/those 'further away in time'.
> *I'm working as a tourist guide **this** summer. I'm pretty busy **these** days.*
> *Do you remember **that** summer we all went to Spain? **Those** were the days.*
> *I can't see you on the third of July. I'm on holiday **that** week.*

To refer back to something that has just happened or was just mentioned, we normally use **that**.
> *What was **that** noise? ~ I didn't hear anything.*
> *Jessica is on a diet. **That's** why she doesn't want to eat out with us.*
> *I've lost my key. ~ Well, **that's** a silly thing to do.*

To refer forward to something that is just going to happen or something that we are going to say, we use **this**.
> ***This** next programme should be quite interesting.*
> *I don't like to say **this**, but I'm not happy with the service here.*

> ▷ 13.4 this week, this year, etc.

Practice

A This, that, these and those (1)

Write each of the words (*this*, *that*, *these*, *those*) in the correct place.

	Near	Further away
Singular	this	
Plural		

B This, that, these and those (1)

Complete the sentences. Use *this*, *that*, *these* and *those*, and these nouns:
car, *dog*, *flowers*, *parcel*, *trees*

▶ That car ... has crashed.
1 Would you like ....? 　3 The house is behind ....
2 I must post .... 　　　4 Whose is ....?

C This, that, these and those (1–3)

Complete the conversations. Use *this*, *that*, *these* and *those*.

▶ Mark:　　　Are we going out ...this... evening?
　Sarah:　　 I can't really. I'll be working late at the office.
1 David:　　 I hear you've got a new flat.
　Rita:　　　 ....'s right. I've just moved in.
2 Mike:　　　What's the matter?
　Harriet:　　It's .... boots. They don't fit properly. They're hurting my feet.
3 Jessica:　 It's so boring here.
　Rachel:　　I know. Nothing ever happens in .... place.
4 Emma:　　 What's happened? You look terrible.
　Vicky:　　　You won't believe ...., but I've just seen a ghost.
5 Laura:　　 What kind of planes are ....?
　Trevor:　　 I don't know. They're too far away to see properly.
6 Matthew:　The match is three weeks from today.
　Daniel:　　Sorry, I won't be able to play for the team. I'll be away all .... week.
7 Mark:　　　Zedco. Can I help you?
　Alan:　　　 Hello. .... is Alan. Can I speak to Fiona, please?
8 Daniel:　　I've had .... bump on my head ever since someone threw a chair at me.
　Natasha:　Someone threw a chair at you? .... wasn't a very nice thing to do.
9 Mark:　　　................. seats aren't very comfortable, are they?
　Sarah:　　 No, I don't think I'll want to sit here very long.

92 My, your, etc. and mine, yours, etc.

1 Introduction

Mark: *Why have you brought **your** work home? We're going out.*
Sarah: *I'll do it later. Let's go now. Shall we take **my** car?*
Mark: *Well, I'd rather not take **mine**. I think there's something wrong with it.*

My, mine, your, etc. express possession and similar meanings. **My car** means the car belonging to me; **your work** means the work you are doing. **My** comes before a noun, e.g. **my car**. We use **mine** on its own.

	MY, YOUR, ETC.	MINE, YOURS, ETC.
First person singular:	*It's **my** car.*	*It's **mine**.*
Second person singular:	*Here's **your** coat.*	*Here's **yours**.*
Third person singular:	*That's **his** room.*	*That's **his**.*
	*It's **her** money.*	*It's **hers**.*
	*The dog's got **its** food.*	
First person plural:	*That's **our** table.*	*That's **ours**.*
Second person plural:	*Are these **your** tickets?*	*Are these **yours**?*
Third person plural:	*It's **their** camera.*	*It's **theirs**.*

2 Its and it's

We use **its** before a noun to express the idea of belonging.
   *The street is around here somewhere, but I've forgotten **its** name.*
It's is a short form of **it is** or **it has**.
   *I think **it's** time to go.* (= it is)   ***It's** got a lot colder today, hasn't it?* (= it has)

3 My, your with parts of the body and clothes

We normally use **my, your**, etc. with parts of the body and with someone's clothes.
   *Emma shook **her** head sadly.* NOT ~~Emma shook the head sadly.~~
   *Someone came up behind me and grabbed **my** arm.*
   *You must take off **your** shoes before you enter a mosque.*
But we usually use **the** in the following structure with a prepositional phrase.

	VERB	PERSON	PREPOSITIONAL PHRASE
Someone	*grabbed*	*me*	*by **the** arm.*
The stone	*hit*	*Mike*	*on **the** head.*

4 Own

We use **own** after **my, your**, etc. to say that something belongs to us and to no one else.
   *Rachel has got **her own** calculator. She doesn't borrow mine.* NOT ~~an own calculator~~
   *I don't share any more. I've got a flat of **my own**.* NOT ~~of mine own~~

5 A friend of mine

Look at these examples.
   *Tom is **a friend of mine**.* (= one of my friends) NOT ~~a friend of me~~
   *Rachel came to the party with **a cousin of hers**.* (= one of her cousins)
   *I borrowed **some magazines of yours**.* (= some of your magazines)
Note also 's in this example: *Rita is a friend of **Melanie's**.*

Practice

A My, your, etc. and mine, yours, etc. (1)

Complete the conversation. Put in the missing words.

Laura: Did you and (▶) ..your........ friends have a nice holiday?

Emma: Yes, it was wonderful. We had the best holiday of (1) .... lives. It didn't start very well, though. Daniel forgot to bring (2) .... passport.

Laura: Oh, dear. So what happened?

Emma: Well, luckily he doesn't live far from the airport. He rang (3) .... parents, and they brought the passport over in (4) .... car, just in time.

Laura: You remembered (5) ...., I hope.

Emma: Yes, I had (6) ...., even though I'm usually the one who forgets things. Actually Rachel thought for a minute that she'd lost (7) .... Luckily it was in (8) .... suitcase. Anyway, in the end we had a marvellous time.

B Its and it's (2)

Put in the correct form.

▶ Unfortunately, the town has lost .its........... only cinema.
▶ The meeting won't last long. I'll see you when .it's........ over.
1 You should return the book to .... owner immediately.
2 We'd like to go out for a walk, but .... raining.
3 I'm not buying this tablecloth because .... got a hole in it.
4 The board has decided that Zedco needs to improve .... image.

C Parts of the body and clothes (3)

Put in *my, your*, etc. or *the*.

▶ I was doing keep-fit exercises when I fell down and hurt .My........... leg.
▶ Matthew served, and the ball hit Daniel on .the.......... knee.
1 A wasp stung me on .... neck. It really hurt.
2 The mother put both .... arms around the child.
3 Aunt Joan kissed Emma on .... cheek.
4 The fans were all shouting at the top of .... voices.
5 Don't just stand there with .... hands in .... pockets.

D My own, a friend of mine, etc. (4–5)

Correct the sentences which have a mistake.

▶ We're lucky. ~~We've got an own garden.~~
   We've got our own garden. ....

1 I met some nice people. ~~Harriet introduced me to a friend of herself.~~
   ....

2 My friends swim every day. ~~They've got their only pool.~~
   ....

3 I enjoy rock-climbing. ~~It's a favourite hobby to me.~~
   ....

4 I hope Matthew will be here. ~~I've got some CDs from his.~~
   ....

5 I don't want to share. ~~I'd like my very room.~~
   ....

93 The possessive form and **of**

1 Form

We use the possessive of a noun in phrases like *the boy's name* and *Vicky's room*.
We form the possessive like this.

Singular noun:	**'s**	*boy* → *boy's*	*Vicky* → *Vicky's*
Plural noun ending in **s**:	**'**	*boys* → *boys'*	*tourists* → *tourists'*
Plural noun not ending in **s**:	**'s**	*men* → *men's*	*children* → *children's*

We can use the possessive form with another noun or on its own.
> I've met **Rachel's family**, but I haven't met **Vicky's**. (*Vicky's* = Vicky's family)

2 **The boy's name** or **the name of the boy?**

Compare these structures.

THE POSSESSIVE FORM	PHRASE WITH **OF**
the **boy's** name	the name **of the boy**
the **boys'** names	the names **of the boys**
the **men's** names	the names **of the men**

Sometimes we can use either the possessive (*the boy's name*) or a phrase with **of** (*the name of the boy*), but often only one is possible. We normally use the possessive with people and animals.
> **my friend's** house   **Claire's** idea   **Daniel's** brother   **our neighbour's** garden   **the dog's** owner
> **the policemen's** uniforms   **the women's** changing room   **the Parkers'** car

We normally use **of** with things, and not the possessive form.
> the side **of the house** NOT *the house's side*
> the result **of the match** NOT *the match's result*
> the day **of the meeting** NOT *the meeting's day*

But we use **of** with people when there is a long phrase.
> the house **of one of our teachers at college**
> the address **of those people we met in Spain**
> NOT *those people who we met in Spain's address*

We can use both structures for places and organizations.
> **London's** museums OR the museums **of London**
> **the earth's** atmosphere OR the atmosphere **of the earth**
> **the company's** future OR the future **of the company**
> **the government's** intentions OR the intentions **of the government**

3 The possessive of time

We can use the possessive to say 'when' or 'how long'.
> **last week's** concert   **today's** TV programmes   **yesterday's** news
> about **a month's** work   **a moment's** silence   **ten minutes'** walk

Note also:
> in **two months'** time (two months from now)
> **a week's** wages (wages for a week)

Practice

A The possessive form (1)

Write descriptions of the things in the photos. Use *boy*, *girl* and *children* and these words:
bike, cat, <u>dog</u>, skateboards, tent, trophies

►   the children's dog ....   3 ....
1   ....   4 ....
2   ....   5 ....

B The possessive form (1)

Laura is showing Melanie her photos. Put in the possessive form of the nouns.

Laura: This was taken in (►) ..my friend's........ (my friend) garden.
           It was (1) .... (the twins) birthday party.
           This is Kerry, (2) .... (Luke) girlfriend.
           And that's (3) .... (Jason) sister Emily.
Melanie: And who are these two?
Laura: That's (4) .... (Debbie) mother.
           She's talking to Monica Davis, (5) .... (her children) teacher.
           And that's (6) .... (the Lanskys) dog sitting on
           (7) .... (Olivia) foot.

C The boy's name or the name of the boy? (2)

Ed Buckman writes detective stories. Here are the titles of some of his stories.
Write the titles using either *of* or a possessive form (with *'s* or *s'*).

►   the mistake / the policeman   The Policeman's Mistake
►   the bottom / the bottle   The Bottom of the Bottle
1   the gun / Mr Hillman   ....
2   the smell / blood   ....
3   the car / the terrorist   ....
4   the middle / the night   ....
5   the death / someone important   ....
6   the money / the gangsters   ....

D The possessive of time (3)

Rewrite the <u>underlined</u> phrases using a possessive form.

►   <u>The prices this year</u> are even lower.   This year's prices
►   From here it's <u>a drive of two hours</u>.   a two hours' drive
1   I read about it in <u>the paper yesterday</u>.   ....
2   I just want <u>a rest for five minutes</u>.   ....
3   It's <u>the special offer for this month</u>.   ....
4   I'll see you <u>in a week</u>.   ....

94 Some and any

1 Basic use

Some and **any** go before a plural or uncountable noun (see Unit 85.1).
> *There was a bowl and **some** cornflakes on the table, but there wasn't **any** milk.*

We can also use **some** and **any** without a noun.
> *Trevor wanted **some** milk, but he couldn't find **any**.*

We normally use **some** in positive sentences and **any** in negative sentences or ones with a negative meaning.

POSITIVE	NEGATIVE
*There's **some** milk in the fridge.*	*I haven't **any** milk. (= I have no milk.)*
*I need **some** stamps. ~ There are **some*** *in the drawer.*	*I haven't got **any** stamps. Have you got **any**?*
*I met **some** interesting people last night.*	*I never meet **any** interesting people nowadays.*
*We'll have **some** fun at Disneyland.*	*We won't have **any** fun without you.*

We can also use **any** in a sentence with **if**.
> *If you have **any** problems, you can discuss them with your group leaders.*
> *I can answer **any** questions. (= <u>If</u> there are any questions, ...)*

In questions we can use either **some** or **any**, but **any** is more common.
We don't know whether the answer will be yes or no.
> *Have we got **any** butter?*   *Will there be **any** food for the guests?*   *Did you buy **any** clothes?*

We normally use **some** in offers and requests to make them sound more positive.
> *Would you like **some** coffee?*   *Could you post **some** letters for me?*

We can use **some** in questions when we think the answer might be yes.
> *Did you buy **some** clothes? (Perhaps I know that you went out to buy some.)*

2 Someone, anything, etc.

We choose between **someone** and **anyone**, **something** and **anything**, and **somewhere** and **anywhere** in the same way as between **some** and **any**.

***Someone** has spilt water everywhere.*	*Did **anyone** see what happened?*
*Would you like **something** to eat?*	*We haven't got **anything** to eat.*
*Let's go out **somewhere**.*	*Is there **anywhere** we can go?*

3 Another use of any

We can use **any** in a positive sentence to mean 'it doesn't matter which'.
> *I'm free all day. Call **any** time you like.*
> ***Any** student will be able to tell you where the college library is.*
> *You can buy these maps at **any** petrol station. They all have them.*

We say *any petrol station* because all petrol stations have the maps. It doesn't matter which one you go to.
They are all equally good.

Look at these examples with **anyone**, **anything** and **anywhere**.
> *It's a very simple puzzle. **Anyone** could solve it. (= It doesn't matter who.)*
> *What shall we have for lunch? ~ Oh, **anything**. I don't mind.*
> *Where do we have to sit? ~ We can sit **anywhere**. It doesn't matter.*

▷ 85.1 A/an and some   ▷ 103 Everyone, something, etc.

Practice

A Basic use (1)

Look at the pictures and say what people have or haven't got. Use *some* or *any*.
Use these words: *cats, money, petrol, poison, sandwiches*

► They've got some sandwiches.
► She hasn't got any money.
1 ....
2 ....
3 ....

B Basic use (1)

Justin Cooper is a radio disc jockey. Complete what he is saying. Put in *some* or *any*.

That was 'I can't find (►) any............ love' by Arlene Black. Now, I've had (►) some........ letters
asking for something by Express. One listener says she hasn't heard (1) .... Express songs
on this programme for months. Well, I'm going to put that right. And this will be our last track because
there isn't (2) .... more time left. We've had (3) .... great songs tonight, and I'll be
here next week to play (4) .... more. Now here's (5) .... music from Express – 'I
never have (6) .... luck'.

C Some, any, someone, anyone, etc. (1–2)

Complete the conversations. Put in *some, any, anyone, someone, something* or *anything*.

► Trevor: We haven't got ..any............ bread.
  Laura: You'd better go to the shop, then. We need ..some........... tomatoes, too.
1 Claire: Would you like .... cheese and biscuits?
  Sarah: Oh, no thank you. That was delicious, but I couldn't eat ....
            else.
2 Harriet: There's .... at the door.
  Mike: Are we expecting .... visitors?
3 Melanie: Has .... offered to help you with the tea?
  Rita: No, but I'd be very grateful for .... help you can give.
4 Vicky: I was looking for ...., and now I can't remember what it was.
  Rachel: You said you were looking for .... matches.

D Another use of **any** (3)

Put in *any* + noun, *anyone* or *anything*.

► The seats aren't reserved. You can have ..any seat........... you like.
► I don't mind what we do today. We can do ..anything.......... you want.
1 If it's your party, you can invite .... you like.
2 All the buses go into the town centre. Take .... that comes along here.
3 This carpet is available in lots of colours. You can have .... you like.
4 My father has the television on all the time. He'll watch ....
5 It doesn't matter which day you phone. Ring .... you like.

95 A lot of, lots of, many, much, (a) few and (a) little

1 Introduction

A lot of, **lots of**, **many** and **much** mean a large quantity.

*Ron Mason owns a chain of supermarkets. He's made **a lot of** money.*

A few and **a little** mean a small quantity.

*I'd better hurry. My bus goes in **a few** minutes.*

Many and **a few** go before plural nouns.	**Much** and **a little** go before uncountable nouns.
***many** places* ***many** problems*	***much** money* ***much** trouble*
***a few** people* ***a few** buildings*	***a little** sunshine* ***a little** food*

A lot of and **lots of** go before both plural and uncountable nouns.

***a lot of** tourists* ***lots of** games*	***a lot of** sugar* ***lots of** fun*

We use these words without a noun if it is clear what we mean.

*I take photos, but not as **many** as I used to. At one time I took **a lot**.*

Note that we say **a lot** without **of**.

2 A lot of, many and much

As a general rule, we use **a lot of** and **lots of** in positive statements and **many** and **much** in negatives and questions.

Positive:	*We get **a lot of** storms here.*	*We get **a lot of** rain here.*
Negative:	*We don't get **many** storms here.*	*We don't get **much** rain here.*
Questions:	*Do you get **many** storms here?*	*Do you get **much** rain here?*
	*How **many** eggs do we need?*	*How **much** salt do we put in?*

We use **many** or **much** (not **a lot of**) after **too**, **so** and **as**.

*There are **too many** cars.* *I've got **so much** work.* *I haven't got **as much** money as you.*

In formal English, we can sometimes use **many** and **much** in a positive statement.

***Many** students have financial problems.* *There is **much** enthusiasm for the idea.*

But this is less usual in conversation, where we normally use **a lot of** or **lots of**.

In informal English, you may hear **a lot of** in a negative or a question.

*I don't have **many** friends/**a lot of** friends.* *Do you eat **much** fruit/**a lot of** fruit?*

3 Few and little with and without a

With **a** the meaning is positive.	Without **a** the meaning is negative.
***A few** customers have come into the shop. It has been fairly busy.*	***Few** customers have come into the shop. It has been quiet.*
*Vicky has made **a little** progress and so is feeling quite pleased.*	*Vicky has made **little** progress and so is not feeling very pleased.*
A few customers = some customers, a small number of customers	*Few customers = not many customers*
A little progress = some progress, a small amount of progress	*Little progress = not much progress*

Few and **little** (without **a**) can be rather formal. In informal speech we can use these structures.

***Not many** customers have come in.* *Vicky **hasn't** made **much** progress.*

***Only a few** customers have come in.* *Vicky has made **only a little** progress.*

Practice

A A lot of, lots of, many, much, a few and a little (1)

Write the sentences correctly.

▶ Mark was only spending one night away. ~~He quickly put a little things into a bag.~~
  He quickly put a few things into a bag.

1 Rachel is learning to drive. ~~She hasn't had much lessons yet.~~

   ....

2 I'm making soup for twenty people. ~~I'll have to make a lot of.~~

   ....

3 I feel really tired. ~~I haven't got many energy.~~

   ....

4 The mixture looks rather dry. ~~Maybe you should add a few water.~~

   ....

5 We're having a big party. ~~We've invited a lots of friends.~~

   ....

B A lot of, many and much (1–2)

Complete the conversation. Put in *a lot of*, *many* or *much*. More than one answer may be correct.

Matthew: There are (▶) .a. lot. of............... athletes taking part in the International Games in
          London. There's been (1) .... coverage in the papers.
Daniel: Our runners haven't won (2) .... medals, have they?
Matthew: No, not as (3) .... as last time. But there's plenty of time. There are
          still (4) .... events to come. I'd like to go and see some of the track
          events, but I haven't got (5) .... time at the moment.
Daniel: No, not with exams coming up.
Matthew: I'm hoping to go at the weekend if I can get a ticket. Apparently there aren't
          (6) .... seats left.
Daniel: I've heard the cheapest tickets are £25. I think that's too (7) ....

C A few, few, a little and little (3)

Put in *a few*, *few*, *a little* or *little*.

▶ I don't think I can lift this box on my own. I need a .little........... help.
▶ .Few................. tourists visited Northern Ireland in the 1980s because of the terrorism there.
1 The postman doesn't often come here. We receive .... letters.
2 The snow was quite deep. There seemed .... hope of completing
   our journey.
3 Trevor isn't finding it easy to fix the shelves. He's having ....
   trouble.
4 Sarah is exhausted. She's having .... days' holiday next week.
5 David quite likes golf, but unfortunately he has .... ability.
6 I can speak .... words of Swedish, but I'm not very fluent.

D Many, few, much and little (2–3)

Complete this paragraph from a travel book. Put in *many*, *few*, *much* or *little*.

The main town on the island is very small and does not have (▶) .many......... important buildings.
The islanders do not have (1) .... money, and they have (2) .... contact with the
outside world. There is not (3) .... chance of the place attracting large numbers of tourists.
The roads are not very good. There are lots of bicycles but not (4) .... cars. And there are
hardly any of the modern facilities which visitors expect. There are (5) .... shops, and there
is (6) .... entertainment.

96 All, half, most, some, no and none

1 All, most and some

We can use **all**, **most** and **some** before a plural or an uncountable noun.

> ***All plants*** *need water.*   ***All matter*** *is made up of atoms.*
> ***Most people*** *would like more money.*   ***Some food*** *makes me ill.*

All plants means 'all plants in general/in the world'. *Most people* means 'most people in this country/in the world'. *Some food* means 'some food but not all food'. Here **some** is pronounced /sʌm/.

2 All of, half of, most of and some of

> Laura: *Why do you keep **all of these clothes**? You never wear **most of them**. You've had **some of your** jackets for ten years. Why don't you throw **them all** out? This one is completely out of fashion.*
> Trevor: *Well, I thought if I waited long enough, it might come back into fashion.*

All of these clothes has a specific meaning. Laura is talking about Trevor's clothes, not about clothes in general.

We can use **all (of)**, **half (of)**, **most of** and **some of**.

> *Have **all (of) the plants** died? ~ No, not **all of them**.*
> ***Most of the people*** *who live around here are students.*
> *I've spent **most of my money** already.*
> ***Half (of) the audience*** *left before the end of the film.*
> ***Some of that food*** *from the party was all right, but I threw **some of it** away.*

We can leave out **of** after **all** or **half**, but not before a pronoun.

> *all of these clothes* OR *all the clothes* BUT *all of them* NOT ~~all them~~
> *half of our group* OR *half our group* BUT *half of us* NOT ~~half us~~

We can also use **all** in mid position (see Unit 113.2) or after a pronoun.

> *These cups **are all** dirty. I'll have to clean **them all**.*
> *The guests **have all gone** now. I think **they all** enjoyed themselves.*

We can use **most** and **some** on their own.

> *The band sang a few songs. **Most** were old ones, but **some** were new.*

3 All meaning 'everything' or 'the only thing'

We can use **all** with a clause to mean 'everything' or 'the only thing'.

> *Tell me **all** you know.   **All** I did was ask a simple question.*

Here *you know* and *I did* are clauses. We do not normally use **all** without the clause.

> *Tell me **everything**.* NOT ~~Tell me all.~~

4 No and none

We use **no** with a noun.

> *We've rung all the hotels, and there are **no rooms** available.*
> *I'm afraid I've got **no money**. (= I haven't got **any** money.)*

We use **none** with **of** or on its own.

> ***None of my friends*** *will be at the party.   Look at these clothes. **None of them** are in fashion now.*
> *I wanted some cake, but there was **none** left.* NOT ~~There was no left.~~

▷ 86 Cars or the cars?   ▷ 94 Some and any   ▷ 103 Everyone, etc.

Practice

A All, most, half, some and none (2, 4)

Read this advertisement for some new flats and then complete the sentences.
Put in *all of them*, *most of them*, *half of them*, *some of them* and *none of them*.

Hartley House is an old manor house which has been converted into thirty one-bedroom and two-bedroom flats. All the flats have a fitted kitchen, bathroom and large living-room. Ten of them have a separate dining-room. Twenty-five of the flats have a view of the sea, and fifteen have a private balcony. All thirty flats are still for sale. Ring us now for more details.

▶ The flats are modern. .All.of..them.... have a fitted kitchen.
1 .... have two bedrooms.
2 From .... you can see the sea.
3 .... have a private balcony.
4 .... have a large living-room.
5 There's also a dining-room in ....
6 .... has been sold yet.

B All, most, some and none (2, 4)

There was a quiz evening yesterday. Six friends took part, and they all answered twenty questions. Did they get all, most, some or none of them right?

▶ Natasha answered all twenty correctly.   She.got.all.of.them.right. ....
▶ Daniel's score was fifteen.   He.got.most.of.them.right. ....
1 Jessica had only eight correct answers.   ....
2 Matthew got them all right except three.   ....
3 Andrew gave twenty correct answers.   ....
4 But poor Vicky didn't get a single one right. ....

C All, most, no and none (1–4)

Complete the conversations. Use the word in brackets with *all*, *all the*, *most*, *most of the*, *no* or *none of the*.

▶ Andrew: I wonder where they make this milk.
  Jessica: It isn't made in a factory, Andrew. .All.milk.. (milk) comes from animals.
▶ Rita: What do you usually do on a Sunday?
  Mike: Not much. We spend .most.of.the.time.. (time) reading the papers.
1 Claire: In general, people aren't interested in politics, are they?
  Mark: I think .... (people) are bored by the subject.
2 Vicky: These new flats are supposed to be for students.
  Rachel: That's ridiculous. .... (student) in the world could possibly afford such a high rent.
3 Tom: Who's paying for the new ice-rink to be built?
  Nick: Well, ... (money) will come from the government, but the city has to pay a quarter of the cost.
4 Melanie: We should ban cars. .... (cars) pollute the air, don't they?
  David: Well, except electric ones, I suppose.
5 Vicky: What kind of fruit should you eat to stay healthy?
  Natasha: I don't think it matters. .... (fruit) is good for you, isn't it?
6 Tom: I knew there had been a power cut because it was so dark everywhere.
  Harriet: Yes, ... (lights) in our street went out.

97 Every, each, whole, both, either and neither

1 Every and each

We use **every** and **each** before a singular noun to talk about a whole group.
> The police questioned *every person/each person* in the building.
> *Every room/Each room* has a number.

In many contexts either word is possible, but there is a difference in meaning.

EVERY	EACH
Every person means 'all the people', 'everyone'.	*Each* person means all the people seen as individuals, one by one.
Every guest watched as the President came in. *I go for a walk every day*.	*Each guest* (*in turn*) shook hands with him. *Each day* seemed to pass very slowly.
Every means three or more, usually a large number.	**Each** is more usual with smaller groups and can mean only two.
There were cars parked along every street in town. (= all the streets)	*There were cars parked along each side of the street.* (= both sides)

We can use **each** (but not **every**) on its own or with **of**.
> *There are six flats. Each has its own entrance.* NOT ~~Every has ...~~
> *Each of the six flats has its own entrance.* NOT ~~Every of the ...~~

We can also say *Each one/Every one* has its own entrance.

We can also use **each** in mid position (see Unit 113.2) or after a pronoun.
> *We've each got our own desk.   They gave us each a desk.*

Compare **every** and **all** before **day**, **morning**, **week**, etc.
> *I travel every day*. (= Monday, Tuesday, Wednesday, ...)
> *I was travelling all day*. (= from morning till evening)

2 Whole

We use **whole** before a singular noun. It means 'all' or 'complete'.
> *The baby cried the whole time.* (= all the time)
> *I've spent my whole life waiting for this moment.* (= all my life)
> *We'll need a whole loaf to make sandwiches for everyone.*

3 Both, either and neither

We use **both**, **either** and **neither** for two things.
> *I've got two bicycles. Both of them are quite old. I've given up cycling, so I don't ride either of them any more. Neither of them is in very good condition, I'm afraid.*

Both means 'the one and the other'. We can use it in the following structures.
> *We had two letters this morning, and both letters/both the letters/both of the letters/both of them are bills.*

We can also use **both** in mid position (see Unit 113.2) or after a pronoun.
> *The letters are both bills. I've opened them both.*

Either means 'the one or the other', and **neither** means 'not the one or the other'.
> *I haven't met either twin/either of the twins/either of them.*
> *Neither shoe fits/Neither of the shoes fit(s)/Neither of them fit(s).*

We can use **both**, **either** and **neither** on their own.
> *The store has two lifts, and both are out of order/neither is working.*

Practice

A Every and each (1)

Complete the dialogue. Put in *every* or *each*. Sometimes both are possible.

Laura: It's a lot bigger than your last house, isn't it? Did you say there are four people living here?
Natasha: Yes, and we (▶) .*each*......... have our own bedroom.
Laura: Does (1) .... person pay a quarter of the rent?
Natasha: That's right. On the first of (2) .... month.
Laura: It must be fantastic for parties.
Natasha: Yes, it is. We don't have one (3) .... week, but almost!
Laura: Isn't that rather expensive?
Natasha: Not if (4) .... guest brings something to eat or drink! Anyway, there'll be no more parties until our exams are over. We're spending (5) .... moment revising.

B Every, all and whole (1–2)

Put in *every*, *all* or *the whole* and the word in brackets. Sometimes more than one answer is possible.

▶ Melanie is a religious person. She goes to church *every Sunday* (Sunday).
1 The weather has been awful today. It's been raining .... (day).
2 I just can't sleep. I spent .... (night) lying awake.
3 Sarah gets the train at half past seven .... (morning).
4 It's eleven o'clock. Are you going to lie in bed .... (morning)?
5 Last Saturday Trevor spent .... (day) putting up some shelves.
6 Why are you in such a hurry .... (time) I see you?

C Both, either and neither (3)

There are two pubs in Brickfield, The White Horse and The Ship. Look at the information and then write the sentences. Use *both of them*, *one of them* or *neither of them*.

THE WHITE HORSE		
MEALS	BAR SNACKS	FAMILY ROOM

THE SHIP	
MEALS	SEPARATE RESTAURANT
BAR SNACKS	NON-SMOKING AREA

▶ (serve meals) *Both of them serve meals.*
1 (have a separate restaurant) ....
2 (serve bar snacks) ....
3 (have a family room) ....
4 (allow pub games) ....
5 (have live music) ....
6 (have a non-smoking area) ....

D Every, each, whole, both, either and neither (1–3)

Complete the conversation. Put in *every*, *each*, *whole*, *both*, *either* or *neither*.

Assistant: These plain sofas come in two different styles.
Sarah: I think (▶) .*both*.. styles are rather old-fashioned. (1) .... of them is really what I want. I don't like (2) .... of them, I'm afraid.
Assistant: What about a patterned fabric? There are some lovely colours here.
Sarah: I feel more and more unsure with (3) .... new fabric I look at.
Mark: We haven't got time to look at (4) .... fabric in the shop. We've been in here a (5) .... hour already, you know.

Test P: This, my, some, a lot of, all, etc.

A

Look at what people are saying and choose the correct meaning.

▶ Polly: Let's sit under these trees, shall we?
  The trees are a) ☑ near Polly.   b) ☐ a long way away from Polly.

1 Martin: My friend and I ate a whole loaf.
  Martin and his friend ate a) ☐ part of the loaf.   b) ☐ all the loaf.

2 Nigel: The girls' dog has gone missing.
  The dog belongs to a) ☐ one girl.   b) ☐ more than one girl.

3 Tessa: My brother has got his own office.
  Tessa's brother a) ☐ works alone in the office.   b) ☐ shares the office with another person.

4 Nancy: The weather looks a little better, I think.
  How does Nancy feel about the weather? a) ☐ Hopeful.   b) ☐ Not very hopeful.

5 Ben: I can't answer either of these questions.
  How many questions is Ben talking about? a) ☐ One.   b) ☐ Two.   c) ☐ More than two.

6 Adrian: The children can keep any tennis balls they find.
  Will they find any tennis balls? a) ☐ Yes.   b) ☐ No.   c) ☐ Adrian doesn't know.

B

Decide which word is correct.

▶ What colour shall we have? ~ I don't mind. Pick ..any.. colour you like.
  a) any   b) some   c) that   d) what

1 Peter has two brothers, but he doesn't speak to .... of them.
  a) any   b) both   c) either   d) neither

2 .... has left a bicycle outside.
  a) Anyone   b) Anything   c) Someone   d) Something

3 I like .... pictures here. ~ Yes, so do I.
  a) that   b) these   c) this   d) those

4 Would you mind waiting .... minutes?
  a) a few   b) a little   c) few   d) little

5 .... countries still have a king or a queen, don't they?
  a) Any   b) Half   c) Part   d) Some

6 Safety should come first. .... lives shouldn't be put at risk.
  a) People   b) Peoples   c) People's   d) Peoples'

7 Nigel isn't very well. ~ Oh, I'm sorry to hear ....
  a) so   b) that   c) this   d) you

8 Mr Jones is an uncle of ....
  a) Polly   b) Pollys   c) Polly's   d) Pollys'

C

Tessa is walking along the street when she sees her old friend Angela.
Read the conversation and write the missing words. Use one word only in each space.

Tessa: Hello, Angela. How are you?

Angela: Tessa! Hello! Shall we have lunch together?

Tessa: I was just going to the bank to get (▶) ..some.. money. I have to be back at the office in (1) .... few minutes. My life's one mad rush.

Angela: So is (2) .... I'm working for Tuffex Plastics now. And my daughter has invited three friends (3) .... hers to stay. I wish I didn't have so (4) .... things to do at once.

Tessa: I'm glad I've run into you. I never see (5) .... else from our old gang.
          (6) .... of them seem to be around any more.
Angela: I think they've (7) .... moved away, except us two. Carol went to Japan.
Tessa: Angela, would you like to come for a meal some time?
Angela: Oh, that would be lovely. We'll certainly have a (8) .... to talk about.
Tessa: Maybe we'll need a (9) .... day. What about the Saturday after next?

D

Each of the sentences has a mistake in it. Write the correct sentence.

►   Are you going on holiday that year?   *Are you going on holiday this year?*
1   That was a very good idea of you.
2   You've got a lot books, haven't you?
3   I don't know the meeting's time.
4   Nigel has hurt the leg.
5   All rooms in the house were cold.
6   Wear everything–it doesn't matter what.
7   Every of the four doors was locked.
8   I live my life, and my sister lives her.
9   The both socks have got holes in them.
10   Here's a copy of this week magazine.
11   This sweater is losing it's colour.
12   I want some paper, but there's no in here.

E

Write a second sentence so that it has a similar meaning to the first. Use the word in brackets.

►   When I was on holiday, it rained all week. (whole)
     When I was on holiday, it rained the whole week.
1   I've lived here more than half my life. (most)

2   All the hotels were full. (every)

3   The house on the corner is bigger than our house. (ours)

4   I've forgotten my doctor's name. (of)

5   We haven't had much warning of the changes. (little)

6   Such a large number of people have applied for the job. (so)

7   I met one of your old boyfriends at a party. (an)

8   Both the chairs are uncomfortable. (neither)

9   My holiday starts ten days from now. (time)

98 Personal pronouns (I, you)

1 The meaning of the pronouns

Vicky:	*Hello, Andrew. Have **you** seen Rachel?*
Andrew:	*I don't think so. No, **I** haven't seen **her** today.*
Vicky:	***We**'re supposed to be going out at half past seven, and **it**'s nearly eight now.*
Andrew:	*Maybe **she**'s just forgotten. **You** know Rachel.*
Vicky:	***We**'re going out for a meal. Matthew and Emma said **they** might come too. I hope **they** haven't gone without **me**.*

I/me means the speaker, and **you** means the person spoken to.
We/us means the speaker and someone else. Here, **we** = Vicky and Rachel.
He/him means a male person and **she/her** a female person. Here, **she** = Rachel.
It means a thing, an action, a situation or an idea. Here, **it** = the time.
They/them is the plural of **he**, **she** and **it** and means people or things.

We can also use **they/them** for a person when we don't know if the person is male or female.
*If anyone calls, ask **them** to leave a message.*

2 Subject and object forms

		FIRST PERSON	SECOND PERSON	THIRD PERSON
Singular	SUBJECT	I	you	he/she/it
	OBJECT	me	you	him/her/it
Plural	SUBJECT	we	you	they
	OBJECT	us	you	them

We use the subject form (**I**, etc.) when the pronoun is the subject and there is a verb.
*__I__ don't think so.   Maybe **she**'s just forgotten.*
We use the object form (**me**, etc.) when the pronoun is the object of a verb or preposition.
*I haven't **seen her** today.   I hope they haven't gone **without me**.*

The pronoun on its own or after **be** usually has the object form.
*Who spilt coffee all over the table? ~ **Me**./Sorry, it was **me**.*
Compare this answer.
*Who spilt coffee all over the table? ~ **I** did.*

3 You, one and they

We can use **you** or **one** to mean 'any person' or 'people in general', including the speaker.
*__You__ shouldn't believe what **you** read in the newspapers.*
OR *__One__ shouldn't believe what **one** reads in the newspapers.*
__You__ don't like/__One__ doesn't like to have an argument in public.
You is normal in conversation. **One** is more formal.

We can use **they** for other people in general.
__They__ say too much sugar is bad for you.
We can also use it for people in authority.
__They__'re going to build a new swimming-pool here.
They is informal and conversational. We use the passive in more formal situations.
*A new swimming-pool **is going to be built** here (see Unit 56.2).*

▷ 99 There and it   ▷ page 379 You and one in British and American English

Practice

A The meaning of the pronouns (1)

Read the conversation between Melanie and Rita. Then say what the <u>underlined</u> pronouns mean.

Melanie: Have (▶) <u>you</u> been in that new shop?
Rita: No, not yet.
Melanie: Nor have I, but (▶) <u>it</u> looks interesting. There's a lovely
dress in the window, and (1) <u>it</u> isn't expensive.
Rita: Laura bought some jeans there. (2) <u>She</u> said
(3) <u>they</u> were really cheap.
Melanie: (4) <u>You</u> ought to go along there and have a look, then.
Rita: (5) <u>We</u>'d better not go now or we'll be late.
(6) <u>I</u> told Mike and Harriet we'd meet
(7) <u>them</u> at half past five.
Melanie: Oh, Tom said (8) <u>he</u>'s coming too.

▶ you = Rita
▶ it = the shop
1 it = ...
2 she = ...
3 they = ...
4 you = ...
5 we = ...
6 I = ...
7 them = ...
8 he = ...

B Subject and object forms (2)

Complete the conversation. Put in the pronouns.

Nick: Did (▶) you say that you and Harriet wanted some coloured lights for your party?
Mike: Yes, but (▶) it 's OK. Melanie's neighbour Jake has got some, and (1) ....'s going to lend (2) .... to (3) ....
Nick: Great. Is Rita coming to the party?
Mike: We've invited (4) .... of course, but (5) .... isn't sure if (6) .... can come or not. Her parents are flying somewhere on Saturday evening, and she might be taking (7) .... to the airport.
Nick: And what about Laura's friend Emily?
Mike: I expect (8) ....'ll be there. And her brother. (9) .... both came to our last party.
Nick: Do (10) .... mean Jason? I don't like (11) .... very much.
Mike: Oh, (12) ....'s OK. But (13) .... don't have to talk to (14) ....

C Subject and object forms (2)

Put in the pronouns.

▶ There's no need to shout. I can hear you .
1 You and I work well together. ....'re a good team.
2 We've got a bit of a problem. Could .... help ...., please?
3 This is a good photo, isn't ....? ~ Is Jessica in ....? ~ Yes, that's ...., look. ....'s next to Andrew.
4 Who did this crossword? ~ .... I did .... this morning.
5 Is this Vicky's bag? ~ No, ... didn't bring one. It can't belong to ....
6 ....'m looking for my shoes. Have .... seen ....? ~ Yes, ...'re here.

D You and they (3)

Complete the conversation. Put in you or they.

Trevor: I'm not going to drive in this weather. It's too icy.
Laura: (▶) You don't want to take any risks. (1) .... can't be too careful.
Trevor: I've just heard the weather forecast and (2) .... say there's going to be more snow. (3) ....'re better off indoors in weather like this.
Laura: I think (4) .... ought to clear the snow off the roads more quickly.

99 There and it

1 There + be

Look at these examples.

*I really ought to phone home. ~ Well, **there's** a phone box round the corner.*
*Could I make myself an omelette? ~ Of course. **There are** some eggs in the fridge.*
***There's** an important meeting at work that I have to go to.*

To talk about the existence of something, we use **there + be**. Be agrees with the following noun.

*There **is** a phone box.* BUT *There **are** some eggs.*

Here are some more examples.

***There's** a bus at ten to five.*   ***There'll be** a meal waiting for us.*
***Is there** a toilet in the building?*   ***Were there** any bargains in the sale?*
***There have been** some burglaries recently.*   ***There might have been** an accident.*

We also use **there** with words like **a lot of, many, much, more, enough** and with numbers.

***There** were **a lot of** problems to discuss.*   ***There's** too **much** noise in here.*
*Will **there** be **enough** chairs?*   ***There** are **thirty** days in April.*

2 Uses of it

We use **it** for a thing, an action, a situation or an idea.

*You've bought a new coat. **It's** very nice. (it = the coat)*
*Skiing is an expensive hobby, isn't **it**?*
*You have to fill in all these stupid forms. **It's** ridiculous.*
*I find astrology fascinating. I'm really interested in **it**.*

We use **it** to mean 'the unknown person'.

*Did someone ring? ~ **It** was Vicky. She just called to say she's arrived safely.*

We use **it** for the time, the weather and distance.

***It's** half past five already.*   ***It's** Sunday tomorrow.*
***It** was much warmer yesterday.*   ***It's** fifty miles from here to Brighton.*

We also use **it** in structures with a to-infinitive or a that-clause (see also Unit 67.2).

***It** was nice **to meet your friends**.*
***It** would be a good idea **to book in advance**.*
***It's** important **to switch off the electricity**.*
***It's** a pity **(that) you can't come with us**.*

This is much more usual than, for example, *To meet your friends was nice.*

3 There or it?

We often use **there** when we mention something for the first time, like the picture in this example.

***There** was a picture on the wall. **It** was an abstract painting.*

We use **it** when we talk about the details. It means *the picture*.

Here are some more examples.

***There's** a woman at the door. ~ Oh, **it's** Aunt Joan.*
***There** was a dog in the field. **It** was a big black one.*
***There's** a new one-way traffic system in the town centre. **It's** very confusing.*

Practice

A There + be (1)

Look at the pictures and comment on what you see. Use these words: *a balloon*, *some boxes*, *the car*, *a dinosaur*, *an elephant*, *some flowers*, *the garden*, *her hat*, *the sky*, *the water*

▶ There's a dinosaur in the water.
▶ There are some flowers on her hat. 2 ....
1 .... 3 ....

B There + be (1)

Put in *there* and a form of *be*, e.g. *is*, *are*, *was*, *have been* or *will be*.
▶ Victor: Are there .... any restaurants here that open on a Sunday?
  Rachel: There's .... a café in the High Street which is open for lunch.
1 Alan: .... a train at twelve thirty, isn't there? Let's catch that one.
  Mark: OK. .... time to finish our discussion on the train.
2 Vicky: What's happened? Why .... so many police cars here?
  Daniel: .... a hold-up at the bank.
3 Tom: Last night .... a party next door. I couldn't get to sleep.
  Melanie: .... must .... a lot of people there.

C Uses of it (2)

Rewrite the sentences in brackets using *it*.
▶ We sometimes go surfing. (Surfing is really good fun.) It's really good fun. ....
1 I bought a shirt in the market. (The shirt was very cheap.) ....
2 Someone rang. (The caller was Vicky.) ....
3 Our heating is out of order.(The situation is a nuisance.)..
4 I've left my coat at home. (The weather is very warm.) ....
5 Don't lose your credit card. (To keep it somewhere safe is important.)
   ....

D There or it? (3)

Put in *there* or *it*.
▶ Is it .... the fifteenth today? ~ No, the sixteenth.
1 The road is closed. ....'s been an accident.
2 Take a taxi. ....'s a long way to the station.
3 .... was a motor bike outside. .... looked very expensive.
4 Will .... be any delays because of the strike? ~ Well, ... would be a good idea
  to ring the airline and check.
5 .... was wet, and .... was a cold east wind. .... was after midnight,
  and .... were few people on the streets.

100 Reflexive pronouns

1 Introduction

Myself is a reflexive pronoun. In the sentence
I've cut myself, the words **I** and **myself** mean
the same thing. **Myself** refers back to the subject, **I**.

> Ow! I've cut **myself**.

2 Form

	FIRST PERSON	SECOND PERSON	THIRD PERSON
Singular	myself	yourself	himself/herself/itself
Plural	ourselves	yourselves	themselves

Compare **yourself** and **yourselves**.

> *Emma, you can dry **yourself** on this towel.*   *Vicky and Rachel, you can dry **yourselves** on these towels.*

3 The use of reflexive pronouns

Here are some examples.

> *Mark made **himself** a sandwich.*   *Vicky had to force **herself** to eat.*
> *We've locked **ourselves** out.*   *The children watched **themselves** on video.*

We cannot use **me**, **you**, **him**, etc. to refer to the subject. Compare these sentences.

> *When the policeman came in, the gunman shot **him**.* (**him** = the policeman)
> *When the policeman came in, the gunman shot **himself**.* (**himself** = the gunman)

We can use a reflexive pronoun after a preposition.

> *The children are old enough to look **after themselves**.*

But after a preposition of place, we can use **me**, **you**, **him**, etc.

> *In the mirror I saw a lorry **behind me**.*   *Mike didn't have any money **with him**.*
> *Laura thought she recognized the woman standing **next to her**.*

4 Idioms with reflexive pronouns

Look at these examples.

> *We really **enjoyed ourselves**.* (= had a good time)
> *I hope the children **behave themselves**.* (= behave well)
> *Just **help yourself** to sandwiches, won't you?* (= take as many as you want)
> *Please **make yourself at home**.* (= behave as if this was your home)
> *I don't want to be left here **by myself**.* (= on my own, alone)

5 Verbs without a reflexive pronoun

Some verbs do not usually take a reflexive pronoun, although they may in other languages.

> *We'd better **hurry**, or we'll be late.* NOT *We'd better hurry ourselves.*
> *Shall we **meet** at the cinema?*   *I **feel** uncomfortable.*   *Just try to **relax**.*

Some of these verbs are: **afford, approach, complain, concentrate, decide, feel** + adjective, **get up, hurry (up), lie down, meet, remember, rest, relax, sit down, stand up, wake up, wonder, worry**

We do not normally use a reflexive pronoun with **change** (clothes), **dress** and **wash**.

> *Daniel **washed** and **changed** before going out.* (See also Unit 54.4.)

But we can use a reflexive pronoun when the action is difficult.

> *My friend is disabled, but she can **dress herself**.*

Practice

A Reflexive pronouns (1–3)

Look at the pictures and write sentences with a reflexive pronoun.
Use these words: *dry, introduce, look at, photograph, teach*

▶ <u>He's photographing himself.</u>

1 She ....   3 ....

2 They ....   4 ....

B Reflexive pronouns (1–3)

Complete the conversations. Put in a reflexive pronoun (*myself, yourself,* etc.).

▶ Matthew: I'll get the tickets, shall I?

    Emma: It's OK. I can pay for .myself............................. .

1 Olivia: I've got lots of photos of my children.

    Linda: Yes, but you haven't got many of ...., Olivia.

2 Rita: Did you have a good time at the Holiday Centre?

    Laura: Well, there wasn't much going on. We had to amuse ....

3 Emma: Why has the light gone off?

    Matthew: It switches .... off automatically.

C Pronouns after a preposition (3 and Unit 98.2)

Put in the correct pronoun (e.g. *me* or *myself*).

▶ We looked up and saw a strange animal in front of .us............ .

▶ Don't tell us the answer to the puzzle. We can work it out for .ourselves..... .

1 It's a pity you didn't bring your camera with ....

2 Mark talked to the woman sitting next to ....

3 The old man is no longer able to look after ....

4 My mother likes to have all her family near ....

5 To be successful in life, you must believe in ....

D Idioms with and without reflexive pronouns (4–5)

Rachel and Vicky are at Mike and Harriet's party. Complete the conversation.
Put in the verbs with or without a reflexive pronoun.

Mike: Have you two (▶) .met.. (met) before?

Rachel: Yes, we have. Vicky and I are old friends.

Mike: Oh, right. Well, I hope you (▶) .enjoy yourselves.......... (enjoy) tonight.

Rachel: I'm sure we will. I (1) .... (feel) just in the mood for a party.

Mike: Well, please (2) .... (help) to a drink. Are you OK, Vicky?

Vicky: Sorry, I've got this awful feeling that I have to do something very important, and I can't
(3) .... (remember) what it is.

Rachel: Vicky, you (4) .... (worry) too much. Come on, just
(5) .... (relax).

101 Emphatic pronouns and each other

1 Emphatic pronouns

*Trevor and Laura are decorating their living-room **themselves**.*

An emphatic pronoun is a word like **myself, yourself**.
It has the same form as a reflexive pronoun (see Unit 100.2).

Here the emphatic pronoun means 'without help'. Trevor and
Laura are decorating the room without help from anyone else.
Compare *They're having the room wallpapered (by a decorator)*
(see Unit 58.1).

Here are some more examples.
*I built this boat **myself**.   My sister designs all these clothes **herself**.*
*Are you doing all the painting **yourselves**?*
When we say these sentences, we stress **self** or **selves**.

Now look at these examples.
*The manager **himself** welcomed us to the hotel.*
(= The manager welcomed us, not someone else.)
*Although she is very rich, the Queen **herself** never carries any money.*
*The house **itself** is small, but the garden is enormous.*
*Of course the children have been to the zoo. You **yourself** took them there last year.*
Here the emphatic pronoun comes after the noun or pronoun it relates to.

2 Each other

Look at this example.
*Andrew and Jessica help **each other** with their work.*
This means that Andrew helps Jessica, and Jessica helps Andrew. Here are some more examples.
*Mark and Alan aren't really friends. They don't like **each other** much.*
*I'm still in touch with Kirsty. We write to **each other**.*
One another has the same meaning.
*We send **each other/one another** Christmas cards every year.*

We can also use the possessive form **each other's**.
*Tom and Mark wrote down **each other's** phone numbers.*
This means that Tom wrote down Mark's number, and Mark wrote down Tom's number.

Compare **each other** and **themselves**.

*They're laughing at **each other**.*

*They're laughing at **themselves**.*

Practice

A Emphatic pronouns (1)

Add a sentence with an emphatic pronoun, e.g. *myself*.
Use these verbs: *bake, clean, decorate, grow, paint, service, type, wash*

▶ I don't take the car to the garage. .I. service. it. myself.
▶ Laura didn't buy those pictures. .She. painted. them. herself.
1 Tom doesn't have his windows cleaned. ....
2 My bread doesn't come from a shop. ....
3 My friends eat lots of fresh vegetables. ....
4 We finished the dining-room yesterday. ....
5 Mark doesn't dictate his letters to a secretary. ....
6 I don't take my car to the car wash. ....

B Emphatic pronouns (1)

Put in an emphatic pronoun, e.g. *myself, yourself*.

▶ Of course I know about Matthew and Emma. You told me .yourself.
1 The princess .... visited the children in hospital.
2 The song .... wasn't very good, but the title of the song became a popular phrase.
3 The visitors were welcomed to the school by the headmaster ....
4 The pilots .... are nervous of flying because of terrorist threats.
5 You all know that no one can take your decisions for you. You .... will have to decide.

C Each other (2)

David and Melanie are in love. Write sentences about them using *each other*.

▶ Melanie often writes notes to David. He also often writes notes to Melanie.
They often write notes to each other.
1 David is always thinking about Melanie. She's just the same. She's always thinking about him.
....
2 Melanie has got lots of photos of David. He's got lots of photos of her, too.
....
3 They love being together. David enjoys Melanie's company, and she enjoys David's company.
....
4 Melanie is crazy about David. He feels the same way. He's crazy about Melanie.
....

D Each other or a reflexive pronoun? (2 and Unit 100)

Put in *each other, ourselves* or *themselves*.

▶ We could all do more to keep healthy. We don't look after .ourselves. properly.
▶ The hostess introduced the two guests to .each other.
1 The two boxers did their best to knock .... out.
2 We talk to .... in French because it's the only language we both know.
3 People who talk to .... may get strange looks from other people.
4 We'd better set off early to give .... plenty of time to get there.
5 The guards who shot a gunman claimed that they were defending ....
6 Luckily we managed to get two seats next to ....

102 The pronoun **one/ones**

1 Introduction

Trevor: *Here's that bottle of mineral water you wanted.*
Laura: *Oh, no, you've got a small **one**. I wanted a big **one**.*
Trevor: *They didn't have any big **ones** at the shop on the corner.*
Laura: *That shop never has what I want. Why didn't you go to
             the **one** in the High Street?*

Here *a small **one*** means 'a small bottle', *big **ones*** means 'big bottles',
and *the **one** in the High Street* means 'the shop in the High Street'.
We use **one** for a singular noun and **ones** for a plural noun.
We use **one** and **ones** to avoid repeating a noun.

We cannot use **one** or **ones** with an uncountable noun, e.g. **water**.
   *There was no hot water. I had to wash in **cold**.*

2 Structures with **one/ones**

Sometimes we can either put in **one/ones** or leave it out.
   *These bowls are nice. What about **this** (**one**)?*
We can do this after **this**, **that**, **these** and **those**; after **each** or **another**; after **which**; or
after a superlative, e.g. **easiest**.
   *I don't like these sweaters. I prefer **those** (**ones**) over there.*
   *I tried all three numbers, and **each** (**one**) was engaged.*
   *The product is available in all these colours. **Which** (**one**) would you like?*
   *The last question is the **most difficult** (**one**).*

Sometimes we cannot leave out **one/ones**.
   *Our house is the **one** on the left.* NOT ~~Our house is the on the left.~~
We cannot leave out **one/ones** after **the** or **every** or after an adjective.
   *The film wasn't as good as **the one** we saw last week.*
   *I rang all the numbers, and **every one** was engaged.*
   *I'd like a box of tissues. A **small one**, please.*
   *I threw away my old trainers and bought some **new ones**.*

3 A small one and one

We can say **a small one**, **a red one**, etc. but NOT ~~a one~~.
   *I've been looking for a coat, but I can't find **a nice one**.*
   *I've been looking for a coat, but I can't find **one**.*
Here we use **one** instead of **a coat**. Here are some more examples.
   *We decided to take a taxi. Luckily there was **one** waiting.*
   *If you want a ticket, I can get **one** for you.*

Now look at these examples with **one**, **some**, **it** and **them**.
   *I haven't got a passport, but I'll need **one**.*   (**one** = a passport)
   *I haven't got any stamps, but I'll need **some**.*   (**some** = some stamps)
   *I've got my passport. They sent **it** last week.*   (**it** = the passport)
   *I've got the stamps. I put **them** in the drawer.*   (**them** = the stamps)
One and **some/any** are like **a**, but **it** and **they/them** are like **the**. We use **one** and **some/any** when we aren't
saying which, and we use **it** and **they/them** to be specific (when we know which).

Practice

A One (1)

Look at the pictures and complete the conversations.

▶ blue ✓ black ✗   1 smart ✗ casual ✓   2 big ✓ small ✗   3 white ✗ brown ✓   4 ordinary ✓ electric ✗

▶	Emma:	Can you lend me a pen, please?
	Matthew:	Do you want <u>a blue one or a black one</u>?
	Emma:	Oh, <u>a blue one</u>, please.
1	Mark:	I might buy a new jacket.
	Sarah:	Do you mean ....?
	Mark:	Oh, ... for when I go on holiday.
2	Jessica:	Could you pass me one of those saucepans, please?
	Andrew:	Do you need ....?
	Jessica:	...., please.
3	Sarah:	Could I have a small envelope?
	Secretary:	Yes, of course. ....?
	Sarah:	...., please. Thanks.
4	Vicky:	I'm looking for a toothbrush, but I can't find any.
	Assistant:	Do you mean ....?
	Vicky:	Oh, ...

B One and ones (1–3)

Rewrite the sentences in brackets so that the noun is not repeated. Use *one* or *ones*.

▶ These cups are nice. <u>Each one is hand-painted.</u> (Each cup is hand-painted.)

1 I need to fill in a form about my driving test, but .... (I haven't got a form.)

2 I've watched all these videos. .... (I must get some new videos.)

3 These photos are good. .... (Have you seen this photo?)

4 I need a dinner-jacket for the party, so .... (I've hired a dinner-jacket.)

5 Those socks are horrible. .... (Can't you find any nice socks?)

6 This map isn't very good. .... (The map in the car is better.)

C One, some, it and them (3)

Put in *one, some, it* or *them*.

▶ I don't know if I'll need any money. I'd better take <u>some</u>, I suppose.

1 If you need an umbrella, I can lend you ....

2 The radio isn't working. Vicky dropped .... on the floor.

3 I'm having a biscuit. Would you like ...., too?

4 I had the matches a minute ago, and now I can't find ....

5 I haven't got any computer disks, but Emma has got ....

103 Everyone, something, etc.

1 Introduction

Look at these examples.

> *Everyone enjoyed the show. It was a great success.*
> *The police searched the house but found **nothing**.*
> *Let's find **somewhere** to eat.*
> ***Nobody** came into the shop all afternoon.*

With **every**, **some** and **no**, we can form words ending in **one**, **body**, **thing** and **where**.

everyone/everybody = all the people	everything = all the things	everywhere = (in) all the places
someone/somebody = a person	something = a thing	somewhere = (in) a place
no one/nobody = no person	nothing /ˈnʌθɪŋ/ = no things	nowhere = (in) no places

Words ending in **thing** can also mean actions or ideas.

> ***Something** awful has happened.*   *You must tell me **everything**.*

2 Someone and anyone, etc.

We can also form words with **any**: **anyone, anybody, anything, anywhere**.
For **some** and **any** see Unit 94.1.

Positive:	*There's **some**one in the phone box.*
Negative:	*I looked round the shops, but I didn't buy **any**thing.*
Question:	*Has **any**one seen today's newspaper?*
Offer/Request:	*Could you do **some**thing for me, please?*

We can also use words with **any** in a positive sentence.

> *This door is always left open. **Any**one could just walk in here.*
> *Where shall we go? ~ **Any**where. I don't mind.*

In these sentences **anyone** means 'it doesn't matter who', and **anywhere** means 'it doesn't matter where'. For more details about **any** see Unit 94.3.

3 Singular and plural

We use a singular verb after **everyone, something, anything**, etc.

> ***Everywhere was** very crowded.*   ***No one knows** how to start the motor.*

After words with **one** or **body**, we normally use **they/them/their**, even though the verb is singular.

> ***Everyone** is having **their** lunch.*   ***Nobody** wants to have **their** coffee yet.*

We can also use **he, she, him, her, his**, etc. with **someone/somebody** when we know the person's sex.

> ***Someone** left **their/her** handbag behind.*

4 Other structures

After **everyone, something**, etc. we can use an adjective.

> *Let's go **somewhere nice**.*   *Is there **anything interesting** in that magazine?*

We can also use **else**.

> *We always play Scrabble. Let's play **something else**. (= a different game)*
> *Henry wore a suit, but **everyone else** had jeans on. (= all the other people)*

Words ending in **one** and **body** have a possessive form (with **'s**).

> ***Someone's** cat is on our roof.*   *I need to be informed about **everybody's** plans.*

▷ page 380 **Someplace**, etc. in American English

A Everyone, something, etc. (1)

Complete the conversations. Put in the correct words.

▶ Melanie: Did you say you found ..<u>something</u>. in the street?
  David: Yes, a diamond ring.
1 Nick: We all know the man is a thief, don't we?
  Tom: Yes, ... knows, but .... dares to say so
       publicly.
2 Mark: Were there any calls for me?
  Secretary: Yes, ... rang while you were out. It was rather strange. He
       refused to give his name, but he wants to discuss .... with you.
3 Melanie: Do you have any plans for the summer?
  Tom: I'd like to go away .... if I can. .... I know
       has invited me to his villa in Portugal, so I may go there.
4 Daniel: Has Matthew got a job yet?
  Emma: No, but he's looked .... He's been to all the job agencies. He
       hates the idea of sitting around doing ....

B Someone and anyone, etc. (2)

Put in *someone*, *anyone*, *something*, *anything*, *somewhere* or *anywhere*.
Rachel: Have you seen my MP3 player? I can't find it (▶) <u>anywhere</u> .
Vicky: No, I haven't. Perhaps (1) ....'s borrowed it.
Rachel: I haven't given (2) .... permission to borrow it. It must be
       (3) .... in this room.
Vicky: Things are in such a mess. It could be (4) ....
Rachel: I know. I can never find (5) .... when I want it.
Vicky: We'll have to do (6) .... about this mess. We'd better tidy it up.

C Singular and plural (3)

Choose the correct form.
▶ We had to wait because someone had lost <u>its/their</u> ticket.
1 One of the policemen had injured <u>his/their</u> arm.
2 One of the guests had brought something wrapped in brown paper. She put <u>it/them</u> on the table.
3 No one <u>likes/like</u> going to the dentist, do <u>he/they</u>?
4 Everyone <u>have/has</u> to leave <u>his/their</u> bags outside.

D Other structures (4)

**Rewrite the sentences using a phrase with *everyone*, *someone*, *something*, *nothing* and
somewhere instead of the phrases in brackets.**
▶ I'd like to buy (a nice thing). <u>I'd like to buy something nice.</u>
▶ Let's go (to another place), shall we? <u>Let's go somewhere else, shall we?</u>
▶ I'll try to remember (the name of everyone). <u>I'll try to remember everyone's name.</u>
1 I once met (a famous person). ....
2 (A person's car) is blocking me in. ....
3 I've got (a different thing) to tell you. ....
4 We know (the opinions of all the people). ....
5 (All the other people) except you are going. ....
6 (No exciting things) ever happen here. ....

Test Q: Pronouns

A

A group of friends are going on a coach trip together. They're meeting at the coach stop.
Complete the conversation. Put in a personal pronoun (*I, me, you,* etc.) or a reflexive pronoun
(*myself, yourself,* etc.).

Polly: Where's Martin?

Rupert: He's ill. I spoke to (▶) .him. yesterday. He was feeling a bit sorry for (1) ....

Polly: Oh, poor Martin. And what about the twins?

Peter: (2) .... came with Janet and me. (3) .... gave (4) ....
           a lift.

Janet: Yes, the twins came with (5) .... in the car.

Tessa: I hope they're going to behave (6) ....

Janet: Oh, I'm sure they will.

Rupert: (7) ....'ll be nice to have a day out. (8) .... say it's going to stay
           sunny.

Polly: I'm sure we'll all enjoy (9) ....

Peter: Where's Anna?

Tessa: Oh, she's here somewhere. I spoke to (10) .... a moment ago. She was
           standing right next to (11) ....

B

Decide which word is correct.

▶ I can't go to a party. I haven't got ..anything. to wear.
    a) anything b) everything c) something d) nothing

1 Take care, won't you, Anna? Look after ....
    a) you b) your c) yours d) yourself

2 Yes, ... would be lovely to see you again.
    a) it b) that c) there d) you

3 If you want some apples, I'll get you .... at the shop.
    a) any b) it c) one d) some

4 We've brought some food with ....
    a) me b) ourselves c) us d) we

5 Who does this CD belong to? ~ .... I've just bought it.
    a) I b) Me c) Mine d) Myself

6 The shop doesn't sell new books. It only sells old ....
    a) of them b) ones c) some d) them

7 Is .... a post office near here, please?
    a) here b) it c) there d) this

8 The two girls often wear .... clothes.
    a) each other b) each other's c) themselves d) themselves'

9 Have you had enough to eat, or would you like something ....?
    a) another b) else c) new d) other

C

Use a pronoun instead of the words in brackets.

▶ Michelle is in hospital. .She. (Michelle) isn't very well.

1 I lost my watch, but it was only a cheap .... (watch).

2 I have to make tea for .... (all the people).

3 Tessa took a photo of .... (Tessa).

4　My flat is the .... (flat) at the top.
5　The phone rang. .... (The caller) was Alex.
6　There was .... (a thing) worrying me.
7　I've got some sweets. Would you like .... (a sweet)?
8　............................ (People in general) can't make an omelette without breaking eggs.
9　We decorated the whole house .... (without help).

D

Complete the text. Write the missing words. Use one word only in each space.
(▶) It was on 20 September 1973 that Bobby Riggs met Billie Jean King on the tennis court. Of all the tennis matches until then, this was probably the (1) .... that attracted the most attention. Riggs had once been a champion, but at 55 he was getting rather old for top-class tennis. But he considered (2) .... a better player than any woman. In fact, he thought women should go home and find (3) .... useful to do in the kitchen. Billie Jean King, on the other hand, was a 29-year-old star of women's tennis and a feminist. Riggs thought that (4) .... would be a good idea to play King. He was sure he could beat (5) .... King agreed to play. (6) .... was a lot of interest in the match, and more or less (7) .... in the country was looking forward to (8) .... On the night of the match, (9) .... were over 30,000 people in the Houston Astrodrome. When Riggs and King came face to face with (10) .... other, they had 50 million people watching (11) .... on TV. The match didn't work out for Riggs, because Billie Jean King defeated (12) .... , 6–4, 6–3, 6–3.

E

Each of these sentences has a mistake in it. Write the correct sentence.
▶　~~I didn't want the fridge, so I sold him.~~
　　I didn't want the fridge, so I sold it.
　　...
1　~~It's a train leaving in ten minutes.~~
　　...
2　~~I think someone are coming up the stairs.~~
　　...
3　~~Let's meet ourselves at eight o'clock, shall we?~~
　　...
4　~~We haven't got a camcorder, but we'd like a.~~
　　...
5　~~Let's do a different something today.~~
　　...
6　~~One is going to build a new motorway through here.~~
　　...
7　~~I'm afraid I haven't done something all day.~~
　　...
8　~~Everyone enjoyed themself at the barbecue.~~
　　...
9　~~If you're buying a loaf, get a nice fresh.~~
　　...
10　~~I've looked in all places for my credit card.~~
　　...
11　~~The two friends still see themselves occasionally.~~
　　...

104 Adjectives

1 Introduction

Henry and Claire are having dinner in a **quiet** *restaurant. It's a* **warm** *evening. The food is* **delicious**. *Henry is feeling* **romantic**.

An adjective is a word like **quiet**, **warm**, **delicious**, **romantic**. The word **quiet** describes the restaurant. It tells us what the restaurant is like.

2 Word order

There are two places where we can use an adjective:
before a noun (*a quiet restaurant*) and after a linking verb (*feeling romantic*).

BEFORE A NOUN	AFTER A LINKING VERB
Claire's got a **new car**.	*Claire's car* **is new**.
It was a **dark night**.	*It was* **getting dark**.
This is **good coffee**.	*This coffee* **tastes good**.
	Some linking verbs are: **appear, be, become, feel, get, look, seem, smell, stay, taste**

We can use two or more adjectives together (see Unit 105).
    It's a **quiet little** *restaurant.*   *Mike was wearing a* **dirty old** *coat.*

We can put a word like **very** or **quite** before an adjective.
    It was a **very dark** *night.*   *Henry was feeling* **quite romantic**.
Very and **quite** are adverbs of degree (see Unit 115).

3 Adjectives used in one position only

We can use most adjectives in both positions – before a noun or after a linking verb. But a few adjectives can go in one position but not in the other.

Here are some examples of adjectives which can only go before a noun.
    Be careful crossing the **main** *road.*   *The* **only** *problem is I've got no money.*
    Chess is an **indoor** *game.*   *The* **former** *footballer now trains young players.*

Some more examples are: **chief** (= main), **elder** (= older), **eldest** (= oldest), **inner**, **outdoor**, **outer**, **principal** (= main), **upper**

Here are some examples of adjectives which can only go after a linking verb.
    At last the baby is **asleep**.   *Emma's two brothers are very* **alike**.
    I'm really **pleased** *to see you.*   *Vicky looked* **ill**, *I thought.*

Some more examples are: **afraid, alone, ashamed, awake, alive, content** (= happy), **fine** (= in good health), **glad, unwell, well**

▷ 82 Two nouns together, e.g. **a colour photo**   ▷ 108 Adjective or adverb?

Practice

A Adjectives (1)

Look at the pictures and write a phrase with an adjective and noun.
Use these nouns: *building, car, cat, chairs, music, power, skirt, weather*

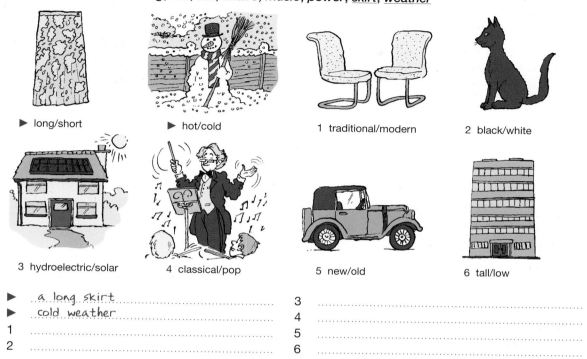

▶ long/short   ▶ hot/cold   1 traditional/modern   2 black/white

3 hydroelectric/solar   4 classical/pop   5 new/old   6 tall/low

▶ a long skirt ....   3 ....
▶ cold weather ....   4 ....
1 ....   5 ....
2 ....   6 ....

B Adjectives (1–2)

<u>Underline</u> all the adjectives in this description of a hotel.

This ▶ <u>comfortable</u> hotel with its pleasant gardens is ideal for people who want a quiet holiday, yet it is only a short distance from the highly popular attractions of the area. There are lovely views from every room. The atmosphere is very friendly, and the staff are always helpful. A holiday here is very good value for money. You can eat your meals at the hotel, where the food tastes marvellous. Or you can of course try some of the excellent local restaurants.

C Adjectives used in one position only (3)

Look at the notes and write the song titles. Sometimes the adjective comes before the noun, and sometimes you need to use *is* or *are*.

▶ your sister / elder   Your elder sister ....
▶ this boy / alone   This boy is alone ....
1 the world / asleep   ....
2 my desire / chief   ....
3 my heart / content   ....
4 the thing to remember / main   ....
5 the night / alive   ....
6 secrets / inner   ....
7 the girl for me / only   ....

105 Adjectives (order)

1 Introduction

*It's **beautiful sunny** weather.*

*Nick has got a **big black** dog.*

We can use more than one adjective before a noun. There is usually one correct order.
We cannot say ~~sunny beautiful weather~~ or ~~a black big dog~~.

2 Adjectives and nouns

We sometimes use two nouns together (see Unit 82).

   *a **glass** door   a **computer** program*

Here we use **glass** like an adjective, to describe the door. When we use another adjective
as well (e.g. **heavy**), it comes before both the nouns.

   *a **heavy** glass door   a **useful** computer program*

3 Word order

We order adjectives according to their meaning. This is the normal order:

	GROUP	EXAMPLES	
1	Opinion (how good?)	***wonderful, nice, great, awful, terrible***	Adjectives that say how good
2	Size (how big?)	***large, small, long, short, tall***	and how big come first.
3	Most other qualities	***quiet, famous, important, soft, wet,*** ***difficult, fast, angry, warm***	Most adjectives come next if they do not belong to another group.
4	Age (how old?)	***new, old***	
5	Colour	***red, blue, green, black***	
6	Origin (where from?)	***American, British, French***	
7	Material (made of?)	***stone, plastic, steel, paper***	Some of these are nouns.
8	Type (what kind?)	*an **electric** kettle, **political** matters, **road** transport*	
9	Purpose (what for?)	*a **bread** knife, a **bath** towel*	

Here are some examples.

   *a **small green** insect* (size, colour)   ***Japanese industrial** designers* (origin, type)
   *a **wonderful new face** cream* (opinion, age, purpose)   ***awful plastic** souvenirs* (opinion, material)
   *a **long boring train** journey* (size, quality, type)   *some **nice easy quiz** questions* (opinion, quality, purpose)
   *a **beautiful wooden picture** frame* (opinion, material, purpose)

We sometimes put commas between adjectives in Groups 1–3

   *a **horrible, ugly** building   a **busy, lively, exciting** city*

Practice

A Adjectives (order) (1–3)

Describe the pictures. Use these words: *boots*, *building*, *car*, *seat*, *singer*

▶ They're leather.
They're big.

1 It's small.
It's white.

2 It's old.
It's attractive.

3 It's wooden.
It's for the garden.
It's expensive.

4 He sings in
the opera.
He's Italian.
He's famous.

▶ big leather boots
1 .... 3 ....
2 .... 4 ....

B Adjectives (order) (1–3)

Write a list of things to be sold at an auction.

▶ basin / sugar, antique, silver .... an antique silver sugar basin
1 vase / glass, old, lovely ....
2 mirror / wall, attractive ....
3 desk / modern, office ....
4 chairs / kitchen, red, metal ....
5 boat / model, splendid, old ....
6 stamps / postage, valuable, Australian ....
7 table / small, coffee, wooden ....

C Adjectives (order) (1–3)

Look at each advertisement and write the information in a single sentence.

▶ This game is new. It's for the family. And it's exciting.
   This is an exciting new family game.

1 This computer is for business. It's Japanese. And it's powerful.
   It's a powerful computer for japanese's business

2 This fire is electric. It's excellent. And it's small.
   It's a small excellent small electric fire

3 This is a chocolate bar. It's new. And it's a big bar.
   This is new big bar chocolate bar

4 This comedy is American. It's for television. And it's terrific.
   This is a terrific comedy american television comedy

5 These doors are aluminium. They're for your garage. And they're stylish.
   These stylish aluminium doors for your garage

6 These shoes are modern. They're for sports. And they're wonderful.
   These wonderful modern sports shoes

7 This phone is a mobile. It's German. And it's very good.
   This very good mobile German mobile phone

106 The old, the rich, etc.

1 Introduction

> These people are protesting. They want equal rights for **the disabled** and more help for **the blind**.

There are some adjectives that we can use with **the** to talk about groups of people in society, e.g. **the disabled, the blind.** Here are some more examples.

> *What can we do to feed **the hungry**?*   ***The rich** can afford to pay more taxes.*
> ***The young** are usually keen to travel.*   *It is our duty to care for **the sick**.*

2 What adjectives can we use?

These are some of the adjectives and other words that we can use in a phrase with **the**.

> To do with social or economic position:
> **the disadvantaged, the homeless, the hungry, the poor, the privileged, the rich, the starving, the strong, the underprivileged, the unemployed, the weak**
>
> To do with physical condition or health:
> **the blind, the deaf, the dead, the disabled, the handicapped, the living, the sick**
>
> To do with age:
> **the elderly, the middle-aged, the old, the over-sixties, the under-fives, the young**

We can sometimes use an adverb before the adjective.

> ***The very poor** are left without hope.*   ***The severely disabled** need full-time care.*

There are some adjectives in this structure that normally have an adverb.

> ***The less fortunate** cannot afford to go on holiday.*
> *Should **the mentally ill** be allowed to live in the community?*

3 The young or the young people?

The young means 'young people in general'.

> ***The young** have their lives in front of them.*

When we mean a specific person or a specific group of people, then we use **man, woman, people,** etc.

> *There was **a young man** standing on the corner.*
> *I know **the young woman** in reception. She lives in our street.*
> *None of **the young people** in the village can find jobs here.*

Practice

A The old, the rich, etc. (1)

Write in the missing words. Use *the* and these adjectives: *homeless, hungry, old, sick, unemployed, young*

▶ Better education for *the young* ....
1 Food for ....
2 Homes for ....
3 Better hospitals for ....
4 Jobs for ....
5 Better pensions for ....

B The old, the rich, etc. (1–2)

Rewrite the sentences using a phrase with *the* and an adjective instead of the <u>underlined</u> phrases.

▶ <u>People who have lots of money</u> have comfortable lives.
The rich have comfortable lives. ....

1 We live near a special school for <u>people who can't hear</u>.
....

2 The old soldiers were holding a service for <u>those who had died</u>.
....

3 The government should do more for <u>people who do not have enough money</u>.
....

4 I'm doing a course on caring for <u>people who are mentally handicapped</u>.
....

C The young or the young people? (3)

Complete these sentences from a newspaper. Use the adjectives in brackets.
Put in e.g. *the hungry* or *the hungry people*.

▶ Rich nations can afford to feed *the hungry* (hungry).
▶ *The homeless people* (homeless) whose story appeared in this paper last week have now found a place to live.

1 .... (sick) need to be looked after, so money must be spent on hospitals.
2 Some of .... (young) at the youth club here are running in a marathon.
3 Life must be hard for .... (unemployed) in our society today.
4 What is the government doing to help .... (poor)?
5 There was a fire at a nursing home in Charles Street, but none of .... (old) who live there were hurt.
6 .... (homeless) usually have great difficulty in getting a job.
7 There is a special television programme for .... (deaf) every Sunday morning.

107 Interesting and interested

1 Introduction

MIKE IS READING ABOUT UFOS.

INTERESTING

The book is full of information. It's very **interesting**.

The word **interesting** tells us what the book does to Mike – it interests him. A book can be **interesting, boring, exciting** or **amusing**, for example.

INTERESTED

Mike is very **interested** in UFOs.

The word **interested** tells us how Mike feels. A person can feel **interested, bored, excited** or **amused**, for example.

2 Adjective pairs

Here are some more examples.

-ING	-ED
Tom told us an **amusing** story.	We were **amused** at Tom's story.
The two-hour delay was **annoying**.	The passengers were **annoyed** about the delay.
I didn't enjoy the party. It was **boring**.	I went to the party, but I felt **bored**.
This computer has some very **confusing** instructions.	I got very **confused** trying to make sense of the instructions.
This wet weather is so **depressing**.	This weather makes me so **depressed**.
It was very **disappointing** not to get the job.	I was very **disappointed** not to get the job.
The game was really **exciting**.	The United fans were **excited**.
Going for a jog with Matthew is **exhausting**.	I'm **exhausted** after jogging all that way.
I thought the programme on wildlife was **fascinating**.	I watched the programme on wildlife. I was absolutely **fascinated**.
For one **frightening/terrifying** moment I thought I was going to fall.	When I got onto the roof, I felt **frightened/terrified**.
I just don't understand. I find the whole thing rather **puzzling**.	I must say I'm **puzzled**. I just don't understand.
Lying in a hot bath is **relaxing**.	I feel **relaxed** when I lie in a hot bath.
I think the way Jessica behaved was quite **shocking**.	I was quite **shocked** to see Jessica behaving like that.
The test results were **surprising**.	I was **surprised** at the test results.
What **thrilling** news this is! Congratulations!	We were **thrilled** to hear your good news.
The journey took all day and night. They found it very **tiring**.	After travelling all day and night they were very **tired**.

Practice

A Interesting and interested (1–2)

What are they saying? Put in these words: *depressing*, *exciting*, *exhausted*, *fascinating*, *interested*

▶ This is a _depressing_ place.

1 I'm absolutely .... 3 Chess is a .... game.
2 I'm .... in astronomy. 4 This is really ....!

B Interesting and interested (1–2)

Complete the conversation. Write the complete word in each space.

Vicky: That was an (▶) _exciting_ (excit...) film, wasn't it?
Rachel: Oh, do you think so? I'm (1) .... (surpris...) you liked it. I thought it
         was rather (2) .... (disappoint...).
Vicky: Well, I was (3) .... (puzzl...) once or twice. I didn't understand the
         whole story. It was (4) .... (confus...) in places. But the end was good.
Rachel: I was (5) .... (bor...) most of the time. I didn't find it very
         (6) .... (interest...).

C Interesting and interested (1–2)

Complete the conversations using a word ending in *-ing* or *-ed*.

▶ David: I'm surprised how warm it is for March.
  Melanie: Yes, all this sunshine is quite _surprising_.
▶ Vicky: I'm not very fit. I was pretty tired after climbing the mountain.
  Natasha: Yes, I think everyone felt _tired_.
1 Trevor: I think I need to relax.
  Laura: Well, lying by the pool should be ....
2 Vicky: It was annoying to lose my ticket.
  Emma: You looked really .... when you had to buy another one.
3 Sarah: The cabaret was amusing.
  Mark: Claire was certainly .... She couldn't stop laughing.
4 Daniel: The museum was interesting, wasn't it?
  Rachel: It was OK. I was quite .... in those old maps.
5 Matthew: I'm fascinated by these old photos.
  Emma: I always find it .... to see what people looked like as children.
6 Rachel: Was it a big thrill meeting Tom Hanks?
  Vicky: You bet. It was just about the most .... moment of my life.
7 Sarah: You look exhausted. You should go to bed.
  Mark: Driving down from Scotland was pretty ....

108 Adjective or adverb? (1)

1 Introduction

Vicky: *I like that song that Natasha sang.*
Rachel: *Yes, it's a **nice** song. And she sang it **nicely**, too.*

An adjective (**nice**) describes a noun (**song**). *The man had a **quiet voice**.* *Claire wears **expensive clothes**.* *The runners made a **slow start**.*	An adverb (**nicely**) describes a verb (**sang**). *The man **spoke quietly**.* *Claire **dresses expensively**.* *They **started** the race **slowly**.* We do NOT say ~~She sang it nice.~~

We can use adverbs in other ways. An adverb like **really** or **very** can be combined with an adjective (**hot**) or another adverb (**carefully**) (see Unit 115).
   *It was **really hot** in the sun.*   *Andrew checked his work **very carefully**.*
An adverb like **fortunately** or **perhaps** says something about the whole situation.
   ***Fortunately** nothing was stolen.*   ***Perhaps** Sarah is working late.*

2 The -ly ending

We form many adverbs from an adjective + **-ly**. For example **politely**, **quickly**, **safely**.
But there are some special spelling rules.

1   We do not leave out **e**, e.g. nice → nicely
    Exceptions are true → truly, whole → wholly.
2   **-y** → **-ily** after a consonant, e.g. easy → easily, lucky → luckily
    Also **angrily, happily, heavily**, etc.
3   **-le** → **-ly**, e.g. possible → possibly
    Also **comfortably, probably, reasonably, sensibly, terribly**, etc.
4   **-ic** → **-ically**, e.g. dramatic → dramatically
    Also **automatically, scientifically**, etc. (Exception: **publicly**)

3 Looked **nice** and looked **carefully**

Compare these two structures.

LINKING VERB + ADJECTIVE	ACTION VERB + ADVERB
*Tom **was hungry**.* *The children **seemed happy**.* *My soup has **got cold**.* An adjective can come after a linking verb such as **be** (see Unit 104.2).	*Paul **ate hungrily**.* *The children **played happily**.* *The man **stared coldly** at us.* We use an adverb when the verb means that something happens.

Some verbs like **look, taste** and **appear** can be either linking verbs or action verbs.

LINKING VERB + ADJECTIVE	ACTION VERB + ADVERB
*Mike **looked angry**.* *The medicine **tasted awful**.* *The man **appeared** (to be) **drunk**.*	*He **looked carefully** at the signature.* *Emma **tasted** the drink **nervously**.* *A waiter **appeared suddenly**.*

▷ page 380 American English

Practice

A Adverbs (1–2)

This is part of a story about a spy called X. Put in adverbs formed from these adjectives:
bright, careful, fluent, immediate, patient, punctual, quiet, safe, secret, slow

The journey took a long time because the train travelled so (▶) .slowly. It was hot, and the sun
shone (1) .... from a clear sky. X could only wait (2) .... for
the journey to end. When the train finally arrived, he had no time to spare, so he
(3) .... took a taxi to the hotel. Y was on time. She arrived
(4) .... at three. No one else knew about the meeting – it was important to meet
(5) .... 'I had a terrible journey,' said Y. 'But luckily the pilot managed to land
(6) ....' Her English was good, and she spoke very (7) ....
X was listening (8) .... to every word. They were speaking very
(9) .... in case the room was bugged.

B The -ly ending (2)

Look at the information in brackets and put in the adverbs. Be careful with the spelling.
▶ (Emma's toothache was terrible.) Emma's tooth ached .terribly.
1 (Henry was angry.) Henry shouted .... at the waiter.
2 (I'm happy sitting here.) I can sit here .... for hours.
3 (The switch is automatic.) The machine switches itself off ....
4 (The debate should be public.) We need to debate the matter ....
5 (Everyone was enthusiastic.) Everyone discussed the idea ....
6 (We should be reasonable.) Can't we discuss the problem ....?
7 (The building has to be secure.) Did you lock all the doors ....?

C Adverb or adjective? (1–2)

Decide what you need to say. End your sentence with an adverb ending in *-ly*.
▶ Tell the police that you can't remember the accident. It isn't very clear in your mind.
  I can't remember the accident very clearly.
1 Tell your friend that United won the game. It was an easy win.
  ....
2 Tell your boss that you've checked the figures. You've been careful.
  ....
3 Tell your neighbour that his dog barked at you. It was very fierce.
  ....
4 You are phoning your friend. Tell him about the rain where you are. It's quite heavy.
  ....

D Adverb or adjective? (1–3)

Vicky is telling Rachel about a dream she had. Choose the correct forms.

I had a (▶) strange/~~strangely~~ dream last night. I was in a garden. It was getting (1) dark/darkly, and it
was (2) terrible/terribly cold. My head was aching (3) bad/badly. I was walking out of the garden when
(4) sudden/suddenly I saw a man. He was sitting (5) quiet/quietly on a seat. He seemed very
(6) unhappy/unhappily. He looked up and smiled (7) sad/sadly at me. I don't know why, but I felt
(8) curious/curiously about him. I wanted to talk to him, but I couldn't think what to say. I just stood
there (9) foolish/foolishly.

109 Adjective or adverb? (2)

1 Friendly, likely, etc.

The ending -**ly** is the normal adverb ending (see Unit 108). But a few adjectives also end in -**ly**.
  *Melanie was very **friendly**.   It was a **lively** party.   We had a **lovely** time.*

Some more examples are: **elderly, likely, lonely, silly, ugly**

The words are adjectives, not adverbs (NOT ~~She spoke to us friendly~~). And we cannot add -**ly**.
There is no such word as ~~friendlily~~. But we can say **in a friendly way/manner**.
  *She spoke to us **in a friendly way**.*
If we need to use an adverb, we often choose another word of similar meaning.
  *It was lovely. Everything went **beautifully**.*

2 Hard, fast, etc.

Compare these sentences.

ADJECTIVE	ADVERB
*We did some **hard** work.*	*We worked **hard**.*
*I came on the **fast** train.*	*The train went quite **fast**.*

We can use these words both as adjectives and as adverbs:
deep, early, fast, hard, high, late, long, low, near, right, straight, wrong (For **hardly, nearly**, etc, see 3.)

In informal English, the adjectives **cheap, loud, quick** and **slow** can be adverbs.

ADJECTIVE	ADVERB
*They sell **cheap** clothes in the market.*	*They sell things **cheap**/cheaply there.*
*Back already! That was **quick**.*	*Come as **quick**/quickly as you can.*

3 Hard, hardly, near, nearly, etc.

There are some pairs of adverbs like **hard** and **hardly** which have different meanings.
Here are some examples.
  *I tried **hard**, but I didn't succeed.*
  *I've got **hardly** any money left.* (*hardly any* = very little, almost none)
  *Luckily I found a phone box quite **near**.   I **nearly** fell asleep in the meeting.* (*nearly* = almost)
  *Rachel arrived **late**, as usual.   I've been very busy **lately**.* (*lately* = in the last few days/weeks)
  *The plane flew **high** above the clouds.   The material is **highly** radioactive.* (*highly* = very)
  *We got into the concert **free**.* (*free* = without paying)
  *The animals are allowed to wander **freely**.* (*freely* = uncontrolled)

4 Good and well

Good is an adjective, and **well** is its adverb. The opposites are **bad** and **badly**.

ADJECTIVE	ADVERB
*Natasha is a **good** violinist.*	*She plays the violin very **well**.*
*Our test results were **good**.*	*We all did **well** in the test.*
*I had a **bad** night.*	*I slept **badly** last night.*

Well can also be an adjective meaning 'in good health', the opposite of **ill**.
  *My mother was very **ill**, but she's quite **well** again now.   How are you? ~ Very **well**, thank you.*

Practice

A Friendly, hard, hardly, etc. (1–3)

Decide if each underlined word is an adjective or an adverb.

▶   That new building is rather <u>ugly</u>.   adjective

▶   I'd like to arrive <u>early</u> if I can.   adverb

1   I haven't seen you for a <u>long</u> time.   ....

2   Why are you wearing that <u>silly</u> hat?   ....

3   Very young children travel <u>free</u>.   ....

4   The temperature is quite <u>high</u> today.   ....

5   We <u>nearly</u> missed the bus this morning.   ....

6   Do you have to play that music so <u>loud</u>?   ....

B Friendly, hard, hardly, etc. (1–3)

Complete the conversation. Decide if you need -ly with the words in brackets.

Mark: How did you get on with Henry today?

Sarah: Oh, we had a nice lunch and some (▶) .lively. (live) conversation. Henry was charming, as usual. He gave me a lift back to the office, but it was (1) .... (hard) worth risking our lives to save a few minutes. He (2) .... (near) killed us.

Mark: What do you mean?

Sarah: Well, we'd sat a bit too (3) .... (long) over our meal, and we were (4) .... (late) getting back to work. Henry drove very (5) .... (fast). I tried (6) .... (hard) to keep calm, but I was quite scared. We went (7) .... (wrong) and missed a left turn, and Henry got annoyed. Then a van came round the corner, and it was coming (8) .... (straight) at us. I don't know how we missed it.

Mark: Well, I'm glad you did. And next time you'd better take a taxi.

C Good and well (4)

Complete the conversation. Put in good, well (x2), bad, badly and ill.

Rachel: How did you and Daniel get on in your tennis match?

Matthew: We lost. I'm afraid we didn't play very (▶) .well.. Daniel made some (1) .... mistakes. It wasn't a very (2) .... day for us. We played really (3) ....

Andrew: I heard Daniel's in bed at the moment because he isn't very (4) ....

Matthew: Yes, I'm afraid he's been (5) .... for several days, but he's better now.

D Friendly, hard, hardly, etc. (1–4)

Complete the conversation. Choose the correct form.

Daniel: Is it true you saw a ghost last night?

Vicky: Yes, I did. I went to bed (▶) <u>late</u>/~~lately~~, and I was sleeping (1) <u>bad/badly</u>. I suddenly woke up in the middle of the night. I went to the window and saw the ghost walking across the lawn.

Daniel: Was it a man or a woman?

Vicky: A woman in a white dress. I had a (2) <u>good/well</u> view from the window, but she walked very (3) <u>fast/fastly</u>. She wasn't there very (4) <u>long/longly</u>. I'd (5) <u>hard/hardly</u> caught sight of her before she'd gone. I (6) <u>near/nearly</u> missed her.

Daniel: You don't think you've been working too (7) <u>hard/hardly</u>? You've been looking a bit pale (8) <u>late/lately</u>.

Vicky: I saw her, I tell you.

Daniel: It isn't very (9) <u>like/likely</u> that ghosts actually exist, you know. I expect you were imagining it.

Test R: Adjectives and adverbs

A

Choose the correct word or phrase.

▶ We walked slow/slowly back to the hotel.
1 We could walk free/freely around the aircraft during the flight.
2 The young/The young man with dark hair is my sister's boyfriend.
3 I'm getting quite hungry/hungrily.
4 The man looked thoughtful/thoughtfully around the room.
5 Have I filled this form in right/rightly?
6 I think Egypt is a fascinated/fascinating country.
7 The two sisters do alike/similar jobs.
8 I'm pleased the plan worked so good/goodly/well.
9 She invented a new kind of wheelchair for the disabled/the disabled people.
10 I'm very confused/confusing about what to do.
11 They performed the experiment scientifically/scientificly.
12 The hostages must be very afraid/frightened people.

B

Put the words in the right order to form a statement.

▶ a / bought / coat / I / new / red
  I bought a new red coat.
1 a / is / nice / place / this
  ....
2 biscuit / can't / find / I / large / the / tin
  ....
3 a / behaved / in / silly / Tessa / way
  ....
4 coffee / cold / getting / is / your
  ....
5 a / house / in / live / lovely / old / stone / they
  ....
6 for / hospital / ill / is / mentally / the / this
  ....

C

Write the words in brackets and add -ly, -ing or -ed only if you need to.

Janet: Is this the (▶) new (new...) car you've just bought?
Nigel: That's right. Well, it's second-hand of course.
Janet: It's (▶) exciting (excit...) buying a car, isn't it?
Nigel: Well, it was a bit of a problem actually because I didn't have much money to spend. But I managed to find one that wasn't very (1) .... (expensive...).
Janet: It looks very (2) .... (nice...), I must say.
Nigel: It's ten years old, so I was (3) .... (surpris...) what good condition it's in. The man I bought it from is over eighty, and he always drove it very (4) .... (careful...), he said. He never took it out if it was raining, which I find (5) .... (amus...).
Janet: I think (6) .... (elder...) people look after their cars better than young people.
Nigel: He was a (7) .... (friend...) old chap. He even gave me all these maps (8) .... (free...).

D

Write a second sentence so that it has a similar meaning to the first. Use the word in brackets.

▶ Jonathan was stupid. (behaved)
~~Jonathan behaved stupidly.~~

1 The drink had a strange taste. (tasted)

....

2 Obviously, sick people need to be looked after. (the)

....

3 The dog slept. (asleep)

....

4 The young woman was polite. (spoke)

....

5 The train was late. (arrived)

....

6 The film's ending is dramatic. (ends)

....

7 Polly gave an angry shout. (shouted)

....

8 Billiards is a game for indoors. (indoor)

....

9 The clown amused people. (amusing)

....

10 There was almost no time left. (any)

....

E

Some of these sentences are correct, but most have a mistake. If the sentence is correct, put a tick (✓). If it is incorrect, cross the sentence out and write it correctly.

▶ Your friend looked rather ill.   ✓

▶ ~~It was a steel long pipe.~~   It was a long steel pipe.

1 I tasted the soup careful.
2 It's a beautiful old English church.
3 Are they asleep children?
4 It's a school for the deaf people.
5 It's a leather new nice jacket.
6 The riches are very lucky.
7 You handled the situation well.
8 He used a green paper thick towel.
9 Our future lies with the young.
10 The course I started was bored.
11 I often talk to the two old next door.
12 The smoke rose highly into the air.
13 It feels warm in here.
14 We felt disappointing when we lost.
15 Everyone seemed very nervously.
16 Tessa drives too fastly.
17 This scenery is really depressing.

110 Comparative and superlative forms

1 The comparison of adjectives

We form the comparative and superlative of short adjectives (e.g. **cheap**) and long adjectives (e.g. **expensive**) in different ways.

	COMPARATIVE	SUPERLATIVE
Short word, e.g. *cheap*:	*cheaper*	(*the*) *cheapest*
Long word, e.g. *expensive*:	*more expensive*	(*the*) *most expensive*

For **less** and **least**, see Unit 112.1.
> *There are some **less expensive** ones here, look.*

2 Short and long adjectives

One-syllable adjectives (e.g. **small**, **nice**) usually have the -**er**, -**est** ending.
> *Your hi-fi is **smaller**.   Emma needs a **bigger** computer.*
> *This is the **nicest** colour.   This room is the **warmest**.*

But we use **more**, **most** before words ending in -**ed**.
> *Everyone was pleased at the results, but Vicky was the **most pleased**.*

We also use **more**, **most** with three-syllable adjectives (e.g. **ex·cit·ing**) and with longer ones.
> *The film was **more exciting** than the book.   This dress is **more elegant**.*
> *We did the **most interesting** project.   This machine is the **most reliable**.*

Some two-syllable adjectives have -**er**, -**est**, and some have **more**, **most**. Look at this information.

TWO SYLLABLE ADJECTIVES

1   Words ending in a consonant + -**y** have -**er**, -**est**, e.g. *happy* → *hap**pier**, hap**piest***.
    Examples are: *busy, dirty, easy, funny, happy, heavy, lovely, lucky, pretty, silly, tidy*
2   Some words have -**er**, -**est** OR *more*, *most*, e.g. *narrow* → *narro**wer**, narro**west*** OR ***more** narrow*, ***most** narrow*.
    Examples are: *clever, common, cruel, gentle, narrow, pleasant, polite, quiet, simple, stupid, tired*
3   The following words have *more*, *most*, e.g. *useful* → ***more** useful*, ***most** useful*.
    a   Words ending in -***ful*** or -***less***, e.g. ***careful**, **helpful**, **useful**; **hopeless***
    b   Words ending in -*ing* or -*ed*, e.g. *boring, willing; annoyed, surprised*
    c   Many others, e.g. *afraid, certain, correct, eager, exact, famous, foolish, frequent, modern, nervous, normal, recent*

---

3 Spelling

There are some special spelling rules for the -er and -est endings.

> 1   -e → -er, -est, e.g. *nice* → *nicer, nicest, large* → *larger, largest*.
>   Also *brave, fine, safe,* etc.
> 2   -y → -ier, -iest after a consonant, e.g. *happy* → *happier, happiest*.
>   Also *lovely, lucky, pretty,* etc.
> 3   Words ending in a single vowel letter + single consonant letter → double the consonant
>   e.g. *hot* → *hotter, hottest, big* → *bigger, biggest*.
>   Also *fit, sad, thin, wet,* etc. (but *w* does not change, e.g. *new* → *newer*)

For more details, see page 371.

4 The comparison of adverbs

Some adverbs have the same form as an adjective, e.g. **early, fast, hard, high, late, long, near.**
They form the comparative and superlative with -er, -est.
> *Can't you run **faster** than that?*   *Andrew works the **hardest**.*

Note also the spelling of **earlier** and **earliest**.

Many adverbs are an adjective + -ly, e.g. **carefully, easily, nicely, slowly.**
They form the comparative and superlative with **more, most.**
> *We could do this **more easily** with a computer.*
> *Of all the players it was Matthew who planned his tactics the **most carefully**.*

In informal English we use **cheaper, cheapest, louder, loudest, quicker, quickest** and **slower, slowest** rather than **more cheaply, the most loudly,** etc.
> *Melanie reacted the **quickest**.*   *You should drive **slower** in fog.*

Note the forms **sooner, soonest** and **more often, most often.**
> *Try to get home **sooner**.*   *I must exercise **more often**.*

5 Irregular forms

Good, well, bad, badly and **far** have irregular forms.

ADJECTIVE/ADVERB	COMPARATIVE	SUPERLATIVE
good/well	*better*	*best*
bad/badly	*worse*	*worst*
far	*farther/further*	*farthest/furthest*

> *You've got the **best** handwriting.*   *How much **further** are we going?*

We can use **elder, eldest** + noun instead of **older, oldest,** but only for people in the same family.
> *My **elder/older** sister got married last year.*

6 Comparing quantities

We use **more, most** and their opposites **less** and **least** to compare quantities.
> *I haven't got many books. You've got **more** than I have.*   *The Hotel Bristol has the **most** rooms.*
> *Trevor spends **less** on clothes than Laura does.*   *Emma made the **least** mistakes.*

▷ 111–112 Comparative and superlative patterns

Practice

A The comparison of adjectives (1–2)

Complete the sentences. Use these adjectives: *beautiful*, <u>*expensive*</u>, *high*, *interesting*, <u>*tall*</u>

▶ The giraffe is taller than the man.
▶ The CD is more expensive. than the cassette.
1 Detective stories .... than algebra.
2 The top of the mountain .... than the clouds.
3 The acrobat .... than the clown.

B The comparison of adjectives (1–2)

Tom is a United fan. He never stops talking about them. Put in the superlative form of the adjectives.
▶ Everyone's heard of United. They're the most famous. (famous) team in the world.
▶ They've got a long history. They're the oldest. (old) club in England.
1 They've got lots of money. They're the .... (rich) club in the country.
2 Their stadium is new. It's the .... (modern) stadium in Europe.
3 United are wonderful. They're the .... (great) club in the world.
4 And what a team! It's the .... (exciting) team ever.
5 They've got lots of fans. They're the .... (popular) team in the country.
6 United have won everything. They're the .... (successful) team ever.
7 They're good to watch. They play the .... (attractive) football.
8 United fans are happy. We're the .... (happy) people in the world.

C The comparison of adjectives (1–3)

Complete the advertisements with the comparative form of the adjective.
▶ Use Get-It-Clean and you'll get your floors cleaner .
▶ Elegant Wallpapers simply look more elegant .
1 Watch a Happy Video and you'll feel ....
2 Wear a pair of Fast Shoes and you'll be a .... runner.
3 Helpful Cookbooks are a .... guide to cooking.
4 Wash your hair with Lovely Shampoo for .... hair.
5 Try a Big-Big Burger and you'll have a .... meal.
6 Restful Beds give you a .... night.
7 Wear Modern Fashions for a .... look.

D The comparison of adverbs (4)

Put in the comparative form of these adverbs: *carefully, early, easily, high, long, loud, often, smartly*

▶ I was too nervous to go .*higher*. than halfway up the tower.
▶ We could have found the place .*more easily*. with a map.
1 Do you have to wear those old jeans, Mike? Can't you dress ....?
2 You needn't go yet. You can stay a bit ....
3 There are lots of break-ins. They happen .... nowadays.
4 If you do it again ...., you won't make so many mistakes.
5 The film starts at eight, but we should get to the cinema a few minutes ....
6 We can't hear. Could you speak a bit ....?

E Irregular forms (5)

Matthew and Emma are walking in the country. Put in *further, furthest, better, best, worse* and *worst*.

Emma: I'm not used to country walks. How much (▶) .*further*. is it?
Matthew: Not far. And it gets better. We've done the (1) .... part. Look, the path
          gets easier. It goes downhill from here. I hope you're feeling (2) ....
          now, Emma.
Emma: I feel dreadful, actually, (3) .... than before.
Matthew: Oh, dear. Do you want to have a rest?
Emma: No, the (4) .... thing would be to get home as soon as we can. I'm
          not very fit, you know. This is the (5) .... I've walked for a long time.

F Comparing quantities (6)

Put in *more, most, less* (x2) and *least*.

Laura: Our new car is smaller, so it uses (▶) .*less*. petrol. They tested some small cars, and this one
           costs the (1) .... to run of all the cars in the test. It's very economical,
           so Trevor likes it. He wants to spend (2) .... on motoring.
Harriet: Can you get three people in the back?
Laura: Not very easily. We had (3) .... room in our old car.
           (4) .... cars take five people, but not this one.

G Comparative and superlative forms (1–6)

Write the correct forms.

▶ You're the ~~luckyest~~ person I know.   *luckiest*
▶ The situation is getting ~~difficulter.~~   *more difficult*
1 I was ~~happyer~~ in my old job.   ....
2 I've got the ~~most small~~ office.   ....
3 This photo is the ~~goodest.~~   ....
4 Last week's meeting was ~~more short.~~   ....
5 Money is the ~~importantest~~ thing.   ....
6 Is Rachel ~~elder~~ than Vicky?   ....
7 This game is ~~excitinger~~ than the last one.   ....
8 Of all the students, Andrew does the ~~more~~ work.   ....
9 This month has been ~~weter~~ than last month.   ....
10 The prices are ~~more low~~ here.   ....
11 I feel more ~~bad than~~ I did yesterday.   ....

111 Comparative and superlative patterns (1)

1 Introduction

Claire, will you marry me?

Henry, I like you very much. You're the **sweetest** man **in the world**. But you're twenty years **older than** me.

There are a number of different sentence patterns with comparative and superlative forms, e.g. **older than me**, **the sweetest man in the world**.

2 The comparative and **than**

We often use a phrase with **than** after a comparative.

*This restaurant is **nicer than** the Pizza House.*
*I had a **bigger** meal **than** you.*
*The steak is **more expensive than** the fish.*

3 The superlative

We normally use **the** before a superlative.

*The **quickest** way is along this path.*   *The last question is **the most difficult**.*

Note the pattern with **one of**.

*Madonna is **one of the most famous** pop singers ever.*

After a superlative we can use **in** or **of**. We use **in** with places and with groups of people, e.g. **team**.

*It's the **most expensive** hotel **in Oxford**.*   *Who is the **best** player **in the team**?*
*This question is the **most difficult of all**.*   *August is the **wettest** month **of the year**.*

We often use a clause after a superlative.

*That was the **most delicious** meal (**that**) **I've ever eaten**.*
*Melanie is the **nicest** person **you could meet**.*

4 As ... as

We use **as ... as** to say that things are equal or unequal.

*Our house is **as big as** yours. They're the same size.* NOT ~~It is so big as yours.~~
*It's warmer today. It **isn't as cold as** yesterday.*

In a negative sentence we can also use **so ... as**, but this is less common than **as ... as**.

*This flat **isn't as big as/so big as** our old one.*

Here are some more examples of **as ... as**.

*The chair is **as expensive as** the table.*   *We can't do crosswords **as quickly as** you do.*
*I don't earn **as much** money **as** I'd like.*

Note also **the same as**.

*The result of the match was **the same as** last year.*

5 Than me/than I am

Compare **than me** and **than I am**. Both are correct, and they have the same meaning.

*You're twenty years older than **me**.*	*You're twenty years older than **I am**.*
*Harriet's husband isn't as tall as **her**.*	*Her husband isn't as tall as **she is**.*
After **than** or **as**, a personal pronoun on its own has the object form, e.g. **me**.	But if the pronoun has a verb after it, then we use the subject form, e.g. **I**.

Practice

A The comparative and **than** (2)

Comment on these situations. Write sentences with a comparative and *than*.
Use these adjectives: *big, expensive, long, old, popular, strong, tall*

▶ The film lasts two and a half hours, but the videotape is only two hours long.
   The film is longer than the videotape.

▶ The water-colour is £85, and the oil-painting is £100.
   The oil-painting is more expensive than the water-colour.

1 The church was built in 1878 and the library in 1925.

   ....

2 Daniel can lift 90 kilos, but Matthew can lift 120 kilos.

   ....

3 Mike is 1.7 metres tall, but Harriet is 1.8 metres.

   ....

4 Andrew hasn't many friends. Claire has lots of friends.

   ....

5 Mark's car has room for five people, but Sarah's has room for only four.

   ....

B The superlative (3)

Write sentences from the notes. Use the superlative form of the adjective.

▶ Melanie / kind person / I know   *Melanie is the kindest person I know.*
1 Friday / busy day / week   .... of the week.
2 the Metropole / nice hotel / town   ....
3 this watch / one / cheap / you can buy   ....
4 this Beatles album / good / they ever made   ....
5 Alan / successful salesman / company   ....

C As ... as (4)

Use the notes and add sentences with *isn't as ... as*.

▶ a car / a motorbike / expensive
   Why don't you buy a motorbike? *A motorbike isn't as expensive as a car.*
1 metal / plastic / strong
   I don't like these plastic screws. ....
2 the armchair / the stool / comfortable
   Oh, don't sit there. ....
3 surfing / swimming / exciting
   I prefer surfing to swimming. ....
4 the post / e-mail / quick
   A letter will take two days. ....

D Than me/than I am (5)

Choose the correct pronoun.

Tom: Why is Luke in our basketball team and not me? Aren't I as good as (▶) ~~he~~/him? Is he taller than (1) I/me? Is he a better player than (2) I am/me am?

Nick: I don't know. I can't understand why I'm in the team. You and Luke are both better than (3) I/me.

Tom: Carl's in the team too, but I've scored a lot more points than (4) he has/him has.

ADJECTIVES AND ADVERBS • PAGE 265

112 Comparative and superlative patterns (2)

1 Less and least

Less and least are the opposites of more and most. We use less and least with both long and short words.

*A bus is **less** expensive than a taxi.*
(= A bus is cheaper than a taxi./A bus isn't as expensive as a taxi.)
*I feel better today, **less** tired.   I'm the **least** musical person in the world, I'm afraid.*
*We go out **less** often these days.   You should do **less** work. You do too much.*

2 Much faster

We can put a word or phrase (e.g. **much, far, a bit**) before a comparative
to say how much faster, cheaper, etc. something is. Look at these examples.

*It's **much faster** by tube.   A bus is **far cheaper** than a taxi.*
*This bed is **a bit more comfortable**.   Business is **rather better** this year.*
*I got up **a little later** than usual.   This month's figures are **slightly less good**.*
*I'll need **a lot more** water.   A computer will do it **much more efficiently**.*

Before a comparative we can use **much, a lot, far; rather; slightly, a bit, a little.**

We can also use **no** and **any**. **No** has a negative meaning.

*Your second throw at the basket was **no nearer** than your first.*

We can use **any** in negatives and questions and with **if**.

*Your second throw wasn't **any nearer** than your first.*
*Are you sleeping **any better** since you've been taking the pills?*
*If we leave **any later** than seven, we'll get caught in the rush hour.*

3 Faster and faster

We use expressions like **faster and faster** and **more and more expensive**
to say that something is increasing all the time.

*The caravan was rolling **faster and faster** down the hill.*
*The queue was getting **longer and longer**.*
*Prices go up and up. Everything gets **more and more expensive**.*
*The crowd are becoming **more and more excited**.*
*The country is rapidly losing its workers, as **more and more** people are emigrating.*

The form depends on whether the comparative is with **-er** (e.g. **louder**) or with **more** (e.g. **more expensive**)
(see Unit 110.2).

We can also use **less and less** for something decreasing.

*As each new problem arose, we felt **less and less enthusiastic**.*

4 The faster, the better

We use this pattern to say that a change in one thing goes with a change in another. Look at these examples.

*There's no time to lose. **The faster** you drive, **the better**.*
***The higher** the price, **the more reliable** the product.*
***The more** the customer complained, **the ruder** and **more unpleasant** the manager became.*
***The sooner** we leave, **the sooner** we'll get there.*
*Are you looking for a cheap holiday? ~ Yes, **the cheaper the better**.*

A Less (1)

Complete the sentences. Use *less* with these words: *attractive, busy, convenient,*
nervous, optimistic, painful, seriously

▶ Laura once hated flying, but now she feels ..*less nervous*.. about it.
1 David says his leg really hurt at first, but now it's ....
2 Mark and Sarah normally have lots to do, but they're .... this week.
3 Rita's old flat was near the shops. Her new place is .... for
   shopping.
4 Claire used to think Henry was very handsome, but now she finds him ....
5 Matthew is always exercising. Maybe he should take his fitness ....
6 With United's best player injured, Tom feels .... about their chances.

B Much faster (2)

Decide what to say. Use a phrase like *a bit better* or *a lot colder*.

▶ You were feeling unwell earlier. Say that you feel better now. A bit, anyway.
   I feel a bit better now.
1 Mention that yesterday was colder than today. A lot colder, in fact.
   ....
2 Say that your coat is longer than is fashionable. A bit, anyway.
   ....
3 You left work earlier than usual this afternoon. Slightly, anyway. Tell your friend.
   ....
4 Say that the shop is more expensive than the supermarket. Much more.
   ....
5 Ask if the new machine is reliable – any more so than the old one.
   ....

C Faster and faster (3)

Vicky works very hard at her studies, but she's worried that she's making no progress.
Complete her sentences.

▶ This subject gets ..*harder and harder*.. (hard) all the time.
▶ I'm just getting ..*more and more confused*.. (confused).
1 It's becoming .... (difficult) for me to keep up.
2 The textbook just gets .... (complicated).
3 I spend .... (more) time on my work.
4 My list of things to do gets .... (long).
5 My problems are just getting .... (bad).

D The faster, the better (4)

Complete each sentence using the information in brackets.

▶ (The rent is high.) The bigger a flat is, *the higher the rent is.*
▶ (You learn quickly.) The younger you are, *the more quickly you learn.*
1 (The roads are quiet.) The earlier you leave, ...
2 (The choice is wide.) The bigger a supermarket is, ...
3 (I get confused.) The more I try to work this out, ...
4 (You can speak fluently.) The more you practise, ...
5 (The beaches get crowded.) The better the weather is, ...

Test S: Comparative and superlative

A

Write the comparative form of the words in brackets.

▶ They've made these chocolate bars ..smaller.. (small).

▶ Sport is ..more..interesting.. (interesting) than politics.

1 Can't you think of anything .... (intelligent) to say?

2 Well, the place looks .... (clean) now.

3 Janet looks .... (thin) than she did.

4 You need to draw it .... (carefully).

5 The weather is getting .... (bad).

6 The programme will be shown at a .... (late) date.

7 I can't stay .... (long) than half an hour.

8 A mobile phone would be a .... (useful) present.

9 I'll try to finish the job .... (soon).

10 It was .... (busy) than usual in town today.

11 I'll be even .... (annoyed) if you do that again.

12 Since the break-in I feel .... (nervous).

B

Write the superlative form of the words in brackets.

▶ It's the ..shortest.. (short) day of the year.

▶ It's the ..most..beautiful.. (beautiful) building in the world.

1 That was the .... (funny) film I've ever seen.

2 It was the .... (horrible) feeling I've ever had.

3 Have you read her .... (recent) book?

4 It's the .... (large) company in the country.

5 It was the .... (boring) speech I've ever heard.

6 You've got the .... (far) to travel.

7 That's the .... (helpful) idea so far.

8 The factory uses the .... (modern) production methods.

9 This is the .... (early) I've ever got up.

10 It was the .... (sad) day of my life.

C

Some of these sentences are correct, and some have a word which should not be there. If a sentence is correct, put a tick (✓). If it is incorrect, cross the unnecessary word out of the sentence and write it in the space.

▶ I've got the least powerful computer in the world.   ✓................

▶ London is ~~more~~ bigger than Birmingham.   more................

1 Silver isn't as expensive as gold.   ....

2 Indian food is the nicer than Chinese, I think.   ....

3 The telephone is one of the most useful inventions ever.   ....

4 I feel a much better now, thank you.   ....

5 The longer you wait, so the harder it'll be.   ....

6 The piano is heavier than the sofa.   ....

7 This is the most quickest way to the hotel.   ....

8 You're taller than he is.   ....

9 Who is the cleverest student in of the class?   ....

10 The weather is getting hotter and more hotter.   ....

D

Read this part of Tessa's letter to her friend Angela about her new job.
Then look at the answers after the letter and write the correct answer in each space.

My new job is great. I like it (▶) .much. better than my old one. The people here are
(1) .... than I expected. Luckily my new boss isn't as rude
(2) .... my old boss, Mrs Crossley, was. I hated her. She was the
(3) .... friendly person I've ever met. Everyone here is older
(4) .... In fact I'm the youngest person (5) ....
the office. But I don't mind.

The good thing about the job is that I get a (6) .... more money, although
not much more than I did before. The bad thing is that the journey isn't (7) ....
simple as it was in my old job, where the bus took me straight there. Now I have to change buses.
But I'm allowed to start work early. The earlier I leave home, (8) .... the
journey is because the buses aren't so crowded.

▶	a) more	b) most	c) much	d) very
1	a) more nice	b) most nice	c) nicer	d) nicest
2	a) as	b) so	c) than	d) that
3	a) least	b) less	c) less and less	d) so
4	a) as I	b) as me	c) than I	d) than me
5	a) from	b) in	c) of	d) out of
6	a) bit	b) less	c) lot	d) much
7	a) as	b) less	c) more	d) same
8	a) more easier	b) more easy	c) the easier	d) the easy

E

Complete the second sentence so that it has a similar meaning to the first. Use the word in brackets.

▶ This train is more convenient than all the others. (most)
This train is. the. most. convenient... .

1 The living-room isn't as big as the kitchen. (bigger)
The kitchen ....

2 I'm not as fit as you. (am)
You're ....

3 The table and the desk are the same size. (big)
The table .... the desk.

4 Prices just get higher all the time. (and)
Prices ....

5 The dress is cheaper than the skirt. (expensive)
The skirt .... the dress.

6 This crossword is the easiest. (difficult)
This crossword ....

7 Their excitement was increasing all the time. (excited)
They were getting ....

8 I've never read a more romantic story. (most)
It's the .... read.

113 Adverbs and word order

1 Where do adverbs go?

There are three places in the sentences where an adverb can go. They are called front position (at the beginning of a sentence), mid position (see 2) and end position (at the end of a sentence).
(But for adverbs of degree see Unit 115.)

FRONT		MID		END
Then	the ship	**slowly**	sailed	**away.**
Outside	it was	**obviously**	raining	**hard.**

2 Mid position

Mid position means close to the verb. Here are some examples of adverbs in mid position.

	AUXILIARY	ADVERB	AUXILIARY	MAIN VERB	
The visitors	are	**just**		leaving.	
Andrew	has	**always**		liked	Jessica.
We	don't	**often**		go	out in the evening.
You	should	**never**		take	unnecessary risks.
The pictures	have	**definitely**	been	stolen.	
I		**really**		hate	housework.
You		**probably**		left	the bag on the bus.

The adverb comes after the first auxiliary, e.g. **are**, **has**, **don't**.
If there is no auxiliary, then the adverb comes before the main verb, e.g. **hate**, **left**.

Note the word order in questions.
> Has Andrew **always** liked Jessica?   Do you **often** go out in the evening?

When the verb **be** is on its own, the adverb usually comes after it.
> The boss is **usually** in a bad temper.   You're **certainly** a lot better today.

When there is stress on the main verb **be** or on the auxiliary, then the adverb usually comes before it.
> You **certainly** <u>are</u> a lot better today.   I **really** <u>have</u> made a mess, haven't I?

3 Verb and object

An adverb does not usually go between the verb and the direct object.
We put it in end position, after the object.

	VERB	OBJECT	ADVERB	
Tom	ate	his breakfast	**quickly.**	NOT ~~Tom ate quickly his breakfast.~~
We	played	volleyball	**yesterday.**	NOT ~~We played yesterday volleyball.~~
I	like	classical music	**very much.**	NOT ~~I like very much classical music.~~

But an adverb can go before a long object.
> Detectives examined **carefully** the contents of the dead man's pockets.

4 Adverbs of manner

An adverb of manner tells us how something happens, e.g. **noisily**, **quickly**. It usually goes in end position, but an adverb which ends in **-ly** can sometimes go in mid position.
> We asked permission **politely**.   We **politely** asked permission.

5 Adverbs of place and time

Adverbs and adverbial phrases of place and time usually go in end position.

*Is there a phone box **nearby**?*   *People didn't have cars **then**.*
*We're meeting **by the entrance**.*   *Trevor wasn't very well **last week**.*
*Did you have a nice time **in New York**?*   *I'll see you **before very long**.*

Sometimes they can go in front position.

*We're really busy this week. **Last week** we had nothing to do.*

Some short adverbs of time can also go in mid position.

*I'll **soon** find out.*   *The train is **now** approaching Swindon.*

For **yet**, **still** and **already** see Unit 114.

6 Adverbs of frequency

An adverb of frequency tells us 'how often'. It usually goes in mid position (see 2).

*Mark is **always** in such a hurry.*   *I **sometimes** feel depressed.*
*I've **often** thought about getting married.*   *Do you **usually** work so late?*

Normally, **usually**, **often**, **sometimes** and **occasionally** can also go in front or end position.

***Normally** Sarah goes by train.*   *I feel depressed **sometimes**.*

Phrases like **every day**, **once a week** or **most evenings** go in front or end position.

***Every day** we go jogging.*   *Rachel has a driving lesson **three times a week**.*
*There's a news summary **every hour**.*   *We watch television **most evenings**.*

7 Sentence adverbs

A sentence adverb is a word or phrase like **certainly**, **perhaps**, **luckily**, **of course**. It says something about the situation described in the sentence. The adverb can go in front, mid or end position.
Sometimes we put a comma after or before the adverb, especially in front or end position.

***Fortunately**, the weather stayed fine.*   ***Maybe** you'll win a free holiday.*
*We'll **probably** have to queue for tickets.*   *Rachel was late, **of course**.*

In a negative sentence, **probably** and **certainly** come before **won't**, **didn't**, etc.

*We **probably** won't get there in time.*   *I **certainly** didn't expect a present!*

Also usually goes in mid position, but **too** and **as well** go in end position.

*Melanie bakes lovely cakes. She **also** makes bread./She makes bread, **too/as well**.*

8 End position

There can be more than one adverb or adverbial phrase in end position. Usually a single-word adverb (e.g. **safely**) comes before a phrase (e.g. **on a small airfield**).

*They landed **safely on a small airfield**.*   *I always eat **here at lunch-time**.*

When there is a close link in meaning between a verb and an adverb, then that adverb goes next to the verb. For example, with verbs of movement like **go**, **come** and **move**, a phrase of place comes before time.

*I usually go **to bed early**.*
*Tom came **here yesterday**.*
*My parents moved **to London in 1993**.*

But often two adverbial phrases can go in either order.

*The concert was held **at the arts centre last night**.*
*The concert was held **last night at the arts centre**.*

Practice

A Adverbs (1–2)

Read each sentence and write down the word which is an adverb.

▶ I'm just finishing an interesting article in this magazine. ...*just*......................
1 We have to leave our dirty shoes outside. ....
2 Perhaps you have to type a password into the computer. ....
3 Someone always leaves this door open. ....
4 Obviously we aren't going to go for a walk in the rain. ....
5 The car rolled silently down the hill. ....
6 Your friend Andrew works hard, doesn't he? ....

B Adverbs and their position (1–2)

Read this true story. Some adverbs are <u>underlined</u>. Say if their position is front, mid or end.

<u>Once</u> a man called Alvin decided to rob a bank in Montgomery, Alabama. Alvin's parents had <u>often</u> told him that good manners were important. So Alvin went to the bank and stood in line. He waited <u>patiently</u>. <u>Soon</u> it was his turn. He <u>dramatically</u> pulled out a gun and threatened the cashier. She <u>politely</u> told him that he was in the wrong line and should go to another counter. Alvin <u>immediately</u> went to the correct place and stood in line <u>again</u>. <u>Suddenly</u> the police rushed in and arrested him. Alvin was amazed. They'd caught him before he'd <u>even</u> done the robbery. The moral of the story is that you shouldn't <u>always</u> do what your parents tell you.

	ADVERB	POSITION			ADVERB	POSITION
▶	once	*front*................				
1	often	....		6	immediately	....
2	patiently	....		7	again	....
3	soon	....		8	suddenly	....
4	dramatically	....		9	even	....
5	politely	....		10	always	....

C Mid position (2)

Complete the conversations using the words in brackets. Put the adverbs in the best place.

▶ Emma: Did you know the man who tried to steal your bag? (certainly / recognize / would)
   Vicky: No, but I ...*would certainly recognize*... him again.

1 David: That was a goal, wasn't it? (clearly / crossed)
   Tom: Yes, the ball .... the line.

2 Mark: The weather is a lot better today. (probably / rain / will)
   Sarah: It said on the radio it .... later.

3 Tom: How do we get to Mike's place? (didn't / fully / understand)
   Nick: I don't know. I .... the directions.

4 Harriet: It's quiet here today, isn't it? (usually / are)
   Laura: Yes, the neighbours .... out on a Sunday.

5 Emma: Have you been to this place before? (it / occasionally / visited)
   Matthew: Yes, I .... as a child.

6 Alan: Did the computers crash this morning? (soon / were / working)
   Mark: Yes, but they .... again.

7 Melanie: Your friend's late, Vicky. (forgotten / has / obviously)
   Vicky: Rachel .... that we arranged to go out.

D Adverbs of frequency (2, 6)

Look at what people are saying and write the information in one sentence.
Put the adverb or adverbial phrase in mid or end position. Choose the best position.

▶ Vicky: I lose my way in London. It always happens.
Vicky always loses her way in London.

▶ Laura: The birds wake me up. It happens every morning.
The birds wake Laura up every morning.

1 David: It rains when I'm on holiday. Well, usually.
....

2 Rita: My friend visits me. She comes most weekends.
....

3 Mark: I get a pay rise. I get one every year.
....

4 Rachel: I don't check my work. I never do that.
....

E Adverbs and word order (1–7)

Put the words in the right order and write the statements. Sometimes there is more than one possible order.

▶ cleaned / every day / is / the office   *The office is cleaned every day.*
1 always / I've / known / your secret   ....
2 afford / can't / certainly / a new car / we   ....
3 didn't / far / the tourists / walk   ....
4 carefully / cut / the paper / Tom   ....
5 also / can / Natasha / play / the violin   ....
6 I / most days / read / the newspaper   ....

F Adverbs in end position (8)

Complete these sentences from a newspaper. Put the words and phrases in the best order.

▶ The Queen has visited the show *regularly since 1985* (regularly / since 1985).
1 The President died .... (at his home / peacefully).
2 The protesters marched .... (through the streets / yesterday).
3 The Prime Minister went .... (last year / to Greece).
4 Henry likes Rome. He spent a week .... (in June / there).

G Adverbs and word order (1–8)

Read the postcard from Olivia to her friend Kirsty and write the sentences. Put the adverbs in the best place.

(▶) Thank you for having us (last weekend). (1) We had a lovely time (in the country). (2) We arrived home at about eight (safely). (3) You must come and visit us (before too long). (4) It's nice to see you and Tony (always). (5) You'll be able to come in the new year (maybe). (6) We'll see you (sometime).

▶ *Thank you for having us last weekend.*
1 ....
2 ....
3 ....
4 ....
5 ....
6 ....

114 Yet, still and already

1 Introduction

Have you booked a holiday **yet**?

No, not **yet**. I'm **still** thinking about it.

I've **already** had a holiday. I went to Corfu.

Yet means that we are expecting something. (It's the time to book a holiday.)
Still means 'going on longer than expected'. (It's late to be thinking about a holiday.)
Already means 'sooner than expected'. (It's early to have had a holiday.)

2 Yet

Yet usually goes at the end of a negative statement or a question.
*Vicky has got a present, but she hasn't opened it **yet**.*   *Wait a minute. I'm not ready **yet**.*
*Have they sent you your cheque **yet**? ~ No, not **yet**. I should get it next week.*

3 Still and already

In a positive statement, **still** and **already** usually go in mid position (see Unit 113.2).
*Sarah isn't home yet. She's **still** at work.*
*We wrote a month ago, and we're **still** waiting for a reply.*
*I've only been at work an hour, and I'm **already** exhausted.*
*There's no need to tell me. I **already** know.*

We can also use **still** in a negative statement. It goes before **haven't**, **can't**, etc.
*It's nearly lunch-time, and you **still** haven't opened your mail.*
*My friend is sixteen, and she **still** can't swim.*
Compare these sentences. The meanings are similar.
*Rita hasn't booked a holiday **yet**.*   *Rita **still** hasn't booked a holiday.*
Still is stronger than **yet**. It often expresses surprise that the situation has gone on for so long.

In a question **still** and **already** usually go after the subject.
*Are you **still** waiting after all this time?*   *Has Tom **already** been on holiday?*

4 No longer and any longer/any more

No longer means that something is finished. It goes in mid position (see Unit 113.2).
*You can't buy these bikes now. They **no longer** make them.*
*I used to belong to the sports club, but I'm **no longer** a member.*

No longer can be a little formal. In informal speech we use **not ... any longer** or **not ... any more**.
*They don't make these bikes **any longer/any more**.*
*Rita has moved. She doesn't live here **any longer/any more**.*
Any longer/any more comes at the end.

▷ 12.1 **Yet** and **already** with the Present Perfect

Practice

A Yet, still and already (1)

Put in *yet*, *still* or *already*.

▶ Mark: I know it isn't lunch-time ..yet., but I'm really hungry.

    Sarah: It's only eleven. And you've ..already. had two coffees since breakfast.

1 Vicky: You've .... got this library book, and it was due back ten days ago.

    Rachel: Well, I haven't finished it ....

2 Nick: Tom is a very slow eater, isn't he? He's .... having his soup.

    David: And we've .... started our pudding.

3 Trevor: Has the postman been ....? I'm expecting a letter from the bank.

    Laura: Yes, he has, but that letter .... hasn't arrived.

B Word order with yet, still and already (1)

Put the word in brackets into one of the sentences.

▶ I've bought some CDs. I haven't played them. (yet)
I haven't played them yet.

▶ This calculator works. I've had it for ages. (still)
This calculator still works.

1 I owe Emma £20. I can't ask her for more. (already)

2 We've spent all our money. And we're only halfway through our holiday. (already)

3 I've cleaned this window. But it looks dirty. (still)

4 Our friend took some photos. We haven't seen them. (yet)

5 I can't understand the rules. I know you explained them to me. (still)

C Still and any more (3–4)

Two people are talking about the place they live in. Write the replies using *still* or *not ... any more*.

Old man:	Young man:
▶ There was a church.	~ Well, there's still a church .
▶ You could see fields.	~ You can't see them any more . Now it's just houses.
1 Children played there.	~ Not now. ....
2 Boats came along the river.	~ Oh, ... Look at them.
3 The view was beautiful.	~ Well, ... It's awful.
4 It was our home.	~ And ....

D Yet, still, already, no longer and any longer/any more (1–4)

Put in *already*, *any more*, *no longer*, <u>still</u> and *yet*.

▶ It's .still. raining, look. How much longer can it go on?

1 The railway closed down years ago, so there's .... a railway station here.

2 They want to build a new hotel here, but they haven't got permission ....

3 Rita isn't going out with Nick. She told him she didn't want to see him ....

4 Those people moved here only three months ago, and they're .... leaving.

115 Adverbs of degree (**very, quite**)

1 Very, quite, a bit, etc.

*Laura is a **bit** tired. She's been working all morning.*

*Mark is **quite** tired. He's been working all day.*

*Sarah is **very** tired. She's had to work late at the office.*

An adverb of degree makes the meaning weaker or stronger. Here are some more examples.

SMALL DEGREE (weaker)	MEDIUM DEGREE	LARGE DEGREE (stronger)
a little late	*fairly* unusual	*absolutely* sure *really* ill
slightly complicated	*pretty* good	*completely* mad
	rather nice	*extremely* cold

2 Very cold, quite quickly, etc.

An adverb of degree (e.g. **very**) goes before an adjective (e.g. **cold**) or an adverb (e.g. **quickly**).

ADVERB + ADJECTIVE	ADVERB + ADVERB
*It's **very cold** today.*	*The time passed **quite quickly**.*
*Rita looked **rather upset**.*	*We go on holiday **fairly soon**.*
*This dress is **absolutely marvellous**.*	*United played **extremely well**.*

Before a comparative we can use **a bit, a little, a lot, far, much, rather** and **slightly**. See also Unit 112.2.
   *I'm feeling **a lot better** today.*   *These new trains go **much faster**.*

3 Really hurting, quite enjoys, etc.

Some adverbs of degree can describe a verb.
They usually go in mid position (close to the verb – see Unit 113.2).
   *My foot is **really hurting**.*   *Laura **quite enjoys** shopping.*   *I **rather like** this cake.*
Some adverbs of degree go at the end of a sentence when they describe a verb.
They are **a bit, a little, a lot, awfully, much** and **terribly**.
   *Mark **travels a lot**.*   *I'll **open** the window **a little**.*   *The animals **suffer terribly**.*

Absolutely, completely and **totally** can go in mid position or at the end.
   *We **completely** lost our way./We lost our way **completely**.*
   *I'm afraid I **totally** disagree./I'm afraid I disagree **totally**.*

4 Much

Now look at these sentences.
Positive: *I like this town **very much**.* NOT *I like this town much.*
Negative: *I don't like this town **very much**.* OR *I don't like this town **much**.*
In a positive statement we use **very much**. In a negative statement we can use either **very much** or **much**.

▷ 116 More about **quite** and **rather**   ▷ 117 **Too** and **enough**

Practice

A Very, quite, a bit, etc. (1)

Write sentences using one of the phrases in brackets.

▶ (quite hungry or very hungry?) He's quite hungry.   3 (quite strong or very strong?) ....
1 (a bit busy or very busy?) ....   4 (fairly happy or extremely happy?) ....
2 (a bit thirsty or really thirsty?) ....
....

B Very, quite and a bit (1)

Put in *very*, *quite* or *a bit*.

▶ The bus service is all right. The buses are ..quite.. frequent.
1 I couldn't sleep because of the awful noise. The disco was .... noisy.
2 The weather was OK – at least it didn't rain. It was .... good.
3 The train was almost on time. It was just .... late.
4 Someone paid a great deal of money for the house. It was .... expensive.
5 There were some very small traces of mud on the boots. They were .... dirty.
6 There was a medium amount of traffic on the road. It was .... busy.

C Very cold, really hurting, etc. (2–4)

Put the adverbs in the right place. Sometimes more than one answer is correct.

▶ These books are old (very).   These books are very old.
▶ I hate travelling by air (really).   I really hate travelling by air.
1 That radio is loud (a bit). ....
2 I like my new job (quite). ....
3 Why don't you slow down (a little)? ....
4 The rain spoilt our day (completely). ....
5 We did the job quickly (fairly). ....
6 I feel better now (a lot). ....
7 We enjoyed the concert (very much). ....
8 My arms ached (terribly). ....

D Adverbs of degree (1–4)

Complete the advertisement for holiday apartments by choosing the correct words.

Why not take this opportunity to buy a wonderful Interlux Timeshare apartment in San Manila? These are (▶) a bit/rather/really luxurious apartments set in this (1) absolutely/slightly magnificent seaside resort, a (2) fairly/really beautiful and unspoilt place, which you'll like (3) much/very/very much. The apartments are (4) extremely/pretty/quite good value. And we are a company with a (5) fairly/quite/very good reputation. This is a (6) bit/slightly/totally safe way of investing your money. But hurry! People are buying up the apartments (7) a lot/very/very much quickly.

116 Quite and rather

1 Quite meaning 'fairly'

Quite usually means 'fairly' or 'a medium amount' (see Unit 115.1).

> I feel **quite** hungry now.   Repairing the machine is **quite** difficult.
> The talk was **quite** interesting.   We were **quite** surprised at the result.

(But see 4 for another meaning of **quite**.)

2 Stress with quite

In speech, whether we stress **quite** or the adjective makes a difference to the meaning.

If we stress **quite**, it means 'fairly but not very'. The meaning is negative.	If we stress the adjective, the meaning is positive (but not as positive as **very**).
The exhibition was <u>quite</u> good, but I've seen better ones.	The exhibition was quite <u>good</u>. I enjoyed looking round it.
I get up <u>quite</u> early, but not as early as you do.	I got up quite <u>early</u>. I had a lot of jobs to do.

3 Quite or rather?

When we make a favourable comment, we usually say **quite**, not **rather**.

> The book was **quite interesting**.   It's **quite warm** now.
> It was **quite nice** walking through the park.

In unfavourable comments, we usually say **rather**, but **quite** is possible.

> The book was **rather boring**/quite boring.
> It was **rather awkward**/quite awkward taking my suitcase on the underground.

Rather in a favourable comment means 'to a surprising or unusual degree'.

> It's **rather warm** for October. (It isn't usually so warm.)
> I didn't know David can cook. He's **rather good** at it.
> I expect Tom's jokes were awful. ~ Actually they were **rather funny**.

We can use **rather** with a comparative but not **quite**.

> The meal took **rather longer** than we expected.

For **quite** and **rather** with a/an, see Unit 89.2.

> It was **quite an interesting** book.

4 Quite meaning 'completely'

With some adjectives, **quite** means 'completely' or 'totally'.

> What you said is **quite wrong**. (= completely wrong)
> The idea is **quite absurd**. (= totally absurd)
> The situation is **quite hopeless**.

Quite means 'completely' with these adjectives: **absurd, alone, amazing, awful, brilliant, certain, dead, different, dreadful, extraordinary, false, hopeless, horrible, impossible, perfect, ridiculous, right, sure, true, useless, wrong**

Compare the uses of **quite**.

I'm **quite tired**. (= fairly) The advice was **quite useful**. I got one or two tips.	I'm **quite exhausted**. (= completely) The advice was **quite useless**. It was absolutely no good at all.

A Stress with quite (2)

Which word do we stress, *quite* or the adjective? Underline the stressed word.

► These pens are <u>quite</u> good but not as good as the ones I usually buy.
► This book is quite <u>exciting</u>. I can't put it down.
1   These fashions are quite new but not the very latest thing.
2   It's quite late. We'd better be going.
3   The sums are quite easy. I can do them in my head.
4   The music was quite good, but I wasn't really impressed.
5   The sun is quite bright. You'll need your sunglasses.

B Quite or rather? (3)

Put in these adjectives: *better, busy, nice, noisy, popular*
Use *quite* or *rather* with each adjective. Sometimes either is possible.

Mark: I didn't like that meal very much.
Sarah: The soup was (►) ..*quite nice*.. though, wasn't it?
Mark: The food was (1) .... the last time we came.
Sarah: It's (2) .... in here, isn't it? Everyone seems to be shouting.
Mark: I wasn't expecting the place to be so full. It's (3) .... for a Monday evening.
Sarah: This restaurant is (4) ...., you know.

C Quite or rather? (3)

Add a sentence expressing the idea in brackets.
Use *quite* or *rather* in your sentence. Sometimes either is possible.

► (It's pleasant by the river.)
   Let's walk along by the river. *It's quite pleasant there.*
► (You think Nick is aggressive.)
   I don't like Nick much. *I think he's rather aggressive.*
1   (Changing trains twice is complicated.)
   We have to change trains twice. ....
2   (Your car is big.)
   I can give you all a lift. ....
3   (The show went on longer than you expected.)
   It was a good show, but ....
4   (You made your decision quickly.)
   It wasn't a difficult decision. ....

D The meanings of quite (1, 4)

Does *quite* mean 'fairly' or 'completely'?

► Try one of these sweets. I think they're <u>quite nice</u>. = *fairly nice*
► The driver walked away unhurt. It was <u>quite amazing</u>. = *completely amazing*
1   I couldn't agree to the idea. It was <u>quite ridiculous</u>. = ...
2   I need some help with this crossword. It's <u>quite difficult</u>. = ...
3   That isn't the same thing at all. It's <u>quite different</u>. = ...
4   I wasn't expecting to get a postcard. I was <u>quite surprised</u>. = ...
5   I bought this guidebook. It looks <u>quite useful</u>. = ...
6   Are you sure you want the job? ~ Yes, I'm <u>quite certain</u>. = ...

117 Too and enough

1 Introduction

Too short and **not long enough** both mean the same thing.

2 Word order with too and enough

Too goes before an adjective or adverb.

*Claire doesn't want to marry Henry. She thinks he's **too old**.*
*Zedco are in trouble. The company reacted **too slowly** to the rise in prices.*

Enough goes after an adjective or adverb.

*The water isn't **hot enough**. It needs to be boiling.* NOT ~~enough hot~~
*You didn't put the screws in **tightly enough**.* NOT ~~enough tightly~~

Too many, **too much** and **enough** go before a noun.

*No wonder you're tired. You've been going to **too many parties**.*
*Andrew spends **too much time** working.*
*There'll be fifteen people for coffee. Have we got **enough cups**?*
*Everything is so expensive. Did you bring **enough money**?*

We use **many** with a plural noun and **much** with an uncountable noun (see Unit 95.1).

Compare these examples with **enough**.
After an adjective: *The coffee isn't **strong enough**.*
Before a noun: *You didn't put **enough coffee** in.*

We leave out the noun if the meaning is clear without it.

*Just add a little water. Not **too much**.   We'll need fifteen cups. Have we got **enough**?*

3 Other structures with too and enough

We can use a phrase with **for** after **too** or **enough**.

*These puzzles are **too** difficult **for children**.   This coat isn't warm **enough for winter**.*
*Have we got **enough** cups **for everyone**?*

We can also use a to-infinitive.

*It's **too** dangerous **to walk** home at this time of night.*
*There are **too** many museums here **to visit** in a single day.*
*Are you fit **enough to run** a marathon?*
*I couldn't get close **enough to see** properly.*
*Vicky didn't bring **enough** money **to buy** two CDs.*

Practice

A Too and enough (1–2)

Look at the pictures and write sentences with *too* and *enough*.
Use these nouns and adjectives: *big*, *gate*, *long*, *low*, *plane*, *sweater*, *ruler*, *warm*, *water*, *wide*

▶ The sweater is too big. ....
▶ The ruler isn't long enough. ....

1 ....
2 ....
3 ....

B Too and enough (1–2)

Look at what people are saying and complete the sentences. Use *too*, *too many*, *too much* or
enough with these words: *clearly, complicated, difficult, expensive, food, hastily, mistakes, rain,
sweet, traffic*

▶ You should have stopped to think first. You acted too hastily. ....
▶ This quiz is rather easy. The questions aren't difficult enough. ....
1 Can I have some more sugar in my coffee, please? It isn't ....
2 I can't afford a new stereo. It would be ....
3 There's a water shortage. There just hasn't been ....
4 I can't read your writing. You don't write ....
5 Try to be more careful, please. You're making ....
6 The roads are very crowded. There's simply ....
7 I can't understand these instructions. They're ....
8 Thousands of people are starving because they can't get ....

C Other structures with too and enough (3)

Comment on the situations. Use *too* or *enough* and a phrase with *for* or a to-infinitive.
▶ A taxi would have been best. But you didn't have the money.
   I didn't have enough money for a taxi. ....
▶ Sarah can't take a day off. She's very busy.
   Sarah is too busy to take a day off. ....
1 A picnic would be nice. But it's wet.
   ....
2 All your guests will need chairs. But you haven't got very many.
   ....
3 You couldn't carry the equipment. You had such a lot.
   ....
4 Natasha wants to be a professional musician. You think she's very good.
   ....

Test T: Adverbs and word order

A

Put each word in brackets into the sentence.

▶ Anna arrives for work. (late)
  Anna arrives late for work.

1 I like old cowboy films. (quite)
   ....

2 Have you finished this magazine? (yet)
   ....

3 This coat is big. (too)
   ....

4 Have the children had their tea? (already)
   ....

5 You don't look ill. (certainly)
   ....

6 We don't go out. (much)
   ....

7 I think everyone works hard. (fairly)
   ....

8 I don't know the date of the meeting. (still)
   ....

9 The others are getting ready. (just)
   ....

10 I have to go to work. (on Saturdays)
   ....

B

Put the words in the right order to form a statement.

▶ I / love / really / these trousers
  I really love these trousers.

1 is / rather / silly / this game
   ....

2 already / I've / paid / the bill
   ....

3 enough / isn't / loud / the alarm
   ....

4 easily / Jonathan / passed / the test
   ....

5 a lot / cards / play / the children
   ....

6 didn't / enough / sell / they / tickets
   ....

7 ask / many / questions / too / you
   ....

8 a member / any more / of the club / I'm / not
   ....

9 enough / it's / outside / to sit / warm
   ....

C

Read the conversation. Then look at the answers below and write the correct answer in each space.

Martin: Hello, Nancy. (►) ..How.. are you? Have you found a job (1) ....?

Nancy: No, I'm afraid not, but I'm (2) .... looking. It's taking (3) ....
longer than I expected. The problem is there just aren't (4) .... jobs. And
there are too (5) .... people looking for jobs.

Martin: I'm old enough (6) .... remember when there was plenty of work.

Nancy: There used to be lots of work, but there isn't (7) .... more. I'm afraid I'm
(8) .... longer as optimistic as I was a few weeks ago. In fact I feel a
(9) .... depressed about it sometimes.

Martin: Don't worry. You'll (10) .... find something, I expect.

►	a) How	b) What	c) Who	d) Why	6	a) for	b) of	c) that	d) to
1	a) longer	b) soon	c) still	d) yet	7	a) any	b) no	c) now	d) some
2	a) already	b) more	c) still	d) yet	8	a) any	b) never	c) no	d) not
3	a) more	b) quite	c) rather	d) some	9	a) bit	b) piece	c) quite	d) slightly
4	a) enough	b) plenty	c) right	d) several	10	a) already	b) yet	c) soon	
5	a) big	b) lot	c) many	d) much		d) before very long			

D

Each of these sentences has a mistake in it. Write the correct sentence.

►	My friend calls always for me.	My friend always calls for me.
1	I didn't last night sleep very well.	....
2	I think I need to rest little.	....
3	I don't work for the company longer.	....
4	The article is fair interesting.	....
5	Tessa locked carefully the door.	....
6	You aren't enough tall to play basketball.	....
7	We went yesterday to town.	....
8	I like this music much.	....

E

Write a second sentence so that it has a similar meaning to the first. Use the word in brackets.

► It's probable that the strike will be over soon. (probably)
  The strike will probably be over soon.

1 We often go to the cinema. (a lot)
  ....

2 Adrian wears jeans all the time. (always)
  ....

3 These shoes are too small. (big)
  ....

4 I don't live in Birmingham any more. (no)
  ....

5 Polly spent more money than she should have done in the sales. (too)
  ....

118 Prepositions of place

1 Meanings

The bird is **in/inside** the cage.

Sarah is diving **in/into** the water.

Tom is getting **out of** the car.

They're waiting **outside** the bank.

The jug is **on** the table.

The case is **on top of** the wardrobe.

Emma is putting her luggage **on/onto** the trolley.

Henry is falling **off** the horse.

Rachel is **at** the bus stop.

The table is **by/beside** the bed.

Jessica is sitting **next to** Andrew.

The airport is **near** Manchester.

The coach is going **to** London.

The letter is **from** Chicago.

Matthew is walking **towards** the sun.

Vicky is running **away from** the fire.

There's a bridge **over** the river.

Tom is **under** the car.

The plane is **above** the clouds.

The temperature is **below** zero.

The cyclist is **in front of** the bus.

The cyclist is **behind** the tractor.

Rita is going **up** the stairs.

Daniel is coming **down** the stairs.

Melanie is running **across** the road.

The cars are going **through** the tunnel.

Trevor is walking **along** the street.

The car is going **past** the house.

The house is **among** the trees.

Jackson is **between** Memphis and New Orleans.

Jessica is sitting **opposite** Andrew.

They're running **around/round** the track.

2 Position and movement

Most of these prepositions can express either position (where something is) or movement (where it is going).

Position: *The coin **was under** the sofa.*
Movement: *The coin **rolled under** the sofa.*

Now look at these examples with **in** and **on** expressing position.
   *The manager was **in** the office.*   *The papers were **on** the floor.*
To express movement, we use **into** and **onto**, but we can also use **in** and **on**, especially in informal English.
   *The manager came **in/into** the office.*   *The papers fell **on/onto** the floor.*

At expresses position, and **to** expresses movement.
Position: *Vicky **was at** the doctor's.*
Movement: *Vicky **went to** the doctor's.*

▷ page 380 British and American English

Practice

A Prepositions of place (1)

Put in the prepositions. Sometimes more than one answer is correct.

▶ Sarah is getting out of the taxi.

1 David is going .... the ladder.

2 The furniture is .... the van.

3 My friend lives in a flat .... a shop.

4 The boss is coming .... the corridor.

5 There's a garage .... the house.

6 We walked .... the lake.

7 There's a statue .... the museum.

8 Tom and Nick are walking .... the stadium.

B Prepositions of place (1)

Complete the conversations. Choose the correct preposition.

1 Vicky: I felt really afraid when I was walking home from/off the club. All the time I could hear someone behind/in front of me, but I didn't dare turn round.

Rachel: I expect you were imagining it.

Vicky: No, I wasn't. I saw him after I'd come in across/through the gate. He was wearing a long black coat that came down well below/under his knees.

2 Daniel: You know Adam, don't you? He's very strange. He walked right along/past me yesterday as I was coming among/down the stairs, but he didn't say hello.

Matthew: The other day he was sitting beside/opposite me at lunch, so I couldn't help looking at him. I said hello, but he didn't speak.

C Between, next to and opposite (1)

Look at the plan and explain where things are. Use *between*, *next to* or *opposite*.

▶ The bank is ..next to. the gift shop.
1 The sports shop is .... the bank.
2 The travel agency is .... the sports shop and the art gallery.
3 The restaurant is .... the art gallery.
4 The gift shop is .... the bank and the restaurant.
5 The art gallery is .... the travel agency.

D Prepositions of place (1–2)

Where did the fly go? Put in these prepositions: *around, into, on, out of, through, under, up*

▶ The fly came in .through. the door.
1 It flew .... the chair.
2 It crawled .... the chair leg.
3 It stopped .... the desk for a moment.
4 It went .... the telephone.
5 It flew .... the drawer.
6 It went .... the window.

E Prepositions of place (1–2)

Put in the correct preposition.
▶ Rachel was lying .on. the grass reading a book.
1 It's my holiday next week. I'm going .... Spain.
2 There was a big crowd .... the shop waiting for it to open.
3 That man is an idiot. He pushed me .... the swimming-pool.
4 I went .... the chemist's just now, but I didn't notice if it was open.
5 David hurt himself. He fell .... his bike.
6 There's a café .... top of the mountain. You can have a coffee there before you
   go down.
7 The sheep got out .... a hole in the fence.
8 Pompeii is quite .... Sorrento. It's only a short train ride.
9 There's such a crowd. You won't find your friend .... all these people.

119 In, on and at (place)

1 Meanings

*Emma is **in** the phone box.*

*Nick's dog is **on** the rug.*

*There's someone **at** the door.*

IN	ON	AT
in the phone box **in** the kitchen work **in** the garden swim **in** the pool	sit **on** the floor walk **on** the pavement a number **on** the door egg **on** your shirt	sit **at** my desk wait **at** the bus stop **at** the crossroads wait **at** the traffic lights
In a street (GB) **in** Shirley Road	On a street (US) **on** Fifth Avenue	At a house/an address **at** Mike's (house) **at** 65 Shirley Road
In a town/country Kate lives **in** York. Atlanta is **in** America.	On a road or river a village **on** this road Paris is **on** the Seine.	At a place on a journey Does this train stop **at** York?
	On a floor (1st, 2nd, etc.) **on** the first floor	At an event **at** the party

2 In and at with buildings

IN	AT
There are 400 seats **in** the cinema. It was raining, so we waited **in** the pub. We use **in** when we mean inside a building.	I was **at** the cinema. (= watching a film) We were **at** the pub. (= having a drink) But we normally use **at** when we are talking about what happens there.

3 Some common phrases

IN	ON	AT
in prison/hospital **in** the lesson **in** a book/newspaper **in** the photo/picture **in** the country **in** the middle **in** the back/front of a car **in** a queue/line/row	**on** the platform **on** the farm **on** the page/map **on** the screen **on** the island/beach/coast drive **on** the right/left **on** the back of an envelope	**at** the station/airport **at** home/work/school **at** the seaside **at** the top/bottom of a hill **at** the back of the room **at** the end of a corridor

▷ 87 In bed, at home, etc.   ▷ 123.3 In the car, on the train, etc.

Practice

A Meanings (1)

Look at the pictures and write the sentences. Use *in*, *on* or *at* and these words:
the bath, *the disco*, *the lights*, *the roof*, *the table*

▶ He's on the table.
1 *He is on the roof.*   3 *He is in the bath.*
2 *They are at the disco.*   4 *He is at the lights.*

B In and at with buildings (2)

Complete each sentence. Use *in* or *at* and these words:
the petrol station, *the restaurant*, *the stadium*, *the station*, *the theatre*, *the zoo*

▶ There's a huge crowd *in the stadium* waiting for the Games to start.
1 Sarah's just rung. She's *at the petrol station* getting some petrol.
2 The children like wild animals. They'd love to spend an afternoon *at the zoo*.
3 It was so hot *in the theatre* that I didn't really enjoy the play.
4 We're quite a large group. There may not be enough room *in the restaurant*
   for all of us to sit together.
5 I saw Daniel while I was *at the station* waiting for a train.

C In, on and at (1, 3)

Put in the preposition *in*, *on* or *at*.

▶ We spent the whole holiday *on* the beach.
1 I read about the pop festival *in* a magazine.
2 My parents' flat is *on* the twenty-first floor.
3 Melanie was holding a small bird *in* her hands.
4 I'll meet you *at* the airport.
5 Natasha now lives *at* 32 The Avenue.
6 I was standing *at* the counter in the baker's shop, waiting to be served.
7 London is *on* the Thames.
8 There weren't many books *on* the shelves.
9 The passengers had to stand *in* a queue.
10 The woman sitting next to me left the train *at* Chesterfield.

120 In, on and at (time)

1 Saying when

Look at these examples.

IN	ON	AT
We bought the flat in 1994.	*The race is on Saturday.*	*The film starts at seven thirty.*
In + year/month/season	On + day/date	At + clock time/meal time
in 1988	*on Wednesday*	*at three o'clock*
in September	*on 15 April*	*at lunch (-time)*
in winter	*on that day*	*at that time*
in the 21st century		*at the moment*
In + a week or more	On + a single day	At + two or three days
in the Easter holiday	*on Easter Monday*	*at Easter/Christmas*
in the summer term	*on Christmas Day*	*at the weekend*
		(US: **on** the weekend)
In + part of day	On + day + part of day	
in the morning	*on Friday morning*	
in the evening	*on Tuesday evening*	

Look at these examples with **night**.

I woke up in the night.	*It happened on Monday night.*	*I can't sleep at night.*
(= in the middle of the night)		(= when it is night)

But we do not use **in**, **on** or **at** before **every**, **last**, **next**, **this**, **tomorrow** and **yesterday**.
  We go to Greece every summer.   *My brother came home last Christmas.*
  I'll see you next Friday.   *I leave school this year.*
  The party is tomorrow evening.   *The group set off yesterday morning.*

2 In time or on time?

IN TIME	ON TIME
In time means 'early enough'.	**On time** means 'at the right time', 'on schedule'.
We'll have to hurry if we want to be in time for the show.	*The plane took off on time.*
We got to the airport in time to have a coffee before checking in.	*I hope the meeting starts on time.*
I was about to close the door when just in time I remembered my key. (= at the last moment)	*Rachel is never on time. She's always late.*

3 Other uses of in

We can use **in** for the time it takes to complete something.
  I did the crossword in five minutes.   *Could you walk thirty miles in a day?*

We can also use **in** for a future time measured from the present.
  Your photos will be ready in an hour. (= an hour from now)
  The building will open in six weeks/in six weeks' time.

▷ 88 On Friday, etc. without the

Practice

A Saying when (1)

Read the information about John F. Kennedy and then answer the questions.
Begin each answer with *in*, *on* or *at*.

John F. Kennedy was born into a famous American family. His date of birth was 29 May 1917. The year 1961 saw him become the 35th President of the US. Kennedy was killed as he drove in an open car through the streets of Dallas, Texas. Friday, 22 November 1963 was a sad day for America. It was 12.30 when a gunman opened fire and shot the President dead.

▶ When was John F. Kennedy born?   *On 29 May 1917.*
1 When did he become President?   ....
2 When was he killed?   ....
3 What time was he shot?   ....

B Saying when (1)

Mark is arranging a business meeting. Decide if you need *in*, *on* or *at*.
If you do not need a preposition, put a cross (*x*).

Mark: I'm sorry I was out when you called (▶) *x* yesterday afternoon, Alice. Look, I'm free
        (▶) *on* the fifteenth of March. Can we meet then?
Alice: I'm pretty busy (1) .... next week, I'm afraid. I can't see you (2) .... Friday.
Mark: I'd like to have a meeting (3) .... this month if possible. I'll be very busy
        (4) .... April.
Alice: I'm going away (5) .... Easter, so how about the week after? Shall we meet
        (6) .... the twenty-seventh? That's a Wednesday.
Mark: I've got an appointment (7) .... the morning but nothing (8) .... the
        afternoon. Let's meet (9) .... Wednesday afternoon (10) .... half past two.

C In time or on time? (2)

Put in the right phrase: *in time* or *on time*.

▶ If the plane is late, we won't get to Paris *in time* for our connecting flight.
1 We were up very early, ... to see the sun rise.
2 How can the buses possibly run .... with all these traffic jams?
3 The post goes at five. I'm hoping to get this letter written ....
4 The coach will be here at 12.13 if it's ....

D In, on or at? (1–3)

Complete the conversations using *in*, *on* or *at*.

▶ Andrew: You only bought that book *on* Saturday. Have you finished it already?
   Jessica: I read it *in* about three hours yesterday evening.
1 Vicky: Will the bank be open .... half past nine?
   Daniel: Yes, it always opens absolutely .... time.
2 Sarah: We're leaving .... half past, and you haven't even changed.
   Mark: It's OK. I can easily shower and change .... ten minutes.
3 Laura: Your mother's birthday is .... Monday, isn't it?
   Trevor: Yes, I just hope this card gets there .... time.
4 Harriet: If we ever go camping again, it's going to be .... summer, not autumn.
   Mike: Never mind. We'll be home .... two days, and then we'll be dry again.

121 For, since, ago and before

1 Introduction

FOR	SINCE	AGO
Mark has spent three hours playing a computer game. He's been sitting there **for three hours**.	It was two o'clock when Mark started the game. He's been playing **since two o'clock**.	Three hours have passed since Mark and Sarah got up from the lunch table. They finished their lunch **three hours ago**.

2 For and since with the Present Perfect

We often use **for** and **since** with the Present Perfect to talk about something continuing up to the present.

FOR	SINCE
We use **for** to say <u>how long</u> something has continued. *I've been waiting **for forty minutes**.* *We've known about it **for two days**.* *Melanie has been living here **for a year** now.*	We use **since** to say <u>when</u> something began. *I've been waiting **since ten past six**.* *We've known about it **since Monday**.* *Melanie has been living here **since last year**.*

We can also use **for** with other tenses.
> *I'm staying in England **for** a year.   We swam for quite a long time.*

We can often leave out **for** (but not from some negative sentences).
> *We've had this car (**for**) six months.   I haven't seen Vicky **for** a day or two.*

3 Ago with the past

We can use the adverb **ago** to talk about a past time measured from the present.
Six months ago means six months before now.
> *I passed my driving test **six months ago**. NOT since six months*
> *Vicky wrote to the company **weeks ago**.   David first met Melanie **a long time ago**.*
> *Have you seen Emma? ~ Yes, just **a few minutes ago**.*

We put **ago** after the phrase of time. NOT ago six months

4 Before with the Past Perfect

We use **before** (not **ago**) with the Past Perfect, e.g. **had done**.
> *I bought a car in August. I'd passed my driving test **three months before**.*
> (= in May, three months before August)
> *Vicky finally received a reply to the letter she had written **weeks before**.*

Practice

A For and since (1–2)

Put in _for_ or _since_.

Daniel: How long have you been learning English?

Ilona: Well, I studied it (▶) ..for.. five years at school, and I've been having evening classes
(1) .... last summer. That's when I left school.

Daniel: And you're staying here (2) .... three months?

Ilona: That's right. I've been here (3) .... the end of April. I'm going to London
(4) .... a week before I go home.

B For and since (1–2)

Look at the pictures and say how long people have been there.
Use these phrases: _at his desk_, _in bed_, _in the garden_, _in the shop_, _on the road_

| ▶ half an hour | 1 three days | 2 breakfast | 3 nine o'clock | 4 five hours |

▶ _She's been in the shop for half an hour._

1 ....

2 ....

3 ....

4 ....

C For, since or ago? (1–3)

Put in a phrase with _for_, _since_ or _ago_.

▶ I got here an hour ago. ~ What! You mean you've been waiting _for an hour_ .... ?

1 The phone last rang at four o'clock. ~ So you've had no calls .... ?

2 I haven't been to the dentist for ten years. ~ You last went to the dentist .... ?

3 I last saw Rachel on Monday. ~ Haven't you seen her .... ?

4 We've had six weeks without rain. ~ Yes, it hasn't rained ....

5 It's three years since Laura got married. ~ Really? Has she been married .... ?

6 It's eight months since my brother had any work. ~ He lost his job .... ?

7 Mrs Miles was taken ill three weeks ago. ~ You mean she's been ill .... ,
and nobody's told me!

D Ago or before? (3–4)

Put in _ago_ or _before_.

▶ This film looks familiar. Didn't we see it at the cinema about two years _ago_ ?

1 The road was wet when the accident happened. It had stopped raining only
half an hour ....

2 My telephone is working now. They repaired it a week ....

3 A young man threw himself off this bridge last year. His girlfriend had left him
two days ....

122 During or while? By or until? As or like?

1 During or while?

Compare these examples.

> I often read **during** a meal.
> It happened **during** the night.
> You'll have to be quiet **during** the performance.
> **During** is a preposition (like **in**). It comes before a phrase like **a meal** or **the night**.

> I often read **while** I'm eating.
> It happened **while** they were asleep.
> Were there any phone calls **while** I was out?
> **While** is a linking word (like **when**). It comes before a clause, e.g. **I'm eating**.

2 By or until?

Compare these examples.

> I'm very busy this week. I have to finish this report **by** Thursday.
> Trevor will be home **by** half past six.
> They hope to build the new bridge **by** next July.
> The post should be here **by** now.

> I'll be busy for most of this week. I won't have any time **until** Friday.
> He'll be at work **until** half past five.
> We won't have another holiday **until** next summer.
> **Till** is more informal than **until**.
> I slept **till** ten o'clock.

We can use **by the time** or **until** before a clause, e.g. **we arrived**.

> There was no food left **by the time** we arrived.
> NOT ~~by we arrived~~

> I'll wait **until** you're ready.
> See Unit 27.2 for the Present Simple after **until**, etc.

3 As, like and as if/as though

Compare these examples.

> She works **as** a fashion model.
> (= She is a model.)
> **As** a beginner you simply have to learn the basics.
> I'm using this tin **as** an ashtray.
> We use **as** to talk about a job or function.

> She dresses **like** a fashion model.
> (= Her clothes are <u>similar</u> to a model's.)
> Mark is a good golfer, but today he played **like** a beginner.
> You look **like** your brother.
> We use **like** to talk about things being similar.

We can also use **as** or **like** before a clause.
> We drive on the left here, **as/like you do in Britain**.
> Mike and Sarah are going to Paris for the weekend, **as/like they did last year**.

Like is more informal than **as** before a clause.

We also use **as** with verbs of speaking and knowing, e.g. **say**, **know**, **expect**.
> **As I said before**, I'm sorry. (= I'm sorry, and I said so before.)
> I haven't much money, **as you know**. (= I haven't much money, and you know it.)
> Rachel arrived late, **as we expected**. (= We expected her to arrive late, and she did.)

We use **as if/as though** before a clause to say how something seems.
> Tom looks really awful. He looks **as if/as though he's been up all night**.
> Nick can be a difficult person. He sometimes behaves **as if/as though he's the only one with problems**.

Practice

A During or while? (1)

Put in *during* or *while*.

▶ Did you take notes ..during... the lecture?
1 Shall we have a coffee .... we're waiting?
2 Try not to make any noise .... the baby is asleep.
3 The fire alarm rang .... yesterday's meeting.
4 Trevor tried to fix the shelves .... Laura was out shopping.

B By or until? (2)

Rachel is talking to her teacher. Put in *by* or *until*.

Mrs Lewis: You'll need to hand your project in (▶) .by. the end of the week. I'd like to have it
(1) .... Friday, ideally.

Rachel: Well, I'm going on a three-day study trip tomorrow. I'll be away (2) .... Thursday.
The project will probably take me (3) .... the middle of next week. I can't finish it
(4) .... the end of this week.

Mrs Lewis: Well, let me have it (5) .... Wednesday of next week, please.

C As or like? (3)

Put in *as* or *like*.

▶ Sarah works in here. She uses this room .as. her study.
1 Matthew worked .... a waiter last summer.
2 The way your sister plays the violin sounds .... two cats fighting.
3 Do you mind using this saucer .... a plate?
4 The body sank .... a stone to the bottom of the river.

D As or as if? (3)

Put in *as* or *as if*.

▶ That poor dog looks .as if. it never gets fed.
1 Rachel failed her driving test, ... she expected.
2 Daniel spends money .... it grows on trees.
3 We shall deliver the goods on the twenty-seventh, ... we promised.
4 From what Emma said, it sounds .... she and Matthew are going to get married.

E While, by the time, until, as and like (1–3)

Decide what to say. Use the word in brackets to join the two ideas together.

▶ Tell Matthew he needs to click on the box. You showed him. (like)
You need to click on the box, like I showed you.

1 Tell Tom that you arrived at his flat, but he'd left. (by the time)
....

2 Tell your friend that Rita went to the party with Tom. Your friend predicted this. (as)
....

3 Tell Claire that you saw her sister. You were shopping in London. (while)
....

4 Tell Vicky she can keep the book. She can finish it. (until)
....

123 Preposition + noun (**on holiday**)

1 Some useful phrases

on holiday, on business, on a journey/a trip/a tour
> *I'm travelling **on business**.   We're **on a coach tour** of Europe.*

in cash, by cheque/credit card
> *It's cheaper if you pay **in cash**.   Can I pay **by credit card**?*

in writing, in pen/biro/felt-tip/ink/pencil
> *Could you confirm that **in writing**?   I'll write the names **in pencil**.*

on television, on the radio/the phone/the Internet
> *I saw the programme **on TV**.   Mark is **on the phone** at the moment.*

for sale, on the market
> *The house next door is **for sale**.   It's the best hi-fi **on the market**.*

on the whole, in general
> ***On the whole** it's a good idea, but there are one or two problems.*
> *People **in general** aren't very interested in politics.*

in advance, up to date, out of date
> *The company wants us to pay for the goods **in advance**.*
> *Oh no! My passport is **out of date**.   These latest figures are **up to date**.*

in my opinion, from my point of view
> *All sport is silly **in my opinion**.*
> *Matthew never sees things **from Emma's point of view**.*

on purpose, by mistake/chance/accident
> *I didn't spill my drink **on purpose**.   I pressed the wrong button **by mistake**.*
> *We didn't arrange to meet. We met **by chance** in the street.*

2 Way and end

On the way = during the journey. *I'm driving into town. I'll get some petrol **on the way**.*	**In the way** = blocking the way. *We couldn't get past because there was a parked car **in the way**.*
In the end = finally, after a long time. *It took Claire hours to decide. **In the end** she chose a long blue dress.*	**At the end** = when something stops. *We all left quickly **at the end** of the meeting.*

3 Transport

We use **by** without **a/the** when we talk about a means of transport.
> *We decided to go to Brussels **by train**.* NOT ~~go by the train~~

We can also use **in** and **on**.
> *It'll be quicker to go **in the car**.   Richard came **on the train**.*

Note that **on foot** means 'walking'.
> *We came all the way **on foot**.* NOT ~~by foot~~

BY:	air, bicycle/bike, boat, bus, car, coach, ferry, helicopter, hovercraft, plane, rail, sea, ship, taxi, train, tube
IN:	the/my/your car, a helicopter, a taxi
ON:	my bicycle/bike, the boat, the bus, the ferry, the hovercraft, the plane, the ship, the train

Practice

A Preposition + noun (1–2)

Put in *by*, *from*, *in* or *on*.

▶ There's something I want to listen to .on. the radio.

1 They've promised me more money, but I haven't got it .... writing.
2 Why can't you look at the problem .... my point of view?
3 Would you mind moving? You're rather .... the way here.
4 I rang the wrong number .... mistake.
5 I booked our seats more than a month .... advance.
6 Sarah's mobile phone was stolen while she was away .... a business trip.
7 Could you be quiet for a minute, please? I'm .... the phone.
8 We've had a few nice days, but .... general it's been a poor summer.
9 I was lucky. I found the solution .... accident.
10 It's a long journey. Let's stop somewhere .... the way and have a meal.
11 I spent ages looking for a phone box. .... the end I found one.
12 Are you here .... holiday or .... business?

B Preposition + noun (1–2)

What would you ask? Use the word in brackets with the correct preposition.
You may also need to use *the* or *your*.

▶ Ask if you can book a cabin before you travel. (advance)
Can I book a cabin in advance?

1 Ask if you can pay in notes. (cash)
Can ....
2 Ask if the information is current. (date)
Is ....
3 Ask your friend if he dropped the ball deliberately. (purpose)
Did ....
4 Ask if there is anything to watch tonight. (television)
Is ....
5 Ask your teacher if he or she will be here on the last day of July. (end)
Will ....
6 Ask Melanie if she thinks nuclear power is a good idea. (opinion)
Is ....
7 Ask Nick if he is selling his car. (sale)
Is ....
8 Ask Sarah if she approves of the plan in general. (whole)
Do ....

C Transport (3)

Complete the conversation. Put in *by*, *in* or *on*.

Sarah: It's a long way to Glasgow. Why don't you go (▶) .on. the train?
Mark: I don't know. I think I'd rather go (1) .... car.
Sarah: How far is your hotel from the station?
Mark: Oh, it's only five minutes (2) .... foot, but with all my luggage,
        I'd probably go (3) .... a taxi.
Sarah: Well, why not? It's less tiring going (4) .... train, isn't it?
Mark: I could go (5) .... air. That would be quickest.

124 Noun + preposition (**trouble with**)

1 Introduction

Read this true story about a prison escape.

Prisoners at a jail in Iowa in the US were trying to think of a **way of** escaping. At last they found an **answer to** their problem. They told the governor about their **interest in** drama and their **need for** creative activities. They put in a **request for** some tunnel-digging equipment for a play about coalminers. They knew that the governor felt **sympathy for** his prisoners and wanted a good **relationship with** them, but they weren't surprised when he said no. But later, when the prisoners mentioned the **importance of** physical fitness, the governor agreed to let them use a trampoline. Their **skill at** trampolining was put to good use when six prisoners bounced over the prison wall and escaped.

Some nouns can have a preposition after them, e.g. **way of, answer to, interest in**.
The preposition often has a phrase with a noun after it.

the answer **to the problem**   *their interest* **in drama**

And the preposition can sometimes have an -ing form after it.

a way **of escaping**   *their skill* **at trampolining**

2 Noun + preposition

Here are some more examples.

your **ability in** maths	an **example of** this	your **opinion of** the film
a cheap **alternative to** leather	some **experience of** selling	the **price of** food
an **attack on** the government	an **expert on** computers	the **reason for** the delay
my **attitude to/towards** him	no **hope of** winning	**respect for** the environment
a **belief in** God	an **invitation to** a party	a **student of** chemistry
the **cause of** the accident	some **knowledge of** Italian	a **substitute for** meat
the **cost of** living	a **lack of** money	**success at** golf/**in** my search
some **damage to** the car	something the **matter with** you	a **tax on** alcohol
a **difficulty over/with** visas	a new **method of** storing data	having **trouble with** my teeth

3 Connection, difference; increase, reduction, etc.

One thing has a <u>link</u> <u>with</u> another.	There is a <u>link</u> <u>between</u> two things.
a **connection with** another crime	a **connection between** the two crimes
Matthew's **relationship with** Emma	the **relationship between** Matthew and Emma
the **contrast with** yesterday's weather	the **contrast/difference between** town and country

Look at these words for increases and decreases. We use **in** before the thing that is increasing or decreasing and **of** before the amount of the increase or decrease.

an **increase/rise in** the price	an **increase/rise of** £10
a **reduction/fall in** the number of unemployed	a **reduction/fall of** 3%

4 Need, wish, etc.

Nouns meaning 'need', 'wish' or 'request' can have **for** after them.

There's a **need for** *more houses.*   *There was no* **demand for** *the product.*

Here are some examples: **appetite for, application for, demand for, desire for, need for, order for, preference for, request for, taste for, wish for**

Practice

A Noun + preposition (1–2)

Complete the conversation. Put in *at*, *in* or *of*.

Daniel: What's the job you've applied for?

Vicky: It's with a travel company. But the advert says that you need some experience (▶) ..of.. work in tourism. I haven't got that. And I don't think my knowledge (1) .... foreign languages will be good enough. I'm having no success at all (2) .... my attempts to get a job.

Daniel: What about your interest (3) .... computers? And your skill (4) .... typing? That's the sort of thing employers are looking for.

B Noun + preposition (1–2)

Complete the sentences. Use a preposition after these nouns:
answer, cause, damage, difficulty, invitation, matter, tax, way

▶ I've had an ..invitation to.. Laura's barbecue.

1 The accident caused some .... the car.
2 I'm trying to think of the best .... getting this piano upstairs.
3 I can't think of an .... the problem, I'm afraid.
4 The .... the accident is still unknown.
5 The government has introduced a new .... luxury goods.
6 Unfortunately there was some .... the arrangements.
7 The television won't come on. What's the .... it?

C Noun + preposition (2–3)

Complete the advertisement for a supermarket. Put in *between*, *for*, *in*, *of* or *with*.

Why not shop at Greenway Supermarket? You'll find the cost (▶) ..of.. your weekly shopping is much lower. There's quite a contrast (1) .... other stores. Here's one example (2) .... this: from today many of our products have a price reduction (3) .... five per cent! But this is not the only reason (4) .... Greenway's success. We're proud of our good relationship (5) .... our customers. We believe there is simply no substitute (6) .... quality. And there is no lack (7) .... choice at Greenway. That's the difference (8) .... Greenway and ordinary stores.

D Noun + preposition (1–4)

What are they saying? Read about each situation and complete the sentence.

▶ A motorist has rung the garage and requested a breakdown truck.
   Mechanic: I've just had a ..request for a breakdown truck...

1 Claude can answer all the quiz questions.
   Claude: I can tell you the ....

2 Matthew doesn't know any French.
   Matthew: Unfortunately I have no ....

3 The Prime Minister greatly desires progress.
   Prime Minister: I have a great ....

4 Vicky thinks the two colours are the same.
   Vicky: I can't see any ....

5 Most people say they prefer Zedco products.
   Zedco: Most people express a ....

125 Adjective + preposition (**proud of**)

1 Introduction

Matthew: *Why are you **angry with** me, Emma?*
Emma: *I'm **tired of** talking to myself. You never listen. I get **annoyed at** the way you behave.*
Matthew: *Sorry, but I have to go now or I'll be **late for** the basketball game.*
Emma: *You aren't **interested in** us, are you? You never worry about our relationship, do you?*

Some adjectives can have a preposition after them, e.g. **angry with, tired of, late for**.
The preposition often has a phrase with a noun or pronoun after it.
   annoyed **at the way** you behave   late **for the game**   angry **with me**
The preposition can sometimes have an -ing form after it.
   tired **of talking** to myself

2 Feelings

Here are some examples of adjective + preposition which are to do with feelings.

***afraid of** the dark*	***excited about** the holiday*	***proud of** our work*
***amazed at/by** the changes*	***fed up with** waiting*	***satisfied with** the result*
***ashamed of** myself*	***fond of** my sister*	***shocked at/by** the violence*
***bored with** doing nothing*	***happy about/with** the*	***surprised at/by** the reaction*
***disappointed with/about** the*	*arrangements*	***tired of** housework*
poor figures	***keen on** sport*	***worried about** money*
***eager for** action*	***nervous of** flying*	

Compare these examples.

*I'm **sorry about** the mistake.*	*I feel **sorry for** poor Melanie.*
*We were **angry at/about** the delay.*	*Sarah was **angry with** Henry.*
*We were **annoyed at/about** the delay.*	*Emma was **annoyed with** Matthew.*
*I was **pleased about** winning.*	*The winner was **pleased with** himself.*
*Vicky is **anxious about** her exam.*	*People are **anxious for** news.*

3 **Good, bad**, etc.

To talk about a person's ability, we use **good at, bad at**, etc.
   good at *tennis*   **brilliant at** *crosswords*   **bad at** *games*   **hopeless at** *cooking*
To talk about whether something makes you healthy or ill, we use **good for** and **bad for**.
   *Oranges are **good for** you.*   *Smoking is **bad for** you.*
For behaviour towards another person, we use **good to, kind to, nice to, polite to** and **rude to**.
   *My friends have been **good to** me.*   *You were very **rude to** the waitress.*

4 Other adjectives

Here are some more expressions with other adjectives.

***accustomed to** the noise*	***fit for** work*	***responsible for** running a business*
***aware of** the facts*	***full of** water*	***safe from** attack*
***capable of** looking after myself*	***guilty of** murder*	*the **same as** before*
***different from** our usual route*	***involved in** a project*	***similar to** my idea*
(see page 381)	***prepared for** action*	***typical of** David*
***famous for** her film roles*	***ready for** the big day*	***used to** the traffic*

▷ 71 Afraid, anxious, ashamed, interested, sorry   ▷ 72 Used to

Practice

A Feelings (1–2)

Say what these people's feelings are. Use the adjectives in brackets and a preposition.

▶ The children are leaving on a trip to the zoo. (excited)
   They're *excited about the trip to the zoo.*

1 Vicky doesn't like the dark. (afraid)
   She's ....

2 Nick was watching a video, but he's going to switch it off. (bored)
   He's ....

3 Emma is reading about computers. (interested)
   She's ....

4 Mark has just heard some news that he didn't expect. (surprised)
   He's ....

5 United have won a victory. (proud)
   They're ....

6 Olivia's children are being very silly. (annoyed)
   She's ....

7 The Zedco staff don't think their pay increase is big enough. (not satisfied)
   ....

B Good, bad, etc. (3)

Complete the conversation. Put in *at, for* or *to*.

Sarah: You were very rude (▶) *to* Henry when you said he needs to lose weight.

Claire: Well, it's true. Exercise would be good (1) .... him. He started jogging and then gave
         it up.

Sarah: Yes, but we can't all be good (2) .... taking physical exercise.

Claire: Anyone can do a bit of jogging. You don't have to be brilliant (3) .... it. And eating
         so much must be bad (4) .... you.

Sarah: Well, you could have been more polite.

Claire: Sorry. I'm not very good (5) .... saying the right thing. I'll try to be nice
         (6) .... him next time I see him.

C Other adjectives (1, 4)

Complete these paragraphs from an email Emma has received from her brother. Use these
adjectives and put a preposition after each one: *aware, different, famous, full, interested, late,
ready, responsible, similar, used*

Everything was strange here at first because this new job is (▶) *different from* any
I've had before. But I've got (▶) *used to* it now, and I'm really enjoying it. I'm mainly
(1) .... controlling the costs of the project. The work is quite hard,
and I must say I feel (2) .... a holiday. The company expect people
to do overtime. I wasn't (3) .... that before
I arrived because they hadn't told me at the interview, but I don't mind.

I've got a nice flat, which is very (4) .... the one I had in London.
The only difference is that my flat here is (5) .... horrible old
furniture. I keep falling over it! I live right by the harbour. It's a pity I've never been
(6) .... boats, because this is a good place for sailing. The noise of
the motor boats wakes me up every morning, so I'm never (7) ....
work. The area is (8) .... its seafood, which is great, because I love
eating fish, as you know.

Test U: Prepositions

A

Write the sentences correctly.

▶ ~~I'll see you at Monday.~~
I'll see you on Monday.

1 ~~The doctor has been working since twelve hours.~~

2 ~~We had a great time in the disco.~~

3 ~~The woman was getting from the car.~~

4 ~~The players had numbers at their shirts.~~

5 ~~The new manager takes over at two weeks' time.~~

6 ~~Anna drove at the garage to get some petrol.~~

7 ~~We were sitting in the back of the room.~~

B

Read Polly's postcard and write the missing words. Use one word only in each space.
Sometimes more than one answer is correct.

This is our first real holiday (▶) for ages, and I'm enjoying it tremendously. I love being
(1) .... an island. We arrived here almost a week (2) ...., and I can't believe the time
is going so fast. We finally completed the journey here (3) .... Friday evening (4) ....
about eleven o'clock. The journey wasn't too bad, but we had to wait ages (5) .... the airport
for our flight.

Our apartment here is fine. It's (6) .... the top floor. The beach isn't far away – we can walk
there (7) .... five minutes. The only problem is that we have to get (8) .... a busy
main road, which can be difficult.

We don't do much (9) .... the day, but we go out every evening. Last night's disco went on
very late, and today we slept (10) .... eleven.

C

Some of these sentences are correct, and some have a word which should not be there.
If the sentence is correct, put a tick (✓). If it is incorrect, cross the unnecessary word out
of the sentence and write it in the space.

▶ The cat was sitting on top of the shed.   ✓

▶ Coventry is near ~~by~~ Birmingham.   by

1 Luckily our train arrived on the time.   ....

2 People were running away from the gunman.   ....

3 It sounds as if the company is in trouble.   ....

4 The car was in the front of a bus.   ....

5 There's a meeting on next Tuesday.   ....

6 Lisa drew a plan on the back of an envelope.   ....

7 I'll be exhausted by the time I get home.   ....

D

Decide which word is correct.

▶ I saw a really funny programme .on. television.   a) at   b) from   c) in   d) on

1 You can see all the information .... the screen.   a) at   b) in   c) inside   d) on
2 Are these pictures .... sale?   a) at   b) for   c) in   d) to
3 Could you let me know .... Friday at the latest?   a) by   b) to   c) up to   d) until
4 The audience clapped .... the end of the show.   a) at   b) for   c) in   d) to
5 I've lived here .... last year.   a) after   b) by   c) for   d) since
6 What's the matter .... your car?   a) by   b) for   c) on   d) with
7 We could see the balloon high .... the town.   a) above   b) on   c) onto   d) up
8 There was a fall .... ten per cent in prices.   a) at   b) by   c) in   d) of
9 The house was burgled .... we were out.   a) at   b) during   c) time   d) while
10 What's the difference .... a boat and a ship?   a) between   b) from   c) under   d) with
11 Rupert's new car looks more .... an aeroplane.   a) as   b) like   c) near   d) similar
12 We're all bored .... this game.   a) about   b) at   c) for   d) with
13 I can't find my keys. I had them a minute ....   a) ago   b) before   c) behind   d) back
14 We get lots of requests .... help.   a) at   b) for   c) of   d) on
15 The babysitter will stay there .... we get home.   a) by   b) for   c) to   d) until
16 I'm going to be late .... the meeting.   a) at   b) for   c) in   d) to
17 We do most of our business .... summer.   a) along   b) at   c) in   d) on
18 The job is similar .... my old one.   a) as   b) at   c) to   d) with

E

Complete the second sentence so that it has a similar meaning to the first. Use the word in brackets.

▶ This is the Glasgow train. (going)
  This train is going to Glasgow.

1 Scott is a resident of Washington. (lives)
  ....

2 I'm travelling to Italy as part of my job. (business)
  ....

3 Friday morning is a busy time for me. (I'm)
  ....

4 They started playing an hour ago. (been)
  ....

5 Jonathan can play tennis very well. (good)
  ....

6 I'm rather busy now. (moment)
  ....

7 We took a plane to Budapest. (air)
  ....

8 Nigel passes the newsagent's every day. (goes)
  ....

9 The company is planning to reduce the workforce. (reduction)
  ....

10 We got to our guest-house early enough for a meal. (time)
  ....

126 Prepositional verbs (**wait for**)

1 Introduction

A prepositional verb is a verb + preposition.

> I'm **waiting for** you.   The dog **belongs to** our neighbours.

The preposition always goes before the object.

> NOT ~~I'm waiting you for.~~

In questions the preposition usually goes at the end of the sentence (see Unit 38).

> Who are you waiting **for**?

Some verbs can go with a number of different prepositions.

> I'm **looking at** these photos. They're really good.   I'm **looking for** my ticket. I can't find it anywhere.
> I'm **looking after** the children while their parents are out.   The police are **looking into** the matter.

2 Some common prepositional verbs

Here are some more examples.

> Yes, I **agree with** you.   Tom's neighbours **apologized for** the noise.
> I **approve of** the new scheme. I think it's a good idea.
> Have you **applied for** the job?   The patient **asked for** a glass of water.
> Do you **believe in** God?   I'm sorry, but I don't **care about** your problems.
> Lots of people **care for** elderly relatives. (= look after)
> I didn't **care for** the film. (= like)   Please **concentrate on** your work.
> The US **consists of** fifty states.   I can **deal with** any enquiries.
> Claire finally **decided on** a holiday in Turkey.
> Whether we go out will **depend on** the weather.   I **feel like** a drink. (= want)
> Everyone **laughed at** the joke.   I was **listening to** the radio.
> Did you **pay for** the coffee?   You can't **rely on** the weather forecast.
> I'll **see to** the matter at once.   Vicky **suffers from** headaches.

We do not normally use a preposition after these verbs:
answer, approach, control, demand, enter, expect, leave, reach, request

> The President is **entering** the building. NOT ~~He is entering into the building.~~

3 About, of and to

We can use **about** after many verbs. Here are some of them:
ask, complain, dream, enquire, hear, know, learn, protest, speak, talk, think, wonder

> Did you **hear about** the accident?   Mark was **talking about** golf.

We do not use **about** after **discuss**.

> We **discussed** the problem. NOT ~~We discussed about the problem.~~

Note the meaning of **dream of, hear of** and **think of**.

> I'd never tell you a lie. I wouldn't **dream of** it.
> Who's Ron Mason? ~ I don't know. I've never **heard of** him.
> Did you like the play? What did you **think of** it?

We can **apologize to, complain to, talk to** and **write to** a person.

> I'm **writing to** my sister.   We **talked to** Natasha about classical music.

We do not use **to** after **phone**.

> I'm **phoning** the office. NOT ~~I'm phoning to the office.~~

> ▷ 70 Verb + preposition + -ing form

Practice

A Prepositions with look (1)

Complete the conversation between Laura and her friend Olivia. Put in *after*, *at*, *for* and *into*.

Laura: Did you say you were looking (▶) .for. an au pair?

Olivia: Yes, I was just looking (1) .... this advertisement. We need someone to look
(2) .... our children.

Laura: Do you have to pay an au pair?

Olivia: I'm not sure. I'll have to look (3) .... how it all works.

B Some common prepositional verbs (2)

This is some news that Melanie has received from an old friend. Put in these verbs and add a
preposition after each one: *agree, applied, ask, care, caring, concentrate, decided, pay, suffering*

I'm working in a hospital now. I (▶) ..applied. for. a nurse's job last July and started in August.
I don't earn much money, and I even had to (1) .... my uniform out of
my own money. Perhaps I should (2) .... a pay rise. But I don't really
(3) .... the money. The work is the important thing. Of course it's very hard
work (4) .... the patients, and at the moment I'm (5) ....
backache. But I knew it would be like this when I (6) .... a career in nursing.
I just try to forget all the problems and (7) .... the job. I think it's a worthwhile
thing to do, and I'm sure you (8) .... me.

C Some common prepositional verbs (2)

Put in the verbs and add a preposition if necessary.

Mark and Sarah had accepted an invitation to Mike and Harriet's party. Sarah had to stay late at work
to (▶) .see. to. (see) one or two things. Her boss really (1) .... (relies) her. It's
usually Sarah who (2) .... (deals) all the little problems. Sarah didn't really
(3) .... (feel) going to a party but thought she ought to keep Mark company.
She decided to go straight to the party instead of going home first. She (4) ....
(reached) the house just after nine. Mark was sitting in his car outside waiting for her. He was
(5) .... (listening) the radio. Sarah (6) .... (apologized)
being late. At the party Mark talked to a strange woman who (7) .... (believed)
ghosts. Sarah met a man who kept (8) .... (laughing) his own jokes.
She managed to get away from him but couldn't avoid a woman who wanted to
(9) .... (discuss) house prices. Mark and Sarah (10) ....
(left) the party early and drove home feeling exhausted.

D About, of and to (3)

Complete the conversation. Put in *about*, *of* or *to*.

David: Did you hear about my experience at the Quick Burger café?

Harriet: No. And I've never heard (▶) .of. the Quick Burger café.

David: Oh, it's near the station. I was just talking (1) .... Melanie about it.
They took at least twenty minutes to bring me a burger. I don't call that quick. I complained
(2) .... the waitress, and she poured a can of cola over me.

Harriet: Really? She must have had a bad day.

David: The manager wasn't there, so I've written (3) .... him to complain (4) ....
the service. It was terrible. I wouldn't go there if I were you.

Harriet: I wouldn't dream (5) .... going there. I hate those burger places.

127 Verb + object + preposition

1 Introduction

We can use some verbs in the structure: verb + object + preposition.

	VERB	OBJECT	PREPOSITION	
People	**admired**	Cleopatra	**for**	her beauty.
The trees	**protect**	the garden	**from**	the wind.

In the passive, the preposition comes after the verb.

> Cleopatra was **admired for** her beauty.   The garden is **protected from** the wind.

2 Verb + object + preposition

Here are some more examples.

> Tom **accused** Nick **of** cheating at cards.   Can I **add** something **to** your list?
> You should never **aim/point** a gun **at** someone.
> The player was **arrested/punished for** hitting an opponent.   Let's **ask** someone **for** directions.
> The passengers **blamed/criticized** the airline **for** the delay.
> I'll have to **borrow** the money **from** my parents.
> If you **compare** these figures **with/to** last year, you can see the improvement.
> I **congratulated** Andrew **on** his excellent exam results.
> Melanie **cut/divided/split** the pudding **into** four portions.
> The cameras **discourage/prevent** motorists **from** speeding.
> You should **insure** your camera **against** theft. It might get stolen.
> Harriet has **invited** us **to** a party.   I **prefer** hot weather **to** cold. I hate the cold.
> The hotel **provided/supplied** us **with** a packed lunch.   Most people **regard** Picasso **as** a great artist.
> The two men **robbed** the woman **of** her savings. They stole £2,000 from her.
> The restaurant was full. We **shared** a table **with** a young Swedish couple.
> Mike doesn't **spend** much money **on** clothes.
> Zedco **suspected** one of their managers **of** selling commercial secrets.
> Don't forget to **thank** Tom **for** his help.   Victor **translated** the letter **into** English.

3 About, of and to

We can use **about** with **tell** and **ask**.

> Did I **tell** you **about** my operation?   **Ask** your travel agent **about** cheap flights.

With **inform** we can use **about** or **of**.

> You should **inform** everyone **about/of** the decision.

Look at these examples with **warn**.

> A sign **warned** motorists **about/of** the danger. (warn **about/of** a danger)
> A sign **warned** motorists **about** the hole in the road. (warn **about** something that might be dangerous)

With **remind**, there is a difference in meaning between **about** and **of**.

> Emma **reminded** me **about** my appointment. (= Emma told me not to forget.)
> Emma **reminds** me **of** my sister. (= Emma is like my sister.)

We can **write**, **describe** or **explain** something **to** a person.

> I've **written** several letters **to** the company.   The woman **described** her attacker **to** the police.

▷ 3 Give something to someone   ▷ 126 Wait for, belong to, etc.

Practice

A Verb + object + preposition (2)

This is a sports commentary at the Olympic Games.
Put in the correct prepositions, e.g. *for*, *from*.

So Australia's Steve Brearley wins the gold medal ahead of Germany's Klaus Schliemann and Ivan Podorosky of Bulgaria. They're just congratulating Brearley (▶) .on. his victory. His speed over the first kilometre split the runners (1) .... two groups, and in the end it was a race between the three leaders. Brearley prevented Schliemann (2) .... overtaking him in a sprint finish. I've always regarded Brearley (3) .... a great athlete, and look how well he's done today. I would even compare him (4) .... the great Emil Kristo himself. There's no doubt now that Brearley will be invited (5) .... Oslo for the next World Championships. So the Australian runner adds another medal (6) .... his collection. And Australia are doing really well in the medals table. In fact, they share second place (7) .... the United States.

B Verb + object + preposition (2)

People are saying some surprising things.
Complete the replies using a verb + object + preposition.

▶ Andrew: I've bought a lot of books. I've spent £300.
  Emma: What? Have you really ~~spent £300 on books?~~
1 Jessica: I don't like wine. I prefer water.
  Daniel: I don't believe that. Do you really ....
2 Melanie: You heard about David's accident. Well, he's blaming Tom.
  Rita: But why? Why is he ....
3 Henry: I gave Claire a present, but she didn't thank me.
  Sarah: Did you say she didn't ....
4 Tom: The police say it's murder. They're accusing the head teacher.
  Rita: What evidence do they have? How can they ....
5 Vicky: We had no towels. The hotel didn't provide them.
  Rachel: Really? Why didn't they ....
6 Natasha: It's my sister's wedding today, but she didn't invite me.
  Emma: What! Do you mean she didn't ....
7 Nick: The team won a great victory, but no one congratulated them.
  Trevor: Oh? And why didn't anyone ....
8 David: A man pointed a gun. Melanie was terrified.
  Harriet: You mean someone ....

C About, of and to (3)

Put in *about*, *of* or *to*.

▶ The interviewer asked Mrs Miles .about. her parachute jump.
1 I've told the police .... people throwing stones at our windows.
2 That man over there reminds me .... someone I know.
3 The man explained .... the court that he had some personal problems.
4 Vicky is writing a letter .... her friends in Toronto.
5 There was a poster warning young people .... the dangers of drugs.
6 Melanie had to remind Nick .... the money he owed her.
7 We would like to inform our customers .... a number of improvements in the service we offer.

128 Phrasal verbs (1)

1 Introduction

A phrasal verb is a verb + adverb, e.g. **come in**, **sit down**, **take off**. There are very many phrasal verbs in English.

Here are some adverbs which are used in phrasal verbs: **about**, **along**, **around**, **away**, **back**, **behind**, **by**, **down**, **forward**, **in**, **off**, **on**, **out**, **over**, **round**, **through**, **up**

Some of these words can also be prepositions. For prepositional verbs see Unit 126.

Hello, Tom.

Hello, Melanie. Good to see you. **Come in** and **sit down**. **Take** your coat **off**.

2 Understanding phrasal verbs

Some phrasal verbs are easy to understand.

*Tom asked Melanie to **come in**.*   *The man in front **turned round** and stared at me.*

The meanings are clear if you know the words **come**, **in**, **turn** and **round**.

But many phrasal verbs are idiomatic. The verb + adverb has a special meaning.

*Fortunately the plan **came off**.* (= succeeded)
*Why did you **turn down** such a good offer?* (= refuse)
*I can't **make out** if it's a man or a woman over there.* (= see clearly)

Sometimes a phrasal verb has the same meaning as a one-word verb.

find out = discover	**leave out** = omit	**send out** = distribute
go back = return	**make up** = invent (a story)	**throw away** = discard
go on = continue	**put off** = postpone	**turn up** = arrive

The phrasal verb is usually more informal than the one-word verb.

3 Word order with phrasal verbs

When a phrasal verb has an object, the object can go either before or after the adverb.

	VERB	OBJECT	ADVERB			VERB	ADVERB	OBJECT
Melanie	**took**	*her coat*	**off.**	OR	*Melanie*	**took**	**off**	*her coat.*
I	**wrote**	*the number*	**down.**	OR	*I*	**wrote**	**down**	*the number.*
Who	**let**	*the cat*	**out?**	OR	*Who*	**let**	**out**	*the cat?*

A long object goes after the adverb.

*The gang have **carried out a number of bank raids** in the last few months.*
*Why don't you **try on that dress in the window**?*

A pronoun (e.g. **it**, **them**) always goes before the adverb.

*Melanie felt hot in her coat, so she **took it off**.*
NOT ~~She took off it.~~
*There have been a number of raids. The police know who **carried them out**.*
NOT ~~The police know who carried out them.~~

Practice

A Understanding phrasal verbs (1–2)

Work out the meaning of these phrasal verbs and put them in the right sentences:
come back, come in, cut out, fall over, get on, give away, go away, let in, lie down, pay back, stay in, take back. (Use a dictionary if you need to.)

▶ Hello. Nice to see you. Come in and sit down.
▶ I didn't have a key, but luckily someone was there to let me in.
1 Can't we go out somewhere? I don't want to .... all evening.
2 Could you lend me ten pounds? I'll .... you .... on Friday.
3 The pavement is very icy. Be careful you don't ....
4 I was feeling so tired I had to .... on the bed for a while.
5 There was an article in the newspaper that I wanted to .... and keep.
6 Mark's gone out, and I don't know when he's going to ....
7 The driver unlocked the coach so that the passengers were able to ....
8 I'll have to .... these books .... to the library.
9 Your brother was being a nuisance, so I told him to ....
10 In order to get publicity, the company decided to .... some of the new sweets free to children.

B One-word verb and phrasal verb (2)

Put in a phrasal verb that means the same as the verb in brackets. Use the correct form of the phrasal verb.

Rachel: I've (▶) found out (discovered) what the problem is with the exam.
Vicky: Oh, good. Tell me.
Rachel: When they printed the papers, they (1) .... (omitted) a page. No one noticed until the papers had all been (2) .... (distributed). Now they'll have to (3) .... (discard) all the papers and (4) .... (postpone) the exam.
Vicky: Are you sure you haven't (5) .... (invented) this whole story?
Rachel: It's true, I tell you. And isn't it good news?
Vicky: I don't know about that. It means we'll have to (6) .... (continue) revising.

C Word order with phrasal verbs (3)

Complete the sentences by putting in the phrasal verbs. Some of the spaces you have to leave empty. Sometimes more than one answer is correct.

▶ The sweater was full of holes, so I threw it away. (threw away).
▶ I've put up (put up) that picture we bought last week.
1 There's always litter here. No one ever .... it .... (pick up).
2 It's quite cold now. I think I'll .... my coat .... (put on).
3 I haven't heard from Rita lately. I might .... her .... (ring up).
4 Daniel has to go into college to .... his project .... (hand in).
5 I can't remember the address. I wish I'd .... it .... (write down).
6 Nick is trying to .... all the money he's just lost .... (win back).
7 I'm not going to have time to .... these dishes .... (wash up).
8 If you don't know the number, you can .... it .... (look up) in the phone book.
9 There was an accident which .... all the traffic coming into town .... (held up).
10 The words 'expect' and 'except' are so similar that I keep .... them .... (mix up).

129 Phrasal verbs (2)

1 Everyday situations

Here are some phrasal verbs in everyday situations.

Come on, *we're going now.*
*Trevor **dug up** an old coin in the garden.*
*You have to **fill in** your name and address.*
*How did you **get on** in the test?*
*I usually **get up** late on Sundays.*
*I'm **going out** for the evening.*
*Melanie poured tea for the guests and **handed** the cakes **round**.*
***Hurry up**. We haven't got much time.*
*David hit his head on a lamppost and **knocked** himself **out**.*
*Mark **picked up** the cassette and put it in the player.*
*You have to **plug** the machine **in** first.*
*I'm going to **throw** these old clothes **away**.*
*We were too tired to **wash up** after the meal.*
*Sarah **woke up** suddenly in the night.*

Look out! It's **boiling over.**

2 Phrasal verbs and one-word verbs

Here are some phrasal verbs with the same meaning as a one-word verb (see also Unit 128.2).

*They're going to **bring in** a new law against drinking and driving.* (= introduce)
*How did the argument **come about**?* (= happen)
*Emma isn't speaking to Matthew. They've **fallen out**.* (= quarrelled)
*We've **fixed up** a meeting for next Tuesday.* (= arranged)
*Trevor **gave up** playing football years ago.* (= stopped)
*I had a pain in my arm, but it's **gone away**.* (= disappeared)
*We heard the bomb **go off** five miles away.* (= explode)
*The traffic was **held up** by road works.* (= delayed)
*The United Nations was **set up** to settle conflicts peacefully.* (= established)
*I'm trying to **work out** how much money I've spent.* (= calculate)

3 Business situations

Here are some examples of phrasal verbs in business situations.

*If we're spending too much money, we'll have to **cut back**.* (= spend less)
*Our lawyers will **draw up** a new contract.* (= write)
*We mustn't **fall behind** in the race to develop new products.* (= be slower than others)
*The two sides were close to an agreement, but it **fell through**.* (= didn't happen)
*The company **fought off** a takeover by ICM Computers.* (= managed to stop)
*I tried to ring Santiago, but I couldn't **get through**.* (= make contact)
*The company has **laid off** two hundred workers because of a lack of new orders.* (= dismissed)
*The computer will **print out** the details.*
*The consultants **put forward** a proposal to reorganize the company.* (= suggested)
*I'll get the information for you. Can I **ring** you **back** in half an hour?* (= phone again)
*Sarah paid a visit to the client to try to **sort out** the difficulties.* (= put right)
*The company boss has **stepped down** after ten years in charge.* (= left the job)
*We are **taking on** the challenge of expanding overseas.* (= accepting)
*Large companies sometimes **take over** smaller ones.* (= take control of)

Practice

A Phrasal verbs in everyday situations (1)

Look at the pictures and say what is happening.
Use these phrasal verbs: *dig up*, *pick up*, *plug in*, *throw away*, *wash up*
Use these objects: *the armchair*, *litter*, *the plates*, *the road*, *the television*

▶   They're throwing the armchair away.

1   3   ....

2   4   ....

B Phrasal verbs and one-word verbs (2)

Rewrite the sentences replacing each underlined verb with a phrasal verb.

▶   We're trying to <u>arrange</u> a holiday together.
    We're trying to fix up a holiday together.

1   Nick says he's <u>stopped</u> smoking.
    ....

2   How did the accident <u>happen</u>?
    ....

3   I think Matthew and Emma have <u>quarrelled</u>.
    ....

4   The problem isn't going to just <u>disappear</u>.
    ....

5   The government is <u>introducing</u> a new tax on computers.
    ....

6   Zedco want to <u>establish</u> a new sales office in Germany.
    ....

C Business situations (3)

Complete the news article about Zedco. Put in these words: *fallen behind, fell through, fight off, laying off, put forward, sort out, step down, taking over, taken on*

Zedco Chief Executive Barry Douglas has (▶) put forward a new plan designed to
(1) .... the company's problems. It is only twelve months since Zedco
tried to strengthen its position by (2) .... Alpha Plastics. But the deal
(3) ...., and Alpha managed to (4) ....
Zedco's attempts to take control. Since then Zedco has performed poorly and has
(5) .... in the race for market share. Managing Director James
Ironside has had to (6) ...., and Barry Douglas has
(7) .... the task of rescuing the company. There are fears that the new
plan will mean (8) .... staff in order to reduce expenditure.

130 Phrasal verbs (3)

Our advertising campaign has pushed sales **up**. I can show you on the screen. I'll just switch the computer **on**.

1 Introduction

Look at the two adverbs in the two phrasal verbs **push up** and **switch on**. Here **up** has the sense of 'increasing', and **on** has the sense of 'connected'. The same meanings can be used with other verbs: for example, sales can **go up**, or a company can **put up** prices. But remember that an adverb can have more than one meaning; **up** can also mean 'completely': *Aren't you going to **eat up** your cornflakes?* There are some examples of adverb meanings in 2.

2 Adverb meanings

down = becoming less
  __turn down__ the music
  __bring down__ the cost of living

down = completely to the ground
  knock a house __down__
  __cut down__ a tree

down = stopping completely
  the car __broke down__
  a factory __closing down__

down = on paper
  __copy down__ the words
  __write down__ the message
  __note down__ the details

off = away, departing
  __set off__ on a journey
  jump in the car and __drive off__
  __see__ Emma __off__ at the station
  the plane __took off__
  the pain is __wearing off__

off = disconnected
  __switch off__ the heater
  __cut off__ our electricity
  the caller __rang off__

on = connected
  __switch on__ the kettle
  __turn on__ the TV
  __leave__ the lights __on__ all night

on = wearing
  __put__ a coat __on__
  __try__ the sweater __on__

on = continuing
  __carry on__ working
  __drive on__ a bit further
  __hang on/hold on__ a minute

out = away, disappearing
  __wash out__ the dirt
  __cross out__ a mistake
  __blow out__ the candle

out = to different people
  __hand out__ free tickets
  __share out__ the winnings

out = aloud
  __read out__ the article
  __call out__ anxiously

out = from start to finish
  __write out__ the whole list
  __work out__ the answer

over = from start to finish
  __check__ your work __over__
  __think__ the problem __over__

up = increasing
  prices are __going up__
  __put up__ taxes
  __speak up__ so we can hear

up = completely
  __eat up__ these chocolates
  __fill up__ with petrol
  __count up__ the money
  __tear up__ the paper

Some phrasal verbs have more than one meaning:
*Can you **turn down** the radio?* (= make less loud)
*I **turned down** the offer.* (= refused)
*How do we **get around** this problem?* (= deal with)
*The news will soon **get around**.* (= be widely communicated)

Practice

A Adverb meanings (2)

Look back at B and then write the meaning of the <u>underlined</u> words in these sentences.

▶ I must get these ideas <u>down</u> in writing. ....on paper.............

1 Daniel finished all the cake <u>up</u>. ....
2 I'm writing in pencil so I can rub <u>out</u> my mistakes. ....
3 Vicky didn't answer. She just went <u>on</u> reading. ....
4 I'll just read <u>over</u> what I've written. ....
5 A woman in the audience shouted something <u>out</u>. ....
6 The water was turned <u>off</u> for about an hour today. ....
7 Nick's aggressive manner frightens people <u>off</u>. ....
8 The company wants to keep its costs <u>down</u>. ....
9 The embassy was burnt <u>down</u> by terrorists. ....
10 Someone will have to type all these figures <u>out</u>. ....
11 Social workers were giving <u>out</u> soup to the hungry. ....
12 Luckily Zedco's sales figures are moving <u>up</u> again. ....
13 The man was tall and dark. He had a blue jacket <u>on</u>. ....
14 Business is so bad that many firms have shut <u>down</u>. ....

B Adverb meanings (2)

Put in the correct adverb.

▶ Melanie: Everything is so expensive. Prices seem to be going ..up.. all the time.
   David: Yes, and the government is supposed to be bringing inflation .down..

1 Laura: You shouldn't leave the television .... all night.
   Trevor: Sorry, I forgot. I usually turn it ....
2 Vicky: I've written the wrong word here.
   Rachel: Well, rub it ....
   Vicky: I can't. It's in biro. I'll have to write the whole thing .... again.
3 Sarah: They're going to pull .... this beautiful old building.
   Mark: I know. Some protesters were handing .... leaflets about it.
4 Emma: Hold .... a minute. I thought I heard someone call ....
   Matthew: I think you must have imagined it.

C Adverb meanings (2)

What are they saying? Put in the phrasal verbs.

▶ I'm afraid the car has broken down.
1 Why don't you .... this coat?
2 Look, the plane is ....
3 I can't hear. Please ....
4 We're just .... on holiday.

131 Verb + adverb + preposition

1 Simple meanings

Look at these examples.

	VERB	ADVERB	PREPOSITION	
So you've	**come**	**in**	**from**	the cold.
The old man	**fell**	**down**	**on**	the pavement.
I couldn't	**get**	**through**	**to**	directory enquiries.
David decided to	**get**	**up**	**onto**	the roof.
It was nice to	**go**	**out**	**into**	the fresh air.
We	**look**	**out**	**over**	the sea.
Everyone	**looked**	**up**	**at**	the aeroplane.
Vicky	**ran**	**away**	**from**	the fire.

2 Idiomatic meanings

A verb + adverb + preposition often has a special, idiomatic meaning which isn't clear from the individual words. Look at these examples.

Tom often **calls in on/drops in on** us without warning. (= pays short visits)
You go on ahead. I'll soon **catch up with** you. (= reach the same place as)
The police are going to **clamp down on** drug dealers. (= take strong action against)
I'm afraid we've **come up against** another difficulty. (= be stopped by)
Did Claire's trip **come up to/live up to** her expectations? (= Was it as good as she expected?)
The country is **crying out for** a new leader. (= in great need of)
We need to **cut back on** our spending. (= reduce)
I'm trying to lose weight. I have to **cut down on** puddings. (= reduce)
They should **do away with** these useless traditions. (= abolish)
You've got to **face up to** your responsibilities. You can't just ignore them. (= not avoid)
If plan A doesn't work, we've got plan B to **fall back on**. (= use if necessary)
I'm tired, Mark. I don't really **feel up to** going out. (= have enough energy for)
We can't go on holiday together if your dates don't **fit in with** mine. (= go together with)
The thief managed to **get away with** about £2,000 in cash. (= steal and take away)
The goods are damaged. We'll have to **get on to** our suppliers. (= contact)
You haven't packed your suitcase yet. You'd better **get on with** it. (= start, continue)
Mark doesn't really **get on with** Alan. They're always arguing. (= have a good relationship with)
I have lots of little jobs to do, but I can never **get round to** actually doing them. (= find the right time for)
I can't make a promise and then **go back on** it, can I? (= break, fail to keep)
Matthew has decided to **go in for** the ten-mile 'Fun Run' this year. (= enter, compete in)
Most of the audience had left in the interval, but the actors decided to **go on with** the show. (= continue)
If you **hold on to** the rope, you'll be perfectly safe. (= keep your hands around)
Daniel was walking so fast I couldn't **keep up with** him. (= go as fast as)
I'm **looking forward to** the trip. (= thinking ahead with pleasure about)
If you're going barefoot, **look out for/watch out for** broken glass. (= be careful about)
I got some money from the insurance company, but nothing could **make up for** losing
  my wedding ring. (= compensate for)
I'm not going to **put up with** this nonsense. (= tolerate)
We've **run out of** milk, I'm afraid. (= We have none left.)
Are you going to **send away for** your free gift? (= write to ask for)

Practice

A Simple meanings (1)

Put in these words: *away from, down on, in from, out into, through to, up at, up onto*

▶ To reach the light bulb, Trevor had to get ..up. onto.. the table.
1 Nick hurt himself when he was skating. He fell .... the ice.
2 It was a very long tunnel, but we finally came .... the sunshine.
3 Wondering if it was going to rain, Vicky looked .... the clouds.
4 People were running .... the gunman as fast as they could.
5 I'm trying to phone my secretary, but I can't get .... the office.
6 When I've come .... the cold, I just want to sit by the fire.

B Idiomatic meanings (2)

Put in a verb + adverb + preposition which means the same as the expression in brackets.

▶ I'm afraid this product doesn't .live. up. to. (be as good as) the claims made in the advertisement.
1 I'll just call at the garage. I don't want to .... (have none left) petrol.
2 If you want a catalogue, I'll .... (write to ask for) one.
3 We'd better .... (be careful about) sheep in the road.
4 I .... (think ahead with pleasure about) seeing you again soon, Emma.
5 The teacher was dictating so fast we couldn't .... (go as fast as) her.
6 Why should we have to .... (tolerate) this awful noise?
7 It's half past twelve. I'd better .... (start) making lunch.
8 Do you think the committee will .... (change) their earlier decision?
9 There was a problem with the cheque, so I decided to .... (contact) my bank immediately.
10 I always like to .... (enter) quiz competitions.
11 I'm trying to .... (reduce) the amount of coffee I drink.
12 I might lose my job. And I haven't got any savings to .... (use if necessary).
13 I've been meaning to reply to Rachel's email, but I haven't managed to .... (find the right time for) it yet.
14 An apology alone cannot .... (compensate for) all the inconvenience.

C Idiomatic meanings (2)

What might you say in these situations? Use the words in brackets.

▶ You're tired. You can't go jogging. (don't feel up)
  I don't feel up to jogging.
1 You like Melanie. The two of you are very friendly. (I get)
  ....
2 You might go and see David. It would be a short visit. (might drop)
  ....
3 You don't mind what you do. You'll do the same as everyone else. (I'll fit)
  ....
4 You are too slow. Matthew is too far ahead of you. (can't catch up)
  ....
5 The sunny weather is nice. Last week was terrible. (is making up)
  ....

Test V: Verbs with prepositions and adverbs

A

Put the words in the right order to form a statement.

▶ I won't forget the titles of the books. down / I've / them / written
I've written them down.

1 I'll give you the money. for / I / must / my ticket / pay

....

2 I have to look smart. going to / I'm / on / put / that expensive grey coat I bought

....

3 Anna rang. invited / lunch / she's / to / us

....

4 Peter's got the photos. at / he's / looking / them

....

5 I wasn't allowed to go. from / leaving / me / prevented / the police

....

6 This programme is boring. going to / I'm / it / off / turn

....

B

Decide which word is correct.

▶ I'm not speaking to Oliver. I've fallen ..*out*. with him.
a) away   b) back   c) out   d) through

1 Everyone complained .... the awful food.
a) about   b) for   c) on   d) over

2 You don't need this word. You should cross it ....
a) down   b) out   c) over   d) up

3 It's late. How much longer are you going to go .... working?
a) along   b) on   c) through   d) with

4 My shoes are dirty. I'd better take them .... before I come in.
a) away   b) off   c) on   d) up

5 The bus journey costs more now. They've put the fares ....
a) down   b) out   c) over   d) up

6 We all laughed .... the cartoon.
a) at   b) for   c) on   d) to

7 We'd all decided to go on holiday together, but the plan fell .... , I'm afraid.
a) away   b) back   c) out   d) through

8 I suppose you're being nice to make .... the awful way you behaved yesterday.
a) away of   b) down on   c) in with   d) up for

C

Write the correct sentence.

▶ Could you be a little quieter, please? ~~I'm trying to concentrate at my work.~~
I'm trying to concentrate on my work.

1 You haven't answered all the questions. ~~You've left one away.~~

....

2 Where is Bigbury? ~~I've never heard about it.~~

....

3 The children were frightened of the dog. ~~They ran out of it.~~

....

4   Michelle has got the job. ~~You must congratulate her for her success.~~

    ....

5   My sister is in computers. ~~She's going to set out her own company.~~

    ....

6   I like Peter. ~~He reminds me about an old school friend of mine.~~

    ....

7   Adrian has a suggestion. ~~He wants to put it ahead at the meeting.~~

    ....

D

Read the story and write the missing words. Use one word only in each space.

This true story is about a policeman in New York City who had a girlfriend he cared (►) .for. very
much. I don't know if you regard New York City (1) .... a dangerous place, but
the hero of our story certainly did, and he warned his girlfriend (2) .... the
danger of walking the streets alone and the need to (3) .... out for muggers.
But as he also believed (4) .... being prepared for the worst, he bought a can of
gas that would protect his girlfriend (5) .... muggers. It certainly seemed
worth spending a few dollars (6) .... The idea is that you point the thing
(7) .... your attacker and spray him with the gas, which knocks him
(8) .... On the day he bought the gas, the policeman and his girlfriend
had arranged to go (9) .... for the evening. So he was looking
(10) .... to giving her the can later on. When he got home from work,
he had a bath and then sprayed some deodorant on himself. He knew nothing more until he
(11) .... up in hospital the next day. He had picked (12) ....
the wrong can and sprayed himself with the gas.

E

Complete the second sentence so that it has a similar meaning to the first. Use the word in brackets.

►   I'm trying to find my diary. (looking)
    I'm looking for my diary. ....

1   You're too young to stop working. (give)

    ....

2   This bag is Janet's. (belongs)

    ....

3   Everyone continued working as usual. (carried)

    ....

4   They talked about the plan. (discussed)

    ....

5   I haven't got any money left. (run)

    ....

6   I told the police what the problem was. (explained)

    ....

7   I wouldn't tolerate such terrible conditions. (put)

    ....

8   They'll have to postpone the game. (off)

    ....

132 Direct speech and reported speech

1 Direct speech

Look at these examples of direct speech.

> Trevor: **I'm tired**.

> Wasn't it Greta Garbo who said, '**I want to be alone**'?

> '**But I don't love you, Henry**,' replied Claire.

We can show that words are direct speech by putting them in quotation marks (' '). See page 373. Sometimes the words are put after the speaker's name, in the script of a play or film, for example. In a picture we can put the words in a speech bubble.

2 Reported speech

In reported speech we give the meaning of what was said rather than the exact words.

> Trevor says **he's tired**.

> Wasn't it Greta Garbo who said **that she wanted to be alone**?

> Claire replied **that she didn't love Henry**.

> The actress Melissa Livingstone and supermarket owner Ron Mason have announced that they are getting married next month. Melissa is sure they will be happy together, she told reporters.

In reported speech we often change the actual words, e.g. '**I'm** tired' → **he's** tired. Sometimes the verb tense changes, e.g. I **want** → she **wanted** (see Unit 134).

In reporting we use verbs such as **announce**, **answer**, **explain**, **mention**, **promise**, **reply**, **say**, **suggest**, **tell**, **warn**. The most common of these are **say** and **tell** (see 3). We can also report thoughts.

> We **think** the meal was expensive.   Nick **knew** Rita wanted to be with someone else.

When we report statements, we often use **that**, but we can sometimes leave it out.

> You promised (**that**) you wouldn't be late.   Sarah was saying (**that**) there's a problem.

3 Tell or say?

TELL	SAY
We use **tell** if we want to mention the hearer (the person spoken to). *Sarah's boss **told her** she could leave early.* NOT *Sarah's boss told she could leave early.* *Daniel **tells me** he's ready.* We use **tell** without an indirect object (e.g. **her**, **me**) only in the expressions **tell a story**, **tell the truth** and **tell a lie**.	When we do not mention the hearer, we use **say**. *Sarah's boss **said** she could leave early.* NOT *Sarah's boss said her she could leave early.* *Daniel **says** he's ready.* We sometimes use **to** after **say**, especially when the words are not reported. *The boss wanted to **say** something **to** Sarah.* *What did Matthew **say to** you?*

Practice

A Reported speech (2)

Why are these people at the doctor's? What do they say is wrong with them?

▶ I get pains in my leg.   1 I can't sleep.   2 I've hurt my back.   3 I feel sick all the time.   4 I fell over and hurt myself.

▶ She says *she gets pains in her leg.*
1 She says ....
2 He says ....
3 ....
4 ....

B Reported speech (2)

Who said what? Match the words to the people and report what they said.
If you can't match them, look at the answers at the bottom of the page.

▶ Mrs Thatcher
1 Stokeley Carmichael
2 Galileo
3 Shakespeare
4 George Orwell

a) 'All the world's a stage.'
b) 'Black is beautiful.'
c) 'Big Brother is watching you.'
d) <u>'There is no such thing as society.'</u>
e) 'The earth moves round the sun.'

▶ *Mrs Thatcher said that there is no such thing as society.* ....
1 ....
2 ....
3 ....
4 ....

C Tell or say? (3)

Put in *tell* or *say*.

▶ All the experts *say* the earth is getting warmer.
▶ Did you *tell* Mark and Sarah how to find our house?
1 The Sales Manager is going to .... everyone about the meeting.
2 Vicky, why don't you just .... what the matter is?
3 They .... they're going to build a new Disney World here.
4 What did Natasha .... about her holiday plans?
5 Could you .... me the way to the train station, please?
6 The company should .... its employees what's going on.
7 You shouldn't .... lies, you know, Matthew.
8 Did you .... anything to Melanie about the barbecue?

133 Reported speech: person, place and time

1 Introduction

It's Friday afternoon. David is at Tom's flat. Tom has decided to have a party for all his friends.

A few minutes later Nick has arrived at the flat. Now David is reporting what Tom said. So instead of Tom's words **I'm having**, David says **he's having**.

The next day David is talking to Harriet. Now David is in a different place from where Tom first told him about the party. So instead of **here**, he says **at his flat**. And a day has passed since he first heard about it. It is now the day of the party. So instead of **tomorrow evening**, David says **this evening**.

2 Changes in reported speech

Changes from direct speech to reported speech depend on changes in the situation.
We may have to make changes when we are reporting something another person has said,
or when we report it in a different place or at a different time. Here are some typical changes.

Person:	I	→	he/she
	my	→	his/her
Place:	here	→	there, at the flat
Time:	now	→	then, at the time
	today	→	that day, on Monday, etc.
	yesterday	→	the day before, the previous day
	tomorrow	→	the next/following day, on Saturday, etc.
	this week	→	that week
	last week	→	the week before, the previous week
	an hour ago	→	an hour before/earlier

Practice

A Changes in reported speech (1–2)

Read what each person says and then complete the sentences.

▶ Vicky: Daniel told me on Friday that he'd had a job interview the previous day.
Daniel had a job interview on ....*Thursday*.......... .

1 Trevor: Laura tells me I need a haircut.
.... needs a haircut.

2 Claire: My brother told me in 2002 that he expected to become Manager the following year.
Claire's brother expected that he would become Manager in ....

3 Alice: I wanted to see Mark in April, but he said he was very busy that month.
Mark was very busy in ....

4 Harriet: I saw Nick last week. He said he'd given up smoking the week before.
Nick gave up smoking .... ago.

B Changes of person (1–2)

Put in the missing words.

C Changes of place and time (1–2)

Put in here, that day, the day before, <u>the next day</u>, the week before.

▶ Rachel (a week ago): I'm taking my driving test tomorrow.
You (today): When I saw Rachel, she said she was taking her driving test *the next day*.

1 Emma (two days ago): I've only had this new computer since yesterday.
You (today): Emma said she'd only had the new computer since ....

2 Matthew (a week ago): I'm meeting a friend at the station later today.
You (today): Matthew said he was meeting a friend at the station later ....

3 Mark (in the street): I'll see you in the office.
You (in the office): Mark said he would see me ....

4 Sarah (a month ago): The conference was last week.
You (today): Sarah told me the conference had taken place ....

134 Reported speech: the tense change

1 When do we change the tense?

After a past-tense verb (e.g. **said**), there is often a tense change.

> 'It really **is** cold today.' → Vicky said it **was** cold.

If the statement is still up to date when we report it, then we have a choice.
We can either leave the tense the same, or we can change it.

> You said you **like/liked** chocolate.   Claire told me her father **owns/owned** a racehorse.
> Sarah said she**'s going**/she **was** going to Rome in April.

We can say that Sarah <u>is</u> going to Rome because it <u>is</u> still true that she will go there.

If the statement is no longer up to date, then we change the tense.

> Claire once told me that her father **owned** a racehorse. (He may no longer own one.)
> Sarah said she **was** going to Rome in April. (Now it is May.)

Now Sarah's trip is over, so it is no longer true that she <u>is</u> going to Rome.

We usually change the tense if we think the statement is untrue or may be untrue.

> You said you **liked** chocolate, but you aren't eating any.
> The Prime Minister claimed that the government **had** made the right decision.

2 Is → was, like → liked, etc.

Look at these examples of the tense change.

DIRECT SPEECH		REPORTED SPEECH
'Andrew **is** working.'	→	Jessica said Andrew **was** working.
'The windows **aren't** locked.'	→	Mark told me the windows **weren't** locked.
'I've fixed the shelves.'	→	Trevor said he**'d** fixed the shelves.
'It's been raining.'	→	We noticed it **had** been raining.
'We**'ve got** plenty of time.'	→	Rachel insisted they **had** plenty of time.
'We **like** the flat.'	→	The couple said they **liked** the flat.

If the verb phrase is more than one word (e.g. **is working**), then the first word changes,
e.g. **is** working → **was** working, **have** fixed → **had** fixed, **don't** know → **didn't** know.
If the verb is already in the past tense, then it can stay the same or change to the Past Perfect.

'We **came** by car.'	→	They said they **came**/they **had come** by car.
'Sorry. I **wasn't** listening.'	→	I admitted I **wasn't** listening/**hadn't** been listening.

If the verb is Past Perfect, it stays the same.

'My money **had run** out.'	→	Daniel said his money **had run** out.

3 Modal verbs: can → could, etc.

Can, may and **will** change to **could, might** and **would.**

'You **can** sit over there.'	→	The steward said we **could** sit here.
'I **may** go to Bali again.'	→	Claire said she **might** go to Bali again.
'I**'ll** help if you like.'	→	Tom said he **would** help.

Could, might, ought to, should and **would** stay the same. But **must** can change to **have to.**

'Sarah **would** love a holiday.'	→	Mark thought Sarah **would** love a holiday.
'I **must** finish this report.'	→	Sarah said she **must** finish/**had to** finish the report.

Practice

A When do we change the tense? (1)

Put in *is* or *was*. Sometimes both are possible.

▶ I heard today that the house ...is... for sale. I wonder who will buy it.

▶ I saw David yesterday. He said he .was. on his way to visit his sister.

1 This wallet is made of plastic not leather. Why did you tell me it .... leather?

2 We had to hurry yesterday morning. Just as we arrived at the station, we heard an announcement that the train .... about to leave.

3 I saw Emma just now. She said her tooth .... still aching.

4 I'm surprised Matthew lost. I thought he .... much better at tennis than Daniel.

5 When he spoke to reporters yesterday, Mr Douglas said that Zedco .... now in a much better financial position.

B The tense change (2)

Complete the replies. The second speaker is surprised at what he or she hears.

▶ Matthew: Emma and I are getting married.
  Rachel: Really? But you said last week *you weren't getting married.*

▶ Rita: I like pop music more than classical music.
  Laura: I'm sure you told me *you liked classical music best.*

1 Vicky: I haven't finished my project.
  Emma: Haven't you? I thought you said ....

2 Rachel: I'm on a diet.
  Natasha: But you told me ....

3 Andrew: I enjoy parties.
  Daniel: Surely I remember you saying ....

4 Matthew: I'm applying for the job.
  Rachel: I thought you told me ....

C The tense change (2–3)

A comedy show called 'Don't Look Now!' has just closed after five years in London's West End. Here's what the critics said when it opened five years ago.

▶ 'It's a marvellous show.' *The Daily Mail*

▶ 'You'll love it.' *The Guardian*

1 'The production is brilliant.' *The Sunday Times*

2 'I can't remember a funnier show.' *Edward Devine*

3 'It made me laugh.' *Robert Walsh*

4 'You must see it.' *The Evening Standard*

5 'It will be a great success.' *The Telegraph*

6 'You might die laughing.' *The Express*

7 'It's the funniest show I've ever seen.' *Susan Proctor*

8 'You shouldn't miss it.' *Time Out*

Now report what the critics said.

▶ The Daily Mail said it was a marvellous show.

▶ The Guardian said people would love it.

1 ....

2 ....

3 ....

4 ....

5 ....

6 ....

7 ....

8 ....

135 Reported questions

1 Wh-questions

We can report questions with verbs like **ask**, **wonder** or **want to know**. Look first at these wh-questions.

DIRECT QUESTION		REPORTED QUESTION
'**When** did you start acting, Melissa?'	→	Guy **asked** Melissa **when** she started acting.
'**What**'s the time?'	→	I just **asked what** the time is.
'**Which** way is the post office?'	→	Someone **wants to know which** way the post office is.
'**How** can we find out?'	→	I was **wondering how** we can find out.
'**Where** can we eat?'	→	They're **asking where** they can eat.

Wh-questions have a word like **when**, **what**, **which** or **how** both in direct speech and in reported speech.

2 Yes/no questions

DIRECT QUESTION		REPORTED QUESTION
'Has the taxi arrived yet?' ~ 'No, not yet.'	→	Someone was **wondering if/whether** the taxi has arrived yet.
'Can we take photos?' ~ 'Yes, of course.'	→	The visitors **want to know if/whether** they can take photos.
'Is there a café nearby?' ~ 'No.'	→	Daniel **asked if/whether** there was a café nearby.

Reported yes/no questions have **if** or **whether**.

3 Word order

In a reported question the subject comes before the verb, as in a statement.

*Guy asked Melissa when **she started** acting.*
NOT ~~Guy asked Melissa when did she start acting~~.
*Someone was wondering if **the taxi has** arrived yet.*
NOT ~~Someone was wondering if has the taxi arrived yet.~~

4 Asking for information

To ask politely for information, we sometimes use a reported question after a phrase like
Could you tell me …? or **Do you know …?**

*   **Could you tell me** what time the concert starts?
*   **Do you know** if there's a public phone in the building?
*   **Have you any idea** how much a taxi would cost?

Note the word order **a taxi would cost** (see 3).

5 The tense change: is → was, etc.

In reported speech there are often changes to the tense, to pronouns and so on.
This depends on changes to the situation since the words were spoken.
For details see Units 133 and 134. Here are some examples of the tense change.

'What's the problem?'	→	We asked what the problem **was**.
'How much money **have** you got, Vicky?'	→	I was wondering how much money Vicky **had**.
'**Does** Nick **need** a lift?'	→	Tom asked if Nick **needed** a lift.
'**Can** you type?'	→	They asked me if I **could** type.

Practice

A Reported questions (1–3)

These people are at the tourist information centre. What do they want to know?

Speech bubbles:
- What are the most interesting sights?
- Have you got a town plan?
- 1 How can I find out about the area?
- 2 Are there guided tours?
- 3 Where can we stay?
- 4 What shows are there?

▶ She wants to know what the most interesting sights are.

▶ He wants to know if the centre has got a town plan.

1 ....

2 ....

3 ....

4 ....

B Asking for information (4)

You need information. Ask for it using *Could you tell me ...?* or *Do you know ...?*

▶ Where are the toilets? (tell)   Could you tell me where the toilets are?

1 Can I park here? (know)   ....

2 How long does the film last? (tell)   ....

3 How often do the buses run? (know)   ....

4 Are we allowed to smoke? (know)   ....

5 What time is the flight? (tell)   ....

6 How much does a ticket cost? (tell)   ....

C The tense change (5)

Barry Douglas, Zedco Chief Executive, is talking to a reporter about his business career.
He can still remember his first job interview after leaving school.

Interviewer:	Barry:
▶ 'Where do you live?'	The interviewer asked me where I lived.
▶ 'Have you worked before?'	She asked me if I had worked before.
1 'Why do you want the job?'	She wanted to know ....
2 'How did you hear about it?'	I remember she asked ....
3 'Are you fit?'	She wondered ....
4 'Can you work on Saturdays?'	Then she asked me ....
5 'How will you travel to work?'	She wanted to know ....
6 'Have you got a bicycle?'	And she asked me ....
7 'How much do you hope to earn?'	She also asked ....
8 'When can you start?'	And finally she asked ....

136 Reported requests, offers, etc.

1 Reported orders and requests

We can use the structure **tell/ask someone to do something**.

DIRECT SPEECH		REPORTED SPEECH
'Please move this car.'	→	A policeman **told me to move** the car.
'You really must be careful.'	→	Melanie is always **telling David to be** careful.
'Would you mind turning the music down?'	→	We **asked our neighbours to turn** the music down.

The negative is **tell/ask someone not to do something**.

'You mustn't leave the door unlocked.'	→	Mr Atkins **told Mark not to leave** the door unlocked.
'Please don't wear those boots in the house.'	→	I **asked you not to wear** those boots in the house.

We can also use the structure **ask to do something**.

'Can I see your ticket, please?'	→	The inspector **asked to see** my ticket.

We use **ask for** when someone asks to have something.

'Can I have some brochures, please?'	→	I **asked** (the travel agent) **for** some brochures.

It is also possible to report an order or request like this.
A policeman told me (that) I had to move the car.
We asked our neighbours if they would mind turning the music down.

2 Reported offers, suggestions, etc.

We can use **agree**, **offer**, **promise**, **refuse** and **threaten** with a to-infinitive.

DIRECT SPEECH		REPORTED SPEECH
'We'll pay for the damage.'	→	We **offered to pay** for the damage.
'I'll definitely finish it by the end of next week.'	→	You **promised to finish** the work by the end of this week.

We can also use an object + to-infinitive after **advise**, **invite**, **remind** and **warn**.

'I think you should take a taxi.'	→	Mark **advised us to take** a taxi.
'Don't forget to ring me.'	→	I **reminded David to ring** me.

We can use an ing-form after **admit**, **apologize for**, **insist on** and **suggest**.

'I really must have a rest.'	→	Emma **insisted on having** a rest.
'Shall we go to a nightclub?'	→	Claire **suggested going** to a nightclub.

3 Admit that, insist that, etc.

We can use a clause with **that** after **admit**, **advise**, **agree**, **insist**, **promise**, **remind**, **suggest** and **warn**.
*Trevor **admitted (that)** he had forgotten the shopping.*
*Claire **insisted (that)** we all went round to her flat for coffee.*
*You **promised (that)** you would finish the work by the end of this week.*
*I **warned** you **(that)** Nick's dog is very fierce.*

▷ 62 Verb + to-infinitive/-ing form   ▷ 65 Verb + object + to-infinitive

Practice

A Tell/ask someone to do something (1)

Trevor isn't feeling very happy. Everyone has been telling him what to do. Report the orders and requests.

► His mother: Can you dig my garden, please, Trevor?

  His mother asked him to dig her garden.

1 The doctor: You must take more exercise.

  ....

2 His boss: Would you mind not playing computer games in the office?

  ....

3 A traffic warden: You can't park your car in the High Street.

  ....

4 Laura: Could you put some shelves up, please, Trevor?

  ....

B Reported offers, suggestions, etc. (2)

Complete the sentences. Report what was said.

► Would you like to stay for lunch, Claire?

► All right. I won't talk about football.

1 You ought to take a break, Andrew.

2 I'm sorry I forgot the shopping.

3 Why don't we sing a few songs?

4 You're going to post the letter, don't forget, Vicky.

5 Yes, I made a mistake.

6 Laura! Don't touch the electric wires!

► Sarah invited *Claire to stay for lunch.* ....

► Tom agreed *not to talk about football.* ....

1 Matthew advised ....

2 Mike apologized ....

3 Tom suggested ....

4 Rachel reminded ....

5 Mr Atkins admitted ....

6 Trevor warned ....

C Admit that, insist that, etc. (3)

Combine each pair of sentences using *that*.

► The roads were dangerous. The police warned us.

  The police warned us that the roads were dangerous. ....

1 Everything will be ready on time. The builders have promised.

  ....

2 We have to check the figures carefully. The boss insists.

  ....

3 Tom's story wasn't completely true. He's admitted it.

  ....

4 Emma's train was about to leave. Matthew reminded her.

  ....

Test W: Reported speech

A

Some of these sentences are correct, and some have a word which should not be there. If the sentence is correct, put a tick (✓). If it is incorrect, cross the unnecessary word out of the sentence and write it in the space.

▶ You promised you wouldn't be late. ....✓........

▶ Susan thought 'That I can't understand what's happening.' ....that....

1 Do you know me what time the coach leaves? ....
2 Robert wanted to know if did the price included breakfast. ....
3 Anna insisted on showing us her photos. ....
4 Someone asked us whether that we had eaten lunch. ....
5 Nancy told me she had started the job the week before. ....
6 Nigel said me he wanted to come with us. ....
7 My friend said she did liked her new flat. ....
8 Martin asked us for not to wake the baby. ....

B

Decide which word is correct.

▶ What did that man say ...to you...?
a) at you   b) for you   c) to you   d) you

1 I rang my friend in Australia yesterday, and she said it .... raining there.
a) is   b) should be   c) to be   d) was

2 The last time I saw Jonathan, he looked very relaxed. He explained that he'd been on holiday the .... week.
a) earlier   b) following   c) next   d) previous

3 I wonder .... the tickets are on sale yet.
a) what   b) when   c) where   d) whether

4 I told you .... switch off the computer, didn't I?
a) don't   b) not   c) not to   d) to not

5 Someone .... me there's been an accident on the motorway.
a) asked   b) said   c) spoke   d) told

6 When I rang Tessa some time last week, she said she was busy .... day.
a) that   b) the   c) then   d) this

7 When he was at Oliver's flat yesterday, Martin asked if he .... use the phone.
a) can   b) could   c) may   d) must

8 Judy .... going for a walk, but no one else wanted to.
a) admitted   b) offered   c) promised   d) suggested

C

Read the news report and write the missing words. Use one word only in each space. Sometimes there is more than one possible answer.

Police have warned people (▶) ..to.. watch out for two men who have tricked their way into an old woman's home and stolen money. The men called on Mrs Iris Raine and said (1) .... were from the water company and wanted to check (2) .... her water was OK. They asked if (3) .... would mind letting them into her house. The woman didn't ask (4) .... see their identity cards. She said she (5) .... know about any problem with the water. The men explained that they (6) .... just discovered the problem but

that it was very simple and (7) .... take long to check. The woman asked
(8) .... the service was free, and they said yes. They (9) ....
to know where the water tank was. While one man ran water in the kitchen, the other went upstairs
and took several hundred pounds from a drawer in a bedroom. The men then left saying that they
would return the (10) .... day to have another look.

D

Complete each sentence by reporting what was said to you yesterday.
Use *said* and change the tense in the reported speech.

▶ Polly: I'm really tired.
When I saw Polly yesterday, *she said she was really tired.*
1 Tessa: I feel quite excited.
When I saw Tessa yesterday, ...
2 Nigel: I can't remember the code word.
When I saw Nigel yesterday, ...
3 Robert: I won't be at the next meeting.
When I saw Robert yesterday, ...
4 The twins: We've got a problem.
When I saw the twins yesterday, ...
5 Michelle: I've been swimming.
When I saw Michelle yesterday, ...
6 Your friends: We would like to be in the show.
When I saw my friends yesterday, ...
7 Adrian: I don't need any help.
When I saw Adrian yesterday, ...
8 Susan: My sister is coming to see me.
When I saw Susan yesterday, ...

E

Report the sentences. They were all spoken last week. Use the verbs in brackets.

▶ Anna to Janet: Don't forget to sign the form. (remind)
Anna reminded Janet to sign the form.
▶ Robert: What time will the office close this evening? (ask)
Robert asked what time the office would close that evening.
1 A policeman to Christopher: Stop shouting. (tell)
....
2 Tessa: It was me. I ate all the cake yesterday. (admit)
....
3 Adrian: I'm sorry I was rude. (apologize)
....
4 Simon to Susan: Would you like to join me for lunch? (invite)
....
5 Martin to Nancy: Did someone ring you an hour ago? (ask)
....
6 Peter: I really must leave. (insist)
....

137 Relative clauses with **who**, **which** and **that**

1 Introduction

Emma: *I saw Natalie the other day.*
Melanie: *Natalie? The girl **who plays the piano**?*
Emma: *No, that's Natasha. Natalie is the student*
              who dropped out of college**, the one **who
              ***never did any studying**. She's working in*
              *Davidson's now, the shop **that sells very***
              ***expensive clothes**.*

The relative clauses in this conversation identify which
person or thing we are talking about. The clause **who
plays the piano** tells us which girl Melanie means. The
clause **that sells very expensive clothes** tells us which
shop Emma means.

Sometimes we can use an adjective or a phrase to identify someone or something.
Adjective: *the **tall** girl   the **new** student   the **red** car*
Phrase: *the man **in the suit**   the shop **on the corner**   the woman **with red hair***
But when we need a longer explanation, we can use a relative clause.
Relative clause: *the woman **who gets up early**   the car **that broke down***

2 Who, which and that

The relative pronouns **who**, **which** and **that** go after the noun and at the beginning of the relative clause.
Who refers to people.
    *Nick is the **man who** owns that enormous dog.   I don't like **people who** tell jokes all the time.*
    *The little **girl who** sat next to me on the coach ate sweets the whole way.*
    *Sarah is pretty annoyed with the **person who** stole her mobile phone.*
We can also use **that**, but it is less usual.
    *Jake is the **man that** plays the guitar.*
    *The **woman that** lived here before us is a romantic novelist.*

That and **which** refer to things. **That** is more usual than **which**, especially in conversation.
    *The **car that** won the race looked very futuristic, didn't it?*
    *They've recaptured all the **animals that** escaped from the zoo.*
    *The children saw the actual **spacecraft that** landed on the moon.*

Which can be a little formal.
    *There are several **restaurants which** do Sunday lunches.*
    *Is Zedco the **company which** was taken over last year?*

We do not use another pronoun like **he** or **it** with the relative pronoun.
    NOT ~~the man who he owns that enormous dog~~
    NOT ~~the actual spacecraft that it landed on the moon~~

In all these sentences **who**, **which** and **that** are the subject of the relative clause.
For **who**, **which** and **that** as object, see Units 138 and 139.

Practice

A Identifying (1)

Look at the information and identify which one is meant.
Use the shortest way of identifying where possible, e.g. *the tall boy*, not *the boy who is tall*.

▶ the boy (he is tall)   → *the tall boy*
▶ the man (he has a beard)   → *the man with a beard*
▶ the woman (she plays golf)   → *the woman who plays golf*
1 the young man (he is at the door)   → ....
2 the man (he plays his stereo at night)   → ....
3 the woman (she is very thin)   → ....
4 the girl (she has green eyes)   → ....
5 the young woman (she is in the office)   → ....
6 the man (he drives a taxi)   → ....
7 the young man (he is smart)   → ....
8 the student (she failed all her exams)   → ....

B Who, which and that (2)

Complete the conversation. Put in *who*, *which* or *that*.
There is always more than one possible answer.

Emma: Shall we have something to eat?
Matthew: Yes, but not here. I don't like cafés (▶) ..*that*.. don't have chairs. I'm not one of those
           people (▶) .*who*. can eat standing up.
Emma: There's another restaurant over there.
Matthew: It looks expensive – one of those places (1) .... charge very high prices. The only
           customers (2) .... can afford to eat there are business executives (3) ....
           get their expenses paid. Anyway, I can't see a menu. I'm not going into a restaurant
           (4) .... doesn't display a menu.
Emma: We just passed a café (5) .... does snacks.
Matthew: Oh, I didn't like the look of that.
Emma: You're one of those people (6) .... are never satisfied, aren't you?

C Relative clauses (1–2)

Combine the information to make news items. Make the sentence in brackets
into a relative clause with *who* or *which*. Start each sentence with *the*, e.g. *The man ...*

▶ A man has gone to prison. (He shot two policemen.)
   The man who shot two policemen has gone to prison.
1 A bomb caused a lot of damage. (It went off this morning.)
   ....
2 A scientist has won the Nobel Prize. (He discovered a new planet.)
   ....
3 A footballer has been banned from playing again. (He took drugs.)
   ....
4 A little girl has been found safe and well. (She had been missing since Tuesday.)
   ....
5 A company has laid off thousands of workers. (It owns Greenway Supermarkets.)
   ....
6 An old lady now wants to swim the English Channel. (She did a parachute jump.)
   ....

138 The relative pronoun as object

1 Subject and object

Harriet is showing David her holiday photos.

Harriet: *That's an old castle **that we visited on holiday**. And those are some people **we met**, a couple **who were staying at the campsite**.*

David: *Mm. They look very friendly.*

A relative pronoun such as **who** or **that** can be the subject of a relative clause.

> *Harriet talked to a couple* | who | *were staying at the camp-site*.
>
>   (| They | were staying at the camp-site.)

> *The postcard* | that | *came this morning was from Harriet.*
>
>   (| It | came this morning.)

A relative pronoun can also be the object of a relative clause.

> *Mike and Harriet are visiting a woman* | who | *they met on holiday*.
>
>   (They met | her | on holiday.)

> *The old castle* | that | *we visited was really interesting.*
>
>   (We visited | it. |)

We do not use another pronoun like **her or** it with the relative pronoun.

NOT ~~a woman who they met her~~   NOT ~~the old castle that we visited it~~

2 Leaving out the relative pronoun

We can leave out the relative pronoun when it is the object of the relative clause. We do this especially in spoken English. Compare these examples.

WITH OBJECT PRONOUN	WITHOUT OBJECT PRONOUN
*The man **who Vicky saw** at the concert is Sarah's boss.*	*The man **Vicky saw** at the concert is Sarah's boss.*
*That's an old castle **that we visited**.*	*That's an old castle **we visited**.*

Here are some more examples of relative clauses without an object pronoun.

> *We don't know the name of the person **the police are questioning**.*
> *The cakes **Melanie baked** were delicious.*
> *That jacket **you're wearing** is falling to pieces, Mike.*

Remember that we cannot leave out a pronoun when it is the subject of a relative clause.

> *The man **who** spoke to Vicky is Sarah's boss.*

3 Who and whom

In formal English, **whom** is sometimes used when the object of the relative clause is a person.

> *The person **who/whom** the police were questioning has now been released.*

But in conversation **whom** is not very common.

Practice

A Subject and object (1)

Comment on the conversations. Add a sentence with *who* or *that* as the subject of the underlined part.

▶ She's Tom's new girlfriend. ~ Who is? ~ That girl. <u>She just said hello.</u>
That's right. The .girl who just said hello is Tom's new girlfriend.

1 The dog has been rescued. ~ What dog? ~ <u>It fell down a hole.</u>
Haven't you heard? The ....

2 The story was untrue. ~ What story? ~ You know. <u>It upset everyone.</u>
Yes, the ....

3 He's a film producer. ~ Who is? ~ That man. <u>He interviewed Natasha.</u>
That's what I heard. The ....

Now comment on these conversations. Add a sentence with *who* or *that* as the object of the underlined part.

4 The accident wasn't very serious. ~ What accident? ~ Oh, <u>Daniel saw it.</u>
Yes, the ....

5 He's a billionaire. ~ Who is? ~ That man. <u>Claire knows him.</u>
It's true. The ....

6 The vase was extremely valuable. ~ What vase? ~ You know. <u>David broke it.</u>
That's right. The ....

7 It's really nice. ~ What is? ~ The jacket. <u>Melanie wore it at the party.</u>
Yes, it is. The ....

B Leaving out the relative pronoun (2)

Complete the script for these TV advertisements. Use a relative clause without a pronoun.

▶ Fresho soap. Beautiful people use it. It's the soap beautiful people use.
1 An Everyman car. You can afford it. ....
2 'Hijack'. People want to see this film. ....
3 Greenway Supermarket. You can trust it. ....
4 'Cool' magazine. Young people read it. ....
5 Jupiter chocolates. You'll love them. ....

C Leaving out the relative pronoun (2)

Look carefully at these sentences. Are they correct without a relative pronoun? Where you see ★, you may need to put in *who*, *which* or *that*. Write the sentences and put in a pronoun only if you have to.

▶ The man ★ paid for the meal was a friend of Tom's.
The man who paid for the meal was a friend of Tom's.

▶ The meeting ★ Mark had to attend went on for three hours.
The meeting Mark had to attend went on for three hours.

1 Somewhere I've got a photo of the mountain ★ we climbed.
....

2 The man ★ repaired my car is a real expert.
....

3 The detective lost sight of the man ★ he was following.
....

4 I thought I recognized the assistant ★ served us.
....

5 I'm afraid the numbers ★ I chose didn't win a prize.
....

RELATIVE CLAUSES • PAGE 333

139 Prepositions in relative clauses

1 Introduction

A relative pronoun (e.g. **that**) can be the object of a preposition (e.g. **for**).

This is the bus │ **that** │ *I've been waiting **for**.*

*I've been **waiting for*** │ *the bus.*

The restaurant │ **that** │ *we normally go **to** is closed today.*

*We normally go **to*** │ *the restaurant.*

In informal spoken English we normally put the preposition at the end of the relative clause. Compare the word order.

> This is the bus that I've been waiting **for**.

> OK. I'll see you sometime.

STATEMENT	RELATIVE CLAUSE
*I've been **waiting for** the bus.* *We go **to** the restaurant.*	*the bus that **I've been waiting for*** *the restaurant that **we go to***

We do not use another pronoun like **it** or **her** after the preposition.

NOT ~~the restaurant that we go to it~~   NOT ~~someone who I work with her~~

2 Leaving out the pronoun

We often leave out the relative pronoun when it is the object of a preposition.

WITH OBJECT PRONOUN	WITHOUT OBJECT PRONOUN
*The bus **that I'm waiting for** is late.* *Is this the article **which you were interested in**?* *That's the man **who I was talking about**.*	*The bus **I'm waiting for** is late.* *Is this the article **you were interested in**?* *That's the man **I was talking about**.*

Here are some more examples of relative clauses without an object pronoun.

*I can't remember the name of the hotel **we stayed at**.*
*This is the colour **we've finally decided on**.*
*The shop **I got my stereo from** has lots of bargains.*

3 A preposition at the beginning

These examples are typical of formal English.

*Was that the restaurant **to which** you normally go?*
*Electronics is a subject **about which** I know very little.*
*The Sales Manager is the person **from whom** I obtained the figures.*

Here the preposition comes at the beginning of the relative clause, before **which** or **whom**.

We cannot put a preposition before **that** or **who**.

a subject (that) I know little about NOT ~~a subject about that I know little~~
the person (who) I got the figures from NOT ~~the person from who I got the figures~~

▷ 138.3 **Whom**

Practice

A A preposition at the end (1–2)

What are they saying? Put in sentences with a preposition at the end.

▶ (Mark has been looking for this letter.) *This is the letter I've been looking for.*

1 (Rachel was talking about that film.) ....

2 (Laura has decided on this wallpaper.) ....

3 (Matthew played tennis with that man.) ....

4 (David fell down those steps.) ....

B A preposition at the end (1–2)

Match the phrases and write the definitions. Put the preposition at the end of the relative clause.

▶	a kitchen	a cupboard	you hit nails with it
1	a hammer	the person	you keep valuable things in it
2	your destination	a piece of furniture	<u>you cook in it</u>
3	a safe	the place	you can either sit or sleep on it
4	your opponent	<u>a room</u>	you're going to it
5	a sofa bed	a tool	you're playing against them

▶ *A kitchen is a room you cook in.*

1 ....

2 ....

3 ....

4 ....

5 ....

C A preposition at the beginning (3)

It's election time. All the politicians are arguing.
Rewrite the first sentence using a preposition at the beginning of a relative clause.

▶ I cannot agree with that statement. I hope I've made that clear.
   That is a statement with which I cannot agree.

1 Our party believes in that idea. I say this from the bottom of my heart. ....
....

2 I am strongly opposed to that policy. And I am not afraid to say so. ....
....

3 No one cares about these people. They are the forgotten people. ....
....

4 Your party should be ashamed of those mistakes. And everyone knows that. ....
....

5 The government is now dealing with that problem. How many times do I have to tell you?
....

140 Relative structures with **whose**, **what** and **it**

1 Whose

Vicky: *What I'd really like is a job in television.*
Daniel: *The other day I met a man **whose sister** works in television.*
Vicky: *Who? What's her name?*
Daniel: *Oh, I don't know. She's the woman **whose car** Tom crashed into.*

Here **whose sister** means <u>his</u> sister (the sister of the man Daniel met), and **whose car** means <u>her</u> car (the car belonging to the woman). Here are some more examples.

> Someone **whose bicycle** had been stolen was reporting it to the police.
> Wayne Johnson is the man **whose goal** won the game for United.

We use **whose** mainly with people, e.g. **someone**, **the man**. But sometimes it goes with other nouns.

> Which is the European **country whose** economy is growing the fastest?
> Round the corner was a **building whose** windows were all broken.
> Melanie was looking after a **dog whose** leg had been broken in an accident.

2 What

We use the relative pronoun **what** without a noun in front of it.

> The shop didn't have **what** I wanted. (= the thing that I wanted)
> **What** we saw gave us quite a shock. (= the thing that we saw)

We can also use **what** to give emphasis to a word or phrase, to make it more important. Compare these examples.

NEUTRAL	EMPHATIC
Rachel's stereo kept me awake.	***What** kept me awake was **Rachel's stereo**.*
Vicky is looking for a job in television.	***What** Vicky is looking for is **a job in television**.*
I want to make a fresh start.	***What** I want to do is **make a fresh start**.*
They booked a holiday together.	***What** they did was **book a holiday together**.*

3 It

We also use **it** + **be** + a relative clause to give emphasis.

NEUTRAL	EMPHATIC
Tom had an accident.	***It was Tom** who had an accident (not David).*
The computer gives me a headache.	***It's the computer** that gives me a headache.*
I'm eating chocolate cake.	***It's chocolate cake** (that) I'm eating.*
Mike's uncle died on Thursday.	***It was on Thursday** that Mike's uncle died.*

We must put in a pronoun when it is the subject of the relative clause (e.g. **who** *had an accident*). If it is the object (e.g. **that** *I'm eating*), then we can leave it out (see Unit 138.2).

A Who or whose? (1)

You are reading a crime story. One of these people has murdered the industrialist Colin Howard.
Look at the detective's notes and write a sentence about each person. Use a relative clause with
who or *whose*.

▶ George Paxton, company director – he had an argument with Colin
George is the company director who had an argument with Colin.

▶ Vera Stokes, politician – her sister once worked for Colin
Vera is the politician whose sister once worked for Colin.

1 Felix Reeves, journalist – his tape recorder was stolen
....

2 Graham Wilshaw, architect – he knew Colin at school
....

3 Rex Carter, farmer – Colin bought his land
....

4 Norman Bridge, lawyer – he looked after Colin's interests
....

5 Sonia Goldman, house guest – her fingerprints were on the door handle
....

B What (2)

Zedco Chief Executive Barry Douglas is telling a group of managers how to run
a business successfully. He emphasizes the underlined words using *what*.

▶ You must pay attention to the details.
What you must pay attention to are the details.

1 You have to think about your profit.
....

2 You must know the needs of your customers.
....

3 You should work towards a realistic target.
....

4 You need to plan ahead.
....

C It (3)

Quiz champion Claude Jennings is answering some questions.
Look at each question and answer and write a sentence with *it* + *be* + a relative clause.

▶ Who invented radio? ~ Marconi.
It was Marconi who *invented radio.*

1 When did Columbus sail to America? ~ In 1492.
It was in 1492 that ....

2 What does Tiger Woods play? ~ Golf.
It's ....

3 Where did the Olympic Games first take place? ~ In Greece.
....

4 Which is nearest the sun, Venus or Mercury? ~ Mercury.
....

141 The use of relative clauses

1 Introduction

There are two kinds of relative clause. Compare this conversation and newspaper report.

Laura: *Art Golding has died.*
Trevor: *Who?*
Laura: *You know. The film star **who played the ship's captain in 'Iceberg'**.*
Trevor: *I don't think I've seen that.*
Laura: *Yes, you have. It's the film **we saw on TV the other night**.*

ART GOLDING DIES

The actor Art Golding, <u>who starred in films such as 'Tornado' and 'Iceberg'</u>, has died after a long illness. He was seventy-eight. Art Golding's most famous role was as the scientist in the film 'Supernova', <u>which broke all box-office records</u>.

The clauses in this conversation identify which film star and which film Laura means. They are called identifying clauses.

The clauses in this report add information about Art Golding and about 'Supernova'. They are called adding clauses, or sometimes non-identifying clauses.

2 Identifying clauses and adding clauses

IDENTIFYING

*The man **who lives next door to Melanie** is rather strange.*
*The river **which flows through Hereford** is the Wye.*
*The picture **which was damaged** is worth thousands of pounds.*

These clauses identify which thing the speaker is talking about. The clause **who lives next door to Melanie** tells us which man. The clause **which flows through Hereford** tells us which river. Without the relative clause the sentence would be incomplete. **The man is rather strange** makes sense only if we know which man.

An identifying clause does not have commas around it.

ADDING

*Jake, **who lives next door to Melanie**, is rather strange.*
*The Wye (**which flows through Hereford**) is a beautiful river.*
*This famous picture – **which was damaged during the war** – is worth thousands of pounds.*

These clauses add extra information about something which is already identified. The clause **who lives next door to Melanie** adds information about Jake. But we can say the sentence on its own without the relative clause. **Jake is rather strange** makes sense because the name **Jake** identifies who we are talking about.

An adding clause has commas around it. Instead of commas, we can use brackets ( ) or dashes – –. If the adding clause is at the end of the sentence, we need only one comma or dash.
That's Jake, who lives next door.

Most relative clauses are identifying. We use them both in speech and in writing.

Adding clauses can be rather formal. We use them mainly in writing. They are common in news reports. In speech we often use two short sentences. *Jake lives next door to Melanie. He's rather strange.*

▷ 137.1 Identifying clauses ▷ 142.1 Pronouns in identifying and adding clauses

A Adding clauses (1)

Match the parts and write sentences with an adding clause. Use *who* or *which*.

▶	The Grand Canyon	He was in prison for 27 years.	He was one of the Beatles.
1	Nelson Mandela	He was killed in 1980.	He became President of South Africa.
2	John Lennon	It is 140 million miles away.	It is one of the wonders of the world.
3	The Titanic	It is over 200 miles long.	It is known as the red planet.
4	Queen Victoria	It sank in 1912.	It stood for 28 years.
5	Mars	It was built in 1961.	It was supposed to be unsinkable.
6	The Berlin Wall	She came to the throne in 1837.	She ruled over the British Empire.

▶ The Grand Canyon, which is over 200 miles long, is one of the wonders of the world.

1 ....
2 ....
3 ....
4 ....
5 ....
6 ....

B Identifying or adding? (2)

Read the news article and then say what each relative clause does.
Does it tell us which one, or does it add information?

The play (▶) that the students put on last week was Oscar Wilde's 'The Importance of Being Earnest', (▶) which was written in 1895. The college theatre, (1) which holds over 400 people, was unfortunately only half full for the Friday evening performance. However, the people (2) who bothered to attend must have been glad they did. Lucy Kellett, (3) who played Lady Bracknell, was magnificent. Unfortunately the young man (4) who played John Worthing forgot his lines twice, but that did not spoil the evening, (5) which was a great success.

▶ It tells us which play.
▶ It adds information about 'The Importance of Being Earnest'.
1 ....
2 ....
3 ....
4 ....
5 ....

C Commas in relative clauses (2)

Put in the relative clauses. You may also need to put in one or two commas.
▶ (that Claire drives) This car is a lot cheaper than the one *that Claire drives* .
▶ (who has twins) Olivia, *who has twins* , often needs a babysitter.
1 (who took Rita to the party) The person .... was Tom.
2 (who has a bad temper) Henry... shouted at the waiter.
3 (which Tom supports) The team .... is United.
4 (who is afraid of heights) We all climbed up except Vicky ....
5 (which is on the tenth floor) My new flat .... has a terrific view.
6 (she bought the sofa from) Sarah can't remember the name of the shop ....

142 Relative pronouns and relative adverbs

1 Pronouns in identifying and adding clauses

There are two kinds of relative clause: identifying and adding (see Unit 141).
Look at the pronouns in these examples.

IDENTIFYING	ADDING
*I'm sure I know the person **who** served us.*	*Natalie, **who** served us, is a friend of Emma's.*
*The pop singer **whom** Guy invited onto his chat show never turned up.*	*Arlene Black, **whom** Guy invited onto his chat show, never turned up.*
*The woman **whose** flat was burgled spent the night at a friend's house.*	*Natasha, **whose** flat was burgled, spent the night at a friend's house.*
*Towns **which/that** attract tourists are usually crowded in the summer.*	*Oxford, **which** attracts many tourists, is often crowded in the summer.*
In an identifying clause we can use **who, whom, whose, which** or **that**.	In an adding clause we can use **who, whom, whose** or **which**. We do NOT use **that**.

2 Leaving out the pronoun

Sometimes we can leave the pronoun out of an identifying clause (see Unit 138.2).	We cannot leave the pronoun out of an adding clause.
*The woman (**who**) you met yesterday works in advertising.*	*Sarah, **whom** you met yesterday, works in advertising.*
*Have you seen the book (**that**) I was reading?*	*That book 'Brighton Rock', **which** I was reading, is really good.*
*Laura couldn't find the box (**that**) she kept her photos in.*	*Laura had a wooden box, **in which** she kept her photos* OR **which** *she kept her photos* **in**.

3 The relative adverbs **where, when** and **why**

Look at these examples.
> *This is the place **where** the accident happened.*
> *Do you remember the day **when** we moved the piano upstairs?*
> *The reason **why** Nick came was that he wanted to see Rita.*

We can leave out **when** or **why**, or we can use **that**.
> *Do you remember the day (**that**) we moved the piano upstairs?*
> *The reason (**that**) Nick came was that he wanted to see Rita.*

There are also adding clauses with **where** and **when**.
> *We went to the Riverside Restaurant, **where** I once had lunch with Henry.*
> *Mark likes to travel at night, **when** the roads are quiet.*

4 A special use of **which**

In an adding clause, we can use **which** relating to a whole sentence, not just to a noun.
> *It rained all night, **which** was good for the garden.*

Here **which** means 'the fact that it rained all night'.

Here are some more examples.
> *David helped me clear up, **which** was very kind of him.*
> *Sarah had to work late again, **which** annoyed Mark.*
> *Tom pushed Nick into the swimming-pool, **which** seemed to amuse everyone.*

Practice

A Who, whom, whose, which, where and why (1, 3)

Complete this advertisement. Put in *who, whom, whose, which, where* or *why*.

The town of Keswick, (▶) .wh̲i̲c̲h̲. lies at the heart of the Lake District, is the perfect place for a holiday, and the Derwent Hotel, (1) .... overlooks the town, is the perfect place to stay. Robin and Wendy Jackson, (2) .... bought this small hotel three years ago, have already won an excellent reputation. Robin, (3) .... cooking is one of the reasons (4) .... the Derwent is so popular, was once Young Chef of the Year. The comfort of the guests, (5) .... the owners treat almost as members of the family, always comes first. Peter Ustinov, (6) .... once stayed at the hotel, described it as 'marvellous'. And the Lake District, (7) .... has so much wonderful scenery and (8) .... the poet Wordsworth lived, will not disappoint you.

B Identifying clauses and adding clauses (1–3)

Put in the relative clauses. Sometimes there is more than one possible answer.

▶ Someone knows all about it – the secretary.
   The person .w̲h̲o̲ ̲k̲n̲o̲w̲s̲ ̲a̲l̲l̲ ̲a̲b̲o̲u̲t̲ ̲i̲t̲. is the secretary.
1 Zedco has 10,000 employees. It's an international company.
   Zedco, ..., is an international company.
2 Vicky's name was missed off the list, so she wasn't very pleased.
   Vicky, ..., wasn't very pleased.
3 Laura painted a picture, and it's being shown in an exhibition.
   The picture .... is being shown in an exhibition.
4 We're all looking forward to a concert. It's next Saturday.
   The concert .... is next Saturday.
5 One week Mike and Harriet went camping. It was the wettest of the year.
   The week .... was the wettest of the year.
6 Aunt Joan is a bit deaf, so she didn't hear the phone.
   Aunt Joan, ..., didn't hear the phone.
7 You'll meet Henry tomorrow. He's also a member of the board.
   Henry, ..., is also a member of the board.
8 I'll see you near the post office. We met there the other day.
   I'll see you near the post office, ...

C A special use of which (4)

Match the sentence pairs and join them with *which*.

▶ My phone is out of order.   It means he can't get about very easily.
1 Rachel's mother paid for the meal. It's made her very depressed.
2 My brother is disabled.   That was rather careless of you.
3 You left the keys in the car.   That caused a traffic jam.
4 Vicky didn't get the job.   It's a real nuisance.
5 The police blocked off the road.   That was very kind of her.

▶ M̲y̲ ̲p̲h̲o̲n̲e̲ ̲i̲s̲ ̲o̲u̲t̲ ̲o̲f̲ ̲o̲r̲d̲e̲r̲,̲ ̲w̲h̲i̲c̲h̲ ̲i̲s̲ ̲a̲ ̲r̲e̲a̲l̲ ̲n̲u̲i̲s̲a̲n̲c̲e̲.
1 ....
2 ....
3 ....
4 ....
5 ....

143 Relative clauses: participle and to-infinitive

1 Relative clauses with a participle

Read this news report about an accident.

> Several people were injured this morning when a lorry **carrying concrete pipes** overturned in the centre of town and hit two cars. Ambulances **called to the scene** took a long time to get through the rush hour traffic. The accident happened in Alfred Road, where road repairs are under way. People who saw the accident say that the lorry hit the cars after it swerved to avoid a pile of stones **left in the road**. The traffic chaos **caused by the accident** has meant long delays for people **travelling to work**.

Carrying concrete pipes, called to the scene, etc. are relative clauses: they relate to a noun. **Carrying concrete pipes** tells us something about **a lorry**.

We can form these clauses with an active participle, e.g. **carrying**, or a passive participle, e.g. **called**. The participles can refer to the present or the past.

ACTIVE	PASSIVE
*There are delays this morning for people **travelling** to work.* (= people **who are travelling** to work) *A lorry **carrying** concrete pipes has overturned.* (= a lorry **which was carrying** pipes) *the path **leading** to the church* (= the path **which leads/led** to the church)	*I have a message for people **delayed** by the traffic chaos.* (= people **who are being delayed**) *We noticed a pile of stones **left** in the road.* (= stones **which had been left** there) *food **sold** in supermarkets* (= food **which is/was sold** in supermarkets)
The active participle means the same as a pronoun + a continuous verb, e.g. **which is/was carrying**, or a pronoun + a simple verb, e.g. **which leads/led**.	The passive participle means the same as a pronoun + a passive verb, e.g. **which is/was sold**.
But we do NOT use the active participle for a single action in the past. *The police want to interview people **who saw** the accident.* NOT ~~people seeing the accident~~	

2 Relative clauses with a to-infinitive

Look at this structure with the to-infinitive.
> *New Zealand was the **first** country **to give** women the vote.*
> (= the first country which gave women the vote)
> *Melanie was the **only** person **to write** a letter of thanks.*
> (= the only person who wrote a letter of thanks)

Here are some more examples.
> *The guest on our show is the **youngest** golfer **to win** the Open.*
> *Emma Thompson is the **most famous** actress **to appear** on stage here.*

We can use a to-infinitive with these words: **first, second,** etc; **next** and **last**; **only**; and superlatives, e.g. **youngest, most famous**.

We can leave out the noun (except after **only**) if the meaning is clear.
> *The captain was the **last to leave** the sinking ship.*

Practice

A Relative clauses with a participle (1)

Complete the definitions. Put in an active or passive participle of these verbs:
add, arrive, block, own, play, take, tell, watch, wear

▶ A competitor is someone .taking. part in a competition.
▶ Your property is everything .owned. by you.
1 Baseball is a game .... mainly in the US.
2 A wrist-watch is a watch .... on your wrist.
3 A latecomer is a person .... late.
4 An instruction is a statement .... you what to do.
5 A spectator is someone .... a game or an event.
6 An extension is a new part .... on to a building.
7 An obstacle is something .... your way.

B Relative clauses with a participle (1)

Write each news item as one sentence. Change the part in brackets into a clause with an active participle (e.g. *costing*) or a passive participle (e.g. *found*).

▶ A new motorway is planned. (It will cost £500 million.)
A new motorway .costing £500 million is planned.
▶ Some weapons belong to the IRA. (They were found at a flat in Bristol.)
Some weapons .found at a flat in Bristol belong to the IRA.
1 Families have been evicted. (They were living in an empty office building.)
Families ....
2 A chemical company has gone bankrupt. (It employed 4,000 people.)
A chemical company ....
3 A bridge has been declared unsafe. (It was built only two years ago.)
A bridge ....
4 People have marched to London. (They are protesting against pollution.)
....
5 Tennis fans have been queuing all night at Wimbledon. (They hope to buy tickets.)
....
6 A new drug may give us eternal youth. (It was developed at a British university.)
....

C Relative clauses with a to-infinitive (2)

Comment on each situation. Use the to-infinitive structure.

▶ David offered his help. No one else did.
David was .the only person to offer his help.
1 Olivia's daughter swam a length of the pool. No other girl as young as her did that.
Olivia's daughter was ....
2 The secretaries got a pay rise. No one else did.
The secretaries were ....
3 The pilot left the aircraft. Everyone else had left before him.
....
4 Mrs Harper became Managing Director. No other woman had done that before.
....
5 Daniel applied for the job. No other candidate as suitable as him applied.
....

Test X: Relative clauses

A

Decide which word or phrase is correct.

▶ ..What.. I really need is a long holiday.
   a) that   b) what   c) which   d) who

1   At last I've found the information that I was looking ....
    a) for   b) for it   c) for that   d) it

2   Everyone .... the building was searched by the police.
    a) enter   b) entered   c) entering   d) enters

3   The plane .... has just taken off is an hour late.
    a) it   b) what   c) which   d) who

4   I had just one reply. Abco was the .... company to reply to my letter.
    a) last   b) most   c) only   d) second

5   My friend Nigel, ... works in the City, earns much more than I do.
    a) that   b) which   c) who   d) whose

6   Martin is someone with .... I usually agree.
    a) him   b) that   c) who   d) whom

7   I'd like to see the photo ....
    a) took   b) you took it   c) that you took   d) that you took it

8   Atlanta is the city .... the Olympic Games were held in 1996.
    a) that   b) when   c) where   d) which

9   It rained all the time, ... was a great pity.
    a) that   b) what   c) which   d) who

10 We passed shops .... windows were decorated for Christmas.
    a) the   b) their   c) which   d) whose

B

Each of these sentences has a mistake in it. Write the correct sentence.

▶ ~~I've found the magazine who was missing.~~
   I've found the magazine that was missing. ....

1   ~~This isn't the train on that I normally travel.~~
    ....

2   ~~The letter that I opened it wasn't for me.~~
    ....

3   ~~The reason because I didn't know was that no one had told me.~~
    ....

4   ~~That we should do is ring the police.~~
    ....

5   ~~I didn't know the name of the man helped me.~~
    ....

6   ~~Rupert knows the family who's house is for sale.~~
    ....

7   ~~Einstein who failed his university entrance exam discovered relativity.~~
    ....

8   ~~The person we talked to were very friendly.~~
    ....

9   ~~It's the President makes the important decisions.~~
    ....

10 ~~I can't find my diary, what is a real nuisance.~~
    ....

11 ~~Outside the door was a pair of boots covering in mud.~~
....

12 ~~Lake Superior, that lies on the US-Canadian border, is the largest lake in North America.~~
....

C

Complete the story about a thief's punishment. Write the missing words. Use one word only in each space.

This is a true story (▶) ...which... is supposed to have happened somewhere in the US. A man
(1) .... was accused of housebreaking appeared in court. He had put his arm through
the window of a house and stolen some money (2) .... was lying on a table inside.
The argument (3) .... the man's lawyer put forward wasn't very impressive. He said that
(4) .... was the man's arm (5) .... had committed the crime and not the man
himself. 'You cannot punish a man for (6) .... his arm has done,' said the lawyer. Now the
judge in (7) .... court the man was appearing wanted to show how stupid the lawyer's
argument was. Instead of finding the man guilty, he found the man's arm guilty and sent it to prison.
'He can go with his arm or not, as he chooses,' the judge added, (8) .... made everyone
laugh. But (9) .... the judge didn't know was that the man had an artificial arm. He took the
arm off, gave it to the judge – (10) .... could hardly believe his eyes – and walked out of the
court.

D

Combine the two sentences into one.
▶ That man was Anna's brother. He just walked past.
   The man who just walked past was Anna's brother.
....
1 The plane was twenty-five years old. It crashed.
   The plane .... twenty-five years old.
2 One day Tessa was ill in bed. Martin rang.
   The day .... ill in bed.
3 Our offices are in Queen Street. They are new.
   Our .... in Queen Street.
4 Some documents have been found. They were stolen from a car.
   The documents .... found.
5 That map is out of date. You were looking at it.
   The map .... out of date.
6 The King's Theatre is in the centre of town. It dates from 1896.
   The King's .... in the centre of town.
7 A woman was terribly upset. Her dog was run over.
   The woman .... terribly upset.
8 Janet solved the puzzle. She did it before everyone else.
   Janet was .... the puzzle.
9 A man was standing outside the building. He was selling newspapers.
   A man .... outside the building.
10 The talk was very interesting. Judy gave it.
   The talk .... very interesting.
11 The house is empty now. I used to live there.
   The house .... is empty now.

144 Conditionals (1)

1 Introduction

Come on, Rachel. **If** we **hurry**, we**'ll** catch the half-past-nine bus.

There's no rush, is there? **If** we **miss** it, there**'ll** be another one in fifteen minutes.

Vicky and Rachel are talking about possible future actions.
They may catch the bus, or they may miss it.

2 First Conditional: **If we hurry, we'll catch the bus**

IF-CLAUSE			MAIN CLAUSE	
If	+	PRESENT SIMPLE		+ will
If we		*hurry,*	*we*	*'ll catch the bus.*
If we		*miss it,*	*there*	*'ll be another one.*
If it		*doesn't rain,*	*we*	*'ll be having a picnic.*
If I		*don't practise my golf,*	*I*	*won't get any better.*

The verb in the if-clause (e.g. **hurry**) is in the Present Simple, not the future.
> NOT ~~If we'll hurry, we'll catch the bus.~~

But we can use **will** in the if-clause when we make a request.
> *If you'll just wait a moment, I'll find someone to help you.* (= Please wait a moment ...)

We can use the Present Continuous (e.g. **are doing**) or the Present Perfect (e.g. **have done**) in the if-clause.
> *If we're expecting visitors, the flat will need a good clean.*
> *If you've finished with the computer, I'll put it away.*

The main clause often has **will**. But we can use other modal verbs (e.g. **can**).
> *If you haven't got a television, you **can't** watch it, can you?*
> *If Henry jogs regularly, he **might** lose weight.*
> *If Matthew is going to a job interview, he **should** wear a tie.*

The if-clause usually comes first, but it can come after the main clause.
> ***If** I hear any news, I'll phone you./I'll phone you **if** I hear any news.*

3 More uses of the First Conditional

We can use First Conditionals in offers and suggestions.
> *If you need a ticket, I can get you one.   If you feel like seeing the sights, we can take a bus tour.*

We can also use them in warnings and threats.
> *If you go on like this, you'll make yourself ill.   If you don't apologize, I'll never speak to you again.*

4 If you heat water, it boils

We sometimes use the Present Simple in both clauses.
> *If you **heat** water, it **boils**.   If Daniel **has** any money, he **spends** it.*
> *If you **press** this switch, the computer **comes** on.*

This means that one thing always follows automatically from another.
Pressing the switch always results in the computer coming on.

Practice

A First Conditional (1–3)

Read the conversation and then choose the correct forms.

Rachel: Have you heard about the pop festival?
Vicky: Yes, (▶) ~~it's~~/it'll be good if Express are playing. They're a great band.
Rachel: Will you be able to go, Nick?
Nick: If (1) <u>I ask/I'll ask</u> my boss, he'll give me some time off work, I expect.
Vicky: How are we going to get there?
Rachel: Well, if (2) <u>there are/there'll be</u> enough people, we can hire a minibus.
Vicky: I won't be going if (3) <u>it's/it'll be</u> too expensive.
Rachel: It (4) <u>isn't costing/won't cost</u> much if we all (5) <u>share/will share</u> the cost.
Nick: If (6) <u>I see/I'll see</u> the others later on tonight, (7) <u>I ask/I'll ask</u> them if they want to go.

B First Conditional (1–3)

Comment on the situations. Use *if* + the present tense + *will/can*.

▶ It might rain. If it does, everyone can eat inside.
  If it rains, everyone can eat inside.
▶ The children mustn't go near Nick's dog. It'll bite them.
  If the children go near Nick's dog, it'll bite them.

1 Rachel might fail her driving test. But she can take it again.

2 United might lose. If they do, Tom will be upset.

3 The office may be closed. In that case Mark won't be able to get in.

4 Nick may arrive a bit early. If he does, he can help Tom to get things ready.

5 The party might go on all night. If it does, no one will want to do any work tomorrow.

6 Emma may miss the train. But she can get the next one.

7 Is Matthew going to enter the race? He'll probably win it.

C Present Simple in both clauses (4)

Match the sentences and join them with *if*.

▶ You lose your credit card.   I can't sleep.
1 You get promoted.   You get a warning letter.
2 I drink coffee late at night.   <u>You have to ring the bank.</u>
3 You don't pay the bill.   Your salary goes up.
4 I try to run fast.   The alarm goes off.
5 Someone enters the building.   I get out of breath.

▶ *If you lose your credit card, you have to ring the bank.*
1
2
3
4
5

145 Conditionals (2)

1 Introduction

Rachel: *Would you like some cake, Jessica?*
Jessica: *No thanks.* **If I ate** *cake, I'd get fat.*
Rachel: *But it's delicious.*
Jessica: *It looks delicious.* **If I had** *your figure, I'd eat the whole lot.*

I ate cake and *I had your figure* are imaginary or unreal situations.
Jessica isn't going to eat the cake, and she hasn't got a figure like Rachel's.

2 Second Conditional: **If I ate cake, I'd get fat**

IF-CLAUSE				MAIN CLAUSE	
If	+	PAST SIMPLE	+	would	
If I		ate cake,	I	'd get fat.	
If I		had your figure,	I	'd eat the whole lot.	
If we		didn't have a car,	we	'd find it difficult to get about.	
If Rachel		got up earlier,	she	wouldn't always be late.	

Note the Past Simple (e.g. **ate**). We do not use **would** in the if-clause. NOT ~~If I'd eat cake.~~
But we can use **would** in the if-clause when we make a request.

> *If you'd like to come this way, the doctor will see you now.* (= Please come this way …)

As well as the Past Simple we can use the Past Continuous (e.g. **was doing**) in the if-clause.

> *If Rachel* **was playing** *her stereo, it wouldn't be so quiet in here.*

In a Second Conditional if-clause we sometimes use **were** instead of **was**, especially in the clause **if I were you.**

> *If Rachel* **were playing** *her stereo, it wouldn't be so quiet in here.*
> *If I* **were** *you, I'd ask a lawyer for some advice.*

The main clause often has **would**. We can also use **could** or **might.**

> *If we had a calculator, we* **could** *work this out a lot quicker.*
> *If Rachel worked harder, she* **might** *do even better at her studies.*

The if-clause usually comes first, but it can come after the main clause.

> **If** *I knew, I'd tell you./I'd tell you* **if** *I knew.*

3 First and Second Conditionals

Compare these examples.

> First: *If you* **have** *a lie-down, you'll feel better.* (See Unit 144.2)
> Second: *If I* **had** *a million pounds, I'd probably buy a yacht.*

The present tense (**have**) refers to a possible future action, something which may or may not happen.
The past tense (**had**) refers to something unreal. *If I had a million pounds* means that I haven't really got a million pounds, but I am imagining that I have. Compare these examples.

> First: *If we* **take** *the car, we'll have to pay for parking.*
> Second: *If we* **took** *the car, we'd have to pay for parking.*

Here both sentences refer to a possible future action. But in the Second Conditional, the action is less probable. *If we took the car* may mean that we have decided not to take it.

We can use Second Conditionals in offers and suggestions.

> *If you needed a ticket, I could get you one.*
> *If you felt like seeing the sights, we could take a bus tour.*

The Second Conditional is less direct than the First Conditional (Unit 144.3). The speaker is less sure that you want to see the sights.

Practice

A Second Conditional (1–2)

Comment on these situations. Use a Second Conditional with *would* or *could*.

► Andrew is such a boring person because he works all the time.
You know, *if Andrew didn't work all the time, he wouldn't be such a boring person.*

► You can't take a photo because you haven't got your camera.
How annoying. *If I had my camera, I could take a photo.*

1 You can't look the word up because you haven't got a dictionary.
I'm sorry. ....

2 You don't write to your friends because you're so busy.
I've got so much to do. ....

3 You can't play tennis because your back is aching.
It's a nuisance. ....

4 Claire won't marry Henry because she doesn't love him.
Of course, ...

5 Nick can't find the way because he hasn't got a map.
Nick's lost, but ....

6 David has so many accidents because he's so clumsy.
You know, ...

B First and Second Conditionals (1–3)

Complete the conversation. Put in the correct form of the verb. You may need to use *will* or *would*.

Matthew: I haven't forgotten your birthday, you know. If you like, (►) *I'll book* (I / book) a table for Thursday at our favourite restaurant.

Emma: My birthday is on Wednesday, Matthew. You're playing basketball then, aren't you? If you cared for me, (1) .... (you / not / play) basketball on my birthday.

Matthew: What's the difference? If (2) .... (we / go) out on Thursday, it'll be just the same. If (3) .... (I / not / play), I'd be letting the team down.

Emma: Yes, I suppose (4) .... (it / be) a disaster if you missed one game. Well, if (5) .... (you / think) more of your friends than you do of me, you can forget the whole thing.

Matthew: I just don't understand you sometimes, Emma.

Emma: If (6) .... (you / think) about it, you'd understand. And I think (7) .... (it / be) better if we forgot all about my birthday.

Matthew: Don't be silly, Emma. If you get into one of your bad moods, (8) .... (it / not / do) any good.

Emma: If you were interested in my feelings, (9) .... (I / not / get) into a bad mood.

C First and Second Conditionals (3)

What does the if-clause mean? Write a sentence with *isn't* or *might*.

► If this room was tidy, I could find things. *The room isn't tidy.*

► If we're late tonight, we can get a taxi. *We might be late tonight.*

1 If the phone was working, I could call you. ....

2 If it rains, can you bring the washing in? ....

3 If Mike was here, he'd know what to do. ....

4 If this spoon was silver, it would be worth a lot. ....

5 If Sarah calls, can you say I'll ring back? ....

146 Conditionals (3)

1 Introduction

David: *How was your camping holiday?*
Mike: *Well, it **would have** been all right if it **hadn't rained** all the time.*
Harriet: *If we**'d gone** two weeks earlier, we**'d have** had better weather.*

If it hadn't rained and *if we'd gone two weeks earlier* are imaginary situations in the past.
It did rain, and they didn't go two weeks earlier.

2 Third Conditional: **If we had gone earlier, we would have had better weather**

IF-CLAUSE			MAIN CLAUSE	
If	+ PAST PERFECT		+ would have	
If we	**'d gone** earlier,	*we*	**'d have** had better weather.
If Matthew	**had phoned** her,	*Emma*	**wouldn't have** been so annoyed.
If you	**hadn't made** that mistake,	*you*	**'d have** passed your test.
If David	**had been** more careful,	*he*	**wouldn't have** fallen.

Note the verb in the Past Perfect (e.g. **had been**). We do not use **would** in the if-clause.
NOT ~~If David would have been more careful, he would have fallen.~~

The main clause often has **would have**. We can also use **could have** or **might have**.
*If I'd had my mobile yesterday, I **could have** contacted you.*
*We just caught the train. If we'd stopped to buy a paper, we **might have** missed it.*

The short form **'d** can be either **had** or **would**.
*If you**'d** rung me, I**'d** have come to see you.* (= If you **had** rung me, I **would** have come to see you.)

3 The use of the Third Conditional

We use the Third Conditional to talk about things in the past happening differently from the way they really happened. This sometimes means criticizing people or pointing out their mistakes.
If you'd been a bit more careful, you wouldn't have cut yourself.
If Matthew had set his alarm clock, he wouldn't have overslept.
We can also use this structure to express regret about the past.
If I hadn't fallen ill and missed the interview, I might have got the job.

4 Second and Third Conditionals

Compare these examples.
Second: *If you **planned** things properly, you **wouldn't** get into a mess.* (You don't plan.)
Third: *If you **had planned** things properly, you **wouldn't have** got into a mess.* (You didn't plan.)
We can mix the Second and Third conditionals.
*If you **had planned** things at the start, we **wouldn't** be in this mess now.*
*If you **hadn't left** all these dirty dishes, the place **would** look a bit tidier.*
*If Matthew **was** more sensible, he **would have** worn a suit to the interview.*
*If I **didn't have** all this work to do, I **would have** gone out for the day.*

Practice

A Third Conditional (1–3)

Complete the conversation. Put in the correct form of the verb. Use the Past Perfect or _would have_.

Nick: United didn't play very well today.

Tom: We were awful. But if Hacker (▶) ..had..taken.. (take) that easy chance,
(▶) ..we would have won.. (we / win).

Nick: We didn't deserve to win. It (1) .... (be) pretty unfair if Rangers
(2) .... (lose).

Tom: Hacker was dreadful. My grandmother (3) .... (score) if
(4) .... (she / be) in that position.

Nick: And if Burley (5) .... (not / be) asleep,
he (6) .... (not / give) a goal away.

Tom: If Johnson (7) .... (not / be) injured when we needed him
most, (8) .... (it / be) different.

Nick: Yes, (9) .... (we / beat) them if (10) ....
(he / be) fit.

B Third Conditional (1–3)

Comment on each situation using a Third Conditional with _if_. Use _would have_, _could have_ or _might have_.

▶ In a bookshop yesterday Daniel saw a book he really wanted. The only problem was that he didn't
have any money. ..Daniel would have bought the book if he had had any money...

▶ Rita often goes to concerts at the town hall, although not to every one. There was one on Saturday,
but she didn't know about it. ..Rita might have gone to the concert if she had known
about it...

1 On Sunday the guests had to have their lunch inside. Unfortunately it wasn't warm enough to
have it outside. ....

2 There was a bomb scare last Tuesday. Sarah wanted to fly to Rome, but she wasn't able to. The
airport was closed. ....

3 Laura has only met Nick once, and it's possible she wouldn't recognize him. He passed her
yesterday, but he had a crash-helmet on. ....

4 Sarah has been quite busy, and she hasn't watered her plants for some time. As a result, they've died.
....

5 Nick likes ice hockey, but he didn't have a ticket to the game last week, so unfortunately he
wasn't able to get in. ....

C Second and Third Conditionals (4)

Complete the conversations. Put in the correct form of the verb.
Use the Past Simple, the Past Perfect, _would_, or _would have_.

▶ Mike: You look tired.
Harriet: Well, if ..you hadn't woken.. (you / not / wake) me up in the middle of the night,
..I wouldn't be.. (I / not be) so tired.

1 Rita: Is Trevor a practical person?
Laura: Trevor? No, he isn't. If .... (he / be) practical,
.... (he / put) those shelves up a bit quicker. It took him ages.

2 Tom: Why are you sitting in the dark?
David: Let's just say that if .... (I / pay) my electricity bill last
month, ... (I / not be) in the dark now.

3 Matthew: Why are you so angry with me? All I did yesterday was play basketball.
Emma: If .... (you / love) me, ...
(you / not / leave) me here all alone on my birthday.

147 Review of conditionals

1 First, Second and Third Conditionals

BEFORE THE GAME.   AFTER THE GAME.

There are three main types of conditional. Study the examples.

First: **if** ... the Present Simple ... **will/can/might**, etc.

> *If we **win** today, we'**ll** go to the top of the league.* (We may win, or we may not.)

Second: **if** ... Past Simple ... **would/could/might**

> *If Johnson **was** in the team, I'**d** feel more confident.* (Johnson isn't in the team.)

Third: **if** ... Past Perfect ... **would have/could have/might have**

> *If Johnson **had** played, we'**d have** won.* (Johnson didn't play.)

Here are some more examples with different verb forms.

First
> *If I'**m** going shopping, I'**ll** need some money.*
> *If the disco **has** finished, we **might** be able to get some sleep.*
> *You **should** stay in bed if you **feel** unwell.*

Second
> *If I **didn't** like this pudding, I **wouldn't** eat it.*
> *If the video recorder **was** working, we **could** watch a film.*
> *The alarm **might** go off if we **tried** to get in through a window.*

Third
> *If we'**d dropped** the piano, it **would have** been a disaster.*
> *If Vicky **had come** to the theme park with us last week, she **might have** enjoyed it.*
> *We **could have** given you a lift if we'**d known** you were coming this way.*

2 Other conditional sentences

As well as the three main types, there are other types of conditional sentence.

For example, we can use two present-tense verbs (see Unit 144.4).

> *If you **ring** this number, no one **answers**.*

We can also use a present-tense verb and an imperative.

> *If you **need** any help, just **ask**.   If you **drink**, **don't drive**.*

We can use **be going to**.

> *If it'**s going to** rain, I'd better take an umbrella.*
> *If they try to cut down the trees, there'**s going to** be a big protest.*

We can mix the Second and Third Conditionals (see Unit 146.4).

> *If Matthew **had booked** a table, we **wouldn't** be standing here in a queue.*
> *If you **needed** help, you **should have** asked me.*

Practice

A First, Second and Third Conditionals (1)

Match the sentences and join them with *if*. Say what type they are.

- ► I went to bed earlier.
- 1 The twins had worn different clothes.
- 2 You tell me what the instructions say.
- 3 People used public transport.
- 4 You don't wear a sweater.
- 5 I hadn't seen the product advertised.

I'll try to follow them.
You might not be warm enough.
I wouldn't have bought it.
I wouldn't sleep.
There'd be less pollution.
We could have told them apart.

- ► If I went to bed earlier, I wouldn't sleep. .... Second
- 1 ....
- 2 ....
- 3 ....
- 4 ....
- 5 ....

B First, Second and Third Conditionals (1)

Adam is a music student. He rents a room from Mr Day. Put in the correct forms.

Mr Day: Can't you stop playing that trumpet? You're making an awful noise.

Adam: Well, if (►) ...I don't practise. (I / not practise), I won't pass my exam.

Mr Day: But why at night? It's half past twelve. If (1) .... (you / play)
it in the daytime, (2) .... (I / not / hear) you because I'd be
at work. If (3) .... (you / tell) me about this trumpet when
you first came here, (4) .... (I / not / let) you have the room.
I'm afraid it's becoming a nuisance. If (5) .... (you / not / play)
so loud, (6) .... (it / not / be) so bad.

Adam: I'm sorry, but you can't play a trumpet quietly.

Mr Day: If (7) .... (I / realize) a year ago what you were going
to do, then (8) .... (I / throw) you out long ago. If
(9) .... (you / go) on making this noise at night,
(10) .... (I / have) to complain to your college.

C Conditionals (1–2)

What might you say in these situations? Use a conditional sentence.

- ► You think Emma should book a seat on the train. The alternative is having to stand.
  If Emma doesn't book a seat on the train, she'll have to stand.
- 1 You didn't know how unpopular Jason was when you invited him to your party.
  ....
- 2 Warn your friend not to put too many tins into the plastic bag or it'll break.
  ....
- 3 You haven't got a pen, so you can't write down the address.
  ....
- 4 You should have started your project earlier. You're so far behind now.
  ....
- 5 Your friend might need some help. If so, tell her to give you a ring.
  ....
- 6 The automatic result of the door opening is the fan coming on.
  ....

148 If, when, unless and in case

1 Present Simple for the future

Look at these examples.

> *You'll be tired tomorrow if you stay up late.*   *Tell me when the water boils.*
> *I won't do anything unless you agree.*   *Write the name down in case you forget it.*

We use the Present Simple for the future after linking words such as **if**, **when**, **unless** and **in case** (see also Units 27 and 144.2).

2 If or when?

If you hear any news, can you ring me immediately? (You <u>might</u> hear some news.) *I'll probably go for a walk later on if it stays fine.* (It <u>might</u> stay fine.)	*When you hear some news, can you ring me immediately?* (You <u>will</u> hear some news.) *I'll make myself an omelette when I get home tonight.* (I <u>will</u> get home tonight.)
We use **if** for something that we think might happen. We use **if** (not **when**) for something impossible or imaginary. *If I were you, I'd refuse.*	We use **when** for something that we know will happen.

We can use either **if** or **when** in contexts where they mean 'every time'.

If you run, you use up energy.	*When you run, you use up energy.*

3 If and unless

If … not means the same as **unless**.

I can't see if I don't wear glasses.	= *I can't see unless I wear glasses.*
The doctor will be here if she isn't called to an emergency.	= *The doctor will be here unless she's called to an emergency.*
If you can't pay your bills, you'll have to leave.	= *Unless you can pay your bills, you'll have to leave.*
I wouldn't say that if I didn't believe it.	= *I wouldn't say that unless I believed it.*

4 In case

Look at these examples.

> *Take a sandwich with you in case you get hungry.*
> *I'd better reserve a seat today in case the train is full tomorrow.*
> *Laura took two photos in case one of them didn't come out.*

We use **in case** to talk about doing something to avoid a possible problem later on.
(For American English, see page 381.)

Compare **if** and **in case**.

I'll bring in the washing if it rains. (= I'll bring it in at the time it starts raining.)	*I'll bring in the washing in case it rains.* (= I'll bring it in now because it might rain later.)

Practice

A If or when? (2)

**Look at the information in brackets and complete the sentences using *if* or *when*
and a verb in the Present Simple.**

▶ (I may see Tom tonight.) ..If.I.see.Tom,.. I'll tell him the news.
▶ (Melanie is coming soon.) ..When.Melanie.comes,. can you let her in, please?
1 (The alarm will ring soon.) .... we all have to leave the building.
2 (I might feel better tomorrow.) .... I'll probably go back to work.
3 (This film finishes at ten.) .... I'll stop the video.
4 (The plan may not work.) .... we'll have to think of something else.

B If and unless (3)

Complete the sentences using *unless* and the information in brackets.

▶ You won't get there in time .unless.you.hurry.. (if you don't hurry)
1 We can't have a picnic .... (if it isn't a nice day)
2 Don't leave the TV on .... (if you aren't watching it)
3 We can't do the job .... (if we don't get help)
4 I wouldn't have bought the picture .... (if I didn't like it)

C If and unless (3)

Which word makes more sense? Put in *if* or *unless*.

▶ Rachel will be pleased .if.. she passes her driving test.
▶ The bus won't stop .unless.. you ring the bell.
1 I can't read your writing .... you print clearly.
2 Emma will be upset .... she doesn't get the job.
3 You can't go into the reception .... you've got a ticket.
4 Don't bother to ring me .... it's important.

D In case (4)

What could you say in these situations? Use *in case*.

▶ You think Vicky had better take a coat. It might get cold.
  You to Vicky: You'd better take a coat in case it gets cold. ....
1 You think you and Mark had better book a table. The restaurant might be busy.
  You to Mark: ....
2 You think Claire ought to insure her jewellery. It might get stolen.
  You to Claire: ....
3 You'll leave David your phone number. He might want to contact you.
  You to David: ....

E If, when, unless and in case (2–4)

Jake lives next door to Melanie. Complete their conversation. Put in *if*, *when* (x2), *unless* or *in case*.

Jake: A man is delivering a washing-machine this morning, but I have to go to work. I won't be
          here (▶) .when. he calls. Could you let him in for me, please, (1) .... you're
          terribly busy?
Melanie: Oh, that's no problem.
Jake: Oh, thanks. (2) .... you could do that, I'd be really grateful. I'll leave a
          message on his answerphone. And (3) .... he doesn't get the message, I'll put
          a note on the door, just to make sure. He'll see it (4) .... he comes.

149 Wish and if only

1 Introduction

If only I wasn't so fat.

I wish you wouldn't say that, Jessica. You aren't fat.

We can use **I wish** or **if only** to express a wish. Jessica wishes she was slimmer.
If only is stronger and more emphatic than **wish**.

We can use a clause with **if only** on its own, or we can add another clause.
> **If only** I wasn't so fat. **If only** I wasn't so fat, I would be able to get into these trousers.

2 Wish ... would

Look at these examples.
> I wish you **would** put those shelves up soon.
> Tom wishes his neighbours **wouldn't** make so much noise.
> If only you**'d** try to keep the place tidy.

Wish/If only ... would expresses a wish for something to happen, or to stop happening.

3 Wish ... the past

Look at these examples.
> I wish I **lived** in a big city. It's so boring in the country.
> We all wish we **had** more money, don't we? If only I **was** taller, I might be better at basketball.

Wish and if only with a past-tense verb express a wish for things to be different.

We can use **were** instead of **was** (see also Unit 145.2).
> If only I **were** taller, I might be better at basketball.

We cannot use **would** in these sentences, but we can use **could**.
> I wish I **could** sing (but I can't). I feel so helpless. If only I **could** speak the language.

Compare **wish** with **would** and with the past.
> I wish something exciting **would** happen. (I wish for an action in the future.)
> I wish my life **was** more interesting. (My life isn't interesting.)

4 Wish ... the Past Perfect

We use **wish** and **if only** with the Past Perfect to express a wish about the past.
> I wish you **had told** me about the dance. I would have gone.
> I wish I**'d got** up earlier. I'm behind with everything today.
> I wish you **hadn't lost** that photo. It was a really good one.
> If only David **had been** a bit more careful, he'd have been all right.

We do not use **would have** for the past, but we can use **could have**.
> I wish I **could have** been at the wedding, but I was in New York.

Practice

A Wish ... would (2)

What might you say in these situations? Begin *I wish ...*

▶ to someone who never answers your emails
I wish you'd answer my emails.

▶ to someone who makes rude remarks about you
I wish you wouldn't make rude remarks about me.

1 to someone who won't hurry up

2 to someone who never does the washing-up

3 to someone who isn't telling you the whole story

4 to someone who blows cigarette smoke in your face

5 to someone who won't tell you what he's thinking

B Wish ... the past (3)

Vicky is fed up. What is she saying? Use *I wish* or *if only*.

▶ (She can't think straight.) *I wish I could think straight.*
1 (She is so tired.)
2 (She gets headaches.)
3 (Her work isn't going well.)
4 (She can't concentrate.)
5 (Life is so complicated.)

C Wish ... the Past Perfect (4)

Complete the sentences. Use these words: *accepted, caught, found, played, saved, stayed*

▶ I spent all my money. I wish now that *I had saved it.*
1 I missed the train. I really wish
2 Rita left the party early. Nick wishes
3 Emma refused the offer. But her parents wish
4 I looked everywhere for the key. I wish
5 The injured player could only watch. He wishes

D Wish and if only (2–4)

Complete the conversation.

Claire: Oh, Henry. You're giving me another present. It's very sweet of you,
  but I wish (▶) *you wouldn't give me* so many presents.

Henry: Claire, I've been thinking. I shouldn't have asked you to marry me. I wish now that
  (1) ....

Claire: Now you're talking nonsense. I wish (2) .... , Henry.

Henry: I'm not a young man, am I? Of course I wish (3) ....

Claire: Why don't you listen? If only (4) .... to me just this once.

Henry: Why couldn't we have met twenty years ago? I wish (5) .... you then.

Claire: Henry, twenty years ago I was just starting school.

Test Y: Conditionals and wish

A

Complete the news report about a protest against a new road. Put in the correct form of the verbs. Sometimes you need *will* or *would*.

Yesterday protesters managed to hold up work on the Oldbury bypass. Protest leader Alison Compton defended the action by members of the Green World group. 'If we don't protest, soon (▶) ..*there'll be*.. (there / be) no countryside left,' she told reporters. The bypass is now well behind schedule, and if the protesters had not held up the work so often, (1) *It would have opened* (it / open) two months ago. 'If these fields (2) ...*disappear*... (disappear), we'll never see them again,' said Ms Compton. 'Why can't we use public transport? If more people (3) ...*travelled*... (travel) on buses and trains, we wouldn't need new roads. If the motor car had never existed, the world (4) ...*would be*... (be) a more pleasant place today.'

But many people in Oldbury want their new bypass. 'If (5) .... (they / not build) it soon, the traffic jams in the town will get worse,' said Asif Mohammed, whose house is beside the busy A34. 'We just can't leave things as they are. If things remained the same, people's health (6) .... (suffer) even more from all the pollution here. It's terrible. If we don't get the traffic out of the town, (7) .... (I / go) mad. If (8) *I had known* (I / know) earlier how bad this problem would get, (9) *I would have moved* (I / move) out years ago. But now it has become impossible to sell this house because of the traffic. The government waited too long. If (10) .... (they / do) something sooner, there would be less traffic today.' And the protest is making the new road even more expensive. 'If this goes on, (11) .... (there / not / be) enough money left to finish the road,' says the Transport Minister.

B

Look at the answers below and write the correct answer in each space.

▶ A: There's always something going wrong with this car.
B: If you had any sense, you'd ..*have sold*.. it long ago.
a) be selling   b) have sold   c) sell   d) sold

1 A: It's a pity the lake wasn't frozen yesterday.
B: Yes, it is. If it .... frozen, we could have gone skating.
a) had been   b) was   c) would be   d) would have been

2 A: Haven't you got enough money for a holiday?
B: Oh yes. I've got some saved up .... I suddenly need it.
a) if   b) in case   c) that   d) unless

3 A: What are you going to do next year?
B: I wish I .... the answer to that question.
a) knew   b) know   c) could know   d) would know

4 A: These figures are too complicated to work out in your head.
B: Yes, if .... we had a calculator.
a) better   b) only   c) really   d) that

5 A: What are you doing later this afternoon?
B: Oh, ... the game finishes, I'll go home, I expect.
a) if   b) in case   c) unless   d) when

6 A: Do you think I should take the job?
B: You shouldn't do anything .... you think it's the right thing to do.
a) if   b) in case   c) unless   d) when

C

Write a second sentence so that it has a similar meaning to the first. Begin with *If ...*

▶ I haven't got a key, so I can't get in.

If I had a key, I could get in.

1 You talk about football and I'm going to be very bored.

....

2 The baby didn't cry, so we had a good sleep.

If the baby had cried, we wouldn't have had a good sleep

3 You may want a chat, so just give me a ring.

....

4 Nigel hasn't got satellite TV, so he can't watch the game.

If Nigel had satellite TV, he would be able to watch the game

5 You go away and I'll miss you.

....

6 I'm not rich or I'd have given up working long ago.

....

7 We should have bought that picture five years ago because it would be quite valuable now.

If we had bought that picture five years ago, it would be quite valuable now.

8 Throw a stone into water and it sinks.

....

D

Write the sentences correctly.

▶ There aren't any eggs. ~~If we have some eggs, I could make an omelette.~~

If we had some eggs, I could make an omelette.

1 The weather doesn't look very good. ~~If it'll rain, I'll stay here.~~

If it rains, I'll stay here.

2 The programme is starting soon. ~~Can you tell me if it starts?~~

Can you tell me when it starts?

3 Could you just listen? ~~I didn't need to repeat things all the time if you listened.~~

I wouldn't need to repeat things all the time if you listened.

4 It's a simple law of science. ~~If air will get warmer, it rises.~~

If air gets warmer, it rises.

5 There's only one key. ~~I'd better get another one made if I lose it.~~

I'd better get another one made just incase I lose it.

6 We were really late. ~~I wish we left home earlier.~~

I wish we had left home earlier

7 I hope the parcel comes today. ~~If it won't arrive today, we'll have to complain.~~

If it doesn't arrive today, we'll have to complain

8 That radio is on loud. ~~I wish someone turns it down.~~

I wish someone would turn it down

9 We must do something. ~~Until we act quickly, it'll be too late.~~

Unless we act quickly, it'll be too late

10 Of course Martin was angry. ~~But he hadn't been angry if you hadn't damaged his stereo.~~

But he wouldn't have been angry if you hadn't damaged his stereo.

150 But, although, in spite of, whereas, etc.

Linking words

1 But, although and however

We can join two sentences with **but**.

> *The café was crowded, **but** we found a table.   Nick has a car, **but** he doesn't often drive it.*

But expresses a contrast or conflict between two ideas. We can also use **although**.

> ***Although** the café was crowded, we found a table.   **Although** Nick has a car, he doesn't often drive it.*

The clause with **although** can come at the end.

> *We found a table, **although** the café was crowded.*

However is a little formal.

> *The new system was supposed to be more efficient. **However**, in practice it caused chaos./In practice,*
> ***however**, it caused chaos.*

2 Though and even though

Though is informal. It means the same as **although**.

> ***Though/Although** I liked the sweater, I decided not to buy it.*

We can also use **though** at the end of a sentence.

> *I liked the sweater. I decided not to buy it, **though**.*

Even though is stronger, more emphatic than **although**.

> *Matthew looked quite fresh, **even though** he'd been playing squash.*
> ***Even though** you dislike Jessica, you should try to be nice to her.*

3 In spite of and despite

We use **in spite of** before a noun or before the ing-form of a verb.

> *Kitty wanted to report on the war **in spite of** the danger.*
> *Mark went on working **in spite of** feeling unwell.*

We use **despite** in exactly the same way as **in spite of** and with the same meaning.

> *She wanted to go **despite** the danger.   He went on working **despite** feeling unwell.*

4 In spite of and although

IN SPITE OF	ALTHOUGH
*I'm no better **in spite of** the pills/**in spite of** taking the pills.*	*I'm no better, **although** I've taken the pills.*
*Laura wants to fly **in spite of** her fear/**in spite of** feeling afraid.* NOT ~~in spite of she feels afraid~~	*Laura wants to fly, **although** she feels afraid.*

We can use **in spite of the fact** (**that**) in the same way as **although**.

> *I'm no better **in spite of the fact that** I've taken the pills.*

5 Whereas, while and on the other hand

We use these words to express a comparison between two ideas.

> *United are top of the league, **whereas** City are bottom.*
> *Yesterday it was freezing cold, **while** today it's quite warm.*
> *The flat is conveniently located. **On the other hand**, there's a lot of noise from the traffic./*
> *There is, **on the other hand**, a lot of noise from the traffic.*

Sometimes either **but** or **whereas** is possible.

> *The red pills make me feel sick, **but/whereas** the blue ones don't.*

Practice

A But (2)

Complete each sentence with *but* and one of these clauses:
it didn't break, it's really quite modern, no one laughed, she turned it down

► I dropped the dish, but it didn't break.

1 The house looks old, ...
2 Emma was offered a job, ...
3 The joke was funny, ...

B In spite of and although (4)

Put in *although* or *in spite of*.

► My sister got the job, although she didn't expect to.

1 .... I told the absolute truth, no one would believe me.
2 Daniel forgot his passport .... having it on his list.
3 .... it was sunny, it was quite a cold day.
4 The goods were never delivered .... the promise we had received.
5 Henry asked Claire to marry him .... the fact that he's a lot older than her.

C But, although, however, even though, in spite of, and despite (1–4)

Complete the report by putting in the correct linking words. There is always more than one possible answer.

(►) Although the ground was very wet, it was decided to go ahead with United's game against City. United were 1–0 winners (1) .... not playing very well. (2) .... the poor conditions, City played some attractive football, (3) .... they just couldn't score. (4) .... they lost, their fans gave them a big cheer.

D Although, even though, in spite of and despite (1–4)

Join each pair of sentences. Be careful where you put the words in brackets.

► Nick used to smoke. He seems to be in good health. (although)
  Although Nick used to smoke, he seems to be in good health.

► I couldn't sleep. I was tired. (despite)
  I couldn't sleep despite being tired.

1 Trevor didn't notice the sign. It was right in front of him. (even though)
  ....

2 Matthew doesn't know any French. It was one of his school subjects. (although)
  ....

3 Henry's friend is a millionaire. He hates spending money. (despite)
  ....

4 We couldn't get tickets. We queued for an hour. (in spite of)
  ....

E Whereas, on the other hand, in spite of and although (4–5)

Put one of the linking words into each of these sentences.

► Although it was rush-hour time, the roads weren't at all busy.

1 I always spend money when I have it. My brother, ..., is very careful.
2 I managed to do some studying .... all the noise.
3 People are friendly in the North, ... in London no one speaks to you.

151 To, in order to, so that and for

1 Introduction

Can we stop soon **so that** I can buy a newspaper? And I'd quite like a walk around **to** stretch my legs.

Good idea. We'll have to stop **for** petrol in any case.

We use **to, in order to, so that** and **for** to express purpose, to say why we do things.
The purpose of stopping is to buy a newspaper.

2 To

We can use the to-infinitive to express purpose.

    *Melanie was hurrying **to catch** her bus.*   *Most people work **to earn** money.*
    *I rang **to find** out the train times.*   *We went to the library **to get** some books.*

3 In order to and so as to

In order to and **so as to** are more formal than **to**.

    *The government took these measures **in order to** reduce crime.*
    *The staff are working at weekends **so as to** complete the project in time.*

We can use the negative **in order not to** or **so as not to**.

    *Melanie was hurrying **in order not to** miss her bus.*
    *The staff are working at weekends **so as not to** delay the project any further.*

We cannot use **not to** on its own.

    *She was hurrying **to catch** her bus.* NOT ~~She was hurrying not to miss her bus.~~

4 So that

Look at this example.

    *I'll post the card today **so that it gets** there on Daniel's birthday.*

After **so that** we use a subject and verb, e.g. *it gets*.
We often use **will** or **can** for a present purpose and **would** or **could** for a past purpose.

    *I'll give you a map **so that** you **can** find/you'**ll** find the way all right.*
    *I gave Nick a map **so that** he **could** find/**would** be able to find the way all right.*

5 To or for?

We can use **for** with a noun to say why we do something.

    *The whole family have gone out **for** a bike ride.*   *Why don't you come over **for** coffee?*

To talk about the purpose of a thing, we use either a to-infinitive or **for** + an ing-form.

    *This heater is **to keep**/**for keeping** the plants warm in winter.*
    *This machine is used **to cut**/**for cutting** plastic.*

But we do not use **for** + an ing-form to talk about a specific action.

    *I put the heater on **to keep** the plants warm.* NOT ~~I put the heater on for keeping the plants warm.~~

A To (2)

Complete each sentence using *to* and these words:
cash a cheque, finance her studies, go to sleep, hear the football results, look smart

▶ Laura went to the bank .to..cash..a..cheque...

1 Mrs Miles sometimes takes a pill ....

2 Tom turned on the radio ....

3 Just this once Mike is going to wear a suit ....

4 Jessica is borrowing some money ....

B In order to and so as to (3)

Alan works for Zedco. He wants to succeed in business, so he is listening to a talk on the subject. Here is what the speaker is showing the audience.

	ACTION		PURPOSE
▶	study the market	→	be more successful
1	get to work earlier	→	impress the boss
2	work harder	→	achieve more
3	take risks	→	be a winner
4	think positively	→	not miss any opportunities

Say what Alan is going to do. Use either *in order to* or *so as to*. Both are correct.

▶ He's going to study the market in order to be more successful.

1 ....

2 ....

3 ....

4 ....

C To, for and so that (2, 4, 5)

Comment on what each person says. Use the word in brackets.

▶ Ilona: I'm learning English. I want to get a better job. (to)
  Ilona is learning English to get a better job.

▶ Claude: I study encyclopedias. Then I can answer quiz questions. (so that)
  Claude studies encyclopedias so that he can answer quiz questions.

▶ Vicky: I'm saving up. I'm planning a holiday. (for)
  Vicky is saving up for a holiday.

1 Nick: I keep a dog. It guards the house. (to)
  ....

2 David: I'm going to be very careful. Then I won't have an accident. (so that)
  ....

3 Jessica: I'm going on a diet. I want to lose weight. (to)
  ....

4 Trevor: I often switch off the heating. It saves money. (to)
  ....

5 Sarah: I had to go to Birmingham. I had a business meeting. (for)
  ....

6 Emma: I wore boots because I didn't want my feet to get wet. (so that)
  ....

152 Review of linking words

1 Time words

Look at these examples with **when, while, as soon as**, etc.

*My leg hurts **when** I walk.* (= **at the time** I walk)
*Mark heard the news on the radio **as/while** he was driving home.* (= **during the time** he was driving)
*We're going to tidy up **after** everyone's gone.* (= **later than** everyone goes)
***As soon as** Laura had left the house, it started to rain.* (= **immediately after** she had left)
*I must get to the post office **before** it closes.* (= **earlier than** it closes)
*You have to wait **until** the light changes to green.* (= **up to the time** it changes)
*David hasn't been able to work **since** he broke his leg.* (= **from the time** he broke his leg)

Remember that we use the Present Simple for future time after **when**, etc.
We say *before it **closes**, until it **changes***, etc. (see Unit 27).

2 If, unless and in case

We use these words to express a condition (see Unit 148).

*Rachel might buy a car **if** she passes her test.* (She may or may not pass her test.)
*You won't learn to use a keyboard properly **unless** you practise.* (= **if** you don't practise)
*We'd better start early **in case** there are traffic hold-ups.* (= **because** there may be hold-ups)

3 But, although and in spite of

We use these words to express the idea of a contrast (see Unit 150).

*The jacket was nice, **but** it was too small for me.*
***Although** the forecast said it would rain, it turned out to be a beautiful day.*
*We still haven't got a sponsor **in spite of** writing/**in spite of the fact that** we've written to dozens of companies.*

4 Reason

Here are some ways of expressing reason.

*I took a taxi **because** I had some luggage.*   ***Since** we've got some time, let's look around the museum.*
***As** there was no evidence against him, the man was released.*   *We hurried on, **for** it was getting late.*
For is rather literary.

We can also use these prepositions.

*The match has been cancelled **because of** the weather.*
*The shop was closed **due to** illness.*
***Owing to** its remote situation, the village has no electricity supply.*
***In view of** the test results, we expect the drug to be approved.*

5 Because and so

We use **because** to express the reason for something and **so** to express the result of something.

*I turned the heating on **because** it was cold.*   *Henry started jogging **because** his doctor told him to.*
*It was cold, **so** I turned the heating on.*   *The stereo didn't work, **so** Vicky took it back to the shop.*

6 To, in order to and so that

We use these words to express purpose (see Unit 151).

*Sarah went to Birmingham **to** meet a client.*
*We're having to borrow money **in order to** pay our bills.*
*I took the bread out of the freezer **so that** it would defrost.*

Practice

A Time words (1)

Arlene Black's new CD is now available in the shops. Write the titles of her songs.
Use these words instead of the ones in brackets: *as soon as, before, since, when, while, until*

▶ Think of me (during the time) I'm away   Think of me while I'm away
1 I'll love you (up to the day) I die   ....
2 I hear music (at the time) I see you   ....
3 Come back (earlier than) I forget you   ....
4 I've been sad (from the time) you left me   ....
5 I fell in love (immediately after) we met   ....

B Linking words (2–5)

Put in these words: *although, because, but, due to, if, in case, in order to, in spite of, so,*
so that, unless

▶ Olivia booked a babysitter *so that* she could go out for the evening.
1 .... it was late, Nick didn't seem in a hurry to leave.
2 They put video cameras in shops .... stop people stealing things.
3 We decided not to go out for a meal .... we were simply too tired.
4 .... you're ready, we can start now.
5 Our room was very small, ... we didn't really mind.
6 No one was watching the television, ... I switched it off.
7 You can't drive a car .... you've got a licence.
8 .... having absolutely no talent, Guy became a popular TV personality.
9 I think my answers are right, but can I just check them with yours ....
   I've made a mistake?
10 The road was closed .... an accident.

C Linking words (1–5)

Complete the conversation. Choose the correct linking word.

Daniel: What are you going to do (▶) <u>after/before</u> you finish college, Rachel?
Rachel: Vicky and I will be off to the States (1) <u>as soon as/in spite of</u> this term is over. We're going to travel around, and we may go to Canada (2) <u>so that/to</u> see some friends of Vicky's. We've been thinking about nothing else (3) <u>since/until</u> we bought our plane tickets.
Daniel: It sounds great. How are you getting around in the States?
Rachel: By Greyhound bus. I know it takes longer than flying, (4) <u>but/in spite of</u> it'll be more interesting. We fly to LA and then we're taking the bus to New York. We're going to buy a special ticket (5) <u>in order/so that</u> we can go anywhere we like on the way.
Daniel: Yes, it's better by bus (6) <u>because/unless</u> you can stop off at interesting places.
Rachel: Of course the bus will probably be tiring.
Daniel: Maybe you should take plenty of money (7) <u>if/in case</u> you decide to fly instead.
Rachel: I'll have to be careful with my money (8) <u>since/so that</u> I've only just got enough. I'm hoping to stay out there (9) <u>unless/until</u> I have to come back and start my job in September. I'm really looking forward to the trip, (10) <u>although/because</u> I'll be sad to leave here. And what about you? What are you doing this summer?
Daniel: I'd go away somewhere (11) <u>if/in case</u> I could afford to. But I'm working. I've got no money, (12) <u>because/so</u> I'll have to earn some.
Rachel: Have you really got no money (13) <u>although/in spite of</u> the fact that you've had a part-time job this term?
Daniel: You know me, Rachel. If I've got money, I spend it.

153 Links across sentences

1 Introduction

Rita: *You go to United's games, don't you, Tom?*
You watch them on TV, **too**.

Tom: *Well, I'm a fan. It's wonderful when United win.*
On the other hand, *it's terrible when they lose.*

Rita: *Why not have a change?* ***After all***, *there are*
other things in life.

Tom: *Such as?*

Rita: *There's music,* ***for example***. *Why don't you go*
to a concert some time?

Tom: *But I don't like classical music.*

Look at the words and phrases **too**, **on the other hand**,
after all and **for example**. They all make a link with
an earlier sentence. When Rita says *There's music,*
for example, she is giving an example of *other things*
in life, which she has already mentioned.

2 Words and phrases meaning 'and', 'but' and 'so'

'And': *Sarah often works late. She works on Saturdays sometimes,* **too/as well**.
Sarah often works late. She **also** *works on Saturdays sometimes.*
Arlene Black has a yacht and a helicopter. **In addition**, *she has five cars.*
I'm not inviting my cousin – I don't like him. **Besides**, *he didn't invite me to his party.*
The buildings are in a very poor condition. **Furthermore**, *there is no money to repair them.*

'But': *I haven't been very well recently.* **Still**, *it could be worse.*
Nick is in love with Rita. Rita, **however**, *is in love with Tom.*
Everyone thought that Emma should accept the offer. **Nevertheless/All the same**, *she turned it down.*
I don't want to be late for the meeting. **On the other hand**, *I don't want to get there too early.*

'So': *The holiday had been a complete disaster. We* **therefore** *decided to fly home early if we could.*
Someone switched the freezer off. **Consequently/As a result**, *all the food was spoilt.*

Some of these words and phrases are rather formal and typical of written English. They are **consequently**,
furthermore, **however**, **in addition**, **nevertheless** and **therefore**.

3 Other linking words and phrases

Rephrasing:	*Jessica isn't the most popular person around here.* **In other words**, *no one likes her.*
Correcting yourself:	*We play basketball.* **I mean/Or rather** *volleyball.*
Contradicting:	*Sarah isn't lazy.* **On the contrary**, *she works extremely hard.*
Picking up a topic:	*I like Natasha. I went on holiday with her. ~* **Talking of** *holidays, what are your plans for this year?*
Changing the subject:	*It's a lovely day, isn't it? ~ Yes, beautiful.* **By the way**, *have you seen Melanie?*
Supporting a statement:	*We don't need to drive to the club, do we?* **After all**, *it's only about 200 metres from here.*
Dismissing something:	*I'm not sure a thank-you letter is really necessary.* **Anyway**, *I can't be bothered to write one.*
Giving an example:	*Yes, I do think Henry is rude. He shouts at waiters,* **for example/for instance**.

Practice

A Words and phrases meaning 'and', 'but' and 'so' (2)

What do the underlined words mean? Write *and*, *but* or *so*.

▶ Daniel's suitcase got left behind. He got it back in the end, <u>however</u>. = <u>but</u> ....
1 I'm too tired to go for a walk. <u>Besides</u>, it looks like rain. = ...
2 The road was under water. The police <u>therefore</u> closed it to traffic. = ...
3 We took lots of photos. We videoed the speeches <u>as well</u>. = ...
4 It was a terrible journey. <u>Still</u>, we got there safely in the end. = ...
5 A strike by air traffic controllers has begun. Many flights have <u>consequently</u> been cancelled. = ...
6 The company has spent millions on computers. <u>Nevertheless</u>, it does not seem to have become more efficient. = ...

B Links across sentences (2–3)

Complete this letter to a local newspaper. Choose the correct word or phrase.

There's been a lot of talk about a 'spaceship' seen over the town at about eleven o'clock on Friday night. (▶) <u>As a result/Nevertheless,</u> hundreds of enthusiastic sky-watchers have arrived in town, hoping that it will return. But was it really a spaceship? About twenty people say they saw it. (1) <u>Consequently/Furthermore</u>, there is a photograph which is supposed to show the object in the sky. We know, (2) <u>however/as a result</u>, that trick photos are easy to produce. (3) <u>By the way/In other words</u>, it is almost certainly a fake. But it would be wrong to treat the whole thing as a joke. (4) <u>All the same/On the contrary</u>, all such reports should be carefully investigated. (5) <u>After all/Anyway</u>, the arrival of a spacecraft from another world would indeed be a serious matter. But usually there is a more simple explanation. Many supposed spaceships turn out to be weather balloons, (6) <u>for example/or rather</u>. A similar mistake probably lies behind the belief that someone from another world really did pay us a visit last Friday.

C Links across sentences (3)

What would you say? Give your answer using a linking word or phrase.

▶ Support Emma's opinion: she might not get another offer.
  Emma: You're right. Maybe I should accept the offer.
           After all, you might not get another one.
1 Rephrase what Rita is saying: she doesn't want to see Nick.
  Rita: I don't know if I'll have time to see Nick.
           ....
2 Change the subject and ask what the time is.
  Tom: I hope Wayne Johnson will be fit to play for United on Saturday.
           ....
3 Dismiss the idea of buying a sweater: they haven't got one in your size.
  Daniel: I'm not sure if that sweater really suits you.
           ....
4 Mention Sarah as an example.
  Claire: Lots of our friends have DVD recorders, don't they?
           ....
5 Contradict what Nick says.
  Nick: Sorry. I persuaded you to see that film and you hated it, didn't you?
           ....

Appendix 1: Word formation

A Introduction

Look at these examples.

> *Lots of people believe that God **exists**.*
> *Lots of people believe in the **existence** of God.*

Exist is a verb and **existence** is a noun. The word **existence** has two parts: **exist-** and **-ence**. We call **-ence** a 'suffix'. We add it to the end of the verb **exist** to form a noun.

We can also use suffixes to form verbs, adjectives and adverbs.

> *The system is being **modernized**. (= made modern)*
> *I grew up in an **industrial** town. (= a town where there is a lot of industry)*
> *The man was behaving **strangely**. (= in a strange way)*

There are many different suffixes, such as **-ence**, **-ize**, **-al**, **-ly**, **-tion** and **-ment**. Some of them can be used to form many different words. For example, there are a lot of nouns ending in **-tion**: **action**, **education**, **explanation**, **information**, **instruction**, etc. There are no exact rules about which suffix you can add to which word. Adding a suffix can also involve other changes to the form of a word.

> *industry → industrial   repeat → repetition   science → scientist.*

Now look at these examples.

> *They're going to **play** the match on Wednesday.*
> *They're going to **replay** the match on Wednesday.*

We can add **re-** to the beginning of the verb **play**. We call **re-** a 'prefix'. A prefix adds something to the meaning of a word. The verb **replay** means 'play again'. We can also add prefixes to nouns and adjectives. See G and H.

B Noun suffixes

-ment	*the prospects for **employment** reach an **agreement***
-ion/-tion/-sion	*take part in a **discussion** increase steel **production** ask for **permission***
-ation/-ition	*an **invitation** to a party people's **opposition** to the idea*
-ence/-ance	*a **preference** for houses rather than flats a **distance** of ten miles*
-ty/-ity	*no **certainty** that we shall succeed keep the door locked for **security***
-ness	*people's **willingness** to help recovering from an **illness***
-ing	*enter a **building** reach an **understanding***

C Nouns for people

-er/-or	*the **driver** of the car a newspaper **editor***
-ist	*a place full of **tourists** a **scientist** doing an experiment*
-ant/-ent	*an **assistant** to help with my work **students** at the university*
-an/-ian	***Republicans** and Democrats the **electrician** rewiring the house*
-ee	*an **employee** of the company (= someone employed)*
	*notes for **examinees** (= people taking an exam)*

We also use **-er** for things, especially machines.

> *a hair-**dryer**   a food **mixer**   a cassette **player***

D Verb suffixes

Many verbs are formed by adding **-ize** or **-ise** to an adjective. Some are formed by adding **-en**.

-ize	*European safety rules are being **standardized**. They **privatized** the company.*
-en	*They're **widening** the road here. Meeting you has really **brightened** my day.*

E Adjective suffixes

Most of these adjectives are formed from nouns.

-al	a **professional** musician Britain's **coastal** waters
-ic	a **metallic** sound a **scientific** inquiry
-ive	an **informative** guidebook an offer **exclusive** to our readers
-ful	a **successful** career feeling **hopeful** about the future
-less	feeling **hopeless** about the future (= without hope) **powerless** to do anything about it
-ous	guilty of **dangerous** driving **luxurious** holiday apartments
-y	a **rocky** path the **salty** taste of sea water
-ly ▷ 109.1	a **friendly** smile a very **lively** person
-able/-ible	an **acceptable** error (= an error that can be accepted) a **comprehensible** explanation
	a **valuable** painting (= worth a lot of money) a **comfortable** chair

F Adverbs

-ly ▷ 108	He looked around **nervously**. I moved here quite **recently**.

G Some common prefixes

anti- (= against)	**anti-roads** protestors **anti-government** troops
inter- (= between)	an **international** match **interstate** highways in the US
mini- (= small)	a **minicomputer** the **minibar** in your hotel room
mis- (= wrongly)	**mishear** what someone says **miscalculate** the amount
multi- (= many)	**multicoloured** lights a **multimillionaire**
over- (= too much)	too fond of **overeating** **overcrowded** roads
post- (= after)	the **post-war** world a **postgraduate** student
pre- (= before)	**pre-match** entertainment in **prehistoric** times
re- (= again)	a **reunion** of old friends **reread** a favourite book
semi- (= half)	**semi-skilled** work sitting in a **semicircle**
super- (= big)	a huge new **superstore** a **supertanker** carrying oil
under- (= too little)	thin and **underweight** **underpaid** work

H Negative prefixes

We can also use a prefix to form an opposite. For example, the opposite of **clear** is **unclear** (= not clear). Un- is the most common negative prefix.

dis-	a **dishonest** way to behave can't help being **disorganized** **dislike** the idea
	disappear from the scene a **disadvantage** of the plan
il- (+ l)	an **illegal** drug an **illiberal** attitude
im- (+ m or p)	an **impossible** task an **impolite** question
in-	an **indirect** route the **invisible** man a great **injustice**
ir- (+ r)	an **irregular** shape an **irrelevant** remark
non-	**non-alcoholic** drinks a **non-stop** flight
un-	an **uncomfortable** chair an **unusual** event an **undated** letter
	uncertain what to do **unpack** your suitcase **unzip** the bag

Appendix 2: The spelling of endings

A Plural nouns

We add -**s** to a noun to form the plural.
a car → two cars   a name → some names

1   After -**s**, -**sh**, -**ch** and -**x** we add -**es** /ɪz/.
glass → glasses   dish → dishes
match → matches   box → boxes

2   A few nouns ending in -**o** have -**es**.
heroes   potatoes   tomatoes
But most have **s**.
discos   kilos   photos   pianos
radios   stereos   studios   zoos

3   When a noun ends in a consonant + -**y**, the -**y**
changes to -**ies**.
penny → pennies   story → stories
We do not change -**y** after a vowel.
day → days   journey → journeys

B The Present Simple -s ending

In the third person singular, a Present Simple
verb ends in -**s**. (See Unit 5.2.)
I know → he knows   I work → she works

1   After -**s**, -**sh**, -**ch** and -**x** we add -**es** /ɪz/.
pass → passes   wash → washes
catch → catches   mix → mixes

2   Some verbs ending in -**o** have -**es**.
go → goes /gəʊz/   *do → does* /dʌz/

3   When a verb ends in a consonant + -**y**,
the -**y** changes to -**ies**.
hurry → hurries   copy → copies
We do not change -**y** after a vowel.
stay → stays   enjoy → enjoys

C The -ed ending

Most verbs have -**ed** in the past tense.
(See Unit 8.2.) Most past participles also end
in -**ed**. (See Unit 11.2.)
look → looked   call → called

1   If the verb ends in -**e**, we add -**d**.
hope → hoped   save → saved

2   When a verb ends in a consonant + -**y**, the -**y**
changes to -**ied**.
hurry → hurried   copy → copied

3   Sometimes we double a final consonant. This
happens when a one-syllable verb ends with one
vowel and one consonant, e.g. *beg*, *plan*.
beg → begged   plan → planned
For more details about doubling, see G.

D The -ing form

1   We normally leave out -**e** when we add -**ing**
to a verb.
take → taking   drive → driving
But we keep a double **e** before -**ing**.
see → seeing   agree → agreeing

2   When a verb ends in -**ie**, it changes to -**ying**.
die → dying   lie → lying
But -**y** does not change.
hurry → hurrying

3   Sometimes we double a final consonant. This
happens when a one-syllable verb ends with one
vowel and one consonant, e.g. *win*, *put*.
win → winning   put → putting
For more details about doubling, see G.

E Adverbs

We form many adverbs from an adjective + -**ly**.
slow → slowly   calm → calmly

1   We do not leave out -**e** before -**ly**.
safe → safely   strange → strangely
But there are a few exceptions.
due → duly   true → truly
whole → wholly

2   When an adjective ends in a consonant + -**y**, the
-**y** changes to -**ily**.
angry → angrily   happy → happily
An exception is *shy → shyly*.

3   When an adjective ends in a consonant + -**le**, the
-**e** changes to -**y**.
probable → probably   sensible → sensibly

4   When an adjective ends in -**ic**, we add -**ally**.
automatic → automatically /ɔːtə'mætɪkli/
romantic → romantically /rəʊ'mæntɪkli/
But there is one exception.
public → publicly

F The comparison of adjectives

We form the comparative and superlative of short adjectives with -**er** and -**est**. (See Unit 110.)

> old → old**er**, old**est**
> quick → quick**er**, quick**est**

1 If the adjective ends in -**e**, we add -**r** and -**st**.

> late → late**r**, late**st**   fine → fine**r**, fine**st**

2 When an adjective ends in a consonant + -**y**, the -**y** changes to -**ier** or -**iest**.

> heavy → heav**ier**, heav**iest**
> lucky → luck**ier**, luck**iest**

3 Sometimes we double a final consonant. This happens when a one-syllable adjective ends with one vowel and one consonant, e.g. *big, flat*.

> big → big**ger**, big**gest**   flat → flat**ter**, flat**test**

For more details about doubling, see G.

G The doubling of consonants

1 When we add -**ed**, -**ing**, -**er** or -**est** to a word, we sometimes double a final consonant. This happens when a one-syllable word ends with one vowel and one consonant, e.g. *stop, get, thin, sad*.

> stop → stop**ped**   get → get**ting**
> thin → thin**ner**   sad → sad**dest**

2 We do not double -**y**, -**w** or -**x**.

> play → play**ed**   new → new**est**
> fax → fax**ing**

We do not double when there are two consonants.

> ask → ask**ing**   short → short**est**
> rich → rich**er**

And we do not double when there are two vowels.

> seem → seem**ed**   shout → shout**ing**
> fair → fair**est**

3 The rule about doubling is also true for words of more than one syllable (e.g. *permit = per + mit*), but only if the last syllable is stressed.

> per'mit → per'mit**ted**
> pre'fer → pre'fer**ring**

We do not usually double a consonant when the syllable is unstressed.

> 'open → open**ed**   'enter → enter**ing**

An exception is that in British English -**l** is usually doubled, even if the syllable is unstressed.

> travel → travel**led** (US: traveled)

Appendix 3: Punctuation

A Full stop (.), question mark (?) and exclamation mark (!)

A sentence ends with one of these punctuation marks.

Full stop:	*It's cold today.*	*The office was closed.*	*Please be careful.*
Question mark:	*Who's that?*	*Did you see the show?*	*Could you wait, please?*
Exclamation mark:	*Oh, no! I don't believe it!*		

In the US a full stop is called a 'period'.

B Semi-colon (;)

We can use a semi-colon between two separate statements which are linked in meaning.

> *Melanie is a very kind person; she visits David in hospital every day.*

We could also use a full stop here.

C Colon (:)

We can use a colon before an explanation or before a list.

> *Vicky felt nervous: she hated the dark.*
> *There wasn't much in the fridge: a couple of sausages, some butter, half a bottle of milk.*

D Dash (–)

A dash is rather informal. It is sometimes used instead of a colon or a semi-colon.

> *I'm having a great time – there's lots to do here.*
> *Vicky felt nervous – she hated the dark.*

E Comma (,)

We often use a comma when we link two statements with **and**, **but** or **or**.

> *Daniel was tired, and his feet were hurting.*   *It's a really good camera, but I can't afford it.*

Note the two subjects in each sentence: *Daniel... his feet* and *It... I.* When there is only one subject, we do not use a comma.

> *Daniel sat down and took his shoes off.*

We can also use a comma when a sentence has a linking word like **when** or **although**.

> *When the office is busy, Sarah has to work late.*

For commas with relative clauses, see Unit 141.

Sometimes a comma can separate off an adverb or a phrase.

> *Sarah, unfortunately, has to work late.*   *On busy days, Sarah has to work late.*

Here the commas separate off *on busy days* and *unfortunately*.

The rules about commas are not very exact. In general, commas are more likely around longer phrases. With a short phrase there is often no comma.

> *On busy days Sarah has to work late.*   *Sometimes she has to work late.*

It is less usual to separate off something at the end of the sentence.

> *Sarah has to work late when the office is busy.*   *She stayed late to get the work done.*

We do not usually put a comma before **to** expressing purpose.

We also use commas in a list of more than two. The last two are linked by **and**, often without a comma.

> *I went out with Rachel, Vicky, Emma and Matthew.*

F Quotation marks (' ')

We put direct speech in quotation marks.

> Laura said, 'You haven't put those shelves up yet.'   'I haven't had time,' replied Trevor.

We normally use a comma to separate the direct speech from the rest of the sentence.
The comma comes before the quotation mark. Quotation marks are also called 'quotes' or
'inverted commas'.

Double quotation marks are sometimes used.

> Laura said, "You haven't put those shelves up yet."

We can put quotation marks around titles.

> Do you watch that American comedy series called 'Roseanne'?

We often use quotation marks when we mention a word or phrase.

> What does 'punctuation' mean?   Rap music is also called 'hip hop'.

G Hyphen (-)

We sometimes use hyphens in these structures.

> Compound noun: *eating ice-cream*
> Compound expression before a noun: *an oven-ready meal*
> Noun formed from a phrasal verb: *ready for take-off*
> Noun + -ing form: *interested in rock-climbing*
> Before the last word of a compound number: *a hundred and twenty-six people*
> After some prefixes: *anti-aircraft guns*

The rules about hyphens are not very exact. For example, you may see a compound noun written as
phonecard, **phone-card** or **phone card**. Hyphens are not very frequent in British English, and they are used
even less in American English. If you are unsure, it is usually safer to write two separate words.

H Apostrophe (')

Look at these examples.

> Today *we're going for a drive in the country.*   *Everyone is looking at Nick's car.*

We use an apostrophe (') in short forms, when there is a missing letter, e.g. **we're** (= we are). See Unit 32. We
also use an apostrophe with **s** to form the possessive of a noun, e.g. **Nick's car**. See Unit 93.

I Capital letters

There are two capital letters (big letters) in this sentence.

> The boss said **I** could leave early.

We use a capital letter at the beginning of a sentence and for the word **I**.

We also use a capital letter to begin the names of people, places, companies, etc.

> *Mark and Sarah*   *New Orleans*   *the High Street*   *Somerset House*   *General Motors*

This includes the names of books, films, magazines, etc. All the important words start with a capital letter.

> *The Spy Who Loved Me*   *Four Weddings and a Funeral*   *Newsweek*

We also use a capital letter for days of the week, months of the year, holidays and festivals,
historical times, nationalities and most abbreviations.

> *Monday*   *August*   *Easter*   *the New Year*   *the Industrial Revolution*
> *some Italian wine*   *the UN* (= the United Nations)

Appendix 4: Pronunciation

A Key to phonetic symbols

VOWELS					CONSONANTS						
iː	tea	ʌ	cup		p	put	f	first	h	house
i	happy	ɜː	bird		b	best	v	van	m	must
ɪ	sit	ə	away		t	tell	θ	three	n	next
e	ten	eɪ	pay		d	day	ð	this	ŋ	song
æ	sad	əʊ	so		k	cat	s	sell	l	love
ɑː	car	aɪ	cry		g	good	z	zoo	r	rest
ɒ	dog	aʊ	now		tʃ	cheese	ʃ	ship	j	you
ɔː	ball	ɔɪ	boy		dʒ	just	ʒ	pleasure	w	will
ʊ	book	ɪə	dear							
u	actual	eə	chair							
uː	fool	ʊə	sure							

B Stress

In books about English, the symbol ' is used before a stressed syllable, the part of the word which is spoken with greater force.

    midnight /ˈmɪdnaɪt/   *about* /əˈbaʊt/   *exercise* /ˈeksəsaɪz/   *belonging* /bɪˈlɒŋɪŋ/

Here the syllables **mid**, **bout**, **ex** and **long** are stressed. It is important to get the stress on the right part of the word. Stressing a word incorrectly can make it difficult to understand.

Now look at these two sentences.

    We want to **protest** /prəˈtest/ *against experiments on live animals.*
    We want to make a **protest** /ˈprəʊtest/ *against experiments on live animals.*

Protest as a verb is stressed on the second syllable. As a noun it is stressed on the first syllable. There are a number of words like this, e.g. **conflict**, **contrast**, **export**, **import**, **increase**, **insult**, **produce**, **progress**, **protest**, **record**, **suspect**, **transfer**, **transport**. Sometimes a change of stress means a change of vowel sound.

    Verbs: *produce* /prəˈdjuːs/, *progress* /prəˈgres/, *record* /rɪˈkɔːd/
    Nouns: *produce* /ˈprɒdjuːs/, *progress* /ˈprəʊgres/, *record* /ˈrekɔːd/

We also use stress to show which are the important words in a sentence.

    'Claire's got a 'lovely 'flat. She 'bought it last 'year. It's 'right in the 'centre of 'town.

Here the important words are **Claire**, **lovely**, **flat** and so on. We do not usually stress 'grammatical words' like **a**, **she**, **the** and **of**.

C Intonation

The voice usually falls or rises on the most important word in the sentence. This word is usually at or near the end of the sentence.

    Claire's got a lovely ↘ flat.

Here the voice falls when saying **flat**, which is the key word.

The symbol ↘ is used for a falling intonation and ↗ for a rising intonation.

    Everything is more or less ↘ ready. (a statement)
    Everything is more or less ↗ ready? (a question)

The voice usually goes down in a statement and up in a yes/no question. In general, a fall means that what we say is complete. A rise means that what we say is incomplete, or it needs an answer. See also Unit 42 for intonation in question tags.

The voice often rises in the first part of a sentence and falls at the end.

If you don't ↗ mind, I ought to be ↘ going.

There is always a fall or rise on the important part of the message. Which word is the key word depends on the meaning. Compare these examples.

My friend is a bit upset. She's just failed her ↘ exam.
I passed my exam last summer, but my friend has just ↘ failed hers.
Lots of people have failed their exams. My ↘ friend has just failed.

D Voicing

Sounds can be voiced or voiceless. Voiced sounds are like those you make when you sing. All the vowels are voiced and some of the consonants. Voiceless sounds are like those you make when you whisper. Some of the consonants are voiceless. Compare these sounds.

VOICED		VOICELESS	
/b/	*bill*	/p/	*pill*
/d/	*down*	/t/	*town*
/g/	*gold*	/k/	*cold*
/z/	*prize*	/s/	*price*

The voiceless sounds are /p/, /t/, /k/, /f/, /θ/, /s/, /ʃ/, /tʃ/ and /h/.

E The -s ending

We sometimes add the ending **-s** or **-es** to a word. For example we can do this to form the plural or the possessive of a noun.

some chairs   the bushes   Mark's car   the woman's name

We can also add **-s** or **-es** to a verb.

It looks nice and sunny.   Tom watches the football on Saturday afternoons.

The pronunciation of **-s/-es** depends on the sound which is before it. The ending is pronounced /s/ after a voiceless sound, /z/ after a voiced sound, and /ɪz/ after a sibilant sound.

Voiceless + /s/	*shops* /ps/	*gets* /ts/	*takes* /ks/
Voiced + /z/	*jobs* /bz/	*hides* /dz/	*bags* /gz/
	Laura's /əz/	*days* /eɪz/	*knows* /əʊz/
Sibilant + /ɪz/	*buses* /sɪz/	*loses* /zɪz/	*crashes* /ʃɪz/

For voiced and voiceless sounds see D. The sibilant sounds are /s/, /z/, /ʃ/, /ʒ/, /tʃ/ and /dʒ/.

F The -ed ending

We add **-ed** or **-d** to a regular verb to form the past tense or past participle.

*We all **walked** home.   They've **closed** the gates.*

The pronunciation of **-ed** depends on the sound coming before it. The ending is pronounced /t/ after a voiceless sound, /d/ after a voiced sound, and /ɪd/ after /t/ or /d/.

Voiceless + /t/	*hoped* /pt/	*worked* /kt/	*increased* /st/
Voiced + /d/	*robbed* /bd/	*begged* /gd/	*raised* /zd/
	played /eɪd/	*allowed* /aʊd/	*cared* /eəd/
/t/ or /d/ + /ɪd/	*wanted* /tɪd/	*landed* /dɪd/	

For voiced and voiceless sounds see D.

G Weak forms

We are using a weak form when we pronounce **is** as /s/ rather than /ɪz/, or we pronounce **from** as /frəm/ rather than /frɒm/. Normally a word like **is** or **from** is not stressed, and so we can use a weak form. (For written short forms see Unit 32.)

	STRONG FORM	WEAK FORM			STRONG FORM	WEAK FORM
a	/eɪ/	/ə/		*is*	/ɪz/	/z/ or /s/
am	/æm/	/əm/ or /m/		*me*	/miː/	/mi/
an	/æn/	/ən/		*must*	/mʌst/	/məst/ or /məs/
and	/ænd/	/ənd/, /ən/ or /n/		*of*	/ɒv/	/əv/ or /v/
are	/ɑː(r)/	/ə(r)/		*shall*	/ʃæl/	/ʃəl/ or /ʃl/
as	/æz/	/əz/		*she*	/ʃiː/	/ʃi/
at	/æt/	/ət/		*should*	/ʃʊd/	/ʃəd/
be	/biː/	/bi/		*some*	/sʌm/	/səm/ or /sm/
been	/biːn/	/bɪn/		*than*	/ðæn/	/ðən/
can	/kæn/	/kən/		*that*	/ðæt/	/ðət/
could	/kʊd/	/kəd/		*the*	/ðiː/	/ði/ or /ðə/
do	/duː/	/du/ or /də/		*them*	/ðem/	/ðəm/ or /əm/
for	/fɔː(r)/	/fə(r)/		*there*	/ðeə(r)/	/ðə(r)/
from	/frɒm/	/frəm/		*to*	/tuː/	/tu/ or /tə/
had	/hæd/	/həd/, /əd/ or /d/		*was*	/wɒz/	/wəz/
has	/hæz/	/həz/, /əz/ or /z/		*we*	/wiː/	/wi/
have	/hæv/	/həv/, /əv/ or /v/		*were*	/wɜː(r)/	/wə(r)/
he	/hiː/	/hi/ or /i/		*will*	/wɪl/	/l/
her	/hɜː(r)/	/hə(r)/ or /ə(r)/		*would*	/wʊd/	/wəd/, /əd/ or /d/
him	/hɪm/	/ɪm/		*you*	/juː/	/ju/
his	/hɪz/	/ɪz/		*your*	/jɔː(r)/	/jə(r)/

Notes on weak forms

1 (r) means that an -r sound is pronounced before a vowel. In the phrase **for a minute**, the words **for a** are pronounced /fərə/.

2 **A, an** and **the** are normally spoken in their weak form.

3 **Some** does not have a weak form when it means 'some but not all'. See Unit 96A.

4 **That** normally has a weak form when it is a linking word, e.g. *I knew **that** /ðət/ it was true.* It does not have a weak form when it means something at a distance from the speaker, e.g. *Look at **that** /ðæt/ car.* (See Unit 91.)

5 **There** normally has a weak form in a sentence like ***There's** /ðəz/ a bookshop in town.* (See Unit 99.) It does not have a weak form when it means 'in that place', e.g. *The bookshop is over **there** /ðeə/.*

6 A verb does not have a weak form in a short answer with **yes**.
   *Are you tired? ~ Yes, **I am** /æm/.*

Appendix 5: American English

The differences between British and American English are mainly matters of pronunciation and vocabulary. There are also a few spelling differences such as British **centre** and **colour** and American **center** and **color**. There are some grammatical differences. Although they are not very great, those points that are most relevant to learners of English are explained here.

A Seem, look, etc.

Compare these examples.

BRITISH

In British English there can be a noun (e.g. **pilot**) after **appear, feel, look, seem** and **sound**.
> She **seemed (to be)** a good pilot.

> It **looks (to be)** a lovely evening.

> I **felt** a fool.

AMERICAN

Americans do not say *She seemed a good pilot.* They use **to be** or **like** after these verbs.
> She **seemed to be** a good pilot.
> OR She **seemed like** a good pilot.
> It **looks to be** a lovely evening.
> OR It **looks like** a lovely evening.
> I **felt like** a fool.

B Present Perfect and Past Simple (Units 11–15)

The British use the Present Perfect for recent actions, and especially with **just, already** and **yet**.
> Bob **has washed** the dishes, look.

> We've already **eaten** our lunch.

> I've just **seen** Elaine.

> **Have** you **corrected** your work yet?

The British normally use the Present Perfect with **ever** and **never**, not the Past Simple.

> **Have** you ever **played** cricket?

> The child **has** never **seen** snow before.

Americans can use either the Present Perfect or the Past Simple in these sentences.
> Bob **has washed** the dishes, look.
> OR Bob **washed** the dishes, look.
> We've already **eaten** our lunch.
> OR We already **ate** our lunch.
> I've just **seen** Elaine.
> OR I just **saw** Elaine.
> **Have** you **corrected** your work yet?
> OR **Did** you **correct** your work yet?
Americans normally use the Past Simple with **ever** and **never,** but the Present Perfect is possible.
> **Did** you ever **play** baseball?
> OR **Have** you ever **played** baseball?
> The child never **saw** snow before.
> OR The child **has** never **seen** snow before.

C Shall (Unit 23.4)

The British use **will** for the future, but they can also use **shall** in the first person.
> I **will**/I **shall** be here tomorrow.
> We **will**/We **shall** contact you.

The British use **shall** to make an offer.
> **Shall** I make the coffee?

The British can use **Shall we ...?** for a suggestion.
> **Shall** we go for a walk?

Americans do not normally use **shall** for the future.
> I **will** be here tomorrow.
> We **will** contact you.

Americans normally use **should.**
> **Should** I make the coffee?

Americans do not normally use **shall** in suggestions.
> **How about** a walk?
> **Would you like** to take a walk?

D Got and gotten

Both **have** and **have got** are used in Britain and in the US.
*He **has** a lot of money./He's **got** a lot of money.* (= He is rich.)

The British do not use **gotten**. *He's **made** a lot of money from his business activities.* *Your driving has **got** better.*	In the US, **have gotten** expresses an action. *He's **gotten/made** a lot of money from his business activities.* Americans also use **gotten** meaning 'become'. *Your driving has **gotten** better.*

E Negatives and questions with **have** (Unit 31)

In Britain there are two different structures. *I **haven't** (**got**) enough time.* OR *I **don't have** enough time.* **Has** *Carol **got** a computer?* OR ***Does** Carol **have** a computer?*	Americans normally use the auxiliary **do**. *I **don't have** enough time.* ***Does** Carol **have** a computer?*

In the past tense, **did** is usual in both countries.
*We **didn't have** tickets.*

F Emphatic **do** (Unit 33.3)

The British can use **do** with an imperative for emphasis. *Have a piece of cake.* OR ***Do** have a piece of cake.*	**Do** with an imperative is less common in the US. *Have a piece of cake.*

G Do for an action

The British can use **do** to refer to an action already mentioned. *I don't practise as often as I should (**do**).* *You'd better take your pill. ~ I already have (**done**).*	Americans do not use **do** in this way. *I don't practice as often as I should.* *You'd better take your pill. ~ **I** already have.*

H Question tags (Unit 42)

Both the British and the Americans can use question tags when talking about facts.

*Blackpool is in Lancashire, **isn't it**?*	*Las Vegas is in Nevada, **isn't it**?*

But in general Americans use tags much less often than the British. They do not use tags to persuade or to argue. A sentence like *You aren't listening to me, are you?* is British but not American. But Americans often use **right?** and **OK?** as tags.

*I'll bring the luggage in, **shall I**?*	*I'll bring the baggage in, **OK**?*

I Can't and **must not** (Unit 46.3)

The British use **can't** to say that something is impossible.

> *I rang, but there's no reply. They **can't** be at home.*

Americans can also use **must not** to say that something is impossible.

> *I called, but there's no reply. They **can't** be home./They **must not** be home.*

J Needn't and **don't need to** (Unit 48)

The British can use either form.

> *You **needn't** see the inspector.*
> OR *You **don't need** to see the inspector.*

Americans do not normally use **needn't**.

> *You **don't need** to see the inspector.*

K Group nouns (Unit 81.2)

In Britain a group noun can usually take either a singular or a plural verb.

> *The crowd **was/were** getting restless.*
> *Sweden **plays/play** Germany tomorrow.*

In the US a group noun takes a singular verb.

> *The crowd **was** getting restless.*
> *Sweden **plays** Germany tomorrow.*

L The (Unit 86.3 and 87.1)

The British use **the** with a musical instrument.
> *I can play **the** piano.*

The British say **in hospital**.
> *My sister is still **in hospital**.*

Americans can leave out **the**.
> *I can play piano/play **the** piano.*

Americans say **in the hospital**.
> *My sister is still **in the hospital**.*

M Numbers

The British use **and** between **hundred** and the rest of the number.

> *six hundred **and** twenty*

Americans can leave out **and**.

> *six hundred twenty*
> OR *six hundred **and** twenty*

N Dates

There are a number of different ways of writing and saying dates, but these are the most common.

BRITISH

> *23 June*
> *'the twenty-third of June'*
> *'June the twenty-third'*

AMERICAN

> *June 23*
> *'June twenty-third'*

The British write 23.6.98, and Americans write 6.23.98.

O You and **one** (Unit 98.3)

The British use **you** for people in general, including the speaker. In more formal English they can use **one**.

> ***You/One** can't be too careful.*

Americans use **you** for people in general. **One** is unusual.

> ***You** can't be too careful.*

P Somewhere and someplace (Unit 103)

In informal American English, **everyplace**, **someplace**, **anyplace** and **no place** can be used as well as **everywhere**, **somewhere**, etc.

*Let's find **somewhere** to eat.*	*Let's find **somewhere/someplace** to eat.*

Q Adjectives and adverbs (Unit 108)

In informal speech we can sometimes use an adjective form instead of an adverb. Americans do this more than the British.

*We had some **really** nice weather.*	*We had some **really** nice/some **real** nice weather.*
*It **certainly** doesn't make things any easier.*	*It **certainly/sure** doesn't make things any easier.*

R Prepositions (Units 118–126)

There are some differences in prepositions.

BRITISH	AMERICAN
round/around *the village*	**around** *the village*
towards/toward *the west*	**toward** *the west*
looking **out of** *the window*	*looking* **out** *the window/***out of** *the window*
outside *the town*	**outside** *the town/***outside of** *the town*

In American English there is a special use of **through** as a preposition of time.

*He'll be on the road **from** Tuesday **to/till** Friday.* *They will stay in Brighton **until** the end of April.*	*He'll be on the road (**from**) Tuesday **through** Friday.* *They will stay in Miami **through** April.*

Note the prepositions after **different**.

BRITISH	AMERICAN
*This cup is different **from/to** the others.*	*This cup is different **from/than** the others.*

Compare these expressions.

BRITISH	AMERICAN
in *Bond Street*	**on** *Fifth Avenue*
at *the weekend,* **at** *weekends*	**on** *the weekend,* **on** *weekends*
stay **at** *home*	*stay home*
a player **in** *the team*	*a player* **on** *the team*
ten minutes **past** *four*	*ten minutes* **past/after** *four*
twenty **to** *seven*	*twenty* **to/of** *seven*
write **to** *me*	*write* **me***/write* **to** *me*
talk **to** *someone*	*talk* **to/with** *someone*
meet someone	*meet* **with** *someone*

S In case (Unit 148.4)

In case can have different meanings.

BRITISH	AMERICAN
Take an umbrella **in case** it rains. (= because it may rain)	**In case** you're sick, you should call the office. (= if you're sick)

T Go and …

Americans can leave out **and** from this structure.

I'll go **and** buy the tickets.	I'll go buy/I'll go **and** buy the tickets.

U The subjunctive

We can use expressions like **I suggest that** … and **It's important that** … to talk about what we want to happen. Look at these examples.

BRITISH	AMERICAN
Tim's parents have suggested that he **gets** a job/that he **should** get a job. It's important that everything **goes**/everything **should** go according to plan.	Tim's parents have suggested that he **get** a job. It's important that everything **go** according to plan.
The British normally use the Present Simple or **should**. (They use the subjunctive only in formal English.)	Americans normally use a form called the 'subjunctive', e.g. **get**, **go**.

V Irregular verbs

In the past tense some verbs can have either an irregular -t ending or the regular -ed ending. These verbs are **burn**, **learn**, **smell**, **spell**, **spill** and **spoil**.

The British prefer the -t ending, although -ed is also possible. They **burnt/burned** the old sofa. You've **spelt/spelled** this word wrong.	Americans normally use the -ed ending. They **burned** the old sofa. You've **spelled** this word wrong.

But we say e.g. *a slice of **burnt** toast* in both British and American English.

In Britain the verbs **dream**, **lean** and **leap** can be regular, or they can have a -t ending.

I **dreamt/dreamed** about you.	I **dreamed** about you.

These three forms ending in -t have the vowel sound /e/. For example, **dreamt** is pronounced /dremt/, and **dreamed** is pronounced /driːmd/.

The verb **dive** is regular in Britain but can be irregular in the US.

Craig **dived** into the water.	Craig **dived/dove** into the water.

Dived is pronounced /daɪvd/, and **dove** is pronounced /dəʊv/.

Appendix 6: Irregular verbs

VERB	PAST TENSE	PAST/PASSIVE PARTICIPLE
arise	arose	arisen
be	was, were	been
bear	bore	borne
beat	beat	beaten
become	became	become
begin	began	begun
bend	bent	bent
bet	bet	bet
		betted
bind	bound	bound
bite	bit	bitten
		bit
bleed	bled	bled
blow	blew	blown
break	broke	broken
breed	bred	bred
bring	brought	brought
broadcast	broadcast	broadcast
build	built	built
burn	burnt	burnt
	burned	burned
burst	burst	burst
buy	bought	bought
catch	caught	caught
choose	chose	chosen
come	came	come
cost	cost	cost
creep	crept	crept
cut	cut	cut
deal /diːl/	dealt /delt/	dealt /delt/
dig	dug	dug
dive	dived	dived
	dove (US)	
do	did	done
draw	drew	drawn
dream /driːm/	dreamt /dremt/	dreamt /dremt/
	dreamed	dreamed
drink	drank	drunk
drive	drove	driven
eat /iːt/	ate /et/	eaten /ˈiːtn/
fall	fell	fallen
feed	fed	fed
feel	felt	felt
fight	fought	fought

VERB	PAST TENSE	PAST/PASSIVE PARTICIPLE
find	found	found
flee	fled	fled
fly	flew	flown
forbid	forbad(e) /fəˈbæd/	forbidden
forget	forgot	forgotten
forgive	forgave	forgiven
freeze	froze	frozen
get	got	got
		gotten (US)
give	gave	given
go	went	gone
grind	ground	ground
grow	grew	grown
hang	hung	hung
have	had	had
hear /hɪə/	heard /hɜːd/	heard /hɜːd/
hide	hid	hidden
hit	hit	hit
hold	held	held
hurt	hurt	hurt
keep	kept	kept
kneel	knelt	knelt
know	knew	known
lay	laid	laid
lead	led	led
lean /liːn/	leant /lent/	leant /lent/
	leaned	leaned
leap /liːp/	leapt /lept/	leapt /lept/
	leaped	leaped
learn	learnt	learnt
	learned	learned
leave	left	left
lend	lent	lent
let	let	let
lie	lay	lain
light	lit	lit
	lighted	lighted
lose	lost	lost
make	made	made
mean /miːn/	meant /ment/	meant /ment/
meet	met	met
mow	mowed	mown
		mowed

VERB	PAST TENSE	PAST/PASSIVE PARTICIPLE	VERB	PAST TENSE	PAST/PASSIVE PARTICIPLE
pay	paid	paid	**stand**	stood	stood
put	put	put	**steal**	stole	stolen
read /riːd/	read /red/	read /red/	**stick**	stuck	stuck
ride	rode	ridden	**sting**	stung	stung
ring	rang	rung	**stink**	stank	stunk
rise	rose	risen		stunk	
run	ran	run	**stride**	strode	stridden
say /seɪ/	said /sed/	said /sed/	**strike**	struck	struck
see	saw	seen	**swear**	swore	sworn
seek	sought	sought	**sweep**	swept	swept
sell	sold	sold	**swim**	swam	swum
send	sent	sent	**swing**	swung	swung
set	set	set	**take**	took	taken
sew	sewed	sewn	**teach**	taught	taught
		sewed	**tear**	tore	torn
shake	shook	shaken	**tell**	told	told
shine	shone	shone	**think**	thought	thought
shoot	shot	shot	**throw**	threw	thrown
show	showed	shown	**tread**	trod	trodden
shrink	shrank	shrunk	**understand**	understood	understood
	shrunk		**wake**	woke	woken
shut	shut	shut		waked	waked
sing	sang	sung	**wear**	wore	worn
sink	sank	sunk	**weave**	wove	woven
sit	sat	sat		weaved	weaved
sleep	slept	slept	**weep**	wept	wept
slide	slid	slid	**win**	won	won
smell	smelt	smelt	**wind**	wound	wound
	smelled	smelled	**write**	wrote	written
speak	spoke	spoken			
speed	sped	sped			
	speeded	speeded			
spell	spelt	spelt			
	spelled	spelled			
spend	spent	spent			
spill	spilt	spilt			
	spilled	spilled			
spin	spun	spun			
spit	spat	spat			
split	split	split			
spoil	spoilt	spoilt			
	spoiled	spoiled			
spread	spread	spread			
spring	sprang	sprung			

The verbs in this list are also irregular when they have a prefix, e.g. **overtake – overtook – overtaken, foretell – foretold – foretold.**

A few verbs have irregular Present Simple forms:

VERB	PRESENT SIMPLE
be	I **am**; you/we/they **are**; he/she/it **is**
do	he/she/it **does** /dʌz/
go	he/she/it **goes** /gəʊz/
have	he/she/it **has**
say	he/she/it **says** /sez/

For **burnt/burned, dreamt/dreamed,** etc. in British and American English see page 382. For **gotten** see page 378.

Key to the exercises

Unit 1

A
1 determiner	8 preposition
2 verb	9 linking word
3 pronoun	10 adverb
4 adverb	11 determiner
5 pronoun	12 adjective
6 verb	13 linking word
7 adjective	14 noun

B
VERB: is, loves
NOUN: Claire, café
ADJECTIVE: wonderful, old, romantic
ADVERB: madly, unfortunately, rather
PREPOSITION: of, for, at
DETERMINER: a, their, some
PRONOUN: He, her, they
LINKING WORD: and, but, so

C
1 verb	6 verb
2 noun	7 verb
3 adjective	8 noun
4 verb	9 adjective
5 noun	10 verb

Unit 2

A
1 subject	4 adverbial
2 verb	5 object
3 complement	6 complement

B 1 e) 2 a) 3 c) 4 d)

C
1 Tom likes football.
2 David had an accident.
3 We moved the piano.
4 Harriet is a tall woman.
5 Everyone sat on the floor.
6 Mike's friends gave him some help.

D
1 also, with several young people
2 first, in 1994
3 naturally, without help
4 fortunately, from the National Lottery

Unit 3

A
1 David gave Melanie a sweater.
2 Laura gave Trevor a scarf.
3 Emma gave Matthew a tennis racket.
4 Henry gave Claire a necklace.

B
1 sold her bike to her sister.
2 told the joke to all his friends.
3 gave her neighbour some help.
4 wrote her teacher a letter.

C 1 for 2 to 3 to 4 for 5 for 6 to

D
1 them to the bottle bank.
2 me a job.
3 them to the police.
4 you my umbrella.

Unit 4

A
1 They're/They are playing basketball.
2 She's/She is taking a photo.
3 He's/He is painting a picture.
4 They're/They are carrying a parcel.

B
1 are trying	5 We aren't spending
2 are you finding	6 It isn't taking
3 is helping	7 are you waiting
4 We're/We are getting	8 I'm/I am correcting

C
1 it's/it is raining.
2 I'm/I am working.
3 you're/you are sitting on my coat.
4 I'm/I am writing an important letter.
5 I'm/I am getting/feeling better.

Unit 5

A
1 a feeling	5 a thought
2 a repeated action	6 a feeling
3 a fact	7 a repeated action
4 a fact	8 a thought

B
1 doesn't speak	6 don't look
2 walk	7 doesn't work
3 needs	8 don't like
4 love	9 wins
5 doesn't eat	10 don't own

C
1 I go	8 does it cost
2 comes	9 I don't know
3 we travel	10 that doesn't matter
4 don't you come	11 I don't want
5 doesn't make	12 Does that annoy
6 do you take	13 it doesn't annoy
7 I love	14 find

Unit 6

A
1 He's/He is talking	8 You know
2 I think	9 I give
3 they're/they are discussing	10 she gives
4 Are you looking	11 She lives
5 Do you know	12 It saves
6 works	13 I agree
7 She doesn't work	14 I'm/I am wasting

B
1 It's/It is snowing, It's/It is coming
2 I start, I'm/I am starting
3 I'm/I am going, I drive
4 rises, we're/we are travelling
5 I'm/I am writing, I promise
6 I want, I'm/I am saving

C 1 she always takes
    2 She's/She is always missing
    3 do you always go
    4 They're/They are always arguing.

Unit 7

A 1 state   4 action
    2 action   5 state
    3 state

B 1 I think   5 you're having
    2 I have   6 you're thinking
    3 it didn't fit   7 I come
    4 I see   8 It weighed

C 1 are being   4 're/are
    2 's/is   5 's being/is being
    3 're being/are being

D 1 And I've still got a chance to win.
    2 It's too expensive to buy.
    3 It uses so much petrol.
    4 I think it's going to be perfect for me.
    5 I've never wanted to change it.

Unit 8

A 1 She swam in the sea.
    2 She had a picnic.
    3 She played volleyball.
    4 She went out dancing.

B 1 were   7 arrived
    2 started   8 fought
    3 saw   9 brought
    4 called   10 entered
    5 tried   11 found
    6 was

C 1 We didn't try   5 I didn't like
    2 did you see   6 did Sarah enjoy
    3 I didn't know   7 I didn't want
    4 did you go

Unit 9

A 1 were watching television
    2 were dancing in the street
    3 was driving his taxi
    4 was writing an essay

B 1 were you doing   4 I was going
    2 I was taking   5 You weren't looking
    3 She was coming   6 you were going

C 1 I was making phone calls all evening.
    2 I was waiting in the rain for half an hour.
    3 I was making sandwiches all afternoon.
    4 I was sitting in a traffic jam for two hours.
    5 My neighbour was playing loud music all night.

Unit 10

A 1 He sat down on a chair while I was painting it.
    2 As he was running for a bus, he collided with a lamppost.
    3 His hair caught fire when he was cooking chips.
    4 When he was holding a beautiful vase, he suddenly dropped it.
    5 He was sitting in the garden when a wasp stung him on the nose.

B 1 We lost   6 were playing
    2 it came   7 I was working
    3 was coming   8 I lost
    4 went   9 I got
    5 fell   10 did

C 1 The train was waiting when we arrived at the station.
    2 I was reading a library book when I found a £10 note in it.
    3 Sarah had an electric shock when she touched the wire.
    4 When the doors opened, the crowd rushed in.
    5 When the campers woke, they saw that the sun was shining.

Unit 11

A 1 She's/She has repaired it.
    2 I've/I have opened the window.
    3 They've/They have arrived.
    4 He's/He has moved it.
    5 We've/We have watched all these.

B 1 He's/He has broken his leg.
    2 They've/They have built a house.
    3 They've/They have seen a film.
    4 She's/She has caught a fish.

C 1 I haven't done   8 I've/I have looked
    2 hasn't made   9 have you done
    3 You haven't put   10 I've/I have painted
    4 I've/I have hurt   11 I've/I have cleaned
    5 you've/you have had   12 We've/We have made
    6 have you put   13 has that brush gone
    7 It's/It has disappeared   14 you've/you have left

Unit 12

A 1 just tidied it.
    2 He's/He has just made some/it.
    3 I've/I have just eaten it.
    4 she's/she has just checked them.
    5 I've/I have just rung her.

B 1 I haven't started it yet.
    2 I've/I have just seen Andrew
    3 he's/he has already done
    4 I haven't finished my plan yet.
    5 You've/You have already begun

6 We've/We have already spent
7 I haven't done any real work yet
8 I've/I have just realized
9 I've/I have just decided

C 1 He hasn't had any fun for a long time.
2 He's/He has had a cold for a week.
3 He hasn't seen his friends for ages.
4 He hasn't done any sport since last year.
5 He's/He has been busy with his studies for months.

D 1 rung her since   4 had one since
2 seen them for   5 played (it) since
3 watched one for

Unit 13

A 1 been 2 been 3 gone

B 1 Have you ever been to San Francisco?
No, I've never been to San Francisco
I've been to Los Angeles.
2 Have you ever played basketball?
No, I've never played basketball
I've played volleyball.
3 Have you ever seen/read (the play) 'Hamlet'?
No, I've never read/seen 'Hamlet'
I've read/seen 'Macbeth'.

C 1 the second time I've lost my bank card.
2 This is the third time the washing-machine has broken down.
3 This is the first time I've been in/to England.
4 This is the second time I've stayed in this hotel.
5 This is (about) the fifth time I've missed the bus.

D 1 I haven't seen her today.
2 we haven't been there this weekend.
3 we haven't had one this term.
4 has rung this evening.

Unit 14

A 1 have arrived   7 We planted
2 repaired   8 have gone
3 I've/I have lost   9 has turned
4 has started   10 I phoned
5 ran   11 I've/I have made
6 earned   12 broke

B 1 The train drivers have gone on strike. They stopped work(ing) at twelve o'clock.
2 The Queen has arrived in Toronto. She flew there in an RAF aircraft.
3 Two men have escaped from Parkhurst Prison. They got away during the night.
4 The actor Howard Bates has died in a car accident. His car crashed into a wall.
5 Linda Jones has won the women's marathon. She ran it in 2 hours 27 minutes.

C 1 haven't taken a photo since
2 weeks since I last saw
3 was the last time we played
4 haven't eaten anything for

Unit 15

A 1 has stood   4 've/have lived
2 was   5 've/have known
3 stayed   6 were

B 1 b) 2 b) 3 a)

C 1 this, last   3 last, this
2 today, yesterday   4 this, yesterday

D 1 What's/What has happened   7 You knew
2 He's/He has had   8 you didn't tell
3 He fell   9 I didn't see
4 broke   10 I haven't seen
5 did it happen   11 He's/He has had
6 told   12 He did

Unit 16

A 1 have you been doing
2 She's/She has been helping
3 have you been studying
4 I've/I have been trying
5 it's/it has been getting

B 1 they've/they have been arguing
2 he's/he has been cooking
3 he's/he has been driving
4 He's/He has been waiting

C 1 Matthew has been swimming for an hour.
2 My friends have been travelling (around the world) for three months.
3 Mark has been working for ten hours.
4 Melanie and Rita have been talking for forty minutes.
5 How long have you been reading the/that/your book?

Unit 17

A 1 's/has left, He's/He has been cleaning, he's/he has finished
2 I've/I have been working, You've/You have done
3 I've/I have heard, have you been doing, We've/We have done

B 1 How many miles have you walked?
2 How long have they/the workmen been digging up the road?
3 How many photos have you taken?
4 How long has it been raining?

C 1 I've/I have been clearing
2 I've/I have found
3 You've/You have been sitting

4 I've/I have been watching
5 You've/You have been
6 I've/I have had
7 They've/They have been
8 I've/I have never had

Unit 18

A 1 b) 2 a) 3 a) 4 b)

B 1 The train had just gone.
2 The rain had stopped.
3 I'd/I had forgotten my ticket.
4 They'd/They had stolen it a week before.
5 I hadn't seen her for ages.
6 I'd/I had just cleaned it.
7 I'd/I had already eaten my sandwiches.

C 1 had left   6 had told
2 've/have finished   7 'd had/had had
3 've/have eaten   8 's/has started
4 'd/had ordered   9 've/have turned
5 've/have made   10 'd/had made

Unit 19

A 1 a) 2 a) 3 b) 4 a)

B 1 When Nick had saved enough money, he
bought a motor bike.
2 Mark put all the dishes away when he'd/he
had dried them.
3 When I'd/I had looked both ways, I pulled
out into the road.
4 The golfers went into the clubhouse when
they'd/they had played the last hole.

C 1 had decided   11 drove
2 We were waiting   12 I met
3 I realized   13 We had
4 I'd/I had forgotten   14 I'd/I had said
5 It was   15 I ran
6 I hurried   16 I got
7 rang   17 were sitting
8 They were working   18 they saw
9 heard   19 started
10 They found

Unit 20

A 1 I'd/I had been working
2 I hadn't been looking
3 she'd/she had been dealing
4 I'd/I had been waiting
5 I'd/I had been reading

B 1 She'd/She had been crying.
2 He'd/He had been driving too fast.
3 They'd/They had been playing with matches.
4 He'd/He had been standing under a tree.

C 1 had been watching
2 'd/had been playing, hadn't won
3 'd/had been walking, 'd/had walked
4 'd/had stopped, was smoking
5 has been aching
6 was lying, 'd/had bought, 'd/had been reading

Unit 21

A 1 She uses it
2 She's/She has lost it
3 We're/We are getting them
4 She's/She is enjoying it
5 I hate it
6 I've/I have checked them
7 They play it
8 You haven't watered them

B 1 I haven't seen you for months.
2 I'm/I am waiting for a (phone) call.
3 I like your (new) jacket.
4 It's/It has been snowing since yesterday.

C 1 a) 2 b) 3 a) 4 b) 5 a) 6 b)

D 1 I've/I have been working
2 she went
3 You've/You have been writing
4 They moved
5 he stopped, I was waiting

E 1 you know   9 I don't often drive
2 David told   10 I don't like
3 haven't been   11 I ride
4 I started   12 bought
5 have you sold   13 was working
6 I've been learning 14 I'd been doing
7 had   15 I'd earned
8 I've had

F 1 I'm/I am speaking
2 knows
3 had heard
4 he'd/he had been taking OR he's/he has been
taking
5 he's/he has answered
6 he arrived
7 were waiting
8 has been reading

Unit 22

A 1 I'll be leaving here at the end of the month.
2 Luckily they'll find a flat for me.
3 The training programme finishes next
summer.
4 They'll decide about that next year.

B 1 future   4 future
2 future   5 present
3 future

C 1 a) 2 a) 3 b) 4 b) 5 a)

Unit 23

A   1 future   4 decision
      2 decision   5 future
      3 future

B   1 I'll answer it/the phone.
      2 I'll have (the) chicken (, please).
      3 I'll carry the/your bag (for you).
      4 I'll post it/the letter (for you),

C   1 Tom will watch the match.
      2 Harriet's party will be fun.
      3 Trevor won't put up the shelves.
      4 Laura will be annoyed.
      5 Andrew will study all weekend.
      6 Rachel won't do any work.

D   1 will   4 will
      2 Shall   5 will
      3 will   6 Shall

Unit 24

A   1 He's/He is going to light the firework.
      2 She's/She is going to hit the ball.
      3 They're/They are going to catch a bus.
      4 She's/She is going to answer the phone.

B   1 I'm/I am going to lend
      2 He's/He is going to take
      3 It's/It is going to be
      4 is he going to keep
      5 are we going to get
      6 He's/He is going to have
      7 We're/We are going to get
      8 it isn't going to get

C   1 I'm/I am going to get wet.
      2 I'm/I am going to be sick.
      3 I'm/I am going to lose.
      4 It's/It is going to crash!
      5 It isn't going to stop.

Unit 25

A   1 's/is going to read
      2 'll have
      3 'll video
      4 are you going to buy

B   1 It's/It is going to attack us/me.
      2 aliens will land on the earth in the next ten years.
      3 she's/she is going to get married.
      4 I'll invite her for a meal.

C   1 We're/We are going to build
      2 will be (or is going to be)
      3 will like (or are going to like)
      4 will be (or are going to be)
      5 We aren't going to cut (or We won't cut)
      6 We're/We are going to have

      7 will be OR is going to be
      8 We're/We are going to stop OR We will stop

Unit 26

A   1 future   4 future
      2 future   5 present
      3 present

B   1 She's/She is working on Saturday.
      2 She's/She is flying to Cairo on 15 May.
      3 He's/He is seeing his boss at four o'clock this afternoon.
      4 They're/They are playing tennis tomorrow afternoon.

C   1 I'm/I am going   5 I'm/I am going
      2 He's/He is staying   6 finishes
      3 gets   7 we're/we are going
      4 are you doing

D   1 's/is about to win   4 're/are about to move
      2 are to go   5 are to take
      3 is to visit

Unit 27

A   1 When Mark sees the boss, he's/he is going to discuss his problem.
      2 When Rachel uses the computer (later), she's/she is going to send an email.
      3 When Tom visits David in hospital, he's/he is going to tell him about United's win.
      4 When Matthew's/Matthew is in town tomorrow, he might buy some new trainers.

B   1 you need   9 I'll/I will be
      2 you get   10 I hear
      3 I hire   11 I'm/I am
      4 it'll/it will be   12 I'll/I will lie
      5 I'll/I will get   13 I go
      6 there's/there is   14 You'll/You will be
      7 I arrive   15 you don't get
      8 I'll/I will ring

C   1 You shouldn't decide until you've/you have thought about it (first).
      2 I'll think of you next week when I'm/I am lying on the beach.
      3 We ought to/We can leave as soon as I've/I have paid the bill.
      4 We can discuss it (later) while we're/we are sitting on the plane together.
      5 You can use the computer when I've/I have finished with it.

Unit 28

A   1 I'll/I will be earning
      2 I'll/I will be doing
      3 will you be doing
      4 I'll/I will be giving

5 who'll/who will be doing
6 you'll/you will be playing

B 1 I'll/I will be seeing her
2 I'll/I will be going there next summer
3 I'll/I will be playing (it/badminton) next weekend.
4 I'll/I will be having lunch/it in the canteen tomorrow. OR I'll/I will be having lunch/it there tomorrow.

C 1 Will you be going to the library today?
2 Will you be writing to Vicky soon?
3 Will you be using your calculator this afternoon?
4 Will you be seeing Daniel tomorrow?
5 Will you be driving to the festival?
6 Will you be phoning your sister soon?

Unit 29

A 1 I'll/I will have had
2 I'll/I will have been the subject of a TV documentary
3 I'll/I will have become world-famous
4 I'll/I will have made millions of pounds from my pictures

B 1 twenty
2 She will/She'll have travelled two hundred miles.
3 He will/He'll have done a/one hundred and fifty (press-ups).

C 1 were going to go
2 was going to pick
3 were going to see

D 1 I was going to paint the door, but I didn't feel very well.
2 I was going to repair the lamp, but I forgot.
3 I was going to wallpaper the bedroom, but I didn't have time.

Unit 30

A 1 It will/It'll be
2 who will/who'll answer OR who will/who'll be answering
3 will be answering
4 he'll/he will still be giving
5 he'll/he will have replied
6 he won't/will not be eating OR he won't/will not eat
7 will be
8 he'll/he will have earned
9 we'll/we will be returning OR we'll/we will return
10 he'll/he will have got

B 1 'm/am going to get up early tomorrow.
2 arrives at ten thirty.
3 I'm/I am seeing my bank manager tomorrow.
4 I'm/I am about to go out.
5 There's/There is going to be trouble.

C 1 I'm/I am spending OR I'm/I am going to spend
2 I'm/I am going to look OR I'll/I will be looking
3 That'll/That will be OR That's/That is going to be
4 I'll/I will be OR I'm/I am going to be
5 Are you staying/Are you going to stay OR Will you be staying/Will you stay
6 I'm/I am staying OR I'm/I am going to stay OR I'll/I will be staying
7 I'm/I am going to see OR I'm/I am seeing OR I'll/I will be seeing OR I'll/I will see
8 I'm/I am going OR I'll/I will be going
9 we might see OR we'll/we will probably see OR we're/we are probably going to see
10 do you leave OR are you leaving OR will you be leaving
11 is
12 I'll/I will see

Unit 31

A 1 She's/She has got a map. OR She has a map.
2 He hasn't got an umbrella. OR He doesn't have an umbrella.
3 They've/They have got a rabbit. OR They have a rabbit.
4 They haven't got a car. OR They don't have a car.

B 1 Has … got   4 didn't have
2 hasn't got   5 haven't got
3 didn't have

C 1 played   3 spent
2 drinks   4 received

D 1 we're/we are having
2 you've/you have got OR you have
3 it hasn't got OR it doesn't have
4 Did you have
5 I had
6 Have you got OR Do you have
7 have
8 I didn't have

Unit 32

A 1 It's a difficult problem.
2 I've seen the results.
3 I don't have any information.
4 We haven't reached a decision.
5 I'm very excited about it.
6 You needn't decide now.

7 It isn't yet certain. OR It's not yet certain.
8 We'll be pleased to see you.
9 Don't worry.
10 I'd like to buy a new computer.
11 We're willing to help.
12 We won't know the result for some time.

B 1 Where's, It's
   2 don't, isn't OR 's not
   3 What's, He's

C 1 I would like a coffee, please.
   2 There has been an accident.
   3 That is correct.
   4 I had seen the film before.
   5 Who has got the key?
   6 We would have stopped if we had seen you.

Unit 33

A 1 I am smiling.
   2 I do like my new portrait.
   3 It is foggy today.
   4 Yes, I did remember the water.

B 1 it did cost   4 I did go
   2 you do look   5 they do quarrel
   3 it does stop

C 1 I did finish the crossword today.
   2 my room does need tidying up.
   3 I do find the work difficult.
   4 I did want to give the course up.
   5 Do have a chocolate.
   6 this place does depress me.

Unit 34

A 1 offering
   2 making a suggestion
   3 asking for information
   4 requesting
   5 inviting
   6 asking for information
   7 asking permission

B 1 Are you a rich man?
   2 Are quizzes your only hobby?
   3 Did you work hard at school?
   4 Have you got/Do you have any other interests?
   5 Is it an interesting life?
   6 Does your wife ask you quiz questions?
   7 Do you answer questions in your dreams?

C 1 Are you going to America?
   2 Does Laura play tennis?
   3 Did you enjoy your holiday?
   4 Shall we (both) go for a walk?
   5 Will you be at the club tonight?
   6 Is the train on time?
   7 Do Mike and Harriet go camping?

8 Could I/Can I/May I borrow your squash racket?
9 Have you got/Do you have a motor bike?

Unit 35

A 1 Yes, I can   5 No, they aren't
   2 Yes, it is   6 Yes, I do
   3 No, he hasn't   7 No, he isn't
   4 Yes, I did   8 No, I haven't

B 1 No, we won't   5 Yes, she does
   2 Yes, I did   6 No, we aren't
   3 Yes, she has   7 No, we can't
   4 No, I didn't   8 No, I'm/I am not

C 1 b) 2 b) 3 b) 4 a) 5 b) 6 a) 7 b) 8 b)

Unit 36

A 1 What's/What is the date (today)?
   2 When does the course finish?
   3 Who have you invited (to your party)?
   4 How can I/we get tickets (to the concert)?
   5 Where are we going to have lunch? OR Where shall we have lunch?

B 1 Where   6 How far
   2 How many   7 How often
   3 When   8 What kind
   4 Who   9 How long
   5 What

C 1 where do you record
   2 How many programmes have you done?
   3 How much money do you earn?
   4 When did you start acting?
   5 What are your plans for the future?

Unit 37

A 1 a) Rita   b) Rita
   2 a) Mark   b) a bus
   3 a) a/the lorry   b) a/the car

B 1 Who is/Who's having a party?
   2 What were you reading?
   3 What have you learnt?
   4 what should we do?
   5 Who is/Who's looking for me?
   6 Who are you looking for?
   7 What is she planning?
   8 Who has/Who's moved in next door?
   9 What is/What's worrying you?
   10 Who do you want to meet?

C 1 photos can I keep?
   2 flowers look lovely?
   3 (money) went missing?
   4 house did you pass (earlier)?
   5 children has the doctor got?/does the doctor have?

6 (money) do doctors earn?
7 uncle has died?
8 wife is coming (later)?

Unit 38

A 1 What are you looking at?
   2 What are you talking about?
   3 What are you waiting for?
   4 What are you pointing at?

B 1 What are you ashamed of?
   2 What is she famous for?
   3 What is he going to complain about?
   4 What is she going to be late for?
   5 What do you feel nervous about?

C 1 What   6 for
   2 for   7 What
   3 What   8 like
   4 like   9 how
   5 what

Unit 39

A 1 Which flight did you take?
   2 Which hotel did you stay at?
   3 What music do you like?
   4 What magazine did you buy?
   5 What company do you work for?
   6 What language are you learning?

B 1 Which   4 What
   2 Which   5 Which
   3 What

C 1 Who   4 What
   2 Which   5 Which
   3 What   6 Who

Unit 40

A 1 wasn't   5 has
   2 had   6 didn't know
   3 don't know 7 isn't
   4 didn't land

B 1 can't   5 wasn't
   2 doesn't 6 isn't
   3 didn't   7 don't
   4 weren't 8 haven't

C 1 doesn't get headaches.
   2 can't relax.
   3 didn't miss a lecture.
   4 isn't a nervous person.
   5 doesn't lose things.
   6 wasn't a happy child.
   7 hasn't decided on a career.

D 1 no   4 no
   2 no   5 No
   3 not   6 not

Unit 41

A 1 Can't you drive, Melanie?
   2 Won't you be at the disco, Rachel?
   3 Haven't you got/Don't you have a television, Nick?

B 1 Don't you feel well? OR Aren't you feeling well?
   2 Haven't they arrived yet?
   3 Didn't she say hello?
   4 Can't you swim?

C 1 No 2 Yes 3 Yes 4 No

D 1 Why didn't the staff know what to do?
   2 Why couldn't they stop the ride?
   3 Why aren't they trained in first aid?
   4 Why wasn't the ambulance called immediately?
   5 Why didn't the doctor have a mobile phone?

Unit 42

A 1 a comment   3 a question
   2 a comment   4 a question

B 1 isn't it?   5 don't they?
   2 are there?   6 can't we?
   3 aren't you? 7 was it?
   4 didn't you?

C 1 don't you?   5 does it?
   2 haven't I?   6 is there?
   3 aren't you? 7 can you?
   4 do you?

D 1 Let's listen to some music, shall we?
   2 Don't do anything silly, will you?
   3 You haven't got a train timetable, have you?
   4 Pass me the salt, can you?/could you? OR You couldn't pass me the salt, could you?

Unit 43

A 1 neither am I   4 so do I
   2 Neither can I 5 Neither have I
   3 so am I   6 so would I

B 1 neither does Emma. 4 neither is Melanie.
   2 so has Emma.   5 so does Emma.
   3 neither can Mark.   6 so does Claire.

C 1 I don't expect so 4 I don't think so
   2 I suppose so   5 I'm afraid not
   3 I hope not

Unit 44

A 1 She can't play the violin.
   2 He can climb trees.
   3 She can juggle.
   4 They can't lift the weights.

B 1 I can walk OR I'm able to walk
   2 I can go OR I'll be able to go
   3 to be able to get
   4 been able to do

C 1 c) 2 a)

D 1 was able to   4 were able to
   2 could   5 couldn't/wasn't able to
   3 could/was able to

Unit 45

A (Can, could and may are all possible.)
   1 Can I borrow your calculator?
   2 May I join you?
   3 Could I look at your notes?

B 1 You can have a picnic.
   2 You can't drop litter.
   3 You can turn left.
   4 You can't play ball games/football.
   5 You can't smoke.

C 1 I wasn't allowed to have
   2 we're/we are allowed to have
   3 we're/we are allowed to do
   4 we'll/we will be allowed to hold

D 1 Am I allowed to   4 Am I allowed to
   2 May I   5 May I
   3 Am I allowed to

Unit 46

A (May and might are both possible.)
   1 she might be   4 She may be having
   2 She may be   5 You might find
   3 She might be sitting   6 She might know

B 1 He may/might win.
   2 I may/might have one.
   3 We may/might get one.
   4 She may/might be late.
   5 They may/might be visiting me.

C 1 mightn't   4 couldn't
   2 mightn't   5 mightn't
   3 couldn't

D 1 can't   4 can't
   2 must   5 might
   3 might   6 must

Unit 47

A 1 I had to pay, did you have to pay
   2 You have to slam, You'll have to fix
   3 do you have to take, I'll have to take
   4 We had to move, We didn't have to look,
      We've/We have had to do
   5 has to start, does he have to get

B 1 You must get to work on time.
   2 has to keep his dog under control.
   3 You must listen carefully.
   4 visitors have to report to the security officer.

C 1 must   5 have to
   2 has to   6 must
   3 have to   7 must
   4 must

Unit 48

A 1 must, mustn't, needn't
   2 mustn't, must
   3 mustn't, needn't
   4 mustn't, must, needn't

B 1 didn't have to wait ages to cross the road.
   2 don't have to work long hours.
   3 doesn't have to work in a factory.
   4 didn't have to lock their doors.
   5 don't have to wash their clothes by hand.

C 1 we didn't need to borrow any money.
   2 I needn't have bothered.
   3 We needn't have left/We didn't need to leave
      so early.
   4 I didn't need to pay to go in.
   5 you needn't have tipped/you didn't need to
      tip the waiter.

Unit 49

A 1 shouldn't   4 shouldn't
   2 ought   5 should
   3 should   6 oughtn't

B 1 We'd better wait (for Rachel).
   2 You'd better lock it/lock your bike.
   3 I'd better tidy my room.
   4 You'd better not drive/We'd better not go too
      fast.
   5 We'd better do some revision.

C 1 I'm/I am supposed to take two before meals.
   2 They're/They are supposed to report to the
      police.
   3 You're/You are supposed to stand in a queue.
   4 They aren't supposed to watch it.

D 1 We had/We'd better hurry. OR We should
      hurry./We ought to hurry.
   2 We had/We'd better not be OR We oughtn't to
      be/We shouldn't be
   3 should arrive/ought to arrive
   4 You shouldn't take/You oughtn't to take
   5 We aren't supposed to get

Unit 50

A 1 Can I have a fork, please?
   2 Could I have a towel, please?
   3 Would you mind answering the phone?

B 1 must   5 Can/Could
   2 have   6 Would
   3 like   7 wonder
   4 want   8 Can/Could

C 1 Can I have a receipt, please?/Can you give me
      a receipt, please?
   2 Could you tell me the time, please?
   3 Can you help me, please?
   4 Could I have a bag, please?/Could you give
      me a bag, please?
   5 Would you mind clearing a space (on the
      table), please?
   6 Could I speak to the manager, please?

Unit 51

A 1 Shall we stop for a minute?
   2 Would you like a game?
   3 I'll post that letter for you.

B 1 Shall   4 Would
   2 Shall   5 Will
   3 could   6 Would

C 1 Would you like a cup of tea? OR Will/Won't
      you have a cup of tea?
   2 What shall/can/should I say in my letter?
   3 Let's have/We could have a cup of coffee. OR
      Shall we have a cup of coffee?
   4 I'll/I can walk home with you. OR Shall/Can I
      walk home with you?
   5 Would you like to visit me one weekend?
      OR Will/Won't you visit me one weekend?

Unit 52

A 1 will   5 would
   2 won't   6 wouldn't
   3 would   7 would
   4 will

B 1 will help   5 would like
   2 wouldn't let   6 wouldn't open
   3 will give   7 won't stand
   4 won't go

C 1 Shall we go to the swimming-pool?
   2 I won't take any risks.
   3 I'd/I would like a shower (, please).
   4 You shouldn't decide in a hurry.
   5 (I think) the world will end in the year 3000.

Unit 53

A 1 b) 2 a) 3 b)

B 1 They shouldn't have left/oughtn't to have left
      litter everywhere.
   2 She should say/ought to say hello to people.
   3 He shouldn't have been/oughtn't to have been
      late for the interview.
   4 She should have looked./She ought to have
      looked.

C 1 he shouldn't have left
   2 might have taken
   3 You must have been
   4 he can't have rung

D 1 someone must have posted it.
   2 she may/might not have heard the alarm.
   3 he shouldn't have driven/oughtn't to have
      driven at 100 miles an hour/so fast.
   4 He can't/couldn't have failed the exam.

Unit 54

A 1 Dinner is being served.
   2 Some houses are being built.
   3 The seals are being fed.
   4 A flag is being raised.

B 1 is owned   4 hadn't been looked
   2 was being used 5 has been done
   3 was bought   6 is used

C 1 will be done/are going to be done
   2 will … be called
   3 can't be bought
   4 should be sold

D 1 got hurt   3 get broken
   2 get lost   4 got divorced

Unit 55

A 1 swept   6 were blocked
   2 burst   7 were brought
   3 were rescued   8 is being done
   4 received   9 said
   5 reached

B 1 my brother   4 the alarm
   2 The water   5 The guide
   3 terrorists   6 The dog

C 1 was won by Claude Jennings.
   2 did a parachute jump last week.
   3 been attacked by a bull.
   4 being built.
   5 likes Jessica.
   6 been thrown away.
   7 been kidnapped by Martians.
   8 was seen by five people.

Unit 56

A 1 was taken
   2 was done
   3 was interviewed by a very nice young police officer
   4 fingerprints were found (by detectives)
   5 burglar was identified (by the police computer).
   6 has been arrested
   7 (he) is being questioned
   8 jewellery hasn't been found

B 1 didn't produce many cars for sale.
   2 production was started by a German called Karl Benz.
   3 is now seen as the father of the motor car.

C 1 People should use them/bicycles for short journeys.
   2 someone has discovered a new source of energy?
   3 they're/they are going to knock it down/knock down this building.
   4 you shouldn't keep them/eggs in a freezer.
   5 people put it/litter in the bin?

Unit 57

A 1 New employees are given special training.
   2 Extra payments are given to staff who perform well.
   3 Most employees are offered company shares.
   4 All Zedco staff are allowed six weeks' holiday.
   5 A full salary is paid to women who leave to have children.

B 1 expected that the soap opera 'Round the Corner' will end next year.
   2 It is supposed that the footballer Wayne Johnson is earning £10 million a year.
   3 It is believed that the Prime Minister and his wife have separated.

C 1 is expected to end next year.
   2 The footballer Wayne Johnson is supposed to be earning £10 million a year.
   3 The Prime Minister and his wife are believed to have separated.

Unit 58

A 1 had his car repaired.
   2 is having her photo taken.
   3 had his windows cleaned.
   4 is having her eyes tested.

B 1 David (has) had his arm bandaged.
   2 Daniel is going to have his tooth filled.
   3 Laura is having her photos developed.

C 1 did you get your arm bandaged, David?
   2 did you get your tooth filled, Daniel?
   3 did you get your photos developed, Laura?

D 1 Tom had his car stolen from outside his house.
   2 Rita had her rent increased by ten per cent.
   3 David has had his electricity cut off.

Unit 59

A 1 He is afraid of being sent away.
   2 He doesn't want to be misunderstood.
   3 He hopes to be offered a job.
   4 He doesn't mind being paid low wages at first.
   5 He is willing to be re-trained.
   6 He would like to be given a chance.

B 1 being used
   2 working
   3 to be treated
   4 to give
   5 to be invited
   6 being taken

C 1 to write
   2 to be tidied
   3 hoovering/to be hoovered
   4 to do
   5 ironing/to be ironed
   6 to finish
   7 missing
   8 to be handed
   9 to be
   10 being told

Unit 60

A 1 Trevor promised to put up the shelves/to put the shelves up (soon).
   2 Claire decided to buy both the dresses.
   3 Melanie offered to cook the meal.
   4 Tom threatened to shoot Nick's dog/the dog.

B 1 They seem to believe
   2 it seems to have improved
   3 She doesn't seem to like
   4 He seems to be working
   5 He doesn't seem to have made
     OR He seems not to have made

C 1 to hang
   2 to come
   3 to be having
   4 to invite
   5 to take
   6 to have left

Unit 61

A 1 I've/I have given up trying. OR I gave up trying.
   2 I can't imagine being
   3 I enjoy watching it on TV.
   4 suggested having a party.

B 1 can't stand lying
   2 couldn't/can't resist having
   3 couldn't face doing
   4 can't help feeling

C   1 trying   5 getting
    2 walking   6 changing
    3 ringing   7 missing
    4 waiting   8 discussing

Unit 62

A   1 to get   6 to go
    2 to leave   7 to hire
    3 staying   8 driving
    4 sitting   9 to spend
    5 touring   10 taking

B   1 taking   6 to repair
    2 losing   7 waiting
    3 to insist   8 to have
    4 arguing   9 to accept
    5 to be   10 saying

C   1 I don't mind asking to see the manager.
    2 Matthew admitted promising to go to
       Scotland.
    3 the band happened to finish playing.

Unit 63

A   1 I'd like to buy this tin.
    2 I like driving this car.
    3 I'd like to see the manager.
    4 I like chasing rabbits.

B   1 he loves watching/to watch
    2 I wouldn't like to work
    3 I'd like to see
    4 I'd prefer to come/go
    5 I hate queuing
    6 He doesn't like cooking
    7 I'd love to fly
    8 I like to have

C   1 to drive/driving   3 to go/going
    2 to make   4 to search

Unit 64

A   1 mentioning   5 to lock
    2 agreeing   6 looking
    3 to call   7 to look
    4 to lock

B   1 running   6 to tell
    2 to make   7 to disappoint
    3 spending   8 phoning
    4 watching   9 to explain
    5 to work   10 going

C   1 Harriet didn't even try to move the piano.
    2 Mike will never forget seeing a spaceship.
    3 The walls need painting.
    4 Natasha didn't mean to be unkind to Jessica.
    5 Andrew went on studying through the night.
    6 Mark stopped to make a phone call.

Unit 65

A   1 Guy invited Kitty to come on his chat show.
    2 Sarah reminded Mark to get the theatre
       tickets.
    3 The dentist told Daniel to give up eating
       sweets.
    4 The police ordered the gunman to come out
       with his hands up.

B   1 don't want her to do a parachute jump
    2 doesn't want him to fall in love with her
    3 would like/'d like her to go (on holiday) with
       them

C   1 The police must stop the suspects leaving the
       country.
    2 The President didn't expect Congress to
       oppose him.
    3 The terrorists forced the hostages to lie down.
    4 The government doesn't mind the pound
       falling in value.

D   1 to travel   3 to use
    2 buying   4 to take

Unit 66

A   1 He can't think what to say.
    2 They're not sure/They aren't sure where to go.
    3 She doesn't know how to stop.

B   1 what to expect   4 what to do
    2 where to go   5 who to contact
    3 how to find

C   1 whether to do
    2 how much (money) to spend
    3 whether to join
    4 which route to take
    5 which (lottery numbers) to choose

Unit 67

A   1 simple to use the computer.
    2 difficult to understand the handbook.
    3 It's easy to run any kind of software.
    4 It's absolutely fascinating to explore the world
       of Compex.
    5 Are you ready to try the ultimate computer
       experience?

B   1 is very simple to use.
    2 isn't difficult to understand.
    3 Any kind of software is easy to run.
    4 The world of Compex is absolutely
       fascinating to explore.

C   1 it's/it is likely to be pretty crowded.
    2 she's/she is certain to be there.
    3 you're/you are unlikely to find it. OR you'll be
       unlikely to find it.

D   1 of   2 for   3 of   4 of   5 for

Unit 68

A
1 (just) can't wait for it to arrive.
2 It would be a mistake for him to marry her.
3 It's important for advertisements to tell the truth.

B
1 There's a fun pool for children to swim in.
2 There are quiet areas for you to relax in.
3 There are regular shows for you to enjoy.
4 There's a giant roller-coaster for you to ride on (if you dare).

C
1 It's/It is too high for her to reach.
2 It's/It is too difficult for us to understand.
3 It wasn't loud enough for them/everyone to hear.
4 It wasn't hot enough for him to drink.

D
1 difficult for the town to attract new industry.
2 very generous of the council to give the land to Sanko.
3 is eager for production to begin soon.

Unit 69

A
1 have something to eat.
2 nice to have a rest.
3 wants Rita to speak to him.
4 Daniel doesn't know how to repair the video.
5 Claire and her sister have decided to go to Bali.
6 Melanie has gone to the hospital to visit David.
7 (Unfortunately) Vicky has to do some studying.
8 It's important for Sarah to ring the office.

B
1 see/read   4 lie/sit/stay
2 drive/go   5 snow
3 cry/weep   6 see/visit

C
1 to visit   8 look
2 to see   9 get
3 to have   10 to leave
4 buy   11 to change
5 to read   12 forget
6 read   13 to get
7 feel

Unit 70

A
1 of buying   3 on buying
2 for breaking   4 like arguing

B
1 blamed Trevor for forgetting the tickets.
2 succeeded in saving the driver's life.
3 The customers complained about not receiving the goods.
4 Emma has accused Matthew of breaking his promise.
5 Melanie is insisting on cooking a meal for David.

6 A new traffic scheme has stopped cars from going into the town centre.
7 Everyone congratulated Claude on winning the quiz competition.
8 Some football fans were arrested for attacking a policeman.

C
1 about seeing   5 from doing
2 about/at getting   6 like writing
3 on travelling   7 with doing
4 for not writing   8 of/about going

Unit 71

A
1 of falling   3 to move
2 of dropping them

B
1 Nick was afraid to jump.
2 Daniel was afraid to argue with the policeman.
3 Matthew is afraid of getting sunburnt.

C
1 to buy   4 to read
2 of getting   5 to book
3 of being

D
1 about being so rude
2 about losing my temper
3 to interrupt you

Unit 72

A
1 We used to like   4 did you use to help
2 used to be   5 I used to look
3 we didn't use to have

B
1 's/is used to flying planes.
2 used to play badminton.
3 's/is used to climbing mountains.

C
1 to living   5 to drinking
2 to stop   6 to being
3 to work   7 to have
4 to be

Unit 73

A
1 by staying up all night.
2 on waking (in the morning).
3 without using a calculator.
4 for carrying the food.
5 in spite of having it on his list.
6 as well as doing the typing.

B
1 before signing   4 after using
2 after eating   5 before changing
3 Before leaving   6 before opening

C
1 He thought carefully before deciding to buy it.
2 He bought the shop despite having little money of his own.
3 He became successful by giving the customers what they wanted.
4 He put the profit back into the business instead of spending it on himself.

5 He was happy when running his own business.
6 He fell ill as a result of working too hard.
7 He has made a lot of money since buying his first shop ten years ago.

Unit 74

A 1 I saw him take it.
2 I watched him leave (the restaurant).
3 I heard him drive away.

B 1 I can hear it ringing.
2 I can see her waving.
3 I can hear them barking.
4 I can smell it burning.

C 1 She felt the building shake.
2 He heard people shouting.
3 She could hear an alarm ringing.
4 They saw the police arrive.
5 He saw a woman crying.

Unit 75

A 1 broke his leg skiing.
2 cut his finger opening a tin.
3 injured her toe running.
4 hurt his back lifting weights.

B 1 Taking a gun out of the drawer, he put it in his briefcase. OR Having taken a gun …
2 Having left the office, he (then) had to wait a while for the lift.
3 Reaching the ground floor, he hurried outside to a taxi. OR Having reached the ground floor …
4 Pulling out a gun, the taxi driver shot Mitchell. OR Having pulled out a gun …

C 1 Having studied the map, Trevor knew which way to go.
2 Feeling cold, Harriet turned on the heating.
3 Not knowing French, Daniel found it hard to communicate.
4 Having finished the book, Andrew took it back to the library.

Unit 76

A 1 uncountable   5 uncountable
2 countable   6 uncountable
3 countable   7 countable
4 uncountable   8 countable

B 1 some biscuits   6 some soap
2 a light bulb   7 a lemon
3 some wine   8 some butter
4 some mineral water 9 some eggs
5 a banana

C 1 a computer   4 many
2 essays   5 money
3 hours   6 food

7 much   10 a few
8 a job   11 pictures
9 some

Unit 77

A 1 a jar of jam
2 a box of matches
3 two loaves of bread
4 a bar of chocolate
5 five kilos of potatoes
6 a box/packet of breakfast cereal
7 two bottles of mineral water
8 a tube of toothpaste

B 1 some   5 some
2 some   6 some
3 some   7 a
4 a   8 some

C 1 beautiful scenery   4 fun
2 good weather   5 an awful journey
3 a meal

Unit 78

A 1 sport   6 a conversation
2 some potatoes   7 some chicken
3 painting   8 war
4 a noise   9 life
5 cheese   10 some egg

B 1 some business
2 an iron
3 a glass, a light
4 a business, some time
5 some experience, an experience

C 1 time   4 a paper
2 an experience   5 an orange
3 a painting   6 fruits

Unit 79

A 1 is   5 has
2 are   6 costs
3 look   7 have
4 are   8 weren't

B 1 was   5 were
2 were   6 were
3 was   7 was
4 were   8 was/were

C 1 is   5 have
2 isn't   6 is
3 are   7 is
4 work   8 has

D 1 Fifteen miles is a long walk.
2 Eight students are travelling on the bus.
3 Three people were waiting for the museum to open.
4 Twenty kilos is the baggage allowance.

Unit 80

A   1 thanks
   2 damages
   3 pain
   4 belongings
   5 saving
   6 goods
   7 damage
   8 savings
   9 pains

B   1 mathematics/maths
   2 history
   3 athletics
   4 economics
   5 geography

C   1 are
   2 is
   3 were
   4 seem
   5 is
   6 was
   7 were

D   1 was
   2 outskirts
   3 headquarters
   4 savings
   5 damage
   6 aren't
   7 crossroads
   8 is
   9 gives

Unit 81

A   1 don't
   2 go
   3 is
   4 fit
   5 look
   6 suit
   7 some
   8 a

B   1 some
   2 pairs
   3 pair
   4 some

C   1 are
   2 have
   3 know
   4 are
   5 want
   6 has

D   1 team is
   2 choir are
   3 crew are
   4 orchestra is
   5 police are
   6 cattle are
   7 population is

Unit 82

A   1 a tennis-racket/a tennis racket
   2 a television camera
   3 an alarm clock
   4 a motor cycle
   5 a luggage trolley

B   1 Have you got any cotton shirts?
   2 What shall I do with this lemonade bottle?
   3 Have you got a shopping bag?
   4 Is there a shoe shop near here?
   5 I'd like a corner table, please.
   6 I'll need some climbing boots.
   7 Are you a computer operator?

C   1 a stone wall
   2 a tourist information centre
   3 a bath-towel/a bath towel
   4 working clothes
   5 a city centre office block

   6 a sales graph
   7 a credit card
   8 a horse-race/a horse race
   9 the Marketing Director
  10 a weekend bicycle tour

Unit 83

A   1 a
   2 the
   3 a
   4 the
   5 The
   6 the
   7 the
   8 a
   9 The
  10 the
  11 the
  12 the
  13 the
  14 a
  15 the
  16 the
  17 an
  18 the
  19 the
  20 the

B   1 Matthew won the race easily.
   2 Suddenly a child ran into the road.
   3 She was watching a film on television.
   4 The bus was half an hour late.
   5 The camera videoed the thief.

C   1 a, the, the
   2 a, the, a
   3 the, the
   4 a, the, The
   5 a, the
   6 a, the
   7 a, the

Unit 84

A   1 an, the
   2 The, a
   3 The, an
   4 an, the
   5 a, the
   6 the, a

B   1 a, a
   2 a, a, the, a
   3 the, a
   4 a, the, an, the
   5 the, a, the, the, a, The, a
   6 the, a, a, the, the

C   1 a DJ
   2 a VIP
   3 an IRA member
   4 a PC
   5 an LA suburb
   6 a UFO
   7 an AGM
   8 an MP

Unit 85

A   1 some luggage
   2 some flowers
   3 a cat
   4 some birds
   5 some fruit

B   1 a   2 One   3 One   4 a

C   1 A violin is a musical instrument.
   2 A queue is a line of people.
   3 An atlas is a book of maps.
   4 A spade is a tool for digging.

D   1 some nuts
   2 mineral water
   3 some clothes
   4 lovely bread
   5 (university) students

Unit 86

A 1 He likes chips.   3 He likes art.
  2 She likes dogs.   4 She likes chemistry.

B 1 dogs, the dogs
  2 cars, pollution, cars, aeroplanes, the pollution
  3 the birds, birds, wildlife
  4 history, the history, museums, old buildings

C 1 the atom   4 television
  2 football   5 the telescope
  3 the guitar

Unit 87

A 1 church, the church
  2 the cinema, the pub
  3 hospital (in American English: the hospital),
    the hospital
  4 school, college

B 1 college   6 bed
  2 the cinema   7 work
  3 the station   8 the church
  4 sea   9 prison
  5 home

C 1 at home   6 to the library
  2 in bed   7 in prison
  3 to the hospital 8 at college
  4 to church   9 in the factory
  5 to work

Unit 88

A 1 Thanksgiving, November
  2 the weekend, Saturday
  3 Christmas, a white Christmas
  4 the summer, 1997
  5 the afternoon, the year
  6 night, the dark, the day

B 1 breakfast   4 the dinner
  2 lunch   5 a marvellous meal
  3 the lunch

C 1 breakfast   6 night
  2 midnight   7 the day
  3 Christmas   8 Wednesday
  4 Wednesday   9 the Wednesday
  5 the morning   10 February

Unit 89

A 1 a very grand hotel
  2 quite a tiring journey
  3 a really big flat
  4 quite a nice meal

B 1 so   2 such   3 such   4 so   5 such   6 so

C 1 The piano was so heavy (that) Mike and
    Harriet couldn't move it.

2 Tom was so annoyed about United losing
  (that) he wouldn't speak to anyone.
3 The band was such a big attraction (that) all
  the tickets sold out.
4 Vicky had such a lot of work to do (that) she
  was sure she'd never finish it.
5 The party made such a (lot of) noise/so much
  noise (that) it kept all the neighbours awake.

D 1 what   2 What a   3 What

Unit 90

A 1 Lake Michigan   5 Tasmania
  2 Italy   6 the West Indies
  3 The Andes   7 The River Nile
  4 The United   8 Brussels
    Kingdom   9 the North

B 1 the Thames
  2 Hyde Park
  3 Heathrow Airport
  4 Trafalgar Square
  5 Westminster Bridge
  6 the Houses of Parliament
  7 Buckingham Palace
  8 West London
  9 The M1 motorway
 10 The Ritz

C 1 New York
  2 the Statue of Liberty
  3 Central Park
  4 the Metropolitan Museum of Art
  5 Broadway
  6 Macy's
  7 Washington Square
  8 New York University
  9 the Paramount
 10 Broadway

D 1 the Little Theatre   4 the High Street
  2 Kingston House   5 the Royal Hotel
  3 Wood Lane

E 1 is in George Street.
  2 The Odeon Cinema is in the Avenue.
  3 The Clarendon Art Gallery is in Newton Lane.
  4 King Edward College is in College Road.
  5 St John's Church is in South Street.
  6 Webster's department store is in the High
    Street.
  7 The Bristol Hotel is in Westville Way.

F 1 A day at Blenheim Palace
  2 A train journey in North Wales
  3 A tour of the White House
  4 A beach on the Riviera
  5 A shopping trip to Harrods
  6 A small town in France
  7 A trip across the Severn Bridge

8 A walk around Lake Windermere
9 A visit to Tower Bridge
10 A journey across the Rockies
11 A look around the National Gallery
12 A boat trip along the Oxford Canal

Unit 91

A

	Near	Further away
Singular		that
Plural	these	those

B 1 these flowers   3 those trees
    2 this parcel   4 that dog

C 1 That   6 that
    2 these   7 This
    3 this   8 this, That
    4 this   9 These
    5 those

Unit 92

A 1 our   5 yours
    2 his   6 mine
    3 his   7 hers
    4 their   8 her

B 1 its   2 it's   3 it's   4 its

C 1 the   4 their
    2 her   5 your, your
    3 the OR her

D 1 Harriet introduced me to a friend of hers.
    2 They've got their own pool.
    3 It's a favourite hobby of mine.
    4 I've got some CDs of his.
    5 I'd like my own room.

Unit 93

A 1 the boy's bike
    2 the girls' tent
    3 the children's skateboards
    4 the girl's cat
    5 the boys' trophies

B 1 the twins'   5 her children's
    2 Luke's   6 the Lanskys'
    3 Jason's   7 Olivia's
    4 Debbie's

C 1 Mr Hillman's Gun
    2 The Smell of Blood
    3 The Terrorist's Car
    4 The Middle of the Night
    5 The Death of Someone Important
    6 The Gangsters' Money

D 1 yesterday's paper
    2 (a) five minutes' rest
    3 this month's special offer
    4 in a week's time

Unit 94

A 1 She's/She has got some cats.
    2 He hasn't got any petrol.
    3 He's/He has got some poison.

B 1 any   4 some
    2 any   5 some
    3 some   6 any

C 1 some, anything
    2 someone, any/some
    3 anyone (or someone), any
    4 something, some

D 1 anyone   4 anything
    2 any bus   5 any day
    3 any colour

Unit 95

A 1 She hasn't had many lessons yet.
    2 I'll have to make a lot (of it).
    3 I haven't got much energy.
    4 Maybe you should add a little water/a few
       drops of water.
    5 We've invited lots of friends/a lot of friends.

B 1 a lot of   5 much/a lot of
    2 many/a lot of   6 many/a lot of
    3 many   7 much
    4 a lot of

C 1 few   4 a few
    2 little   5 little
    3 a little   6 a few

D 1 much   4 many
    2 little   5 few
    3 much   6 little

Unit 96

A 1 Some of them   4 All of them
    2 most of them   5 some of them
    3 Half of them   6 None of them

B 1 She got some of them right.
    2 He got most of them right.
    3 He got all of them right.
    4 She got none of them right.

C 1 most people
    2 No student/No students
    3 Most of the money
    4 All cars
    5 All fruit/Most fruit
    6 All (of) the lights

Unit 97

A 1 each   4 each/every
    2 each/every   5 every
    3 every

B   1 all day/the whole day
    2 all night/the whole night
    3 every morning
    4 all morning/the whole morning
    5 all day/the whole day
    6 every time

C   1 One of them has a separate restaurant.
    2 Both of them serve bar snacks.
    3 One of them has a family room.
    4 Neither of them allows/allow pub games.
    5 Neither of them has/have live music.
    6 One of them has a non-smoking area.

D   1 Neither   4 every
    2 either   5 whole
    3 each (or every)

Unit 98

A   1 the dress   5 Rita and Melanie
    2 Laura   6 Rita
    3 the jeans   7 Mike and Harriet
    4 Rita   8 Tom

B   1 he   8 she
    2 them   9 They
    3 us/me   10 you
    4 her   11 him
    5 she   12 he
    6 she   13 you/we
    7 them   14 him

C   1 We   4 Me, it
    2 you, us   5 she, her
    3 it, it, her, She   6 I, you, them, they

D   1 You 2 They 3 You 4 they

Unit 99

A   1 There's/There is a balloon in the sky.
    2 There are some boxes on the car.
    3 There's/There is an elephant in the garden.

B   1 There's/There is, There'll be
    2 are there, There's/There has been OR There was
    3 there was, There … have been

C   1 It was very cheap.
    2 It was Vicky.
    3 It's/It is a nuisance.
    4 It's/It is very warm.
    5 It's/It is important to keep it somewhere safe.

D   1 There   4 there, it
    2 It   5 It, there, It, there
    3 There, It

Unit 100

A   1 's/is looking at herself (in the mirror).
    2 're/are introducing themselves.

---

    3 He's/He is teaching himself Arabic.
    4 She's/She is drying herself (on/with a towel).

B   1 yourself   2 ourselves   3 itself

C   1 you   4 her
    2 him   5 yourself
    3 himself

D   1 feel   4 worry
    2 help yourselves 5 relax
    3 remember

Unit 101

A   1 He cleans them himself.
    2 I bake it myself.
    3 They grow them themselves.
    4 We decorated it ourselves.
    5 He types them himself.
    6 I develop them myself.

B   1 herself   4 themselves
    2 itself   5 yourselves
    3 himself

C   1 They're/They are always thinking about each other.
    2 They've/They have got lots of photos of each other.
    3 They enjoy each other's company.
    4 They're/They are crazy about each other.

D   1 each other   4 ourselves
    2 each other   5 themselves
    3 themselves   6 each other

Unit 102

A   1 a smart one OR a casual one, a casual one
    2 a big one OR a small one, A big one
    3 A white one OR a brown one, A brown one
    4 an ordinary one OR an electric one, an ordinary one

B   1 I haven't got one.
    2 I must get some new ones.
    3 Have you seen this one?
    4 I've hired one.
    5 Can't you find any nice ones?
    6 The one in the car is better.

C   1 one   4 them
    2 it   5 some
    3 one

Unit 103

A   1 everyone/everybody, no one/nobody
    2 someone/somebody, something
    3 somewhere, Someone/somebody
    4 everywhere, nothing

B 1 someone   4 anywhere
   2 anyone   5 anything
   3 somewhere   6 something

C 1 his   3 likes, they
   2 it   4 has, their

D 1 I once met someone famous.
   2 Someone's car is blocking me in.
   3 I've got something else/something different to
      tell you.
   4 We know everyone's opinions/opinion.
   5 Everyone else except you is going.
   6 Nothing exciting ever happens here.

Unit 104

A 1 modern chairs   4 classical music
   2 a black cat   5 an old car
   3 solar power   6 a tall building

B pleasant, ideal, quiet, short, popular, lovely,
   friendly, helpful, good, marvellous, excellent, local

C 1 The world is asleep
   2 My chief desire
   3 My heart is content
   4 The main thing to remember
   5 The night is alive
   6 Inner secrets
   7 The only girl for me

Unit 105

A 1 a small white car
   2 an attractive old building
   3 an expensive wooden garden seat
   4 a famous Italian opera singer

B 1 a lovely old glass vase
   2 an attractive wall mirror
   3 a modern office desk
   4 red metal kitchen chairs
   5 a splendid old model boat
   6 valuable Australian postage stamps
   7 a small wooden coffee table

C 1 This is a powerful Japanese business
      computer.
   2 This is an excellent small electric fire.
   3 This is a big new chocolate bar.
   4 This is a terrific American television comedy.
   5 These are stylish aluminium garage doors.
   6 These are wonderful modern sports shoes.
   7 This is a very good German mobile phone.

Unit 106

A 1 the hungry   4 the unemployed
   2 the homeless   5 the old
   3 the sick

B 1 We live near a special school for the deaf.
   2 The old soldiers were holding a service for the
      dead.
   3 The government should do more for the poor.
   4 I'm doing a course on caring for the mentally
      handicapped.

C 1 The sick   5 the old people
   2 the young people   6 The homeless
   3 the unemployed   7 the deaf
   4 the poor

Unit 107

A 1 exhausted   3 fascinating
   2 interested   4 exciting

B 1 surprised   4 confusing
   2 disappointing   5 bored
   3 puzzled   6 interesting

C 1 relaxing   5 fascinating
   2 annoyed   6 thrilling
   3 amused   7 exhausting
   4 interested

Unit 108

A 1 brightly   6 safely
   2 patiently   7 fluently
   3 immediately   8 carefully
   4 punctually   9 quietly
   5 secretly

B 1 angrily   5 enthusiastically
   2 happily   6 reasonably
   3 automatically   7 securely
   4 publicly

C 1 United won the game easily.
   2 I've/I have checked the figures carefully.
   3 Your dog barked at me very fiercely.
   4 It's/It is raining quite heavily (here).

D 1 dark   6 unhappy
   2 terribly   7 sadly
   3 badly   8 curious
   4 suddenly   9 foolishly
   5 quietly

Unit 109

A 1 adjective   4 adjective
   2 adjective   5 adverb
   3 adverb   6 adverb

B 1 hardly   5 fast
   2 nearly   6 hard
   3 long   7 wrong
   4 late   8 straight

C 1 bad   4 well
   2 good   5 ill
   3 badly

D 1 badly   6 nearly
   2 good   7 hard
   3 fast   8 lately
   4 long   9 likely
   5 hardly

Unit 110

A 1 are more interesting
   2 is higher
   3 is more beautiful

B 1 richest   5 most popular
   2 most modern   6 most successful
   3 greatest   7 most attractive
   4 most exciting   8 happiest

C 1 happier   5 bigger
   2 faster   6 more restful
   3 more helpful   7 more modern
   4 lovelier

D 1 more smartly   4 more carefully
   2 longer   5 earlier
   3 more often   6 louder/more loudly

E 1 worst   4 best
   2 better   5 furthest
   3 worse

F 1 least 2 less 3 more 4 Most

G 1 happier   7 more exciting
   2 smallest   8 most
   3 best   9 wetter
   4 shorter   10 lower
   5 most important   11 worse
   6 older

Unit 111

A 1 The church is older than the library.
   2 Matthew is stronger than Daniel.
   3 Harriet is taller than Mike.
   4 Claire is more popular than Andrew.
   5 Mark's car is bigger than Sarah's.

B 1 Friday is the busiest day
   2 The Metropole is the nicest hotel in (the) town.
   3 This watch is one of the cheapest (watches) you can buy.
   4 This Beatles album is the best (one) they ever made.
   5 Alan is the most successful salesman in the company.

C 1 Plastic isn't as strong as metal.
   2 The stool isn't as comfortable as the armchair.
   3 Swimming isn't as exciting as surfing.
   4 The post isn't as quick as e-mail.

D 1 me 2 I am 3 me 4 he has

Unit 112

A 1 less painful   4 less attractive
   2 less busy   5 less seriously
   3 less convenient   6 less optimistic

B 1 Yesterday was a lot colder than today.
   2 My coat is a bit longer than is fashionable.
   3 I left work slightly earlier than usual this afternoon.
   4 The shop is much more expensive than the supermarket.
   5 Is the new machine any more reliable than the old one?

C 1 more and more difficult
   2 more and more complicated
   3 more and more
   4 longer and longer
   5 worse and worse

D 1 the quieter the roads (are).
   2 the wider the choice (is).
   3 the more confused I get.
   4 the more fluently you can speak.
   5 the more crowded the beaches get.

Unit 113

A 1 outside   4 Obviously
   2 Perhaps   5 silently
   3 always   6 hard

B 1 mid   5 mid   9 mid
   2 end   6 mid   10 mid
   3 front   7 end
   4 mid   8 front

C 1 clearly crossed
   2 will probably rain
   3 didn't fully understand
   4 are usually
   5 occasionally visited it/visited it occasionally
   6 were soon working
   7 has obviously forgotten

D 1 It usually rains when David is on holiday.
   2 Rita's friend visits her most weekends.
   3 Mark gets a pay rise every year.
   4 Rachel never checks her work.

E 1 I've always known your secret.
   2 We certainly can't afford a new car.
     OR Certainly we can't afford a new car.
   3 The tourists didn't walk far.
   4 Tom cut the paper carefully./Tom carefully cut the paper.
   5 Natasha can also play the violin.
     OR Natasha can play the violin also.
   6 I read the newspaper most days./Most days I read the newspaper.

F 1 peacefully at his home
  2 through the streets yesterday
  3 to Greece last year
  4 there in June

G 1 We had a lovely time in the country.
  2 We arrived home safely at about eight.
  3 You must come and visit us before too long. OR Before too long you must come and visit us.
  4 It's always nice to see you and Tony.
  5 Maybe you'll be able to come in the New Year./You'll be able to come in the New Year maybe. OR You'll maybe be able to come in the New Year.
  6 We'll see you sometime.

Unit 114

A 1 still, yet
  2 still, already
  3 yet, still

B 1 I already owe Emma £20.
  2 We've already spent all our money./We've spent all our money already.
  3 But it still looks dirty. OR But it looks dirty still.
  4 We haven't seen them yet. OR We haven't yet seen them.
  5 I still can't understand the rules.

C 1 They/Children don't play there any more
  2 they/boats still come along the river
  3 it/the view isn't beautiful any more
  4 it's/it is still our home OR it's/it is our home still

D 1 no longer   3 any more
  2 yet   4 already

Unit 115

A 1 She's very busy.   3 He's very strong.
  2 She's a bit thirsty.   4 He's extremely happy.

B 1 very   4 very
  2 quite   5 a bit
  3 a bit   6 quite

C 1 That radio is a bit loud.
  2 I quite like my new job.
  3 Why don't you slow down a little?
  4 The rain completely spoilt our day./The rain spoilt our day completely.
  5 We did the job fairly quickly.
  6 I feel a lot better now.
  7 We enjoyed the concert very much. OR We very much enjoyed the concert.
  8 My arms ached terribly.

D 1 absolutely   5 very
  2 really   6 totally
  3 very much   7 very
  4 extremely

Unit 116

A 1 quite   4 quite
  2 late   5 bright
  3 easy

B 1 rather better
  2 rather noisy
  3 rather/quite busy
  4 quite popular

C 1 It's/It is rather/quite complicated.
  2 My car is quite big.
  3 it went on rather longer than I expected.
  4 I made it quite quickly.

D 1 completely ridiculous
  2 fairly difficult
  3 completely different
  4 fairly surprised
  5 fairly useful
  6 completely certain

Unit 117

A 1 The plane is too low.
  2 The gate isn't wide enough.
  3 The water isn't warm enough.

B 1 sweet enough.   5 too many mistakes.
  2 too expensive.   6 too much traffic.
  3 enough rain.   7 too complicated.
  4 clearly enough.   8 enough food

C 1 It's too wet for a picnic/too wet to have a picnic.
  2 I/We haven't got enough chairs for all my/our guests.
  3 I had too much equipment to carry.
  4 (I think) Natasha is good enough to be a professional musician.

Unit 118

A 1 up   5 by/beside/next to
  2 in/inside   6 around/round
  3 above/over   7 in front of
  4 along   8 away from/out of
     OR down

B 1 behind, through, below
  2 past, down, opposite

C 1 opposite   4 between
  2 between   5 next to
  3 opposite

D 1 under   4 around
   2 up   5 into
   3 on   6 out of

E 1 to   6 on
   2 outside   7 through
   3 in/into   8 near
   4 past/by   9 among
   5 off

Unit 119

A 1 He's/He is on the roof.
   2 They're/They are at the disco.
   3 He's/He is in the bath.
   4 She's/She is at the lights

B 1 at the petrol station   4 in the restaurant
   2 at the zoo   5 at the station
   3 in the theatre

C 1 in   2 on   3 in   4 at   5 at
   6 at   7 on   8 on   9 in   10 at

Unit 120

A 1 In 1961.
   2 On 22 November 1963.
   3 At 12.30.

B 1 8   6 on
   2 on   7 in
   3 8   8 in
   4 in   9 on
   5 at   10 at

C 1 in time   3 in time
   2 on time   4 on time

D 1 at, on   2 at, in   3 on, in   4 in, in

Unit 121

A 1 since   2 for   3 since   4 for

B 1 He's/He has been in bed for three days.
   2 They've/They have been in the garden since breakfast.
   3 He's/He has been at his desk since nine o'clock.
   4 She's/She has been on the road for five hours.

C 1 since four o'clock   4 for six weeks
   2 ten years ago   5 for three years
   3 since Monday/   6 eight months ago
     since then   7 for three weeks

D 1 before   2 ago   3 before

Unit 122

A 1 while   2 while   3 during   4 while

B 1 by   2 until   3 until   4 by   5 by

C 1 as   2 like   3 as   4 like

D 1 as   2 as if   3 as   4 as if

E 1 By the time I arrived at your flat, you'd/you had left.
   2 Rita went to the party with Tom, as you predicted.
   3 I saw your sister while I was shopping in London.
   4 You can keep the book until you've/you have finished it OR you finish it.

Unit 123

A 1 in   7 on
   2 from   8 in
   3 in   9 by
   4 by   10 on
   5 in   11 In
   6 on   12 on, on

B 1 I pay in cash?
   2 the information up to date?
   3 you drop the ball on purpose?
   4 there anything (to watch) on television tonight?
   5 you be here at the end of July?
   6 nuclear power a good idea in your opinion?
   7 your car for sale?
   8 you approve of the plan on the whole?

C 1 by   2 on   3 in   4 by   5 by

Unit 124

A 1 of   3 in
   2 in   4 at (or in)

B 1 damage to   5 tax on
   2 way of   6 difficulty with
   3 answer to   7 matter with
   4 cause of

C 1 with   5 with
   2 of   6 for
   3 of   7 of
   4 for   8 between

D 1 answers to all the (quiz) questions
   2 knowledge of French
   3 desire for progress
   4 difference between the (two) colours
   5 preference for our/Zedco products

Unit 125

A 1 afraid of the dark.
   2 bored with the video.
   3 interested in computers.
   4 surprised at/by the news.
   5 proud of the/their victory.
   6 annoyed with her/the children.
   7 They're not/They aren't satisfied with their pay increase.

B   1 for   2 at   3 at   4 for   5 at   6 to

C   1 responsible for   5 full of
    2 ready for   6 interested in
    3 aware of   7 late for
    4 similar to   8 famous for

Unit 126

A   1 at   2 after   3 into

B   1 pay for   5 suffering from
    2 ask for   6 decided on
    3 care about   7 concentrate on
    4 caring for   8 agree with

C   1 relies on   6 apologized for
    2 deals with   7 believed in
    3 feel like   8 laughing at
    4 reached   9 discuss
    5 listening to   10 left

D   1 to   2 to   3 to   4 about   5 of

Unit 127

A   1 into   5 to
    2 from   6 to
    3 as   7 with
    4 with/to

B   1 prefer water to wine?
    2 blaming Tom for the/his accident?
    3 thank you for the/her present?
    4 accuse him/the head teacher of murder?
    5 provide you with towels?
      OR provide towels for you?
    6 invite you to her wedding?
    7 congratulate them on the/their (great)
      victory?
    8 pointed a gun at Melanie?

C   1 about   5 about/of
    2 of   6 about
    3 to   7 about/of
    4 to

Unit 128

A   1 stay in   6 come back
    2 pay … back   7 get on
    3 fall over   8 take … back
    4 lie down   9 go away
    5 cut out   10 give away

B   1 left out   4 put off
    2 sent out   5 made up
    3 throw away   6 go on /carry on

C   1 picks … up   6 win back
    2 put on/put … on   7 wash up/wash … up
    3 ring … up   8 look … up
    4 hand in/hand … in   9 held up
    5 written … down   10 mixing … up

Unit 129

A   1 She's picking litter up./She's picking up litter.
    2 They're digging the road up./They're digging
      up the road.
    3 He's washing the plates up./He's washing up
      the plates.
    4 She's plugging the television in./She's
      plugging in the television.

B   1 Nick says he's/he has given up smoking.
    2 How did the accident come about?
    3 I think Matthew and Emma have fallen out.
    4 The problem isn't going to just go away.
    5 The government is bringing in a new tax on
      computers.
    6 Zedco want to set up a new sales office in
      Germany.

C   1 sort out   5 fallen behind
    2 taking over   6 step down
    3 fell through   7 taken on
    4 fight off   8 laying off

Unit 130

A   1 completely
    2 away/disappearing
    3 continuing
    4 from start to finish
    5 aloud
    6 disconnected
    7 away/departing
    8 becoming less
    9 completely to the ground
   10 from start to finish
   11 to different people
   12 increasing
   13 wearing
   14 stopping completely

B   1 on, off   3 down, out
    2 out, out   4 on, out

C   1 try on   3 speak up
    2 taking off   4 setting off

Unit 131

A   1 down on   4 away from
    2 out into   5 through to
    3 up at   6 in from

B   1 run out of   8 go back on
    2 send away for   9 get on to
    3 look/watch out for   10 go in for
    4 look forward to   11 cut down on
    5 keep up with   12 fall back on
    6 put up with   13 get round to
    7 get on with   14 make up for

C 1 I get on (well) with Melanie. OR Melanie and
      I get on (well).
   2 I might drop in on David.
   3 I'll fit in with everyone else.
   4 I can't catch up (with) Matthew.
   5 The sunny weather is making up for last week.

Unit 132

A 1 she can't sleep.
   2 he's/he has hurt his back.
   3 She says she feels sick all the time.
   4 He says he fell over and hurt himself.

B 1 Stokeley Carmichael said (that) black is
      beautiful.
   2 Galileo said (that) the earth moves round the
      sun.
   3 Shakespeare said (that) all the world's a stage.
   4 George Orwell said (that) Big Brother is
      watching you.

C 1 tell   5 tell
   2 say   6 tell
   3 say   7 tell
   4 say   8 say

Unit 133

A 1 Trevor   3 April
   2 1998   4 (about) two weeks

B 1 you   3 he, you
   2 he, your

C 1 the day before/the previous day
   2 that day
   3 here
   4 the week before/the previous week

Unit 134

A 1 was   4 was
   2 was   5 was OR is
   3 is OR was

B 1 you had finished it/your project.
   2 you weren't on a diet.
   3 you didn't enjoy them/parties.
   4 you weren't applying for it/the job.

C 1 The Sunday Times said the production was
      brilliant.
   2 Edward Devine said he couldn't remember a
      funnier show.
   3 Robert Walsh said it (had) made him laugh.
   4 The Evening Standard said you/people had to
      see it. OR The Evening Standard said
      you/people must see it.
   5 The Telegraph said it would be a great
      success.
   6 The Express said you/people might die
      laughing.

   7 Susan Proctor said it was the funniest show
      she'd/she had ever seen.
   8 Time Out said you/people shouldn't miss it.

Unit 135

A 1 She wants to know how she can find out
      about the area.
   2 He wants to know if/whether there are any
      guided tours.
   3 They want to know where they can stay.
   4 They want to know what shows there are.

B 1 Do you know if I can park here?
   2 Could you tell me how long the film lasts?
   3 Do you know how often the buses run?
   4 Do you know if we are/we're allowed to smoke?
   5 Could you tell me what time the flight is?
   6 Could you tell me how much a ticket costs?

C 1 why I wanted the job.
   2 how I (had) heard about it.
   3 if/whether I was fit.
   4 if/whether I could work on Saturdays.
   5 how I would/I'd travel to work.
   6 if/whether I had (got) a bicycle.
   7 how much I hoped to earn.
   8 when I could start.

Unit 136

A 1 The doctor told him to take more exercise.
   2 His boss asked/told him not to play computer
      games in the office.
   3 A traffic warden told him not to park his car
      in the High Street.
   4 Laura asked him to put some shelves up.

B 1 Andrew to take a break.
   2 for forgetting the shopping.
   3 singing a few songs.
   4 Vicky to post a/the letter.
   5 making a mistake.
   6 Laura not to touch the electric wires.

C 1 The builders have promised that everything
      will be ready on time.
   2 The boss insists that we (have to) check the
      figures carefully.
   3 Tom has admitted that his story wasn't
      completely true.
   4 Matthew reminded Emma that her train was
      about to leave.

Unit 137

A 1 the young man at the door
   2 the man who plays his stereo at night
   3 the very thin woman
   4 the girl with green eyes
      (or the green-eyed girl)
   5 the young woman in the office

6 the man who drives a taxi
7 the smart young man
8 the student who failed all her exams

B 1 that/which   4 that/which
   2 who/that   5 that/which
   3 who/that   6 who/that

C 1 The bomb which went off this morning caused a lot of damage.
   2 The scientist who discovered a new planet has won the Nobel Prize.
   3 The footballer who took drugs has been banned from playing again.
   4 The little girl who had been missing since Thursday has been found safe and well.
   5 The company which owns Greenway Supermarkets has laid off thousands of workers.
   6 The old lady who did a parachute jump now wants to swim the English Channel.

Unit 138

A 1 dog that fell down a hole has been rescued.
   2 story that upset everyone was untrue.
   3 man who interviewed Natasha is a film producer.
   4 accident that Daniel saw wasn't very serious.
   5 man who/that Claire knows is a millionaire.
   6 vase that David broke was extremely valuable.
   7 jacket Melanie wore at the party is really nice.

B 1 It's/It is the car you can afford.
   2 It's/It is the film people want to see.
   3 It's/It is the supermarket you can trust.
   4 It's/It is the magazine young people read.
   5 They're/They are the chocolates you'll love.

C 1 Somewhere I've got a photo of the mountain we climbed.
   2 The man who/that repaired my car is a real expert.
   3 The detective lost sight of the man he was following.
   4 I thought I recognized the assistant who/that served us.
   5 I'm afraid the numbers I chose didn't win a prize.

Unit 139

A 1 That's/That is the film (that/which) I was talking about.
   2 This is the wallpaper (that/which) I've/I have decided on.
   3 That's/That is the man (who/that) I played tennis with.
   4 Those are the steps (that/which) I fell down.

B 1 A hammer is a tool (that/which) you hit nails with.
   2 Your destination is the place (that/which) you're/you are going to.
   3 A safe is a cupboard (that/which) you keep valuable things in.
   4 Your opponent is the person (who/that) you're/you are playing against.
   5 A sofa bed is a piece of furniture you can either sit OR sleep on.

C 1 That is an idea in which our party believes.
   2 That is a policy to which I am strongly opposed.
   3 These are people about whom no one cares.
   4 Those are mistakes of which your party should be ashamed.
   5 That is a problem with which the government is now dealing.

Unit 140

A 1 Felix Reeves is the journalist whose tape recorder was stolen.
   2 Graham Wilshaw is the architect who knew Colin at school.
   3 Rex Carter is the farmer whose land Colin bought.
   4 Norman Bridge is the lawyer who looked after Colin's interests.
   5 Sonia Goldman is the house guest whose fingerprints were on the door handle.

B 1 What you have to think about is your profit.
   2 What you must know are the needs of your customers.
   3 What you should work towards is a realistic target.
   4 What you need to do is (to) plan ahead.

C 1 Columbus sailed to America.
   2 golf that Tiger Woods plays.
   3 It was in Greece that the Olympic Games first took place.
   4 It's/It is Mercury that is nearest the sun.

Unit 141

A 1 Nelson Mandela, who was in prison for 27 years, became President of South Africa.
   2 John Lennon, who was killed in 1980, was one of the Beatles.
   3 The Titanic, which sank in 1912, was supposed to be unsinkable.
   4 Queen Victoria, who came to the throne in 1837, ruled over the British Empire.
   5 Mars, which is 140 million miles away, is known as the red planet.
   6 The Berlin Wall, which was built in 1961, stood for 28 years.

B 1 It adds information about the college theatre.
2 It tells us which people.
3 It adds information about Lucy Kellett.
4 It tells us which young man.
5 It adds information about the evening.

C 1 who took Rita to the party
2 , who has a bad temper,
3 which Tom supports
4 , who is afraid of heights.
5 , which is on the tenth floor,
6 she bought the sofa from

Unit 142

A 1 which 5 whom/who
2 who 6 who
3 whose 7 which
4 why 8 where

B 1 which has ten thousand employees
2 whose name was missed off the list
3 (that/which) Laura painted
4 (that/which) we're/we are all looking forward
to OR to which we're/we are all looking forward
5 (that/when) Mike and Harriet went camping
6 who is a bit deaf
7 whom/who you'll meet tomorrow
8 where we met the other day

C 1 Rachel's mother paid for the meal, which was
very kind of her.
2 My brother is disabled, which means he can't
get about very easily.
3 You left the keys in the car, which was rather
careless of you.
4 Vicky didn't get the job, which has made her
very depressed.
5 The police blocked off the road, which caused
a traffic jam.

Unit 143

A 1 played 5 watching
2 worn 6 added
3 arriving 7 blocking
4 telling

B 1 living in an empty office building have been
evicted.
2 employing four thousand people has gone
bankrupt.
3 built only two years ago has been declared
unsafe.
4 People protesting against pollution have
marched to London.
5 Tennis fans hoping to buy tickets have been
queuing all night at Wimbledon.
6 A new drug developed at a British university
may give us eternal youth.

C 1 the youngest girl to swim a length of the pool.
2 the only people to get a pay rise.
3 The pilot was the last person to leave the
aircraft.
4 Mrs Harper was the first woman to become
Managing Director.
5 Daniel was the most suitable candidate to
apply for the job.

Unit 144

A 1 I ask 5 share
2 there are 6 I see
3 it's 7 I'll ask
4 won't cost

B 1 If Rachel fails her driving test, she can take it
again.
2 If United lose, Tom will be upset.
3 If the office is closed, Mark won't be able to
get in.
4 If Nick arrives a bit early, he can help Tom to
get things ready.
5 If the party goes on all night, no one will
want to do any work tomorrow.
6 If Emma misses the train, she can get the next
one.
7 If Matthew enters the race, he'll probably win
it.

C 1 If you get promoted, your salary goes up.
2 If I drink coffee late at night, I can't sleep.
3 If you don't pay the bill, you get a warning
letter.
4 If I try to run fast, I get out of breath.
5 If someone enters the building, the alarm
goes off.

Unit 145

A 1 If I had a dictionary, I could look the word
up.
2 If I wasn't so busy, I'd/I would write to my
friends.
3 If my back wasn't aching, I could play tennis.
4 if Claire loved Henry, she'd/she would marry
him.
5 if he had a map, he could find the way.
6 if he/David wasn't so clumsy, he wouldn't
have so many accidents.

B 1 you wouldn't play 6 you thought
2 we go 7 it'd be/it would be
3 I didn't play 8 it won't do
4 it'd be/it would be 9 I wouldn't get
5 you think

C 1 The phone isn't working.
2 It might rain.
3 Mike isn't here.

4 The/This spoon isn't silver.
5 Sarah might call.

Unit 146

A 1 would have been
2 had lost
3 would have scored
4 she'd been/she had been
5 hadn't been
6 wouldn't have given
7 hadn't been
8 it would have been
9 we'd have beaten/we would have beaten
10 he'd been/he had been

B 1 The guests could/would have had their lunch outside if it had been warm enough/if it hadn't been so cold.
2 Sarah could/would have flown to Rome if the airport hadn't been closed/had been open.
3 Laura might have recognized Nick if he hadn't had a crash-helmet on.
4 Sarah's plants wouldn't have died/might not have died if she'd/she had watered them.
5 Nick could/would have got in (to the ice hockey game) if he'd/he had had a ticket.

C 1 he was/were, he'd/he would have put
2 I'd/I had paid, I wouldn't be
3 you loved, you wouldn't have left

Unit 147

A 1 If the twins had worn different clothes, we could have told them apart. type 3
2 If you tell me what the instructions say, I'll try to follow them. type 1
3 If people used public transport, there'd be less pollution. type 2
4 If you don't wear a sweater, you might not be warm enough. type 1
5 If I hadn't seen the product advertised, I wouldn't have bought it. type 3

B 1 you played
2 I wouldn't/couldn't hear
3 you'd/you had told
4 I wouldn't have let
5 you didn't play
6 it wouldn't be/it might not be
7 I'd/I had realized
8 I would have thrown
9 you go
10 I'll have

C 1 If I'd/I had known how unpopular Jason was, I wouldn't have invited him (to my party).
2 If you put too many tins into the plastic bag, it'll break.

3 If I had a pen, I could write down the address.
4 If I'd/I had started my project earlier, I wouldn't be so far behind (now).
5 If you need some/any help, give me a ring.
6 If the door opens, the fan comes on.

Unit 148

A 1 When the alarm rings,
2 If I feel better tomorrow,
3 When this film finishes,
4 If the plan doesn't work,

B 1 unless it's/it is a nice day.
2 unless you're/you are watching it.
3 unless we get help.
4 unless I liked it.

C 1 unless 2 if 3 unless 4 unless

D 1 We'd/We had better book a table in case the restaurant is busy.
2 You ought to insure your jewellery in case it gets stolen.
3 I'll leave you my phone number in case you want to contact me.

E 1 unless 2 If 3 in case 4 when

Unit 149

A 1 I wish you'd/you would hurry up.
2 I wish you'd/you would do the washing-up.
3 I wish you'd/you would tell me the whole story.
4 I wish you wouldn't blow cigarette smoke in my face.
5 I wish you'd/you would tell me what you're thinking.

B 1 I wish/If only I wasn't so tired.
2 I wish/If only I didn't get (these) headaches.
3 I wish/If only my work was going well/better.
4 I wish/If only I could concentrate.
5 I wish/If only life wasn't so complicated.

C 1 I'd/I had caught it.
2 she'd/she had stayed (there).
3 she'd/she had accepted it.
4 I'd/I had found it. OR I could have found it.
5 he could have played

D 1 I hadn't asked you (to marry me)
2 you wouldn't talk nonsense
3 I was a young man
4 you would/you'd listen
5 I'd/I had met you OR I could have met you

Unit 150

A 1 but it's really quite modern.
2 but she turned it down.
3 but no one laughed.

B 1 Although 4 in spite of
   2 in spite of 5 in spite of
   3 Although

C 1 in spite of/despite
   2 In spite of/Despite
   3 but/although/though
   4 Even though/Although/Though

D 1 Trevor didn't notice the sign even though it was right in front of him.
   2 Matthew doesn't know any French although it was one of his school subjects.
   3 Despite being a millionaire, Henry's friend hates spending money.
   4 We couldn't get tickets in spite of queuing for an hour.

E 1 on the other hand
   2 in spite of (or despite)
   3 whereas

Unit 151

A 1 to go to sleep.
   2 to hear the football results.
   3 to look smart.
   4 to finance her studies.

B 1 He's/He is going to get to work earlier in order to/so as to impress the boss.
   2 He's/He is going to work harder in order to/so as to achieve more.
   3 He's/He is going to take risks in order to/so as to be a winner.
   4 He's/He is going to think positively in order not to/so as not to miss any opportunities.

C 1 Nick keeps a dog to guard the house.
   2 David is going to be very careful so that he doesn't/won't have an accident.
   3 Jessica is going on a diet to lose weight.
   4 Trevor often switches off the heating to save money.
   5 Sarah had to go to Birmingham for a business meeting.
   6 Emma wore boots so that her feet wouldn't get wet.

Unit 152

A 1 I'll love you until I die
   2 I hear music when I see you
   3 Come back before I forget you
   4 I've been sad since you left me
   5 I fell in love as soon as we met

B 1 Although   6 so
   2 in order to   7 unless
   3 because   8 In spite of
   4 If   9 in case
   5 but

C 1 as soon as   7 in case
   2 to   8 until
   3 since   9 although
   4 but   10 if
   5 so that   11 so
   6 because   12 in spite of

Unit 153

A 1 and   4 but
   2 so   5 so
   3 and   6 but

B 1 Furthermore   4 On the contrary
   2 however   5 After all
   3 In other words 6 for example

C 1 In other words, you don't want to see him.
   2 By the way, what's the time/what time is it?
   3 Anyway, they haven't got one in my size.
   4 Sarah ('s got one/has one), for example.
   5 On the contrary, I loved/liked it.

Key to the tests

The numbers after the answer tell you which unit and unit section of the book has information and practice on that grammar point. For example, the numbers 4.2 refer to Unit 4, section 2.

Test A

A
1 aren't 4.2
2 does 5.3
3 Do 5.3
4 don't 5.3
5 are 4.2
6 doesn't 5.3
7 isn't 4.2

B
1 is 4.2
2 do 5.3
3 sitting 4.2
4 don't 5.3
5 doesn't 5.3, 7.1
6 go 5.1-2
7 being 7.2
8 get 5.3
9 gets 5.2
10 means 5.3, 7.1
11 always 6.4
12 costing 4.2, 7.3

C
1 The girls are playing tennis at the moment. 4.2
2 Both my brothers like sport. 5.2
3 Anna is wearing her new coat today. 4.2
4 What colour do you like best? 5.3
5 My suitcase weighs ten kilos. 7.2
6 At the moment I'm staying at a hotel. 6.3
7 Robert catches the same bus every morning. 5.2
8 What does this word here mean? 5.3, 6.2

D
1 I'm thinking 7.2, cost 7.3, It's/It is getting 4.3
2 look 7.2, they don't fit 7.2, I don't know 7.2
3 are you doing 6.1, I'm/I am weighing 7.2, I need 7.1
4 I think 7.2, is going 6.1, I agree 5.1
5 I like 7.3, Are you enjoying 7.3, I'm/I am loving 7.3
6 I'm/I am always falling 6.4, do you go 6.1, it doesn't make 6.1
7 I'm living 6.3, I'm looking 4.3, I promise 5.1
8 do you want 6.2, I don't understand 6.2, you're/you are being 7.2

Test B

A
1 left 8.2
2 were 8.2
3 died 8.4
4 had 8.2
5 didn't like 8.3
6 went 8.4
7 happened 8.2
8 wasn't 8.3
9 knew 8.4

B
1 I was wearing my old coat. 9.2, 9.3
2 We were (both) on holiday. 8.2
3 I didn't make a mistake. 8.3
4 The boys were playing (a game of) cards. 9.2, 9.3
5 I didn't know about the change of plan. 8.3, 8.4
6 My friend won the competition. 8.2
7 Did the Romans build this wall? 8.3

C
1 shining 9.1
2 was 9.2
3 wasn't 9.2
4 didn't 8.3
5 hated/detested 8.2, 8.4
6 walked/went 8.2, 8.4
7 were 9.2
8 sat 8.2, 8.4
9 had 8.2, 8.4
10 was 9.2
11 took 8.2, 8.4
12 didn't 8.3
13 wanted/hoped/had/intended 8.2, 8.4
14 When 10.2
15 was 8.2

D
1 It was peaceful and the birds were singing. 9.2
2 I was washing my hair when the phone rang. 10.2
3 You didn't come to the club last night. 8.3
4 It took ages to get home. 8.2
5 We tried to keep quiet because the baby was sleeping. 9.2
6 As I was watching him, the man suddenly ran way. 10.2
7 We passed a petrol-station two minutes ago. 8.2
8 Everything seemed OK. 10.1
9 Where did you buy that bag? 8.3
10 When I heard the alarm, I left the room immediately. 10.2

E
1 was lying 10.2, rang 10.2, stopped 10.1
2 was 10.1, left 10.2, was falling 10.3
3 came 10.1, seemed 10.1, enjoyed 10.1
4 saw 10.2, was standing 10.2, had 10.1
5 opened 10.2, fell 10.2
6 was walking 10.2, felt 10.2, didn't know 10.1
7 were going 10.1, heard 10.1, drove 10.1
8 happened 10.1, was driving 10.1, saw 10.1

Test C

A
1 washed 11.2
2 eaten 11.4
3 opened 11.2
4 written 11.3
5 made 11.3
6 had 11.3
7 scored 11.2
8 landed 11.1
9 broken 11.4
10 been 11.3
11 sold 11.3
12 finished 11.2

B
1. 's/has opened 11.2
2. 's/has drawn 11.3
3. 's/has broken 11.3
4. have won 11.3
5. 've/have drunk/finished 11.3/11.2
6. 've/have washed/cleaned 11.2
7. 've/have learnt/learned 11.3/11.2
8. have arrived/come 11.2/11.3
9. haven't finished 12.1

C
1. already 12.1
2. yet 12.1
3. been 13.1
4. ever 13.2
5. this 13.4
6. long 12.2
7. gone 13.1
8. since 12.2
9. time 13.3
10. never 13.2

D
1. have 14.1
2. ✔ 14.1
3. have 14.3
4. ✔ 14.3
5. ✔ 14.1
6. has 14.1
7. ✔ 14.1
8. ✔ 14.1
9. has 14.2
10. have 14.2

E
1. went 14.3
2. 've/have never seen 15.2
3. did 14.3
4. has won 14.1
5. worked 15.1
6. did you get 15.3
7. has been 15.2
8. has come 14.1
9. did you get 14.3
10. haven't ridden 14.3
11. was 15.2
12. Have you ever baked 15.2
13. was 15.1
14. rang 14.2
15. Have you seen 15.3
16. 've/have been 15.1

Test D

A
1. been 16.2
2. I've 18.3
3. were 19.3
4. been 20.2
5. hadn't 18.3
6. Have 18.3
7. was 19.2
8. went 19.2
9. I've 16.2

B
1. The doctor has been working since six o'clock. 16.3
2. Rupert had forgotten his credit card. 18.1
3. I didn't want to go until I'd/I had taken a photo. 19.4
4. Nancy has written the report. 17.1
5. I've/I have been waiting in the queue (for) forty minutes (so far). 16.3
6. When we arrived, everyone was dancing. 19.3

7. I've had/I have had the computer for four years. 17.2
8. When we were having/eating lunch, there was a knock at the door. 19.3
9. Nigel felt sick because he'd/he had eaten too many cakes. 20.3

C
1. I'd/I had been on holiday. 19.4
2. I've/I have been playing badminton. 16.3
3. I'd had/I had had a shock. 17.1
4. How long have you been working? 16.4
5. Lots of people were walking along the street outside. 19.2
6. She's/She has been practising her English since last summer. 16.3
7. I've/I have passed my exam. 17.1
8. She'd/She had been lying in the sun for too long. 20.3
9. But the coach had already gone. 18.1

D
1. I've/I have finished 18.3
2. have we been waiting 17.1, We've/We have been 17.2
3. we'd/we had drunk, she hurried 19.4
4. I was having, I heard 19.3
5. have you been doing 16.4, We've/We have done 17.1
6. she'd/she had been crying 20.3, she'd had/she had had 18.1
7. heard, threw 19.4

Test E

A
1. I'm/I am living 21.2, I've/I have found 21.3
2. I think, it belongs 21.2
3. I'm/I am using 21.2, I want 21.2, I've/I have started 21.3
4. You leave 21.2, I've had/I have had 21.4, I've/I have been rushing 21.4

B
1. heard 21.5
2. thought 21.5
3. was 21.5
4. called/rang/phoned 21.6
5. stopped 21.6
6. was 21.5
7. had 21.6
8. knocked 21.6
9. got/come 21.6
10. been 21.7

C
1. It's/It has been raining for ten hours. 21.4
2. I think it's the right thing to do. 21.2
3. We've moved our/the sofa. 21.3
4. I was having/eating (some/my) breakfast when Susan rang. 21.5
5. They always play badminton on Tuesday. 21.2

D
1. I was looking 21.5
2. I'm going 21.2
3. I've been trying 21.4
4. I'd spent 21.6
5. They opened 21.3

E
1. ✔ 21.2
2. been 21.7
3. was 21.5
4. are 21.2
5. have 21.3
6. ✔ 21.7
7. been 21.4
8. ✔ 21.6

F
1. failed 21.3
2. lives 21.2
3. left 21.3
4. had made 21.7
5. were walking 21.5
6. saw 21.5
7. has seen 21.4
8. hadn't arrived 21.6
9. had been waiting 21.7/were waiting 21.5
10. have been trying/have tried 21.4
11. have had 21.4
12. are taking 21.2
13. believe 21.2
14. want 21.2

Test F

A
1. going 24.1
2. will 23.2 OR won't
3. see 27.1
4. not 23.3
5. to 26.3
6. Shall 23.4
7. is 24.2
8. getting 26.1
9. has 27.3
10. about OR going/ready

B
1. What time does it get to London? 26.2
2. I'll tell her when I see her this evening. 27.1
3. He's about to fall asleep. 26.3
4. We're/We are meeting in town later. OR We're/We are going to meet in town later. 26.1
5. I'll send you a postcard. 23.2
6. I can read a book while I'm waiting. 27.3
7. I'm/I am going to lie down. 24.1
8. All your friends will be there. 23.4
9. No one can go into the building until the police have searched it. 27.3

C
1. will 25.1
2. is 27.1
3. will 25.1
4. going 24.1
5. to 24.2
6. have 27.3
7. will 25.1
8. having/holding 26.1
9. starts/begins 26.2
10. will 25.1

D
1. leaves 26.2
2. I'm going to apply 25.1
3. I'll help 25.2
4. it's about to open 26.3
5. I go 27.1
6. Are you doing 26.1

E
1. I'm/I am going to have a rest. 24.1
2. (The) term starts on 6 September. 26.2
3. There will be a world war in five years' time. 23.2
4. Judy and I are/We're playing tennis tomorrow. 26.1
5. Prices will probably fall. 25.3 OR Prices are probably going to fall.
6. The car is/We're going to crash! 24.3

Test G

A
1. going 24.3
2. be 28.3
3. will 23.1
4. don't 26.2
5. was 29.2
6. are 26.1
7. to 24.2
8. about 26.3

B
1. is 26.2
2. ✔ 26.3
3. be 23.3
4. for 26.3
5. ✔ 28.3
6. ✔ 29.2
7. will 27.2
8. to 29.1

C
1. 'll/will be having 28.2
2. was going to drive 29.2
3. 'll/will be working 28.2
4. 'll/will have done 29.1
5. were going to buy 29.2
6. 'll/will have had 29.1

D
1. I'm/I am going 26.1 OR I'm/I am going to go 24.1
2. I'm/I am leaving 26.1 OR I leave 26.2 OR I'm going to leave 24.1
3. I'm/I am visiting 26.1 OR I'm/I am going to visit 24.1
4. That'll/That will be 25.1
5. starts 26.2/is starting 26.1
6. you get 27.2
7. I'll/I will send 23.2

E
1. We'll wait for you. 23.2
2. This train stops at Bath. 26.2
3. My friend was going to meet us. 29.2
4. Adrian is having a job interview on 17 October. 26.1
5. We'll/We will have finished our meal by eight o'clock. 29.1
6. I might go on the trip. 30.3
7. The fire is about to go out. 26.3

F 1 I'm going to move 24.1
2 I'll take 23.2
3 we're going 26.1
4 He's going to jump 24.3
5 I'll be using 28.3

Test H

A 1 Where have you been? 36.2
2 Do you sell postcards? 34.2
3 Who does this calculator belong to? 39.1
4 How long are you staying here? 36.3
5 What is your new office like? 38.2
6 Which of the flights are full? 39.2
7 What time does the carnival start? 36.3
8 What holiday has Nancy decided on? 38.1

B 1 How old 36.3   7 Who 39.2
2 What colour 36.3   8 How 38.2
3 Whose 37.2   9 How far 36.3
4 How much 36.3   10 How often 36.3
5 Which 39.1   11 What 39.1
6 What kind 36.3

C 1 Are you a student here? 34.2
2 How many cakes have you eaten? 37.2
3 Did you enjoy your walk? 34.2
4 Where have your friends gone? 36.2
5 What kind of music do you like? 36.3
6 Does Peter play tennis? 34.2
7 What are you talking about? 38.1
8 What has happened? 37.1

D 1 Where did you buy your coat? 36.2
2 Can Amy swim? 34.2
3 Which band do you like best? 37.2
4 Who am I speaking to? 38.1
5 How much do video recorders cost? 36.3
6 May/Can I come in (, please)? 34.1
7 How long does the journey take? 36.2
8 What did you lock the door for? 38.2
9 What happens next? 37.1
10 Shall we (all) go out together? 34.1

E 1 How many cars have the Smiths got/do the Smiths have? 36.3
2 Where does Janet work? 36.2
3 Why is Andrea learning English? 36.1
4 What was the film like? 38.2
5 When will the meeting take place? 36.2
6 Who switched off the computer? 37.1
7 Whose burglar alarm was ringing? 37.2
8 Who did Anna go to the dance with? 38.1

Test I

A 1 Who's 37.1   7 they 42.2
2 don't 42.2   8 Which 39.2
3 not 40.2   9 don't 40.2
4 has 35.2   10 neither 42.1
5 Haven't 41.2   11 doesn't 41.2
6 so 43.2   12 Let's 42.3

B 1 Where do you live? 36.2
2 What are you thinking about? 38.1
3 Would you like to come to my room? 34.1
4 Didn't you watch the football match on television? 41.3
5 May I take a photo (, please)? 34.1
6 Have you seen Polly? 34.2
7 How many letters have you written? 37.2
8 Who is/Who's coming to your party? 37.1
9 How often does Martin cook? 36.3
10 What will the weather be (like) tomorrow? 38.2

C 1 No, it hasn't. 35.2
2 No, I hate it./Yes, I love it. 41.4
3 Yes, I expect so. 43.2
4 It isn't very nice, is it? 42.2
5 Yes, please. 35.3
6 So am I./I am too. 43.1
7 I hope not. 43.2
8 Neither did the second. 43.1

D 1 How old are you? 36.3
2 Did you go to college? 34.2
3 What are your interests? 39.1
4 Which company do you work for? 38.1
5 What don't you like about your job? 41.5

E 1 doesn't 40.2   9 will 42.3
2 course 35.3   10 far 36.3
3 neither/nor 43.1   11 so 43.2
4 No 41.4   12 don't 41.5
5 for 38.2   13 Which 39.1
6 did 42.2   14 so 43.1
7 won't 35.2   15 hasn't 41.5
8 not 43.2   16 Which 40.2

Test J

A 1 mustn't 48.1   5 needn't 48.1
2 Would 51.3   6 Shall 51.2
3 might 46.2   7 had 49.3
4 would 52.1   8 wouldn't 52.3

B
1 ✔ 51.3
2 ✔ 47.1
3 to 44.3
4 for 50.1
5 be 46.1
6 ✔ 52.1
7 been 53.2
8 ✔ 49.4
9 ✔ 48.2
10 be 45.3

C
1 We ought to be careful. 49.2
2 I was able to finish all my work. 44.3
3 It must have been a terrible experience for you. 53.4
4 Players aren't allowed/are not allowed to have a drink. 45.3
5 You'd/You had better sit down. 49.3
6 The report has to be on my desk tomorrow morning. 47.1
7 Joanne mightn't have/might not have received my message. 53.3
8 Martin can't be jogging in this weather. 46.3
9 Tessa would like a cup of coffee. 52.2
10 Nancy didn't need to clean the flat. 48.3

D
1 asking permission 45.1
2 giving an order 50.2
3 asking for advice 49.2
4 inviting 51.3
5 offering to help 51.2
6 making a suggestion 51.1
7 refusing permission 45.2
8 making a request 50.1
9 expressing a wish 47.2

E
1 have/need 48.2
2 may/might OR could 46.1
3 has 47.1
4 can 44.1
5 allowed 45.3
6 supposed 49.4
7 shouldn't 49.2 OR mustn't 48.1
8 able 44.2

Test K

A
1 The film may be banned. 54.3
2 Nancy was offered a pay increase. 57.1
3 The mistakes need correcting/need to be corrected. 59.2
4 The situation was reported to be under control. 57.3
5 The new drug is being tested. 54.2
6 The machine hasn't been used for ages. 55.2

B
1 is 54.2
2 by 55.2
3 be 54.3/get 54.4
4 were 54.2
5 it 57.2
6 been 54.2
7 have 58.2
8 to 57.3
9 being 59.1

C
1 The song was sung by Pavarotti. 55.2
2 Nigel had his passport stolen. 58.4
3 Doctors are paid a lot of money. 57.1
4 I hope to be interviewed for the job. 59.1
5 The floor was being cleaned. 54.2
6 Judy is having her car repaired. 58.2
7 Tessa got lost. 54.4
8 It was agreed that the plan should go ahead. 57.2
9 When did you get your kitchen decorated? 58.3
10 Exercise is said to be good for you. 57.3

D
1 b) 55.1
2 b) 55.1
3 a) 55.1
4 a) 55.1
5 b) 55.1

E
1 The story was written by Agatha Christie. 55.2
2 Baseball is played at this stadium. 54.2
3 This shirt needs ironing/needs to be ironed. 59.2
4 I got my hair cut yesterday. 58.3
5 It is believed that there is going to be a war. 57.2
6 My parents got divorced last year. 54.4
7 I've got a report to write. 59.2
8 The winner was given a prize. 57.1
9 This man on TV is supposed to be the tallest person in the world. 57.3

Test L

A
1 to organize 62.2
2 wearing 62.2
3 to approve 62.2
4 to be 62.2
5 reminding 62.2
6 to be 62.2
7 working 62.2
8 to buy 62.2
9 waiting 62.2

B
1 We must avoid wasting so much time. 61.1
2 Sometimes a country refuses to take part in the Olympics. 62.2
3 I'd/I would like to see the Rocky Mountains some day. 63.2
4 I meant to give Judy a nice welcome yesterday. 64.5
5 I always like to see my doctor once a year. 63.1
6 The buses usually stop running before midnight. 64.4
7 I can't face getting up at five tomorrow. 61.3
8 Last year we made an agreement to work together. 60.4
9 Yesterday you promised to carry on shooting the film. 62.2
10 My father seems to be getting better now. 60.2

C
1 wait 62.3
2 to 60.1
3 seeing/meeting 61.1
4 would 63.2
5 need 64.7 OR have/ought
6 not 61.1
7 help 61.3 OR stop 64.4
8 to 62.4
9 on 61.4

D
1 We've finished decorating the flat. 61.1
2 I regret saying what I did. 64.2
3 Tessa decided not to go to work. 60.1
4 Do you mind helping me? 61.2
5 I'm beginning to get worried. 63.3
6 I can't afford to buy a new car. 60.1
7 I hope to avoid making things worse. 62.5
8 Peter seems to have gone away already. 60.2

E
1 The children couldn't wait to see their presents. 62.3
2 I can't stand getting up in the dark. 61.3
3 I happened to see your brother yesterday. 62.4
4 The shop tends to open ten minutes late. 60.3
5 Do you fancy going for a walk? 62.3
6 The police carried on watching the house. 61.4
7 I'll/I will never forget seeing Nelson Mandela. 64.1

Test M

A
1 for 67.2
2 in 75.1
3 ✔ 70.3
4 ✔ 66.3
5 ✔ 65.4
6 to 69.2(3)
7 enough 68.3
8 for 74.3
9 them 67.3
10 ✔ 73.2

B
1 to get 71.2
2 making 70.2
3 reaching 70.2
4 running 65.4
5 dreaming 73.1
6 to happen 65.3
7 ordering 73.2
8 to follow 68.2
9 to be 67.4
10 to do 65.2
11 respect 69.2(3)
12 to do 65.2
13 buying 65.5
14 order 69.2(2)

C
1 We saw Rupert looking in a shop window. 74.1
2 I remember the clown falling over. 65.4
3 Tessa wasn't sure which way to go. 66.3
4 The porter just stood there expecting a tip. 75.1
5 How about going to the barbecue? 73.2
6 Susan is used to (always) living in the country. 72.2
7 I'm afraid of hurting myself. 71.1

8 Christopher apologized for forgetting to pay. 70.2
9 The food was too cold for Michelle to eat. 68.3
10 It was silly of Polly to give away the secret. 67.5 OR Polly was silly to give away the secret.

D
1 after 73.3
2 to 65.2
3 used 72.1
4 to 71.2
5 having/eating 70.2
6 of 67.5
7 to 68.4
8 to 72.2
9 how 66.2
10 of 71.1
11 for 68.1
12 by 73.2
13 Having 75.2
14 put 74.4

E
1 breaking 70.3, knock 74.4
2 to see 69.1(8), to forget 68.4
3 doing 73.3, to write 69.1(2)
4 to bother 71.3, to ask 66.2
5 to play 72.1, watch 69.2(2)

Test N

A
1 a 77.2
2 ✔ 76.1
3 ✔ 77.2
4 a 76.1
5 ✔ 77.2
6 some 77.1
7 an 78.3
8 an 78.3

B
1 much 76.3
2 clothes 80.1
3 pairs 81.1
4 fun 76.1
5 is/was 79.5
6 saving 80.1
7 doesn't 79.3
8 was 79.1
9 was 79.1
10 piece/slice 78.1

C
1 Every window was broken. 79.2
2 My earnings aren't enough to live on. 80.1
3 There was litter everywhere. 77.2
4 We went to the hotel to get some food. 76.1
5 Judy bought a pair of binoculars. 81.1
6 I need a new cheque book. 82.2
7 I'll have a glass of orange juice, please. 78.3
8 The reporter needed two pieces/bits/items of information. 77.2

D
1 We can't sit here because the grass is wet. 79.1
2 Do you want (some) butter on your bread? 76.1
3 All my belongings were stolen. 80.1
4 Do you have any information about hotels? 77.2
5 The police are questioning two men. 81.3
6 Can we have two coffees/two cups of coffee, please? 78.4
7 The news isn't very good, I'm afraid. 80.2

8 I just want to go into this shoe shop. 82.2
9 It's only a short journey by train. 79.2

E 1 wears 79.2
   2 a piece of advice 77.2
   3 the football match 82.1
   4 customs 80.1
   5 are 81.2
   6 many 76.3
   7 is 79.5
   8 these glasses 81.1
   9 steelworks 80.3
  10 any 77.2
  11 meat 76.1
  12 were 80.1
  13 A noise 78.2
  14 were 81.3
  15 is 79.3
  16 light 78.3
  17 sports club 82.2
  18 means 80.3
  19 woods 78.4
  20 has 79.2

Test O

A 1 a 83.2
   2 the 84.3
   3 the 88.2
   4 The 83.2
   5 the 90.5
   6 a 85.3
   7 The 83.2
   8 the 83.2
   9 the 84.2
  10 the 83.2
  11 a 89.2
  12 a 83.2
  13 one 85.2
  14 the 83.2
  15 The 83.2

B 1 work 87.2
   2 quite a difficult 89.2
   3 Golf 86.2
   4 School 87.1
   5 a really nice 89.2
   6 some photos 85.4
   7 the violin 86.3
   8 breakfast 84.6
   9 an X-ray 84.4
  10 the radio 86.3
  11 the environment 84.2
  12 such terrible 89.3

C 1 ✗ 86.2
   2 a 89.2
   3 ✗ 88.2
   4 an 84.4
   5 a 83.2
   6 the 90.3
   7 ✗ 90.6
   8 a 83.2
   9 ✗ 88.4
  10 some 85.4/the 83.2 OR ✗
  11 a 83.2
  12 a 84.3
  13 one 85.2
  14 a 83.2 OR one
  15 the 83.2
  16 What 89.4 OR Such

17 so 89.3
18 the 84.3

D 1 ✔ 87.2
   2 ✔ 88.6
   3 The 86.2
   4 the 89.4
   5 ✔ 85.4
   6 the 88.5
   7 ✔ 87.1
   8 A 85.2
   9 ✔ 89.3
  10 ✔ 90.10
  11 ✔ 86.3

E 1 a beautiful city 84.3
   2 The weather 84.2
   3 Easter 88.3
   4 Princes Street 90.7
   5 the Royal Scottish Museum 90.9
   6 the Highlands 90.4
   7 mountains 86.2
   8 a thing 89.3
   9 the sea 87.2
  10 Corfu 90.2
  11 some sunshine 85.4 OR sunshine
  12 beach holidays 88.2

Test P

A 1 b) 97.2
   2 b) 93.1
   3 a) 92.4
   4 a) 95.3
   5 b) 97.3
   6 c) 94.1

B 1 either 97.3
   2 Someone 94.2
   3 these 91.1
   4 a few 95.3
   5 Some 96.1
   6 People's 93.1
   7 that 91.2
   8 Polly's 92.5

C 1 a 95.3
   2 mine 92.1
   3 of 92.5
   4 many 95.2
   5 anyone 94.2
   6 None 96.4
   7 all 96.2
   8 lot 95.1
   9 whole 97.2

D 1 That was a very good idea of yours. 92.5
   2 You've got a lot of books, haven't you? 95.1
   3 I don't know the time of the meeting. 93.2
   4 Nigel has hurt his leg. 92.3
   5 All (of) the rooms in the house were cold. 96.2
   6 Wear anything - it doesn't matter what. 94.3
   7 Each of the four doors was locked. 97.1
   8 I live my life, and my sister lives hers. 92.1
   9 Both socks/Both the socks/Both of the socks have got holes in them. 97.3
  10 Here's a copy of this week's magazine. 93.3
  11 This sweater is losing its colour. 92.2
  12 I want some paper, but there's none in here. 96.4

E 1 I've lived here most of my life. 96.2
2 Every hotel was full. 97.1
3 The house on the corner is bigger than ours. 92.1
4 I've forgotten the name of my doctor. 93.1
5 We have had/We've had little warning of the changes. 95.3
6 So many people have applied for the job. 95.2
7 I met an old boyfriend of yours at a party. 92.5
8 Neither of the chairs is/are comfortable. 97.3
9 My holiday starts in ten days' time. 93.3

Test Q

A
1 himself 100.3
2 They 98.2
3 We 98.2
4 them 98.2
5 us 98.2
6 themselves 100.4
7 It 99.2
8 They 98.3
9 ourselves 98.4
10 her 98.2
11 me 98.2

B
1 yourself 100.3
2 it 99.2
3 some 102.3
4 us 100.3
5 Me 98.2
6 ones 102.2
7 there 99.1
8 each other's 101.2
9 else 103.4

C
1 one 102.3
2 everyone/everybody 103.1
3 herself 100.3
4 one 102.2
5 It 99.2
6 something 103.1
7 one 102.3
8 You 98.3
9 ourselves 101.1

D
1 one 102.3
2 himself 100.4
3 something 103.1
4 it 99.2
5 her 98.2
6 There 99.1
7 everyone/everybody 103.3
8 it 99.2
9 there 99.1
10 each 101.2
11 them 98.2
12 him 98.2

E 1 There's/There is a train leaving in ten minutes. 99.3
2 I think someone is/someone's coming up the stairs. 103.3
3 Let's meet at eight o'clock, shall we? 100.5
4 We haven't got a camcorder, but we'd like one. 102.3
5 Let's do something different/something else today. 103.4
6 They are/They're going to build a new motorway through here. 98.3

7 I'm afraid I haven't done anything all day. 103.2
8 Everyone enjoyed themselves at the barbecue. 100.2, 100.4
9 If you're buying a loaf, get a nice fresh one. 102.2
10 I've looked everywhere for my credit card. 103.1
11 The two friends still see each other/see one another occasionally. 101.2

Test R

A
1 freely 109.3
2 The young man 106.3
3 hungry 104.2
4 thoughtfully 108.3
5 right 109.2
6 fascinating 107.2
7 similar 104.3
8 well 109.4
9 the disabled 106.2
10 confused 107.2
11 scientifically 108.2
12 frightened 104.3

B
1 This is a nice place. 104.2
2 I can't find the large biscuit tin. 105.2
3 Tessa behaved in a silly way. 109.1
4 Your coffee is getting cold. 104.2
5 They live in a lovely old stone house. 105.3
6 This hospital is for the mentally ill. 106.2

C
1 expensive 104.2
2 nice 104.2
3 surprised 107.2
4 carefully 108.1
5 amusing 107.2
6 elderly 109.1
7 friendly 109.1
8 free 109.3

D
1 The drink tasted strange. 108.3
2 Obviously, the sick need to be looked after. 106.1
3 The dog was asleep. 104.3
4 The young woman spoke politely. 108.1
5 The train arrived late. 109.3
6 The film ends dramatically. 108.2
7 Polly shouted angrily. 108.2
8 Billiards is an indoor game. 104.3
9 The clown was amusing. 107.2
OR People found the clown amusing.
10 There was hardly any time left. 109.3

E 1 I tasted the soup carefully. 108.3
2 ✔ 105.3
3 Are the children asleep? 104.3
4 It's a school for the deaf/for deaf people. 106.3
5 It's a nice new leather jacket. 105.3

6   The rich are/Rich people are very lucky. 106.1
7   ✔ 109.4
8   He used a thick green paper towel. 105.3
9   ✔ 106.1
10 The course I started was boring./I was bored with the course I started. 107.2
11 I often talk to the two old people/men/women next door. 106.3
12 The smoke rose high into the air. 109.3
13 ✔ 104.2
14 We felt disappointed when we lost. 107.2
15 Everyone seemed very nervous. 108.3
16 Tessa drives too fast. 109.2
17 ✔ 107.2

Test S

A   1   more intelligent 110.2
    2   cleaner 110.2
    3   thinner 110.3
    4   more carefully 110.4
    5   worse 110.5
    6   later 110.3
    7   longer 110.4
    8   more useful 110.2
    9   sooner 110.4
    10 busier 110.3
    11 more annoyed 110.2
    12 more nervous 110.2

B   1   funniest 110.3   6   farthest/furthest 110.5
    2   most horrible 110.2   7   most helpful 110.2
    3   most recent 110.2   8   most modern 110.2
    4   largest 110.3   9   earliest 110.4
    5   most boring 110.2   10 saddest 110.3

C   1   ✔ 111.4   6   ✔ 111.2
    2   the 111.2   7   most 110.1
    3   ✔ 111.3   8   ✔ 111.5
    4   a 112.2   9   of 111.3
    5   so 112.4   10 more 112.3

D   1   nicer 111.2   5   in 111.3
    2   as 111.4   6   bit 112.2
    3   least 112.1   7   as 111.4
    4   than me 111.5   8   the easier 112.4

E   1   is bigger than the living-room 111.2
    2   fitter than I am 110.3, 111.2
    3   is as big as 111.4
    4   just get higher and higher 112.3
    5   is more expensive than 110.1, 111.2
    6   is the least difficult 112.1
    7   more and more excited 112.3
    8   most romantic story I've ever 111.3

Test T

A   1   I quite like old cowboy films. 115.3
    2   Have you finished this magazine yet? 114.2
    3   This coat is too big. 117.2
    4   Have the children already had their tea?/Have the children had their tea already? 114.3
    5   You certainly don't look ill. 113.7
    6   We don't go out much. 115.4
    7   I think everyone works fairly hard. 115.2
    8   I still don't know the date of the meeting. 114.3
    9   The others are just getting ready. 113.2
    10 I have to go to work on Saturdays./On Saturdays I have to go to work. 113.8

B   1   This game is rather silly. 115.2
    2   I've already paid the bill./I've paid the bill already. 114.3
    3   The alarm isn't loud enough. 117.2
    4   Jonathan passed the test easily./Jonathan easily passed the test. 113.3
    5   The children play cards a lot. 115.3
    6   They didn't sell enough tickets. 117.2
    7   You ask too many questions. 117.2
    8   I'm not a member of the club any more. 114.4
    9   It's warm enough to sit outside. 117.3

C   1   yet 114.2
    2   still 114.3
    3   rather 116.3
    4   enough 117.2
    5   many 117.2
    6   to 117.3
    7   any 114.4
    8   no 114.4
    9   bit 115.1
    10 soon 113.5

D   1   I didn't sleep very well last night./Last night I didn't sleep very well. 113.5
    2   I think I need to rest a little. 115.3
    3   I don't work for the company any longer. 114.4
    4   The article is fairly interesting. 115.1
    5   Tessa locked the door carefully./Tessa carefully locked the door.113.3
    6   You aren't tall enough to play basketball.117.2
    7   We went to town yesterday./Yesterday we went to town. 113.8
    8   I like this music very much./I very much like this music. 115.4

E 1 We go to the cinema a lot. 115.3
2 Adrian always wears jeans. 113.6
3 These shoes aren't big enough. 117.1
4 I no longer live in Birmingham. 114.4
5 Polly spent too much money in the sales. 117.2

Test U

A 1 The doctor has been working for twelve hours. 121.2
2 We had a great time at the disco. 119.2
3 The woman was getting out of the car. 118.1
4 The players had numbers on their shirts. 119.1
5 The new manager takes over in two weeks' time. 120.3
6 Anna drove to the garage to get some petrol. 118.2
7 We were sitting at the back of the room. 119.3

B 1 on 119.3
2 ago 121.3
3 on 120.1
4 at 120.1/by 122.2
5 at 119.3
6 on 119.1
7 in 120.3
8 across 118.1
9 during 122.1/in
10 until/till 122.2

C 1 the 120.2
2 ✔ 118.1
3 ✔ 122.3
4 the 118.1
5 on 120.1
6 ✔ 119.3
7 ✔ 122.2

D 1 on 119.3
2 for 123.1
3 by 122.2
4 at 123.2
5 since 121.2
6 with 124.2
7 above 118.1
8 of 124.3
9 while 122.1
10 between 124.3
11 like 122.3
12 with 125.2
13 ago 121.3
14 for 124.4
15 until 122.2
16 for 125.1
17 in 120.1
18 to 125.4

E 1 Scott lives in Washington. 119.1
2 I'm travelling to Italy on business. 120.1
3 I'm busy on Friday morning. 120.1
4 They've/They have been playing (for) an hour. 121.1
5 Jonathan is very good at tennis. 125.3
6 I'm rather busy at the moment. 120.1
7 We went/travelled to Budapest by air. 123.3
8 Nigel goes past the newsagent's every day. 118.1
9 The company is planning (to make) a reduction in the workforce. 124.3
10 We got to our guest house in time for a meal. 120.2

Test V

A 1 I must pay for my ticket. 126.2
2 I'm going to put on that expensive grey coat I bought. 128.3
3 She's invited us to lunch. 127.2
4 He's looking at them. 126.1
5 The police prevented me from leaving. 127.2
6 I'm going to turn it off. 128.3

B 1 about 126.3
2 out 130.2
3 on 128.2
4 off 128.1
5 up 130.2
6 at 126.2
7 through 129.3
8 up for 131.2

C 1 You've left one out. 128.2
2 I've never heard of it. 126.3
3 They ran away from it. 131.1
4 You must congratulate her on her success. 127.2
5 She's going to set up her own company. 129.2
6 He reminds me of an old school friend of mine. 127.3
7 He wants to put it forward at the meeting. 129.3

D 1 as 127.2
2 about/of 127.3
3 look/watch 131.2
4 in 126.2
5 from 127.1
6 on 127.2
7 at 127.2
8 out 129.1 OR over
9 out 125.1
10 forward 131.2
11 woke 129.1
12 up 129.1

E 1 You're too young to give up working. 129.2
2 This bag belongs to Janet. 126.1
3 Everyone carried on working as usual. 130.2
4 They discussed the plan. 126.3
5 I've/I have run out of money. 131.2
6 I explained the problem to the police./I explained to the police what the problem was. 127.3
7 I wouldn't put up with such terrible conditions. 131.2
8 They'll have to put off the game/put the game off. 128.2

Test W

A 1 me 135.4
2 did 135.3
3 ✔ 136.2
4 that 135.2

5 ✔ 133.2
6 me 132.3
7 did 134.2
8 for 136.1

B 1 was 134.2
2 previous 133.2
3 whether 135.2
4 not to 136.1

5 told 132.3
6 that 133.2
7 could 134.3
8 suggested 136.2

C 1 they 133.2
2 that/if/whether 132.2
3 she 133.2
4 to 132.1
5 didn't 134.2
6 had 134.2
7 wouldn't/didn't 134.3
8 if/whether 135.2
9 wanted/needed/had 135.1
10 next/following/same 134.2

D 1 she said she felt quite excited. 133.2, 134.2
2 he said he couldn't remember the code word. 133.2, 134.3
3 he said he wouldn't be at the next meeting. 133.2, 134.3
4 they said they had/they'd got a problem. 133.2, 134.2
5 she said she'd been swimming/she had been swimming. 133.2, 134.2
6 they said they would like to be in the show. 133.2, 134.3
7 he said he didn't need any help. 133.2, 134.2
8 she said her sister was coming to see her. 133.2, 134.2

E 1 A policeman told Christopher to stop shouting. 136.1
2 Tessa admitted eating all the cake/having eaten all the cake the day before/the previous day. 133.2, 136.2
3 Adrian apologized for being rude/for having been rude. 136.2
4 Simon invited Susan to join him for lunch. 133.2, 136.2
5 Martin asked Nancy if/whether someone rang her/someone had rung her an hour before. 133.2, 135.2
6 Peter insisted on leaving. 136.2

Test X

A 1 for 139.1
2 entering 143.1
3 which 136.2
4 only 143.2
5 who 142.1
6 whom 139.3
7 that you took 138.1
8 where 142.3
9 which 142.4
10 whose 140.1

B 1 This isn't the train on which I normally travel. 139.3/This isn't the train (that/which) I normally travel on. 139.2
2 The letter that I opened wasn't for me. 137.2
3 The reason (why/that) I didn't know was that no one had told me. 142.3
4 What we should do is ring the police. 140.2
5 I didn't know the name of the man who/that helped me. 138.2
6 Rupert knows the family whose house is for sale. 140.1
7 Einstein, who failed his university entrance exam, discovered relativity. 141.2
8 The person we talked to was very friendly./ The people we talked to were very friendly. 138.2

9 It's the President who makes the important decisions. 140.3
10 I can't find my diary, which is a real nuisance. 142.4
11 Outside the door was a pair of boots covered in mud. 143.1
12 Lake Superior, which lies on the US-Canadian border, is the largest lake in North America. 142.1

C 1 who 133.2 OR that
2 that/which 133.2
3 that/which 135.1
4 it 136.3
5 that/which 133.2
6 what 136.2
7 whose 136.1
8 which 138.4
9 what 136.2
10 who 138.1

D 1 that/which crashed was 137.2/, which crashed, was 142.1
2 (when/that) Martin rang (,) Tessa was 142.3
3 new offices are 133.1/offices, which are new, are 142.1
4 stolen from a car have been 143.1/that/which were stolen from a car have been 137.2
5 (that/which) you were looking at is 139.1-2
6 Theatre, which dates from 1896, is 142.1
7 whose dog was run over was 140.1
8 the first (person) to solve 143.2/the first (person) who solved 137.2
9 selling newspapers was standing 143.1/who was selling newspapers was standing 137.2
10 (that/which) Judy gave was 138.1–2/, which Judy gave, was 142.1
11 where I used to live is 142.3/(that/which) I used to live in 139.1-2/in which I used to live 139.3

Test Y

A 1 it would have opened 146.2
2 disappear 144.2
3 travelled 145.2
4 would be 147.2
5 they don't build 144.2
6 would suffer 145.2
7 I'll go 144.2/I'm going to go 147.2
8 I'd/I had known 146.2
9 I'd/I would have moved 146.2
10 they'd/they had done 147.2
11 there won't be/there might not be 144.2

B 1 had been 146.2
2 in case 148.4
3 knew 149.3
4 only 149.1
5 when 148.2
6 unless 148.3

C 1 If you talk about football, I'm going to be very bored. 147.2
2 If the baby had cried, we wouldn't have had a good sleep. 146.2
3 If you want a chat, just give me a ring. 147.2
4 If Nigel had satellite TV, he could watch/would be able to watch the game. 145.2
5 If you go away, I'll miss you. 144.2
6 If I was/were rich, I'd/I would have given up working long ago. 146.4
7 If we'd/we had bought that picture five years ago, it would be quite valuable now. 146.4
8 If you throw a stone into water, it sinks. OR If you throw a stone into water, it'll/it will sink.

144.4

D 1 If it rains, I'll stay here. 144.2
2 Can you tell me when it starts? 148.2
3 I wouldn't need to repeat things all the time if you listened. 145.2
4 If air gets warmer, it rises. 144.4
5 I'd better get another one made in case I lose it. 148.4
6 I wish we'd/we had left home earlier. 149.4
7 If it doesn't arrive today, we'll have to complain. 144.2
8 I wish someone would turn it down. 149.2
9 Unless we act quickly, it'll be too late. 148.3
10 But he wouldn't have been angry if you hadn't damaged his stereo. 146.2

Exit test

This test will help you to find out if there are parts of the book that you should look at again. Choose the correct answer – a), b), c) or d).

Words and sentences

1 We gave .... a meal.
   a) at the visitors b) for the visitors c) the visitors d) to the visitors

Verbs

2 I'm busy at the moment. .... on the computer.
   a) I work b) I'm work c) I'm working d) I working

3 My friend .... the answer to the question.
   a) is know b) know c) knowing d) knows

4 I think I'll buy these shoes. .... really well.
   a) They fit b) They have fit c) They're fitting d) They were fitting

5 Where .... the car?
   a) did you park b) did you parked c) parked you d) you parked

6 At nine o'clock yesterday morning we .... for the bus.
   a) wait b) waiting c) was waiting d) were waiting

7 When I looked round the door, the baby .... quietly.
   a) is sleeping b) slept c) was sleeping d) were sleeping

8 Here's my report. .... it at last.
   a) I finish b) I finished c) I'm finished d) I've finished

9 I've .... made some coffee. It's in the kitchen.
   a) ever b) just c) never d) yet

10 We .... to Ireland for our holidays last year.
   a) goes b) going c) have gone d) went

11 Robert .... ill for three weeks. He's still in hospital.
   a) had been b) has been c) is d) was

12 My arms are aching now because .... since two o'clock.
   a) I'm swimming b) I swam c) I swim d) I've been swimming

13 I'm very tired. .... over four hundred miles today.
   a) I drive b) I'm driving c) I've been driving d) I've driven

14 When Martin .... the car, he took it out for a drive.
   a) had repaired b) has repaired c) repaired d) was repairing

15 Janet was out of breath because ....
   a) she'd been running b) she did run c) she's been running d) she's run

16 Don't worry. I .... be here to help you.
   a) not b) shall c) willn't d) won't

17 Our friends .... meet us at the airport tonight.
   a) are b) are going to c) go to d) will be to

18 .... a party next Saturday. We've sent out the invitations.
   a) We had b) We have c) We'll have d) We're having

19 I'll tell Anna all the news when .... her.
   a) I'll see b) I'm going to see c) I see d) I shall see

20 At this time tomorrow .... over the Atlantic.
   a) we flying b) we'll be flying c) we'll fly d) we to fly

21 Where's Robert? .... a shower?
   a) Does he have b) Has he c) Has he got d) Is he having

22 I .... like that coat. It's really nice.
   a) am b) do c) very d) yes

Questions, negatives and answers

23 What's the weather like in Canada? How often .... there?
   a) does it snow b) does it snows c) snow it d) snows it

24 Which team .... the game?
   a) did it win b) did they win c) won d) won it

25 What did you leave the meeting early ....? ~ I didn't feel very well.
   a) away b) because c) for d) like

26 Unfortunately the driver .... the red light.
   a) didn't saw b) didn't see c) no saw d) saw not

27 You haven't eaten your pudding. .... it?
   a) Are you no want b) Do you no want c) Don't want you d) Don't you want

28 I really enjoyed the disco. It was great, ...?
   a) is it b) isn't it c) was it d) wasn't it

29 Are we going the right way? ~ I think ....
   a) indeed b) it c) so d) yes

Modal verbs

30 The chemist's was open, so luckily I .... buy some aspirin.
   a) can b) can't c) did can d) was able to

31 Susan has to work very hard. I .... do her job, I'm sure.
   a) can't b) couldn't c) don't d) shouldn't

32 We had a party last night. .... spend all morning clearing up the mess.
   a) I must have b) I've been to c) I've had to d) I've must

33 There was no one else at the box office. I .... in a queue.
   a) didn't need to wait b) mustn't wait c) needn't have waited d) needn't wait

34 .... I carry that bag for you? ~ Oh, thank you.
   a) Do b) Shall c) Will d) Would

35 I've lost the key. I ought .... it in a safe place.
   a) that I put b) to be putting c) to have put d) to put

The passive

36 We can't go along here because the road is ....
   a) been repaired b) being repaired c) repair d) repaired

37 The story I've just read .... Agatha Christie.
   a) was written b) was written by c) was written from d) wrote

38 Some film stars .... be difficult to work with.
   a) are said b) are said to c) say d) say to

39 I'm going to go out and ....
   a) have cut my hair b) have my hair cut c) let my hair cut d) my hair be cut

The infinitive and the -ing form

40 The driver was arrested for failing .... an accident.
   a) of report b) report c) reporting d) to report

41 Someone suggested .... for a walk.
   a) go b) going c) of going d) to go

42 I can remember .... voices in the middle of the night.
   a) hear b) heard c) hearing d) to hear

43 The police want .... anything suspicious.
   a) that we report b) us reporting c) us to report d) we report

44 We weren't sure .... or just walk in.
   a) should knock b) to knock c) whether knock d) whether to knock

45 It was too cold .... outside.
   a) the guests eating b) for the guests to eat c) that the guests should eat d) that the guests eat

46 Did you congratulate Tessa .... her exam?
   a) of passing b) on passing c) passing d) to pass

47 I didn't like it in the city at first. But now .... here.
   a) I got used to living b) I'm used to living c) I used to live d) I used to living

48 They raised the money simply .... for it. It was easy.
   a) asking b) by asking c) of asking d) with asking

49 As we walked past, we saw Nigel .... his car.
   a) in washing b) to wash c) wash d) washing

Nouns and articles (a/an and the)

50 I need to buy ....
   a) a bread b) a loaf bread c) a loaf of bread d) breads

51 My father is not only the town mayor, he runs ...., too.
   a) a business b) a piece of business c) business d) some business

52 The .... produced at our factory in Scotland.
   a) good are b) good is c) goods are d) goods is

53 I'm looking for .... to cut this string.
   a) a pair scissors b) a scissor c) a scissors d) some scissors

54 I was watching TV at home when suddenly .... rang.
   a) a doorbell b) an doorbell c) doorbell d) the doorbell

55 I've always liked ....
   a) Chinese food b) food of China c) some food of China d) the Chinese food

56 In England most children go .... at the age of five.
   a) school b) to school c) to some schools d) to the school

57 We haven't had a holiday for .... time.
   a) a so long b) so a long c) such a long d) such long

58 Our friends have a house in ....
   a) a West London b) the West London c) West London d) West of London

This, my, some, a lot of, all, etc.

59 It's so boring here. Nothing ever happens in .... place.
   a) that b) these c) this d) those

60 Is that my key, or is it ....?
   a) the yours b) the your's c) your d) yours

61 Adrian takes no interest in clothes. He'll wear ....
   a) a thing b) anything c) something d) thing

62 There's .... use in complaining. They probably won't do anything about it.
   a) a few b) a little c) few d) little

63 I don't want to buy any of these books. I've got ....
   a) all b) all them c) everything d) them all

Pronouns

64 Let's stop and have a coffee. .... a café over there, look.
   a) Is b) It's c) There d) There's

65 Everyone in the group shook hands with ....
   a) each other b) one other c) one the other d) themselves

66 The washing-machine has broken down again. I think we should get ....
   a) a new b) a new one c) new d) new one

67 All the guests were dancing. .... having a good time.
   a) All were b) Every was c) Everyone was d) Someone were

Adjectives and adverbs

68 The house was .... building.
   a) a nice old stone b) a nice stone old c) a stone old nice d) an old nice stone

69 The government is doing nothing to help ....
   a) poor b) the poor c) the poors d) the poor ones

70 The young man seems very ....
   a) sensible b) sensiblely c) sensibley d) sensibly

71 I .... missed the bus. I was only just in time to catch it.
   a) mostly b) near c) nearest d) nearly

72 This detailed map is .... the atlas.
    a) more useful as b) more useful than c) usefuller as d) usefuller than

73 This place gets .... crowded with tourists every summer.
    a) always more b) crowded and more c) from more to more d) more and more

74 Yes, I have got the report. .... it.
    a) I just am reading b) I'm just reading c) I'm reading just d) Just I'm reading

75 I've read this paragraph three times, and I .... understand it.
    a) can't still b) can't yet c) still can't d) yet can't

76 We're really sorry. We regret what happened ....
    a) a bit b) much c) very d) very much

Prepositions

77 The village is .... Sheffield. It's only six miles away.
    a) along b) by c) near d) next

78 You can see the details .... the computer screen.
    a) at b) by c) in d) on

79 I've got a meeting .... Thursday afternoon.
    a) at b) in c) on d) to

80 We've lived in this flat .... five years.
    a) ago b) already c) for d) since

81 This car is ...., if you're interested in buying it.
    a) for sale b) in sale c) at sale d) to sell

82 Polly wants to cycle round the world. She's really keen .... the idea.
    a) about b) for c) on d) with

Verbs with prepositions and adverbs

83 I prefer dogs .... cats. I hate cats.
    a) from b) over c) than d) to

84 My father used the money he won to set .... his own company.
    a) forward b) on c) out d) up

85 Don't go too fast. I can't keep .... you.
    a) on to b) on with c) up to d) up with

Reported speech

86 Someone .... the tickets are free.
    a) said me b) said me that c) told me d) told to me

87 Last week Justin said 'I'll do it tomorrow.' He said he would do it ....
    a) the following day b) the previous day c) tomorrow d) yesterday

88 I don't know why Nancy didn't go to the meeting. She said she .... definitely going.
   a) be b) is c) was d) would

89 The librarian asked us .... so much noise.
   a) don't make b) not make c) not making d) not to make

Relative clauses

90 What's the name of the man .... gave us a lift?
   a) he b) what c) which d) who

91 What was that notice ....?
   a) at that you were looking b) you were looking at c) you were looking at it d) which you were looking

92 Susan is the woman .... husband is in hospital.
   a) her b) hers the c) whose d) whose the

93 York, ... last year, is a nice old city.
   a) I visited b) that I visited c) which I visited d) whom I visited

94 The accident was seen by some people .... at a bus stop
   a) waited b) waiting c) were waiting d) who waiting

Conditionals and wish

95 If .... my passport, I'll be in trouble.
   a) I lose b) I'll lose c) I lost d) I would lose

96 I haven't got a ticket. If .... one, I could get in.
   a) I'd have b) I had c) I have d) I've got

97 If the bus to the airport hadn't been so late, we .... the plane.
   a) caught b) had caught c) would catch d) would have caught

98 If only people .... keep sending me bills!
   a) don't b) shouldn't c) weren't d) wouldn't

Linking words

99 I just had to take the dog out .... of the awful weather.
   a) although b) despite c) even though d) in spite

100 Anna put the electric fire on .... warm.
   a) for getting b) in order get c) so she gets d) to get

Key to the exit test

The number after the answer tells you which unit of the book has information and practice on that grammar point.

1	c) 3	51	a) 78
2	c) 4, 6	52	c) 80
3	d) 5, 6	53	d) 81
4	a) 7	54	d) 83, 84
5	a) 8	55	a) 86
6	d) 9	56	b) 87
7	c) 9, 10	57	c) 89
8	d) 11	58	c) 90
9	b) 12, 13	59	c) 91
10	d) 14	60	d) 92
11	b) 15	61	b) 94
12	d) 16	62	d) 95
13	d) 17	63	d) 96
14	a) 18, 19	64	d) 99
15	a) 20	65	a) 100, 101
16	b) 23	66	b) 102
17	b) 24, 25	67	c) 103
18	d) 26	68	a) 105
19	c) 27	69	b) 106
20	b) 28	70	a) 108
21	d) 31	71	d) 109
22	b) 33	72	b) 110, 111
23	a) 34, 36	73	d) 112
24	c) 37	74	b) 113
25	c) 38	75	c) 114
26	b) 40	76	d) 115
27	d) 41	77	c) 118
28	d) 42	78	d) 119
29	c) 43	79	c) 120
30	d) 44	80	c) 121
31	b) 46	81	a) 123
32	c) 47	82	c) 124, 125
33	a) 48	83	d) 126, 127
34	b) 51, 52	84	d) 128–130
35	c) 49, 53	85	d) 131
36	b) 54	86	c) 132
37	b) 55, 56	87	a) 133
38	b) 57	88	c) 134
39	b) 58	89	d) 136
40	d) 60, 62	90	d) 137
41	b) 61, 62	91	b) 139
42	c) 64	92	c) 140
43	c) 65	93	c) 141, 142
44	d) 66	94	b) 143
45	b) 68	95	a) 144, 147
46	b) 70	96	b) 145, 147
47	b) 72	97	d) 146, 147
48	b) 73	98	d) 149
49	d) 74	99	d) 150
50	c) 76, 77	100	d) 151

Index

The numbers in this index are unit and section numbers unless they have the letter 'p' for 'page.'